# A History of Art for Beginners and Students: Painting, Sculpture, Architecture

Clara Erskine Clement Waters

A

# HISTORY OF ART

FOR

## BEGINNERS AND STUDENTS

### PAINTING — SCULPTURE — ARCHITECTURE

WITH

*COMPLETE INDEXES AND NUMEROUS ILLUSTRATIONS*

BY

mrs CLARA ERSKINE CLEMENT Waters

AUTHOR OF "HANDBOOK OF LEGENDARY AND MYTHOLOGICAL ART," "PAINTERS, SCULPTORS, ENGRAVERS, ARCHITECTS AND THEIR WORKS," "ARTISTS OF THE NINETEENTH CENTURY," ETC.

NEW YORK
FREDERICK A. STOKES
SUCCESSOR TO WHITE, STOKES, & ALLEN
1887

# PART I.

# ·PAINTING·

# CONTENTS.

## CHAPTER I.



## CHAPTER II.



## CHAPTER III.

# LIST OF ILLUSTRATIONS.

# PAINTING.

## CHAPTER I.

### ANCIENT PAINTING, FROM THE EARLIEST TIMES TO THE CHRISTIAN ERA.

IN speaking of art we often contrast the useful or mechanical arts with the Fine Arts; by these terms we denote the difference between the arts which are used in making such things as are necessary and useful in civilized life, and the arts by which ornamental and beautiful things are made.

The fine arts are Architecture, Sculpture, Painting, Poetry, and Music, and though we could live if none of these existed, yet life would be far from the pleasant experience that it is often made to be through the enjoyment of these arts.

In speaking of Painting, just here I wish to include the more general idea of pictures of various sorts, and it seems to me that while picture-making belongs to the fine or beautiful arts, it is now made a very useful art in many ways. For example, when a school-book is illustrated, how much more easily we understand the subject we are studying through the help we get from pictures of objects or places that we have not seen, and yet wish to know about. Pictures of natural scenery bring all countries before our eyes in such a way that by looking at them, while reading books of travel, we may know a great deal more about lands we have never seen, and may never be able to visit.

Who does not love pictures? and what a pleasure it is to open a magazine or book filled with fine illustrations. St. Augustine, who wrote in the fourth century after Christ, said that "pictures are the books of the simple or unlearned;" this is just as true now as then, and we should regard pictures as one of the most agreeable means of education. Thus one of the uses of pictures is that they give us a clear idea of what we have not seen; a second use is that they excite our imaginations, and often help us to forget disagreeable circumstances and unpleasant surroundings. The cultivation of the imagination is very important, because in this way we can add much to our individual happiness. Through this power, if we are in a dark, narrow street, in a house which is not to our liking, or in the midst of any unpleasant happenings, we are able to fix our thoughts upon a photograph or picture that may be there, and by studying it we are able to imagine ourselves far, far away, in some spot where nature makes everything pleasant and soothes us into forgetfulness of all that can disturb our happiness. Many an invalid—many an unfortunate one is thus made content by pictures during hours that would otherwise be wretched. This is the result of cultivating the perceptive and imaginative faculties, and when once this is done, we have a source of pleasure within ourselves and not dependent on others which can never be taken from us.

It often happens that we see two persons who do the same work and are situated in the same way in the world who are very different in their manner; one is light-hearted

FIG. 1.—HARP-PLAYER. *From an Egyptian painting.*

and happy, the other heavy and sad. If you can find out the truth, it will result that the sad one is matter-of-fact, and has no imagination—he can only think of his work and what concerns him personally; but the merry one would surprise you if you could read his thoughts—if you could know the distances they have passed over, and what a vast difference there is between his thought and his work. So while it is natural for almost every one to exclaim joyfully at the beauty of pictures, and to enjoy looking at them simply, I wish my readers to think of their uses also, and understand the benefits that may be derived from them. I have only hinted at a few of these uses, but many others will occur to you.

When pictures are composed of beautiful colors, such as we usually think of when we speak of the art of painting, the greatest charm of pictures is reached, and all civilized people have admired and encouraged this art. It is true that the remains of ancient art now existing are principally those of architecture or sculpture, yet there are a sufficient number of pictures in color to prove how old the art of painting is.

## EGYPT.

Egyptian painting is principally found on the walls of temples and tombs, upon columns and cornices, and on small articles found in burial places. There is no doubt that it was used as a decoration; but it was also intended to be useful, and was so employed as to tell the history of the country;—its wars, with their conquests and triumphs, and the lives of the kings, and many other stories, are just as distinctly told by pictures as by the hieroglyphics or Egyptian writings. We can scarcely say that Egyptian painting is beautiful; but it certainly is very interesting.

The Egyptians had three kinds of painting: one on flat surfaces, a second on bas-reliefs, or designs a little raised

FIG. 2.—KING RAMESSES II. AND HIS SONS STORMING A FORTRESS. *From Abousimbel.*

and then colored, and a third on designs in *intaglio*, or hollowed out from the flat surface and the colors applied to the figures thus cut out. They had no knowledge of what we call perspective, that is, the art of representing a variety of objects on one flat surface, and making them appear to be at different distances from us—and you will see from the illustrations given here that their drawing and their manner of expressing the meaning of what they painted were very crude. As far as the pictorial effect is concerned, there is very little difference between the three modes of Egyptian painting; their general appearance is very nearly the same.

The Egyptian artist sacrificed everything to the one consideration of telling his story clearly; the way in which he did this was sometimes very amusing, such as the making one man twice as tall as another in order to signify that he was of high position, such as a king or an officer of high rank. When figures are represented as following each other, those that are behind are frequently taller than those in front, and sometimes those that are farthest back are ranged in rows, with the feet of one row entirely above the heads of the others. This illustration of the storming of a fort by a king and his sons will show you what I mean. The sons are intended to be represented as following the father, and are in a row, one above the other (Fig. 2).

For the representation of water, a strip of blue filled in with perpendicular zigzag black lines was used. From these few facts you can understand how unformed and awkward Egyptian pictures seem if we compare them with the existing idea of what is beautiful. There appear to have been certain fixed rules for the use of colors, and certain objects were always painted in the colors prescribed for them. The background of a picture was always of a single, solid color; Egyptian men were painted in a reddish brown, and horses were of the same shade; women were generally yellow, sometimes a lighter brown than the men; negroes were black, the Asiatic races yellow, and but one instance is known of a white skin, blue eyes, and yellow hair. The draperies about the figures were painted in pleasing colors, and were sometimes transparent, so that the figures could be seen through them.

The execution of Egyptian paintings was very mechanical. One set of workmen prepared the plaster on the wall for the reception of the colors; another set drew all the outlines in red; then, if chiselling was to be done, another class performed this labor; and, finally, still others put on the colors. Of course nothing could be more matter-of-fact than such painting as this, and under such rules an artist of the most lofty genius and imagination would find it impossible to express his conceptions in his work. We know all this because some of these pictures exist in an unfinished condition, and are left in the various stages of execution; then, too, there are other pictures of the painters at their work, and all these different processes are shown in them. The outline drawing is the best part of Egyptian painting, and this is frequently very cleverly done.

As I have intimated, the greatest value of Egyptian painting is that it gives us a clear record of the habits and customs of a very ancient people—of a civilization which has long since passed away, and of which we should have a comparatively vague and unsatisfactory notion but for this picture-history of it. The religion, the political history, and the domestic life of the ancient Egyptians are all placed before us in these paintings. Through a study of them we know just how they hunted and fished, gathered their fruits, tilled the soil, and cooked the food, played games, danced, and practised gymnastics, conducted their scenes of festivity and mourning—in short, how they lived under all circumstances. Thus you see that Egyptian painting is a very important example of the way in which pictures can teach us; you will also notice that it is not even necessary that they should be pretty in order that we may learn from them.

Another use made of Egyptian painting was the illustration of the papyrus rolls upon which historical and other documents were written. These rolls, found in the tombs, are now placed in museums and collections of curious things; the paintings upon them may be called the oldest book illustrations in the world. Sometimes a single color is used, such as red or black; but others are in a variety of colors which have been put on with a brush. Indeed, some rolls exist which have pictures only, and are entirely without hieroglyphics or writing characters; one such is more than twenty yards long, and contains nothing but pictures of funeral ceremonies.

The ancient Egyptians were so serious a people that it is a pleasant surprise to find that some of these pictures are intended for jokes and satires, somewhat like those of the comic papers of to-day; for example, there is one in the British Museum, London, representing cats and rats fighting, which is intended to ridicule the soldiers and heroes of the Egyptian army.

One cannot study Egyptian painting without feeling sorry for the painters; for in all the enormous amount of work done by them no one man was recognized—no one is now remembered. We know some of the names of great Egyptian architects which are written in the historical rolls; but no painter's name has been thus preserved. The fact that no greater progress was made is a proof of the discouraging influences that must have been around these artists, for it is not possible that none of them had imagination or originality: there must have been some whose souls were filled with poetic visions, for some of the Egyptian writings show that poetry existed in ancient Egypt. But of what use could imagination be to artists who were governed by the laws of a narrow priesthood, and hedged about by a superstitious religion which even laid down rules for art?

For these reasons we know something of Egyptian art and nothing of Egyptian artists, and from all these influences it follows that Egyptian painting is little more than an illuminated alphabet or a child's picture-history. In the hieroglyphics, or writing characters of Egypt, it often occurs that small pictures of certain animals or other objects stand for whole words, and it appears that this idea was carried into Egyptian painting, which by this means became simply a picture chronicle, and never reached a point where it could be called truly artistic or a high art.

## ASSYRIA.

The remains of Assyrian painting are so few that they scarcely serve any other purpose than to prove that the Assyrians were accustomed to decorate their walls with pictures. Sometimes the walls were prepared with plaster, and the designs were painted on that; in other cases the painting was done upon the brick itself. The paintings on plaster were usually on the inner walls, and many of these which have been discovered during the excavations have disappeared when exposed to the air after their long burial from the sight and knowledge of the world.

Speaking of these pictures, the writer on art, J. Oppert, says that some paintings were found in the Palace of Sargon; they represented gods, lions, rosettes, and various other designs; but when he reached Nineveh, one year after these discoveries, the pictures had all disappeared—the colors which had been buried twenty-five hundred years lasted but a few days after they were uncovered.

Assyrian tile-painting was more durable than the wall-painting; but in all the excavations that have been made these have been found only in fragments, and from these

FIG. 3.—FRAGMENT OF AN ASSYRIAN TILE-PAINTING.

fragments no complete picture has been put together. The largest one was found at Nimrud, and our illustration is taken from it. It represents a king, as we know by the tiara he wears, and two servants who follow him. The pictures to which the existing fragments belong could not have been large: the figures in our picture are but nine inches high. A few pieces have been found which must have belonged to larger pictures, and there is one which shows a part of a face belonging to a figure at least three feet high; but this is very unusual.

The Assyrian paintings have a broad outline which is of a lighter color than the rest of the picture; it is generally white or yellow. There are very few colors used in them. This does not accord with our notions of the dresses and stuffs of the Assyrians, for we suppose that they were rich and varied in color—probably they had so few pigments that they could not represent in their paintings all the colors they knew.

No one can give a very satisfactory account of Assyrian painting; but, judging from the little of it which remains, and from the immense number of Assyrian sculptures which exist, we may conclude that the chief aim of Assyrian artists was to represent each object they saw with absolute realism. The Dutch painters were remarkable for this trait and for the patient attention which they gave to the details of their work, and for this reason Oppert has called the Assyrians the Dutchmen of antiquity.

## BABYLON.

In Babylon, in the sixth century B.C., under the reign of Nebuchadnezzar, the art of tile-painting reached a high state of perfection. The Babylonians had no such splendid alabaster as had the Assyrians, neither had they lime-stone; so they could not make fine sculptured slabs, such as are found at Nineveh and in other Assyrian ruins. But the Babylonians had a fine clay, and they learned how to use it to the best advantage. The city of Babylon shone with richly colored tiles, and one traveller writes : "By the side of Assyria, her colder and severer sister of the North, Babylon showed herself a true child of the South,—rich, glowing, careless of the rules of taste, only desiring to awaken admiration by the dazzling brilliance of her appearance."

Many of the Babylonish tiles are in regular, set patterns in rich tints ; some are simply in solid colors. These last are found in the famous terrace-temple of Borsippê, near Babylon. We know from ancient writings that there were decorative paintings in Babylon which represented hunting scenes and like subjects, and, according to the prophet Ezekiel, chap. xxiii., verse 14, there were "men portrayed upon the wall, the images of the Chaldeans portrayed with vermilion, girded with girdles upon their loins, exceeding in dyed attire upon their heads, all of them princes to look to, after the manner of the Babylonians of Chaldea, the land of their nativity." Some writers assume that this must have been a description of tapestries ; but most authorities believe them to have been glazed tile-paintings.

A whole cargo of fragments of Babylonish tile-paintings was once collected for the gallery of the Louvre at Paris, and, when on board a ship and ready to be sent away, by some accident the whole was sunk. From the descriptions of them which were written, we find that there were portions of pictures of human faces and other parts of the body, of animals, mountains, and forests, of water, walls, and trees.

Judging from what still remains, the art of painting was far less important and much less advanced among the Eastern or Oriental nations than were those of architecture and sculpture. It is very strange that these peoples, who seem to have observed nature closely, and to have mastered the mathematical sciences, made no steps toward the discovery of the laws of perspective; neither did they know how to give any expression of thought or feeling to the human face. In truth, their pictures were a mere repetition of set figures, and were only valuable as pieces of colored decorations for walls, adding a pleasing richness and variety by their different tints, but almost worthless as works of art.

## ANCIENT GREECE AND ITALY.

The painting of Greece and that of ancient Italy are so much the same that it is almost impossible to speak of them separately; the art of painting was carried from Greece to Italy by the Etruscans, and the art of ancient Rome was simply that of Greece transplanted. If Greek artists were employed by Romans, certainly their works were Greek; and if Romans painted they aimed to imitate the Greeks exactly, so that Italian painting before the time of the Christian era must be considered together with that of Greece.

In architecture and sculpture the ancient Greeks accepted what had been done by the Egyptians and Assyrians as a foundation, and went on to perfect the work of the older nations through the aid of poetic and artistic imaginations. But in painting the Greeks followed nothing that had preceded them. They were the first to make pictures which were a life-like reproduction of what they saw about them: they were the first to separate painting from sculpture, and to give it such importance as would permit it to have its own place, quite free from the influence of any other art, and in its own way as grand and as beautiful as its sister arts.

There are writers who trace the origin and progress of Greek painting from the very earliest times; but I shall begin with Apollodorus, who is spoken of as the first Greek painter worthy of fame, because he was the first one who knew how to make his pictures appear to be real, and to follow the rules of perspective so as to have a background from which his figures stood out, and to shade his colors and soften his outlines. He was very famous, and was called *skiagraphos*, which means shadow painter.

Apollodorus was an Athenian, and lived at about the close of the fifth century B.C. Although he was a remarkable artist then, we must not fancy that his pictures would have satisfied our idea of the beautiful—in fact, Pliny, the historian, who saw his pictures six hundred years later, at Pergamos, says that Apollodorus was but the gatekeeper who threw open the gates of painting to the famous artists who lived after him.

Zeuxis was a pupil of Apollodorus, and a great artist also. He was born at Heraclea, probably in Lower Italy. When young he led a wandering life; he studied at Athens under Apollodorus, and settled in Ephesus. He was in the habit of putting his pictures on exhibition, and charging an admittance fee, just as artists do now: he called himself "the unsurpassable," and said and did many vain and foolish things. Near the end of his life he considered his pictures as beyond any price, and so gave them away. Upon one of his works he wrote, "Easier to carp at than to copy." It is said that he actually laughed himself to death from amusement at one of his own pictures, which represented an old woman.

Zeuxis had a rival in the painter Parrhasius, and their names are often associated. On one occasion they made trial of their artistic skill. Zeuxis painted a bunch of grapes so naturally that the birds came to peck at them. Then Parrhasius painted a hanging curtain, and when his picture was exposed to the public Zeuxis asked him to draw aside his curtain, fully believing it to be of cloth and concealing a picture behind it. Thus it was judged that Parrhasius was the best artist, for he had deceived Zeuxis, while the latter had only deceived the birds.

From these stories it appears that these artists tried to imitate objects with great exactness. Parrhasius, too, was a vain man, and went about in a purple robe with a gold wreath about his head and gold clasps on his sandals; he painted his own portrait, and called it the god Hermes, or Mercury; he wrote praises of himself in which he called himself by many high-sounding names, for all of which he was much ridiculed by others.

However, both these artists were surpassed by Timanthes, according to the ancient writers, who relate that he engaged in a trial of skill with Parrhasius, and came off the victor in it. The fame of his picture of the "Sacrifice of Iphigenia" was very great, and its one excellence seems to have been in the varied expression of its faces. The descriptions of this great work lead to the belief that this Pompeian wall-painting, from which we give a cut, closely resembles that of Timanthes, which no longer exists.

The story of Iphigenia says that when her father, King Agamemnon, killed a hart which was sacred to Diana, or Artemis, that goddess becalmed his fleet so that he could not sail to Troy. Then the seer, Calchas, advised the king to sacrifice his daughter in order to appease the wrath of Diana. Agamemnon consented; but it is said that the goddess was so sorry for the maiden that she bore her away to Tauris, and made her a priestess, and left a hart to be sacrificed instead of Iphigenia. In our cut you see Calchas on the right; two men are bearing the maiden to her doom, while her father stands on the left with his head veiled from sight (Fig. 4).

Zeuxis, Parrhasius, and Timanthes belonged to the Ionian school of painting, which flourished during the Peloponnesian war. This school was excelled by that of Sikyon, which reached its highest prosperity between the end of the

FIG. 4.—SACRIFICE OF IPHIGENIA. *From a Pompeian wall-painting.*

Peloponnesian war and the death of Alexander the Great. The chief reason why this Dorian school at Sikyon was so fine was that here, for the first time, the pupils followed a regular course of study, and were trained in drawing and mathematics, and taught to observe nature with the strictest attention. The most famous master of this school was Pausias; some of his works were carried to Rome, where they were much admired. His picture of the garland-weaver, Glykera, gained him a great name, and by it he earned the earliest reputation as a flower-painter that is known in the history of art.

Nikomachos, who lived at Thebes about 360 B.C., was famous for the rapidity with which he painted pictures that were excellent in their completeness and beauty. Aristides, the son or brother of Nikomachos, was so good an artist that Attalus, king of Pergamos, offered more than twenty thousand pounds, or about one hundred thousand dollars, for his picture of Dionysus, or Bacchus. This wonderful picture was carried to Rome, and preserved in the temple of Ceres; but it no longer exists. Euphranor was another great painter, and was distinguished for his power to give great expression to the faces and a manly force to the figures which he painted.

Nikias, the Athenian, is said to have been so devoted to his art that he could think of nothing else: he would ask his servants if he had bathed or eaten, not being able to remember for himself. He was very rich, and when King Ptolemy of Egypt offered him more than sixty thousand dollars for his picture of Ulysses in the under-world, he refused this great sum, and gave the painting to his native city. Nikias seems to have greatly exalted and respected his art, for he contended that painters should not fritter away time and talent on insignificant subjects, but ought rather to choose some grand event, such as a battle or a sea-fight. His figures of women and his pictures of animals, especially those of dogs, were much praised. Some of his paintings were encaustic, that is to say, the colors were burned in; thus they must have been made on plaster or pottery of some sort. Nikias outlived Alexander the Great, and saw the beginning of the school of painters to which the great Apelles belonged—that which is called the Hellenic school, in which Greek art reached its highest point.

Apelles was the greatest of all Greek painters. He was born at Kolophon; but as he made his first studies at Ephesus he has been called an Ephesian: later he studied in the school of Sikyon, but even when a pupil there he was said to be the equal of all his instructors. Philip of Macedon heard of his fame, and persuaded Apelles to remove to his capital city, which was called Pella. While there Apelles became the friend of the young Alexander, and when the latter came to the throne he made Apelles his court-painter, and is said to have issued an edict forbidding all other artists from painting his portrait. Later on Apelles removed to Ephesus.

During the early part of his artistic life Apelles did little else than paint such pictures as exalted the fame of Philip, and afterward that of Alexander. He painted many portraits of both these great men; for one of Alexander he received nearly twenty-five thousand dollars; in it the monarch was represented as grasping the thunderbolt, as Jupiter might have done, and the hand appeared to be stretched out from the picture. This portrait was in the splendid temple of Diana, or Artemis, at Ephesus. Alexander was accustomed to say of it, "There are two Alexanders, one invincible, the living son of Philip—the other immutable, the picture of Apelles."

Later in his life Apelles painted many pictures of mythological subjects. He visited Alexandria, in Egypt; he did not win the favor of King Ptolemy, and his enemies in the Egyptian court played cruel practical jokes upon him. On one occasion he received an invitation to a feast at which the king had not desired his presence. The monarch was angry; but Apelles told him the truth, and appeased his wrath by sketching on the wall the exact likeness of the servant who had carried the invitation to him. However, Ptolemy remained unfavorable to him, and Apelles painted a great picture, called Calumny, in which he represented those who had been his enemies, and thus held them up to the scorn of the world. Apelles visited Rhodes and Athens, but is thought to have died in the island of Kos, where he had painted two very beautiful pictures of the goddess Venus. One of these is called the Venus Anadyomene, or Venus rising from the sea. The emperor Augustus carried this picture to Rome, and placed so high a value on it that he lessened the tribute-money of the people of Kos a hundred talents on account of it. This sum was about equal to one hundred thousand dollars of our money.

The art of Apelles was full of grace and sweetness, and the finish of his pictures was exquisite. The saying, "leave off in time," originated in his criticism of Protogenes, of whom he said that he was his superior except that he did not know when to leave off, and by too much finishing lessened the effect of his work. Apelles was modest and generous: he was the first to praise Protogenes, and conferred a great benefit upon the latter by buying up his pictures, and giving out word that he was going to sell them as his own. Apelles was never afraid to correct those who were ignorant, and was equally ready to learn from any one who could teach him anything. It is said that on one occasion, when Alexander was in his studio, and talked of art, Apelles advised him to be silent lest his color-grinder should laugh at him. Again, when he had painted a picture, and exposed it to public view, a cobbler pointed out a defect in the shoe-latchet; Apelles changed it, but when the man next proceeded to criticise the leg of the figure, Apelles replied, "Cobbler, stick to your last." These sayings have descended to our own day, and have become classical. All these anecdotes from so remote a time are in a sense doubtful; but they are very interesting—young people ought to be familiar with them, but it is also right to say that they are not known to be positively true.

Protogenes of Rhodes, to whom Apelles was so friendly, came to be thought a great painter. It is said that when Demetrius made war against Rhodes the artist did not trouble himself to leave his house, which was in the very midst of the enemy's camp. When questioned as to his fearlessness he replied, "Demetrius makes war against the Rhodians, and not against the Arts." It is also said that after hearing of this reply Demetrius refrained from burning the town, in order to preserve the pictures of Protogenes.

The ancient writers mention many other Greek painters, but none as important as those of whom we have spoken. Greek painting never reached a higher point than it had gained at the beginning of the Hellenistic age. Every kind of painting except landscape-painting had been practised by Greek artists; but that received no attention until figure-painting had declined. Vitruvius mentions that the ancients had some very important wall-paintings consisting of simple landscapes, and that others had landscape backgrounds with figures illustrating scenes from the poems of Homer. But we have no reason to believe that Greek landscape-painting was ever more than scenic or decorative work, and thus fell far short of what is now the standard for such painting.

The painting of the early Romans was principally derived from or through the early Etruscans, and the Etruscans are believed to have first learned their art from Greek artists, who introduced plastic art into Italy as early as B.C. 655, when Demaratus was expelled from Corinth—and later, Etruscan art was influenced by the Greek colonies of Magna Græcia. So it is fair to say that Etruscan art and early Roman art were essentially Greek art. The earliest artists who are known to have painted in Rome had Greek names, such as Ekphantos, Damophilos, and Gargasos. Later on in history there are painters mentioned with Latin names, but there is little of interest related concerning them; in truth, Ludius (who is also called by various authors Tadius and Studius) is the only really interesting ancient Roman painter of whom we know. He lived in the time of Augustus, and Pliny said of him: "Ludius, too, who lived in the age of the divine Augustus, must not be cheated of his fame. He was the first to bring in a singularly delightful fashion of wall-painting—villas, colonnades, examples of landscape-gardening, woods and sacred groves, reservoirs, straits, rivers, coasts, all according to the heart's desire—and amidst them passengers of all kinds on foot, in boats, driving in carriages, or riding on asses to visit their country properties; furthermore fishermen, bird-catchers, hunters, vintagers; or, again, he exhibits stately villas, to which the approach is through a swamp, with men staggering under the weight of the frightened women whom they have bargained to carry on their shoulders; and many another excellent and entertaining device of the same kind. The same artist also set the fashion of painting views—and that wonderfully cheap—of seaside towns in broad daylight."

We cannot think that Ludius was the first painter, though he may have been the first Roman painter, who made this sort of pictures, and he probably is the only one of whose work any part remains. Brunn and other good authorities believe that the wall-painting of Prima Porta, in Rome, was executed by Ludius. It represents a garden, and covers the four walls of a room. It is of the decorative order of painting, as Pliny well understood, for he speaks

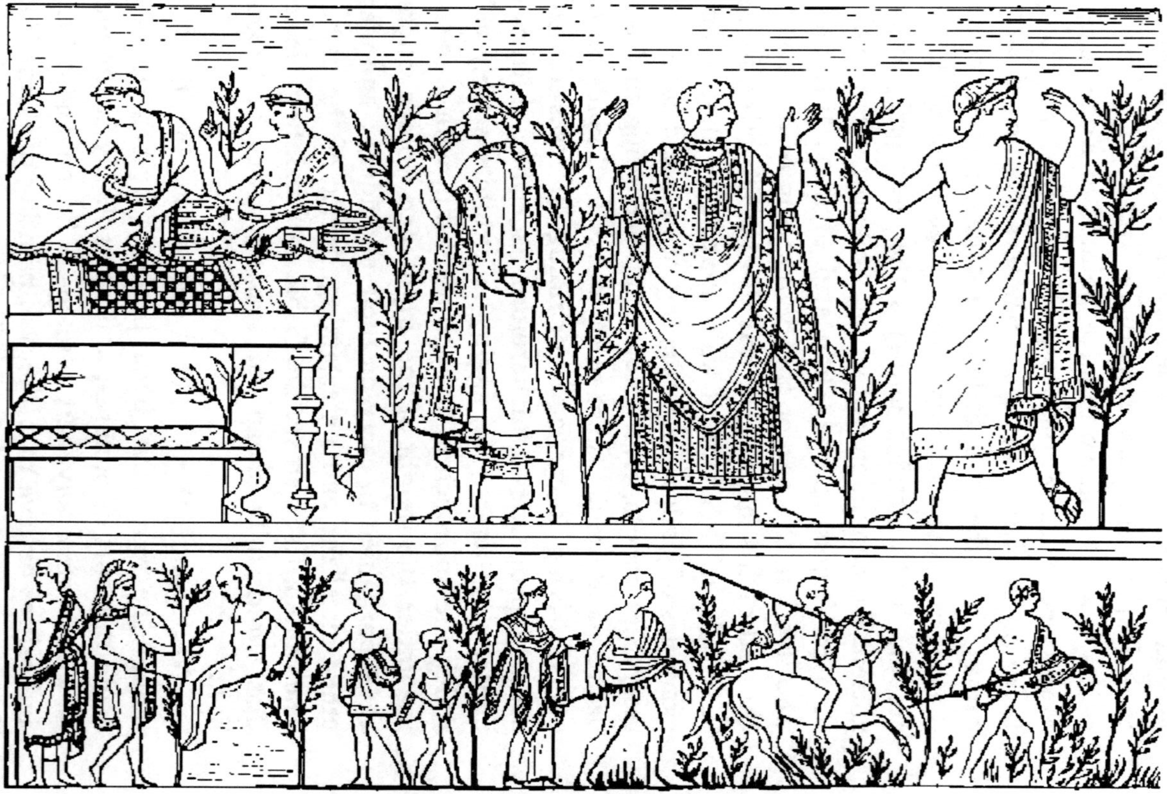

FIG. 5.—ETRUSCAN WALL-PAINTING.

of the difference between the work of Ludius and that of the true artists who painted panel pictures and not wall-paintings. After the time of Ludius we can give no trustworthy account of any fine, Roman painter.

The works of the ancient painters which still remain in various countries are wall-paintings, paintings on vases, mosaics, paintings on stone, and certain so-called miniatures; and besides these principal works there are many small articles, such as mirrors, toilet-cases, and other useful objects, which are decorated in colors.

We will first speak of the mural, or wall-paintings, as they are the most important and interesting remains of ancient painting. We shall only consider such as have been found in Italy, as those of other countries are few and unimportant.

The Etruscan tombs which have been opened contain many beautiful objects of various kinds, and were frequently decorated with mural pictures. They often consist of several rooms, and have the appearance of being prepared as a home for the living rather than for the dead. I shall give you no long or wordy description of them; because if what I tell you leads you to wish to know more about them, there are many excellent books describing them which you can read. So I will simply give you two cuts from these Etruscan paintings, and tell you about them.

Fig. 5 is in a tomb known as the *Grotta della Querciola.* The upper part represents a feast, and the lower portion a boar-hunt in a wood, which is indicated by the few trees and the little twigs which are intended to represent the underbrush of the forest. If we compare these pictures with the works of the best Italian masters, they seem very crude and almost childish in their simplicity; but, if we contrast them with the paintings of the Egyptians and Assyrians, we see that a great advance has been made since the earliest paintings of which we know were done.

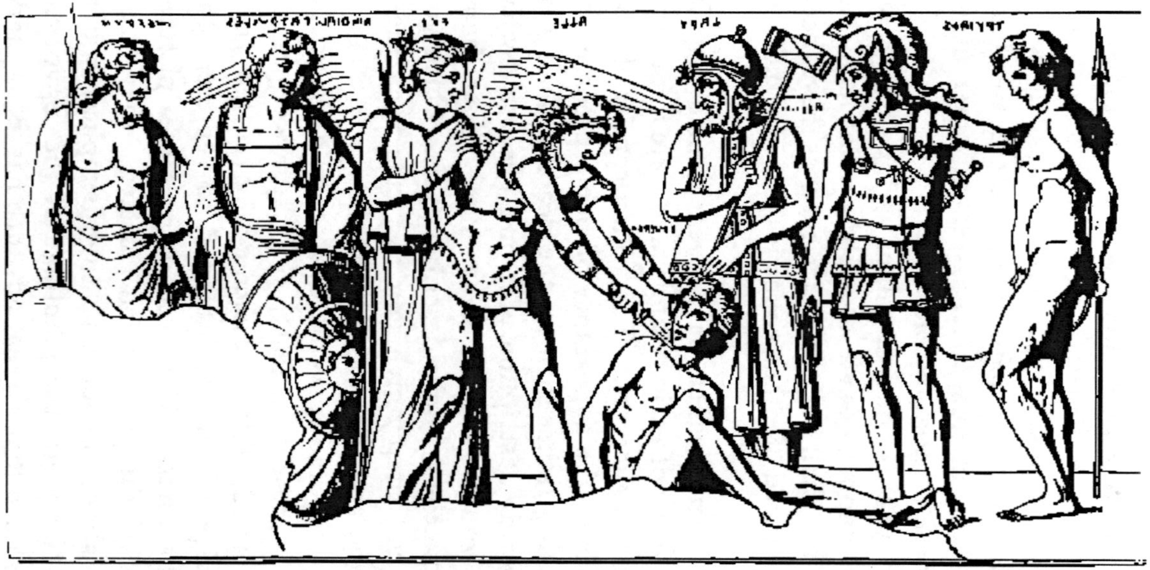

**Fig. 6.—Human Sacrifice Offered by Achilles to the Shade of Patroklos.** *From an Etruscan wall-painting.*

The pose and action of the figures and their grace of movement, as well as the folding of the draperies, are far better than anything earlier than the Greek painting of which there is any knowledge; for, as we have said, these Etruscan works are essentially Greek.

Fig. 6 belongs to a later period than the other, and is taken from a tomb at Vulci which was opened in 1857 by François. This tomb has seven different chambers, several of which are decorated with wall-paintings of mythological subjects. A square chamber at the end of the tomb has the most important pictures. On one side the human sacrifices which were customary at Etruscan funerals are represented: the pictures are very painful, and the terror and agony of the poor victims who are being put to death make them really repulsive to see. On an opposite wall is the painting from which our cut is taken. This represents the sacrifices made before Troy by Achilles, on account of the death of his dear friend Patroklos. The figure with the hammer is Charon, who stands ready to receive the sacrifice which is intended to win his favor. Your mythology will tell you the story, which is too long to be given here. The realism of this picture is shocking in its effect, and yet there is something about the manner of the drawing and the arrangement of the whole design that fixes our attention even while it makes us shudder.

The ancient wall-paintings which have been found in Rome are far more varied than are those of Etruria; for, while some of the Roman pictures are found in tombs, others are taken from baths, palaces, and villas. They generally belong to one period, and that is about the close of the Republic and the beginning of the Empire. Modern excavations have revealed many of these ancient paintings; but so many of them crumble and fade away so soon after they are exposed to the air, that few remain in a condition to afford any satisfaction in seeing them. But fortunately

FIG. 7.—THE ALDOBRANDINI MARRIAGE. *From a wall-painting in the Vatican.*

drawings have been made of nearly all these pictures before they fell into decay.

Some of the ancient paintings have been carefully removed from the walls where they were found, and placed in museums and other collections. One of the finest of these is in the Vatican, and is called the Aldobrandini Marriage. It received this name from the fact that Cardinal Aldobrandini was its first possessor after its discovery, near the Arch of Gallienus, in 1606.

As you will see from Fig. 7, from it, there are three distinct groups represented. In the centre the bride veiled, with her head modestly bowed down, is seated on a couch with a woman beside her who seems to be arranging some part of her toilet, while another stands near holding ointment and a bowl. At the head of the couch the bridegroom is seated on a threshold. The upper part of his figure is bare, and he has a garland upon his head. On the right of the picture an ante-room is represented in which are three women with musical instruments, singing sacrificial songs. To the left, in another apartment, three other women are preparing a bath. This is charming on account of the sweet, serious way in which the whole story is placed before us ; but as a painting it is an inferior work of art—not in the least above the style which we should call house decoration.

Although ancient writers had spoken of landscape paintings, it was not until 1848–1850, when a series of them was discovered on the Esquiline in Rome, that any very satisfactory specimens could be shown. These pictures number eight : six are complete, of the seventh but half remains, and the eighth is in a very imperfect state. They may be called historical landscapes, because each one has a complete landscape as well as figures which tell a story. They illustrate certain passages from the Odyssey of Homer. The one from which our cut is taken shows the visit of Ulysses to the lower world. When on the wall the pictures were

[illegible] ILLUSTRATION TO THE ODYSSEY. *From a wall-painting discovered on the Esquiline at Rome.*

divided by pilasters, and finished at the top by a border or frieze. The pilasters are bright red, and the chief colors in the picture are a yellowish brown and a greenish blue. In this scene the way in which the light streams through the entrance to the lower world is very striking, and shows the many figures there with the best possible effect. Even those in the far distance on the right are distinctly seen. This collection of Esquiline wall-paintings is now in the Vatican Library.

Besides the ancient mural paintings which have been placed in the museums of Rome, there are others which still remain where they were painted, in palaces, villas, and tombs. Perhaps those in the house of Livia are the most interesting; they represent mythological stories, and one frieze has different scenes of street life in an ancient town. Though these decorations are done in a mechanical sort of painting, such as is practised by the ordinary fresco painters of our own time, yet there was sufficient artistic feeling in their authors to prevent their repeating any one design.

One circumstance proves that this class of picture was not thought very important when it was made, which is that the name of the artist is rarely found upon his work: in but one instance either in Rome or Pompeii has this occurred, namely, in a chamber which was excavated in the gardens of the Farnesina Palace at Rome, and the name is Seleucus.

We have not space to speak of all the Italian cities in which these remains are discovered, and, as Pompeii is the one most frequently visited and that in which a very large proportion of the ancient pictures have been found, I will give a few illustrations from them, and leave the subject of ancient, mural paintings there. Many of the Pompeian pictures have been removed to the Museum of Naples, though many still remain where they were first painted.

The variety of subjects at Pompeii is large: there are landscapes, hunting scenes, mythological subjects, numerous kinds of single figures, such as dancing girls, the hours, or seasons, graces, satyrs, and many others; devotional pictures, such as representations of the ancient divinities, lares, penates, and genii; pictures of tavern scenes, of

FIG. 9.—THE FLIGHT OF ÆNEAS. *From a wall-painting.*

mechanics at their work; rope-dancers and representations of various games, gladiatorial contests, *genre* scenes from the lives of children, youths, and women, festival ceremonies, actors, poets, and stage scenes, and last, but not least, many caricatures, of which I here give you an example (Fig. 9).

The largest dog is Æneas, who leads the little Ascanius by the hand and carries his father, Anchises, on his shoulder. Frequently in the ancient caricatures monkeys are made to take the part of historical and imaginary heroes.

Fig. 11 shows you how these painted walls were some-

FIG. 10.—DEMETER ENTHRONED. *From a Pompeian wall-painting.*

times divided; the principal subjects were surrounded by ornamental borders, and the spaces between filled in with all sorts of little compartments. The small spaces in this picture are quite regular in form; but frequently they are of varied shapes, and give a very decorative effect to the

FIG. 11.—POMPEIAN WALL-PAINTING.

whole work. The colors used upon these different panels, as they may be called, were usually red, yellow, black, and white—more rarely blue and green. Sometimes the entire decoration consisted of these small, variously colored spaces, divided by some graceful little border, with a very small figure, plant, or other object in the centre of each space.

Fig. 10, of Demeter, or Ceres, enthroned is an example of such devotional paintings as were placed above the altars and shrines for private worship in the houses of Pompeii, or at the street corners, just as we now see pictures and sacred figures in street shrines in Roman Catholic countries. In ancient days, as now, these pictures were often done in a coarse and careless manner, as if religious use, and not art, was the object in the mind of the artist.

Fig. 12, of a Nest of Cupids is a very interesting example of Pompeian painting, and to my mind it more nearly resembles pictures of later times than does any other ancient painting of which I know.

## MOSAICS.

The pictures known as mosaics are made by fitting together bits of marble, stone, or glass of different colors and so arranging them as to represent figures and objects of various kinds, so that at a distance they have much the same effect as that of pictures painted with brush and colors. The art of making mosaics is very ancient, and was probably invented in the East, where it was used for borders and other decorations in regular set patterns. It was not until after the time of Alexander the Great that the Greeks used this process for making pictures. At first, too, mosaics were used for floors or pavements only, and the designs in them were somewhat like those of the tile pavements of our own time.

This picture of doves will give you a good idea of a mosaic; this subject is a very interesting one, because it is said to have been first made by Sosos in Pergamos. It was often repeated in later days, and that from which our cut is taken was found in the ruins of Hadrian's villa at Tivoli, near Rome; it is known as the Capitoline Doves, from the fact that it is now in the Capitoline Museum in Rome. Few works of ancient art are more admired and as frequently copied as this mosaic: it is not unusual to see ladies wear brooches with this design in fine mosaic work.

A few examples of ancient mosaics which were used for wall decorations have been found; they may almost be said not to exceed a dozen; but pavement mosaics are very

FIG. 13.—DOVES SEATED ON A BOWL. *From a mosaic picture in the Capitol, Rome.*

numerous, and are still seen in the places for which they were designed and where they have been during many centuries, as well as in museums to which they have been removed. They are so hard in outline and so mechanical in every way that they are not very attractive if we think of them as pictures, and their chief interest is in the skill and patience with which mosaic workers combine the numberless particles of one substance and another which go to make up the whole.

Mosaic pictures, as a rule, are not large; but one found at Palestrina, which is called the Nile mosaic, is six by five metres inside. Its subject is the inundation of a village on the river Nile. There are an immense number of figures and a variety of scenes in it; there are Egyptians hunting the Nile horse, a party of revellers in a bower draped with vines, bands of warriors and other groups of men occupied in different pursuits, and all represented at the season when the Nile overflows its banks. This is a very remarkable work, and it has been proved that a portion of the original is in the Berlin Museum, and has been replaced by a copy at Palestrina.

## PAINTINGS ON STONE.

It is well known that much of the decoration of Greek edifices was in colors. Of course these paintings were put upon the marble and stone of which the structures were made. The Greeks also made small pictures and painted them on stone, just as canvas and panels of wood are now used. Such painted slabs have been found in Herculaneum, in Corneto, and in different Etruscan tombs; but the most important and satisfactory one was found at Pompeii in 1872. Since then the colors have almost vanished; but Fig. 14, from it, will show you how it appeared when found. It represents the mythological story of the punishment of Niobe, and is very beautiful in its design.

## VASE-PAINTING.

Vase-painting was another art very much practised by the ancients. So much can be said of it that it would require more space than we can give for its history even in outline. So I shall only say that it fills an important place

FIG. 14.—NIOBE. *From a picture on a slab of granite at Pompeii.*

in historic art, because from the thousands of ancient vases that have been found in one country and another, much has been learned concerning the history of these lands and the manners and customs of their people ; occasionally inscriptions are found upon decorated vases which are of great value to scholars who study the history of the past.

The Dodwell vase shows you the more simple style of decoration which was used in the earlier times. Gradually the designs came to be more and more elaborate, until whole stories were as distinctly told by the pictures on vases as if they had been written out in books. The next

FIG. 15.—THE DODWELL VASE. *At Munich.*

cut, which is made from a vase-painting, will show what I mean.

The subject of Fig. 16 is connected with the service of the dead, and shows a scene in the under world, such as accorded with ancient religious notions. In the upper portion the friends of the deceased are grouped around a little temple. Scholars trace the manufacture of these vases back to very ancient days, and down to its decline, about two centuries before Christ. I do not mean that vase-painting ceased then, for its latest traces come down to 65 B.C.; but like all other ancient arts, it was then in a state of de-

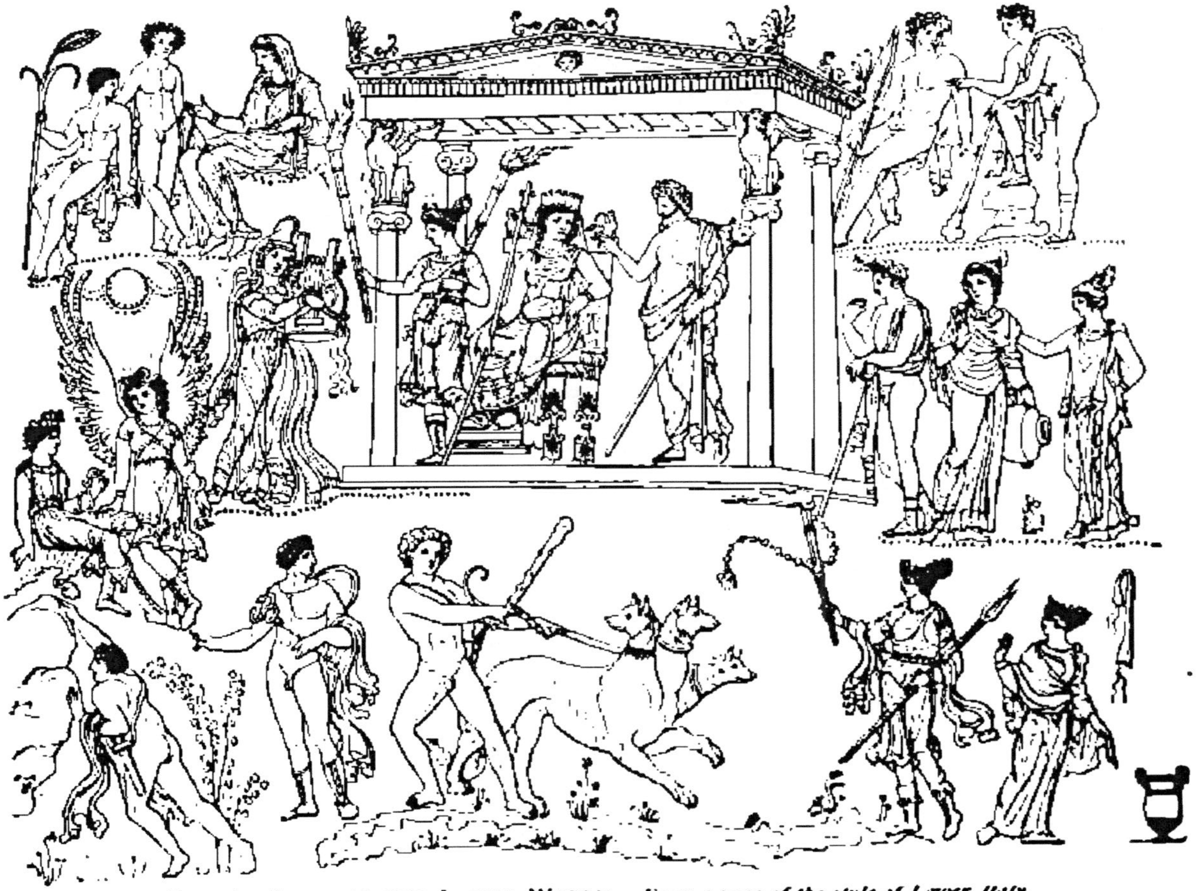

FIG. 16.—SCENE IN THE LOWER WORLD. *From a vase of the style of Lower Italy.*

cadence. Though vase-painting was one of the lesser arts, its importance can scarcely be overestimated, and it fully merits the devoted study and admiration which it receives from those who are learned in its history.

From what we know of ancient Greek painting we may believe that this art first reached perfection in Greece. If we could see the best works of Apelles, who reached the highest excellence of any Greek painter, we might find some lack of the truest science of the art when judged by more modern standards ; but the Greeks must still be credited with having been the first to create a true art of painting. After the decline of Greek art fifteen centuries elapsed before painting was again raised to the rank which the Greeks had given it, and if, according to our ideas, the later Italian painting is in any sense superior to the Greek, we must at least admit that the study of the works of antiquity which still remained in Italy, excited the great masters of the Renaissance to the splendid achievements which they attained.

## CHAPTER II.

### MEDIÆVAL PAINTING, FROM THE BEGINNING OF THE CHRISTIAN ERA TO THE RENAISSANCE.

THE Middle Ages extend from the latter part of the fifth century to the time of the Renaissance, or about the fifteenth century. The painting of this period has little to attract attention if regarded only from an artistic standpoint, for we may truly say that, comparing it with the Greek art which had preceded it, or with the Italian art which followed it, that of the Middle Ages had no claim to the beautiful. On the other hand, it is full of interest to students, because it has its part in the history of art; therefore I shall give a mere outline of it, so that this link in the chain which unites ancient and modern painting may not be entirely wanting in our book.

Early mediæval painting, down to about A.D. 950, consists principally of paintings in burial-places, mosaics (usually in churches), and of miniatures, or the illustration and illumination of *MSS.*, which were the books of that time, and were almost without exception religious writings. This period is called the Early Period of the Middle Ages, and the pictures are often called the works of Early Christian Art.

About 1050 a revival of intellectual pursuits began in some parts of Europe, and from that time it may be said that the Renaissance, or new birth of art and letters, was in its A B Cs, or very smallest beginnings. The period between 950 and 1250 is often called the Central or Romanesque Period of the Middle Ages, and it was during this time that glass-painting originated; it is one of the most interesting features of art in mediæval times.

From 1250 to 1400 comes the Final or Gothic Period of the Middle Ages, and this has some very interesting features which foretell the coming glory of the great Renaissance.

## THE EARLY PERIOD.

The paintings of the catacombs date from the third and fourth centuries after Christ. The catacombs, or burial-places of the early Christians, consist of long, narrow, subterranean passages, cut with regularity, and crossing each other like streets in a city. The graves are in the sides of these passages, and there are some larger rooms or chambers into which the narrow passages run. There are about sixty of the catacombs in and near Rome; they are generally called by the name of some saint who is buried in them. The paintings are in the chambers, of which there are sometimes several quite near each other. The reason for their being in these underground places was that Christians were so persecuted under the Romans, that they were obliged to do secretly all that they did as Christians, so that no attention should be attracted to them.

The principal characteristics of these pictures are a simple majesty and earnestness of effect; perhaps spirituality is the word to use, for by these paintings the early Christians desired to express their belief in the religion of Christ, and especially in the immortality of the soul, which was a very precious doctrine to them. The catacombs of Rome were more numerous and important than those of any other city.

Many of the paintings in the catacombs had a symbolic meaning, beyond the plainer intention which appeared at the first sight of them: you will know what I mean when I

FIG. 17.—MOSES. *From a painting in the Catacomb of S. Agnes.*

say that not only was this picture of Moses striking the rock intended to represent an historical fact in the life of Moses, but the flowing water was also regarded as a type of the blessing of Christian baptism.

The walls of the chambers of the catacombs are laid out

FIG. 18.—DECORATION OF A ROOF. *Catacomb of S. Domitilla.*

in such a manner as to have the effect of decorated apartments, just as was done in the pagan tombs, and sometimes the pictures were a strange union of pagan and Christian devices.

The above cut, from the Catacomb of S. Domitilla, has in

the centre the pagan god Orpheus playing his lyre, while in the alternate compartments of the border are the following Christian subjects: 1, David with the Sling; 2, Moses Striking the Rock; 3, Daniel in the Lion's Den; 4, The Raising of Lazarus. The other small divisions have pictures of sacrificial animals. These two cuts will give you an idea of the catacomb wall-paintings.

The mosaics of the Middle Ages were of a purely ornamental character down to the time of Constantine. Then, when the protection of a Christian emperor enabled the Christians to express themselves without fear, the doctrines of the church and the stories of the life of Christ and the histories of the saints, as well as many other instructive religious subjects, were made in mosaics, and placed in prominent places in churches and basilicas. Mosaics are very durable, and many belonging to the early Christian era still remain.

The mosaics at Ravenna form the most connected series, and are the best preserved of those that still exist. While it is true in a certain sense that Rome was always the art centre of Italy, it is also true that at Ravenna the works of art have not suffered from devastation and restoration as have those of Rome. After the invasion of the Visigoths in A.D. 404, Honorius transferred the imperial court to Ravenna, and that city then became distinguished for its learning and art. The Ravenna mosaics are so numerous that I shall only speak of one series, from which I give an illustration (Fig. 19).

This mosaic is in the church of S. Vitalis, which was built between A.D. 526 and 547. In the dome of the church there is a grand representation of Christ enthroned; below Him are the sacred rivers of Paradise; near Him are two angels and S. Vitalis, to whom the Saviour is presenting a crown; Bishop Ecclesius, the founder of the church, is also represented near by with a model of the church in his hand.

On a lower wall there are two pictures in which the Emperor Justinian and the Empress Theodosia are represented: our cut is from one of these, and shows the emperor and empress in magnificent costumes, each followed by a train of attendants. This emperor never visited Ravenna; but he sent such rich gifts to this church that he and his wife are represented as its donors.

After the time of Justinian (A.D. 527–565) mosaics be-

FIG. 19.—JUSTINIAN, THEODORA, AND ATTENDANTS. *From a mosaic picture at S. Vitalis, Ravenna.*

gan to be less artistic, and those of the later time degenerated, as did everything else during the Middle or Dark Ages, and at last all works of art show less and less of the Greek or Classic influence.

When we use the word miniature as an art term, it does not mean simply a small picture as it does in ordinary conversation; it means the pictures executed by the hand of an illuminator or *miniator* of manuscripts, and he is so called from the *minium* or cinnabar which he used in making colors.

In the days of antiquity, as I have told you in speaking of Egypt, it was customary to illustrate manuscripts, and during the Middle Ages this art was very extensively practised. Many monks spent their whole lives in illuminating religious books, and in Constantinople and other eastern cities this art reached a high degree of perfection. Some manuscripts have simple borders and colored initial letters only; sometimes but a single color is used, and is generally red, from which comes our word rubric, which means any writing or printing in red ink, and is derived from the Latin *rubrum*, or red. This was the origin of illumination or miniature-painting, which went on from one step to another until, at its highest state, most beautiful pictures were painted in manuscripts in which rich colors were used on gold or silver backgrounds, and the effect of the whole was as rich and ornamental as it is possible to imagine.

Many of these old manuscripts are seen in museums, libraries, and various collections; they are very precious and costly, as well as interesting; their study is fascinating, for almost every one of the numberless designs that are used in them has its own symbolic meaning. The most ancient, artistic miniatures of which we know are those on a manuscript of a part of the book of Genesis; it is in the Imperial Library at Vienna, and was made at the end of the fifth century. In the same collection there is a very extraordinary manuscript, from which I give an illustration.

This manuscript is a treatise on botany, and was written by Dioskorides for his pupil, the Princess Juliana Anicia, a granddaughter of the Emperor Valentine III. As this princess died at Constantinople A.D. 527, this manuscript dates from the beginning of the sixth century. This picture from it represents Dioskorides dressed in white robes and seated in a chair of gold; before him stands a woman in a gold tunic and scarlet mantle, who represents the genius of discovery; she presents the legendary mandrake root, or mandragora, to the learned man, while between them is the dog that has pulled the root, and falls dead, according to the fabulous story. This manuscript was painted by a masterly

FIG. 20.—THE DISCOVERY OF THE HERB MANDRAGORA. *From a MS. of Dioskorides, at Vienna.*

hand, and is curious and interesting; the plants, snakes, birds, and insects must have been painted from nature, and the whole is most skilfully done.

During the Middle Ages the arts as practised in Rome were carried into all the different countries in which the Romans made conquests or sent their monks and missionaries to establish churches, convents, and schools. Thus the mediæval arts were practised in Gaul, Spain, Germany, and Great Britain. No wall-paintings or mosaics remain from the early German or Celtic peoples; but their illuminated manuscripts are very numerous: miniature-painting was extensively done in Ireland, and many Irish manuscripts remain in the collections of Great Britain.

When Charlemagne became the king of the Franks in 768, there was little knowledge of any art among his northern subjects; in 800 he made himself emperor of the Romans, also, and when the Franks saw all the splendor of Rome and other parts of Italy, it was not difficult for the great emperor to introduce the arts into the Frankish portion of his empire. All sorts of beautiful objects were carried from Italy by the Franks, and great workshops were established at Aix-la-Chapelle, the capital, and were placed under the care of Eginhard, who was skilled in bronze-casting, modelling, and other arts; he was called Bezaleel, after the builder of the Tabernacle. We have many accounts of the wall-paintings and mosaics of the Franks; but there are no remains of them that can be identified with positive accuracy.

Miniature-painting flourished under the rule of Charlemagne and his family, and reached a point of great magnificence in effect, though it was never as artistic as the work of the Italian miniators; and, indeed, gradually everything connected with art was declining in all parts of the world; and as we study its history, we can understand why the terms Dark Ages and Middle Ages are used to denote the same epoch, remarkable as it is for the decay and extinction of so many beautiful things.

## THE CENTRAL, OR ROMANESQUE PERIOD.

During the Romanesque Period (950–1250) architecture was pursued according to laws which had grown out of the achievements and experiences of earlier ages, and had reached such a perfection as entitled it to the rank of a noble art. But this was not true of painting, which was then but little more than the painting of the Egyptians had been, that is, a sort of picture-writing, which was principally used to illustrate the doctrines of religion, and by this means to teach them to peoples who had no books, and could not have read them had they existed.

During all this time the art of painting was largely under the control of the priests. Some artists were priests themselves, and those who were not were under the direction of some church dignitary. Popes, bishops, abbots, and so on, were the principal patrons of art, and they suggested to the artists the subjects to be painted, and then the pictures were used for the decoration of churches and other buildings used by the religious orders. The monks were largely occupied in miniature-painting; artists frequented the monasteries, and, indeed, when they were engaged upon religious subjects, they were frequently under the same discipline as that of the monks themselves.

Next to the influence of the church came that of the court; but in a way it was much the same, for the clergy had great influence at court, and, although painting was used to serve the luxury of sovereigns and nobles, it was also true that these high personages often employed artists to decorate chapels and to paint altar-pieces for churches at their expense, for during the Romanesque period there was some painting on panels. At first these panel-pictures were placed on the front of the altar where draperies had formerly been used: later they were raised above the altar.

and also put in various parts of the church. The painting of the Romanesque period was merely a decline, and there can be little more said of it than is told by that one word.

Glass-painting dates from this time. The very earliest specimens of which we know are from the eleventh century. Before that time there had been transparent mosaics made by putting together bits of colored glass, and arranging them in simple, set and ornamental patterns. Such mosaics date from the earliest days of Christianity, and were in use as soon as glass was used for windows. From ancient writings we know that some windows were made with pictures upon them as long ago as A.D. 989; but nothing now remains from that remote date.

FIG. 21—KING DAVID. *From a window in Augsburg Cathedral.*

There is a doubt as to whether glass-painting originated in France or Germany. Some French authors ascribe its invention to Germany, while some German writers accord the same honor to France. Remains of glass-painting of the eleventh century have been found in both these countries; but it is probable that five windows in the Cathedral of Augsburg date from 1065, and are a little older than any others of which we know. This picture of David is from one of them, and is probably as old as any painted window in existence.

The oldest glass-painting in France is probably a single fragment in the Cathedral of Le Mans. This cathedral was completed in 1093, but was badly burned in 1136, so that but a single piece of its windows remains; this has

FIG. 22.—WINDOW. *From the Cathedral of St. Denis.*

been inserted in a new window in the choir, and is thus preserved. With the beginning of the twelfth century, glass-painting became more frequent in Europe, and near the end of this century it was introduced into England, together with the Gothic style of architecture. Very soon a highly decorative effect was given to glass-painting, and the designs upon many windows were very much like those used in the miniatures of the same time. The stained glass in the Cathedral of St. Denis, near Paris, is very important. It dates from about 1140–1151, and was executed under the care of the famous Abbot Suger. He employed both French and German workmen, and decorated the entire length of the walls with painted windows. St. Denis was the first French cathedral in the full Gothic style of architecture. The present windows in St. Denis can scarcely be said to be the original ones, as the cathedral has suffered much from revolutions; but some of them have been restored as nearly as possible, and our illustration (Fig. 22) will give you a good idea of what its windows were.

The stripes which run across the ground in this window are red and blue, and the leaf border is in a light tone of color. There are nine medallions; the three upper ones have simply ornamental designs upon them, and the six lower ones have pictures of sacred subjects. The one given here is an Annunciation, in which the Abbot Suger kneels at the feet of the Virgin Mary. His figure interferes with the border of the medallion in a very unusual manner.

Perhaps the most important ancient glass-painting remaining in France is that of the west front of the Cathedral of Chartres. It dates from about 1125, when this front was begun; there are three windows, and their color is far superior to the glass of a later period, which is in the same cathedral. The earliest painted glass in England dates from about 1180. Some of the windows in Canterbury Cathedral correspond to those in the Cathedral of St. Denis.

In the Strasbourg Cathedral there are some splendid remains of painted glass of the Romanesque period, although they were much injured by the bombardment of 1870. Fig. 23 is from one of the west windows, and represents King Henry I.

This is an unusually fine example of the style of the period before the more elaborate Gothic manner had arisen; the quiet regularity of the drapery and the dignified air of the whole figure is very impressive.

An entirely different sort of colored windows was used in the churches and edifices which belonged to the Cistercian order of monks. The rule of this order was severe, and while they wished to soften the light within their churches, they believed it to be wrong to use anything which denoted pomp or splendor in the decoration of the house of God. For these reasons they invented what is called the *grisaille* glass: it is painted in regular patterns in gray tones of color. Sometimes these windows are varied by a leaf pattern in shades of green and brown, with occasional touches of bright color; but this is used very sparingly. Some of these *grisaille* windows are seen in France; but the finest are in Germany in the Cathedral of Heiligenkreuz: they date from the first half of the thirteenth century.

## THE FINAL, OR GOTHIC PERIOD.

The Gothic order of architecture, which was perfected during this period, had a decided influence upon the painting and sculpture of the time; but this influence was not felt until Gothic architecture had reached a high point in its development. France was now the leading country of the world, and Paris came to be the most important of all cities: it was the centre from which went forth edicts as to the customs of society, the laws of dress and conduct, and even of the art of love. From France came the codes of chivalry,

FIG. 23.—FIGURE OF HENRY I. IN WEST WINDOW OF STRASBOURG CATHEDRAL.

and the crusades, which spread to other lands, originated there. Thus, for the time, Paris overshadowed Rome and the older centres of art, industry, and science, with a world-wide influence.

Although the painting of this period had largely the same characteristics as that of the Romanesque period, it had a different spirit, and it was no longer under the control of the clergy. Before this time, too, painters had frequently been skilled in other arts; now it became the custom for them to be painters only, and besides this they were divided into certain classes of painters, and were then associated with other craftsmen who were engaged in the trade which was connected with their art. That is, the glass-painters painted glass only, and were associated with the glass-blowers; those who decorated shields, with the shield or scutcheon makers, and so on; while the painters, pure and simple, worked at wall-painting, and a little later at panel-painting also. From this association of artists and tradesmen there grew up brotherhoods which supported their members in all difficulties, and stood by each other like friends. Each brotherhood had its altar in some church; they had their funerals and festivals in common, and from these brotherhoods grew up the more powerful societies which were called guilds. These guilds became powerful organizations; they had definite rights and duties, and even judicial authority as to such matters as belonged to their special trades.

All this led to much greater individuality among artists than had ever existed before: it came to be understood that a painter could, and had a right to, paint a picture as he wished, and was not governed by any priestly law. Religious subjects were still painted more frequently than others, and the decoration of religious edifices was the chief employment of the artists; but they worked with more independence of thought and spirit. The painters studied

FIG. 24.—BIRTH OF THE VIRGIN. *From the Grandes Heures of the Duc de Berri.*

more from nature, and though the change was very slow, it is still true that a certain softness of effect, an easy flow of drapery, and a new grace of pose did appear, and about A.D. 1350 a new idea of the uses and aims of painting influenced artists everywhere.

About that time they attempted to represent distances, and to create different planes in their works; to reproduce such things as they represented far more exactly than they had done before, and to put them in just relations to surrounding places and objects; in a word, they seemed to awake to an appreciation of the true office of painting and to its infinite possibilities.

During this Gothic period some of the most exquisite manuscripts were made in France and Germany, and they are now the choicest treasures of their kind in various European collections.

Fig. 24, of the birth of the Virgin Mary, is from one of the most splendid books of the time which was painted for the Duke de Berry and called the Great Book of the Hours. The wealth of ornament in the border is a characteristic of the French miniatures of the time. The Germans used a simpler style, as you will see by Fig. 25, of the Annunciation.

The influence of the Gothic order of architecture upon glass-painting was very pronounced. Under this order the windows became much more important than they had been, and it was not unusual to see a series of windows painted in such pictures as illustrated the whole teaching of the doctrines of the church. It was at this time that the custom arose of donating memorial windows to religious edifices. Sometimes they were the gift of a person or a family, and the portraits of the donors were painted in the lower part of the window, and usually in a kneeling posture; at other times windows were given by guilds, and it is very odd to see craftsmen of various sorts at work in a cathedral window: such pictures exist at Chartres, Bourges, Amiens, and other places.

About A.D. 1300 it began to be the custom to represent architectural effects upon colored windows. Our cut is

FIG. 25.—THE ANNUNCIATION. *From the Mariale of Archbishop Arnestus of Prague.*

from a window at Konigsfelden, and will show exactly what I mean (Fig. 26.)

This style of decoration was not as effective as the earlier ones had been, and, indeed, from about this time glass-painting became less satisfactory than before, from the fact that it had more resemblance to panel-painting, and so lost a part of the individuality which had belonged to it.

Wall-paintings were rare in the Gothic period, for its architecture left no good spaces where the pictures could be

FIG. 26.—PAINTED WINDOW AT KONIGSFELDEN.

placed, and so the interior painting of the churches was almost entirely confined to borders and decorative patterns scattered here and there and used with great effect. In Germany and England wall-painting was more used for the decoration of castles, halls, chambers, and chapels; but as a whole mural painting was of little importance at this time in comparison with its earlier days.

About A.D. 1350 panel pictures began to be more numerous, and from this time there are vague accounts of schools of painting at Prague and Cologne, and a few remnants exist which prove that such works were executed in France and Flanders; but I shall pass over what is often called the Transitional Period, by which we mean the time

FIG. 27.—PORTRAIT OF CIMABUE.

in which new influences were beginning to act, and hereafter I will tell our story by giving accounts of the lives of separate painters; for from about the middle of the thirteenth century it is possible to trace the history of painting through the study of individual artists.

GIOVANNI CIMABUE, the first painter of whom I shall tell you, was born in Florence in 1240. He is sometimes called the "Father of Modern Painting," because he was the first who restored that art to any degree of the beauty to which it had attained before the Dark Ages. The Cimabui were a noble family, and Giovanni was allowed to follow his own taste, and became a painter; he was also skilled in mosaic work, and during the last years of his life held the office of master of the mosaic workers in the Cathedral of Pisa, where some of his own mosaics still remain.

Of his wall-paintings I shall say nothing except to tell you that the finest are in the Upper Church at Assisi, where one sees the first step in the development of the art of Tuscany. But I wish to tell the story of one of his panel pictures, which is very interesting. It is now in the Rucellai Chapel of the Church of Santa Maria Novella, in Florence, and it is only just in me to say that if one of my readers walked through that church and did not know about this picture, it is doubtful if he would stop to look at it—certainly he would not admire it. The story is that when Cimabue was about thirty years old he was busy in painting this picture of the Madonna Enthroned, and he would not allow any one to see what he was doing.

It happened, however, that Charles of Anjou, being on his way to Naples, stopped in Florence, where the nobles did everything in their power for his entertainment. Among other places they took him to the studio of Cimabue, who uncovered his picture for the first time. Many persons then flocked to see it, and were so loud in their joyful expressions of admiration for it that the part of the city in which the studio was has since been called the *Borgo Allegri*, or the "joyous quarter."

When the picture was completed the day was celebrated as a festival; a procession was formed; bands of music played joyful airs; the magistrates of Florence honored the occasion with their presence; and the picture was borne in triumph to the church. Cimabue must have been very happy at this great appreciation of his art, and from that time he was famous in all Italy.

FIG. 28.—THE MADONNA OF THE CHURCH OF SANTA MARIA NOVELLA.

Another madonna by this master is in the Academy of Florence, and one attributed to him is in the Louvre, in Paris.

Cimabue died about 1302, and was buried in the Church of Santa Maria del Fiore, or the Cathedral of Florence. Above his tomb these words were inscribed: "Cimabue thought himself master of the field of painting. While living, he was so. Now he holds his place among the stars of heaven."

Other artists who were important in this early time of the revival of painting were ANDREA TAFI, a mosaist of Florence, MARGARITONE OF AREZZO, GUIDO OF SIENA, and of the same city DUCCIO, the son of Buoninsegna. This last painter flourished from 1282 to 1320; his altarpiece for the Cathedral of Siena was also carried to its place in solemn procession, with the sound of trumpet, drum, and bell.

GIOTTO DI BONDONE was the next artist in whom we have an unusual interest. He was born at Del Colle, in the commune of Vespignano, probably about 1266, though the date is usually given ten years later. One of the best reasons for calling Cimabue the "Father of Painting" is that he acted the part of a father to Giotto, who proved to be so great an artist that from his time painting made a rapid advance. The story is that one day when Cimabue rode in the valley of Vespignano he saw a shepherd-boy who was drawing a portrait of one of his sheep on a flat rock, by means of a pointed bit of slate for a pencil. The sketch was so good that Cimabue offered to take the boy to Florence, and teach him to paint. The boy's father consented, and henceforth the little Giotto lived with Cimabue, who instructed him in painting, and put him to study letters under Brunetto Latini, who was also the teacher of the great poet, Dante.

The picture which we give here is from the earliest work

FIG. 29—PORTRAIT OF DANTE, PAINTED BY GIOTTO.

5

by Giotto of which we have any knowledge. In it were the portraits of Dante, Latini, and several others. This picture was painted on a wall of the Podestà at Florence, and when Dante was exiled from that city his portrait was covered with whitewash; in 1841 it was restored to the light, having been hidden for centuries. It is a precious memento of the friendship between the great artist and the divine poet, who expressed his admiration of Giotto in these lines:—

"In painting Cimabue fain had thought
To lord the field; now Giotto has the cry,
So that the other's fame in shade is brought."

Giotto did much work in Florence; he also, about 1300, executed frescoes in the Lower Church at Assisi; from 1303–1306 he painted his beautiful pictures in the Cappella dell' Arena, at Padua, by which the genius of Giotto is now most fully shown. He worked at Rimini also, and about 1330 was employed by King Robert of Naples, who conferred many honors upon him, and made him a member of his own household. In 1334 Giotto was made the chief master of the cathedral works in Florence, as well as of the city fortifications and all architectural undertakings by the city authorities. He held this high position but three years, as he died on January 8, 1337.

Giotto was also a great architect, as is well known from his tower in Florence, for which he made all the designs and a part of the working models, while some of the sculptures and reliefs upon it prove that he was skilled in modeling and carving. He worked in mosaics also, and the famous "Navicella," in the vestibule of St. Peter's at Rome, was originally made by him, but has now been so much restored that it is doubtful if any part of what remains was done by Giotto's hands.

The works of Giotto are too numerous to be men-

FIG. 30.—GIOTTO'S CAMPANILE AND THE DUOMO. *Florence.*

tioned here, and his merits as an artist too important to be discussed in our limits; but his advance in painting was so great that he deserved the great compliment of Cennino, who said that Giotto "had done or translated the art of painting from Greek into Latin."

I shall, however, tell you of one excellent thing that he did, which was to make the representation of the crucifix far more refined and Christ-like than it had ever been. Before his time every effort had been made to picture physical agony alone. Giotto gave a gentle face, full of suffering, it is true, but also expressive of tenderness and resignation, and it would not be easy to paint a better crucifix than those of this master.

In person Giotto was so ugly that his admirers made jokes about it; but he was witty and attractive in conversation, and so modest that his friends were always glad to praise him while he lived, and since his death his fame has been cherished by all who have written of him. There are many anecdotes told of Giotto. One is that on a very hot day in Naples, King Robert said to the painter, "Giotto, if I were you, I would leave work, and rest." Giotto quickly replied, "So would I, sire, *if I were you.*"

When the same king asked him to paint a picture which would represent his kingdom, Giotto drew an ass bearing a saddle on which were a crown and sceptre, while at the feet of the ass there was a new saddle with a shining new crown and sceptre, at which the ass was eagerly smelling. By this he intended to show that the Neapolitans were so fickle that they were always looking for a new king.

There is a story which has been often repeated which says, that in order to paint his crucifixes so well, he persuaded a man to be bound to a cross for an hour as a model; and when he had him there he stabbed him, in order to see such agony as he wished to paint. When the Pope saw the picture he was so pleased with it that he wished to have it for his own chapel; then Giotto confessed what he had done, and showed the body of the dead man. The Pope was so angry that he threatened the painter with the same death, upon which Giotto brushed the picture over so that it seemed to be destroyed. Then the Pope so regretted the loss of the crucifix that he promised to pardon Giotto if he would paint him another as good. Giotto exacted the promise in writing, and then, with a wet sponge, removed the wash he had used, and the picture was as good as before. According to tradition all famous crucifixes were drawn from this picture ever after.

When Boniface VIII. sent a messenger to invite Giotto to Rome, the messenger asked Giotto to show him something of the art which had made him so famous. Giotto, with a pencil, by a single motion drew so perfect a circle that it was thought to be a miracle, and this gave rise to a proverb still much used in Italy:—*Piu tondo che l'O di Giotto*, or, "Rounder than the O of Giotto."

Giotto had a wife and eight children, of whom nothing is known but that his son Francesco became a painter. Giotto died in 1337, and was buried with great honors in the Church of Santa Maria del Fiore. Lorenzo de Medici erected a monument to his memory. The pupils and followers of Giotto were very numerous, and were called Giotteschi; among these TADDEO GADDI, and his son AGNOLO, are most famous: others were MASO and BERNARDO DI DADDO; but I shall not speak in detail of these artists.

While Giotto was making the art of Florence famous, there was an artist in Siena who raised the school of that city to a place of great honor. This was SIMONE MARTINI, who lived from 1283 to 1344, and is often called SIMONE MEMMI because he married a sister of another painter, LIPPO MEMMI. The most important works of Simone which remain are at Siena in the Palazzo Pubblico and in the Lower Church at Assisi. There is one beautiful work of his in the Royal Institution, at Liverpool, which illustrates the text, "Behold, thy father and I have sought Thee, sorrowing."

While the Papal court was at Avignon, in 1338, Simone removed to that city. Here he became the friend of Petrarch and of Laura, and has been praised by this poet as Giotto was by Dante.

Another eminent Florentine artist was ANDREA ORCAGNA, as he is called, though his real name was ANDREA ARCAGNUOLO DI CIONE. He was born about 1329, and died about 1368. It has long been the custom to attribute to Orcagna some of the most important frescoes in the Campo Santo at Pisa; but it is so doubtful whether he worked there that I shall not speak of them. His father was a goldsmith, and Orcagna first studied his father's craft; he was also an architect, sculptor, mosaist, and poet, as well as a painter. He made an advance in color and in the painting of atmosphere that gives him high rank as a painter; as a sculptor, his tabernacle in the Church of Or San Michele speaks his praise. Mr. C. C. Perkins thus describes it: "Built of white marble in the Gothic style, enriched with every kind of ornament, and storied with bas-reliefs illustrative of the Madonna's history from her birth to her death, it rises in stately beauty toward the roof of the church, and, whether considered from an architectural, sculptural, or symbolic point of view, must excite the warmest admiration in all who can appreciate the perfect unity of conception through which its bas-reliefs, statuettes, busts, intaglios, mosaics, and incrustations of *pietre dure*, gilded glass, and enamels are welded into a unique whole."

But perhaps it is as an architect that Orcagna is most interesting to us, for he it was who made the designs for the Loggia de Lanzi in Florence. This was built as a place for public assembly, and the discussion of the topics of the day in rainy weather; it received its name on account of its nearness to the German guard-house which was called that of the Landsknechts (in German), or Lanzi, as it was given in Italian. Orcagna probably died before the Loggia was completed, and his brother Bernardo succeeded him as architect of the commune. This Loggia is one of the most interesting places in Florence, fully in sight of the Palazzo Signoria, near the gallery of the Uffizi, and itself the storehouse of precious works of sculpture.

There were also in these early days of the fourteenth century schools of art at Bologna and Modena; but we know so little of them in detail that I shall not attempt to give any account of them here, but will pass to the early artists who may be said to belong to the true Renaissance in Italy.

## CHAPTER III.

### PAINTING IN ITALY, FROM THE BEGINNING OF THE RENAISSANCE TO THE PRESENT CENTURY.

THE reawakening of Art in Italy which followed the darkness of the Middle Ages, dates from about the beginning of the fifteenth century and is called the Renaissance. The Italians have a method of reckoning the centuries which differs from ours. Thus we call 1800 the first year of the nineteenth century, but they call it the first of the eighteenth; so the painters of what was to us the fifteenth century are called by Italians the "*quattrocentisti*," or men of the fourteenth century, and while to us the term "*cinquecento*" means the style of the sixteenth century, to the Italians the same century, which begins with 1500, is the fifteenth century.

I shall use our own method of reckoning in my writing; but this fact should be known to all who read or study art.

The first painter of whom I shall now speak is known to us as FRA ANGELICO. His name was Guido, the son of Pietro, and he was born at Vicchio in the province of Mugello, in the year 1387. We know that his family was in such circumstances that the young Guido could have led a life of ease; but he early determined to become a preaching friar. Meantime, even as a boy, he showed his taste for art, and there are six years in his life, from the age of fourteen to twenty, of which no one can tell the story.

However, from what followed it is plain that during this time he must somewhere have devoted himself to the study of painting and to preparation for his life as a monk.

Before he was fully twenty years old, he entered the convent at Fiesole, and took the name of Fra, or Brother Giovanni; soon after, his elder brother joined him there, and became Fra Benedetto. Later on our artist was called Fra Angelico, and again *Il Beato Angelico*, and then, according to Italian custom, the name of the town from which he came was added, so that he was at last called *Il Beato Giovanni, detto Angelico, da Fiesole*, which means, "The Blessed John, called the Angelic, of Fiesole." The title *Il Beato* is usually conferred by the church, but it was given to Fra Angelico by the people, because of his saintly character and works.

It was in 1407 that Fra Angelico was admitted to the convent in Fiesole, and after seven years of peaceful life there he was obliged to flee with his companions to Foligno. It was at the time when three different popes claimed the authority over the Church of Rome, and the city of Florence declared itself in favor of Alexander V.; but the monks of Fiesole adhered to Gregory XII., and for this reason were driven from their convent. Six years they dwelt at Foligno; then the plague broke out in the country about them, and again they fled to Cortona. Pictures painted by Fra Angelico at this time still remain in the churches of Cortona.

After an absence of ten years the monks returned to Fiesole, where our artist passed the next eighteen years. This was the richest period of his life: his energy was untiring, and his zeal both as an artist and as a priest burned with a steady fire. His works were sought for far and wide, and most of his easel-pictures were painted during this time. Fra Angelico would never accept the money which was paid for his work; it was given into the treasury of his convent;

FIG. 31.—FRA ANGELICO. *From the representation of him in the fresco of the "Last Judgment," by Fra Bartolommeo, in Santa Maria Nuova, Florence.*

neither did he accept any commission without the consent of the prior. Naturally, the monk-artist executed works for the adornment of his own convent. Some of these have been sold and carried to other cities and countries, and those which remain have been too much injured and too much restored to be considered important now.

He painted so many pictures during this second residence at Fiesole, not only for public places, but for private citizens, that Vasari wrote: "This Father painted so many pictures, which are dispersed through the houses of the Florentines, that sometimes I am lost in wonder when I think how works so good and so many could, though in the course of many years, have been brought to perfection by one man alone."

In 1436 the great Cosimo de Medici insisted that the monks of Fiesole should again leave their convent, and remove to that of San Marco, in Florence. Most unwillingly the brethren submitted, and immediately Cosimo set architects and builders to work to erect a new convent, for the old one was in a ruinous state. The new cloisters offered a noble field to the genius of Fra Angelico, and he labored for their decoration with his whole soul; though the rule of the order was so strict that the pictures in the cells could be seen only by the monks, he put all his skill into them, and labored as devotedly as if the whole world could see and praise them, as indeed has since been done. His pictures in this convent are so numerous that we must not describe them, but will say that the Crucifixion in the chapter-room is usually called his masterpiece. It is nearly twenty-five feet square, and, besides the usual figures in this subject, the Saviour and the thieves, with the executioners, there are holy women, the founders of various orders, the patrons of the convent, and companies of saints. In the frame there are medallions with several saints and a Sibyl, each bearing an inscription from the prophecies relating to

Christ's death; while below all, St. Dominic, the founder of the artist's order, bears a genealogical tree with many portraits of those who had been eminent among his followers. For this reason this picture has great historic value.

At last, in 1445, Pope Eugenius IV., who had dedicated the new convent of San Marco and seen the works of Angelico, summoned him to Rome. It is said that the Pope not only wished for some of his paintings, but he also desired to honor Angelico by giving him the archbishopric of Florence; but when this high position was offered him, Fra Angelico would not accept of it: he declared himself unequal to its duties, and begged the Pope to appoint Fra Antonino in his stead. This request was granted, and Angelico went on with his work as before, in all humility fulfilling his heaven-born mission to lead men to better lives through the sweet influence of his divine art.

The honor which had been tendered him was great—one which the noblest men were striving for—but if he realized this he did not regret his decision, neither was he made bold or vain by the royal tribute which the Pope had paid him.

From this time the most important works of Fra Angelico were done in the chapel of Pope Nicholas V., in the Vatican, and in the chapel which he decorated in the Cathedral of Orvieto. He worked there one summer, and the work was continued by Luca Signorelli. The remainder of his life was passed so quietly that little can be told of it. It is not even known with certainty whether he ever returned to Florence, and by some strange fate the key to the chapel which he painted in the Vatican was lost during two centuries, and the pictures could only be seen by entering through a window. Thus it would seem that his last years were passed in the quiet work which he best loved.

When his final illness was upon him, the brethren of

FIG. 32.—AN ANGEL. *In the Uffizi, Florence.* *By Fra Angelico.*

Santa Maria Sopra Minerva, where he resided, gathered about him, and chanted the *Salve Regina*. He died on the 18th of February, 1455, when sixty-seven years old. His tombstone is in the church of Santa Maria Sopra Minerva, in Rome; on it lies the figure of a Dominican monk in marble. Pope Nicholas V. wrote his epitaph in Latin. The following translation is by Professor Norton:

> "Not mine be the praise that I was a second Apelles,
> But that I gave all my gains to thine, O Christ!
> One work is for the earth, another for heaven.
> The city, the Flower of Tuscany, bore me—John."

In the Convent of San Marco in Florence there are twenty-five pictures by this master; in the Academy of Florence there are about sixty; there are eleven in the chapel of Nicholas V., and still others in the Vatican gallery. The Church of Santa Maria Novella, Florence, the Cathedral of Orvieto, the Church of St. Domenico in Perugia, and that of Cortona, are all rich in his works. Besides these a few exist in some of the principal European galleries; but I love best to see them in San Marco, where he painted them for his brethren, and where they seem most at home.

The chief merit of the pictures of Fra Angelico is the sweet and tender expression of the faces of his angels and saints, or any beings who are holy and good; he never succeeded in painting evil and sin in such a way as to terrify one; his gentle nature did not permit him to represent that which it could not comprehend, and the very spirit of purity seems to breathe through every picture.

Two other Florentine artists of the same era with Fra Angelico were MASOLINO, whose real name was PANICALE, and TOMMASO GUIDI, called MASACCIO on account of his want of neatness. The style of these two masters was much the same, but Masaccio became so much the greater that little is said of Masolino. The principal works of Masaccio are a series of frescoes in the Brancacci Chapel in Florence. They represent "The Expulsion from Paradise," "The Tribute Money," "Peter Baptizing," "Peter Curing the Blind and Lame," "The Death of Ananias," "Simon Magus," and the "Resuscitation of the King's Son." There is a fresco by Masolino in the same chapel; it is "The Preaching of Peter." Masaccio was in fact a remarkable painter. Some one has said that he seemed to hold Giotto by one hand and reach forward to Raphael with the other; and considering the pictures which were painted before his time, his works are as wonderful as Raphael's are beautiful. He died in 1429.

PAOLO UCCELLO (1396–1479) and FILIPPO LIPPI (1412–1469) were also good painters, and SANDRO BOTTICELLI (1447–1515), a pupil of Filippo, was called the best Florentine painter of his time. FILLIPINO LIPPI (1460–1505) was a pupil of Botticelli and a very important artist. ANDREA VERROCCHIO, LORENZO DI CREDI, and ANTONIO POLLAJUOLO were all good painters of the Florentine school of the last half of the fifteenth century.

Of the same period was DOMENICO GHIRLANDAJO (1449–1494), who ranks very high on account of his skill in the composition of his works and as a colorist. He made his pictures very interesting also to those of his own time, and to those of later days, by introducing portraits of certain citizens of Florence into pictures which he painted in the Church of Santa Maria Novella and other public places in the city. He did not usually make them actors in the scene he represented, but placed them in detached groups as if they were looking at the picture themselves. While his scenes were laid in the streets known to us, and his architecture was familiar, he did not run into the fantastic or lose the picturesque effect which is always pleasing. Without being one of the greatest of the Italian masters Ghirlandajo was a very important painter. He was also a teacher of the great Michael Angelo.

Other prominent Florentine painters of the close of the fifteenth century were FRANCISCO GRANACCI (1477–1543), LUCA SIGNORELLI (1441–1521), BENOZZO GOZZOLI (1424–1485), and COSIMO ROSSELLI (1439–1506).

Some good painters worked in Venice from the last half of the fourteenth century; but I shall begin to speak of the Venetian school with some account of the Bellini. The father of this family was JACOPO BELLINI (1395–1470), and his sons were GENTILE BELLINI (1421–1507) and GIOVANNI BELLINI (1426–1516).

The sketch-book of the father is one of the treasures of the British Museum. It has 99 pages, 17 by 13 inches in size, and contains sketches of almost everything—still and animal life, nature, ancient sculpture, buildings and human figures, stories of the Scriptures, of mythology, and of the lives of the saints are all illustrated in its sketches, as well as hawking parties, village scenes, apes, eagles, dogs, and cats. In this book the excellence of his drawing is seen; but so few of his works remain that we cannot judge of him as a colorist. It is certain that he laid the foundation of the excellence of the Venetian school, which his son Giovanni and the great Titian carried to perfection.

The elder son, Gentile, was a good artist, and gained such a reputation by his pictures in the great council-chamber of Venice, that when, in 1479, Sultan Mehemet, the conqueror of Constantinople, sent to Venice for a good painter, the Doge sent to him Gentile Bellini. With him he sent two assistants, and gave him honorable conduct in galleys belonging to the State. In Constantinople Gentile was much honored, and he painted the portraits of many remarkable people. At length it happened that when he had finished a picture of the head of John the Baptist in a charger, and showed it to the Sultan, that ruler said that the neck was not well painted, and when he saw that Gentile did not agree with him he called a slave and had his head instantly struck off, to prove to the artist what would be the true action of the muscles under such circumstances. This act made Gentile unwilling to remain near the Sultan, and after a year in his service he returned home. Mehemet, at parting, gave him many gifts, and begged him to ask for whatever would best please him. Gentile asked but for a letter of praise to the Doge and Signoria of Venice. After his return to Venice he worked much in company with his brother. It is said that Titian studied with Gentile: it is certain that he was always occupied with important commissions, and worked until the day of his death, when he was more than eighty years old.

FIG. 33.—CHRIST. *By Gio. Bellini.*

But Giovanni Bellini was the greatest of his family, and must stand as the founder of true Venetian painting. His works may be divided into two periods, those that were done before, and those after he learned the use of oil colors. His masterpieces, which can still be seen in the Academy and the churches of Venice, were painted after he was sixty-five years old. The works of Giovanni Bellini are numerous in Venice, and are also seen in the principal galleries of Europe. He did not paint a great variety of subjects, neither was his imagination very poetical, but there was a moral beauty in his figures; he seems to have made humanity as elevated as it can be, and to have stopped just on the line which separates earthly excellence from the heavenly. He often painted the single figure of Christ, of which Lübke says: "By grand nobleness of expression, solemn bearing, and an excellent arrangement of the drapery, he reached a dignity which has rarely been surpassed." Near the close of his life he painted a few subjects which represent gay and festive scenes, and are more youthful in spirit than the works of his earlier years. The two brothers were buried side by side in the Church of SS. Giovanni e Paolo, in Venice.

There were also good painters in Padua, Ferrara, and Verona in the fifteenth century.

ANDREA MANTEGNA, of Padua (1430–1506), was a very important artist. He spent the best part of his life in the service of the Duke of Mantua; but his influence was felt in all Italy, for his marriage with the daughter of Jacopo Bellini brought him into relations with many artists. His services were sought by various sovereigns, whose offers he refused until Pope Innocent VIII. summoned him to Rome to paint a chapel in the Vatican. After two years there he returned to Mantua, where he died. His pictures are in all large collections; his finest works are madonnas at the Louvre, Paris, and in the Church of St. Zeno at Verona. Mantegna was a fine engraver also, and his plates are now very valuable.

In the Umbrian school Pietro Perugino (1446–1524) was a notable painter; he was important on account of his own work, and because he was the master of the great Raphael. His pictures were simple and devout in their spirit, and brilliant in color; in fact, he is considered as the founder of the style which Raphael perfected. His works are in the principal galleries of Europe, and he had many followers of whom we have not space to speak.

FRANCISCO FRANCIA (1450–1518) was the founder of the school of Bologna. His true name was Francisco di Marco Raibolini, and he was a goldsmith of repute before he was a painter. He was also master of the mint to the Bentivoglio and to Pope Julius II. at Bologna. It is not possible to say when he began to paint; but his earliest known work is dated 1490 or 1494, and is in the Gallery of Bologna. His pictures resemble those of Perugino and Raphael, and it is said that he died of sorrow because he felt himself so inferior to the great painter of Urbino.

FIG. 34.—MADONNA. *By Perugino. In the Pitti Gallery, Florence.*

Raphael sent his St. Cecilia to Francia, and asked him to care for it and see it hung in its place; he did so, but did not live long after this. It is well known that these two masters were good friends and corresponded, but it is not certain that they ever met. Francia's pictures are numerous; his portraits are excellent. Many of his works are still in Bologna.

We come now to one of the most celebrated masters of

Italy, LEONARDO DA VINCI (1452–1519), the head of the Lombard or Milanese school. He was not the equal of the great masters, Michael Angelo, Raphael, and Titian; but he stands between them and the painters who preceded him or those of his own day.

In some respects, however, he was the most extraordinary man of his time. His talents were many-sided; for he was not only a great artist, but also a fine scholar in mathematics and mechanics; he wrote poetry and composed music, and was with all this so attractive personally, and so brilliant in his manner, that he was a favorite wherever he went. It is probable that this versatility prevented his being very great in any one thing, while he was remarkable in many things.

When still very young Leonardo showed his artistic talent. The paper upon which he worked out his sums was frequently bordered with little pictures which he drew while thinking on his lessons, and these sketches at last attracted his father's attention, and he showed them to his friend Andrea Verrocchio, an artist of Florence, who advised that the boy should become a painter. Accordingly, in 1470, when eighteen years old, Leonardo was placed under the care of Verrocchio, who was like a kind father to his pupils: he was not only a painter, but also an architect and sculptor, a musician and a geometer, and he especially excelled in making exquisite cups of gold and silver, crucifixes and statuettes such as were in great demand for the use of the priesthood in those days.

Pietro Perugino was a fellow-pupil with Leonardo, and they two soon surpassed their master in painting, and at last, when Verrocchio was painting a picture for the monks of Vallambrosa, and desired Leonardo to execute an angel in it, the work of his pupil was so much better than his own that the old painter desired to throw his brush aside forever. The picture is now in the Academy of Florence, and

FIG. 35.—LEONARDO DA VINCI. *From a drawing in red chalk by himself. In the Royal Library, Turin.*

represents "The Baptism of Christ." With all his refinement and sweetness, Leonardo had a liking for the horrible. It once happened that a countryman brought to his father a circular piece of wood cut from a fig-tree, and desired to have it painted for a shield; it was handed over to Leonardo, who collected in his room a number of lizards, snakes, bats, hedgehogs, and other frightful creatures, and from these painted an unknown monster having certain characteristics of the horrid things he had about him. The hideous creature was surrounded by fire, and was breathing out flames. When his father saw it he ran away in a fright, and Leonardo was greatly pleased at this. The countryman received an ordinary shield, and this *Rotello del Fico* (or shield of fig-tree wood) was sold to a merchant for one hundred ducats, and again to the Duke of Milan for three times that sum. This shield has now been lost for more than three centuries; but another horror, the "Medusa's Head," is in the Uffizi Gallery in Florence, and is a head surrounded by interlacing serpents, the eyes being glassy and deathlike and the mouth most revolting in expression.

While in Florence Leonardo accomplished much, but was at times diverted from his painting by his love of science, sometimes making studies in astronomy and again in natural history and botany; he also went much into society, and lived extravagantly. He had the power to remember faces that he had seen accidentally, and could make fine portraits from memory; he was also accustomed to invite to his house people from the lower classes; he would amuse them while he sketched their faces, making good portraits at times, and again ridiculous caricatures. He even went so far, for the sake of his art, as to accompany criminals to the place of execution, in order to study their expressions.

After a time Leonardo wished to secure some fixed income, and wrote to the Duke of Milan, Ludovico Sforza, called Il Moro, offering his services to that prince. This resulted in his going to Milan, where he received a generous salary, and became very popular with the Duke and all the court, both as a painter and as a gentleman. The Duke governed as the regent for his young nephew, and gathered about him talented men for the benefit of the young prince. He also led a gay life, and his court was the scene of constant festivities. Leonardo's varied talents were very useful to the Duke ; he could assist him in everything—by advice at his council, by plans for adorning his city, by music and poetry in his leisure hours, and by painting the portraits of his favorites. Some of these last are now famous pictures—that of Lucrezia Crevelli is believed to be in the Louvre at Paris, where it is called "La Belle Ferronière."

The Duke conferred a great honor on Leonardo by choosing him to be the founder and director of an academy which he had long wished to establish. It was called the "Academia Leonardi Vinci," and had for its purpose the bringing together of distinguished artists and men of letters. Leonardo was appointed superintendent of all the fêtes and entertainments given by the court, and in this department he did some marvellous things. He also superintended a great work in engineering which he brought to perfection, to the wonder of all Italy : it was no less an undertaking than bringing the waters of the Adda from Mortisana to Milan, a distance of nearly two hundred miles. In spite of all these occupations the artist found time to study anatomy and to write some valuable works. At length Il Moro became the established duke, and at his brilliant court Leonardo led a most agreeable life ; but he was so occupied with many things that he painted comparatively few pictures.

At length the Duke desired him to paint a picture of the Last Supper on the wall of the refectory in the Convent of the Madonna delle Grazie. This was his greatest work

FIG. 36.—THE LAST SUPPER. *By Leonardo da Vinci.*

in Milan and a wonderful masterpiece. It was commenced about 1496, and was finished in a very short time. We must now judge of it from copies and engravings, for it has been so injured as to give no satisfaction to one who sees it. Some good copies were made before it was thus ruined, and numerous engravings make it familiar to all the world. A copy in the Royal Academy, London, was made by one of Leonardo's pupils, and is the size of the original. It is said that the prior of the convent complained to the Duke of the length of time the artist was spending upon this picture; when the Duke questioned the painter he said that he was greatly troubled to find a face which pleased him for that of Judas Iscariot; he added that he was willing to allow the prior to sit for this figure and thus hasten the work; this answer pleased the Duke and silenced the prior.

After a time misfortunes overtook the Duke, and Leonardo was reduced to poverty; finally Il Moro was imprisoned; and in 1500 Leonardo returned to Florence, where he was honorably received. He was not happy here, however, for he was not the one important artist. He had been absent nineteen years, and great changes had taken place; Michael Angelo and Raphael were just becoming famous, and they with other artists welcomed Leonardo, for his fame had reached them from Milan. However, he painted some fine pictures at this time; among them were the "Adoration of the Kings," now in the Uffizi Gallery, and a portrait of Ginevra Benci, also in the same gallery. This lady must have been very beautiful; Ghirlandajo introduced her portrait into two of his frescoes.

But the most remarkable portrait was that known as Mona Lisa del Giocondo, which is in the Louvre, and is called by some critics the finest work of this master. The lady was the wife of Francesco del Giocondo, a lovely woman, and some suppose that she was very dear to Leonardo. He worked upon it for four years, and still thought it unfinished: the face has a deep, thoughtful expression—the eyelids are a little weary, perhaps, and through it all there is a suggestion of something not quite understood—a mystery: the hands are graceful and of perfect form, and the rocky background gives an unusual fascination to the whole picture. Leonardo must have loved the picture himself, and it is not strange that he lavished more time upon it than he gave to the great picture of the Last Supper. (Fig. 37.)

Leonardo sold this picture to Francis I. for nine thousand dollars, which was then an enormous sum, though now one could scarcely fix a price upon it. In 1860 the Emperor of Russia paid twelve thousand dollars for a St. Sebastian by Leonardo, and in 1865 a madonna by him was sold in Paris for about sixteen thousand dollars. Of course his pictures are rarely sold; but, when they are, great sums are given for them.

In 1502 Cæsar Borgia appointed Leonardo his engineer and sent him to travel through Central Italy to inspect his fortresses; but this usurper soon fled to Spain, and in 1503 our painter was again in Florence. In 1504 his father died. From 1507 to 1512 Leonardo was at the summit of his greatness. Louis XII. appointed him his painter, and he labored for this monarch also to improve the water-works of Milan. For seven years he dwelt at Milan, making frequent journeys to Florence. But the political troubles of the time made Lombardy an uncongenial home for any artist, and Leonardo, with a few pupils, went to Florence and then on to Rome. Pope Leo X. received him cordially enough, and told him to "work for the glory of God, Italy, Leo X., and Leonardo da Vinci." But Leonardo was not happy in Rome, where Michael Angelo and Raphael were in great favor, and when Francis I. made his successes in Italy in 1515, Leonardo hastened to Lombardy to meet him. The new king of France restored him to the office to which Louis XII. had appointed him, and gave him an annual pension of seven hundred gold crowns.

FIG. 37.—MONA LISA.—"LA BELLE JOCONDE."

When Francis returned to France he desired to cut out the wall on which the Last Supper was painted, and carry it to his own country: this proved to be impossible, and it is much to be regretted, as it is probable that if it could have been thus removed it would have been better preserved. However, not being able to take the artist's great work, the king took Leonardo himself, together with his favorite pupils and friends and his devoted servant. In France, Leonardo was treated with consideration. He resided near Amboise, where he could mingle with the court. It is said that, old though he was, he was so much admired that the courtiers imitated his dress and the cut of his beard and hair. He was given the charge of all artistic matters in France, and doubtless Francis hoped that he would found an Academy as he had done at Milan. But he seems to have left all his energy, all desire for work, on the Italian side of the Alps. He made a few plans; but he brought no great thing to pass, and soon his health failed, and he fell into a decline. He gave great attention to religious matters, received the sacrament, and then made his will, and put his worldly affairs in order.

The king was accustomed to visit him frequently, and on the last day of his life, when the sovereign entered the room, Leonardo desired to be raised up as a matter of respect to the king: sitting, he conversed of his sufferings, and lamented that he had done so little for God and man. Just then he was seized with an attack of pain—the king rose to support him, and thus, in the arms of Francis, the great master breathed his last. This has sometimes been doubted; but the modern French critics agree with the ancient writers who give this account of his end.

He was buried in the Church of St. Florentin at Amboise, and it is not known that any monument was erected over him. In 1808 the church was destroyed; in 1863 Arsine Houssaye, with others, made a search for the grave of

Leonardo, and it is believed that his remains were found. In 1873 a noble monument was erected in Milan to the memory of Da Vinci. It is near the entrance to the Arcade of Victor Emmanuel: the statue of the master stands on a high pedestal in a thoughtful attitude, the head bowed down and the arms crossed on the breast. Below are other statues and rich bas-reliefs, and one inscription speaks of him as the "Renewer of the Arts and Sciences."

Many of his writings are in the libraries of Europe in manuscript form: his best known work is the "Trattato della Pittura," and has been translated into English. As an engineer his canal of Mortesana was enough to give him fame; as an artist he may be called the "Poet of Painters," and, if those who followed him surpassed him, it should be remembered that it is easier to advance in a path once opened than to discover a new path. Personally he was much beloved, and, though he lived when morals were at a low estimate, he led a proper and reputable life. His pictures were pure in their spirit, and he seemed only to desire the progress of art and science, and it is a pleasure to read and learn of him, as it is to see his works.

Other good artists of the Lombard school in the fifteenth century were BERNARDINO LUINI (about 1460–1530), who was the best pupil of Leonardo, GIOVANNI ANTONIO BELTRAFFIO (1467–1516), GAUDENZIO FARRARI (1484–1549), AMBROGIO BORGOGNONE (works dated about 1500), and ANDREA SOLARIO, whose age is not known.

We return now to the Florentine school at a time when the most remarkable period of its existence was about to begin. We shall speak first of FRA BARTOLOMMEO or BACCIO DELLA PORTA, also called IL FRATE (1469–1517). He was born at Savignano, and studied at Florence under Cosimo Rosselli, but was much influenced by the works of Leonardo da Vinci. This painter became famous for the beauty of his pictures of the Madonna, and at the time when the great Savonarola went to Florence Bartolommeo was employed in the Convent of San Marco, where the preacher lived. The artist became the devoted friend of the preacher, and, when the latter was seized, tortured, and burned, Bartolommeo became a friar, and left his pictures to be finished by his pupil Albertinelli. For four years he lived the most austere life, and did not touch his brush: then his superior commanded him to resume his art; but the painter had no interest in it. About this time Raphael sought him out, and became his friend; he also instructed the monk in perspective, and in turn Raphael learned from him, for Fra Bartolommeo was the first artist who used lay figures in arranging his draperies; he also told Raphael some secrets of colors.

About 1513 Bartolommeo went to Rome, and after his return to his convent he began what promised to be a wonderful artistic career; but he only lived four years more, and the amount of his work was so small that his pictures are now rare. His madonnas, saints, and angels are holy in their effect; his representations of architecture are grand, and while his works are not strong or powerful, they give much pleasure to those who see them.

MICHAEL ANGELO BUONARROTI was born at the Castle of Caprese in 1475. His father, who was of a noble family of Florence, was then governor of Caprese and Chiusi, and. when the Buonarroti household returned to Florence, the little Angelo was left with his nurse on one of his father's estates at Settignano. The father and husband of his nurse were stone-masons, and thus in infancy the future artist was in the midst of blocks of stone and marble and the im plements which he later used with so much skill. For many years rude sketches were shown upon the walls of the nurse's house made by her baby charge, and he afterward said that he imbibed a love for marble with his earliest food

At the proper age Angelo was taken to Florence and

FIG. 38.—PORTRAIT OF MICHAEL ANGELO BUONARROTI.

placed in school; but he spent his time mostly in drawing, and having made the acquaintance of Francesco Granacci, at that time a pupil with Ghirlandajo, he borrowed from him designs and materials by which to carry on his beloved pursuits. Michael Angelo's desire to become an artist was violently opposed by his father and his uncles, for they desired him to be a silk and woollen merchant, and sustain the commercial reputation of the family. But so determined was he that finally his father yielded, and in 1488 placed him in the studio of Ghirlandajo. Here the boy of thirteen worked with great diligence; he learned how to prepare colors and to lay the groundwork of frescoes, and he was set to copy drawings. Very soon he wearied of this, and began to make original designs after his own ideas. At one time he corrected a drawing of his master's: when he saw this, sixty years later, he said, "I almost think that I knew more of art in my youth than I do in my old age."

When Michael Angelo went to Ghirlandajo, that master was employed on the restoration of the choir of Santa Maria Novella, so that the boy came at once into the midst of important work. One day he drew a picture of the scaffolding and all that belonged to it, with the painters at work thereon: when his master saw it he exclaimed, "He already understands more than I do myself." This excellence in the scholar roused the jealousy of the master, as well as of his other pupils, and it was a relief to Michael Angelo when, in answer to a request from Lorenzo de Medici, he and Francesco Granacci were named by Ghirlandajo as his two most promising scholars, and were then sent to the Academy which the duke had established. The art treasures which Lorenzo gave for the use of the students were arranged in the gardens of San Marco, and here, under the instruction of the old Bertoldo, Angelo forgot painting in his enthusiasm for sculpture. He first copied the face of a faun; but he changed it somewhat, and opened the moutn so that the teeth could be seen. When Lorenzo visited the garden he praised the work, but said, "You have made your faun so old, and yet you have left him all his teeth; you should have known that at such an advanced age there are generally some wanting." The next time he came there was a gap in the teeth, and so well done that he was delighted. This work is now in the Uffizi Gallery.

Lorenzo now sent for the father of Angelo, and asked that the son might live in the Medici palace under his own care. Somewhat reluctantly the father consented, and the duke gave him an office in the custom-house. From this time for three years, Angelo sat daily at the duke's table, and was treated as one of his own family; he was properly clothed, and had an allowance of five ducats a month for pocket-money. It was the custom with Lorenzo to give an entertainment every day; he took the head of the table, and whoever came first had a seat next him. It often happened that Michael Angelo had this place. Lorenzo was the head of Florence, and Florence was the head of art, poetry, and all scholarly thought. Thus, in the home of the Medici, the young artist heard learned talk upon all subjects of interest; he saw there all the celebrated men who lived in the city or visited it, and his life so near Lorenzo, for a thoughtful youth, as he was, amounted to an education.

The society of Florence at this time was not of a high moral tone, and in the year in which Michael Angelo entered the palace, a monk called Savonarola came to Florence to preach against the customs and the crimes of the city. Michael Angelo was much affected by this, and throughout his long life remembered Savonarola with true respect and affection, and his brother, Leonardo Buonarroti, was so far influenced that he withdrew from the world and became a Dominican monk.

Michael Angelo's diligence was great; he not only studied sculpture, but he found time to copy some of the fine old frescoes in the Church of the Carmine. He gave great attention to the study of anatomy, and he was known throughout the city for his talents, and for his pride and bad temper. He held himself aloof from his fellow-pupils, and one day, in a quarrel with Piètro Torrigiano, the latter gave Angelo a blow and crushed his nose so badly that he was disfigured for life. Torrigiano was banished for this offence and went to England; he ended his life in a Spanish prison.

In the spring of 1492 Lorenzo de Medici died. Michael Angelo was deeply grieved at the loss of his best friend; he left the Medici palace, and opened a studio in his father's house, where he worked diligently for two years, making a statue of Hercules and two madonnas. After two years there came a great snow-storm, and Piero de Medici sent for the artist to make a snow statue in his court-yard. He also invited Michael Angelo to live again in the palace, and the invitation was accepted; but all was so changed there that he embraced the first opportunity to leave, and during a political disturbance fled from the city with two friends, and made his way to Venice. There he met the noble Aldovrandi of Bologna, who invited the sculptor to his home, where he remained about a year, and then returned to his studio in Florence.

Soon after this he made a beautiful, sleeping Cupid, and when the young Lorenzo de Medici saw it he advised Michael Angelo to bury it in the ground for a season, and thus make it look like an antique marble; after this was done, Lorenzo sent it to Rome and sold it to the Cardinal Riario, and gave the sculptor thirty ducats. In some way the truth of the matter reached the ears of the Cardinal, who sent his agent to Florence to find the artist. When Michael Angelo heard that two hundred ducats had been paid for his Cupid, he knew that he had been deceived. The Cardinal's agent invited him to go to Rome, and he gladly went. The oldest existing writing from the hand of Michael Angelo is the letter which he wrote to Lorenzo to inform him of his arrival in Rome. He was then twenty-one years old, and spoke with joy of all the beautiful things he had seen.

Not long after he reached Rome he made the statue of the "Drunken Bacchus," now in the Uffizi Gallery, and then the Virgin Mary sitting near the place of the cross and holding the body of the dead Christ. The art-term for this subject is "La Pietà." From the time that Michael Angelo made this beautiful work he was the first sculptor of the world, though he was but twenty-four years old. The Pietà was placed in St. Peter's Church, where it still remains. The next year he returned to Florence. He was occupied with both painting and sculpture, and was soon employed on his "David," one of his greatest works. This statue weighed eighteen thousand pounds, and its removal from the studio in which it was made to the place where it was to stand, next the gate of the Palazzo Vecchio, was a difficult undertaking. It was at last put in place on May 18, 1504; there it remained until a few years ago, when, on account of its crumbling from the effect of the weather, it was removed to the Academy of Fine Arts by means of a railroad built for the purpose.

About this time a rivalry sprang up between Michael Angelo and Leonardo da Vinci. They were very unlike in their characters and mode of life. Michael Angelo was bitter, ironical, and liked to be alone; Leonardo loved to be gay and to see the world; Michael Angelo lived so that when he was old he said, "Rich as I am, I have always lived like a poor man;" Leonardo enjoyed luxury, and kept a fine house, with horses and servants. They had entered into a competition which was likely to result in serious trouble, when Pope Julius II. summoned Michael Angelo to Rome. The Pope gave him an order to build him a splendid tomb; but the enemies of the sculptor made trouble for him, and one morning he was refused admission to the Pope's palace. He then left Rome, sending this letter to the Pope: "Most Holy Father, I was this morning driven from the palace by the order of your Holiness. If you require me in future you can seek me elsewhere than at Rome."

Then he went to Florence, and the Pope sent for him again and again; but he did not go. Meantime he finished his design, and received the commission that he and Leonardo had striven for, which was to decorate the hall of the Grand Council with pictures. At last, in 1506, the Pope was in Bologna, and again sent for Michael Angelo. He went, and was forgiven for his offence, and received an order for a colossal statue of the Pope in bronze. When this was finished in 1508, and put before the Church of St. Petronio, Michael Angelo returned to Florence. He had not made friends in Bologna; his forbidding manner did not encourage others to associate with him; but we now know from his letters that he had great trials. His family was poor, and all relied on him; indeed, his life was full of care and sadness.

In 1508 he was again summoned to Rome by the Pope, who insisted that he should paint the ceiling of the Sistine Chapel, in the Vatican. Michael Angelo did not wish to do this, as he had done no great painting. It proved to be one of his most famous works; but he had a great deal of trouble in it. On one occasion the Pope threatened to throw the artist from the scaffolding. The Pope complained also that the pictures looked poor; to this the artist replied: "They are only poor people whom I have painted there, and did not wear gold on their garments." His subjects were from the Bible. When the artist would have a leave of absence to go to Florence, the Pope got so angry that he struck him; but, in spite of all, this great painting was finished in 1512. Grimm, in his life of Michael Angelo, says: "It needed the meeting of these two men; in the one such perseverance in requiring, and in the other such power of fulfilling, to produce this monument of human art."

It is impossible here to follow, step by step, the life and works of this master. Among the other great things which he did are the tomb of Julius II. in the Church of S. Pietro

FIG. 39.—THE PROPHET JEREMIAH. *By M. Angelo. From the Sistine Chapel.*

in Vincoli, in Rome, of which the famous statue of Moses makes a part. (Fig. 40.)

He made the statues in the Medici Chapel in the Church of San Lorenzo, in Florence, the painting of the Last Judgment on a wall of the Sistine Chapel, and many works as an architect; for he was called upon to attend to fortifications both in Florence and Rome, and at last, as his great-

FIG. 40.—STATUE OF MOSES. *By M. Angelo.*

est work of this sort, he was the architect of St. Peter's at Rome. Many different artists had had a share in this work ; but as it now is Michael Angelo may be counted as its real architect. His works are numerous and only a small part of them is here mentioned ; but I have spoken of those by which he is most remembered. His life, too, was a stormy one for many reasons that we have not space to tell. While he lived there were wars and great changes in Italy ; he served also under nine popes, and during his life thirteen men occupied the papal chair. Besides being great as a painter, an architect, and a sculptor, he was a poet, and wrote sonnets well worthy of such a genius as his. His whole life was so serious and sad that it gives one joy to know that in his old age he formed an intimate friendship with Vittoria Colonna, a wonderful woman, who made a sweet return to him for all the tender devotion which he lavished upon her.

Italians associate the name of Michael Angelo with those of the divine poet Dante and the painter Raphael, and these three are spoken of as the three greatest men of their country in what are called the modern days. Michael Angelo died at Rome in 1564, when eighty-nine years old. He desired to be buried in Florence ; but his friends feared to let this be known lest the Pope should forbid his removal. He was therefore buried in the Church of the Holy Apostles ; but his nephew, Leonardo Buonarroti, conveyed his remains to Florence secretly, disguised as a bale of merchandise. At Florence, on a Sunday night, his body was borne to Santa Croce, in a torchlight procession, and followed by many thousands of citizens. There his friends once more gazed upon the face which had not been seen in Florence for thirty years ; he looked as if quietly sleeping. Some days later a splendid memorial service was held in San Lorenzo, attended by all the court, the artists, scholars, and eminent men of the city. An oration was pronounced ;

rare statues and paintings were collected in the church; all the shops of the city were closed; and the squares were filled with people.

Above his grave in Santa Croce, where he lies near Dante, Machiavelli, Galileo, and many other great men, the Duke and Leonardo Buonarroti erected a monument. It has statues of Painting, Sculpture, and Architecture, and a bust of the great man who sleeps beneath.

In the court of the Uffizi his statue stands together with those of other great Florentines. His house in the Ghibelline Street now belongs to the city of Florence, and contains many treasured mementoes of his life and works; it is open to all who wish to visit it. In 1875 a grand festival was held in Florence to celebrate the four hundredth anniversary of his birth. The ceremonies were very impressive, and at that time some documents which related to his life, and had never been opened, were, by command of Victor Emmanuel, given to proper persons to be examined.

Thus it is that the great deeds of great men live on and on, through all time, and it is a joy to know that though the fourscore and nine years of the life of this artist had much of care and sorrow in them, his name and memory are still cherished, and must continue to be, while from his life many lessons may be drawn to benefit and encourage others—lessons which we cannot here write out; but they teach patience, industry, and faithfulness to duty, while they also warn us to avoid the bitterness and roughness which are blemishes on the memory of this great, good man.

DANIELE DE VOLTERRA (1509–1566) was the best scholar of Michael Angelo. His principal pictures are the "Descent from the Cross," in the Church of Trinità di Monti, in Rome, and the "Massacre of the Innocents," in the Uffizi Gallery; both are celebrated works.

The next important Florentine painter was ANDREA DEL SARTO (1488-1530). His family name was Vannucchi; but because his father was a tailor, the Italian term for one of his trade, *un sarto*, came to be used for the son. Early in life Andrea was a goldsmith, as were so many artists; but, when he was able to study painting under Pietro di Cosimo, he became devoted to it, and soon developed his own style, which was very soft and pleasing. His pictures cannot be called great works of art, but they are favorites with a large number of people. He succeeded in fresco-painting, and decorated several buildings in Florence, among them the Scalzo, which was a place where the Barefooted Friars held their meetings, and was named from them, as they are called *Scalzi*. These frescoes are now much injured; but they are thought his best works of this kind.

Probably Andrea del Sarto would have come to be a better painter if he had been a happier man. His wife, of whom he was very fond, was a mean, selfish woman who wished only to make a great show, and did not value her husband's talents except for the money which they brought him. She even influenced him to desert his parents, to whom he had ever been a dutiful son. About 1518 Francis I., king of France, invited Andrea to Paris to execute some works for him. The painter went, and was well established there and very popular, when his wife insisted that he should return to Florence. Francis I. was very unwilling to spare him, but Andrea dared not refuse to go to his wife; so he solemnly took an oath to return to Paris and bring his wife, so that he could remain as long as pleased the king, and then that sovereign consented. Francis also gave the artist a large sum of money to buy for him all sorts of beautiful objects.

When Andrea reached Florence his wife refused to go to France, and persuaded him to give her the king's money. She soon spent it, and Andrea, who lived ten years more, was very unhappy, while the king never forgave him, and to this day this wretched story must be told, and continues

FIG. 41.—THE MADONNA DEL SACCO. *By Andrea del Sarto.*

the remembrance of his dishonesty. After all he had sacrificed for his wife, when he became very ill, in 1530, of some contagious disease, she deserted him. He died alone, and with no prayer or funeral was buried in the Convent of the Nunziata, where he had painted some of his frescoes.

His pictures are very numerous; they are correct in drawing, very softly finished, and have a peculiar gray tone of color. He painted a great number of Holy Families, one of which is called the "Madonna del Sacco," because St. Joseph is leaning on a sack (Fig. 41). This is in the convent where he is buried. His best work is called the "Madonna di San Francesco" and hangs in the tribune of the Uffizi Gallery. This is a most honorable place, for near it are pictures by Michael Angelo, Raphael, Titian, and other great painters, as well as some very celebrated statues, such as the "Venus de Medici" and the "Dancing Faun." Andrea del Sarto's pictures of the Madonna and Child are almost numberless; they are sweet, attractive works, as are also his St. Barbara, St. Agnes, and others of his single figures.

We will now leave the Florentine school of the sixteenth century, and speak of the great master of the Roman school, RAPHAEL SANZIO, or SANTI (1483–1520), who was born at Urbino on Good Friday. His father was a painter, and Raphael showed his taste for art very early in life. Both his parents died while he was still a child, and though he must have learned something from seeing his father and other painters at their work, we say that Perugino was his first master, for he was but twelve years old when he entered the studio of that painter in Perugia.

Here he remained more than eight years, and about the time of leaving painted the very celebrated picture called "Lo Sposalizio," or the Marriage of the Virgin, now in the Brera at Milan. This picture is famous the world over, and is very important in the life of the painter, because it shows the highest point he reached under Perugino, or during what is called his first manner in painting. Before this he had executed a large number of beautiful pictures, among which was the so-called "Staffa Madonna." This is a circular picture and represents the Virgin walking in a springtime landscape. It remained in the Staffa Palace in Perugia three hundred and sixty-eight years, and in 1871 was sold to the Emperor of Russia for seventy thousand dollars.

In 1504 Raphael returned to Urbino, where he became the favorite of the court, and was much employed by the ducal family. To this time belong the "St. George Slaying the Dragon" and the "St. Michael Attacking Satan," now in the gallery of the Louvre. But the young artist soon grew weary of the narrowness of his life, and went to Florence, where, amid the treasures of art with which that city was crowded, he felt as if he was in an enchanted land. It is worth while to recount the wonderful things he saw; they were the cathedral with the dome of Brunelleschi, the tower of Giotto, the marbles and bronzes of Donatello, the baptistery gates of Ghiberti, the pictures of Masaccio, Ghirlandajo, Fra Angelico, and many other older masters, while Michael Angelo and Leonardo were surprising themselves and all others with their beautiful works.

At this time the second manner of Raphael begun. During his first winter here he painted the so-called "Madonna della Gran Duca," now in the Pitti Gallery, and thus named because the Grand Duke of Tuscany, Ferdinand III., carried it with him on all his journeys, and said his prayers before it at morning and evening. He made a visit to Urbino in 1505, and wherever he was he worked continually, and finished a great number of pictures, which as yet were of religious subjects with few and unimportant exceptions.

When he returned to Florence in 1506, the cartoon of Leonardo da Vinci's "Battle of the Standard" and Michael Angelo's "Bathing Soldiers" revealed a new world of art

FIG. 42.—PORTRAIT OF RAPHAEL. *Painted by Himself.*

to Raphael. He saw that heroic, exciting scenes could be represented by painting, and that vigor and passion could speak from the canvas as powerfully as Christian love and resignation. Still he did not attempt any new thing immediately. In Florence he moved in the best circles. He received orders for some portraits of nobles and wealthy men, as well as for madonnas and Holy Families. Before long he visited Bologna, and went again to Urbino, which had become a very important city under the reign of Duke Guidobaldo. The king of England, Henry VIII., had sent to this duke the decoration of the Order of the Garter. In return for this honor, the duke sent the king rich gifts, among which was a picture of St. George and the Dragon by Raphael.

While at Urbino, at this time, he painted his first classic subject, the "Three Graces." Soon after, he returned the third time to Florence, and now held much intercourse with Fra Bartolommeo, who gave the younger artist valuable instruction as to his color and drapery. In 1508, among a great number of pictures he painted the madonna which is called "La Belle Jardinière," and is now one of the treasures of the Louvre. The Virgin is pictured in the midst of a flowery landscape, and it has been said that a beautiful flower-girl to whom Raphael was attached was his model for the picture. This picture is also a landmark in the history of Raphael, for it shows the perfection of his second manner, and the change that had come over him from his Florentine experience and associations. His earlier pictures had been full of a sweet, unearthly feeling, and a color which could be called spiritual was spread over them; now his madonnas were like beautiful, earthly mothers, his colors were deep and rich, and his landscapes were often replaced by architectural backgrounds which gave a stately air where all before had been simplicity. His skill in grouping, in color, and in drapery was now marvellous, and when in 1508 the Pope, who had seen some of his works, summoned him to Rome, he went, fully prepared for the great future which was before him, and now began his third, or Roman manner of painting.

This pope was Julius II., who held a magnificent court and was ambitious for glory in every department of life—as a temporal as well as a spiritual ruler, and as a patron of art and letters as well as in his office of the Protector of the Holy Church. He had vast designs for the adornment of Rome, and immediately employed Raphael in the decoration of the first of the Stanze, or halls of the Vatican, four of which he ornamented with magnificent frescoes before his death. He also executed wall-paintings in the Chigi Palace, and in a chapel of the Church of Santa Maria della Pace.

With the exception of a short visit to Florence, Raphael passed the remainder of his life in Rome. The amount of work which he did as an architect, sculptor, and painter was marvellous, and would require the space of a volume to follow it, and name all his achievements, step by step, so I shall only tell you of some of his best-known works and those which are most often mentioned.

While he was working upon the halls of the Vatican Julius II. died. He was succeeded by Leo X., who also was a generous patron to Raphael, who thus suffered no loss of occupation from the change of popes. The artist became very popular and rich; he had many pupils, and was assisted by them in his great frescoes, not only in the Vatican, but also in the Farnesina Villa or Chigi Palace. Raphael had the power to attach men to him with devoted affection, and his pupils gave him personal service gladly; he was often seen in the street with numbers of them in attendance, just as the nobles were followed by their squires and pages. He built himself a house in a quarter of the city called the Borgo, not far from the Church of St. Peter's, and during the remainder of his life was attended by prosperity and success.

One of the important works which he did for Leo X. was the making of cartoons, or designs to be executed in tapestry for the decoration of the Sistine Chapel, where Michael Angelo had painted his great frescoes. The Pope ordered these tapestries to be woven in the looms of Flanders, from the richest materials, and a quantity of gold thread was used in them. They were completed and sent to Rome in 1519, and were exhibited to the people the day after Christmas, when all the city flocked to see them. In 1527, when the Constable de Bourbon allowed the French soldiers to sack Rome, these tapestries were carried away. In 1553 they were restored; but one was missing, and it is believed that it had been destroyed for the sake of the gold thread which was in it. Again, in 1798, the French carried them away and sold them to a Jew in Leghorn, who burned one of the pieces; but his gain in gold was so little that he preserved the others, and Pius VII. bought them and restored them to the Vatican. The cartoons, however, are far more important than the tapestries, because they are the work of Raphael himself. The weavers at Arras tossed them aside after using them, and some were torn; but a century later the artist Rubens learned that they existed, and advised King Charles I. of England to buy them. This he did, and thus the cartoons met with as many ups and downs as the tapestries had had. When they reached England they were in strips; the workmen had cut them for their convenience. After the king was executed Cromwell bought the cartoons for three hundred pounds. When Charles II. was king and in great need of money he was sorely tempted to sell them to Louis XIV., who coveted them, and wished to add them to the treasures of France; but Lord Danby persuaded Charles to keep them. In 1698 they were barely saved from fire at Whitehall, and finally,

FIG. 43. THE SISTINE MADONNA.

by command of William III., they were properly repaired and a room was built at Hampton Court to receive them, by the architect, Sir Christopher Wren. At present they are in the South Kensington Museum, London. Of the original eleven only seven remain.

Both Henry VIII. and Francis I. had received presents of pictures by Raphael: we have told of the occasion when the St. George was sent to England. The "Archangel Michael" and the "Large Holy Family of the Louvre" were given to Francis I. by Lorenzo de Medici, who sent them overland on mules to the Palace of Fontainebleau. Francis was so charmed with these works that he presented Raphael so large a sum that he was unwilling to accept it without sending the king still other pictures; so he sent the sovereign another painting, and to the king's sister, Queen Margaret of Navarre, he gave a picture of St. Margaret overcoming the dragon. Then Francis gave Raphael many thanks and another rich gift of money. Besides this he invited Raphael to come to his court, as did also the king of England; but the artist preferred to remain where he was already so prosperous and happy.

About 1520 Raphael painted the famous Sistine Madonna, now the pride of the Dresden Gallery. It is named from St. Sixtus, for whose convent, at Piacenza, it was painted: the picture of this saint, too, is in the lower part of the picture, with that of St. Barbara. No sketch or drawing of this work was ever found, and it is believed that the great artist, working as if inspired, sketched it and finished it on the canvas where it is. It was originally intended for a *drappellone*, or procession standard, but the monks used it for an altar-piece (Fig. 43).

While Raphael accomplished so much as a painter, he by no means gave all his time or thought to a single art. He was made superintendent of the building of St. Peter's in 1514, and made many architectural drawings for that church; he was also much interested in the excavations of ancient Rome, and made immense numbers of drawings of various sorts. As a sculptor he made models and designs, and there is in the Church of Santa Maria del Popolo, in Rome, a statue of Jonah sitting on a whale, said to have been modelled by Raphael and put into marble by Lorenzetto Latti.

Raphael was also interested in what was happening outside the world of art; he corresponded with scholars of different countries, and sent men to make drawings of places and objects which he could not go to see. He was also generous to those less fortunate than himself, and gave encouragement and occupation to many needy men.

At one time he expected to marry Maria de Bibiena, a niece of Cardinal Bibiena; but she died before the time for the marriage came.

While Raphael was making his great successes in Rome, other famous artists also were there, and there came to be much discussion as to their merits, and especially as to the comparative worth of Michael Angelo and Raphael. At last, when this feeling of rivalry was at its height, the Cardinal Giulio de Medici, afterward Pope Clement VII., gave orders to Raphael and Sebastian del Piombo to paint two large pictures for the Cathedral of Narbonne. The subject of Sebastian's picture was the "Raising of Lazarus," and it has always been said that Michael Angelo made the drawing for it.

Raphael's picture was the "Transfiguration," and proved to be his last work, for before it was finished he was attacked by fever, and died on Good Friday, 1620, which was the thirty-seventh anniversary of his birth. All Rome mourned for him; his body was laid in state, and the Transfiguration was placed near it. Those who had known him went to weep while they gazed upon his face for the last time.

He had chosen his grave in the Pantheon, near to that of Maria Bibiena, his betrothed bride. The ceremonies of his burial were magnificent, and his body was followed by an immense throng dressed in mourning. Above his tomb was placed an inscription in Latin, written by Pietro Bembo, which has for its last sentence these words: "This is that Raphael by whom Nature feared to be conquered while he lived, and to die when he died." Raphael had also requested Lorenzo Lorenzetti to make a statue of the Virgin to be placed above his resting-place. He left a large estate, and gave his works of art to his pupils Giulio Romano and Francesco Penni; his house to Cardinal Bibiena; a sum to buy another house, the rent of which should pay for twelve masses to be said monthly, for the repose of his soul, from the altar near his grave; this was observed until 1705, when the income from the house was not enough to support these services.

For many years there was a skull at the Academy of St. Luke, in Rome, which was called that of Raphael; but there was no proof of this, and in 1833 some antiquarians received the consent of the Pope to their searching for the bones of Raphael in his grave in the Pantheon. After five days of careful work, and removing the pavement in several places, the skeleton of the great master was found, and with it such proofs of its being his as left no room for doubt. Then a second great funeral service was held; the Pope, Gregory XVI., gave a marble sarcophagus in which the bones were placed, and reverently restored to their first resting-place. More than three thousand persons were present at the service, including artists of all nations, as well as Romans of the highest rank. They moved in procession about the church, bearing torches in their hands, and keeping time to beautiful chants from an invisible choir.

Raphael left two hundred and eighty-seven pictures and five hundred and seventy-six studies and drawings, and all

Fig. 44.—Saint Cecilia Listening to the Singing of Angels. *By Raphael.*

done in so short a life. In considering him and the story of his life, we find that it was not any one trait or talent that made his greatness; but it was the rare union of gifts of genius with a personal charm that won all hearts to him. His famous picture of "St. Cecilia," with its sweetness of expression and lovely color—its union of earthly beauty with spiritual feeling, is a symbol of the harmonious and varied qualities of this prince of painters (Fig. 44).

GIULIO ROMANO (1492–1556) was the favorite pupil of Raphael, and the heir of a part of his estate; but his remaining works would not repay us for a study of them.

Of course, the influence of so great a master as Raphael was felt outside of his own school, and, in a sense, all Italian art of his time was modified by him. His effect was very noticeable upon a Sienese painter, BAZZI, or RAZZI, called IL SODOMA (1477–1549), who went to Rome and was under the immediate influence of Raphael's works. He was almost unrivalled in his power to represent beautiful female heads.

His important works were frescoes, many of which are in the churches of Siena. Doubtless Bazzi was lost in the shadow of the great Raphael, and had he existed at a time a little more distant from that great man, he would have been more famous in his life.

During the sixteenth century the Venetian school reached its highest excellence. The great difference between it and the school of Florence was, that the latter made beauty of form the one object of its art, while the Venetian painters combined with grace and ease the added charm of rich, brilliant color.

GIORGIO BARBARELLI, called GIORGIONE (1477–1511), was the first great artist of Venice who cast off the rigid manner of the Bellini school, and used his brush and colors freely, guided only by his own ideas, and inspired by his own genius.

He was born at Castelfranco, and was early distinguished for his personal beauty. Giorgione means George the Great, and this title was given him on account of his noble figure. He was fond of music, played the lute well, and composed many of the songs he sang ; he had also an intense love of beauty—in short, his whole nature was full of sentiment and harmony, and with all these gifts he was a man of pure life. Mrs. Jameson says of him : " If Raphael be the Shakspeare, then Giorgione may be styled the Byron of painting."

There is little that can be told of his life. He was devoted to his art, and passionately in love with a young girl, of whom he told one of his artist friends, Morto da Feltri. This last proved a traitor to Giorgione, for he too admired the same girl, and induced her to forsake Giorgione, and go away with him. The double treachery of his beloved and his friend caused the painter such grief that he could not overcome his sadness, and when the plague visited Venice in 1511, he fell a victim to it in the very flower of his age.

Much of the work of Giorgione has disappeared, for he executed frescoes which the damp atmosphere of Venice has destroyed or so injured that they are of no value. His smaller pictures were not numerous, and there is much dispute as to the genuineness of those that are called by his name. He painted very few historical subjects ; his works are principally portraits, sibyls, and religious pictures. Among the last, the altar-piece at Castelfranco holds the first place ; it represents the Virgin and Child between Sts. Francis and Liberale, and was painted before 1504.

Giorgione gave an elevated tone to his heads and figures ; it seemed as if he painted only the beings of a superior race, and as if they must all be fitted to do great deeds. His fancy was very fruitful, and in some of his works he pictured demons, sea-monsters, dogs, apes, and such creatures with great effect. In clearness and warmth of color Giorgione is at the head of the Venetian painters; in truth, it seems as if the color was within them and showed itself without in a deep, luminous glow.

The most important of Giorgione's scholars was called FRA SEBASTIANO DEL PIOMBO; his real name was *Luciani*, and he was a native of Venice (1485–1547). This artist excelled in his coloring and in the effect he gave to the atmosphere of his work, making it a broad *chiaro-scuro*, or clear-obscure, as it really means. This is an art term which is frequently used, and denotes a sort of mistiness which has some light in it, and is gradually shaded off, either into a full light or a deep shadow. But from the earliest efforts of this artist, it was plain that he had no gift of composition, neither could he give his pictures an elevated tone or effect. For this reason his portraits were his best works, and these were very fine.

A portrait of his in the National Gallery, London, and another in the Städel Gallery at Frankfort, are both said to be of Giulia Gonzaga, the most beautiful woman of her day in Italy. In 1553, Ippolito de Medici, who was madly in love with her, sent Sebastian with an armed force to Fondi to paint her portrait; it was finished in a month, and was said to be the best ever painted by Sebastian. It was sent to France as a gift to Francis I., and its present abiding-place is not known.

While Raphael was at the height of his fame in Rome, the banker Chigi invited Sebastian to that city, and in the Farnesina he painted works which were very inferior beside Raphael's. Then Sebastian tried to improve by study under Michael Angelo. This last great master would not compete with Raphael himself, but he was very jealous of the fame of the younger man, and it is said that he aided Sebastian, and even made his designs for him, in the hopes that thus he might eclipse Raphael. We have spoken of one large picture of the "Raising of Lazarus" said to have been made from Michael Angelo's design, which Sebastian colored; it was painted in competition with Raphael's Transfiguration, and even beside that most splendid work the Lazarus was much admired. This is now in the National Gallery, London.

After Raphael's death Sebastian was called the first painter in Rome, and was made a *piombatore*. It was necessary to be an ecclesiastic to hold this office, and it is on account of this that he gave up his real name, and became a friar. He wrote to Michael Angelo: "If you were to see me as an honorable lord, you would laugh at me. I am the finest ecclesiastic in all Rome. Such a thing had never come into my mind. But God be praised in eternity! He seemed especially to have thus decreed it. And, therefore, so be it." It is not strange that he should have been so resigned to a high office and a salary of eight hundred scudi a year!

Another Venetian, of the same time with Giorgione, was JACOPO PALMA, called IL VECCHIO, or the elder (about 1480–1528). He was born near Bergamo, but as an artist he was a Venetian. We do not know with whom he studied, and he was not a very great man, nor was he employed by the state—but he dwelt much in the palaces of noble families and did much work for them. When he died he left forty-four unfinished paintings.

His female figures are his best works, and one of his fine pictures at Dresden, called the "Three Graces," is said to represent his daughters. The work which is usually called his masterpiece is an altar-piece in the Church of Santa Maria Formosa, in Venice; the St. Barbara in the centre is very beautiful, and is said to have been painted from his daughter Violante.

The greatest master of the Venetian school is called TITIAN, though his real name was TIZIANO VECELLI, and sometimes Cadore is added to this, because of his having

FIG. 45.—PORTRAIT OF TITIAN. *From the etching by Agostino Caracci.*

been born in that village (1477–1576). His family was noble and their castle was called Lodore, and was in the midst of a large estate surrounded by small houses; in one of these last, which is still preserved, the painter was born.

As a child he was fond of drawing, and so anxious to color his pictures that he squeezed the juices from certain flowers, and used them as paints. When but nine years old he was taken to Venice to study, and from this time was called a Venetian; he is said by some writers to be the first portrait-painter of the world.

He first studied under Sebastian Zuccato, and then under the Bellini, where he was a fellow-pupil with Giorgione, and the two became devoted friends, at the time when they were just coming to be men and were filled with glad hopes of future greatness. After a time, when Titian was about thirty years old, the two were employed on the "Fondaco dei Tedeschi," or the exchange for German merchants in Venice. Here the frescoes of Titian were more admired than those of Giorgione, and the latter became so jealous that they ceased to live together, as they had done, and there is cause for believing that they were never good friends again. But after the early death of Giorgione, Titian completed the works he had left unfinished, and, no doubt, sincerely mourned for him.

One of the most celebrated pictures by Titian is the Presentation in the Temple, which was painted for the Church of the Brotherhood of Charity, called in Italian "La Scuola della Carità;" this church is now the Academy of Fine Arts in Venice, where the picture still remains. It represents the Virgin Mary when three years old entering the temple and the high priest receiving her at the entrance. All around below the steps is a company of friends who have been invited by her father and mother to attend them on this important occasion. The picture is full of life and action, and is gorgeous in its coloring. Several of the figures are said to be portraits, one being that of Titian himself.

Among his female portraits, that of Caterina Cornaro, Queen of Cyprus, is celebrated; also one called "Flora;" both of these are in the Uffizi Gallery, in Florence, while near by, in the Pitti, is "La Bella," or the beautiful lady of Titian. He also made many portraits of his daughter Lavinia, who was very beautiful; sometimes he represented her as a fruit or flower-girl, again as Herodias and in various characters (Fig. 46). One of the finest of these is at Berlin, where she is in a very rich dress, and holds up a plate of fruit; it is one of his best works.

Titian's fame extended throughout Italy, and even all over Europe, and the Duke of Ferrara invited him to his court. The artist went, and there painted two very famous mythological pictures, besides portraits and other works. One of these important subjects was "Bacchus and Ariadne," and it is now in the National Gallery, London; the second was a Venus, surrounded by more than sixty children and cupids; some are climbing trees, others shoot arrows in the air, while still others twine their arms around each other; this is now in Madrid.

While at Ferrara the Pope, Leo X., asked Titian to go to Rome; but he longed for his home—he wished for his yearly visit to Cadore, and he declined the honorable invitation, and returned to Venice. In 1530 Titian's wife died, leaving him with two sons, Pomponio and Orazio, and his daughter, Lavinia. In this same sad year the Emperor Charles V. and Pope Clement VII. met at Bologna. All the most brilliant men of Germany and Italy were also there, and Titian was summoned to paint portraits of the two great heads of Church and State, and of many of the notable men among their followers.

When the painter returned to Venice he was loaded with honors and riches. He bought a new house at Beri-

FIG. 46.—PORTRAIT OF LAVINIA. *By Titian.*

grande, opposite the island of Murano; it commanded fine views and its garden was beautiful. The landscapes of his pictures soon grew better than they had been, and no wonder, when he could always see the Friuli Alps in the distance with their snow-capped peaks rising to the clouds; nearer him was the Murano, like another city with its towers and domes, and then the canals, which at night were gay with lighted gondolas bearing fair ladies hither and thither. Here Titian entertained many people, and some of them were exalted in station. The house was called "Casa Grande," and on one occasion, when a cardinal and others invited themselves to dine with him, Titian flung a purse to his steward, saying, "Now prepare a feast, since all the world dines with me."

While living at "Casa Grande," the artist saw the most glorious years of his life. It seemed that every person of note in all Europe, both men and women, desired their portraits at his hand. One only, Cosmo I., Grand Duke of Florence, refused to sit to him. If these pictures could be collected together, most of the famous persons of his time would be represented in them.

After he was sixty years old Titian made a second journey to Ferrara, Urbino, and Bologna. This time he painted a portrait of Charles V., with a favorite dog by his side. After this, in 1545, at an invitation from Pope Paul III., the great master went to Rome; while there he painted many wonderful pictures—among them, one of the pope with his two grandsons was very remarkable; it is now in the Museum of Naples. He left Rome when he was sixty-nine years old.

In 1548 Charles V. summoned Titian to Augsburg, and while there made him a count, and gave him a yearly pension of two hundred gold ducats. The emperor was very fond of Titian, and spent a good deal of time with him. On one occasion the painter dropped his brush; the emperor picked it up, and returned it to him. The etiquette of courts forbade any one to receive such a service from the sovereign, and Titian was much embarrassed, when Charles said, "Titian is worthy to be served by Cæsar," this being one of the great ruler's titles. Charles continued his favors to Titian through life, and when he resigned his crown, and retired to the monastery of Yuste, he took nine pictures by this master into his solitude. One of these, a portrait of the Empress Isabella, was so hung that the emperor gazed upon it when dying; this is now in the museum at Madrid, where are also many fine works by Titian, for Philip II. was his patron as his father had been.

When eighty-five years old he finished his wonderful picture of the "Martyrdom of St. Lawrence" for the Church of the Jesuits in Venice, and his old age was one of strength and mental clearness. Though he had seen great prosperity and received many honors, he had not escaped sorrow. After the death of his wife, his sister Orsa, who was very dear to him, had kept his house; she too sickened and died; his son Pomponio was a worthless fellow, and caused him much grief; Lavinia had married, and the old man was left with Orazio alone, who was a dutiful son. He also was an artist, but painted so frequently on the same canvas with his father that his works cannot be spoken of separately.

At length Titian's work began to show his years, and some one told him that his "Annunciation" did not resemble his usual pictures. He was very angry, and, seizing a pencil, wrote upon it, "*Tizianus fecit fecit*"—meaning to say by this, "Truly, Titian did this!" When he was ninety-six years old he was visited by Henry III. of France, attended by a train of princes and nobles. The aged painter appeared with such grace and dignity as to excite the admiration of all, and when the king asked the price of some pictures, Titian presented them to him as one sovereign might make a gift to another who was his equal, and no more.

In 1576 the plague broke out in Venice, and both Titian and Orazio fell victims to it. Naturally the man of ninety-eight years could not recover, and, though Orazio was borne off to the hospital and cared for as well as possible, he also died. After Titian was left alone robbers entered his house while he still lived, and carried away jewels, money, and pictures. He died August 27th, and all Venice mourned for him.

There was a law that no person who died of the plague in Venice should be buried within the city; but Titian was so much honored and beloved that exception was made, and he was buried in the Church of Santa Maria Gloriosa de Frari; or as it is usually called, "the Frari." He had painted a great picture of the Assumption for this church, which has since been removed to the Academy of Venice; but another work of his, called the Pesaro altar-piece, still remains near his grave. His burial-place is marked by a simple tablet, inscribed thus: "Here lies the great Tiziano di Vecelli, rival of Zeuxis and Apelles."

A little more than two centuries after his death the citizens of Venice determined to erect a monument to Titian, and Canova made a design for it; but political troubles interfered, and prevented the execution of the plan. In 1852 the Emperor of Austria, Ferdinand I., placed a costly monument near his grave; it consists of a Corinthian canopy beneath which is a sitting statue of the painter, while several other allegorical figures are added to increase its magnificence. This monument was dedicated with imposing ceremonies, and it is curious to note that not far away from it the sculptor Canova is buried, and his own monument is made from the design which he made for that of Titian.

Some writers consider the "Entombment of Christ," in the Manfrini Palace, as the greatest work of Titian. At all events, it is the best existing representation of this subject, and is a picture which has had a great effect upon art; its chief feature is the general expression of sorrow which pervades the whole work.

Titian gave a new importance to landscape-painting by making backgrounds to his pictures from natural scenery, and that not as if it was merely for the sake of a background, but in a manner which showed his love for Nature, and, in fact, he often rendered it with poetical significance.

The works of Titian are very seldom sold. One subject which he oftentimes repeated was that of "Danäe" with the shower of gold falling about her; one of these was purchased by the Emperor of Russia for six hundred thousand francs. One of the most important of his religious pictures was that of "St. Peter Martyr;" this was burned in the Church of SS. Giovanni e Paolo in Venice in 1868. An excellent copy of it had been for a long time in the Museum of Florence, and this was presented to the Venetians in order to repair their loss as far as possible. Victor Amadeus of Sardinia presented nine pictures by Titian to the Duke of Marlborough, and these were all destroyed in 1861 when the château of Blenheim was burned. Kugler says: "In the multifariousness of his powers Titian takes precedence of all other painters of his school; indeed, there is scarcely a line of art which in his long and very active life he did not enrich." His last work was not quite completed by himself, and is now in the Academy of Venice. It is a Pietà, and although the hand of ninety-eight years guided the brush uncertainly, yet it has the wonderful light this master threw around his figures, and the whole is conceived with his accustomed animation.

The pupils and followers of Titian were too numerous to be spoken of one by one, and none of them were so great as to require their mention in detail here; yet they were so good that, while the other schools of Italy were decreasing in importance during the sixteenth century, that of Venice was flourishing, and some great masters still existed there. Among these was JACOPO ROBUSTI (1512–1594), who was called, and is best known as Tintoretto, which name was given him because his father was a dyer. He studied under Titian for a time, and then he attempted to follow Michael Angelo, and it is said that his motto was, "The coloring of Titian, the drawing of Michael Angelo." His best pictures are slightly treated, and others are coarse and unfinished in the manner of painting. His portraits seem to be his best works, probably because they are more carefully finished.

Several works of his are simply enormous; one is seventy-four by thirty feet; the school of St. Roch has fifty-seven large pictures by him, in many of which the figures are of life size. His two most famous works are the "Miracle of St. Mark," in the Academy of Venice, and the "Crucifixion," in the school of St. Roch. The last is, for every reason, his best work; there are crowds of people in it, on foot and on horseback, while their faces show every possible kind of expression, and their movements are infinitely varied. The immense painting mentioned above is in the Doge's Palace, and is called "Paradise." His daughter, MARIETTA ROBUSTI (1560–1590), was a pupil of her father's, and became so good a portrait-painter that she was invited to the Court of Spain by Phillip II., but her father could not consent to a separation from her. Some excellent pictures of hers still exist, and her portraits of Marco dei Vescovi and the antiquarian Strada were celebrated pictures. When the Emperor Maximilian and the Archduke Ferdinand, each in turn, desired her presence at their courts, her father hastened to marry her to Mario Augusti, a wealthy German jeweller, upon the condition that she should remain in her father's house. She was celebrated for her beauty, had fine musical talents, and was sprightly and enthusiastic; her father was so fond of having her with him that he sometimes allowed her to dress as a boy, and go with him to study where young girls were not admitted.

When but thirty years old Marietta Robusti died; she was buried in the Church of Santa Maria dell Orto, where are several works by her father. Both he and her husband mourned for her all their remaining days. Many pictures of Tintoretto painting his daughter's portrait after her death have been made by later artists.

PAOLI CAGLIARI, or CALIARI, called PAUL VERONESE (1528–1588), was born at Verona, but as he lived mostly at Venice, he belongs to the school of that city. He was an imitator of Titian, whom he did not equal; still he was a fine painter. His excellences were in his harmonious color, his good arrangement of his figures in the foreground, and his fine architectural backgrounds. He tried to make his works magnificent, and to do this he painted festive scenes, with many figures in splendid costumes. He is buried in the Church of St. Sebastian, where there are many of his works.

In the gallery of the Louvre is his "Marriage at Cana." It is thirty by twenty feet in size, and many of its figures are portraits. His pictures are numerous and are seen in the European galleries. The "Family of Darius," in the National Gallery, London, cost that institution the enormous sum of thirteen thousand six hundred and fifty pounds; it was formerly in the Pisani Palace, Venice, and was said to have been left there by Veronese as payment for his entertainment during a visit he had made in the palace. In 1868, at the Demidoff sale, a portrait of his daughter sold for two thousand five hundred and twenty-four pounds.

At the close of the sixteenth century a family of a father and four sons were busy painting what may rightfully be termed the earliest *genre* pictures of Italy. This term is used to denote pictures that stand between historical and utterly imaginary subjects; that is to say, the representation of something that seems real to us because it is so familiar to our imagination, or because it is something that we know might have happened, that it has all the naturalness of an actual reproduction of a fact. There may be interior or landscape *genre* pictures. The first represent familiar in-door scenes—the latter are landscapes with animals or figures to give a life element and to tell a story.

The name of the family of which I speak was Da Ponte, but it was called Bassano, from the birth-place of JACOPO DA PONTE BASSANO (1510–1592), the father, who was the most important of the family. He studied in Venice, but returned to his native town. His portraits are fine; among them are those of the Doge of Venice, Ariosto, and Tasso. His works are very numerous and are seen in all galleries. He introduced landscapes and animals into most of his pictures, sometimes with great impropriety.

We come now to ANTONIO ALLEGRI, called CORREGGIO (1493–1534), who was born at the end of the fifteenth, but did his work in the beginning of the sixteenth century. His name of Correggio is that of his birth-place, and as he was not born at any of the great art centres, and did not adopt the precise manner of any school, he, with his followers, stand by themselves, and yet, because his principal works were done at Parma, he is sometimes said to be of the school of Parma.

When Correggio was thirteen years old he had learned to draw well. He studied under Andrea Mantegna and his son Francesco Mantegna. From these masters he learned to be very skilful in drawing, especially in foreshortening, or in representing objects seen aslant. But though he learned much of the science of art from his teachers, his grace and movement and his exquisite light

FIG. 47.—PORTRAIT OF CORREGGIO.

and shade are all his own, for they did not possess these qualities.

Foreshortening is so important that I must try to explain it; and, as Correggio is said to be the greatest master in this art since the days of the Greeks, it is quite proper for me to speak of it in connection with him. The art of foreshortening is that which makes different objects painted on a plane or flat surface appear as if they were at different distances from the eye of the person who is looking at the picture, or as scenes in nature appear, where one part is much farther off than another. To produce this effect it is often necessary to make an object—let us say, for example, an arm or a leg, look as if it was stretched forward, out of the canvas, directly toward the person who is looking at it. Now, the truth is that in order to produce this effect the object is often thrown backward in the drawing; sometimes also it is doubled up in an unnatural manner, and occupies a small space on the canvas, while it appears to be of life size when one looks at it. A "Christ in Glory" painted by Correggio in the cupola of the Church of San Giovanni Evangelista, in Parma, is a fine piece of foreshortening. The head is so thrown back, and the knees are so thrown forward, that the whole figure seems to be of life size; yet if the space from the top of the head to the soles of the feet were measured, it would be found to be much less than the height of the same figure would be if it were drawn in an erect position.

I have already explained the meaning of chiaro-scuro, and this delicate manner of passing from light to shade was another quality in the works of Correggio. It is even seen in his early works, as, for instance, in the beautiful Madonna di San Francesco, now at Dresden, which he painted when he was but eighteen years old.

When this master was twenty-six years old he married Girolama Nurlini, and about the same time he was summoned to Mantua by the Duke Federigo Gonzaga. During eleven years after his marriage he was occupied with works in Mantua, and with his great frescoes at Parma. In 1530 he returned to Correggio, and there passed the remainder of his life. That he held a high position is proved by certain records of his life, among which is the fact that in 1533 he was invited to be one of the witnesses of the marriage of the Lord of Correggio.

It is said that when this painter saw one of the great works of Raphael, he exclaimed, enthusiastically and thankfully, "I, too, am a painter!" and no doubt he then felt himself moved to attempt such works as should make his name known to all the world through future centuries. When Titian saw Correggio's frescoes at Parma, he said: "Were I not Titian, I should wish to be Correggio." Annibale Caracci, also a great artist, said of Correggio, more than a hundred years after his death, "He was the only painter!" and declared that the children he painted seemed to breathe and smile with such grace that one was forced to smile and be happy with them.

In 1534 Correggio died of a fever, and was buried in his family tomb in the Franciscan Convent of his native city. His grave is simply marked with his name and the date of his death.

Some of his oil-paintings are very famous. One at Dresden, representing the "Nativity of the Saviour," is called the "Notte," or night, because the only light on the picture comes from the halo of glory around the head of the Holy Child. Correggio's "Reading Magdalen" is in the same gallery; probably no one picture exists which has been more universally admired than this.

There was a large work of his representing "The Shepherds Adoring the Infant Saviour," at Seville, in Spain. During the Peninsular War (1808–14) the people of that city sent many valuable things to Cadiz for safety, and this

FIG. 48.—UPPER PART OF A FRESCO BY CORREGGIO.

picture, on account of its size, was cut in two. By some accident the two parts were separated; but both were sold, and the purchaser of each was promised that the other portion should be given him. From this much trouble arose, because both purchasers determined to keep what they had, and each claimed that the whole belonged to him, and as they were equally obstinate, the two parts of the same work have never been reunited. Fortunately, each half makes a picture by itself.

The frescoes at Parma are the greatest works of this master, and it is very interesting to visit that quaint old city; his works are in the Cathedral, the Church of St. John the Evangelist, and in the parlor of the Convent of the Benedictine Nuns. This last is a wonderful room. The ceiling is arched and high, and painted to represent an arbor of vines with sixteen oval openings, out of which frolicsome children are peeping, as if, in passing around behind the vines, they had stopped to look down into the room. The pictures here will make you understand the effect (Figs. 48 and 49). Beneath each of these openings or lunettes is a half-circular picture of some mythological story or personage. Upon the wall of the parlor, above the mantel, there is a picture of Diana, the goddess of the moon and the protector of young animals, which is a beautiful picture.

When Correggio worked on the frescoes at the Church of St. John, he lived much in the monastery connected with it. The monks became very fond of him, and made him a member of the Congregation Cassinensi; the poet Tasso also was a member of this fraternity. This membership gave him the right to share in the masses, prayers, and alms of the community, and after his death the same offices for the repose of his soul would be performed as if he had been a true monk.

The works of Correggio are very rarely sold. The madonna in the National Gallery, London, known as "*La*

Fig. 49.—Lower Part of a Fresco by Correggio.

*Vierge au Panier*," was formerly in the Royal Gallery at Madrid. During the French invasion of Spain, Mr. Wallace, an English artist, obtained it. It is painted on a panel, and is 13½ inches high by 10 inches wide. In 1813 it was offered for sale in London at twelve hundred pounds. In 1825 it was sold in Paris for eighty thousand francs, and soon after sold to the National Gallery for thirty-eight hundred pounds, or nearly nineteen thousand dollars.

A copy of the "Reading Magdalen" was sold to Earl Dudley for sixteen hundred pounds, or more than seven thousand dollars.

Correggio had but few pupils, but he had many imitators. The one most worthy of mention was FRANCESCO MAZZUOLI (1503–1540), called IL PARMIGIANO, or PARMIGIANINO. He was not a great painter. The "Vision of St. Jerome," in the National Gallery, London, is one of his best works. It is said that during the sack of Rome, in 1527, he was painting the figures of the Virgin and Child in this picture, and was so engrossed by his work that the invaders entered his studio, and surrounded him before he was aware of their approach. And they, for their part, were so moved by what they saw that they went away, and left him undisturbed.

Art writers often use the term "early masters." This denotes Michael Angelo, Raphael, and other men so great that they were very prominent in the history of art, and were imitated by so many followers that they had an unusual effect upon the world. Titian may be called the last of these great masters of the early school, and his life was so long that he lived to see a great decline in art.

The painters of the close of the sixteenth century are called "Mannerists," which means that they adopted or imitated the manner or style of some great master who had preceded them—and this was done in so cold and spiritless a way that it may be said that true artistic inspiration was dead in

Italy. No one lived who, out of his own imagination, could fix upon the wall or the canvas such scenes as would befit a poet's dream or serve to arouse the enthusiasm of those who saw the painted story born in the artist's brain.

About 1600, the beginning of the seventeenth century, there arose a new movement in Italian art, which resulted in forming two schools between which there came to be much bitterness of feeling, and even deadly hatred. On one side there were those who wished to continue the study and imitation of the works of the old masters, but with this they united a study of nature. These men were called "Eclectics," because they elected or chose certain parts of different systems of painting, and from these formed a new manner of their own.

Opposed to the Eclectics were the "Naturalists," who insisted that nature only should be studied, and that everything should be represented in the most realistic way, and made to appear in the picture exactly as it did in reality, not being beautified or adorned by any play of fancy or imagination.

The chief school of the Eclectics, of whom I will first speak, was at Bologna, and is known also as the "school of the Caracci," because LUDOVICO CARACCI (1555–1619) was at the head of a large academy there, and was assisted by his nephews, AGOSTINO CARACCI (1558–1601) and ANNIBALE CARACCI (1560–1609), the latter being the greatest artist of the three. The lives of the Caracci are not of such interest as to require an account of them here, neither are their works so interesting that we may not leave these artists by saying that they have great consideration as the heads of the Eclectic Academy, and for the work they did in it at an important era in the history of Italian art; but the fruits of their work are shown in that of their scholars rather than in their own paintings, and in this view their influence can scarcely be overvalued.

The greatest of their scholars was DOMENICO ZAMPIERI (1581–1641), called DOMENICHINO, who was born at Bologna, and was instructed by Denis Calvert, who forbade his drawing after the works of Annibale Caracci. Domenico disobeyed this command, and was so severely treated by Calvert that he persuaded his father to take him from that master, and place him in the school of the Caracci. When he entered the Academy he was so dull that his fellow-pupils nicknamed him "The Ox;" but Annibale Caracci said: "Take care: this ox will surpass you all by and by, and will be an honor to his art." Domenichino soon began to win many prizes in the school, and left it well trained and prepared for a brilliant career.

He gave much thought to his art, shunned private society, and if he went out at all he frequented public places where large numbers of people were gathered, thus affording him an opportunity to study their varying expressions. He also tried to feel in himself the emotions of the person he was painting. For instance, it is said that when he was painting the "Scourging of St. Andrew," he threw himself into a passion, and used threatening gestures and high words. In the midst of this his master, Annibale Caracci, surprised him, and was so impressed with his method that he threw his arms about his pupil's neck, exclaiming, "Today, my Domenichino, thou art teaching me!"

The most celebrated work by Domenichino is the "Communion of St. Jerome," in the Vatican. It is universally considered the second picture in Rome, the "Transfiguration," by Raphael, being the only one that is placed before it. The scene it represents is just before the death of the saint, when he was borne into the chapel to receive the sacrament of the communion for the last time (Fig. 50).

Domenichino was made very unhappy in Rome, on account of the jealousy of other artists, and he returned to Bologna. However, his fame had reached the court at

FIG. 50.—COMMUNION OF ST. JEROME.

Naples, and the viceroy of that city invited the artist to decorate the Chapel of St. Januarius. There was in Naples at that time an association of artists who had determined that no strange artist should be allowed to do work of any account in their city. As soon as Domenichino began his work, therefore, he received letters threatening his life. His colors were spoiled by having ruinous chemicals mixed with them, his sketches were stolen from his studio, and all sorts of insults and indignities were heaped upon him.

After a time, the painter was so disheartened that he fled to Rome; but the viceroy sent for him and took every precaution possible to protect him and enable him to work in peace. But just as all seemed to be going well he sickened and died, and it has always been said that he was poisoned. Be this as it may, there is no doubt that the fear, vexation, and anxiety of his life caused his death, and on this account his tormentors were his murderers.

The works of Domenichino are not numerous, and are not seen in as many galleries as are those of some Italian painters; but there are a considerable number scattered over Europe and very beautiful ones in several galleries in Rome.

The next painter of importance in the Eclectic school was GUIDO RENI (1575–1642), born at Bologna, and the son of a professor of music. His father intended that Guido also should be a musician, and the poor boy was much persecuted on account of his love for drawing. But after many struggles the boy came into the Caracci school, and was soon a favorite pupil there.

When still young he listened with great attention to a lecture from Annibale, in which he laid down the rules which should govern a true painter. Guido resolved to follow these rules closely, and soon he painted so well that he was accused of trying to establish a new system of painting. At last Ludovico Caracci turned against him and dismissed him from his school.

FIG. 51.—AURORA. *By Guido Reni.*

The young artist went to Rome; but his persecutions did not cease, and it seemed to be his fate to excite the jealousy of other painters. Now, when so much time has elapsed, we know that Guido was not a very great master, and had he painted in the days of Michael Angelo he would not have been thought so. But art had lowered its standard, and Guido's works were suited to the taste of his time; he had a high conception of beauty, and he tried to reach it in his pictures.

In the course of his career Guido really painted in three styles. His earliest pictures are the strongest; those of his middle period are weaker, because he seemed only to strive to represent grace and sweetness; his latest pictures are careless and unequal in execution, for he grew indifferent to fame, and became so fond of gaming that he only painted in order to get money to spend in this sinful folly.

His masterpiece in Rome was the "Aurora," on a ceiling of the Rospigliosi Palace; it represents the goddess of the dawn as floating before the chariot of Apollo, or Phœbus, the god of the sun. She scatters flowers upon the earth, he holds the reins over four piebald and white horses, while Cupid, with his lighted torch, floats just above them. Around the chariot dance seven graceful female figures which represent the Hours, or Horæ. I have been asked why seven was the number; the ancients had no fixed number for the Hours; sometimes they were spoken of as two, again three, and even in some cases as ten. It has always seemed to me that ten was the number chosen by Guido, for in that case there would naturally be three out of sight, on the side of the chariot which is not seen (Fig. 51).

The portrait of Beatrice Cenci is another very celebrated picture by Guido; it is in the gallery of the Barberini Palace, in Rome (Fig. 52). The interest in the portrait of this unhappy girl is world-wide. She was the daughter of a

FIG. 52.—BEATRICE CENCI.

wealthy Roman noble, who after the death of her mother married a second time, and treated the children of his first marriage in a brutal way. It is even said that he hired assassins to murder two of his sons on their return from a journey to Spain. The story also relates that his cruelty to Beatrice was such that, with the aid of her stepmother and her brother, she killed him. At all events, these three were accused of this crime and were executed for it in 1599. Other accounts say that he was murdered by robbers, and his wife and children were made to appear as if guilty. Clement VII. was the pope at that time, and in spite of his knowledge of the cruelty of the father he would not pardon them, though mercy was implored of him for this lovely girl. The reason given for this action of the pope's is that he wished to confiscate the Cenci estates, which he could do if the family suffered the death penalty. So many reproductions of this sad face have been made that it is very familiar to us, and almost seems to have been the face of some one whom we have known.

Guido did not paint his St. Michael for the Cappucini in Rome until after he returned to his native city. When he sent the picture to the monks, he wrote: "I wish I had the wings of an angel to have ascended into Paradise, and there to have beholden the forms of those beatified spirits from which I might have copied my archangel; but not being able to mount so high, it was in vain for me to search for his resemblance here below, so that I was forced to make an introspection into my own mind, and into that idea of beauty which I have formed in my own imagination."

We are told that he always tried to paint his ideal of beauty rather than to reproduce any human beauty that he had seen. He would pose his color-grinder, and draw his outlines from him, and then fill in with his own conceptions of what the head he was painting should be; this accounts for the sameness in his heads and faces.

His passion for gaming degraded the close of his life. It led him into great distresses, and for the sake of money he painted many pictures which are not worthy of his name. He had always received generous prices for his pictures, but he left many debts as a blot upon his memory. His works are seen in the galleries of Europe, and are always admired for their feeling, beauty, and grace.

FRANCESCO ALBANI (1578–1660), born at Bologna, was another scholar of the Caracci school, and a friend of Guido Reni. There are many works of his in Rome. His pictures of landscapes with figures were his best works, and beauty was his characteristic. His own home had all the advantages for painting such works as he best succeeded in, such as Venus and the Loves, maids and boys, children and Cupids in unending variety.

His villa was surrounded by charming views. His wife was very handsome, and they had twelve lovely children, so lovely that it is said that other artists besides himself made use of them for models.

There were several other Eclectics of some importance of whom we shall not speak, but shall leave them with an account of ELISABETTA SIRANI (1640–1665), who also was born at Bologna, and is worthy of attention on account of her talents, while the story of her life adds another interest than that which she has as an artist.

She was an imitator of the attractive manner of Guido Reni. The heads of her madonnas and magdalens are charming, and, indeed, all her work speaks of the innate refinement of her nature. Her industry was marvellous, since she made one hundred and fifty pictures and etchings in a period of about ten years. Much has been said of the rapidity with which she worked, and one story relates that on a certain day the Duchess of Brunswick, the Duchess of Mirandola, and the Duke Cosimo de Medici, with other persons, met in her studio, and she sketched and shaded drawings of subjects which they named to her, with a skill and celerity which astonished and delighted her guests.

Her masterpiece is a picture of "St. Anthony Adoring the Virgin and Child," which is in the Pinacoteca of Bologna. There are pictures by her in the Belvedere and Lichtenstein Galleries at Vienna, in the Hermitage at St. Petersburg, and in the Sciarra Palace, Rome.

In person Elisabetta Sirani was beautiful, and her character commanded the affection of all who knew her. She was a sweet singer, and her biographers increase her virtues by praising her taste in dress, and even her moderation in eating! She was skilful in domestic affairs, and was in the habit of rising early to perform her share in the household duties, never allowing her art to displace any occupation which properly made a part of her life. Her name has come down through more than two centuries as one whose "devoted filial affection, feminine grace, and artless benignity of manner added a lustre to her great talents, and completed a personality which her friends regarded as an ideal of perfection."

She died very suddenly, and the cause of her death has never been known; but the theory that she was poisoned has been generally accepted. Several reasons for the crime have been given; one is that she was the victim of jealous artists, as Domenichino had been; another, that a princely lover whom she had scorned thus revenged himself. A servant-girl in her family was suspected of the crime, tried, and banished; but after a time she was recalled to Bologna at the request of the father of Elisabetta, for he saw no proof of the girl's guilt. Thus the mystery was never solved, but the whole city of Bologna was saddened by her death. The day of her burial was one of public mourning; her funeral was attended with great pomp, and she was buried beside Guido Reni in the splendid church of the Dominicans. Poems and orations in her praise were numerous, and a book was published, called "Il Penello Lagrimate," which contained these, with odes, anagrams, and epitaphs, in both Latin and Italian, all setting forth her charms and virtues. Her portrait in the Ercolani Gallery at Bologna represents her when occupied in painting her father's portrait; according to this picture she had a tall, elegant figure, and a very pretty face. She had two sisters, Barbara and Anna Maria, who also were artists, but her fame was so much greater than theirs that she quite overshadowed them.

The earliest master of the Naturalists was MICHAEL ANGELO AMERIGI, called CARAVAGGIO, from the name of his birth-place (1569–1609). His life and character was not such as to make him an attractive study. His subjects and his manner of representing them combined in producing what has been called "the poetry of the repulsive." He was wild in his nature and lived a wild life. His religious subjects, even, were coarse, though his color was vivid and his figures arranged with good effect. His "False Players" is one of his best works; it represents two men playing cards, while a third looks over the shoulder of one as if advising him what to play.

Naturally, his manner of painting was best suited to scenes from common life, though he made those coarse and sometimes painful; but when he attempted subjects of a higher order his works are positively offensive. Some of his sacred pictures were removed from the altars for which they were painted on account of their coarseness. His most celebrated work is the "Entombment of Christ," at the Vatican; in the Gallery of the Capitol in Rome there is a "Fortune Teller," which is also a fine work.

Next to Caravaggio came GIUSEPPE RIBERA, called IL SPAGNOLETTO (1588–1656). He was a native of Valencia, and when very young made his way to Rome, so that, although his education as an artist was wholly Italian, his familiar name arose from his Spanish origin. While living in miserable poverty in Rome, and industriously copying such frescoes as he could gain access to, he attracted the attention of a cardinal, who took him to his home, and made him comfortable. But the young painter soon ran away, and returned to his street life. The cardinal sougnt him out, and called him an "ungrateful little Spaniard;" but Ribera excused his conduct by saying that as soon as he was made comfortable and was well fed he lost all ambition to work, adding that it would require the spur of poverty to make him a good painter. The cardinal respected his courage, and the story being repeated to other artists, much interest was attracted to him.

Later he went to Naples, and joined the cabal there which had agreed to persecute the strange artists who should come to work in that city. If Ribera did not actually commit many of the crimes which were done there, he was responsible for them through his influence. His works are frequently so brutal in their subjects and treatment that one feels that he who painted them must have lost all the kindliness of his nature.

He married the daughter of a rich picture dealer, and became very rich himself. In 1630 he was made a member of the Academy of St. Luke, at Rome, and in 1648 Pope Innocent X. sent him the cross of the Order of Christ. Few Italian artists were better known in their own country, and many of his pictures were sent to Spain. His greatest excellence was in his knowledge of anatomy, and he painted subjects that enabled him to show this. Among his famous works are a "Descent from the Cross;" "The Flaying of St. Bartholomew;" "Ixion on the Wheel;" and "Cato of Utica." His works are in all the famous galleries of the world.

Ribera's greatest pupil was SALVATOR ROSA (1615–1673), the landscape painter, who was a very gifted man, being a poet and musician as well as an artist. His father was an educated man, and with his other relatives encouraged his son in his taste for art. When twenty years old he went to Rome, and with the exception of some intervals remained there during his life.

It is said that as a youth he associated much with bandits, and, when one considers the wildness of many of his scenes and the character of the figures in their midst, it is not difficult to believe that this may have been true. It is certain that he painted the portrait of the famous Masaniello more than once, and he is believed to have joined the *Compagnia della Morte*, of which Falcone, one of his masters, was the captain.

Salvator made many enemies by his independence and his inclination to satire. He wrote satires on various subjects which were not published until after his death, but it was known that he had written them. He married a Florentine woman, who was the mother of his two sons. When he died he was buried in the Church of Santa Maria degli Angeli, where a monument is erected to his memory.

He painted some historical subjects and portraits in which he followed the Naturalists, but his principal works were landscapes. Jagged rocks and mountains, wild dells and lonely defiles, with here and there robbers, hermits, or soldiers, make his most effective pictures. There is a deep sense of desolation, almost of fear, in them which is very impressive. Sometimes he painted serene landscapes and poetic figures; but his best works are not of this sort. His pictures are in the principal public and in some private galleries. He also left about ninety etchings which are masterly in execution and full of expression in the heads, while the atmosphere is soft. When his works are sold they bring great prices. A large landscape with Apollo and the Sibyl in the foreground brought eight thousand five hundred dollars in England years ago, and is now worth much more than that.

Early in the eighteenth century an artist named ANTONIO CANALE (1697–1768), called CANALETTO, began to make views of the city of Venice and scenes on the canals. He had two followers, BERNARDO BELLOTTI (1720–1780), who was his nephew, and FRANCESCO GUARDI (1712–1793), and these three painters executed a large number of these pictures, which are found in many European galleries, and it is not always easy to distinguish their authorship. There is no doubt that many which were once attributed to the first master were really painted by his pupils.

Before the commencement of the eighteenth century the decline of the Renaissance school in Italy had begun; in fact, the painting of the seventeenth century came to be mere mechanical realism. For this reason the portraits were the best pictures of the time, as in them it was requisite to be true to the object represented.

Late in the eighteenth century a new impulse was given to Italian painting, chiefly through the influence of foreign artists such as Raphael Mengs, and the French painter David. In the beginning of our own century LORENZO BENVENUTI (1769–1844) executed some excellent frescoes in Florence, Siena, and Arezzo, which was his native city. He decorated the ceiling of the Medici Chapel in the Church of San Lorenzo in Florence, and Leopold II., Grand Duke of Tuscany, erected a tomb to this painter in the same church where he had spent so much time and talent. His portrait, painted by himself, is in the gallery of the Uffizi, at Florence. VINCENZIO CAMMUCCINI (1775–1844), too, was a celebrated master of his time. He was a Roman by birth, and became President of the Academy of St. Luke; he was also a member of the Institute of France, and received decorations from sovereigns of various countries. He made many copies from the works of the great masters. His portraits were so much admired as to be compared to those of Rubens and Tintoretto, and his ceiling frescoes in the Torlonia Palace, Rome, were among his important works, as was a "Presentation of Christ in the Temple," painted for the Church of San Giovanni in Piacenza.

But there has been no true restoration of Italian art. The painting of Italy in our time has been largely a commercial enterprise rather than an outcome from artistic genius or impulse, and the few works which are exceptions to this rule are not sufficient to encourage the hope that this nation can again attain to her former rank or regain the fame of her past in the history of modern art.

## CHAPTER IV.

### PAINTING IN FLANDERS, HOLLAND, AND GERMANY.

FLANDERS formerly embraced a larger part of Belgium than is contained in the present Belgian provinces of East and West Flanders. It also covered a portion of Holland and some territory in the northwest of France. The principal Flemish towns connected with the story of Flemish art were Bruges, Tournai, Louvain, Ghent, Antwerp, Brussels, Mechlin, Liege, and Utrecht.

There are some records of Flemish painting much earlier than the fifteenth century, but they are so vague and uncertain that I shall pass them over, and begin with the family of Van Eyck, in which there were four painters—three brothers and a sister. The eldest, HUBERT VAN EYCK (1366–1426), effected a great change in the art of his time and country. Very little is known of him as a young man, or indeed of his personal history at all, except that he passed his middle life at Bruges and his later years at Ghent. The subjects of his pictures were mostly scriptural. I do not suppose that the pictures of this master would seem very beautiful to you if you saw them, but they are of great value. His greatest work was an altar-piece for Judocus Vyts and his wife Lisabetta; it was for the decoration of their funeral chapel in the Church of St. Bavon in Ghent. It was an immense work, with a centre-piece and wings that could be closed; the inside was divided into twelve different pictures, and the outside also was painted. We do not know how much of this was completed when Hubert died and left it to be finished by his brother John. Philip I. of Spain wished to buy this altar-piece, and when he could not do so, he employed Michael Coxie to copy it; this artist spent two years on the work, and was paid four thousand florins. Of the original work, a large portion remains in the Church of St. Bavon; the wings, consisting of six beautiful, tall panels, are in the Berlin Museum, and two outer compartments are in the Brussels Museum. The picture of holy men who have served God is on one of the wings of this altar-piece (Fig. 53).

But the principal interest attached to Hubert van Eyck comes from the fact that he made such discoveries in the use of colors as led to what we call the "Invention of Oil-Painting," and this invention is always attributed to the Van Eycks, for it is probable that the discoveries of Hubert were perfected by JAN VAN EYCK (1390–1440), who became a celebrated painter. Oil-painting had been known, it is true, a long time, but the manner of preparing the colors and the varnish used before the time of the Van Eycks was very unsatisfactory, and the improvement of these substances was the work of these masters.

The pictures of Hubert van Eyck are stronger than those of Jan, who was really the founder of a school remarkable for delicacy and fine finish rather than for power. It was after the death of Hubert that the fame of the new colors spread abroad, and thus it happened that it was to Jan that other artists went to learn his secrets.

Jan van Eyck was something of a diplomat as well as a painter, for when he was in the service of Philip the Good, Duke of Burgundy, he was sent on several secret missions, and in 1428 he accompanied the ambassadors of the duke to Portugal in order to paint the portrait of Isabella of Portugal, who was betrothed to the duke. There is a goodly number of works by Jan van Eyck in various galleries. The

FIG. 53.—THE ANCHORITES. *In S. Bavon at Ghent.*

portrait of himself and wife in the National Gallery, London, is very interesting; they stand hand in hand, with a terrier dog at their feet; their dress and all the details of their surroundings are painted with great care. It is said that the Princess Mary, sister of Charles V., gave a barber who owned it a position with a handsome salary in exchange for the picture. Jan van Eyck, being twenty years younger than his brother Hubert, naturally learned all that the elder knew, and the story of his life gives him the appearance of being the more important artist, though in point of highest merit he was not the superior.

Of LAMBERT VAN EYCK very little is known. It is believed that he made the copy of Hubert's great work which is in the Antwerp Museum; another work called by his name is in Louvain. MARGARETHA VAN EYCK is said to have been a skilful artist, but no one picture can be ascribed to her; she was buried beside her brother Hubert in the Cathedral of Ghent.

Of course the van Eycks had many followers. Among them were PETRUS CHRISTUS (records 1444–1471), GERARD VAN DER MEIRE (records 1447–1474), HUGO VON DER GOES (1405?–1482), and JUSTUS OF GHENT (1468–?), all of whom were good artists, but I shall pass to a more important one, ROGIER VAN DER WEYDEN (1400–1464), who was himself the head of a school of as great importance as was that of the van Eycks. His realism was his chief characteristic, and this was so great as to make some of his works repulsive, especially his martyrdoms, in which he detailed horrors with great exactness. He also loved to paint pictures which illustrated the myths of the Middle Ages. Our illustration is from one of these works (Fig. 54).

This picture is from the story that when the Roman Senate decreed divine honors to the Emperor Augustus, he consulted the Tiburtine Sibyl as to whether he ought to receive them or no. She replied to him that it was more becoming for him to go away silently, and told him that a Hebrew child should be born who should reign over the gods themselves, or that a king should come from heaven whose power should never end. Another version, which is the one this picture represents, says that the heavens opened, and a vision of the Virgin with the Saviour in her arms, standing on an altar, was shown the emperor. He worshipped it, and heard a voice saying, "Haec ara filii Dei" (This is the altar of the Son of God). Augustus reported this to the Senate, and erected an altar upon the spot in Rome where the Church of Santa Maria in Capitolio, or the "Ara Cœli," now stands.

FIG. 54.—THE SIBYL AND THE EMPEROR AUGUSTUS. *By Rogier van der Weyden. In the Berlin Museum.*

Many pictures by Van der Weyden are seen in European galleries. He was also a fine miniaturist. He was official painter to the city of Brussels, and was buried in its cathedral.

His son, ROGIER VAN DER WEYDEN the younger, became very rich and benevolent. He died at Brussels in 1529. His works are not numerous in public galleries.

The elder Van der Weyden had a pupil, HANS MEMLING (records 1450–1499), who became the greatest master in Belgium. I shall not give you a long account of him; but shall tell you of his greatest work, which was the Shrine of St. Ursula, at the Hospital of Bruges, and is the best example of this type of early Flemish art which still exists. It is divided into six compartments, with two ends, and other panels on top, all of which are finished with the greatest care, and give the whole story of St. Ursula and her eleven thousand virgins, which is that Ursula was a daughter of a king of Brittany who was a Christian. The young girl was educated with the greatest care, and the fame of her beauty and wisdom spread all over Europe. At length the king of England asked for her to be the wife of his son. The princess replied that she would wed him on three conditions: first, that he should give her ten virgins of noble blood for her companions, then to each of these virgins and to herself he should give a thousand maidens as attendants; second, he should allow her three years with these companions, with whom she should visit the shrines where the bodies of the saints repose; and third, the English king and his court should receive baptism.

I cannot give space for all the details of this story, which is of great interest; but the result was that Ursula received all that she asked, and started on her journey to Rome, in the course of which she and the eleven thousand maidens met with many adventures. At last, having reached Cologne on their return, they encountered an army of barbarians which was besieging the city, and all were slain.

The subjects of the pictures as they were painted by Memling were: 1, the first landing at Cologne in the beginning of the journey; 2, the landing at Basle; 3, the arrival in Rome; 4, the second arrival at Basle on her return toward home; 5, commencement of the martyrdom, when Ursula and her train are first seen by the barbarians; 6, death of Ursula.

The works of Memling which still remain are numerous, and are seen in many public galleries. After the death of this master the purity of Flemish painting declined. Many artists visited Italy, and the manner of Flemish painters was influenced by association with Italian art and artists. I shall, therefore, pass over a period when no very important masters appeared, and speak next of a great man, QUINTIN MATSYS (1466–1529), who began life as a blacksmith. He was born at Antwerp, and there are specimens of iron work there said to have been executed by him. It is said that he fell in love with the daughter of an artist who refused to allow him to marry her because he was not a painter; for this reason Matsys devoted himself to the study of art, and became the best Belgian master of his time. His pictures of religious subjects are full of tender earnestness and deep feeling, and his most important work was an altarpiece which is now in the Museum of Antwerp. His scenes from common life, his misers and lovers are spirited and truthful.

His portrait and that of his second wife, both painted by himself, are in the gallery of the Uffizi in Florence. His works are not very numerous, but they are seen in the principal galleries. He was buried in the Cathedral of Antwerp, and a slab is inserted in the wall which tells his story; one sentence is, "*Connubialis amor de mulcibre fecit Apellene*" (True love changed the smith to an Apelles).

Rubens is the next great master of whom I shall speak, but I wish to say that during the last part of the sixteenth century there were many Flemish painters of considerable note whose pictures are seen in galleries, and are well worth consideration, but whose lives had no circumstances of especial interest. Among the best of these artists were

ANTONIO MORO, PETER POURBUS (1510-1583), and his son and grandson, both named Frans, PIETER BREUGHEL (1530-1569), and his sons Jan and Pieter the younger, and PAUL BRIL, an early Flemish landscape painter.

All the early Flemish pictures are very interesting, but in the beginning of the seventeenth century a new manner of painting was introduced through the genius of PETER PAUL RUBENS (1577-1640). This master was descended from two good families: his mother was of the distinguished family Pypeling, and his father, John Rubens, was one of the two principal magistrates of Antwerp. This city was the home of Rubens, although he was born at Siegen, in the county of Nassau, during a time when his father was in exile on account of a civil war which was then raging. He was born June 29th, the feast of Sts. Peter and Paul, and hence was named for those apostles.

He was a bright, scholarly boy, and soon showed his love for drawing. When he began to study art under Adam van Noort he had already a good education. During the four years he passed with this teacher he learned thoroughly all the technical part of painting; then, in another four years under Otto Vænius, he cultivated his taste and the more poetical elements of his nature, for Vænius was a very learned and elegant man. In 1598, when twenty-one years old, Rubens was admitted to the guild of painters in Antwerp. Two years later he went to Venice, and, after studying the works of Titian and Paul Veronese there, he entered the service of the Duke of Mantua, to whom he had been recommended by the governor of the Netherlands.

While in Mantua he painted some fine pictures, and the duke sent him to Rome to copy celebrated works there. Rubens also executed some other orders in Rome, from which place he was recalled by the duke, who wished to send an envoy to Spain, and had chosen the young artist for that duty. He showed great political ability in the way he

FIG. 55.—RUBENS AND HIS SECOND WIFE.

conducted his embassy, and through his personal charms made many friends.

After his return from Spain he went again to Rome and then to Genoa, and finally, on account of the illness of his mother, he returned to Antwerp, having been absent seven years. His mother died before he reached her. He then decided to remain in Antwerp, and built himself a fine house with a charming studio. He soon married his first wife, Isabella Brant, and during the next fifteen years led a very regular and industrious life, and executed many important works. He also received a large number of pupils into his studio, and he has been accused of allowing them to paint pictures which he called by his own name; but it is true that Rubens, with his own hand, completed pictures of almost every kind, and so proved his power as an artist.

He was fond of study, and could read and speak seven languages. He was in the habit of having some one read aloud to him while he painted, and preferred books of history and poetry. In 1620 he was invited to France by Marie de Medicis, for whom he executed many works. Among them the most important were scenes illustrating the life of this queen which decorate some apartments in the Louvre.

In 1628 the Infanta Isabella sent him on a second mission to Spain, and while there he painted many grand and important pictures, which are fine examples of his gorgeous coloring. He proved himself so good a diplomatist that he was sent to England to try to make peace between that country and Flanders, in which he was successful. He was knighted by King Charles in 1630, and received the same honor from the king of Spain.

In 1630 he married Helena Forment, a niece of his first wife, who was but sixteen years old. She became the mother of five children; he had two sons by his first marriage, to whom Gevartius was tutor. Rubens made so many portraits of both his wives and so often used them as models in painting his large pictures, that their faces are familiar to all the world (Fig. 55).

Rubens made a valuable collection of all sorts of beautiful objects, and lived luxuriously. After his death a portion of his collection was sold at private sale for more than seventy-five thousand dollars. His death occurred in 1640, and he was buried in a private chapel in the Church of St. James in Antwerp; he had decorated this chapel with some works of his own. His family erected a monument to him, upon which an epitaph written by Gevartius was inscribed.

In painting Rubens was almost a universal genius, for he left a great variety of works as well as a great number. About one thousand eight hundred are ascribed to him: doubtless his pupils did much work on these; but there is something of himself in all. They include historical, scriptural, and mythological subjects, portraits, animals, *genre* pictures, and landscapes. His style is a strange mingling of northern and southern elements. His handling and his arrangement of his subjects was like that of the Italians; but his figures, even when he represented Christ and the holiest men, were like Spanish kings or German peasants, or somebody whom he had seen.

We have not space to speak in detail of the works of Rubens. Some critics insist that one class of his pictures is best, and some another. Of course this depends largely upon the taste of those who make the judgment. It is certain that he was a wonderful painter, and many of his pictures give great pleasure to those who visit the galleries where they are seen.

His pictures of children were so painted that they seem to have been done from pure love of the work. His portraits are splendid, his *genre* scenes delightful, and his landscapes fine; in short, the amount and variety of his work is a proof of his great genius and industry, such as can scarcely

FIG. 56.—THE RETURN FROM EGYPT. *By Rubens.*

be equalled in the history of painting. Yet it cannot be denied that there is much incorrect drawing, unnatural coloring, and coarse, bad taste in some of his works. On the other hand, the fertility of his imagination, his bold design and effective execution, as well as his brilliant color, are all to be admired, and the name of Rubens stands high on the list of Flemish artists who are famous the world over.

FRANS SNYDERS (1579–1657) was born at Antwerp and lived in the time of Rubens. He was a famous painter of animals, and it sometimes happened that they worked together, Rubens painting the landscapes and figures and Snyders the animals in the same pictures. Snyders, like Rubens, excelled in representing animals in the most exciting moment of the combat or the chase, and his pictures are full of life. They are seen in all large European galleries, and are much prized.

JAN FYT (1609–1661), also born at Antwerp, is the greatest Flemish animal painter after Snyders. His greyhounds cannot be equalled, while his live dogs are wonderful; but his best pictures represent dead game. The fur and feathers in his paintings are marvellously done, and his pictures are among the best in the world in which such subjects are treated.

JACOB JORDAENS (1593–1678), another native of Antwerp, studied under Adam van Noort at the same time with Rubens, but later in life he became a follower and a sort of assistant of his former fellow-pupil. He married a daughter of their old master and never visited Italy. His color was fine; in truth, he sometimes excelled Rubens himself in the "golden glow" which is much admired in his works. Many sacred pictures by Jordaens are seen in the churches of Flanders. A fine historical work of his represents scenes from the life of Prince Frederick Henry of Orange, and is in the House of the Wood, near the Hague; but the larger part of his pictures represent the manners and customs of the common people, and are seen in public galleries.

The greatest artist among the pupils of Rubens, as well as one of the greatest of Flanders, was ANTHONY VANDYCK (1599–1641). He was born in Antwerp, and was the son of a silk merchant, this having been the occupation of the Vandycks for several generations. The mother of the painter was extremely skilled in various kinds of embroidery, and had such artistic tastes as enabled her to make many original designs, which she worked out with her needle in delicate and elaborate tapestry work.

Some people believe that to this taste and talent of his mother's Vandyck owed the instinct for drawing which he early showed ; at all events, she did all she could to develop his taste, and when he was still a boy she persuaded her husband to place him under the teaching of Henry van Balen.

He was still quite young when he entered the studio of Rubens, and was soon so much trusted by the master as to be allowed to make drawings from his works for the use of the engravers. This sort of drawing must be done with great care and exactness, and Vandyck must have had much skill to be fitted for it. His fellow-pupils also had great faith in him, as is shown by the story that one day, when Rubens had gone out, the young student bribed his old servant to show them the painting with which the master was then occupied. While jostling each other it happened that one of them hit the fresh picture, and injured it. They were much alarmed, and begged Vandyck to repair it. After some hesitation he did so, and was so successful that at first Rubens did not detect the fact that another had worked on the picture. When he did discover it, and learned the truth about it he forgave the offence heartily.

When Vandyck was nineteen years old he was admitted to the Society of Artists in Antwerp, an unusual honor to one of his age. In 1620 Vandyck went to England, having been invited there through the Earl of Arundel. Little is known of this visit, and two years later he was invited to the Hague, where he spent several months.

When Vandyck was passing through Haarlem he went to the studio of Franz Hals, who was at a tavern just then. A message was sent him saying that a stranger desired to have his portrait made, and had but two hours to spare for it. Hals hastened home and dashed off the portrait within the time stated. Vandyck then said, "Portrait-painting seems to be a simple thing; take my place, and give me the brush for awhile." Hals complied with the request and Vandyck made his portrait with great celerity. Seeing this, Hals cried out, "You are Vandyck; he alone can do such work."

The young artist was suddenly called to the death-bed of his father, who commanded him to paint a picture for the Dominican Sisters who had cared for his father in his illness. Seven years later Vandyck presented the Sisters with a Crucifixion. At the foot of the cross was a rock upon which was inscribed, in Latin, "Lest the earth should be heavy upon the remains of his father, Anthony Vandyck moved this rock to the foot of the cross, and gave it to this place." When the monasteries were broken up, this picture was purchased for two thousand seven hundred dollars for the Antwerp Academy, where it now is.

At length Vandyck prepared to set out for Italy. When he paid his farewell visit to Rubens he presented the master with three of his pictures, and in return Rubens gave him one of his finest horses. As Vandyck was on his way from Antwerp to Brussels he halted at the village of Saventhem, where he fell in love with Anna van Ophem, and so stayed on in the lovely valley of Flanders, week after week, as if he had forgotten that Italy existed. Anna persuaded him to paint a picture for the village church, and he executed a

Holy Family in which the Virgin was a portrait of Anna, and St. Joachim and St. Anna were drawn from her father and mother. This picture pleased the church authorities so much that they gave the young painter an order for another, which represented St. Martin dividing his cloak with beggars. In this work the saint was a portrait of Vandyck, and the horse on which he rode was like that which Rubens had given him.

This picture has quite a history. In 1758 the priest agreed to sell it to a collector from the Hague for one thousand eight hundred dollars; but when the villagers knew of it they surrounded the church with clubs and pitchforks, and drove the purchaser away. In 1806, when the French invaders tried to carry it away, the people again prevented it, and they were forced to call more soldiers from Brussels before they succeeded in taking it. The St. Martin was placed in the Gallery of the Louvre, at Paris, but was restored to Saventhem in 1815. About 1850 a rich American offered twenty thousand dollars for the picture, no matter who brought it to him. Upon this a set of rogues tried to steal it at night; but the dogs of the village gave such an alarm that the town was roused, and the robbers escaped with difficulty. Since then a guardian sleeps in the church, and the St. Martin is still there.

The news that Vandyck was thus lingering on his way to Italy reached the ears of Rubens, and he sent such urgent messages to his pupil as induced him to continue his journey, and he also sent him letters of introduction to artists and to nobles whom the master had known when he made his studies beyond the Alps.

Vandyck went first to Venice, where he worked hard to copy and learn to imitate the rich color and refined manner of Titian and other Venetian masters. He also painted some original pictures in Venice, and made many portraits which gave him fame in that and other cities. He was asked to go to other places for the painting of portraits; but he remained in Venice until his money was spent, and then went to Genoa, where he was well received and generously employed by the old friends of Rubens. His works are still to be seen in some of the palaces of that city, while some have been sold and carried to other countries—they were so fine that they still maintain the name which they gained for him when they were executed. The principal work done in Genoa was a picture of the Lomellini family which is now in Edinburgh; it is about nine feet square. His different visits to Genoa during his absence in Italy make up a period of about three years, and he did a vast amount of work there.

When he first went to Rome Vandyck was invited to the house of Cardinal Bentivoglio, who had been papal nuncio to Flanders, and for whom our artist made a picture of the Crucifixion. The full-length portrait which Vandyck painted of the cardinal is now in Florence; a copy of it is in one of the halls of Harvard College. It is one of the finest among the many splendid portraits by this great master.

Vandyck was fascinated with Rome, but he was so unpopular with the other Flemish painters there that he shortened his stay in the Eternal City in order to escape the vexations he there received. The artists disliked him for his ostentation, and he was called *Il pittore cavalieresco*—and he offended them by declining to associate with them at taverns or to join their coarse festivities. After leaving Rome he visited Palermo, from which place he was driven away by the appearance of the plague. He returned to Genoa, visited Florence and other cities in the north of Italy, and finally returned to Antwerp after an absence of four years.

During the first years after his return he met with small success—Rubens was so great that he filled all the space about him—but at last, in 1628, Vandyck began to receive important commissions, and from this time was constantly busy with works for the churches of the Low Countries. He also painted portraits of many notable persons, and made great numbers of them in brown and white for the use of engravers. While Vandyck was thus executing great numbers of fine pictures for the embellishment of Flanders, he became so unpopular and his rivals said such hard things of him that he determined to go away. One of his unfortunate experiences was in the house of the bishop, who had sent for him to paint his portrait. Vandyck had first sent his implements to the care of the porter of the palace. When he went himself he was taken into the presence of the bishop, who was reclining on a sofa, and gave little attention to the artist. At last the bishop asked if he had not come to paint his portrait. Vandyck declared himself to be quite at the service of his lordship. "Why, then," said the bishop, "do you not go for your implements? Do you expect me to fetch them for you?" Vandyck calmly replied, "Since you have not ordered your servants to bring them I supposed that you wished to do it yourself." Then the bishop leaped up in anger and cried out, "Anthony, Anthony, you are a little asp, but you have a great deal of venom!" Vandyck thought it safe to make his escape, and after he crossed the threshold he called back, "My lord Van der Burch, you are a voluminous personage, but you are like the cinnamon tree. The bark is the best part of you."

In 1629 Vandyck went to England with the hope of being employed by King Charles I.; but he was not able even to get an introduction to the sovereign, and went to the continent filled with mortification. At length, however, Charles called him to London, whither he went in 1632, and soon became the friend of the king as well as his favorite artist. He was assigned a city and a country residence, and within three months of the time of his arrival at court the king knighted him, and gave him a gold chain with a portrait of himself set in brilliants suspended from it. Charles was in the habit of passing much time with Vandyck, and the studio of the court-painter became one of the most fashionable resorts in London for the courtiers and other distinguished people.

Vandyck kept up a fine establishment, and lived luxuriously. He had a habit of asking his sitters to dinner; thus he could study their faces and retouch their portraits with the more natural expressions of their conversational hours, for it is rare that one is natural when posing before an artist who is painting one's portrait. But in the midst of his busy life as an artist and his gay life as a man of the world, Sir Anthony did not forget the needs of his brother painters. There was at that time no club or place where artists met socially to consult and aid each other in their profession. Vandyck founded the Club of St. Luke; it met at the Rose Tavern, and all painters of talent living in London joined it. One of the more personal acts of kindness which are related of him is that having seen by chance a picture which was painted by William Dobson, Vandyck sought him out, found him in a poor garret, instructed him with great care, introduced him to the king, and, in short, by his kind offices so prepared the way that Dobson was made sergeant-painter to the king after Vandyck's death, and won the title of "the English Tintoretto."

The portraits which Vandyck executed in England are numbered by hundreds and are magnificent pictures. Those of the royal family are very numerous and important, and there is scarcely a man or woman belonging to this period whose name has come down to us in history or literature, whose portrait he did not paint. He also made thirteen portraits of himself which are still preserved. He was very skilful in painting horses and dogs, and frequently introduced these animals into his portrait groups.

There is a large collection of the pictures of Vandyck at Windsor Castle; there are many also in the private galleries of Great Britain and other countries, besides a goodly number in the public galleries of Europe. He executed at least thirty-six portraits of Charles I., as many as twenty-five of Queen Henrietta Maria, and he also painted several groups of the children of the royal pair. Prince Rupert of the Rhine and Thomas Wentworth, Earl of Strafford, were also frequently portrayed by him, and one of his most important large works was a family picture of the Earl of Pembroke and his household. It is called the Wilton Family, as it is in a salon at Wilton House; it contains eleven figures, and has been called "the first and most magnificent historic portraiture in the world." Again, it is said to be stiff, wanting in harmony, bad in color, and so on, but after all it still remains a splendid monument to the skill and genius of Vandyck. The picture is twenty feet long by twelve feet high.

Vandyck painted no portraits of the Puritans nor popular leaders of his day; neither did he of the literary men who flourished at that time, with the exception of the court poets, Sir John Suckling and Thomas Carew.

I shall not give a list of Vandyck's historical and religious pictures, though they are quite numerous. They are not as interesting as his portraits, and we have not space to give them. His ambition, however, was never satisfied, for he wished to do some great historical work. At one time his opportunity seemed to have come, for the great banqueting-room of Whitehall Palace, the ceiling of which Rubens had painted, still remained with plain walls. Vandyck desired to paint on them the history of the Order of the Garter. The project was laid before the king, and he desired sketches to be made for the work, and one of them, the "Procession of the Knights of the Garter," was sold after the execution of the king for five pounds. It was owned by Sir Peter

Lely and Sir Joshua Reynolds, and is now at Belvoir in the collection of the Duke of Rutland. We cannot help being sorry for Vandyck's great disappointment when he knew that his work could not be done. He was weak in health and much in debt, for the king could not pay him his pension nor what he owed him for pictures. The artist grew sad and discouraged. He sought relief in the study of alchemy, and indulged the vain hope of discovering some chemical means of making gold from base metals. All this wasted his time and means, and it is to be regretted that he was less wise than his master, for when an alchemist tried to interest Rubens in the same subject, that great artist replied: "You come too late, my good fellow; I have long since discovered the philosopher's stone. My palette and brushes are worth far more than any other secret."

The king and all Vandyck's friends were troubled by his state of health and mind, and a marriage was brought about for him with the hope that he would be a happier man. His wife was Maria Ruthven, a lovely Scotch girl who held a high position among the attendants of the queen. Not long after his marriage Vandyck took her to Flanders, where he enjoyed much the honorable reception which he met with in revisiting the scenes of his childhood and youth. But having learned that Louis XIII. was about to adorn a large gallery in the Louvre, Vandyck hastened to Paris hoping to obtain the commission. He was too late—the work had been given to Poussin, and Vandyck returned to London greatly disheartened.

While at Antwerp he had received much attention, as, indeed, had been the case before, for in 1634 he had been elected Dean of the Confraternity of St. Luke and a great feast was held in his honor. When he came now to London the social atmosphere was full of sadness. The political troubles, which were finally so terrible in England, had already become alarming. In a few months the Earl of Strafford was executed, and Vandyck saw the royal family, to whom he was so much attached, surrounded with danger and at last separated.

His physical health was already delicate, and his sorrows brought on a disease from which he soon died. He continued to work until the very last days of his life. Eight days before his death his daughter was born; she was named Justiniana, and when she grew up married an English baronet, Sir John Stepney.

A short time before Vandyck died the king came from the North to London, and though he was overburdened with his own cares and griefs he found time to sorrow for the condition of his friend and artist. He offered his physician three hundred pounds if he would save the life of Sir Anthony; but nothing availed to baffle his disease, and he died December 9, 1641. Two days later he was buried in St. Paul's Cathedral. It is said that many nobles and artists attended his funeral, which was conducted with impressive ceremony. The fire which destroyed St. Paul's made it impossible to say exactly where Vandyck was laid, but his coffin-plate was found at the time of the burial of Benjamin West.

There were no artists of importance after the time of Rubens and his followers whom we call Flemish artists. There were good painters, certainly, belonging to the schools of Flanders; but these schools had reached their highest excellence and were on the decline, and so we pass to the Dutch school, or the painters of Holland.

There was doubtless a very early school of Dutch painters, dating back to the fourteenth century even; but the records of it are so imperfect, and so few pictures remain from its early days, that for our purpose it is best to pass over the fifteenth century and say that during the sixteenth century the painters of Holland gave up the painting of sacred subjects very largely, and began to take on the characteristics of what is generally known now as the Dutch School. This school is distinguished for its portraits, which form a large and important part of its painting; next for its domestic scenes, which are realistic and true to life in an astonishing degree.

At the beginning of the seventeenth century Holland had obtained a position as a nation that freed its artists from the influence of the Romish Church and the fear of the Inquisition, and they soon used their freedom to establish a national art, and one which became very important to the world. FRANZ HALS (1584–1666) was the most noteworthy of the portrait-painters. He was born at Mechlin, but passed most of his life at Haarlem. There was a custom in Holland of painting portraits of the members of guilds and societies in groups, and some such works of his at Haarlem are very fine. I have told a story of his rapid manner in the sketch of Vandyck. He was the first master to introduce that free, bold, sleight-of-hand manner which was afterward used by the Dutch masters, and is so strong in its effect. This painter led a merry, careless life. His portraits of single heads or figures are rare, and his small *genre* subjects still more so. In the Hôtel de Ville at Haarlem there are as many as eight of his large works, most of them having ten or a dozen portraits.

The Dutch painters of still-life—flowers, dead game and poultry, and metals, glass, and other beautiful objects—were very skilful, and have never been surpassed. The names of these masters would make a long list. There is little to be told of the circumstances of their lives, though their works are seen in most European galleries, and well repay one for careful examination.

Another form of Dutch art is the representation of scenes from peasant life, and there were some very eminent painters who devoted themselves to these subjects entirely.

The interiors of inns with men smoking and drinking, playing cards or making jokes, were subjects many times repeated; dancing villagers, fêtes, and fairs were often pictured, and in all these scenes everything was given exactly to the life. It follows that these pictures of coarse, vulgar people engaged in rude amusements cannot be beautiful;

FIG. 57.—PORTRAIT OF AN OFFICER. *By Franz Hals.*

but they are oftentimes wonderful. Among the most noted names in this kind of painting are those of Adrian Brauwer, the Van Ostades, the Teniers, and Jan Steen. Most of these artists executed small pictures only. I shall speak particularly of but one of these Dutch *genre* painters—DAVID TENIERS the younger (1610–1694), who became the greatest painter of his time of scenes from common life.

This is very great praise, because there were many Dutch and several Flemish painters who were noted for such pictures. This Teniers studied with his father, but his works show that he was much influenced by Rubens. He excelled in guard-house scenes and peasant life in every aspect. In representations of the alchemist also he was unequalled, as well as in fairs and festivals of every sort. He sometimes painted sacred subjects, but they are the least praiseworthy of all his works.

The pictures of Teniers are very numerous. One author describes nine hundred of his works which are known to be genuine, and it is believed that there may be one hundred more. He often represented a great number of figures on one canvas. At Schleissheim there was a large picture, thirteen and a half feet by ten feet in size, which contained one thousand one hundred and thirty-eight figures. It was not unusual for him to paint from one hundred and fifty to three hundred figures in a single picture of moderate size. He had a light, brilliant touch, his color was exquisite, and his arrangement of his subjects was very picturesque. His chief fault was a resemblance in his heads, and for this reason those pictures with the fewest figures are his best works.

Teniers had several royal patrons, and earned sufficient money to live in handsome style in his home in Perck, not far from Mechlin. He chose this place in order to be near the peasant classes, whose life was his chief study. He also excelled in his ability to imitate the styles of other masters. In the Vienna Gallery there is a curious work of his which represents the walls of a room hung with fifty pictures, imitating those of various Italian masters; in the foreground are portraits of Teniers and the Archduke Leopold William, who are represented as conversing with each other.

Teniers reached his excellence early in life, and was but twenty-two years old when he was admitted to the Guild of Painters at Antwerp. That Rubens was his friend is proved by the fact that when Teniers married the daughter of Jan Breughel, in 1637, that great master was one of the witnesses to the ceremony. In 1656 he married his second wife, the daughter of the Secretary of State for Brabant. By his artistic and personal merits Teniers gained a higher place in society than was ever held by any other *genre* painter of the Flemish or Dutch schools. He was eighty-four years old when he died, and was active and industrious up to the close of his life.

Although Teniers had such good fortune during his life, I fancy he would have been surprised if he could have known what his fame would be now, or what prices would be paid for his pictures about two centuries after his death. The "Flemish Kermes" was bought for the Brussels Museum in 1867 for twenty-five thousand dollars, and at the San Donato sale, in 1880, the "Prodigal Son" sold for sixteen thousand two hundred dollars, and the "Five Senses" for fifteen thousand dollars. It is difficult to distinguish the etchings of the son from those of the father, David Teniers the elder, though it is well known that the son executed such works.

GERARD HONTHORST (1592–1660) was also a painter of *genre* scenes, and many of his works had figures of life size. His chief distinction, however, was that of painting the effects of artificial lights. He was famous in England and Italy as well as in his own country, and the Italians called him "*Gherardo della Notte*," or Gerard of the Night, because he painted so many night-scenes lighted by candles, lamps, and torches.

Then there was a class of Dutch artists who represented the interiors of fine houses—rooms with all sorts of beautiful furniture and ornaments, with ladies and gentlemen in splendid costumes. They tried to show the effects of light upon satins, glass, metals, and other shining objects. They painted with great care, and finished their pictures in the most perfect manner. GERHARD TERBURG (1608–1681), GERHARD DOW (1613–1675), and GABRIEL METSU (1615–after 1667) were all remarkable for works of this kind.

PIETER DE HOOGE, who worked from 1628 to 1671, and of whose life little is known, painted similar pictures of courtyards as well as of rooms in houses. The list of the names of all these Dutch masters cannot be given here, and I hasten to tell you of one whose name and fame is so great that when we hear of Dutch art we always think first of him, because he stands out as its head.

REMBRANDT VAN RYN (1607–1669) was born at Leyden, and was educated by his parents with the hope that he would be a scholar and a prominent man in Leyden. But his taste for drawing and painting would not be put aside, and in 1620 he entered the studio of J. J. van Swanenburg, where he learned the first lessons in his art, and was then placed under the teaching of Pieter Lastman in Amsterdam, where he remained only six months, after which he returned to his father's house, and there lived for seven years. He was not far from seventeen years old when he thus left the usual course of study. From this time he gave himself up to close observation of nature in every form.

He studied broad landscapes—farms, groves, gardens, rivers, canals, sunshine, clouds, and shadows, and with and above all these, the human faces that he saw, as well as the varying forms, movements, and peculiarities of the men and women about him. That nothing escaped his observation is proved by the works he did in later life.

In 1630 Rembrandt settled in Amsterdam, which was called the "Venice of the North," and was the centre of northern commerce, civilization, and the activity of political and intellectual life. Rembrandt was no sooner established in his studio on one of the western quays than he was pressed with orders for pictures and applications from young men who desired his instructions. The years following were crowded with work—with painting and engraving. Rembrandt is called the "Prince of Etchers," and he used the etching-needle most skilfully, but he also employed the dry-point and even the graver in finishing. Thus he may be said to have established a new school of engraving of great excellence.

FIG. 58.—ONE OF REMBRANDT'S PORTRAITS OF HIMSELF.

It would seem that in these early years one of his amusements was to make etchings of himself. In one year, 1630–31, he made nineteen of these portraits in different costumes and positions, with as many kinds of expression on his face. He often repeated the portrait of his mother also.

In 1632 he painted the "School of Anatomy," now one

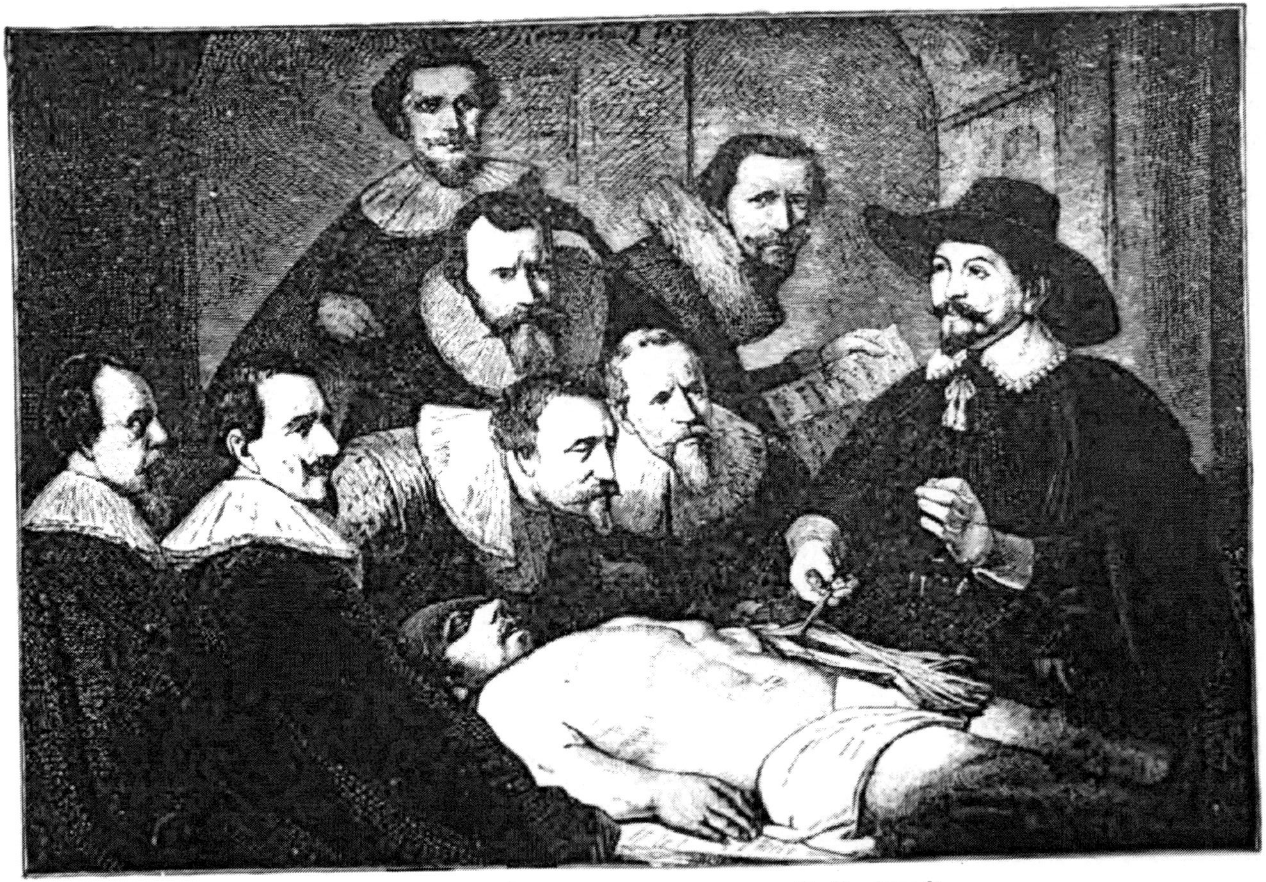

Fig. [illegible].—THE LECTURE ON ANATOMY. By Rembrandt.

of the gems of the fine gallery at the Hague. It represents a lecture by Professor Tulp, who is dissecting the arm of a dead body and explaining its structure to seven other surgeons. It is a wonderful picture and one of the most famous works of this great master. In 1828 it was sold for the benefit of the fund for surgeons' widows, and the Dutch Government paid thirty-two thousand florins for it. This picture is in a certain way a portrait picture, and comes within the class of Dutch pictures of which I have spoken as portraits of guilds and societies; for Tulp was very famous, and Rembrandt probably attended his lectures, and was chosen by him to be the painter of this celebrated portrait of himself surrounded by members of his guild.

Rembrandt's influence upon the art of his time was very great almost from the beginning of his career. About 1634 he introduced his manner of portrait-painting, with dark backgrounds and deep shadows on the face, with a bright light on the cheek and nose passing down to the shoulder, and immediately other artists adopted this manner. They considered it a necessity to imitate him, so much was he admired.

In 1634 Rembrandt married Saskia van Ulenburg, who was very beautiful and of an aristocratic and wealthy family. She was only twenty-one years of age when she married, and Rembrandt painted many portraits of her besides making her his model for beautiful figures in his mythological and sacred subjects. She lived but eight years after her marriage, which were the happiest of the artist's life. She left but one child, a son named Titus, and showed her confidence in her husband by leaving all her fortune to him, with the single stipulation that their son should be properly educated.

After the death of Saskia it seems that the only thought of the master was to work without rest, and in this way to drown the remembrance of his sorrow. There is little material for a story of his life—it is told in his pictures. The house in which Saskia lived was very fine, and Rembrandt was so fond of collecting all sorts of curious and beautiful objects that he finally made himself poor, and his collection was sold. He never travelled, and some writers have said that he was ignorant of classic art; but the list of his collections proves that he had busts of Homer and Socrates and copies of ancient sculptures, such as the "Laöcoon," a "Cupid," and so on. He also had pictures of some of the best Italian masters. After the sale of his home and all his rare objects he hired a house on the Rosengracht near the West Church. This house still stands, and has a shield dated 1652, though the artist did not live there until 1658.

His life here was not lonely or desolate. He had many friends in Amsterdam who did not forget him. He was near the bastions of the city, and had not far to go to sketch, as he loved to do, and he was busy with his brush until 1662, when he did nothing of which we know. In 1666 he executed four pictures. Among his works of 1667 there is a portrait of himself which is of great interest. In October, 1668, Rembrandt died after a short illness. He was buried in the West Church, and his funeral was so simple that its cost was registered as only fifteen florins.

Rembrandt's pictures are so numerous and so varied in their subjects that no adequate list or account of them can be given here. And his numerous engravings are as interesting as his pictures, so that a volume would scarcely suffice to do him justice; but I will try to tell something of his style. His management of light was his most striking characteristic. He generally threw a strong, vivid light upon the central or important object, whether it was a single figure or a group, and the rest of the picture was in shadow. This is true of all his works, almost without exception—portraits, pictures both large and small, and etchings.

Rembrandt loved to paint unusual things. We are apt

to think that an unusual thing is not natural; but if we closely observe nature, especially the effect of light and shade, we shall find that no imagination could make pictures more wonderful than the reality we see. Rembrandt had that keen observation that helped him to seize upon the sharp features—the strong points in a scene or a person—and then he had the skill to reproduce these things on his canvas with great truth.

His etchings are much prized. One of the most famous represents Christ healing the sick, and is called the "Hundred Guilders Print," because that sum was the price he fixed for it; now a good impression of it is worth ten times as much. At his death he left about six hundred pictures and four hundred engravings. His landscapes are his rarest subjects. Most of these are in private collections, but I have seen one in the Cassel Gallery; the color of it is bright and glowing—the sky magnificent. In the foreground there is a bridge, and on an eminence are the ruins of a castle.

Some fine works by Rembrandt are in England, and very large prices have been paid for them. In 1867 "Christ Blessing Little Children" was sold for seven thousand pounds. At the San Donato sale in Florence, in 1880, "Lucretia" brought twenty-nine thousand two hundred dollars, and a "Portrait of a Young Woman" nearly as much.

Among Rembrandt's pupils Gerbrandt van der Eeckhout holds a high rank, and his pictures are seen in many galleries.

Among the landscape painters of Holland ALBERT CUYP (1605–1691) is very famous. He sometimes introduced figures and animals into his pictures, but they were of secondary importance; the scenery was his chief thought. His works are in many galleries, and the increase in their value is marvellous. Sir Robert Peel bought a landscape, twelve by twenty inches in size, for which he paid three hundred and fifty guineas: it was originally sold in Holland for about one English shilling! During the first century after his death no picture by Cuyp brought more than thirty florins; now they cost almost their weight in gold.

Other fine landscape painters were Jan and Andries Both, Jan van Goyen, Jan Wynants, Adrian van de Velde, and, finally, PHILIP WOUVERMAN (1619–1668), who introduced much life into his works. He painted battles, hunting parties, and such subjects as allowed him to introduce white horses, for which he became noted. His works, as well as those of the other painters last mentioned, are valuable. There are so many in galleries which are attributed to Wouverman that it is doubtful if they are all genuine. He had animation and fine feeling for the picturesque. His execution was light and delicate, and there is much tenderness shown in his works. There were many excellent Dutch landscape painters whom we have not mentioned.

PAUL POTTER (1625–1654) was born at Enkhuysen, and though he died young he made himself a great and enduring reputation by his pictures of animals. "Paul Potter's Bull," which is in the gallery at the Hague, is as well known as any one picture the world over. He left one hundred and eight pictures and eighteen etchings. He was most successful in representing cattle and sheep; his horses are not as fine. He never crowded his pictures; they have an open landscape, but few animals, and perhaps a shepherd, and that is all. Some of his pictures have been valued as high as fifty thousand dollars.

JACOB RUYSDAEL (1625–1681) was born in the same year with Paul Potter. His birth-place was Haarlem. He came to be the very best of all Dutch landscape painters, and though most of his pictures represent the dull, uninteresting scenery of Holland, they are so skilfully drawn and painted that they are really most attractive, if not cheerful. His works number about four hundred and forty-eight pictures and seven fine, spirited etchings. He was fond of giving a broad, expansive effect to his pictures, and frequently placed church spires in the distance. He painted a few marine views with rough seas and cloudy skies. Though many of his works are gloomy, he sometimes painted sunshine with much effect. Some of his finest works are in the Dresden Gallery.

MINDERT HOBBEMA was a pupil of Jacob Ruysdael, and this is almost all that is known of him personally; but his pictures show that he was a great landscape painter. They sell for enormous sums, and many of the best are in England. Most of those seen in the continental galleries are not those he should be judged by. At the San Donato sale in Florence, his picture of the "Wind-Mills" sold for forty-two thousand dollars.

The number of reputable Dutch painters is very large, but I shall mention no more names. After the great men whom we have spoken of there comes an army of those who are called "little Dutch masters," and their principal work was making copies from the pictures of the greater artists.

In the history of what we know as German art we find a very early school at Cologne, but the records of it are so scarce and imperfect that I shall give no account of it here. At Augsburg there was an important school of art which commenced with the Holbeins. The first Hans Holbein is known as "Old Holbein," and so little is known of him that I shall merely give his name. The second HANS HOLBEIN, called the elder (1460–1523), painted a great number of religious pictures, which are seen in various churches and galleries in Germany. Some of the best are in the Cathedral of Augsburg. In one salon of the Munich Pinakothek there are sixteen panels painted by him. But it was HANS HOLBEIN the third, known as "the younger," who reached the perfection of his school (1495-1543). This painter was instructed by his father and by Hans Burgkmair. He was but fifteen years of age when he began to receive commissions for pictures. When he was about twenty-one years old he removed to Basle, and there he painted many pictures, though not nearly as many as have been called by his name.

About a year after Holbein went to Basle he was called to Lucerne to decorate a house, and he executed other works there and at Altorf. In 1519, when he had been three years in Basle, he became a citizen of that town and a member of its guild of painters. His works at Basle were mostly decorative, and he painted few easel pictures there.

Holbein married a widow with one son; her name was Elizabeth Schmid. She had a very bad temper. It is said that she made Holbein's life so miserable that he left Basle for that reason. He visited her sometimes, and always gave her money, but lived away from her. In 1526 Holbein went to England, and his friend Erasmus said that he went because he had so little to do in Basle. He carried a letter to Sir Thomas More, who received him with great kindness, and the artist made many portraits of Sir Thomas and his family. There is a story about one of these portraits of that nobleman. He had refused to be present at the marriage of Anne Boleyn to King Henry VIII., and she never forgave him. On the day that More was executed she looked at one of Holbein's portraits of the ex-chancellor and exclaimed, "Ah, me! the man seems to be still alive;" and seizing the picture she threw it into the street.

In 1530 Holbein returned to Basle to complete some unfinished frescoes, and this being done he went again to London. About this time he began to be employed by the king, and did many pictures for him from time to time. In 1538 Henry sent Holbein to Brussels to make a portrait of the Duchess of Milan, of whom the king was thinking for his fourth wife. No citizen of Basle was allowed to enter the service of a foreign sovereign without the consent of the council, so in 1538 the artist went home to ask permission to serve the King of England. Great efforts were made to keep him in Basle, but at last he received permission to remain two years in England: the artist never went again to Basle. Henry VIII. became fond of Holbein, and was generous to him, even giving him a painting-room in the palace of Whitehall.

In 1539 the artist was sent to paint a portrait of Anne of Cleves, whom the king married the next year. It has been said that the picture was so flattering that when the king saw the lady he was disappointed; we know that he was soon divorced from her.

In 1543 the plague raged in London, and on the 7th of October Holbein prepared his will. He died before the 29th of November, but the facts concerning his death and burial are not known.

There are several interesting anecdotes of Holbein. One relates that when passing through Strasburg he visited the studio of an artist, and finding him out, painted a fly on a picture which was on an easel. When the painter saw the fly he tried to brush it away, and when he found who had painted it he searched the city for Holbein; but he had already left for England. Another story shows the regard which Henry VIII. had for him. One day a nobleman went to Holbein's studio, and insisted upon entering, though the artist told him that he was painting the portrait of a lady by his Majesty's orders. The nobleman persisting, Holbein threw him down the stairs with great violence, and then rushed to the king, and told him what he had done. Soon after the nobleman was borne to the presence of the king; he was unable to walk, and was loud in his complaints. The king ridiculed him, and the noble-

FIG. 60.—BURGOMASTER MEIER MADONNA. *By Holbein. Dresden Gallery.*

man was angry, and threatened to punish the artist legally. Then Henry got angry, and said: "Now you have no longer to deal with Holbein, but with me, your king. Do you think that this man is of so little consideration with us? I tell you, my lord, that out of seven peasants I can make seven earls in a day; but out of seven earls I could not make one such artist as Hans Holbein."

At Basle one may see some of the most important of the early portraits of Holbein; these are in the gallery where are also his ten well-known scenes from the Passion of Christ. While at Basle he probably made the designs for the "Dance of Death." For a long time it was believed that he painted this subject both at Basle and at Bonn, but we now know that he only made designs for it. He also decorated the Town Hall at Basle; of this work, however, but little remains.

The most celebrated work by Holbein is the "Meyer Madonna" in the royal palace of Darmstadt, of which there is a copy in the Dresden Gallery. It takes its name from that of the Burgomaster Meyer, for whom it was painted. The Madonna, with the infant Jesus in her arms, stands in a niche in the centre of the picture; the burgomaster and his family kneel before her. This is what is called a votive picture, which means a picture made in the fulfilment of a vow, in gratitude for some signal blessing or to turn away some danger. Many of these works commemorate an escape from accident or a recovery from sickness.

The picture is very beautiful, and it seems as if the Virgin wished to share her peace with the kneeling family, so sweet is the expression of her face, while the child seems to bestow a blessing with his lifted hand. The original was probably painted for a "Chapel of Our Lady."

His "Dance of Death" was very curious, the idea being that Death is always near us and trying to strike down his prey. The pictures represent a skeleton clutching at his victims, who are of all ages and occupations, from the lovely young bride at the altar to the hard-working pedlar in the cut we give here, and all of them are hurried away by this frightful figure which stands for Death itself.

Holbein made many wood engravings, but none so important as these. When the set is complete there are fifty-three cuts, but it is rare to find more than forty-six.

FIG. 61.—FROM HOLBEIN'S DANCE OF DEATH.

Holbein was one of the foremost of German masters. All his pictures are realistic, and many of them are fantastic; he gave graceful movement and beauty of form to many of his subjects; his drapery was well arranged; his color and manner of painting were good. He painted in fresco and oil colors, executed miniatures and engravings. His portraits were his best works, and in them he equalled the greatest masters. The most reliable portrait of this artist is in the Basle Museum. It is done in red and black chalk, and represents him as a man with regular, well-shaped features, with a cheerful expression which also shows decision of character.

There were other good artists in the Augsburg school after the time of the Holbeins; but I shall pass immediately to the Franconian school, or that of Nuremburg, and to its great master, ALBERT DÜRER (1471–1528), whose life was very interesting, and who stands, as an artist, among the greatest painters of the world. The city of Nuremburg was a grand, rich old place even in Dürer's time, and as a boy he was familiar with its scenery and architecture, which helped him to cultivate his artist tastes, and to make him the great man that he became. He was an author of books as well as an architect, sculptor, painter, and engraver.

His father was a goldsmith, and Albert was apprenticed to the same trade; but he was so anxious to study painting that at length his father placed him as apprentice to the painter Michael Wohlgemuth. At this time Albert was fifteen years old, and the two years he had spent with the goldsmith had doubtless been of great advantage to him; for in that time he had been trained in the modelling of small, delicate objects, and in the accurate design necessary in making the small articles in precious metals which are the principal work of that trade.

Albert Dürer had a very strong nature, and Michael Wohlgemuth was not a man who could gain much influence over such a youth. During the three years which Dürer passed under his teaching he learned all the modes of preparing and using colors, and acquired much skill in handling the brush; he also learned the first lessons in wood-engraving, in which he afterward reached so high a perfection that a large part of his present fame rests upon his skill in that art.

One of the earliest portraits painted by Dürer is in the Albertina at Vienna, and bears this inscription: "This I have drawn from myself from the looking-glass, in the year 1484, when I was still a child. ALBERT DÜRER." Six years later he painted the beautiful portrait of his father which is now in the gallery at Florence; and it is a question whether this is not as finely executed as any portrait of his later years.

When Dürer left Wohlgemuth he started upon the student journey which was then the custom with all German youths, and is still practised in a modified degree. These youths, after serving their apprenticeship in the occupation they were to follow, travelled, and worked at their trade or profession in the cities of other countries. Dürer was absent four years, but we know little of what he did or saw, for in his own account of his life he says only this : "And when the three years were out my father sent me away. I remained abroad four years, when he recalled me ; and, as I had left just after Easter in 1490, I returned home in 1494, just after Whitsuntide."

In the same year, in July, Dürer was married to Agnes Frey. He was also admitted to the guild of painters, and we may say that he was now settled for life. It is a singular fact that, although Dürer painted several portraits of his father and himself, he is not known to have made any of his wife. Some of his sketches are called by her name, but there is no good reason for this.

Dürer was so industrious, and executed so many pictures, copper-plates, and wood engravings within the six years next after his return to Nuremburg, that it is not possible to give an exact account of them here. In 1500 an event occurred which added much to his happiness and to his opportunities for enlarging his influence. It was the return to Nuremburg of Willibald Pirkheimer, one of the friends of Dürer's childhood, between whom and himself there had always existed a strong affection. Pirkheimer was rich and influential, and at his house Dürer saw many eminent men, artists, scholars, reformers, and theologians, and in their society he gained much broader knowledge of the world, while he received the respect which was due to his genius and character.

Dürer's health was not good, and his continual work proved more than he could bear. His father died in 1502, and this loss was a deep grief to the artist. So little money was left for his mother and younger brother that their sup-

FIG. 62.—A SCENE FROM DÜRER'S WOOD ENGRAVINGS OF THE LIFE OF THE VIRGIN MARY.

port came upon him. At length, in 1505, he made a journey to Venice, partly for his health, and in order to study Venetian painting. He was well received by the painters of Venice. Giovanni Bellini and Carpaccio were the leading painters of that time. They were both quite old, but Giorgione and Titian were already coming into notice and preparing to fill the places of the older men. Bellini was especially delighted with the exquisite manner in which Dürer painted hair, and asked the German to give him the brush he used for that purpose. Dürer gave him all his brushes, but Bellini insisted upon having *the one* for painting hair. Dürer took a common brush, and painted a long tress of fine hair: Bellini declared that had he not seen this done he could not have believed it.

While in Venice Dürer received an order to paint a picture for the Fondaco de' Tedeschi, or German Exchange. It is believed that this work was the famous "Feast of Rose Garlands," now in the Monastery at Strahow, in Bohemia. The Emperor Rudolph II. bought it, and had it carried from Venice to Prague on men's shoulders. In 1782 it was purchased for the Abbey of Strahow, and was almost lost to the world for many years. It is a beautiful picture, and the praise it received was a great pleasure to Dürer, because heretofore many painters had said that he was a good engraver, but could not use colors. Dürer wrote to Pirkheimer: "There is no better picture of the Virgin Mary in the land, because all the artists praise it, as well as the nobility. They say they have never seen a more sublime, a more charming painting."

The Venetian Government offered Dürer a handsome pension if he would remain in Venice, and he declined many orders for the sake of returning to Germany, which he believed to be his duty. From the time of his return, in 1507, to 1520, there is very little to tell of the personal history of this artist. Almost all that can be said is that he labored with great industry; it was the golden period of his art; he had many young men in his studio, which was the centre of art to Nuremburg. At this time he probably executed the best carvings which he ever did. During seven years he made forty-eight engravings and etchings and more than a hundred wood-cuts. The large demand for these works was a source of good income to Dürer, and gave him a position of comfort. The Reformation was at hand, and Dürer's Virgins and Saints and his pictures of the sufferings of Christ were very well suited to the religious excitement of that period.

The house in which Dürer lived and worked for many years is still preserved in Nuremburg as public property, and is used as an art gallery. The street on which it stands is now called the Albrecht-Dürer Strasse. On the square before the house stands a bronze statue of the master which was erected by the Nuremburgers on the three hundredth anniversary of his death.

About 1509 Dürer occupied himself considerably in writing poetry; but, although there was much earnest feeling in his verse, it was not such as to give him great fame as a poet. It was at the same period that he carved the wonderful bas-relief of the "Birth of John the Baptist," now in the British Museum. It is cut out of stone, is seven and one-half by five and one-half inches in size, and is a marvellous piece of work. Two thousand five hundred dollars were paid for it nearly a century ago. He made many exquisite little carvings in stone, ivory, and boxwood, and in these articles the result of his work as a goldsmith is best seen.

In 1512 Dürer was first employed by the Emperor Maximilian, and for the next seven years there was a close relation between the sovereign and the artist; but there are few records concerning it. It is said that one day when the painter was making a sketch of the emperor the latter took a charcoal crayon, and tried to draw a picture himself: he constantly broke the crayon, and made no progress toward his end. After watching him for a time Dürer took the charcoal from Maximilian, saying, "This is my sceptre, your Majesty;" and he then taught the emperor how to use it.

Dürer executed some very remarkable drawings and engravings. Among them was the "Triumphal Arch of Maximilian," composed of ninety-two blocks. The whole cut is ten and one-half feet high by nine feet wide. It shows all the remarkable events in the emperor's life, just as such subjects were carved upon the triumphal arches of the Romans and other nations. Hieronymus Rösch did the engraving of this great work from Dürer's blocks, and while it was in progress the emperor went often to see it. During one of these visits several cats ran into the room, from which happening arose the proverb, "A cat may look at a king."

The emperor granted Dürer a pension; but it was never regularly paid, and after the emperor's death the Council of Nuremburg refused to pay it unless it was confirmed by the new sovereign, Charles V. For the purpose of obtaining this confirmation Dürer made a journey to the Netherlands in the year 1520. His wife and her maid Susanna went with him. His diary gives a quaint account of the places they visited, the people whom they met, and of the honors which were paid him. In Antwerp he was received with great kindness, and the government of the city offered him a house and a liberal pension if he would remain there; but his love for his native town would not allow him to leave it.

After several months Dürer received the confirmation of his pension and also the appointment of court-painter. This last office was of very little account to him. The emperor spent little time at Nuremburg, and it was not

FIG. 63.—THE FOUR APOSTLES. *By Dürer.*

until he was older that he was seized with the passion of having his portrait painted, and then Dürer had died, and Titian was painter to the court.

When Dürer returned to his home there was quite an excitement over the collection of curious and rare objects which he had made while absent. Some of these he had bought, and many others were gifts to him, and he gave much pleasure to his friends by displaying them. There had been a great change in Nuremburg, for the doctrines of the Reformation were accepted by many of its people, and it was the first free city that declared itself Protestant. The change, too, was quietly made; its convents and churches were saved from violence, and the art treasures of the city were not destroyed. Among the most important Lutherans was Pirkheimer, Dürer's friend. We do not know that Dürer became a Lutheran, but he wrote of his admiration for the great reformer in his diary, and it is a meaning fact that during the last six years of his life Dürer made no more pictures of the Madonna.

These last years were not as full of work as the earlier ones had been. A few portraits and engravings and the pictures of the Four Apostles were about all the works of this time. He gave much attention to the arrangement and publication of his writings upon various subjects connected with the arts. These books gave him much fame as a scholar, and some of them were translated into several languages.

As an architect Dürer executed but little work; but his writings upon architectural subjects prove that he was learned in its theories.

During several years his health was feeble, and he exerted himself to make provision for his old age if he should live, or for his wife after his death. He was saddened by the thought that he had never been rewarded as he should have been for his hard, faithful labors, and his latest letters were sad and touching. He died in April, 1528, after a brief illness, and was buried in the cemetery of St. John, beyond the walls, where a simple epitaph was inscribed upon his monument. This cemetery is an interesting place, and contains the graves of many men noted in the chronicles of Nuremburg.

On Easter Sunday in 1828, three hundred years after his death, a Dürer celebration was held in Nuremburg. Artists came from all parts of Germany. A solemn procession proceeded to his grave, where hymns were sung, and the statue by Rauch, near Dürer's house, was dedicated.

I can give you no description of Dürer's many works, and although it is true that he was a very great master, yet it is also true that his pictures and engravings are not noted for their beauty so much as for their strength and power. His subjects were often ugly and repulsive rather than beautiful, and his imagination was full of weird, strange fancies that can scarcely be understood. Indeed, some of them never have been explained, and one of his most famous engravings, called "The Knight, Death, and the Devil," has never yet been satisfactorily interpreted, and many different theories have been made about it.

Many of the principal galleries of Europe have Dürer's paintings, though they are not as numerous as his engravings, and, indeed, his fame rests more upon the latter than the former, and very large sums are paid by collectors for good impressions of his more important plates.

Dürer had several followers. His most gifted scholar was Lucas Sunder (1472–1553), who is called Lucas Cranach, from the place of his birth. He established a school of painting in Saxony, and was appointed court-painter. Although there were a goodly number of German painters late in the sixteenth century, there were none of great eminence, and, in truth, there have been few since that time whose lives were of sufficient interest to be recounted here, so I shall tell you of but one more before passing to the artists of Spain.

ANGELICA KAUFFMAN (1742–1808) was a very interesting woman who gained a good reputation as an artist; but there is such a difference of opinion among judges as to her merits as a painter that it is difficult to decide what to say of her. As a person, she excited an interest in her lifetime which has never died out, and Miss Thackeray's novel, "Miss Angel," tells what is claimed to be her story, as nearly as such stories are told in novels.

She was born at Coire, in the Grisons. Her father was an artist, a native of Schwarzenburg, and when Angelica was born he was occupied in executing some frescoes at Coire. When the child was a year old he settled at Morbegno, in Lombardy, and ten years later, when she had shown a taste for music, her parents again removed to Como, where there were better opportunities for her instruction. Her progress in music was remarkable, and for a time she was unable to say whether she loved this art or that of painting the better. Later in life she painted a picture in which she represented herself, as a child, standing between allegorical figures of Music and Painting.

The beautiful scenery about Como, the stately palaces and charming villas, the lake with its pleasure boats, and all the poetry of the life there, tended to develop her talents rapidly, and, though she remained but two years, the recollection of this time was a pleasure to her through all her life. She was next taken to Milan, where a world of art was opened to her, and she saw pictures which excelled all her imaginations. The works of Leonardo and other great Lombard masters stirred her soul to its very depths. She soon attracted attention by her pictures, and Robert d'Este became her patron, and placed her under the care of the Duchess of Carrara. She was now daily associated with people of culture and elegance, and thus early in her life acquired the modest dignity and self-possession which enabled her in her future life to accept becomingly the honors and attentions which were paid her.

Her mother's death occurred at Milan, and her father returned to Schwarzenburg. The people about her were so coarse and disagreeable to Angelica that she passed much of her time in the grand forests. At this time she painted frescoes of the Twelve Apostles, copied from the engravings after Piazetta. Her father was not content to remain away from Italy, and they went again to Milan, then to Florence, and at last to Rome. She was now eighteen years old, and found much profit in the friendship of the great scholar Winckelmann, who allowed her to paint his portrait. Angelica visited Naples and Bologna also, and finally Venice, where she met Lady Wentworth, who became her friend, and afterward took her to England.

She had a most brilliant career in London, where her friends were in the highest rank of society. De Rossi described her appearance at this time, and said that she was not very tall, but had a slight, elegant figure. Her complexion was dark and clear, her mouth well formed, her teeth white and even, and all her features good. He speaks of her azure eyes, so placid and bright that their expression had a charm which could not be described. No one felt like criticising her. Other artists paid her many honors, and she was made a member of the Academy of Arts. It has been said that Fuseli, the learned art critic, and Sir Joshua Reynolds, the great artist, both asked her hand in marriage. Some members of the royal family became her friends, and she was at the height of honorable success and of happiness.

It is painful to turn from this bright picture of her life to all the sorrow and darkness which followed it. She made an unhappy marriage, her husband proving to be an adventurer who had assumed a distinguished name. For a time she was crushed by this sorrow; but her friends remained true to her, and she found relief in absolute devotion to her art. For twelve years she supported herself and her father; then his health failed, and it was thought best for him to go to Italy. Angelica was now forty years old, and before leaving England she married Antonio Zucchi, an artist who had long been her friend. He devoted himself to her and to her father with untiring affection, and when the old man died he was happy in the thought that his beloved daughter had so true a friend as Zucchi.

From this time their home was in Rome, where Angelica was the centre of an artistic and literary society of a high order. Among her visitors were such men as Herder and Goethe. The latter wrote of her: "The light and pleasing in form and color, in design and execution, distinguish the numerous works of our artist. No living painter excels her in dignity or in the delicate taste with which she handles the pencil." She was very industrious, and her life seems to have been divided between two pleasures, her work and the society of her friends, until the death of her husband, which occurred in 1795. She lived twelve years longer, but they were years of great sadness. She made journeys in order to regain her spirits. She visited the scenes of her childhood, and remained some time in Venice with the family of Signor Zucchi.

Even after her last return to Rome she worked as much as her strength would permit, but her life was not long. She was mourned sincerely in Rome; her funeral was attended by the members of the Academy of St. Luke; and her latest works were borne in the procession. She was buried beside her husband in the Church of St. Andrea dei Frati. Her bust was placed in the Pantheon.

Various critics have praised her works in the most liberal manner; others can say nothing good of them. For myself, I cannot find the extreme of praise or blame a just estimate of her. No one can deny the grace of her design, which was also creditably correct. Her portraits were good; her poetical subjects are very pleasing; her historical pictures are not strong; her color was as harmonious and mellow as that of the best Italians, excepting a few of the greatest masters, and in all her pictures there is something which wins for her a certain fondness and praise, even while her faults are plainly seen. Her pictures are to be found in galleries in Rome, Florence, Vienna, Munich, and England; many are also in private collections. She painted several portraits of herself; one in the Uffizi, at Florence, is very pleasing. She represents herself seated in a solitary landscape, with a portfolio in one hand and a pencil in the other. She has an air of perfect unconsciousness, as if she thought of her work only. Her etchings are much valued, and sell for large prices. Many of her pictures were engraved by Bartolozzi, and good prints of them are rare. On one of her pictures she wrote: "I will not attempt to express supernatural things by human inspiration, but wait for that till I reach heaven, if there is painting done there."

## CHAPTER V.

### PAINTING IN SPAIN.

SPANISH painting had its birth during the reign of Ferdinand and Isabella, and may be said to have been derived from Italy, through the influence of the Italian painters who went to Spain, and the Spanish artists who made their studies in Italy. But in spite of this strong Italian influence Spanish painting has its own characteristics which separate it from all other schools, and give it a high position on its own merits. ANTONIO DEL RINCON (1446–1500) was the first Spanish painter of whom we know. If any works of his remain they are portraits of his august sovereigns now in the Cathedral of Granada; but it is probable that these pictures are copies of the originals by Rincon.

Dating the beginning of the Spanish school from the last half of the fifteenth century, it is the third school in Europe as to age, it being about two centuries later than the Italian, and one century later than the Flemish school. Its importance is only exceeded by that of Italy. The distinguishing feature of Spanish art is its gravity, or we may almost say its strictly religious character, for, excepting portraits, there were few pictures of consequence that had not a religious meaning. Some artists were also priests, and, as the officers of the Inquisition appointed inspectors whose duty it was to report for punishment any artist who did not follow the rules of the Inquisition, it is easy to understand that the painters were careful to keep within the rules fixed for them. Whatever flights of imagination one might have in secret, he would scarcely run the risk of being excommunicated from the church, sent into exile for a year, and fined one thousand five hundred ducats for the pleasure of putting his fancies on canvas.

Pacheco, who was an inspector at Seville, published minute rules for the representation of sacred subjects and persons, and other writers did the same. There was a long and grave discussion over the propriety of painting the devil with horns and a tail. It was decided that he should have horns because, according to the legend of St. Theresa, he had horns when he appeared to that saint; and he was allowed to have a tail because it was thought to be a suitable appendage to a fallen angel who had lost his wings. One very strict rule was that the feet of the Virgin Mary should be covered, and nude figures or portions of the figure were strictly forbidden.

Another important influence upon the Spanish artists was their belief that the Virgin Mary and other holy spirits appeared to inspire them and aid them in painting their pictures. In fact, the church was the chief patron of art, and the artist was one of her most valuable teachers. A learned Spanish writer said: "For the ignorant, what master is like painting? They may read their duty in a picture though they may not search for it in books."

The painters of Spain were divided between the schools of Castile, Seville, and Valencia. That of Castile was founded at Toledo early in the fifteenth century, and was maintained about two hundred years. Claudio Coello was of this school; he died in 1693, and has well been called "the last of the old masters of Spain."

ALONZO BERREGUETTE (1480–1561), born at Parades de Nava, in Castile, was the most eminent Spanish artist of his time. He is called the Michael Angelo of Spain, because he was painter, sculptor, and architect. He was painter to

Philip I. Later he went to Italy, and journeyed from Florence to Rome with Michael Angelo in 1505. He studied in Italy many years. He was appointed painter and sculptor to the Emperor Charles V. Berreguette received four thousand four hundred ducats for the altar in the Church of St. Benito el Real in Valladolid, where he settled. When he was almost eighty years old he went to Toledo to erect a monument in the Hospital of St. John Baptist. He was lodged in the hospital, and died there. He left a large fortune, and was buried with splendid ceremonies at the expense of the emperor.

Luis de Morales (1510–1586) was called "the divine." He belonged to the school of Castile, and very little is known of his early life. When he was fifty-five years old Philip II. invited him to court. When Morales appeared he was so splendidly dressed that the king was angry, and gave orders that he should be paid a certain sum and dismissed. But the poor painter explained that he had spent all that he had in order to come before the king in a dress befitting Philip's dignity. Then Philip pardoned him, and allowed him to paint one picture; but as this was not hung in the Escorial, Morales was overcome by mortification, and almost forsook his painting, and fell into great poverty. In 1581 the king saw Morales at Badajoz, in a very different dress from that he had worn at court. The king said: "Morales, you are very old." "Yes, sire, and very poor," replied the painter. The king then commanded that he should have two hundred ducats a year from the crown rents with which to buy his dinners. Morales hearing this, exclaimed, "And for supper, sire?" This pleased Philip, and he added one hundred ducats to the pension. The street in Badajoz on which Morales lived bears his name.

Nearly all his pictures were of religious subjects, and on this account he was called "the divine." He avoided ghastly, painful pictures, and was one of the most spiritual of the artists of Spain. Very few of his pictures are seen out of Spain, and they are rare even there. His masterpiece is "Christ Crowned with Thorns," in the Queen of Spain's Gallery at Madrid. In the Louvre is his "Christ Bearing the Cross." At the sale of the Soult collection his "Way to Calvary" sold for nine hundred and eighty pounds sterling.

ALONSO SANCHEZ COELLO (about 1515–1590) was the first great portrait painter of Spain. He was painter-in-ordinary to Philip II., and that monarch was so fond of him that in his letters he called him "my beloved son." At Madrid the king had a key to a private entrance to the apartments of Coello, so that he could surprise the painter in his studio, and at times even entered the family rooms of the artist. Coello never abused the confidence of Philip, and was a favorite of the court as well as of the monarch. Among his friends were the Popes Gregory XIII. and Sixtus V., the Cardinal Alexander Farnese, and the Dukes of Florence and Savoy. Many noble and even royal persons were accustomed to visit him and accept his hospitality. He was obliged to live in style becoming his position, and yet when he died he left a fortune of fifty-five thousand ducats. He had lived in Lisbon, and Philip sometimes called him his "Portuguese Titian."

Very few of his portraits remain; they are graceful in pose and fine in color. He knew how to represent the repose and refinement of "gentle blood and delicate nurture." Many of his works were burned in the Prado. His "Marriage of St. Catherine" is in the Gallery of Madrid. A "St. Sebastian" painted for the Church of St. Jerome, at Madrid, is considered his masterpiece. Lope de Vega wrote Coello's epitaph, and called his pictures

> "Eternal scenes of history divine,
> Wherein for aye his memory shall shine."

JUAN FERNANDEZ NAVARRETE (1526–1579), called El Mudo, because deaf and dumb, is a very interesting painter. He was not born a mute, but became deaf at three years of age, and could not learn to speak. He studied some years in Italy, and was in the school of Titian. In 1568 he was appointed painter to Philip II. His principal works were eight pictures for the Escorial, three of which were burned. His picture of the "Nativity" is celebrated for its lights, of which there are three; one is from the Divine Babe, a second from the glory above, and a third from a torch in the hand of St. Joseph. The group of shepherds is the best part of the picture, and when Tibaldi saw the picture he exclaimed, "O! gli belli pastori!" and it has since been known as the "Beautiful Shepherds."

His picture of "Abraham and the Three Angels" was placed near the door where the monks of the Escorial received strangers. The pictures of Navarrete are rare. After his death Lope de Vega wrote a lament for him, in which he said,

> "No countenance he painted that was dumb."

When the "Last Supper" painted by Titian reached the Escorial, it was found to be too large for the space it was to occupy in the refectory. The king ordered it to be cut, which so distressed El Mudo that he offered to copy it in six months, in reduced size, and to forfeit his head if he did not fulfil his promise. He also added that he should hope to be knighted if he copied in six months what Titian had taken seven years to paint. But Philip was resolute, and the picture was cut, to the intense grief of the dumb Navarrete. While the painter lived Philip did not fully appreciate him; but after his death the king often declared that his Italian artists could not equal his mute Spaniard.

JUAN CARREÑO DE MIRANDA (1614–1685) is commonly

called Carreño. He was of an ancient noble family. His earliest works were for the churches and convents of Madrid, and he acquired so good a name that before the death of Philip IV. he was appointed one of his court-painters. In 1671 the young king Charles gave Carreño the cross of Santiago, and to his office of court-painter added that of Deputy Aposentador. He would allow no other artist to paint his likeness unless Carreño consented to it. The pictures of Carreño were most excellent, and his character was such as to merit all his good fortune. His death was sincerely mourned by all who knew him.

It is said that on one occasion he was in a house where a copy of Titian's "St. Margaret" hung upon the wall, and those present united in saying that it was abominably done. Carreño said: "It has at least one merit; it shows that no one need despair of improving in art, for I painted it myself when I was a beginner."

Gregorio Utande, a poor artist, had painted a "Martyrdom of St. Andrew" for the nuns of Alcalà, and demanded one hundred ducats for it. The nuns thought the price too much, and wished to have Carreño value the work. Utande took the picture to Carreño, and first presenting the great master with a jar of honey, asked him to touch up his St. Andrew for him. Carreño consented, and, in fact, almost repainted Utande's picture. A short time after Carreño was asked to value the St. Andrew, but declined. Then Herrera valued it at two hundred ducats, which price the nuns paid. After Utande received his money he told the whole story, and the picture was then known as "La Cantarilla de Miel," or "the pot of honey."

CLAUDIO COELLO (1635–1693), who, as we have said, has been called the last of the old Spanish masters, was intended by his father for his own profession, that of bronze-casting. But Claudio persuaded his father to allow him to study painting, and before the close of his life he became the most famous painter in Madrid. He was not only the court-painter, but also the painter to the Cathedral of Toledo and keeper of the royal galleries. It was not strange that he should feel that he merited the honor of painting the walls of the Escorial, and when this was refused him and Luca Giordano was selected for the work, Coello threw aside his brushes and paints, grew sad, then ill, and died a year later. His masterpiece is now in the Escorial; it represents the "Collocation of the Host." His own portrait painted by himself is in the gallery of the Hermitage at St. Petersburg.

The school of Seville was the most important school of Spain. It is also known as the school of Andalusia. It dates from the middle of the fifteenth century, and its latest master, Alonso Miguel de Tobar, died in 1758.

Luis de Vargas (1502–1568), one of the earliest of the painters of the school of Seville, was a devout and holy man. He was accustomed to do penance, and in his room after his death scourges were found with which he had beaten himself, and a coffin in which he had been accustomed to lie and meditate upon death and a future life. It is said that Vargas studied twenty-eight years in Italy. His pictures were fine. His female heads were graceful and pure, his color good, and the whole effect that of grand simplicity. His picture of the "Temporal Generation of Our Lord" is his best work in Seville. Adam is kneeling in the foreground, and his leg is so well painted that the picture has been called "La Gamba." In spite of his seriousness Vargas was a witty man. On one occasion he was asked to give his opinion of a very poor picture of "Christ on the Cross." Vargas replied: "He looks as if he were saying, 'Forgive them, Lord, for they know not what they do!'"

Pablo de Cespedes (1538–1608) was born at Cordova, and is an important person in the history of his time, for he was a divine, a poet, and a scholar, as well as an architect, sculptor, and painter. He was a graduate of the University of Alcalà, and excelled in Oriental languages. He studied art in Rome, and while there made a head of Seneca in marble, and fitted it to an antique trunk; on account of this work he was called "Victor il Spagnuolo." Zuccaro was asked to paint a picture for the splendid Cathedral of Cordova; he declined, and said that while Cespedes was in Spain they had no need of Italian artists. The pictures of Cespedes which now remain are so faded and injured that a good judgment can scarcely be formed of them; but they do not seem to be as fine as they were thought to be in his day. His "Last Supper" is in the Cathedral of Cordova. In the foreground there are some jars and vases so well painted that visitors praised them. Cespedes was so mortified at this that he commanded his servant to rub them out, and only the most judicious admiration for the rest of the picture and earnest entreaty for the preservation of the jars saved them from destruction. He left many writings upon artistic subjects and an essay upon the antiquity of the Cathedral of Cordova. He was as modest as he was learned, and was much beloved. He was made a canon in the Cathedral of Cordova, and was received with "full approbation of the Cordovese bishop and chapter."

FRANCISCO PACHECO (1571–1654) was born at Seville. He was a writer on art, and is more famous as the master of Velasquez and on account of his books than for his pictures. He established a school where younger men than himself could have a thorough art education. Pacheco was the first in Spain to properly gild and paint statues and bass-reliefs. Some specimens of his work in this specialty still exist in Seville.

FRANCISCO DE HERRERA, the elder (1576–1656), was a very original painter. He was born at Seville, and never studied out of Andalusia. He had so bad a temper that he drove his children and his pupils away from him. He knew how to engrave on bronze, and made false coins; when his forgery was discovered, he took refuge with the Jesuits. While in their convent Herrera painted the history of St. Hermengild, one of the patron saints of Seville. When Philip IV. saw his picture he forgave him his crime, and set him at liberty.

FRANCISCO ZURBARAN (1598–1662) was one of the first among Spanish painters. He was skilful in the use of colors, and knew how to use sober tints and give them a brilliant effect. He did not often paint the Madonna. His female saints are like portraits of the ladies of his day. He was very successful in painting animals, and his pictures of drapery and still-life were exact in their representation of the objects he used for models. He painted historical and religious pictures, portraits and animals; but his best pictures were of monks. Stirling says: "He studied the Spanish friar, and painted him with as high a relish as Titian painted the Venetian noble, and Vandyck the gentleman of England."

Zurbaran was appointed painter to Philip IV. before he was thirty-five years old. He was a great favorite with Philip, who once called Zurbaran "the painter of the king, and king of painters." Zurbaran's finest works are in the Museum of Seville. He left many pictures, and the Louvre claims to have ninety-two of them in its gallery.

DIEGO RODRIGUEZ DE SILVA Y VELASQUEZ (1599–1660) was born at Seville, and died at Madrid. His parents were of noble families; his father was Juan Rodriguez de Silva, and his mother Geronima Velasquez, by whose name, according to the custom of Andalusia, he was called. His paternal grandfather was a Portuguese, but so poor that he was compelled to leave his own country, and seek his fortune at Seville, and to this circumstance Spain owes her greatest painter. Velasquez's father became a lawyer, and lived in comfort, and his mother devoted herself to his education. The child's great love of drawing induced his father to place young Velasquez in the school of Herrera, where the pupil acquired something of his free, bold style. But Velasquez soon became weary, and entered the school of Francisco Pacheco, an inferior painter, but a learned and polished gentleman. Here Velasquez soon learned that untiring industry and the study of nature were the surest guides to perfection for an artist. Until 1622 he painted pictures from careful studies of common life, and always with the model or subject before him—adhering strictly to form, color, and outline. He is said to have kept a peasant lad for a study, and from him executed a variety of heads in every posture and with every possible expression. This gave him wonderful skill in taking likenesses. To this period belong the "Water Carrier of Seville," now at Apsley House, several pictures of beggars, and the "Adoration of the Shepherds," now in the Louvre, where is also a "Beggar Boy munching a piece of Pastry." At Vienna is a "Laughing Peasant" holding a flower (Fig. 64), and in Munich another "Beggar Boy." In 1622 his strong desire to see the paintings in the Royal Galleries led him to Madrid. Letters which he carried gave him admission to the works of art; but excepting securing the friendship of Fonesca, a noted patron of art, and an order to paint a portrait of the poet Gongora, he was unnoticed, and so he returned in a few months to Seville. Subsequently Fonesca interested the minister Olivarez in his behalf. This resulted in a letter summoning Velasquez to court, with an enclosure of fifty ducats for the journey. He was attended by his slave, Juan Pareja, a mulatto lad, who was his faithful attendant for many years, and who became an excellent painter. His former instructor, Pacheco, now his father-in-law, also accompanied him. His first work at the capital, naturally, was a portrait of his friend Fonesca, which so pleased the king, Philip

FIG. 64.—LAUGHING PEASANT. *Velasquez.*

IV., that he appointed Velasquez to his service, in which he remained during his life. This gave him full opportunity to perfect himself, for the king was never weary of multiplying pictures of himself. Velasquez also painted many portraits of the other members of the royal family, in groups and singly. His life was even and prosperous, and he made steady advances toward perfection. He was sent to Italy to study and to visit the galleries and works in all the cities. A second time the king sent him to Italy to purchase works of art, with orders to buy anything he thought worth having. He was everywhere received with consideration and kindness. The pope sat to him for his portrait; the cardinals Barberini and Rospigliosi; the sculptors Bernini and Algardi; the painters Nicolas Poussin, Pietro da Cortona, Claude and Matteo Prete were his friends and associates. Upon his return to Madrid, Velasquez was appointed aposentador-major, with a yearly salary of three thousand ducats, and a key at his girdle to unlock every door in the palace. He superintended the ceremonies and festivals of the royal household; he arranged in the halls of the Alcazar the bronzes and marbles purchased in Italy; he also cast in bronze the models he brought from abroad, and he yet found time to paint his last great picture, "Las Meniñas," or the "Maids of Honor," which represents the royal family, with the artist, maids of honor, the dwarfs, and a sleeping hound. It is said that when the king saw the picture he declared but one thing was wanting, and with his own hand significantly painted the cross of Santiago upon the breast of the artist. When the courts of France and Spain met on the Isle of Pheasants for the betrothal of the Infanta Maria Teresa to Louis XIV., Velasquez superintended all the ceremonies and all the festivities. These were of surpassing splendor, for these two courts were at this time the most luxurious in Europe. Stirling says the fatigues of the life of Velasquez shortened his days. He arrived at

FIG. 65.—THE TOPERS. *By Velasquez.*

Madrid on his return, on June 26th, and from that time was gradually sinking. He died August 6th. He was buried with magnificent ceremonies in the Church of San Juan. His wife survived him but eight days; she was buried in the same grave.

The character of Velasquez was a rare combination of freedom from jealousy, power to conciliate, sweetness of temper, strength of will and intellect, and steadfastness of purpose. He was the friend of Rubens and of Ribera, the protector of Cano and Murillo, who succeeded and were, next to him, the greatest painters of Spain. As the favorite of Philip IV., in fact, his minister for artistic affairs, he filled his office with purity and disinterestedness.

JUAN DE PAREJA (1610–1670) was born in Spanish South America. He was never a great artist; but the circumstances of his life make him interesting. He was the slave of Velasquez, and was employed as color-grinder. He studied painting secretly, and at last, on an occasion when the king visited the studio of his master, Pareja showed him a picture of his own painting, and throwing himself at Philip's feet begged pardon for his audacity. Both Philip and Velasquez treated him very kindly. Velasquez gave Pareja his freedom; but it is said that he continued to serve his old master faithfully as long as he lived. Pareja succeeded best as a portrait painter. His works are not numerous, and are seen in few collections out of Spain.

BARTOLOMÉ ESTÉBAN MURILLO (1618–1682) was born at Seville. His parents were Gaspar Estéban and Maria Perez, and the name of his maternal grandmother, Elvira Murillo, was added to his own, according to Andalusian custom. From childhood he showed his inclination for art, and although this at first suggested to his parents that he should be educated as a priest, the idea was soon abandoned, as it was found that his interest in the paintings which adorned the churches was artistic rather than religious.

He was therefore, at an early age, placed in the studio of his maternal uncle, Juan de Castillo, one of the leaders of the school of art of Seville. Castillo was then about fifty years old, and had as a student with Louis Fernandez acquired the Florentine style of the sixteenth century—combining chaste designing with cold and hard coloring. Murillo was thus early instructed not only in grinding colors and in indispensable mechanical details, but was thoroughly grounded in the important elements of purity of conception and dignity of treatment and arrangement. Seville at this time was the richest city in the Spanish empire. Its commerce with all Europe, and especially with Spanish America, was at its height. The Guadalquivir was alive with its shipping. Its palaces of semi-Moorish origin were occupied by a wealthy and luxurious nobility. The vast cathedral had been finished a century before. The tower "La Giralda," three hundred and forty feet in height, is to this day one of the greatest marvels in Christendom, and with its Saracenic ornament and its "lace work in stone" is beyond all compare. The royal palace of the Alcazar, designed by Moorish architects, rivalled the Alhambra, and was filled with the finest workmanship of Grenada. There were one hundred and forty churches, of which many had been mosques, and were laden with the exquisite ornaments of their original builders. Such a city was sure to stimulate artists and be their home. The poorer ones were in the habit of exposing their works on balconies, on the steps of churches or the cathedral, or in any place where they would attract attention. Thus it often happened on festival days that a good work would command fame for an artist, and gain for him the patronage of some cathedral chapter or generous nobleman. Castillo removed to Cadiz in 1640, and Murillo, who was very poor, could only bring himself before the public, and earn sufficient for the bare necessities of life by thus exposing his pictures in the market of the Feria, as it was called, in front of the Church of All Saints. He struggled along in this way for two years. Early in 1640, Murillo met with an old fellow-pupil, Moya, who had been campaigning in Flanders in the Spanish army, and had there become impressed with the worth of the clear and strong style of the Flemish masters. Especially was he pleased with Vandyck, so that he followed him to England, and there studied as his pupil during the last six months of Vandyck's life. Moved by Moya's romancing stories of travel, adventure, and study, Murillo resolved to see better pictures than were to be found at Seville, and, if possible, to visit Italy. As a first step he painted a quantity of banners, madonnas, flower-pieces—anything and everything—and sold them to a ship owner, who sent them to Spanish America; and it is said that this and similar trades originated the story that Murillo once visited Mexico and other Spanish-American countries. Thus equipped with funds, and without informing his friends (his parents were dead), he started on foot across the mountains and the equally dreaded plains for Madrid, which he entered at the age of twenty-five, friendless and poor. He sought out Velasquez, and asked him for letters to his friends in Rome. But Velasquez, then at the height of his fame and influence, was so much interested in the young enthusiast that he offered him lodgings and an opportunity to study and copy in the galleries of Madrid. The Royal Galleries contained carefully selected pictures from the Italian and Flemish schools, so that Murillo was at once placed in the very best possible conditions for success. Murillo thus spent more than two years, mostly under the direction of Velasquez, and worked early and late. He copied from the Italian and Flemish masters, and drew from casts and from life. This for a time so influenced his style that even now connoisseurs are said to discern reminiscences of Vandyck and Velasquez in the pictures painted by him on his first return to Seville. At the end of two years Velasquez advised Murillo to go to Rome, and offered to assist him. But Murillo decided first to return to Seville, and perhaps had come to the resolution not to go to Italy ; but this may be doubted. He knew the progress he had made ; he was reasonably certain that, if not the superior, he was the equal of any of the artists he had left behind in Seville. He was sure of the wealth, and taste, and love for art in his native city. His only sister was living there. The rich and noble lady he afterward married resided near there. And so we can hardly wonder that the artist gave up a cherished journey to Italy, and returned to the scene of his early struggles with poverty.

The first works which Murillo painted after his return were for the Franciscan Convent. They brought him little money but much fame. They were eleven in number, but even the names of some are lost. One represents St. Francis resting on his iron bed, listening in ecstacy to the notes of a violin which an angel is playing to him ; another portrays St. Diego of Alcalá, asking a blessing on a kettle of broth he is about to give to a group of beggars clustered before him ; another represents the death of St. Clara of Assisi, in the rapturous trance in which her soul passed away, surrounded by pale nuns and emaciated monks looking upward to a contrasting group of Christ and the Madonna, with a train of celestial virgins bearing her shining robe of immortality. The companion picture is a Franciscan monk who passes into a celestial ecstacy while cooking in the convent kitchen, and who is kneeling in the air, while angels perform his culinary tasks. These pictures brought Murillo into speedy notice. Artists and nobles flocked to see them. Orders for portraits and altar-pieces followed in rapid succession, and he was full of work. Notwithstanding the fact that he was acknowledged to be at the head of his profession in Seville, his style at this time was cold and hard. It is called *frio* (cold), to distinguish it from his later styles. The Franciscan Convent pictures were carried off by Marshal Soult, and fortunately; for the convent was burned in 1810. His second style, called *calido*, or warm, dated from about the time of his marriage, in 1648, to a lady of distinguished family, named Doña Beatriz de Cabrera y Sotomayor. She was possessed of considerable property, and had lived in the village of Pilas, a few leagues southwest of Seville. Her portrait is not known to exist; but several of Murillo's madonnas which resemble each other are so evidently portraits, that the belief is these idealized faces were drawn from the countenance of the wife of the master.

His home now became famous for its hospitable reunions, and his social position, added to his artistic merits, procured for him orders beyond his utmost ability to fill. One after another in quick succession, large, grand works were sent out from his studio to be the pride of churches and convents. At this time his pictures were noted for a portrait-like naturalness in their faces, perhaps lacking in idealism, but withal pure and pleasing; the drapery graceful and well arranged, the lights skilfully disposed, the tints harmonious, and the contours soft. His flesh tints were heightened by dark gray backgrounds, so amazingly true that an admirer has said they were painted in blood and milk. The *calido*, or warm manner, was preserved for eight or ten years. In this style were painted an "Immaculate Conception," for the Franciscan Convent; "The Nativity of the Virgin," for the high altar of the Seville Cathedral; a "St. Anthony of Padua" for the same church, and very many others equally famous. In 1874 the St. Anthony was stolen from the cathedral, and for some time was unheard of, until two men offered to sell it for two hundred and fifty dollars to Mr. Schaus, the picture dealer in New York. He purchased the work and turned it over to the Spanish Consul, who immediately returned it to the Seville Cathedral, to the great joy of the Sevillians. In 1658 Murillo turned his attention to the founding of an Academy of Art, and, though he met with many obstacles, the institution was finally opened for instruction in 1660, and Murillo was its first president. At this time he was taking on his latest manner, called the *vaporoso*, or vapory, which was first used in some of his pictures executed for the Church of Sta. Maria la Blanca. In this manner the rigid outlines of his first style is gone; there is a feathery lightness of touch as if the brush had swept the canvas smoothly and with unbroken evenness: this softness is enhanced by frequent contrasts with harder and heavier groups in the same picture.

But the highest point in the art was reached by Murillo in the eleven pictures which he painted in the Hospital de la Caridad. Six of these are now in their original places; five were stolen by Soult and carried to France; some were returned to Spain, but not to the hospital.

The convent of the Capuchins at Seville at one time possessed twenty pictures by this master. The larger part of them are now in the Museum of Seville, and form the finest existing collection of his works. This museum was once a church, and the statue of Murillo is placed in front of it. Although the lighting of this museum is far inferior to that of Madrid and many others, yet here one must go to realize fully the glory of this master. Among the pictures is the "Virgen de la Sevilletá," or Virgin of the Napkin. It is said that the cook of the convent had become the friend of the painter, and begged of him some memento of his good feeling; the artist had no canvas, and the cook gave him a napkin upon which this great work was done.

Murillo's representation of that extremely spiritual and mystical subject called the Immaculate Conception, has so far excelled that of any other artist that he has sometimes been called "the painter of the Conception." His attention

FIG 66.—THE IMMACULATE CONCEPTION. *By Murillo. In the Louvre.*

was especially called to this subject by the fact that the doctrine it sets forth was a pet with the clergy of Seville, who, when Pope Paul V., in 1617, published a bull making this doctrine obligatory, celebrated the occasion with all possible pomp in the churches; the nobles also gave entertainments, and the whole city was alive with a fervor of religious zeal and a desire to manifest its love for this dogma. The directions given by the Inspector of the Holy Office for the representation of this subject were extremely precise; but Murillo complied with them in general effect only, and disregarded details when it pleased him: for example, the rules prescribed the age of the Virgin to be from twelve to thirteen, and the hair to be of golden hue. Murillo sometimes pictured her as a dark-haired woman. It is said that when he painted the Virgin as very young his daughter Francesca was his model; later the daughter became a nun in the convent of the Madre de Dios.

The few portraits painted by Murillo are above all praise; his pictures of humble life, too, would of themselves have sufficed to make him famous. No Spanish artist, except Velasquez, has painted better landscapes than he. But so grand and vast were his religious works that his fame rests principally on them. It is true, however, that in England and in other countries out of Spain he was first made famous by his beggar boys and kindred subjects.

Murillo and Velasquez may be said to hold equivalent positions in the annals of Spanish Art—Murillo as the painter for the church, and Velasquez as that of the court. As a delineator of religious subjects Murillo ranked only a very little below the greatest Italian masters, and even beside them he excels in one direction; for he is able more generally and fully to arouse religious emotions and sympathies. This stamps his genius as that of the first order, and it should also be placed to his credit, in estimating his native talent, that he never saw anything of all the Classic Art which was such a source of inspiration to the artists of Italy. Stirling says: "All his ideas were of home growth; his mode of expression was purely national and Spanish; his model—nature, as it existed in and around Seville."

While painting a marriage of St. Catherine for the Capuchin Church of Cadiz, Murillo fell from the scaffold, and soon died from his injuries: he was buried in the Church of Sta. Cruz, and it is a sad coincidence that this church and that of San Juan, at Madrid, in which Velasquez was interred, were both destroyed by the French under the command of Soult.

The character of Murillo was such as to command the greatest respect, and though he was not associated with as many royal personages as Velasquez, he was invited to court, and received many flattering acknowledgments of his genius. His fame was not confined to his own country, and his portrait was engraved in Flanders during the last year of his life. He had many strong personal friends, and his interest in the academy and his generosity to other artists prove him to have been above all mean jealousies: he loved Art because it was Art, and did all in his power for its elevation in his own country. It is probable that since his death more money has been paid for a single picture by him than he received for the entire work of his life. The Immaculate Conception, now in the Louvre, was sold from the Soult collection for six hundred and fifteen thousand three hundred francs, or more than one hundred and twenty-three thousand dollars. At the time of its sale it was believed to be the largest price ever paid for a picture.

SEBASTIAN GOMEZ (about 1620) was a mulatto slave of Murillo's, and like Pareja he secretly learned to paint. At last one day when Murillo left a sketch of a head of the Virgin on his easel Gomez dared to finish it. Murillo was glad to find that he had made a painter of his slave, and though the pictures of Gomez were full of faults his color was much like that of his master. Two of his pictures are in the Museum of Seville. He did not live long after Murillo's death in 1682.

DON ALONSO MIGUEL DE TOBAR (1678–1758) never attained to greatness. His best original pictures were portraits. He made a great number of copies of the works of Murillo, and was chiefly famous for these pictures. There is little doubt that many pictures attributed to Murillo are *replicas*, or copies by the hand of Tobar.

The school of Valencia flourished from 1506 to 1680. VICENTE DE JOANES (about 1506–1579) was a painter of religious pictures who is scarcely known out of Spain, and in that country his pictures are, almost without exception, in churches and convents. He was very devout, and began his works with fasting and prayer. It is related that on one occasion a Jesuit of Valencia had a vision in which the Virgin Mary appeared to him, and commanded him to have a picture painted of her in a dress like that she then wore, which was a white robe with a blue mantle. She was to be represented standing on a crescent with the mystic dove floating above her; her Son was to crown her, while the Father was to lean from the clouds above all.

The Jesuit selected Joanes to be the painter of this work, and though he fasted and prayed much he could not paint it so as to please himself or the Jesuit. At last his pious zeal overcame all obstacles, and his picture was hung above the altar of the Immaculate in the convent of the Jesuits. It was very beautiful—the artists praised it, the monks believed that it had a miraculous power, and it was known as "La Purisima," or the perfectly pure one.

Joanes excelled in his pictures of Christ. He seemed to have conceived the very Christ of the Scriptures, the realization of the visions of St. John, or of the poetry of Solomon. In these pictures he combined majesty with grace and love with strength. Joanes frequently represented the Last

Supper, and introduced a cup which is known as the Holy Chalice of Valencia. It is made of agate and adorned with gold and gems, and was believed to have been used by Christ at his Last Supper with his disciples. Some of the portraits painted by Joanes are very fine. In manner and general effect his works are strangely like those of the great Raphael.

FRANCISCO DE RIBALTA (1550–1628) was really the head of the school of Valencia, and one of the best historical painters of Spain. He studied his art first in Valencia, and there fell in love with the daughter of his master. The father refused him his suit, and the young couple parted in deep sorrow. Ribalta went to Italy, where he made such progress, and gained such fame that when he returned to Valencia he had no trouble in marrying his old master's daughter. Valencia has more pictures by Ribalta than are found elsewhere. Out of Spain they are very rare. One of his works is at Magdalene College, Oxford.

One peculiarity of the Spanish painters was that they painted the extremes of emotion. Their subjects represented the ecstacy of bliss or the most excruciating agony. They did not seem to have as much middle ground or to know as much of moderate emotions as the painters of other nations. Ribalta was no exception to this rule, and some of his pictures are painful to look at. His portraits are fine, and represent the most powerful men of Valencia of the time in which he lived.

JOSEF DE RIBERA was a native of Valencia, but lived and studied in Italy, and so became more of an Italian than a Spanish master. I have spoken of him in connection with the Naturalists and their school at Naples.

ALONSO CANO (1601–1667) was a very important artist, and cannot be said to belong to any school. He was born at Granada, and studied under masters of Seville, both in painting and sculpture. He became the best Spanish artist who studied in Spain only. He was something of an architect also, and his various talents acquired a high place for him among artists ; but his temper was such as to cause him much trouble, and it so interfered with his life that he did not attain to the position to which his artistic gifts entitled him.

In 1637 he fought a duel, and was obliged to flee from Madrid, and in 1644 his wife was found murdered in her bed. Cano was suspected of the crime, and although he fled he was found, and brought back, and put to the torture. He made no confession, and was set at liberty; but many people believed in his guilt. He still held his office as painter to the king, and was sometimes employed on important works; but he determined to remove to his native Granada and become a priest. Philip IV. appointed him canon, and after he held this office he was still employed as a painter and sculptor by private persons, as well as by religious bodies, and was even sent to Malaga to superintend improvements in the cathedral there. But his temper led him into so many broils that at length, in 1659, the chapter of Granada deprived him of his office. He went to the king with his complaints, and was again made a canon; but he was so angry that he never would use his brush or his chisel in the service of the Cathedral of Granada.

His life was now devoted to charity and good works. He gave away all his money as soon as he received it. When his purse was empty he would go into a shop, and beg a pencil and paper, and sketching a head or other design would mark the price on it, and give it to a beggar with directions for finding a purchaser for it. After his death large numbers of these charity works were collected.

One of his strong characteristics was hatred of the Jews. He would cross the street, in order not to meet one of them, and would throw away a garment that had brushed against one of the race. One day he went home, and found his housekeeper bargaining with a Jew; he chased him away with great fury, sent the woman off to be purified, repaved the spot where the Jew had stood, and gave the shoes in which he had chased him to a servant. When about to die Cano would not receive the sacrament from the priest who was present, because he had communicated with Jews, and when a rude crucifix was held before him he pushed it away. When he was reproved for this he said: "Vex me not with this thing; but give me a simple cross that I may adore it, both as it is, and as I can figure it in my mind." When this was done, it is said that he died in a most edifying manner.

Very few of Cano's architectural works remain; a few drawings of this sort are in the Louvre which are simple and elegant in style. The finest carving by him is a small figure of the Virgin, now in the Cathedral of Granada. Eight of his pictures are in the Queen of Spain's gallery at Madrid, and the Church of Getafe, the Cathedral of Granada and that of Malaga have his works. A beautiful madonna, which was one of his latest works, is in the chapel of the Cathedral of Valencia, and is lighted by votive tapers only. His pictures are rare out of Spain. One of his portraits is in the Louvre. Other works are in Berlin, Dresden, Munich, and the Hermitage, St. Petersburg.

The last Spanish painter of whom I shall speak belongs to a much later period. FRANCISCO GOYA Y LUCIENTES (1746–1828) was a student in Rome, and after his return to Spain lived in fine style in a villa near Madrid. He was painter to Charles IV., and was always employed on orders from the nobility. He painted portraits and religious pictures, but his chief excellence was in painting caricatures. He was never weary of painting the priests and monks in all sorts of ridiculous ways. He made them in the form of apes and asses, and may be called the Hogarth of Spain, so well did he hold up the people about him to ridicule. He painted with great boldness and could use a sponge or stick in place of a brush. Sometimes he made a picture with his palette-knife, and put in the fine touches with his thumb. He executed engravings also, and published eighty prints which he called "Caprices." These were very famous; they were satires upon all Spanish laws and customs. He also made a series of plates about the French invasion, thirty-three prints of scenes in the bull-ring, and etchings of some of the works of Velasquez. Portraits of Charles IV. and his queen by Goya are in the museum at Madrid. Works of his are in the Louvre and in the National Gallery in London. His pictures sell for large prices. In 1870 his picture of Charlotte Corday sold for five hundred and eighty-four pounds.

## CHAPTER VI.

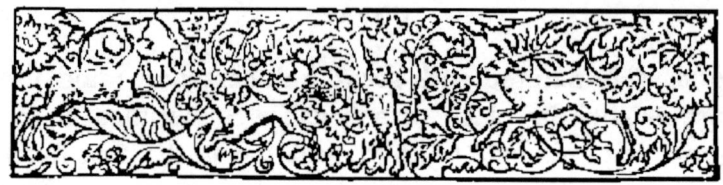

### PAINTING IN FRANCE.

THE French school of painting does not date earlier than the sixteenth century, and the painters of that time were few in number, and little is known of them. Before the time when a French school could be said to exist the kings of France employed foreign artists to decorate their palaces and churches, and they naturally turned to the Italians for all that they needed. Hence it happened that in its earliest days the French school was almost entirely under Italian influence, and I shall first speak of French masters who studied in Italy.

NICHOLAS POUSSIN (1594–1665) may be said to belong to the seventeenth century, since he was born so late in the preceding one. Poussin was born in Normandy, and early began to draw and paint. He studied somewhat in France, and when thirty years old went to Rome, where, in reality, his artistic career began. He was a pupil of Andrea Sacchi, and received some instruction from Domenichino also; but he formed his style principally by studying the works of the ancients and those of the great Raphael. He was so devoted to the study of the habits and customs of the Greeks that he almost became one of them in his modes of thought.

He was very poor when he first went to Rome; but he worked hard, and began to be known and to receive orders for pictures. Louis XIII. heard of Poussin, and invited him

FIG. 67.—ARCADIAN SHEPHERDS. *Poussin.*

to Paris, where he gave him apartments in the Tuileries. But the artist longed to return to Rome, and made a plea of going for his wife. Soon after he left, Louis died, and Poussin never returned to France. Poussin was always busy; but he asked such moderate prices that he was never rich, and, when a great man pitied the artist because he had so few servants, Poussin pitied him in return for having so many. His portrait painted by himself is in the Louvre, where are many of his mythological pictures. His love for the classic manner makes these subjects his best works. His paintings are seen in many European galleries.

CLAUDE LORRAINE (1600–1682), whose real name was Claude Gelée, was born in Champagne in Lorraine. His parents were very poor, and died when he was still young: he was apprenticed to a pastry-cook, and so travelled to Rome as servant to some young gentlemen. Not long after his arrival he engaged himself to the painter Agostino Tassi, for whom he cooked, and mixed colors. After a time he himself began to paint. Nature was his teacher; he studied her with unchanging devotion; he knew all her changes, and was in the habit of sitting for a whole day watching one scene, so that he could paint from memory its different aspects at the various hours of the day. His works brought him into notice when he was still young. He received many orders, and when about twenty-seven years old some pictures he painted for Pope Urban VIII. established his fame as an artist of high rank. His character was above reproach, and his feelings were as tender as many of his pictures. He was attractive in person, though his face was grave in its expression. It would seem that he should have left a large fortune, but he did not. This was partly because he suffered much from gout, and was often unable to paint; but a better reason probably is that he gave so much to his needy relations that he could not save large sums.

Claude Lorraine has been called the prince and poet of landscape painters. Lübke, the German art writer, praises him very much, and his praise is more valuable than it would be if it came from one of Claude's own countrymen. He says: "Far more profoundly than all other masters did Claude Gelée penetrate into the secrets of nature, and by the enchanting play of sunlight, the freshness of his dewy foregrounds, and the charm of his atmospheric distances, he obtained a tone of feeling which influences the mind like an eternal Sabbath rest. In his works there is all the splendor, light, untroubled brightness, and harmony of the first morning of creation in Paradise. His masses of foliage have a glorious richness and freshness, and even in the deepest shadows are interwoven with a golden glimmer of light. But they serve only as a mighty framework, for, more freely than with other masters, the eye wanders through a rich foreground into the far distance, the utmost limits of which fade away in golden mist."

His two great charms are the immense space which he represents in his pictures and his beautiful color. The latter appears as if he had first used a silvery gray, and then put his other colors over that, which gives his works a soft, lovely atmospheric effect, such as no other artist has surpassed. When he introduced buildings into his pictures they were well done; but his figures and animals were so imperfect that he was accustomed to say that he sold the landscape, and gave away the figures.

Before his death his pictures were so much valued that other artists tried to imitate them, and he was accustomed to keep a book of sketches by which his works could be proved. He called this book "Liber Veritatis," and before his death it reached six volumes; one of these containing two hundred drawings is at Chatsworth. A catalogue of his works describes more than four hundred landscapes. All the principal galleries of Europe have his pictures, and there are a great number of them in England, both in public and private collections.

SEBASTIAN BOURDON (1616–1671), who was born at Montpelier, made his studies in Rome. He brought himself into notice by a picture of the Crucifixion of St. Peter, which is now in the Louvre. He was one of the earliest members of the French Academy. Bourdon resided in Sweden for some years; but was in Paris, and held the position of Rector of the Academy when he died. He painted a few *genre* subjects, and two of his portraits by himself are in the Louvre; but his best works were landscapes, and in these his style was like that of Salvator Rosa. It has been said that Rigaud assisted him in his portraits of himself. Bourdon made some engravings, and collectors prize his plates very much.

There were other French painters who studied in Italy, but those that I have mentioned are the important ones. Of those who studied in their own country only, EUSTACHE LE SUEUR (1617–1655) was the first of any importance; but his life was short and uneventful, and he was not appreciated. His most important works are in the Louvre.

CHARLES LE BRUN (1619–1690) was very prominent in his day. His father was a sculptor, and was employed by the Chancellor Segnier. This nobleman's attention was attracted to the son, and he at length sent the young Le Brun to Italy to study. He remained there six years, and after his return to Paris he was made painter to the king, and became the favorite of the court. He used his opportunities to persuade Louis XIV. to found the Royal Academy at Paris, which was done in 1648. All his principal pictures are in the Louvre.

PIERRE MIGNARD (1612–1695) has been called "the Roman," because he lived in Rome twenty-two years, and while there was patronized by three successive popes. In 1664 he was made President of the Academy of St. Luke in

Rome. At length Louis XIV. invited him to return to France. In 1690 he succeeded Le Brun as court painter, and was made Chancellor of the Academy. His portraits are his best works, and these are seen in the galleries of various European countries.

HYACINTHE RIGAUD (1659–1743) became the most distinguished French portrait painter of his time; but his pictures are not very attractive or interesting in our day. He finished them too much, and so gave them an artificial appearance. Then, too, the costume of his day was such that his portraits seem to be the portraits of wigs and not of people. They are very numerous. He often painted the portrait of Louis XIV., and had illustrious people from all parts of Europe among his sitters.

ANTOINE WATTEAU (1684–1721) was the first to practise a new style of painting. The habit of the French court was to pass much time in elegant out-door amusements. Watteau represented the scenes of the *fêtes galantes* and reunions then so much in fashion. His pictures are crowded with figures in beautiful costumes. There are groups of ladies and gentlemen promenading, dancing, love-making, and lounging in pleasant grounds with temples and fountains and everything beautiful about them. The pictures of Watteau are fine, and are seen in many galleries. His color is brilliant, and to their worth as pictures is added the historical interest which belongs to them, because they give us the best idea of court life, dress, and manners of the reign of Louis XIV. which can be had from any paintings.

The followers of Watteau were numerous, but are not of great importance. There were a few painters of animals and fowers in the French school; but we shall pass to the *genre* painters, among whom JEAN-BAPTISTE GREUZE (1725–1805) was important. He painted very beautiful pictures of young girls and children. His color is very agreeable, and some of his works are finished as finely as if they were done on ivory. Most of his pictures are in private galleries, but they are seen in some public collections. Probably the "Broken Jug," in the Louvre, is his best known work. His pictures sell for very large prices. At the Forster sale in 1876, "A Little Girl with a Lap Dog in her Arms" brought six thousand seven hundred and twenty pounds; in 1772 the same picture was sold for three hundred pounds, and in 1832 it was again sold for seven hundred and three pounds. Thus we see that in fifty-four years its value had increased to more than nine times its price, and in one hundred and four years it brought twenty-two times as much as it was first sold for.

CLAUDE JOSEPH VERNET (1714–1789) was the best marine painter of the French school. Louis XV. commissioned him to paint the seaports of France. Fifteen of these pictures are in the Louvre. There have been many engravings after his works. His pictures of Italian seaports and views near Rome and Tivoli are among his best paintings. His color has little variety; but his drawing is correct, and his finish is very careful and fine. Vernet also made a few etchings.

In the early part of the eighteenth century JOSEPH MARIE VIEN (1716–1809) returned to the classic style of painting, and created a feeling against the pretty manner which had been the chief feature of French pictures for some time. His pictures are very numerous in the churches and galleries of Paris. He was not a great painter, but he marks a change in the spirit of French painting. Vien was the teacher of JACQUES LOUIS DAVID (1748–1825), who was considered the first painter in modern art at the close of the eighteenth century. He was so devoted to the classic style that he took the remains of ancient art as models for the figures in his pictures. His groups are like groups of statues, and his flesh looks like marble, it is so hard and lifeless. During the time of the first Napoleon

FIG. 68.—THE SABINE WOMEN. *David.*

this style was carried to excess in everything connected with the arts. David was such a favorite with the emperor that after the return of the Bourbons he was banished, and his family were not allowed to bury him in France. He lived in Brussels, and executed many of his best pictures there.

ANTOINE JEAN GROS (1771–1835) was a great admirer of David, and first attracted attention in 1801 by a picture of "Bonaparte on the Bridge of Arcola." After this Gros painted many such works, and principally represented military events. Many of his pictures are very coarse. The "Plague at Jaffa" and the "Field of Eylau" are of this type, and the first is disgusting. Among his best works is "Francis I. and Charles V. visiting the Tombs at St. Denis." But although he received many honors, and was made a baron by Charles X., he could not bear the criticism which was made upon his pictures, and finally drowned himself in the Seine near Meudon.

PAUL DELAROCHE (1797–1856) was born at Paris, and studied under Baron Gros. He became a celebrated artist and was made a member of the Institute of France, a Professor in l'École des Beaux-Arts, and an officer of the Legion of Honor. His principal works represent scenes of important historical interest, and he so arranged them that they appeal to one's sympathies with great power. Among these pictures are the "Condemnation of Marie Antoinette," the "Death of the Duke of Guise," "Cromwell Contemplating the Remains of Charles I.," and other similar historical incidents. His design was according to academical rules; but he was not entirely conventional, and in some of his religious pictures there was much expression and deep feeling.

His largest and most famous work is the "Hemicycle," in l'École des Beaux-Arts, Paris. He was occupied with this painting during three years; it contains seventy-five figures of life size. The arts of different countries and ages

are represented in it by portraits of the artists of the times and nations typified. Thus it is very interesting when considered merely as a great collection of portraits. Delaroche married the daughter of Horace Vernet, and it is said that the figure which stands for Gothic Architecture is a portrait of her. The Hemicycle is richly colored, and has a great deal of fine painting in it; but from its very nature it has no dramatic power, and does not arouse any deep sentiment in one who studies it. Delaroche was paid only about fifteen thousand dollars for this great labor, and refused to have any further reward.

Perhaps none of his works are more powerful than the "Death of the Duke of Guise." You will easily recall the circumstances of his assassination: the painter has so represented it that one really forgets that it is a picture, and can only remember the horror of the crime. The corpse of the duke is on one side of the immense chamber, near the bed; the assassins are in a terrified group on the other side, and with them the cowardly king, who was absolutely afraid of the dead body of his victim. The picture is a remarkable instance of the power that may be given to what is sometimes called historical-genre art. This picture was sold in 1853 for ten thousand five hundred dollars (Fig. 69).

JEAN LOUIS GÉRICAULT (1791–1824). He was born at Rouen, and studied first under Guérin and then in Rome. He was the first master of any power who entirely dismissed the influence of the art of David with its marble flesh and statuesque effect. The one great work by which he is known is the "Wreck of the Medusa," which is in the Louvre, and which may be said to mark the advent of the modern French school.

EUGENE DELACROIX (1799–1863) was the son of a Minister of Foreign Affairs, and was born to position and wealth. But through misfortunes all this was changed, and he was forced to work hard for his living. At last he managed to study under Guérin, and in the studio of the master became the friend of Géricault. The first work which brought Delacroix fame was a picture of a scene from Dante's "Inferno," in which Dante sees some of his old acquaintances who were condemned to float upon the lake which surrounds the infernal city. This work was exhibited in 1822, and was bought for the Gallery of the Luxembourg. Baron Gros tried to be his friend; but Delacroix wished to follow his own course, and for some time had but small success.

He travelled in Spain, Algiers, and Morocco, and at length was commissioned by Thiers to do some decorative work in the throne-room of the Chamber of Deputies. He was much criticised, but at length was accepted as a great artist, and was made a member of the Institute in 1857. He received another important order for the Chamber of Peers. Some of his works are at Versailles, and others are seen in various churches of Paris. When they are considered as a whole they are effective, but they do not bear examination; his design was free and spirited and his color good, and he painted a variety of subjects, and was able to vary the expression of his work to suit the impression he wished to produce.

ÉMILE JEAN HORACE VERNET (1789–1863) was born in the Louvre. He studied under his father, Carle Vernet, who was the son of Claude Joseph Vernet. Carle was a witty man, and it is said that when he was dying he exclaimed, "How much I resemble the Grand Dauphin—son of a king, father of a king, and never a king myself!" In spite of his being less than his father or his son, he was a good painter of horses. When Horace Vernet was but fifteen years old he supported himself by drawing; he studied with Vincent, and drew from living models. In 1814 he showed such bravery at the Barriere of Clichy that he was decorated with the Cross of the Legion of Honor:

before he died he was a grand officer of the order on account of his artistic merits. He was also a member of the Institute and Director of the Academy of Rome.

His best works were executed in Rome, where he spent seven years; he travelled in Algiers, Syria, Egypt, Palestine, Russia, and England, and was everywhere received with the honors which his genius merited. His works embraced a great variety of subjects, and it is said that he often finished his picture the first time he went over it, and did not retouch it. There is no doubt that in certain ways the excellence of Vernet has been over-estimated, and he has been too much praised; but his remarkable memory, which enabled him truthfully to paint scenes he had witnessed, and his facility of execution, are worthy of honorable mention.

When twenty years old Vernet was married, and from this time he kept an expense account in which all the prices he received for his works are set down. The smallest is twenty-four sous for a tulip; the largest is fifty thousand francs for the portrait of the Empress of Russia.

About 1817 Vernet became the favorite of the Duke of Orleans, and was therefore unpopular with the royal party. In 1820 he had made himself so displeasing to the king by some lithographs which were scattered among the people, that it was thought best for him to leave Paris. However, he overcame all this, and four years later Charles X. sat to him for his portrait. From this time orders and money flowed in from all sides.

The Vernets had originated in Avignon, and in 1826, when the museum there was opened, Horace and his father were invited to be present. Every honor was shown them; poems were read in their praise; they were conducted to the home of their ancestors, which they piously saluted, and inscribed their names upon the door-posts. After they returned to Paris they received rich gifts in return for the pictures they had given to Avignon. The Gallery Vernet, which contains works by Antoine, François, Joseph, Carle, and Horace Vernet, is regarded as a sacred place by the people of that region.

When Horace Vernet was Director of the Academy in Rome he held *salons* weekly; they were very gay, and all people of distinction who lived in Rome or visited that city were seen at these receptions, dancing and amusing themselves in the lively French manner. But after 1830 he felt that the Villa Medici was a prison. He wished to follow the French army in the East, and three years later did go to Algiers. In the same year the king decided to convert the palace at Versailles into an historical museum, and from this time Vernet had but two ideas, the East and Versailles. Almost every work he did was connected with these two thoughts.

Louis Philippe now desired him to paint four battle-pieces; but Vernet objected that no room was large enough to please him: for this reason a floor was removed, two stories turned into one, and the grand Gallery of Battles made. At length he had a difficulty with the king and went to Russia; but hearing that his father was dying he returned to Paris, and was made welcome back to Versailles, where he was really necessary.

We cannot stay to recount the honors which were showered upon him, and which he always received with great modesty of demeanor. He went from one triumph to another until 1848, when the Revolution almost broke his heart; he worked on, but his happiness was over. In the great Exposition of 1855 he had a whole *salon* devoted to his works, and men from all the world came to see and to praise. He lived still eight years; he made pictures of incidents in the Crimean War; he painted a portrait of Napoleon III., but he wrote of himself: "When time has worn out a portion of our faculties we are not entirely destroyed; but it is necessary to know how to leave the first rank and content one's self with the fourth."

His industry and the amount of work he did are simply marvellous. He loved excitement and adventure, and the works which have these elements were his best—and he liked best to do them. His color cannot be praised; he had no lofty intellectual aims; he was clever to a high degree, but he was not great; he was one to whom the happy medium of praise should be given, for he neither merits severity of criticism nor immoderate praise; he was simply a gifted painter and "the greatest and last of the Vernets."

He is also the last French painter of whom we shall speak, as we do not propose to take up the excellent artists of our own day, who would require a volume devoted strictly to themselves.

## CHAPTER VII.

### PAINTING IN ENGLAND.

IN early days in England there were miniature-painters, and in the last half of the sixteenth century there were some very important English painters of this kind. Before the days of Charles I. the English kings were much in the habit of inviting foreign artists to England, and commissions were given to them. The painters who were most prominent in England were of the Flemish school, and even under Charles I., as we have seen, Rubens and Vandyck were the principal painters in England. But in the reign of this king some native artists made names for themselves, and what we call the English school of painting may really be dated from this time.

Before speaking of painters I must mention one miniaturist whose works were in demand in other countries, as well as in England. SAMUEL COOPER (1609–1672) has been called "the Vandyck in little," and there is far more breadth in his works than is usual in miniature. He painted likenesses of many eminent persons, and his works now have an honorable place in many collections.

WILLIAM DOBSON (1610–1646) has been mentioned in our account of Vandyck as a painter whom the great master befriended and recommended to Charles I. He became a good portrait-painter, and after Vandyck's death was appointed sergeant-painter to the king. His portraits are full of dignity; the face shadows are dark, and his color ex-

FIG. 70.—SIR JOSHUA REYNOLDS.

cellent. He did not excel in painting historical subjects. Vandyck was succeeded at court by two foreign artists who are so closely associated with England that they are always spoken of as English artists.

PETER VAN DER FAES (1618–1680), who was born in Westphalia, is known to us as Sir PETER LELY. He became the most celebrated portrait-painter after Vandyck, and his "Beauties at Hampton Court" are pictures which are known the world over. He has been accused of not painting eyes as he ought; but the ladies of his day had an affectation in the use of their eyes. They tried to have "the sleepy eye that spoke the melting soul," so Sir Peter Lely was not to blame for painting them as these ladies wished them to be. He was knighted by Charles II., and became very rich. His portraits of men were not equal to those of women. When Cromwell gave him a commission to paint his portrait, he said: "Mr. Lely, I desire you will use all your skill to paint my picture truly like me, and not flatter me at all; but remark all these roughnesses, pimples, warts, and everything as you see me, otherwise I will never pay you a farthing for it." Sir Peter Lely was buried in Covent Garden, where there is a monument to his memory with a bust by Gibbon.

Sir GODFREY KNELLER (1646–1723), born at Lübeck, was a rival to Sir Peter Lely, and had the honor of painting the portraits of eight crowned heads and a very great number of other people of importance. He had studied both the Dutch and Italian manner; for he was the pupil of Rembrandt and Bol, of Carlo Maratti and Bernini. Some critics praise his pictures very much, while others point out many defects in them. He painted very rapidly, and he sometimes hurried his pictures off for the sake of money; but his finished works are worthy of remark. He especially excelled in painting hair; his drawing was correct; some of his groups of children are fine pictures; and some madonnas that he painted, using his sitters as models, are works of merit. His monument was made by Rysbrach, and was placed in Westminster Abbey.

Both Sir Peter Lely and Sir Godfrey Kneller had pupils and followers; but there was no original English artist before the time of WILLIAM HOGARTH (1697–1764), and he may really be named as the first master of a purely English school of painting. When Hogarth was fifteen years old he was apprenticed to a silversmith, and the grotesque designs which he copied for armorial bearings helped to increase his natural love for all that was ridiculous and strange. After 1718 he was much occupied in engraving for booksellers, and at length he began to paint small *genre* pictures and some portraits, in which he made good success, but he felt that he was fitted for other work. In 1730 he married the daughter of the artist, Sir James Thornhill, without the consent of her father.

Soon after this he began his series of pictures called the "Harlot's Progress," and when Sir James saw them he was so satisfied with the talent of Hogarth that he declared that such an artist could support a wife who had no dower, and the two painters were soon reconciled to each other. Before 1744 Hogarth had also painted the series of the "Rake's Progress" and "Marriage à la Mode" (Fig. 71).

These are all pictures which hold up the customs of the time to ridicule and satire, and his works of this kind are almost numberless. He explains as follows the cause of his painting in this way: "The reasons which induced me to adopt this mode of designing were that I thought both critics and painters had, in the historical style, quite overlooked that intermediate species of subjects which may be placed between the sublime and the grotesque. I therefore wished to compose pictures on canvas similar to representations on the stage; and further hope that they will be tried by the same test and criticised by the same criticism."

FIG. 71.—THE MARRIAGE CONTRACT. *No. 1 of The Marriage à la Mode. By Hogarth. In the National Gallery.*

It was in this sort of picture that Hogarth made himself great, though he supported himself for several years by portrait-painting, in which art he holds a reputable place. Most of his important pictures are in public galleries.

Hogarth was a fine engraver, and left many plates after his own works, which are far better and more spirited than another artist could have made them. The pictures of Hogarth have good qualities aside from their peculiar features. He made his interiors spacious, and the furniture and all the details were well arranged; his costumes were exact, as was also the expression of his faces; his painting was good, and his color excellent. In 1753 he published a book called the "Analysis of Beauty."

Ever after his first success his career was a prosperous one. He rode in his carriage, and was the associate and friend of men in good positions. Hogarth was buried in Chiswick Churchyard, and on his tombstone are these lines, written by David Garrick:

> "Farewell, great painter of mankind!
> Who reach'd the noblest point of Art,
> Whose pictur'd morals charm the mind,
> And through the eye, correct the heart.
> If Genius fire thee, reader, stay;
> If Nature touch thee, drop a tear;
> If neither move thee, turn away,
> For Hogarth's honour'd dust lies here."

The next important English painter was RICHARD WILSON (1713–1782), and he was important not so much for what he painted as for the fact that he was one of the earliest landscape-painters among English artists. He never attained wealth or great reputation, although after his return from studying in Italy he was made a member of the Royal Academy.

We come now to Sir JOSHUA REYNOLDS (1723–1792),

who was born at Plympton, in Devonshire. His father was a clergyman and the master of the grammar school at Plympton. Joshua was destined for the medical profession by his parents; but his love of drawing was so marked that, as the opportunity offered for him to go to London and study under Hudson, his father allowed him to do so. After various changes, in 1749 he was able to go to Rome, and remained in Italy three years (Fig. 70).

When he returned to England he soon attracted attention to his pictures, and it was not long before both fame and fortune were secured to him. His life was a very quiet one, with little of incident that can be related here. His sister kept his house for him, and he lived generously, having company to dinner almost daily. His friends were among the best people of the time, including such persons as Dr. Johnson, Percy, Goldsmith, Garrick, the Burkes, and many others. The day before Johnson died he told Reynolds that he had three requests to make of him: that he would forgive him thirty pounds which he had lent him, would read the Scriptures daily, and would not paint on Sunday. Sir Joshua promised to do these things, and remembered his promise.

Sir Joshua was skilful in compliments. When he painted his famous picture of Mrs. Siddons as the "Tragic Muse" he put his name on the border of her garment. The actress went near the picture to examine it, and when she saw the name she smiled. The artist said: "I could not lose the opportunity of sending my name to posterity on the hem of your garment."

Sir Joshua Reynolds' fame rests upon his portraits, and in these he is almost unrivalled. His pictures of children are especially fine. It was his custom to receive six sitters daily. He kept a list of those who were sitting and of others who waited for an opportunity to have their portraits made by him. He also had sketches of the different por-

FIG. 72.—"MUSCIPULA." *By Reynolds.*

traits he had painted, and when new-comers had looked them over and chosen the position they wished, he sketched it on canvas and then made the likeness to correspond. In this way, when at his best, he was able to paint a portrait in about four hours. His sitters' chairs moved on casters, and were placed on a platform a foot and a half above the floor. He worked standing, and used brushes with handles eighteen inches long, moving them with great rapidity.

In 1768 Sir Joshua was made the first President of the Royal Academy, and it was then that he was knighted by the king. He read lectures at the Academy until 1790, when he took his leave. During these years he sent two hundred and forty-four pictures to the various exhibitions. In 1782 he had a slight shock of paralysis, but was quite well until 1789, when he feared that he should be blind, and from this time he did not paint. He was ill about three months before his death, which occurred in February, 1792. His remains were laid in state at the Royal Academy, and then buried in St. Paul's Cathedral, near the tomb of Sir Christopher Wren.

It is to be regretted that the colors used by Sir Joshua Reynolds are now much faded in many of his pictures. Those in the National Gallery, in London, are, however, in good preservation. Naturally, since so many of his pictures were portraits they are in the collections of private families in England, and but few of them are seen in European galleries. There is an excellent opportunity to study his manner in the pictures at the South Kensington Museum, where there are several portraits, some pictures of children, and the "Graces Decorating a Statue of Hymen."

It is very satisfactory to think of a great artist as a genial, happy man, who is dear to his friends, and has a full, rich life outside of his profession. Such a life had Sir Joshua Reynolds, and one writer says of him: "They made him a knight—this famous painter; they buried him 'with an empire's lamentation;' but nothing honors him more than the 'folio English dictionary of the last revision' which Johnson left to him in his will, the dedication that poor, loving Goldsmith placed in the 'Deserted Village,' and the tears which five years after his death even Burke could not forbear to shed over his memory."

THOMAS GAINSBOROUGH (1727-1788) was born in Sudbury, in Suffolk, and when still quite young went to London, and studied under Francis Hayman, who was not an eminent painter. Gainsborough became one of the most important masters of the English school, especially in landscape painting and the representation of rustic figures. His portraits were not as good in color as those of Sir Joshua Reynolds; they have a bluish-gray hue in the flesh tints; but they are always graceful and charming. His landscapes are not like those of any other master. They are not exact in the detail of leaves and flowers—a botanist could find many faults in them—but they are like nature in spirit: they seem to have the air blowing through them, they are fresh and dewy when it is morning in them, and quiet and peaceful when evening comes under his brush. In many of his pictures he put a cart and a white animal.

His rustic figures have the true country life in them: they seem to have fed upon the air, and warmed themselves in the sun until they are plump and rosy as country lads and lasses should be. His best *genre* pictures are the "Cottage Girl," the "Woodman and Dog in a Storm," the "Cottage Door," and the "Shepherd Boy in a Shower." He painted a picture of a "Girl and Pigs," for which Sir Joshua Reynolds paid him one hundred guineas.

In character Gainsborough was very attractive, though somewhat contradictory in his moods. He was generous and genial, lovable and affectionate; he was also contradictory and impulsive, not to say capricious. His wife and he had little quarrels which they settled in this wise: When

Gainsborough had spoken to her unkindly, he would quickly repent, and write a note to say so, and address it to his wife's spaniel, called "Tristram," and sign it with the name of his pet dog, "Fox." Then Margaret Gainsborough would answer: "My own, dear Fox, you are always loving and good, and I am a naughty little female ever to worry you as I too often do, so we will kiss, and say no more about it; your own affectionate Tris." Like Reynolds, Gainsborough had many warm friends, and when he died Sir Joshua himself watched by his bedside, and bent to catch his last word, which was the name of Vandyck.

JOHN SINGLETON COPLEY (1737–1815) was born in Boston, Mass., U. S., to which place his parents are said to have immigrated from Limerick, Ireland. The father was descended from the Copleys of Yorkshire, England, and the mother from the Singletons of County Clare, both families of note. When young Copley was eleven years old his mother was married to Peter Pelham, a widower with three sons—Peter, Charles, and William—and who subsequently became the father of another son, Henry, by this second marriage. Mr. Pelham was a portrait painter and a mezzotint engraver of unusual merit. One authority calls him "the founder of those arts in New England." Mr. Pelham was also a man of education, a land surveyor, and a mathematician. He was thus well qualified to educate, assist, and stimulate young Copley in the pursuit of studies so natural and congenial to him. He is said to have been studious and quiet, and to have made rapid advances. When he was fifteen years old he painted a portrait of his step-brother, Charles Pelham, now in the family of a great-grandson, Mr. Charles Pelham Curtis, of Boston. At sixteen he published an engraving of Rev. William Welsteed, from a portrait painted by himself. The same year he painted the portrait of a child—afterward Dr. de Mountfort—now owned in Detroit. In 1754 he painted an allegorical picture of Mars,

Venus, and Vulcan, thirty inches long by twenty-five wide, now owned in Bridgewater, Mass. The next year he painted a miniature of George Washington, who was on a visit to Governor Shirley at the time. This picture now belongs to the family of the late George P. Putnam, of New York City. In 1756 he painted a three-quarters length portrait of General William Brattle, life size, signed and dated, and now owned by Mr. William S. Appleton. He now improved rapidly. A crayon portrait of Miss Rebecca Gardiner, afterward Mrs. Philip Dumaresq, an oil painting of Mrs. Edmund Perkins, a portrait of Rebecca Boylston, afterward wife of Governor Gill, portraits of Colonel and Mrs. Lee, grandparents of General William Raymond Lee, all exist and attest the continued growth of his powers. These date between 1763 and 1769. During this time he had access to and was a visitor in houses where were portraits by Saribest, Blackburn, Liopoldt, and even by Vandyck and Sir Godfrey Kneller. Mr. Augustus Thorndike Perkins, in his carefully written monograph on Copley, says that our artist must have seen all these pictures, since, as Dr. Gardiner says, "his genial disposition and his courtly manners make him a welcome guest everywhere." Mr. Perkins remarks that Copley must have studied with Blackburn; that he imitated, but in some respects surpassed him. "Both frequently used, either as the lining of a dress or as drapery, a certain shade of mauve pink; Blackburn uses this shade feebly, while Copley dashes it on with the hand of a master." On November 16, 1769, Copley married Susan (or Susannah, as it is sometimes written), the daughter of Mr. Richard Clarke, a distinguished merchant of Boston, to whom, as agent of the East India Company of London, was consigned the tea thrown overboard in Boston harbor. From all accounts he soon began to live in good style; and as, in 1771, Colonel Trumbull found him living opposite the Common, it is probable that he purchased at about that time the property which afterward became so valuable, although long after Copley had ceased to be the owner. In 1773, says the late eminent conveyancer, Nathaniel Ingersoll Bowditch, "Copley owned all the land bounded on the west by Charles River, thence by Beacon Street to Walnut Street, thence by Walnut Street to Mt. Vernon Street, thence by Mt. Vernon Street to Louisburg Square, thence by Louisburg Square to Pinckney Street, thence by Pinckney Street to the water, containing about eleven acres of land." This land is now covered with handsome residences, and is of great value. An agent of Copley's sold his property after he went abroad without being authorized to do so, and, although his son came over in 1795 to look into the matter, he was only able to secure a compromise by which a further sum of three thousand guineas was paid in final settlement.

Soon after his marriage Copley painted his picture of a "Boy with a Squirrel," which he sent anonymously to Benjamin West, in London, for exhibition. West judged from the wood on which the picture was stretched and from the kind of squirrel that the work was American, and so excellent was the painting that a rule of the institution was set aside, and the picture exhibited. This picture is now in the possession of Mrs. James S. Amory, of Boston, a granddaughter of the artist. The boy in the picture was his half-brother Henry. The picture was so favorably received that Copley was advised to go to England. He sailed in 1774, and never returned.

Mr. Copley, soon after his arrival in London, passed over to the Continent, and through Italy, studying in Parma and in Rome. He visited Naples and Pæstum also. It is said that he studied so diligently that he was with difficulty persuaded to paint two portraits in Rome. In 1775 he travelled and studied in Germany, in Holland, and in France. This same year his wife and family joined him in England. These consisted of his wife, his son, John Singleton, who afterward became the famous Lord Chancellor Lyndhurst; his daughter Elizabeth, afterward married to a distinguished merchant in Boston, and who survived to a great age; Mary Copley, who lived unmarried to the great age of ninety-four; and another son who died young. In 1777 he was made an Associate of the Royal Academy, and six years later an Academician. He was now in the full tide of success. He was offered five hundred guineas to paint a family group of six persons. The well-known group of Copley's family, called the "Family Picture," the "Death of Lord Chatham," and "Watson and the Shark," were on his easel in 1780. The picture of Lord Chatham falling senseless in the House of Lords was commenced soon after his death in 1778. It was engraved by Bartolozzi, and twenty-five hundred copies were sold in a few weeks. Copley exhibited the picture, to his own profit as well as fame.

In 1781 occurred the death of Major Pierson, shot in the moment of victory over the French troops who had invaded the island of Jersey. His death was instantly avenged by his black servant, and of this scene Copley made one of his finest pictures. He took pains, with his usual honesty, to go to St. Helier's, and make a drawing of the locality. The picture is thoroughly realistic, although painful. His large picture of the "Repulse and Defeat of the Spanish Floating Batteries at Gibraltar" was painted on commission from the city of London. It is twenty-five feet long by twenty-two and a half feet high; but there are so many figures and so much distance to be shown in the painting that the artist really needed more room. Of the commander, Lord Heathfield, Sir Robert Royd, Sir William Green, and some twelve or fifteen others, the artist made careful portraits.

The story told by Elkanah Watson shows Copley's strong sympathy for America. In 1782 Watson was in London, and Copley made a full-length portrait of him, and in his journal Watson says: "The painting was finished in most exquisite style in every part, except the background, which Copley and I designed to represent a ship bearing to America the acknowledgments of our independence. The sun was just rising upon the stripes of the Union streaming from her gaff. All was complete save the flag, which Copley did not deem proper to hoist under the present circumstances, as his gallery was the constant resort of the royal family and the nobility. I dined with the artist on the glorious 5th of December, 1782. After listening with him to the speech of the king formally recognizing the United States of America as in the rank of nations, previous to dinner, and immediately after our return from the House of Lords, he invited me into his studio, and there, with a bold hand, a master's touch, and, I believe, an American heart, he attached to the ship the stars and stripes. This was, I imagine, the first American flag hoisted in Old England."

Copley purchased, for a London residence, the mansion-house in George Street belonging to Lord Fauconburg. It afterward became more widely known as the residence of his son, Lord Lyndhurst. Lord Mansfield's residence was near by, and among the many commissions from public men was one to paint his lordship's portrait. Perhaps one of the most interesting of all his commissions was one to paint the picture of Charles I. demanding the five obnoxious members from the Long Parliament, for which a number of gentlemen in Boston paid one thousand five hundred pounds. It is said that every face in this great picture was taken from a portrait at that time extant; and Mrs. Gardiner Greene narrates that she and her father were driven in a post-chaise over a considerable part of England, visiting every house in which there was a picture of a member of the famous Parliament, and were always received as honored guests. Copley's painting of the death of Lord Chatham was much admired. So numerous were the subscriptions for the engraving that it is said Copley must have received nearly, or quite, eleven thousand pounds for the picture and the engraved copies. It was quite natural for Copley to be popular with New Englanders; indeed, almost every Bostonian, at one time, on visiting London, made a point to bring home his portrait by Copley, if possible. There are known to exist in this country two hundred and sixty-nine oil-paintings, thirty-five crayons, and fourteen miniatures by him. These pictures are carefully cherished, as are indeed all memorials of this generous and kindly gentleman. Although his life was mostly passed in England, where he obtained wealth and renown, yet in a strong sense he could be claimed for Boston, as it was there he was born; it was there he received his artistic bias and education; it was there he was married, and had three children born to him; and, finally, it was there that he acquired a fair amount of fame and property solely by his brush. It will be worth while for the readers of this volume to take pains to see some of the more noteworthy Copleys.

A portrait of John Adams, full length, painted in London in 1783, is now in possession of Harvard College. A portrait of Samuel Adams, three-quarters length, spirited and beautiful, standing by a table, and holding a paper, hangs in Faneuil Hall. Another picture of Samuel Adams is in Harvard College, which also owns several other Copleys. A portrait of James Allen, a man of fortune, a patriot, and a scholar, is now owned by the Massachusetts Historical Society. The "Copley Family," one of the artist's very best pictures, is now owned in Boston by Mr. Amory, and, in fact, Mrs. James S. Amory owns a number of his best works.

Copley was a man of elegance and dignity, fond of the beautiful, particular in his dress, hospitable, and a lover of poetry and the arts. His favorite book was said to be "Paradise Lost." His last picture was on the subject of the Resurrection.

BENJAMIN WEST (1738–1820) was born at Springfield, Pennsylvania, of Quaker parentage. In the various narratives of his successful life many stories are told which appear somewhat fabulous, and most of which have nothing to do with his subsequent career. He is said to have made a pen-and-ink portrait of his little niece at the age of seven years; to have shaved the cat's tail for paint brushes; to have received instruction in painting and archery from the Indians; to have so far conquered the prejudices of his relatives and their co-religionists to his adoption of an artist's life that he was solemnly consecrated to it by the laying on of hands by the men, and the simultaneous kissing of the women. His love for art must have been very strong, and he was finally indulged, and assisted in it by his relatives, so that at the age of eighteen he was established as a portrait-painter in Philadelphia. By the kindness of friends in that city and in New York he was enabled to go to Italy, where he remained three years, making friends and reputation everywhere. Parma, Florence, and Bologna elected him a member of their Academies. He was only twenty-five years old when he went to England, on his way back to America. But he was so well received that he finally determined to remain in England, and a young lady named Elizabeth Shewell, to whom he had become engaged before going abroad, was kind and judicious enough to join him in London, where she became his wife, and was his faithful helpmate for fifty years. In 1766 he exhibited his "Orestes and Pylades," which on account of its novelty and merit produced a sensation. He painted "Agrippina weeping over the Urn of Germanicus," and by the Archbishop of York was introduced to George III. as its author. He immediately gained favor with the king, and was installed at Windsor as the court-painter with a salary of one thousand pounds per annum. This salary and position was continued for thirty-three years. He painted a series of subjects on a grand scale from the life of Edward III. for St. George's Hall, and twenty-eight scriptural subjects, besides nine portrait pictures of the royal family. In 1792, on the death of Reynolds, he was elected President of the Royal Academy, a position which, except a brief interregnum, he held until his death in March, 1820. He was greatly praised in his day, and doubtless thought himself a great artist. He painted a vast number of portraits and quite a number of pictures of classical and historical subjects. His "Lear" is in the Boston Athenæum; his "Hamlet and Ophelia" is in the Longworth collection in Cincinnati; "Christ Healing the Sick" is in the Pennsylvania Hospital; and the "Rejected Christ" is or was owned by Mr. Harrison, of Philadelphia. There are two portraits of West, one by Allston and one by Leslie, in the Boston Athenæum, and a full-length, by Sir Thomas Lawrence, in the Wadsworth Gallery in Hartford, Conn. One of West's pictures did a great deal for his reputation, although it was quite a departure from the treatment and ideas then in vogue; this was the "Death of General Wolfe" on the Plains of Abraham. When it was known to artists and amateurs that his purpose was to depict the scene as it really might have happened he was greatly ridiculed. Even Sir Joshua Reynolds expressed an opinion against it; but when he saw the picture he owned that West was right. Hitherto no one had painted a scene from contemporary history with figures dressed in the costume of the day. But West depicted each officer and soldier in his uniform, and gave every man his pigtail who wore one. The picture is spirited and well grouped. West was just such a practical, thoughtful, and kindly man as we might expect from his ancestry and surroundings.

GEORGE ROMNEY (1734–1802), born in Beckside, near Dalton, in Cumberland. He married when he was twenty-two, and in his twenty-seventh year went to London with only thirty pounds in his pocket, leaving his wife with seventy pounds and two young children. He returned home to die in 1799, and in the meantime saw his wife but twice. The year after his arrival in London he carried off the fifty-guinea prize on the subject of the "Death of Wolfe" from the Society of Arts. Through the influence of Sir Joshua Reynolds this was reconsidered, and the fifty-guinea prize was awarded to Mortimer for his "Edward the Confessor," while Romney was put off with a gratuity of twenty-five guineas. This produced a feud between the two artists. Romney showed his resentment by exhibiting in a house in Spring Gardens, and never sending a picture to the Academy, while Reynolds would not so much as mention his name, but spoke of him as "the man in Cavendish Square." This was after his return from the Continent; but before going to Italy he was distinctly the rival of Sir Joshua, so much so that there were two factions, and Romney's studio, in Great Newport Street, was crowded with sitters, among whom was the famous Lord Chancellor Thurlow, whose full-length portrait is the pride of its possessor. At this time he was making about twelve hundred pounds a year, a very good income for those days. In 1773 he went to Rome with a letter to the Pope from the Duke of Richmond. His diary, which he kept for a friend, shows how conscientious and close was his observation and how great his zeal. He made a copy of the "Transfiguration," for which he refused one hundred guineas, and which finally sold for six guineas after his death. On his return to London in 1775 he took the house in Cavendish Square, where he had great success. He painted a series of portraits of the Gower family, the largest being a group of children dancing, which Allan Cunningham commended as being "masterly and graceful." Some of his portraits have a charm beyond his rivals. He painted portraits of Lady Hamilton, the friend of Lord Nelson—"the maid of all work, model, mistress, ambassadress, and pauper"—

scores of times, and in different attitudes and a variety of characters, as Hebe, a Bacchante, a Sibyl, as Joan of Arc, as "Sensibility," as a St. Cecilia, as Cassandra, as Iphigenia, as Constance, as Calypso, as Circe, and as Mary Magdalen, and in some of these characters many times. He often worked thirteen hours a day, and did his fancy sketches when sitters disappointed him. He would paint a portrait of a gentleman in four sittings. He was extremely fond of portraying Shakespeare's characters, and contributed to the Shakespeare Gallery formed by Alderman Boydell. He went to Paris in 1790, where Lord and Lady Gower introduced him to Louis Philippe, and through him to all the art treasures of the French capital. On his return to London he formed a plan of an art museum, to be furnished with casts of the finest statues in Rome, and spent a good deal of money in the erection of a large building for the purpose. His powers as an artist gradually waned. He left his Cavendish Square residence in 1797, and in 1799 returned to his family and home at Kendall. From this time to the close of his life in 1802 he was a mere wreck, and his artist life was over.

GEORGE MORLAND (1763–1804) was born in London, and the son of an artist. His father was unsuccessful, and poor George was articled to his father, after the English fashion, and was kept close at home and at work. It is said that his father stimulated him with rich food and drink to coax him to work. He was very precocious, and really had unusual talents. His subjects were those of rustic life, and his pictures contain animals wonderfully well painted, but his pigs surpass all. His character was pitiful; he was simply, at his best, a mere machine to make pictures. As for goodness, truth, or nobleness of any sort, there is not a syllable recorded in his favor. Strange to say, the pictures of his best time are masterpieces in their way, and have been sold at large prices.

Sir THOMAS LAWRENCE (1769–1830), born at Bristol, England, in the White Hart Inn, of which his father was landlord. He was wonderfully precocious, and as a child of five years would recite odes, and declaim passages from Milton and Shakespeare. Even at this early period he made chalk or pencil portraits, and at nine he finally decided to become a painter from having seen a picture by Rubens. At this period he made a colored chalk portrait of the beautiful Georgiana, Duchess of Devonshire, which still hangs in Chiswick House, in the room in which Charles Fox died. His father was the son of a clergyman, and was bred a lawyer, but had never prospered; still his culture and education gave a certain zest and tone to the mind of young Lawrence, and made him, with his elegant figure and handsome face, the successful courtier that he afterward became. He worked hard, with considerable success, and with but little instruction until, at the age of eighteen, he went to London for the first time. At that period he was described as being extremely handsome in person, with fine, regular features, brilliant eyes, and long, chestnut-colored hair falling to his shoulders. He lodged close by Sir Joshua Reynolds—then near the end of his career, and from him received much valuable advice. During Lawrence's first years in London he attempted pictures illustrating classic art, but without much success. Indeed he was never successful in large, imaginative pictures, and during most of his career of more than forty years, confined himself to portraits. The time was propitious for him: Gainsborough was dead; Reynolds was almost blind, and had given up painting; and Romney had no hold on the court and the leaders of fashion. Lawrence raised his prices, and had all he could do. He adopted a more expensive style of dress, and in fact lived so extravagantly that he never arrived at what may be called easy circumstances—his open-handed generosity contributed to this result. He early received commissions from the royal family. In 1791 he was elected an Associate, and in 1794 an Academician. The next year George III. appointed him painter in ordinary to his Majesty. He was thus fairly launched on a career that promised the highest success. In a certain sense he had it, but largely in a limited sense. He painted the portraits of people as he saw them ; but he never looked behind the costume and the artificial society manner. He reproduced the pyramidically shaped coats and collars, the overlapping waistcoats of different colors, the Hessian boots, and the velvet coats, adorned with furs and frogs, of the fine gentlemen ; and the turbans with birds-of-Paradise feathers, the gowns without waists, the bare arms and long gloves, the short leg-of-mutton sleeves, and other monstrosities of the ladies. And for thirty years his sitters were attired in red, or green, or blue, or purple. He absolutely revelled in the ugliness of fashion. Occasionally Lawrence did some very good things, as when he painted the Irish orator and patriot, Curran, in one sitting, in which, according to Williams, " he finished the most extraordinary likeness of the most extraordinary face within the memory of man." He always painted standing, and often kept his sitters for three hours at a stretch, and sometimes required as many as nine sittings. On one occasion he is said to have worked all through one day, through that night, the next day, and through all the night following ! By command of the prince regent he painted the allied sovereigns, their statesmen, princes, and generals—all the leading personages, in fact, in alliance against Napoleon. His pictures in the exhibition of 1815 were Mrs. Wolfe, the Prince Regent, Metternich, the Duke of Wellington, Blucher, the Hetman Platoff, and Mr. Hart Davis. During the Congress that met at Aix-la-Chapelle in 1818, Lawrence was commissioned by the Prince Regent to paint its principal heads for an especial gallery. He thus had for sitters nearly all the leading statesmen of Europe. From Aix-la-Chapelle he went to

Vienna, and thence to Rome in 1819, where among others he painted likenesses of the Pope, of Cardinal Gonsalvi, and of Canova. Of the latter, Canova cried out, "Per Baccho, che nomo e questo!" It was considered a marvellous likeness; and without violating good taste he worked into the picture crimson velvet and damask, gold, precious marble, and fur, with a most brilliant effect. Before reaching home in London he was elected President of the Royal Academy. At this time he had been elected a member of the Roman Academy of St. Luke's, of the Academy of Fine Arts in Florence, and of the Fine Arts in New York. He continued to improve as a painter, and between 1825 and the year of his death, painted and exhibited some of his finest works. He usually exhibited eight pictures each year, and although without a rival, gave evidence of anxious care to sustain his reputation. He was especially successful with children, and many of these pictures—as well as of celebrities—were engraved, and have thus become known all over the world. Of his eight pictures exhibited in 1829—the last he ever contributed—Williams says: "It is difficult to imagine a more undeviating excellence, an infallible accuracy of likeness, with an elevation of art below which it seemed impossible for him to descend." Lawrence died on the morning of the 7th of January, 1830, with but little warning, from ossification of the heart; he was buried with much pomp and honor in St. Paul's Cathedral, by the side of Sir Joshua Reynolds.

JOSEPH M. W. TURNER, R.A. (1775-1851).—It is believed, by those who have investigated the question most carefully, that this eminent artist and most remarkable man was born in Maiden Lane, London, April 3, 1775, although the artist himself has stated that he was born in Devonshire, April 23, 1769. Turner's father, William Turner, was a native of Devonshire, but came to London while young, and did a fair business in the Covent Gar-

FIG. 73.—PORTRAIT OF TURNER.

den district as a hair-dresser, wig-maker, and in shaving people. The father was garrulous, like the traditional hair-dresser, with a pleasant laugh, and a fresh, smiling face. He had a parrot nose and a projecting chin. Turner's mother was a Miss Mallord (or Marshall), of good family, but a violent-tempered woman, with a hawk nose and a fierce visage. Her life ended in a lunatic asylum. The artist, who was always impatient of inquiry into his domestic matters, resented any allusion to his mother, and never spoke of her. The manifest peculiarities of his parents had an impression upon Turner, and would have made him eccentric had there been no other influences of a kindred nature. The parents were under-sized, and of limited mental range; they were of very little personal assistance to their gifted son, although the father in later years busied himself in mixing colors, adjusting pictures to frames, and sometimes he was entrusted with certain rough work at filling in backgrounds. When Turner was but five years old he is said to have made, from memory, a fair copy of a lion rampant engraved on a silver salver, which he had seen while accompanying his father to the house of a customer. Presently the boy began to copy pictures in water-colors, and then to make sketches from nature of scenes along the river Thames. In his ninth year he drew a picture of Margate Church. When he was ten years old he was sent to school at Brentford-Butts, where he remained two years, boarding with his uncle, the local butcher. His leisure hours were spent in dreamy wanderings and in making countless sketches of birds, trees, flowers, and domestic fowls. He acquired a smattering of the classics and some knowledge of legends and ancient history. On his return to London he received instruction from Palice in painting flowers, and, after a year or two, was sent to Margate, in Kent, to Coleman's school. Here he had more scope and a wider range, and made pictures of the sea, the chalk cliffs, the undulations of the coast, and the glorious effects of cloud scenery. On his return from Margate he began to earn money by coloring engravings and by painting skies in amateurs' drawings and in architects' plans at half a crown an evening. He always deemed this good practice, as he thus acquired facility and skill in gradations. His father at one time thought to make an architect of him, and sent him to Tom Malton to study perspective. But he failed in the exact branch of the profession, and neither with Malton nor with the architect Hardwick did he give satisfaction. While with Hardwick he drew careful sketches of old houses and churches, and this practice must have been of much use to him in after-life. His father finally sent him to the Royal Academy, where he studied hard, drawing from Greek models and the formal classic architecture. About this time he was employed, at half a crown an evening, with supper thrown in, to make copies of pictures by Dr. Munro, of Adelphi Terrace. Munro was one of the physicians employed in the care of George III. when he had a crazy spell, and owned many valuable pictures by Salvator-Rosa, Rembrandt, Snyder, Gainsborough, Hearne, Cozens, and others. He had also portfolios full of drawings of castles and cathedrals, and of Swiss and Italian scenery, and of sketches by Claude and Titian. Turner was also employed to sketch from nature in all directions about London. In these tasks he had for a constant companion "Honest Tom Girtin," a young fellow of Turner's own age, who afterward married a wealthy lady, had rich patrons, and died before he was thirty. Had he lived to mature years, Girtin would have been a powerful rival to Turner. They were most excellent friends, and when Girtin died in Rome, Turner was one of his most sincere mourners. Toward the close of Sir Joshua Reynolds' life, Turner frequented his studio, copied pictures, and acquired some art secrets. He began to teach water-color drawing in schools, while still a boy, at from a crown to a guinea a lesson. He made hundreds of sketches in a part of London now built over compactly with houses in streets and squares, but then picturesque in hills and dells, in wooded fields and green lanes. With all his baggage tied in a handkerchief on the end of his walking-stick, he made a sketching tour through the towns of Rochester, Canterbury, Margate, and others, in Kent, in 1793, and about this time began to paint in oil. His first contribution to the Royal Academy was a water-color sketch in 1790. Within the next ten years he exhibited over sixty pictures of castles, cathedrals, and landscapes. All through his life he made sketches. Wherever he was, if he saw a fine or an unusual effect, he treasured it up for use. He sketched on any bit of paper, or even on his thumb-nail, if he had nothing better. Nothing escaped his attention, whether of earth, or sea, or sky. Probably no artist that ever lived gave nature such careful and profound study. His studies of cloud scenery were almost a revelation to mankind. In all this Turner drew his instruction as well as his inspiration from nature. The critics did nothing for him; he rather opened the eyes of even such men as Ruskin to the wonders of the natural world. But these results all came later, and were the fruit of and resulted from his constant and incessant studies.

In 1794 and 1795 he made elaborate drawings of Rochester, Chepstow, Birmingham, Worcester, Guildford, Cambridge, and other towns, for magazines. In 1796 he did the same for Chester, Bristol, Leith, Peterborough, and Windsor. Within the next four years he completed the circuit of twenty-six counties in England and Wales, and he also exhibited twenty-three highly finished drawings of cathedrals and churches. He was slow to undertake oil-painting, preferring the more rapid touch and the light-and-shade effect of the crayon, or the delicate and beautiful

FIG. 74.—NANTES. *By Turner.*

effects of water-colors. He was always greater as a painter in water-colors than in oils, and it is claimed by Redgrave that "the art all but began with him," and that his water-color paintings "epitomize the whole mystery of landscape art." Some of his paintings in this line have been sold at enormous prices, and even in his own day his water-color picture of Tivoli sold for eighteen hundred guineas. Turner became as fond of Northern Yorkshire—which he first visited in 1797—as he was of Southern Kent. He found there a great variety of scenery, from the sweet and peaceful to the ennobling and grand. He visited and made studies from all the old cathedrals, castles, and abbeys, and in 1798 he exhibited pictures of Fountain and Kirkstall Abbeys, Holy Island Cathedral, Buttermere Lake, Dunstanborough Castle, as well as "Morning Among the Corriston Fells." He found in Yorkshire also some of his warmest friends and most munificent patrons, notably Mr. Hawkesworth Fawkes, of Farnley Hall, whose house was adorned with fifty thousand dollars' worth of Turner's pictures. Some additions to Farnley Hall were designed by Turner, and he was always a welcome visitor. Here he sketched, and at intervals enjoyed himself greatly in hunting and fishing. It is said that the Farnley portfolios still contain sketches not only of the hall and its precincts, but of coast scenes, Swiss views, drawings of birds, illustrations of the Civil War, and, more especially, of fifty-three remarkable drawings of the Rhineland regions, done at the rate of three a day; these last were offered by Turner to Mr. Fawkes on his return from the Continent for the sum of five hundred pounds, and the bargain was closed at once. When Mr. Fawkes visited London he spent hours in Turner's private gallery, but was never shown into the painting-room. Indeed, very few persons were ever allowed there. Once, when Turner dined at a hotel with Mr. Fawkes, the artist took too much wine, and reeled about, exclaiming, "Hawkey, I am the real lion—I am the great lion of the day, Hawkey." When Mr. Fawkes died, ended Turner's visits to Farnley. He never went there again, but when the younger Fawkes brought the Rhine drawings up to London for him to see again, he passed his hand over the "Lorelei Twilight," saying, with tears in his eyes, "But Hawkey! but Hawkey!" When Mr. Wells, an artist of Addiscomb, died he mourned his loss bitterly, and exclaimed to his daughter: "Oh, Clara, Clara, these are iron tears! I have lost the best friend I ever had in my life!" In this family all the children loved him. He would lie on the floor, and play with them, and the oldest daughter afterward said: "Of all the light-hearted, merry creatures I ever knew, Turner was the most so." But in 1797 Turner had a bitter disappointment which warped and distorted all his after-life. A young lady to whom he had become attached while a schoolboy at Margate, was engaged to be married to him. He had been absent for two years on sketching tours, and the step-mother of the young lady had intercepted and destroyed his letters, so that at last she believed the representations made that Turner had deserted her. She became engaged to another, and was about to be married, when Turner appeared, and pleaded passionately that she would return to him. She thought that she had been trifled with, and held by her refusal, and did not find out the wrongs done by the step-mother until it was too late. This disappointment led to greater self-concentration and stingy money-getting until it became the absorbing passion of his life, so that the artist passion was dominated by it.

It would take up too large a portion of this book to describe even briefly Turner's travels and works. Only a bare outline can be given. In 1800 he became an Associate of the Royal Academy. He moved into a more commodious house at 64 Harley Street. During this year he exhibited pictures of Caernarvon Castle and the "Fifth

Plague of Egypt;" also fine views of Fonthill Abbey, the new palace of Beckford, with whom he spent much time. The only portrait for which Turner ever sat was painted in 1800 by George Dance. It shows a handsome young man, with a full but receding forehead, arched eyebrows, a prominent nose, a massive chin, and a sensual mouth. His thick and wiry hair is tied behind, and he wears a coat with an immense cape. By this time full-bottomed wigs had gone out of fashion, and the old barber abandoned his business to go and live with his artist son. In 1801 Turner exhibited pictures of St. Donat's Castle and Pembroke Castle in Wales, the Salisbury Chapter-house, an autumn morning in London, the destruction of the Median army, and Dutch fishing-boats in a gale. He had begun his contest with Claude by painting pictures of classical subjects in Claude's manner. Turner was elected Royal Academician in 1802, and exhibited several notable oil-paintings, signed with all his initials, which he thenceforth used. The Academy had been quick to recognize Turner's genius, and he was always its faithful, conservative, and zealous friend. As an auditor, councillor, or a visitor he was scrupulous, and he attended general meetings and formal dinners with the same promptitude and certainty with which for forty-five years he sent his pictures to the annual exhibitions. He was a peacemaker in debates, but in business he was irresolute. In 1802 he visited the Continent for the first time, travelling in France, Switzerland, and Italy, and everywhere making sketches. At this time he carried sketch-books in which he jotted everything—all manner of drawings and outlines of nature and architecture, notes of local gossip, chemical memoranda, notes of expenses, tavern bills, views of coasts and cities, ruins, castles, manufacturing works, and detached figures. One book gives views about the Simplon Pass, another the sea-coast from Nice to Genoa, another contains countless jottings from the pictures in the Vatican, another is taken up with views in Paris and Rouen, and several are devoted to Scottish scenery.

In 1806 Turner began his *Liber Studiorum*, in rivalship of Claude's *Liber Veritatis;* it was issued in parts in dark blue covers, each part containing five plates. It was discontinued in 1814, after seventy plates had been issued. Although not remunerative at the time, in later days as high as three thousand pounds has been paid for a single copy of the *Liber*, while the subscription price was only seventeen pounds ten shillings; even before Turner died a copy of it was worth over thirty guineas. Charles Turner, the engraver, used the proofs for kindling-paper; but some years later Colnaghi, the print dealer, paid him fifteen hundred pounds for his remaining "rubbish," as he considered it. "Good God!" cried the old engraver; "I have been burning bank-notes all my life!" In 1878 Professor Norton, of Harvard University, published a set of thirty-three of the best of the *Liber* studies, reproduced in Boston by the heliotype process. The *Liber Studiorum* was intended to manifest Turner's command of the whole compass of the landscape art, and was divided into six heads: historical, pastoral, elegant pastoral, mountain, marine, and architectural.

In 1808 Turner was appointed Professor of Perspective in the Royal Academy. During two or three years only, out of the thirty in which he held the professorship, did he deliver lectures. He spoke in a deep and mumbling voice, was confused and tedious in manner, and frequently became hopelessly entangled in blind mazes of obscure words. Sometimes when he had written out his lectures he was unable to read them. Once, after fumbling in his pockets, he exclaimed: "Gentlemen, I've been and left my lecture in the hackney-coach." Still he was interested in this work, and Ruskin says: "The zealous care with which Turner endeavored to do his duty is proved by a large existing series of drawings, exquisitely tinted, and often completely colored, all by his own hand, of the most difficult perspective subjects—illustrating not only directions of light, but effects of light, with a care and completion which would put the work of any ordinary teacher to utter shame." During this year he took a house at Hammersmith, Upper Mall, the garden of which ran down to the Thames, but still retained his residence in Harley Street. In 1812 he first occupied the house No. 47 Queen Anne Street, and this house he retained for forty years. It was dull, dingy, unpainted, weather-beaten, sooty, with unwashed windows and shaky doors, and seemed the very abode of poverty, and yet when Turner died his estate was sworn as under one hundred and forty thousand pounds—seven hundred thousand dollars. When Turner's father died in 1830 he was succeeded by a withered and sluttish old woman named Danby. The whole house was dreary, dirty, damp, and full of litter. The master had a fancy for tailless—Manx—cats, and these made their beds everywhere without disturbance. In the gallery were thirty thousand fine proofs of engravings piled up and rotting. His studio had a fair north light from two windows, and was surrounded by water-color drawings. His sherry-bottle was kept in an old second-hand buffet.

About 1813 or 1814 Turner purchased a place at Twickenham; he rebuilt the house, and called it Solus Lodge. The rooms were small, and contained models of rigged ships which he used in his marine views; in his jungle-like garden he grew aquatic plants which he often copied in foregrounds. He kept a boat for fishing and marine sketching; also a gig and an old cropped-eared horse, with which he made sketching excursions. He made at this time the acquaintance of Rev. Mr. Trimmer, the rector of the church at Heston, who was a lover of art, and often took journeys with Turner. While visiting at the rectory Turner regularly attended church in proper form; and finally he wrote a note to Mr. Trimmer, alluding to his affection for one of the rector's kinswomen, and suggesting: "If Miss —— would but waive bashfulness, or in other words make an offer instead of expecting one, the same [Lodge] might change occupiers." But Turner was doomed to disappointment, and never made another attempt at matrimony. In 1814 Turner commenced his contributions of drawings to illustrate "Cook's Southern Coast," and continued this congenial work for twelve years, making forty drawings at the rate of about twenty guineas each; the drawings were returned to the artist after being engraved. In 1815 he exhibited the "Dido Building Carthage," and in 1817 a companion picture, the "Decline of the Carthaginian Empire," and for these two pictures the artist refused five thousand pounds, having secretly willed them to the National Gallery.

Ruskin divides Turner's art life into three periods: that of study, from 1800 to 1820; that of working out art theories toward an ideal, from 1820 to 1835; and that of recording his own impressions of nature, from 1835 to 1845, preceded by a period of development, and followed by a period of decline, from 1845 to 1850. Besides his pictures painted on private commission, Turner exhibited two hundred and seventy-five pictures at the Academy. The "Rivers of England" was published in 1824, with sixteen engravings after Turner; another series contained six illustrations of the "Ports of England"—second-class cities. In 1826 the "Provincial Antiquities of Scotland" was published, with thirteen illustrations by Turner. The same year he sold his house at Twickenham, because, he said, "Dad" was always working in the garden, and catching abominable colds. In 1827 Turner commenced the "England and Wales" on his own account, and continued it for eleven years. It consisted of a hundred plates, illustrating ports, castles, abbeys, cathedrals, palaces, coast views, and lakes. In 1828 Turner went to Rome by way of Nismes, Avignon, Marseilles, Nice, and Genoa; and this year painted his

"Ulysses Dividing Polyphemus," of which Thornbury says: "For color, for life and shade, for composition, this seems to me to be the most wonderful and admirable of Turner's realisms." Ruskin calls it his central picture, illustrating his perfect power.

Of Turner's wonderful versatility, Ruskin says: "There is architecture, including a large number of formal 'gentlemen's seats;' then lowland pastoral scenery of every kind, including nearly all farming operations, plowing, harrowing, hedging and ditching, felling trees, sheep-washing, and I know not what else; there are all kinds of town life, courtyards of inns, starting of mail coaches, interiors of shops, house-buildings, fairs, and elections; then all kinds of inner domestic life, interiors of rooms, studies of costumes, of still-life and heraldry, including multitudes of symbolical vignettes; then marine scenery of every kind, full of local incident—every kind of boat, and the methods of fishing for particular fish being specifically drawn—round the whole coast of England; pilchard-fishing at St. Ives, whiting-fishing at Margate, herring at Loch Fyne, and all kinds of shipping, including studies of every separate part of the vessels, and many marine battle-pieces; then all kinds of mountain scenery, some idealized into compositions, others of definite localities, together with classical compositions; Romes and Carthages, and such others by the myriad, with mythological, historical, or allegorical figures; nymphs, monsters, and spectres, heroes and divinities. . . . Throughout the whole period with which we are at present concerned, Turner appears as a man of sympathy absolutely infinite—a sympathy so all-embracing that I know nothing but that of Shakespeare comparable with it. A soldier's wife resting by the roadside is not beneath it; Rizpah watching the dead bodies of her sons, not above it. Nothing can possibly be so mean as that it will not interest his whole mind and carry his whole heart; nothing so great or solemn but that he can raise himself into harmony with it; and it is impossible to prophesy of him at any moment whether the next he will be in laughter or tears."

In 1832 Turner made a will in which he bequeathed the bulk of his estate for the founding of an institution "for the Maintenance and Support of Poor and Decayed Male Artists being born in England and of English parents only, and of lawful issue." It was to be called "Turner's Gift," and for the next twenty years the artist pinched, and economized to increase the fund for his noble purpose. At this time he was entering upon his third manner—that of his highest excellence, when he "went to the cataract for its iris, and the conflagration for its flames; asked of the sky its intensest azure, of the sun its clearest gold." It is remarked by Ruskin, who has made most profound study of Turner's works, that he had an underlying meaning or moral in his groups of foreign pictures; in Carthage, he illustrated the danger of the pursuit of wealth; in Rome, the fate of unbridled ambition; and in Venice, the vanity of pleasure and luxury. The Venetian pictures began in 1833, with a painting of the Doge's Palace, Dogana, Campanile, and Bridge of Sighs; and with these were exhibited "Van Tromp Returning from Battle," the "Rotterdam Ferry-boat," and the "Mouth of the Seine." In 1830 or 1831 he made, on commission from the publisher Cadell, twenty-four sketches to illustrate Walter Scott's poems—published in 1834—and while doing this he was entertained royally at Abbotsford, and made excursions with Scott and Lockhart to Dryburgh Abbey and other points of interest. He went as far north as the Isle of Skye, where he drew Loch Corriskin, and nearly lost his life by a fall. About this time he made a series of illustrations for Scott's "Life of Napoleon." Turner spent some time in Edinburgh, frequently sketching with Thomson, a clergyman

FIG. 75.—ILLUSTRATION FROM ROGERS'S POEMS.

and local artist, who was preferred by some of the Scotch amateurs to Turner. He one day called at Thomson's house to examine his paintings, but instead of expected praises he merely remarked, "You beat me in frames." Turner made thirty-three illustrations for Rogers's "Poems" (Fig. 75), and seventeen for an extended edition of Byron. He was in the habit at this time of frequently walking to Cowley Hall, the residence of a Mr. Rose, where he was kindly welcomed. He was there called "Old Pogey." One day Mrs. Rose asked him to paint her favorite spaniel; in amazement he cried, "My dear madam, you do not know what you ask;" and always after this the lady went by the title of "My dear madam." Mr. Rose tells how he and Turner sat up one night until two o'clock drinking cognac and water, and talking of their travels. When Mrs. Rose and a lady, a friend, visited Turner in a house in Harley Street, in mid-winter, they were entertained with wine and biscuits in a cold room, without a fire, where they saw seven tailless cats, which Turner said were brought from the Isle of Man.

For three years Turner travelled in France, and made studies and sketches up and down its rivers. These were first published as "Turner's Annual Tour," but were afterward brought out by Bohn as "Liber Fluviorum." These sketches have been highly praised by Ruskin; but Hamerton, who certainly knows French scenery far more accurately than Ruskin, while praising the exquisite beauty of Turner's work, challenges its accuracy, and especially as to color, saying that "Turner, as a colorist, was splendid and powerful, but utterly unfaithful." Leitch Ritchie, who was associated with Turner in this work, could not travel with him, their tastes were so unlike; and he says that Turner's drawings were marvellously exaggerated, that he would make a splendid picture of a place without a single correct detail, trebling the height of spires and throwing in imaginary accessories. Turner always claimed the right to change the groupings of his landscapes and architecture at will, preferring to give a general and idealized view of the landscape rather than a precise copy thereof.

In 1835 he exhibited "Heidelberg Castle in the Olden Time," "Ehrenbreitstein," "Venice from the Salute Church," and "Line-fishing off Hastings." In 1836 he exhibited a "View of Rome from the Aventine Hill," and the "Burning of the House of Lords and Commons," which last was almost entirely painted on the walls of the exhibition. At this time it was the custom to have what were called "varnishing days" at the exhibition, during which time artists retouched, and finished up their pictures. They were periods of fun and practical jokes, and Turner always enjoyed, and made the most of them. He frequently sent his canvas to the Academy merely sketched out and grounded, and then coming in as early as four in the morning on varnishing days, he would put his nose to the sketch and work steadily with thousands of imperceptible touches until nightfall, while his picture would begin to glow as by magic. About this time he exhibited many pictures founded on classical subjects, or with the scenes laid in Italy or Greece, as "Apollo and Daphne in the Vale of Tempe," "Regulus Leaving Rome to Return to Carthage," the "Parting of Hero and Leander," "Phryne Going to the Public Baths as Venus," the "Banishment of Ovid from Rome, with Views of the Bridge and Castle of St. Angelo." A year later he exhibited pictures of "Ancient Rome," a vast dreamy pile of palaces, and "Modern Rome," with a view of the "Forum in Ruins."

One of the most celebrated of Turner's pictures was that of the "Old Téméraire," an old and famous line-of-battle ship, which in the battle of Trafalgar ran in between and captured the French frigates Redoubtable and Fougueux. Turner saw the Téméraire in the Thames after she had become old, and was condemned to be dismantled. The scene is laid at sunset, when the smouldering, red light is vividly reflected on the river, and contrasts with the quiet, gray and pearly tints about the low-hung moon. The majestic old ship looms up through these changing lights, bathed in splendor. The artist refused a large price for this picture by Mr. Lennox, of New York, and finally bequeathed it to the nation. In 1840 Turner exhibited the "Bacchus and Ariadne," two marine scenes, and two views in Venice; also the well-known "Slavers Throwing Overboard the Dead and Dying, a Typhoon Coming On" (Fig. 76), which is now in the Museum of Fine Arts of Boston. Of this picture Thackeray says: "I don't know whether it is sublime or ridiculous." But Ruskin, in "Modern Painters," says: "I believe if I were reduced to test Turner's immortality upon any single work, I should choose the 'Slave Ship.' Its daring conception, ideal in the highest sense of the word, is based on the purest truth, and wrought out with the concentrated knowledge of a life. Its color is absolutely perfect, not one false or morbid hue in any part or line, and so modulated that every square inch of canvas is a perfect composition; its drawing as accurate as fearless; the ship buoyant, bending, and full of motion; its tones as true as they are wonderful; and the whole picture dedicated to the most sublime of subjects and impressions (completing thus the perfect system of all truth which we have shown to be formed by Turner's works), the power, majesty, and deathfulness of the open, deep, illimitable sea."

No painter of modern times, or perhaps of any time, has ever provoked the discussion of his merits which Turner did. When he was at his best his great merits and his originality procured for him the strongest defenders, and finally brought his pictures into favor with the wealthy middle class of England, so that he obtained high prices, and since his death these prices have doubled, and even quadrupled. At

FIG. 76.—THE SLAVE SHIP. *By Turner.*

a sale of Mr. Bicknell's collection in 1836, ten of Turner's pictures, which had been bought for three thousand seven hundred and forty-nine pounds, were sold for seventeen thousand and ninety-four pounds. As Turner grew older and his manner deteriorated he was assailed by the wits, the art critics, and the amateurs with cruel badinage, and to these censures Turner was morbidly sensitive. But even Ruskin admits that the pictures of his last five years are of "wholly inferior value," with unsatisfactory foliage, chalky faces, and general indications of feebleness of hand.

Wornum, in his *Epochs of Painting*, said: "In the last ten years of his career, and occasionally before, Turner was extravagant to an extreme degree; he played equally with nature and with his colors. Light, with all its prismatic varieties, seems to have been the chief object of his studies; individuality of form or color he was wholly indifferent to. The looseness of execution in his latest works has not even the apology of having been attempted on scientific principles; he did not work upon a particular point of a picture as a focus and leave the rest obscure, as a foil to enhance it, on a principle of unity; on the contrary, all is equally obscure and wild alike. These last productions are a calamity to his reputation; yet we may, perhaps, safely assert that since Rembrandt there has been no painter of such originality and power as Turner." Dr. Waagen says in his *Treasury of Art in Great Britain:* "No landscape painter has yet appeared with such versatility of talent. His historical landscapes exhibit the most exquisite feeling for beauty of hues and effect of lighting, at the same time that he has the power of making them express the most varied moods of nature."

Toward the last part of his life Turner's peculiarities increased; he became more morose, more jealous. He was always unwilling to have even his most intimate friends visit his studio, but he finally withdrew from his own house and home. Of late years he had frequently left his house for months at a time, and secreted himself in some distant quarter, taking care that he should not be followed or known. When the great Exhibition of 1851 opened, Turner left orders with his housekeeper that no one should be admitted to see his pictures. For twenty years the rain had been streaming in upon them through the leaky roof, and many were hopelessly ruined. He sent no pictures to the exhibition of that year, and he was hardly to be recognized when he appeared in the gallery. Finally his prolonged absence from the Academy meetings alarmed his friends; but no one dared seek him out. His housekeeper alone, of all that had known him, had the interest to hunt up the old artist. Taking a hint from a letter in one of his coats, she went to Chelsea, and, after careful search, found his hiding-place, with but one more day of life in him. It is said that, feeling the need of purer air than that of Queen Anne Street, he went out to Chelsea and found an eligible, little cottage by the side of the river, with a railed-in roof whence he could observe the sky. The landlady demanded references from the shabby, old man, when he testily replied, "My good woman, I'll buy the house outright." She then demanded his name—"in case, sir, any gentleman should call, you know." "Name?" said he, "what's your name?" "My name is Mrs. Booth." "Then I am Mr. Booth." And so he was known, the boys along the river-side calling him "Puggy Booth," and the tradesmen "Admiral Booth," the theory being that he was an old admiral in reduced circumstances. In a low studded, attic room, poorly furnished, with a single roof window, the great artist was found in his mortal sickness. He sent for his favorite doctor from Margate, who frankly told him that death was at hand. "Go down stairs," exclaimed Turner, "take a glass of sherry, and then look at me again." But no stimulant could change the verdict of the physician. An hour before he died he was wheeled to the window for a last look at the Thames, bathed in sunshine and dotted with sails. Up to the last sickness the lonely, old man rose at daybreak to watch, from the roof of the cottage, the sun rise and the purple flush of the coming day. The funeral, from the house in Queen Anne Street, was imposing, with a long line of carriages, and conducted with the ritual of the English Church in St. Paul's Cathedral. Dean Milman read the service, and at its conclusion the coffin was borne to the catacombs, and placed between the tombs of James Barry and Sir Joshua Reynolds. Turner's will, with its codicils, was so confused and vague that the lawyers fought it in the courts for four years, and it was finally settled by compromise. The real estate went to the heir-at-law, the pictures and drawings to the National Gallery, one thousand pounds for a monument in St. Paul's Cathedral, and twenty thousand pounds to the Royal Academy for annuities to poor artists. Turner's gift to the British nation included ninety-eight finished paintings and two hundred and seventy pictures in various stages of progress. Ruskin, while arranging and classifying Turner's drawings, found more than nineteen thousand sketches and fragments by the master's hand, some covered with the dust of thirty years.

Sir DAVID WILKIE (1785–1841) has been called the "prince of British *genre* painters." His father was a minister, and David was placed in the Trustees' Academy in Edinburgh in 1799. In 1805 he entered the Royal Academy in London, and was much noticed on account of his "Village Politicians," exhibited the next year. From this time his fame and popularity were established, and each new work was simply a new triumph for him. The "Card Players," "Rent Day," the "Village Festival," and others were rapidly painted and exhibited.

In 1825 Wilkie went to the Continent, and remained three years. He visited France, Germany, Italy, and Spain, and after his return he painted a new class of subjects in a new manner. He made many portraits, and his other works were historical subjects. His most celebrated works in this second manner were "John Knox Preaching," "Napoleon and the Pope at Fontainebleau," and "Peep-o'-Day Boy's Cabin." The portrait of the landscape painter William Daniell is a good picture.

In 1830 Wilkie succeeded Sir Thomas Lawrence as painter to the king, as he had been limner to the King of Scotland since 1822. He was not knighted until 1836. In 1840 he visited Constantinople, and made a portrait of the sultan; he went then to the Holy Land and Egypt. While at Alexandria, on his way home, Wilkie complained of illness, and on shipboard, off Gibraltar, he died, and was buried at sea. This burial is the subject of one of Turner's pictures, and is now in the National Gallery.

The name of Landseer is an important one in British art. JOHN LANDSEER (1761–1852) was an eminent engraver; his son THOMAS (1795–1880) followed the profession of his father and arrived at great celebrity in it. CHARLES, born in 1799, another son of John Landseer, became a painter and devoted himself to a sort of historical genre line of subjects, such as "Cromwell at the House of Sir Walter Stewart in 1651," "Surrender of Arundel Castle in 1643," and various others of a like nature. Charles Landseer travelled in Portugal and Brazil when a young man; he was made a member of the Royal Academy in 1845; from 1851 to 1871 he was keeper of the Academy, and has been an industrious and respected artist. But the great genius of the family was

Sir EDWIN LANDSEER (1802–1873), the youngest son of John Landseer, the engraver. He received his first drawing lessons from his father, and from a very early age showed a great talent for sketching and that love for the brute creation which have been his chief characteristics as an artist. He had the power to understand his dumb subjects as well as if they spoke some language together, and then he had the ability to fix the meaning of all they had told him upon his canvas, by means of the sketching lines which gave the precise form of it all and by his finishing shades which put in the expression. If his animals were prosperous and gladsome, he represented their good fortune with hearty pleasure; if they were suffering, sad, or bereaved, he painted their woes with a sympathy such as none but a true friend can give.

When Edwin and Thomas were old enough that their father thought other instruction than his own should be given them, he placed them with Haydon, and in these early days the master predicted that Edwin Landseer would be the Snyders of England. Edwin sent his first picture to the Royal Academy when he was but thirteen years old, and during the following fifty-eight years there were but six exhibitions to which he did not contribute. When he began his studies at the Royal Academy he was fourteen years old, and already famous as an animal painter. He was a bright, curly-headed, manly lad, and the aged Fuseli, then keeper of the Academy, grew to be very fond of him; he would often ask, "Where is my little dog-boy?"

Edwin Landseer now worked on diligently and quietly; his works were constantly praised, and he received all the patronage that he desired. Through the advice of his master, Haydon, he had the habit of dissecting animals, and learning their anatomy with all the exactness with which other artists study that of human beings. About 1820 a lion died in the Exeter Change Menagerie, and Edwin Landseer secured the body for dissection. He then painted three large pictures of lions, and during the year in which he became eighteen years old, he exhibited these pictures and others of horses, dogs, donkeys, deer, goats, wolves, and vultures.

When nineteen, in 1821, he painted "Pointers, To-ho!" a hunting scene, which was sold in 1872, the year before his death, for two thousand and sixteen pounds. In 1822 Landseer gained the prize of the British Institution, one hundred and fifty pounds, by his picture of "The Larder Invaded." He made the first sketch for this on a child's slate, which is still preserved as a treasure. But the most famous of this master's early works is the "Cat's Paw," in which a monkey uses a cat's paw to draw chestnuts from a hot stove. Landseer was paid one hundred pounds; its present value is three thousand pounds, and it is kept at the seat of the Earl of Essex, Cashiobury.

This picture of the "Cat's Paw" had an important result for the young artist, as it happened that it was exhibited when Sir Walter Scott was in London, and he was so much pleased with it that he made Landseer's acquaintance, and invited him to visit Abbotsford. Accordingly, in 1824, Landseer visited Sir Walter in company with Leslie, who then painted a portrait of the great novelist, which now belongs to the Ticknor family of Boston. It was at this time that Sir Walter wrote in his journal: "Landseer's dogs were the most magnificent things I ever saw, leaping, and bounding, and grinning all over the canvas." Out of this visit came a picture called "A Scene at Abbotsford," in which the dog Maida, so loved by Scott, was the prominent figure; six weeks after it was finished the dog died.

At this time Sir Walter was not known as the author of the "Waverley Novels," but in later years Landseer painted a picture which he called "Extract from a Journal whilst at Abbotsford," to which the following was attached: "Found the great poet in his study, laughing at a collie dog playing with Maida, his favorite old greyhound, given him by Glengarry, and quoting Shakespeare—'Crabbed old age and youth cannot agree.' On the floor was the cover of a proof-sheet, sent for correction by Constable, of the novel then in progress. N. B.—This took place before he was the acknowledged author of the 'Waverley Novels.'" Landseer early suspected Scott of the authorship of the novels, and without doubt he came to this conclusion from what he saw at Abbotsford.

Landseer repeated his visits to Scotland for many years, and saw all parts of that country at various seasons. From the time of his first visit there was a new feeling in his works —a breadth and power was in them which he gained from nature, and a refinement and elevation which he undoubtedly received from his friendship with Sir Walter and the impetus it gave him. He also became so interested in the Gaelic people that he painted good pictures of them. At first these men did not know what to make of a huntsman who would throw away his gun when fine game appeared, and draw out pencils and paper to make pictures of what others were so eager to shoot. This tendency made him a poor hunter; but he was intensely interested in the chase, and especially in deer-stalking. He insisted that deer had intelligence, and the question was whether the game or the hunter happened to have the superior mind. When in London the artist was a quiet, society gentleman; but each year he broke away from all city habits, and went to the Highlands, where he divided his days between the chase and painting portraits of his friends there with their children and pets, or putting frescoes on the walls of their houses.

Landseer continued to live in his father's house long after he was a famous man. The senior artist conducted all business matters—sold pictures, and took the money for them as if his son was still a boy. At length, through the advice of a friend, Edwin Landseer removed to No. 1 St. John's Wood Road, to which he gave the name of Maida Vale; he enlarged, and improved this home from time to time, and had no other for nearly fifty years.

In 1826 Landseer painted "Chevy Chase;" it was the only

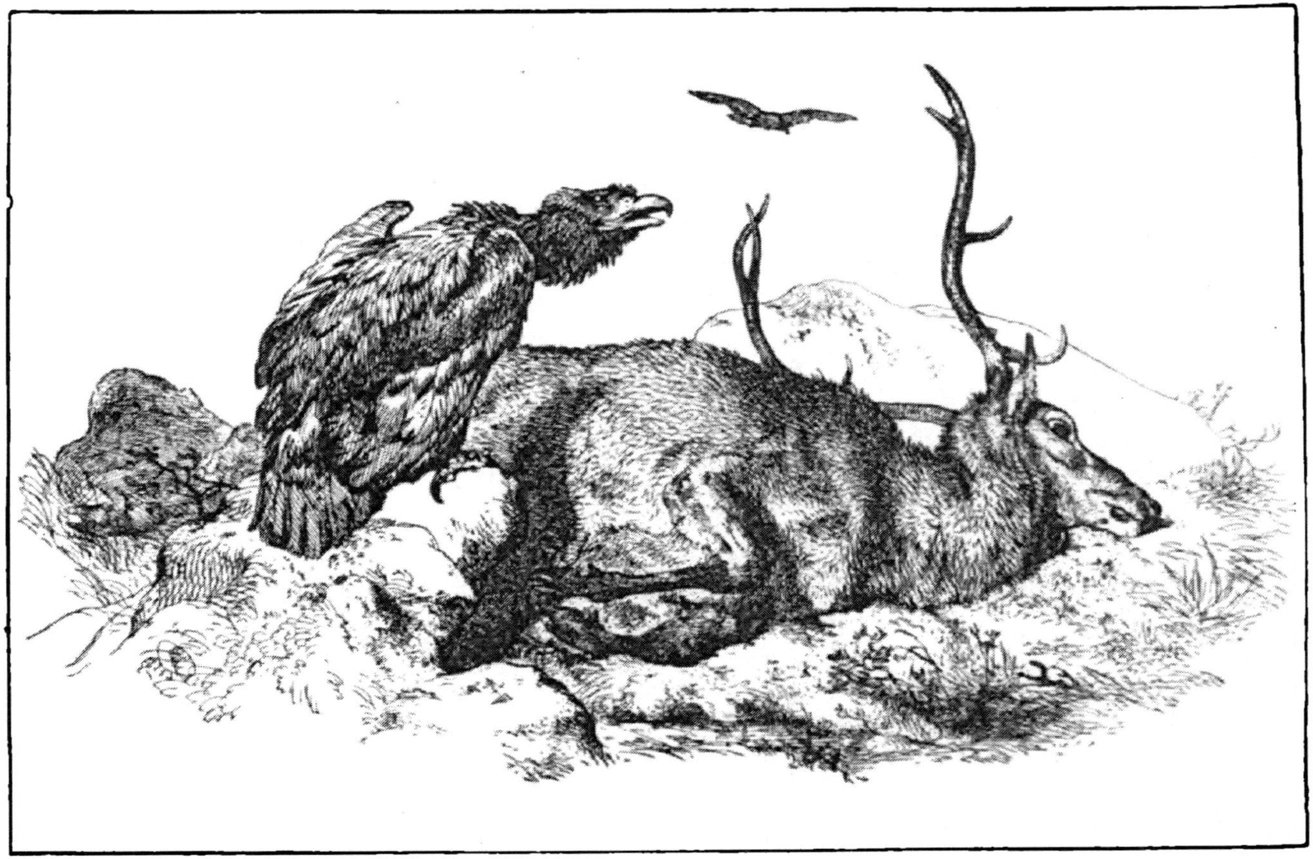

FIG. 77.—THE EAGLE AND DEAD STAG. *By Landseer.*

historical painting he ever did, and still remains at Woburn Abbey, where it originally went. The animals in the picture are excellent of course, but this sort of painting was not that in which Landseer showed his best. This year of 1826 was an important one to this master. He was twenty-four years old, and was immediately admitted an Associate of the Royal Academy. No one can be a candidate for this honor at a younger age, and very few others have attained it so early. Before he was thirty Landseer was a full member, and his diploma picture, "The Dead Warrior" is in the Royal Academy. But this year saw a great change in his pictures, as may be seen in that of "The Chief's Return from Deer-stalking," which he sent to the next exhibition. It was free, broad, and effective beyond any previous work, and this manner was his best. Many judges fix the year 1834 as the very prime in the art of Landseer, and one of the works of that year, called "Bolton Abbey in the Olden Time," is very famous. It represents the vassals of the abbey bringing in their tributes of game, fish, and fruits, which the jolly, old monks gladly receive.

There is no question but that Landseer's best pictures are of dogs, and we can but echo the words of Hamerton when he says: "The best commentators on Landseer, the best defenders of his genius, are the dogs themselves; and so long as there exist terriers, deer-hounds, blood-hounds, his fame will need little assistance from writers on art."

Landseer had a long and happy intimacy with Queen Victoria and the royal family. He painted portraits of the various members of the queen's household in all possible ways, with dogs and on horseback, in fancy dress and hunting costume—in short, these portraits are far too numerous to be mentioned in detail. Ever after 1835 Landseer was called upon to paint pictures of the pets of the royal family, and these works became very numerous. While he was thus favored as an artist he was also a friend of the queen and her immediate family; he was often summoned to play billiards with Prince Albert. The queen's Journal of Life in the Highlands frequently mentions him, and we are sure that if we could read Landseer's diary it would tell us many interesting things of the queen and her family. Naturally it followed that an artist thus favored by the queen would be patronized by the nobility, and it is true that much of Landseer's time, both as an artist and as a gentleman of society, was passed in the company of people of the highest positions in Great Britain; and with the one exception of Sir Joshua Reynolds, no artist in England was ever visited by so many people of rank. His house was really a social centre, and no one felt above accepting his hasty invitations to his parties, which were almost always gotten up on an impulse and the guests invited at the last possible moment.

Among Landseer's friends were Dickens and Thackeray, and Sydney Smith was very fond of the artist; and it is said that when the great wit was asked to sit to Landseer for his portrait, he replied in the words of the haughty Syrian: "Is thy servant a *dog* that he should do this thing?"

When at his best Landseer had a facility in drawing and painting that was marvellous. He could draw two entirely different objects at the same moment, his left hand being equally skilful with the right. He was seen to draw a horse's head with one hand and a stag's head with antlers at exactly the same time—and this at an evening party to prove that it could be done. He once sent to an exhibition a picture of rabbits under which he wrote, "Painted in three-quarters of an hour." He painted a life-size picture of a fallow-deer in three hours, and it required no retouching. One of his comrades said: "Sir Edwin has a fine hand, a correct eye, refined perceptions, and can do almost anything but dance on the slack wire. He is a fine billiard player, plays at chess, sings when with his intimate friends, and has considerable humor."

We have passed over the best and most pleasant part of the life of this great painter, for in 1840 he had an attack of illness from which he never recovered. He travelled, and endeavored in every way to go on with his work; but he was always subject to attacks of depression which were sometimes so serious that his friends feared loss of reason. Of course there was a different tone in his works—a seriousness and pathos, and at times a religious element, which was very acceptable to some persons, and he gained admirers where he had not found them before. But it can scarcely be said that his last days were his best days, though he executed some famous pictures.

In 1866 he exhibited a model of a stag at bay which was afterward cast in bronze. The lions at the base of the Nelson monument in Trafalgar Square may be called the work of Sir Edwin, for he modelled one of the colossal beasts from which the others were formed with but slight changes, and the whole were cast under the care of Baron Marochetti.

In 1872 he painted "The Font," which is a religious subject. It represents the sheep and lambs of the Gospel gathering round a font, upon the edge of which are doves. A rainbow spans the sky; on the sides of the font are a mask of the face of Christ and the symbols of the Atonement. This is a painful picture, for while it is exquisite in conception its execution shows the weakness of the painter, who so soon after he made it was released from all his darkness and suffering.

Sir Edwin Landseer was buried in St. Paul's Cathedral with all the honors which his genius and character merited. His works are known to almost every child in America by means of the engravings which have been made from them. His brother Thomas engraved hundreds of the designs of Edwin and made them popular all over the world, and a large part of this success was due to the skill and sympathy which Thomas devoted to what was largely a work of love. Of course many other engravers have worked after Landseer, and almost all his pictures have been reproduced in one style of engraving or another.

There are nine portraits of Sir Edwin Landseer in existence—one by J. Hayter when Landseer was thirteen years old and is represented as a cricketer; one painted a year later by Leslie, in which Edwin Landseer is the Rutland in the work called "Henry VI." It is owned by the Philadelphia Academy. The next were not made until 1843, when Count d'Orsay painted two portraits of him; in 1830 Dupper had made a drawing, and in 1835 a photograph was taken; Baron Marochetti made a bust portrait of Landseer which is in the Royal Academy, and in his picture called the "Connoisseurs" Sir Edwin painted his own portrait, with dogs on each side who stand as critics of his work. This was painted in 1865.

Sir Edwin Landseer left an estate of two hundred and fifty thousand pounds, and the works unsold at his death brought about seventy thousand pounds. His will made but a few bequests, and the remainder of this large sum was divided between his brother and three sisters. With the account of Sir Edwin I shall close the account of painters given in this volume.

We have seen how few actual remains of the painting of ancient nations are now in existence. Almost nothing is left even from the times of the Greeks; in truth, there is more upon the tombs of Egypt than in the land of Hellas. We read accounts of classic painting which arouse our deepest interest one moment, only to remember in the next that we can see but the merest scraps of all this wealth of beauty which moved the cultured Greeks to write of it with such enthusiasm.

After the days of classic art we have endeavored to trace painting through a period when it could scarcely be termed an art, so little of it was done, and that little was so far below our ideal. Again, this decline was followed by a Renaissance—an awakening—and from that day in the fourteenth century when the Madonna of Cimabue was carried in triumph through the streets of Florence, this art moved on with progressive steps until Michael Angelo, Leonardo, Raphael, Titian, and others highly gifted, had set up the standards which have remained as beacons and guides to all the world.

In tracing this progress we have seen that Italy, the German nations, Spain, France, and England have all striven to dream dreams of beauty and grandeur, of tenderness and love, and to fix them in fitting colors where all the world could see them.

The past is always fascinating. No stories are so pleasantly begun as those that say, "A long time ago there lived," etc. One can have the most complete satisfaction in the study of what has happened so far in the past that we can see all its effects and judge of it by the tests which time is sure to bring to everything. It is such a study that has been made in these pages, and I would suggest that it has a second use scarcely less important than the study of history—that is, the preparation it affords for judging of what is done in the present. A knowledge of what has been achieved enables us by comparison to decide upon the merits of new works.

The painting of to-day offers an immense field for investigation. When we remember that five centuries ago the painters of the world could be counted by tens, and are told that now there is an average of twenty-five hundred painters in some foreign cities, we see that a lifetime is scarcely sufficient in which to study the painting of our own era.

Have we not reason to hope that works are now being produced which shall be studied and admired in the future as we study and admire those of the past? Is it not true that the artistic works of any period show forth the spirit of the time? If, then, the close of the Dark Ages and the dawn of a better life could bring forth the treasures which remain from those days, what ought to be the result of the more universal learning and the advancing civilization of the nineteenth century? And so, in leaving this book, I hope that it may be useful to all who read it for one purpose that I have suggested or the other; either to present an outline of what has been done in the past, or aid in the understanding of the painting of the present.

# INDEX.

By L. E. JONES.

FINIS.

PART II.

# ·SCULPTURE·

FIG. 58.—THE VENUS OF MILO. (*See page* 87.)

# CONTENTS.

CHAPTER I.



CHAPTER II.



CHAPTER III.



CHAPTER IV.



CHAPTER V.



CHAPTER VI.

## CHAPTER VII.



## CHAPTER VIII.



## CHAPTER IX.

# LIST OF ILLUSTRATIONS.

# SCULPTURE.

## CHAPTER I.

### ANCIENT SCULPTURE.

#### EGYPT.

NO one can speak with exactness as to the time when sculpture was first practised by the Egyptians; we only know that it was a very long time ago. But we do know that in the time of the twelfth dynasty, which dates from 2466 B.C., sculpture had reached a stage of excellence such as could only have resulted from the experience of many years of training and practice in this art.

In the Egyptian collection of the Louvre, at Paris, there is the memorial stone of an old Egyptian sculptor which has an inscription that reads as if he had written it himself; this was the way by which Egyptians made these inscriptions sound as if the dead themselves spoke to those who were still alive. This sculptor's name was Martisen, and he lived about forty-four centuries ago. Brugsch-Bey, a very learned writer on Egypt, says: "He calls himself 'a master among those who understand art, and a plastic artist,' who 'was a wise artist in his art.' He relates in succession his knowledge in the making of statues, in every position, according to prescribed use and measure ; and brings forward, as his particular invention, an etching with colors, if I have rightly understood the expression, 'which can neither be injured by fire nor washed off by water ; ' and, as a further explanation of this, states that 'no man has arisen who has been able to do this except himself alone and the eldest son of his race, whom God's will has created. He has arisen able to do this, and the exercise of his hand has been admired in masterly works in all sorts of precious stones, from gold and silver to ivory and ebony.' "

There is no doubt but that Martisen and his son, who was named Usurtasen, were sculptors at the time when Egyptian art reached its highest point.

The earliest works of Egyptian sculpture are the bas-reliefs found in the chambers of the tombs ; the walls are almost covered with them, and they are painted with colors which are still bright and fresh, though more than four thousand years have passed since they were put on. The subjects of these reliefs are taken from the life of the persons buried in the tombs, and even their possessions and occupations are thus represented. These sculptures were made by tracing the designs on the stone and then cutting it away between the figures. The mode of arrangement in these reliefs does not satisfy our ideas of what it should be. It seems as if the artists had no plan of their work in their minds—no aim as to what the effect should be when finished. On the contrary, the reliefs impress us as if the sculptors made one figure, and then added another and another in such a way as to represent the fact they wished to tell without any attention to the beauty of the whole ; and so it does not seem as if there was any unity in them, but as if the large bas-reliefs were made up of disjointed parts which in one sense really have no relation to each other.

The same is true of the Egyptian statues. It appears as if the different parts might have been made separately or even by different sculptors, and then joined together. All this is because the Egyptians seemed to think of an object in parts and not as a whole. Then, too, the position of the early statues was so unnatural and awkward. The arms were placed close to the sides of the body, and there was no separation between the legs; and though in some of their articles of furniture, their pottery, and in the details of their architecture, the Egyptians made a great advance, they did not equally improve in their sculpture.

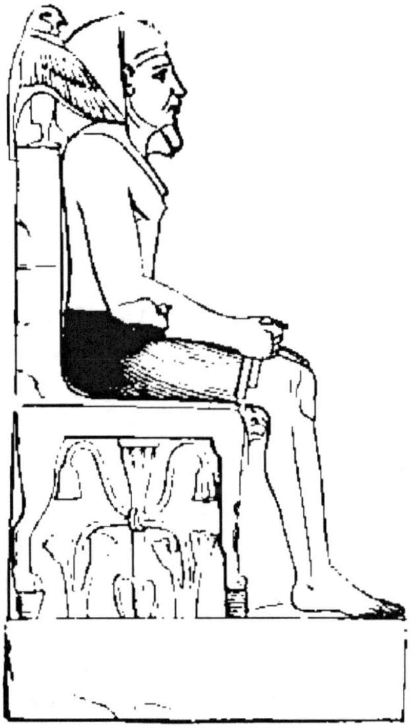

FIG. 1.—STATUE OF CEPHREN IN THE MUSEUM AT CAIRO.

One great hindrance to the progress of Egyptian sculpture was the fact that figures were never represented in action. They were not figures moving and living in stone; they were like figures petrified and fixed: they were *statues*, and no one can forget this for a moment while looking at them. I can learn of but one Egyptian figure sculptured as if in action; this is a quoit-thrower in the Tombs of the Kings. A sitting statue, whether of a man or a woman, had the hands rested on the knees or held across the breast (Fig. 1).

There were very few groups in Egyptian sculpture, and these seldom had more than two figures. It was customary to represent a husband and wife sitting on the same chair holding each other's hands, or having their arms around one another's waists or shoulders. Sometimes the principal figure is of large size, and the inferior persons are made much smaller and placed at the sides of the larger figure. In short, very few attitudes are represented in Egyptian sculpture, and it almost seems as if there must have been fixed rules for a certain limited number of positions after which all sculptured figures were made.

In spite of this sameness and stiffness, Egyptian sculpture is remarkable, and it is probable that if they had not been fettered by prejudices and rules the Egyptians would have excelled both in sculpture and painting.

The sides of obelisks and, more especially, the walls of temples were covered with sculptures which gave the history of kings—of their wars and conquests, and of their great works in their kingdoms. The sculptures upon the temple walls could be estimated by square rods, or even acres, better than by lesser measures. Their amount and the labor it required to make them are simply marvellous.

I will describe the subjects depicted upon one inner wall in the palace-temple of Medemet Haboo, and will quote from Wilkinson's "Egypt and Thebes." On the west wall "the Egyptian princes and generals conduct the 'captive chiefs' into the presence of the king. He is seated at the back of his car, and the spirited horses are held by his attendants on foot. Large heaps of hands are placed before him, which an officer counts, one by one, as the other notes down their number on a scroll; each heap containing three thousand, and the total indicating the returns of the enemy's slain. The number of captives, reckoned one thousand in each line, is also mentioned in the hieroglyphics above, where the name of the Rebo points out the nation against whom this war was carried on. Their flowing dresses, striped horizontally with blue or green bands on a white ground, and their long hair and aquiline noses give them the character of an Eastern nation in the vicinity of

Assyria and Persia, as their name reminds us of the Rhibii of Ptolemy, whom he places near the Caspian." . . .

The suite of this historical subject continues on the south wall. The king, returning victorious to Egypt, proceeds slowly in his car, conducting in triumph the prisoners he has made, who walk beside and before it, three others being bound to the axle. Two of his sons attend as fan-bearers, and the several regiments of Egyptian infantry, with a corps of their allies, under the command of these princes, marching in regular step and in the close array of disciplined troops, accompany their king. He arrives at Thebes, and presents his captives to Amen-Ra and Mut, the deities of the city, who compliment him, as usual, on the victory he has gained, and the overthrow of the enemy he has "trampled beneath his feet."

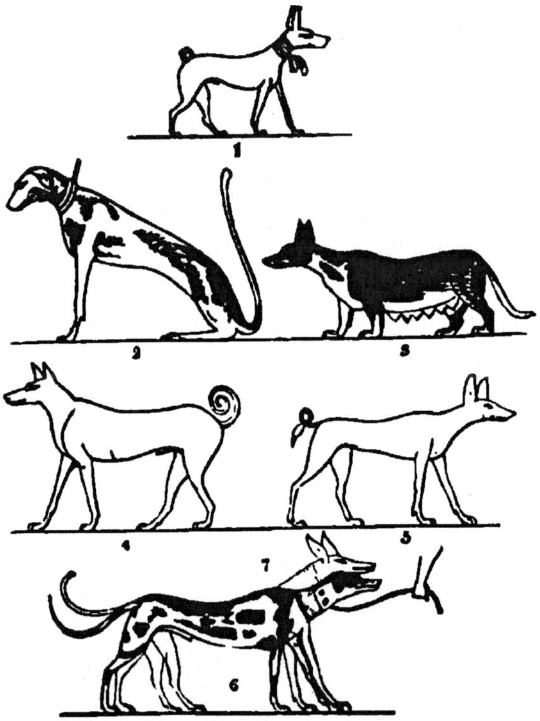

FIG. 2.—VARIOUS KINDS OF DOGS.

This description of these bas-reliefs, which are usually painted, will give an idea of the great works of Egyptian sculptors.

The representation of the animals in these sculptures is as successful as any part of them. There being no intellectual expression required, they are more pleasing than the human beings, with their set, unchanging features and expression. The Egyptians had several breeds of dogs, and the picture here (Fig. 2) is made up from the dogs found in the sculptures—No. 1, hound; 2, mastiff; 3, turnspit; 4, 5, fox-dogs; 6, 7, greyhounds.

FIG. 3.—ANDROSPHINX.

One of the figures often repeated by the sculptors of Egypt was the Sphinx. The colossal and most famous one (Fig. 5) is not far from the great pyramid, and has the form of a recumbent lion with a human head. It is one hundred and seventy-two feet long, and is *the* Sphinx of the world; but there were great numbers of these strange figures in Egypt—in some cases there were avenues leading to the temples bordered by them on each side. The form of the Sphinx was intended to express some spiritual thought to the Egyptians, and the stories about it are very interesting. Its form certainly denotes the union of physical and mental power. The form of which we have spoken as being that of the great Sphinx is called the *androsphinx* (Fig. 3). Another has the body of the lion with the head of the ram, and is called the *kriosphinx* (Fig. 4); still another has the same body and the head of a hawk; this is called the *hieracosphinx* (Fig. 6). They all typified the king, without

FIG. 4.—KRIOSPHINX.

Fig. 5.—The Great Sphinx.

doubt, and it is probable that the various heads were so given to show respect for the different gods who were represented with the heads of these creatures. Sometimes the androsphinx has human hands in place of the lion's paws. The winged Sphinx has been found in Egypt, but it is rare.

The colossal statues of Egypt are very wonderful on account of their vast weight and size. The most famous are two which stand on the west bank of the Nile at Thebes (Fig. 7). Each of these colossi is made from a single block of stone such as is not found within several days' journey of the place where they stand. They are forty-seven feet high, and contain eleven thousand five hundred cubic feet each. But a third is still larger; it represents the King Rameses II., and, when whole, was of a single stone, and weighed eight hundred and eighty-seven tons. It was brought from Assouan to Thebes, a distance of one hundred and thirty-eight miles. It is wonderful to think of moving such a vast weight over such a distance, and one would naturally wish to know also how the sculptors could work on such a statue. The plate here given (Fig. 8) shows the process of polishing a statue, and the following one (Fig. 9) illustrates the mode of moving one when finished. These representations are found in tombs and grottoes, and tell us plainly just what we wish to know about these things.

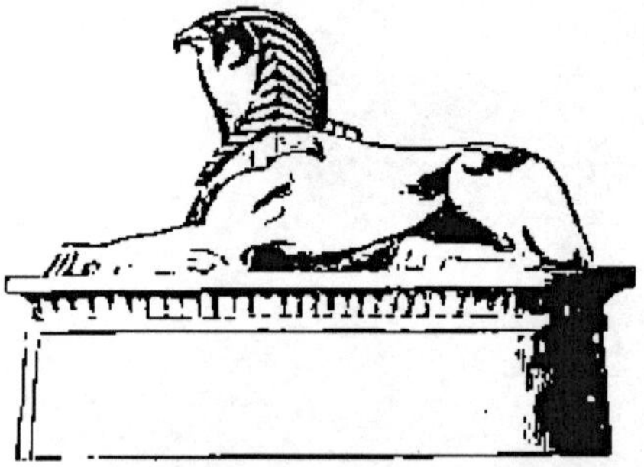

FIG. 6.—HIERACOSPHINX.

I have now pointed out the marked peculiarities of Egyptian sculpture, and before leaving the subject will call your attention to the fact that in most cases it was used in connection with and almost as a part of Egyptian archi-

FIG. 7.—THE COLOSSI AT THEBES.

tecture. In the tombs the bas-reliefs are for the decoration of the walls and to finish the work of the architect, while at the same time they are an interesting feature of the art of the nation and period. In the temple palaces this is also true — though the reliefs serve the purpose of telling the history of the kings; they are, as it were, framed into and make a part of the architectural effect. The obelisks, colossal figures and Sphinxes were placed before the grand buildings, and made a part of them architecturally. In general terms we may say that sculpture never became an independent art in Egypt, but was essentially wedded to architecture; and this fact largely accounts for that other truth that sculpture never reached the perfection in Egypt that it promised, or the excellence that would have seemed to be the natural result of its earliest attainments.

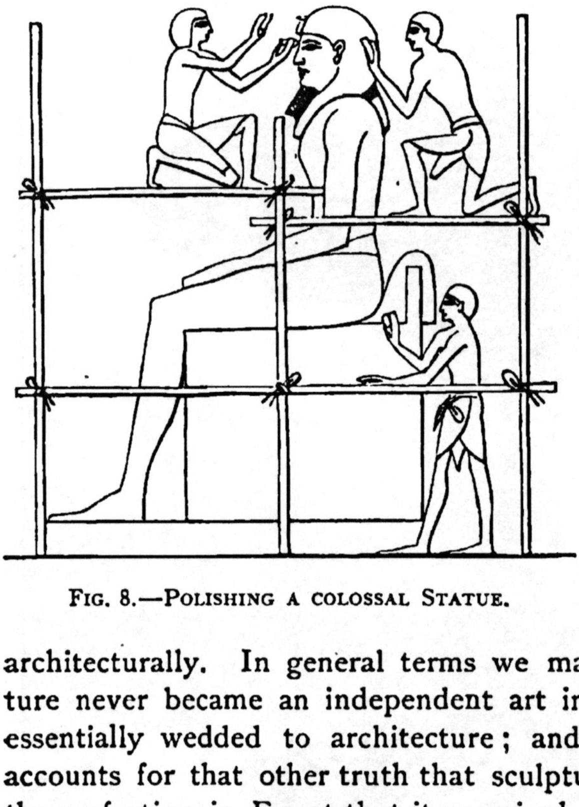

FIG. 8.—POLISHING A COLOSSAL STATUE.

## ASSYRIA.

The works of sculpture in Assyria consisted of statues, bas-reliefs, statuettes in clay, carvings in ivory, metal castings, and some smaller works, such as articles for jewelry, made in minute imitation of larger works in sculpture.

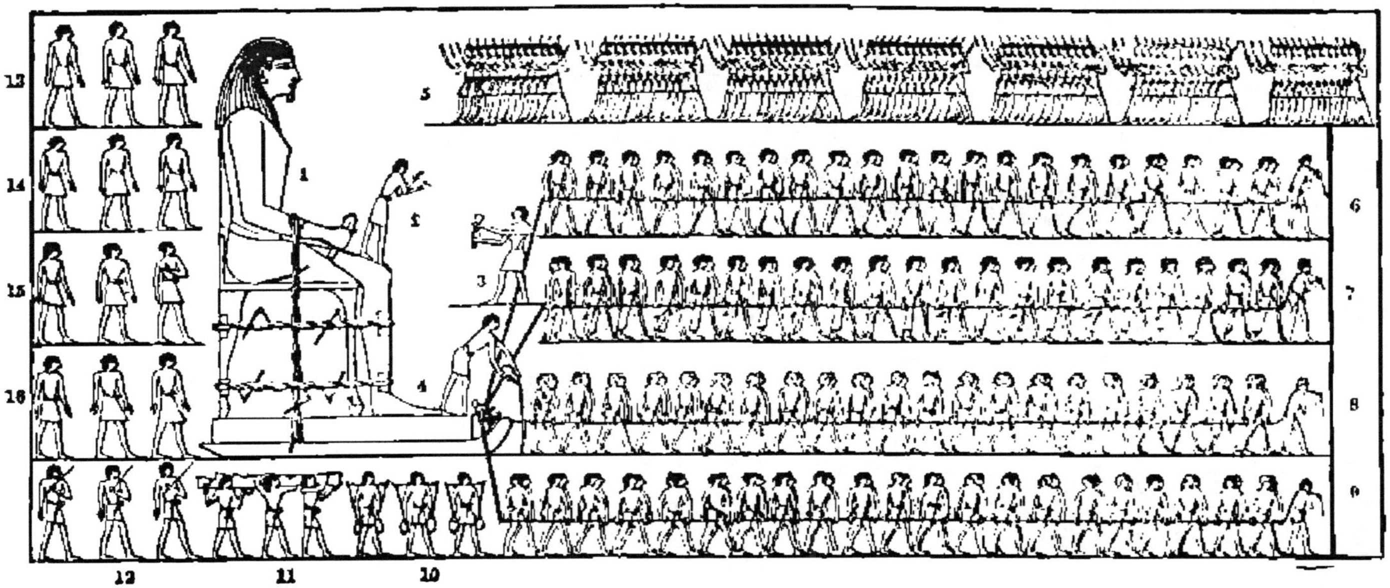

FIG. 9.—MODE OF TRANSPORTING A COLOSSUS FROM THE QUARRIES. *From a Lithographic Drawing.*

In a Grotto at Dayr E'Shake, near El Bersheh.

1. The statue bound upon a sledge with ropes. It is of a private individual, not of a king, or a deity.
2. Man probably beating time with his hands, and giving out the verse of a song, to which the men responded; though 3 appears as if about to throw something which 2 is preparing to catch, or striking crotala.
4. Pouring a liquid, perhaps grease, from a vase.
5. Egyptian soldiers, carrying boughs. 6, 7, 8, 9. Men, probably captives and convicts, dragging the statue.
10. Men carrying water, or grease. 11. Some implements.
12. Taskmasters. 13, 14, 15, 16. Reliefs of men.

The statues found in Assyria are by no means beautiful, according to our idea of beauty. They are as set and stiff in design as the Egyptian works of this sort, and they have suffered so much injury from the weather and from violence that we cannot judge of the manner in which they were originally finished.

The number of Assyrian statues that have been found is small ; this one given here (Fig. 10), of Sardanapalus I., is in the best state of preservation of any of them. It is smaller than life size, being about forty-two inches high. The statuettes of the Assyrians are less artistic than the statues. They are made from a clay which turned red in baking, and are colored so as to resemble Greek pottery. They are almost always of a grotesque appearance, and usually represent gods or genii. They also combine human and animal forms in a less noble and artistic way than is done in the Egyptian representation of the Sphinx. There are also small figures of animals in terra-cotta, principally dogs and ducks. But the large and small statues of the Assyrians are their most unimportant works in sculpture. It is in their bas-reliefs that their greatest excellence is seen, and in them alone their progress in art can be traced. This sort of sculpture seems to have been used by the Assyrians just as painting was used in Italy after the Renaissance. It was their mode of expressing everything. Through it they gave expression to their religious feeling ;

FIG. 10.—STATUE OF SARDANAPALUS I. *From Nimrud.*

they told the history of their nation, and glorified their kings; they represented the domestic scenes which now make the subjects of *genre* pictures; and even imitated vegetables and fruits, as well as to reproduce landscapes and architecture in these pictures cut from stone. In truth, it is chiefly from the bas-reliefs that we learn the history of Assyria, and in this view their sculptures are even more important than when they are considered merely from an artistic view.

The most ancient palaces at Nimrud furnish the earliest examples of bas-relief. These date at about the end of the

FIG. 11.—LION-HUNT. *From Nimrud.*

tenth century B.C. One striking peculiarity in the design is that all the figures, both men and animals, are given in exact profile. In spite of this sameness of position they have much spirit and action. The picture of a lion-hunt given here (Fig. 11) is one of the very best of these reliefs, and you will notice that the animal forms are much superior to those of the human beings. This is true of all Assyrian art in all its stages. In these oldest bas-reliefs there are no backgrounds; but later on these are added, and mountains, hills, streams, trees, and wild animals are all introduced as details of the general design. The highest state of this art was reached about 650 B.C. At this period the various forms seem to be more varied and less arranged according to some rule. The human faces and figures are more delicately finished, and there is an air of freedom and a spirit in the handling of the subjects that is far better than that of any other time. The plants and trees are far more beautiful than before.

The figures of animals, too, are full of life and action in this period. I shall only give one illustration, and shall choose the head of a lion, probably the best specimen of animal drawing which is yet known in Assyrian art. It represents the head of a wounded lion, who, in his agony, rushes upon a chariot and seizes the wheel with his teeth. The drawing of this head, as a portrayal of agony and fierceness, compares favorably with anything of the same kind belonging to any age of art, either classic or modern (Fig. 12).

There is a question which has not yet been decided as to the amount of color used on the Assyrian bas-reliefs. From the traces of color remaining on those that are found in the excavations, and from what we know of the use of colors on the buildings to which the bas-reliefs belonged, we may be sure that colors were used on them; but to what extent cannot be told. It may have been applied with the freedom of the Egyptians, or it may have been sparingly used, as was the manner of the ancient Greeks. The colors that have been found in the ruins of Assyria are white, black, red and blue.

Next to the sculpture, the metal work of the Assyrians was the most important of their arts. This work was done in three ways: I. Whole figures or parts of figures cast in a solid shape. II. Castings of low bas-reliefs. III. Embossed designs made chiefly with the hammer, but finished with the graver. In the solid castings there are only animal forms, and lions are far more numerous than any other creature. Many of them have a ring fastened to the back,

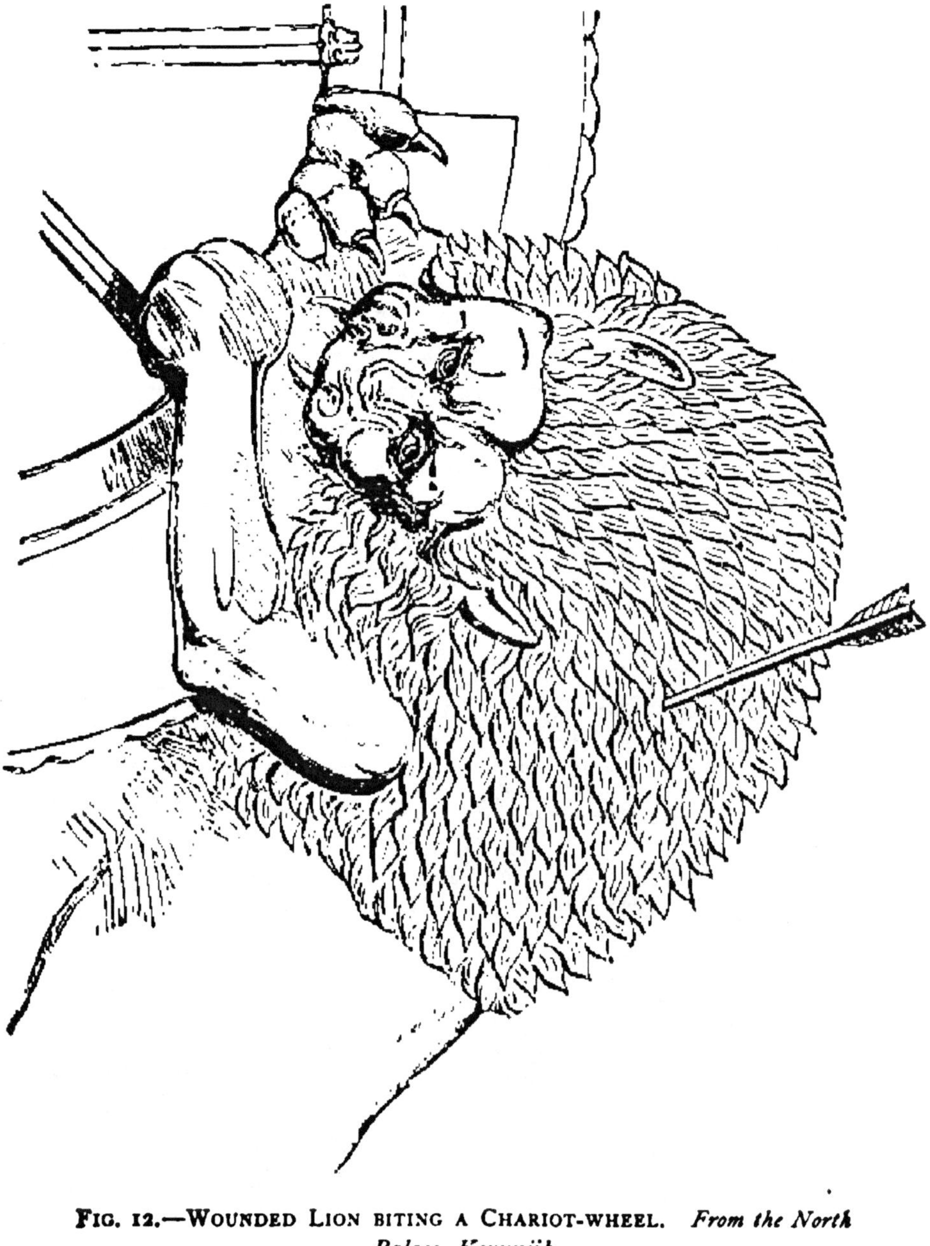

Fig. 12.—Wounded Lion biting a Chariot-wheel. *From the North Palace, Koyunjik.*

which indicates that they were used for weights. These castings are all small and their form good ; but we have no reason to think that the Assyrians could make large metal castings.

The castings in relief were used to ornament thrones, furniture, and perhaps chariots. They were fastened in their places by means of small nails. They had no great merit. The embossed or hammered work, on the contrary, is artistic and very curious. Large numbers of embossed bowls and dishes have been found, and this work was used for the end of sword-sheaths, the sides of chairs and stools, and various other ornamental purposes. It is probable that the main part of the tables, chairs, and so on were of wood, with the ornaments in embossed metals. All this shows the Assyrians to have been an artistic people, and to have reached an interesting stage in their arts, though their works are coarse and imperfect when judged by Greek standards or by our own idea of what is beautiful. If we had the space to consider all the various designs of the bas-reliefs in detail, you would learn from them a great many interesting facts concerning the domestic life of this ancient and interesting people. From them we can learn all about the costumes worn by the king and those of lesser rank ; can see how their wars were carried on, and

FIG. 13.—ARM-CHAIR OR THRONE.
*Khorsabad.*

what their chariots, weapons, and equipments were. Their games, amusements, musical instruments, agricultural pursuits, food, and, in short, everything connected with their daily life is plainly shown in these sculptures, and, as I have said before, the whole history of Assyria is better studied from them than from any other one source. For this reason their great value cannot be over-estimated (Fig. 13).

Other very ancient nations had sculptors, and a few remains of their arts still exist. This is true of the Medes, Babylonians, and Persians; but the general features of their arts resembled those of the Assyrians, though they were less advanced than that nation, and have left nothing as interesting as the Egyptian and Assyrian remains which we have considered. I shall therefore leave them and pass to the sculpture of Greece.

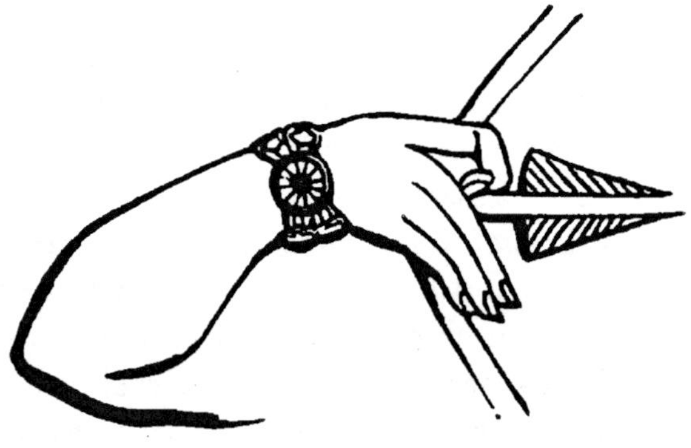

FIG. 14.—MODE OF DRAWING THE BOW. *Koyunjik.*

## CHAPTER II.

### GREEK SCULPTURE.

WE have seen that the Egyptians and Assyrians were skilful in sculpture, but at the same time their works have not moved us as we wish to be moved by art ; there is always something beyond them to be desired, and it remained for the Greeks to attain to that perfection in sculpture which satisfies all our nature and fills our highest conceptions of beauty and grace. In truth, in Greece alone has this perfection in plastic art existed, and since the time of its highest excellence there no other nation has equalled the examples of Greek sculpture which still exist, though we have reason to believe that its finest works have perished, and that those remaining are of the second grade.

There are many reasons for the high artistic attainments of the Greeks, and a discussion or even a simple statement of them would require an essay far too learned and lengthy for the scope of this book ; but I will speak of one truth that had great influence and went far to perfect Greek art —that is, the unbounded love of beauty, which was an essential part of the Greek nature. To the Greek, in fact, beauty and good had the same meaning—*beauty was good*, and the good must be beautiful.

Sculpture deals almost exclusively with the form of man, and the other features in it have some relation to the human element of the design ; and it would have been impossible for a true Greek to represent the human form otherwise than beautiful. A writer on this point says: "The chief aim of the enlightened Greek, his highest ambition and his greatest joy, was to be a *man* in the fullest sense of the word—man in the most complete development of his bodily strength and beauty, in the active exercise of the keenest senses, in the greatest because tempered enjoyment of sensual pleasure, in the free and joyous play of an intellect strong by nature, graced and guided by the most exquisite taste, and enlightened by the sublimest philosophy." Thus, beauty was so important to the Greek that every parent prayed that his children might have this gift, and the names of beautiful persons were engraved upon pillars set where all could read them; and at times there were competitions for the prize of beauty.

The religion of the Greek, too, taught that the body was the beautiful and godlike temple of his soul; and the truth that human beings have something in common with a higher power than their own gave him a great respect for humanity, and, in truth, he felt that if he could escape death he should be content and almost, if not quite, a god. For we must remember that the gods of the Greek were not all-wise, all-powerful, and all-good, as we believe our God to be. If you read their mythology you will find that with the power of the god much imperfection and weakness were mingled. They did not believe that Zeus had been the greatest god from the beginning, but that there was a time when he had no power. He was not omniscient nor omnipresent, and was himself subject to the decrees of Fate, as when he could not save his loved Sarpedon from death. Not knowing all things, even the gods are sometimes represented as depending upon mortals for information, and all these religious views tended to make the human form far more noble to the Greek than it can be to the Christian, with his different views of the relations of God and man.

Greek sculpture existed in very early days, and we have

vague accounts of a person called DÆDALUS, who seems to have been a wood-carver. Many cities claimed to have been his birthplace, and no one can give any clear account of this ancient artist. He is called the inventor of the axe, saw, gimlet, plummet-line, and a kind of fish-glue or isinglass. He is also said to have been the first sculptor who separated the arms from the bodies of his statues, or made the feet to step out; he also opened their eyes, and there is a legend that the statues of Dædalus were so full of life that they were chained lest they should run away.

We call the time to which Dædalus belonged the prehistoric period, and his works and those of other artists of his day have all perished. Two very ancient specimens of sculpture remain—the Lion Gate of Mycenæ and the Niobe of Mount Sipylus; but as their origin is not known, and they may not be the work of Greek artists, it is best for us to pass on to about 700 B.C., when the records of individual artists begin.

Among the earliest of these was DIBUTADES, of whom Pliny said that he was the first who made likenesses in clay. This author also adds that Dibutades first mixed red earth with clay, and made the masks which were fastened to the end of the lowest hollow tiles on the roofs of temples. Pliny relates the following story of the making of the first portrait in bas-relief.

Dibutades lived in Sicyon, and had a daughter called sometimes Kora, and again Callirhoe. She could not aid her father very much in his work as a sculptor, but she went each day to the flower-market and brought home flowers, which gave a very gay and cheerful air to her father's little shop. Kora was very beautiful, and many young Greeks visited her father for the sake of seeing the daughter. At length one of these youths asked Dibutades to take him as an apprentice; and when this request was granted the young man made one of the family of the sculptor. Their life was one of simple content. The young man could play upon the reed, and his education fitted him to be the instructor of Kora. After a time, for some reason that Pliny does not mention, it was best for the youth to go away from the artist's home, and he then asked Kora if she would be his wife. She consented, and vows of betrothal were exchanged, while they were sad at the thought of parting.

The last evening of his stay, as they sat together, Kora seized a coal from the brazier, and traced upon the wall the outline of the face that was so dear to her; and she did this so correctly that when her father saw it he knew instantly from what face it had been drawn. Then he wished to do his part, for he also loved the young man. So he brought his clay and filled in the outline which Kora had drawn, and so went on to model the first portrait in bas-relief that was ever made. Thus did this great art grow out of the love of this beautiful maiden of Sicyon, about twenty-five hundred years ago.

After this beginning Dibutades went on to perfect his art. He made medallions and busts, and decorated the beautiful Grecian structures with his work, and work in bas-relief became the most beautiful ornamentation of the splendid temples and theatres of Greece. He also founded a school for modelling at Sicyon, and became so famous an artist that several Greek cities claim the honor of having been his birthplace.

The bas-relief made from Kora's outline was preserved in the Nymphæum at Corinth for almost two hundred years, but was then destroyed by fire. She married her lover, and he became a famous artist at Corinth.

We have said that accounts of individual artists exist from about 700 B.C.; but these accounts are of so general a character and so wanting in detail that I shall pass on about two hundred years, after saying a few words of the advance made in the arts of sculpture, and mentioning a few of the examples which remain from that early time, which is called the Archaic period. This expression not only means an ancient period of art, but carries also the idea of an obsolete art — of something that is not only ancient, but something that is no longer practised in the same manner or by the same people as existed in this ancient or archaic time. During this archaic period a beginning was made in many branches of plastic art. There were statues in metal and marble, bas-reliefs in various kinds of stone and marble, as well as some chryselephantine statues. This kind of work is often said to have been invented by Phidias, but the truth seems to be that he was not its inventor, but carried it to great perfection. These chryselephantine statues were made of wood and then covered with ivory and gold; the ivory was used for the flesh parts of the statue, and gold for the drapery and ornaments of the figure, and the finished work was very brilliant in its effect.

The principal subjects represented in the sculpture of the archaic period were connected with the religion of the Greeks, which is known to us as mythology. Most statues were of the gods, but portrait statues were not unknown, and the custom of setting up statues of the victors in the Greek games dates back to this very early time. This was a custom which afforded a large field for sculptors to work in, and must have had a great influence to give life and progress to their art.

FIG. 15.—LION DEVOURING DEER.

Of the remains of this art very interesting things have been written, but I shall speak only of a few such objects of which pictures can be given to aid you in understanding

FIG. 16.—HERACLES, TRITON, AND NEREIDS.

about them. Among the earliest reliefs that have been preserved are those now in the Museum of the Louvre, at Paris, which were found in the ruins of a Doric temple at Assos (Fig. 15).

FIG. 17.—HERACLES AND THE CECROPS.

The various designs upon these marbles seem to have no connection with each other, and are executed in a rude manner. The most interesting one represents Heracles, or Hercules, struggling with a Triton (Fig. 16).

The female figures represent Nereids, who are terrified by seeing Heracles in contest with the sea-monster. There are many proofs that these reliefs belong to a very ancient day.

An interesting relief from the temple of Selinus represents Heracles striding off with a pole across his shoulders, to which are hung two Cecrops who had robbed and tormented him (Fig. 17).

A very fine work is also from Selinus, and represents Actæon torn by his dogs. The mythological story was that Zeus, or Jupiter, was angry with Actæon because he wished to marry Semele, and the great god commanded Artemis, or Diana, to throw a stag's skin over Actæon, so that his own dogs would tear him. In the relief Artemis stands at the left (Fig. 18).

FIG. 18.—ACTÆON AND HIS DOGS.

There is in the British Museum a monument which was discovered at Xanthos in 1838. It is thought to have been made about 500 B.C., and is called "The Harpy Monument." It is a tower, round the four sides of which runs a frieze at a height of about twenty-one feet from the ground. The frieze is of white marble, and is let into the frieze which is of sandstone. The Lycians, in whose country it was found, were accustomed to bury their dead at the top of such towers.

There is very great difference of opinion among scholars and critics concerning the meaning of the various scenes in these sculptures; and as all their writing is speculation, and no one knows the truth about it, I shall only say that it is a very interesting object in the history of art, and shall speak of the four corner figures on the shortest parts of the frieze, from which the whole work takes its name. The Harpies are very curious; they had wings, and arms like human arms, with claws for hands, and feathered tails. Their bodies are egg-shaped, which is a very strange feature in their formation. We cannot explain all these different things, but there is little doubt that, with the little forms which they have in their arms, they represent the messengers of death bearing away the souls of the deceased. In the Odyssey, Homer represents the Harpies as carrying off the daughters of King Pandareus and giving them to the cruel Erinnyes for servants. For this reason the Harpies were considered as robbers, and whenever a person suddenly disappeared it was said that they had been carried off by Harpies (Fig. 19).

FIG. 19.—*From the Harpy Monument, London.*

Before leaving this subject of existing sculptures from the fifth century B.C., I will speak of the two groups which belonged to the temple of Minerva in Ægina, and are now in the Glyptothek at Munich. The city of Ægina was the principal city of the island of Ægina, which was in the gulf of the same name, near the south-west coast of Greece. This city was at the height of its prosperity about 475 B.C., at which time a beautiful temple was built, of which many columns are still standing, though much of it has fallen down. In 1811 some English and German architects visited this place, and the marbles they obtained are the most remarkable works which still exist from so early a period. Thorwaldsen, the Danish sculptor, restored these reliefs, and the King of Bavaria bought them.

Upon the western pediment there were eleven figures which represented an episode in the Trojan war; it was the struggle of Ajax, Ulysses, and other Greek warriors to obtain the dead body of Achilles, which was held by the Trojans. The story is that the goddess Thetis had dipped her son Achilles in the river Styx for the purpose of making him invulnerable, or safe from wounds by weapons. But as she held him by the ankles they were not wetted, and so he could be wounded in them. During the siege of Troy Apollo guided the arrow of Paris to this spot, and the great leader of the Greeks was killed. It is believed that the warrior in this picture who is about to send his arrow is Paris. In the central or highest part of the pediment the goddess Minerva stands and tries to cover the fallen body of Achilles with her shield. These figures are on the side where the space grows narrower. You can judge of what the action and spirit of the whole must be when these smaller figures have so much. We are sure that the arrow will shoot out with such force as must carry death to its victim, and the second warrior, who braces himself on his feet and knee, will thrust his lance with equal power (Fig. 20).

There are traces of color and of metal ornaments upon these Æginetan statues; the weapons, helmets, shields, and quivers were red or blue; the eyes, hair, and lips were

FIG. 20.—*Figures from the Pediment of the Temple of Minerva, at Ægina.*

painted, and there are marks upon the garments of the goddess that show that she must have had bronze ornaments. There was a famous sculptor of Ægina named Callon, who lived about the time that this temple was built ; and though it is not known to be so, yet many critics and scholars believe that he may have been the sculptor of these works, because they resemble the written descriptions of his statues and reliefs.

There was a period which we call archaistic, and by this we indicate a time when it was the fashion for the sculptors to imitate as nearly as possible the works of the true archaic period. It has constantly happened in the history of society that fashion has ordained this same thing, though the objects of imitation have varied with the different ages and nations. This archaistic "craze" to imitate old sculptures was at its height in the times of the Roman emperors Augustus and Hadrian ; but here in America we have seen the same passion manifested in the desire to have such furniture as Queen Anne and her people admired, or such as "came over in the Mayflower ;" and when the true original articles were no longer to be found in garrets and out-of-the-way places, then manufacturers began to imitate the old in the new, and one can now buy all sorts of ancient-looking furniture that is only just from the workmen's hands.

But among the Greeks there was a second motive for reproducing the works of the earlier artists, which was the fact that the images of the gods and such articles as belonged to religious services were sacred in their earliest forms, and were venerated by the people. Thus it followed that the advance and change in the taste of the people and the skill of the artists was more suited to other subjects, while the religious images were made as nearly as possible like the older ones. If it happened that a rude ancient image of a god was placed side by side with a modern and more beautiful statue of the same deity, the pious Greek would prefer the ugly one, while he could well admire the most lovely. You should remember that these temple images were really objects of actual worship.

FIG. 21.—ARCHAISTIC ARTEMIS AT NAPLES.

Many of these archaistic works are in various museums of art.

This is a very beautiful temple image, and was discovered at Pompeii in 1760. It was found in a small temple or chapel, of which it must have been the principal deity. It is in excellent preservation; the only parts which are wanting are the fingers of the right hand and the object which it held. Like many of these statues, it is less than life-size—four feet and two inches in height. When it was first discovered there were many traces of color about it. The hair was gilded to represent the blonde hair which the poets ascribed to Artemis (Diana). There was considerable red about the garments, and some flowers were upon the border of the drapery. There is an archaic stiffness about this statue, but the flowing hair, the form of the eyes, and the free style of the nude parts all show that it belongs to the archaistic period (Fig. 21).

It would be pleasant and satisfying if we could trace step by step the progress of Greek sculpture from the rude archaic manner to that of the Periclean age, or from such art as is seen in the sculpture of Ægina to the perfections of the reliefs of the Parthenon. This we cannot do; but we know some of the causes that led to this progress, and can give accounts of a few sculptors who, while they did not equal the great Phidias, were at least the forerunners of such a type of art as his.

The chief cause of the progress of art was the greater freedom of the artist in the choice and treatment of his subjects. So long as the subjects were almost entirely religious there could be little variety in the manner of treating them. Each god or goddess had its own attributes, which must be rendered with exact care; and any new mode of portraying them was almost a sacrilege. But as time passed on and the Panhellenic games and the national Pantheon at Olympia grew into their great importance, new subjects were furnished for the artists, which allowed them to show their originality and to indulge their artistic imaginations to their fullest extent. The victors in the games were heroes, and regarded even as demi-gods, and statues were allowed to be erected to them, although this had hitherto been considered a divine honor and was accorded to the gods alone. When these heroes were represented, the artists, not being bound by any laws, could study their subjects and represent them to the life as nearly as they were able to do. This exaltation of the Olympian victors gave an opportunity for the development of sculpture such as cannot be over-estimated in its influence and results.

Another characteristic of the art of the time we are now

considering was the almost universal use of bronze. This metal is excellent for displaying the minute features of the nude parts of statues, but it is not equal to marble in the representation of draperies or for giving expression to the face. PYTHAGORAS OF RHEGIUM was a famous artist who worked entirely in bronze. The only copies from his works of which we know are on two gems, one of which is in the Berlin Museum. He made exact studies of the body in action, and gave new importance to the reproduction of the veins and muscles. It is also claimed that Pythagoras was the first to lay down clearly the laws of symmetry or proportion which is governed by strict mathematical rules.

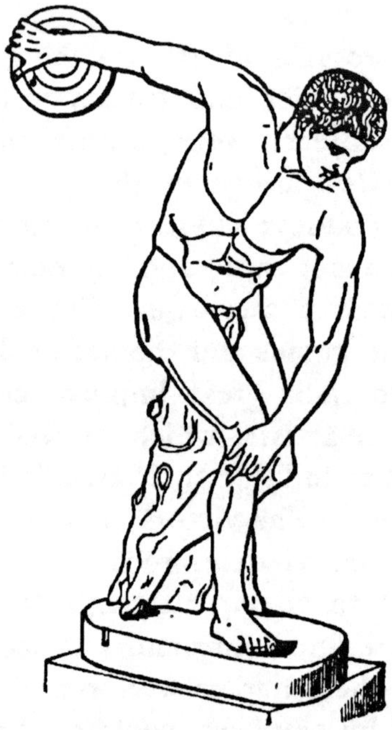

FIG. 22.—THE DISCOBOLUS.

MYRON OF ELEUTHERÆ flourished about 500 to 440 B.C., and was reckoned among Athenian artists because, though not born at Athens, he did most of his works there, and his most famous work, the statue of a cow, stood on the Acropolis of that city. This cow was represented as in the act of lowing, and was elevated upon a marble base. It was carried from Athens to Rome, where it stood in the Forum of Peace. Many writers mentioned this work of Myron's, and thirty-seven epigrams were written concerning it.

Though the cow was so much talked of, the artistic fame of Myron rests more upon the "Discobolus," or quoit-thrower. The original statue does not exist, but there are several copies of it. That in the Massimi Villa is a very accurate one, and was found on the Esquiline Hill at Rome in A.D. 1782; our illustration is made from this statue. Myron's great skill in representing the human figure in excited action is well shown in the quoit-thrower. To make such a figure as this requires great power in a sculptor. No model could constantly repeat this action, and if he could there is but a flash of time in which the artist sees just the position he reproduces. This figure, however, is so true to life that one feels like keeping out of the range of the quoit when it flies (Fig. 22). There are several other existing works attributed to Myron: they are a marble copy of his statue of Marsyas, in the Lateran at Rome; two torsi in the gallery at Florence; a figure called Diomed, and a bronze in the gallery at Munich.

Myron made statues of gods and heroes, but he excelled in representing athletes. His works were very numerous, and a list of those which are only known through the mention of them by various writers would be of little value here. While Myron reproduced the form and action of the body with marvellous effect, he made no advance in representing the expression of the face, nor in the treatment of the hair. He was daring in his art, for he not only imitated what he saw in life, but he also represented grotesque imaginary creatures, and in many ways proved that he had a rich creative fancy.

A third sculptor of this time was CALAMIS, who was in his prime about B.C. 450. He was not born in Athens, but he worked there. Calamis added to the exact representations of Pythagoras and Myron the element of grace beyond their powers in that direction. He made a greater variety of figures than they, for to gods and heroes he added heroines, boys and horses. His works were in bronze, gold and ivory, as well as marble. But what we know of Calamis is gathered from the writings of Greek authors rather than from works, or copies of works, by him still existing;

indeed, no statue remains known to be his own, though there are some which critics fancy may be so. But we may be certain of his great excellence from the many praises sung and said of him, and Lucian, who knew all the best works of all the greatest masters of Greece, puts Calamis before them all for elegance and grace, and for the finer expression of faces; when imagining a beautiful statue of a young girl he declares that he would go to Calamis to impart to it a chaste modesty and give it a sweet and unaffected smile.

PHIDIAS is the most famous of all Greek sculptors, and as Greek sculpture is the finest sculpture of which we have any knowledge, it follows that Phidias was the first sculptor of the world. And yet, in spite of his fame, we do not know the time of his birth. We know that he was the son of Charmidas, but we know nothing of the father except that he had a brother who was a painter, and this makes it probable that the family of Phidias were artists.

As nearly as can be told, Phidias was born about B.C. 500. This would have made him ten years old at the time of the battle of Marathon and twenty years old when Salamis was fought, while he came of age at the time of Platæa. He seems to have begun his artistic life as a painter, and we know nothing of him as an independent sculptor until the administration of Cimon, about B.C. 471. But his finest works belong to the time of Pericles, who was his friend as well as patron, and made him the master over all the great public works at Athens during what we speak of as the Periclean age.

It seems that the favor of Pericles was a dear privilege to Phidias, for it exposed him to bitter envy and hatred; and those who feared to attack Pericles himself avenged themselves upon Phidias, and accused him of dishonesty in obtaining the gold for the robe of the statue of Minerva which he made for the Parthenon. He proved himself innocent of this, but he was accused of other crimes, and one account says that he was thrown into prison and died there of disease or poison. Another account relates that the great sculptor went into exile at Elis, where he made his most famous statue, the Olympian Zeus, and that he was there convicted of theft and put to death. With such contradictory stories we cannot know the exact truth ; but we do know that he went to Elis accompanied by distinguished artists. He was received with honor, and for a long time the studio that he occupied there was shown to strangers. The Olympians also allowed him an honor which the Athenians never extended to him—that is, to inscribe his name upon the base of the statue of Zeus, which he was not permitted to do in the case of the Minerva (or Athena) of the Parthenon.

It often happens in the case of a very great man that the events which have preceded his manhood have prepared the way for him and his work in so striking a manner that it seems as if he could not have been great at any other time, and that he could not avoid being so, when everything had been shaped to his advantage. This was true of Phidias. When he came to be a man the dreadful wars which had ravaged Greece were over, and the destruction of the older structures prepared the way for the rebuilding of Athens. Large quantities of "marble, bronze, ivory, gold, ebony and cypress wood" were there, and a great number of skilful workmen were at hand to work under his command. The Athenians were ablaze with zeal to rebuild the temples and shrines of their gods, who, as they believed, had led them to their victories, and not only the public, but the private means were used to make Athens the grandest and most beautiful city of the world.

The first great work with which the name of Phidias was connected was the building of the temple of Theseus, called also the Theseion. This was a very important temple, and was constructed in obedience to the command of an oracle in this wise: In B.C. 470 the island of Scyros had been taken by the Athenians, and upon this island Theseus had been buried. After the battle of Marathon, in which he had aided the Athenians, Theseus was much regarded by them, and in B.C. 476 they were directed to remove his bones to Athens and build over them a shrine worthy of so great a champion. Just then a gigantic skeleton was discovered at Scyros by Cimon, and was brought to Athens with great ceremony, and laid to rest with pompous respect, and the splendid temple dedicated to Theseus was begun, and Phidias was commissioned to make its plastic ornaments. The precincts of this temple later became a sanctuary where the poor man and the slave could be safe from the oppressor.

Phidias executed many works under the patronage of Cimon, the greatest of which was the colossal statue of Minerva, which stood on the Acropolis. It was called the "Minerva Promachos," and was so gigantic that "the crest of her helmet and the point of her spear could be seen by the mariner off the promontory of Sunium glittering in the sunlight as a welcome to her own chosen people, and an awful warning to her foes." The meaning of Promachos may be given as champion or guardian, and we know from existing descriptions that, with its pedestal, it must have been at least seventy feet in height. It was made from the spoils taken at Marathon; its pedestal was found, in 1840, standing between the Parthenon and the Erechtheium. It has been called the "Pallas with the golden spear," for this goddess was known as Athena, Minerva, and Pallas, and it is said that

Fig. 23.—Athenian Coins with the Minerva Promachos.

Alaric was so impressed by its awful aspect that he shrank from it in horror. The only representations of this statue now in existence are upon Athenian coins, and the position of the goddess differs in these, as you will see by the illustration (Fig. 23); there are reasons for believing that the one in which the shield rests upon the ground is correct, one of which is that some years after the death of Phidias the inside of the shield was ornamented by a relief of the battle of the Centaurs.

Though Phidias proved himself to be a great artist during the reign of Cimon, it was not until the time of Pericles that he reached the glorious height of his genius. Pericles and Phidias seem to have been two grand forces working in harmony for the political and artistic grandeur of Athens, and, indeed, of all Attica, for within a period of twenty years nearly all the great works of that country were begun and completed. Plutarch writes of these wonders in these words: "Hence we have the more reason to wonder that the structures raised by Pericles should be built in so short a time, and yet built for ages. For as each of them, as soon as it was finished, had the venerable air of antiquity, so now that they are old they have the freshness of a modern building. A bloom is diffused over them which preserves their aspect untarnished by time, as if they were animated with a spirit of perpetual youth and unfading elegance."

It is quite impossible that I should speak here of the works of Phidias in detail, and I have decided to speak only of the frieze of the Parthenon, because the Elgin marbles enable us to give illustrations from it and to know more about this than of the other works of the great masters about whom whole volumes might be written with justice. But, first, I will give a picture of a coin which shows the great Olympian Zeus, or Jupiter, which Phidias made at Elis, after he was an exile from Athens (Fig. 24). When

FIG. 24.—COIN OF ELIS WITH THE OLYMPIAN ZEUS.

Phidias was asked how he had found a model for this Jupiter, he quoted the lines from Homer:

> "He said, and nodded with his shadowy brows,
> Waved on the immortal head the ambrosial locks,
> And all Olympus trembled at the nod."

The writings of the ancients have almost numberless references to this statue, and its praise is unending. It was colossal in size and made of ivory and gold, and one historian says that though the temple had great height, yet the Jupiter was so large that if he had risen from his throne he must have carried the roof away. It is related that when the work was completed Phidias prayed to Jupiter to give him a sign from heaven that he might know whether his work was pleasing to the great god or not. This prayer was answered, and a flash of lightning came which struck the pavement in front of the statue. This statue was reckoned among the seven wonders of the world, and it is believed that the magnificent bust called the "Jupiter Otricoli" is a copy from the Olympian statue (Fig. 25).

I shall speak in another volume (upon Architecture) of the former glory and the present ruin of the Parthenon at Athens, and tell how upon its decoration Phidias lavished his thought and care until it surpassed in beauty any other structure of which we have knowledge. Early in the present century Lord Elgin, the English Ambassador to the Porte, interested himself in having the sculptures found in the ruins taken to England. In 1812 eighty chests containing these priceless works of the greatest sculptor who ever lived were placed in Burlington House, and a few years later Parliament purchased them for £35,000, and they were placed in the British Museum, where they now are. There is a great number of them, and all are of great interest; but I shall pass over the metopes and the pediments, and shall pass to the frieze after speaking of this one figure of Theseus, which is from the sculptures of the eastern pediment. The sculptures upon this pediment represented the story of the birth of Athena, and it was proper that Theseus should be present, as he was king over Athens, of which city Athena, or Minerva, was the protecting goddess. Torso is a term used in sculpture to denote a mutilated figure, and many such remains of ancient sculpture exist which are so beautiful, even in their ruin, that they are the pride of the museums where they are, and serve as studies for the artists of all time. This figure of Theseus is wonderful for the majesty and grace of its attitude, for perfection of its anatomical accuracy, and for

FIG. 25.—BUST OF JUPITER FOUND AT OTRICOLI.

the appearance of elasticity of muscle with which it impresses one, even though made of marble. It really seems as if the skin could be moved upon it, so soft does its surface look to be. It is ranked as the greatest miracle of sculpture. Though it is called a Theseus, I ought to state that some critics take exceptions to this name, and believe it to be Hercules or Bacchus ; but by almost general consent it is called a Theseus (Fig. 26).

FIG. 26.—TORSO OF A STATUE OF THESEUS (?).

We may imagine that the representation upon this eastern pediment must have been magnificent. Of course the chosen goddess of Athens would be made to appear with great glory. The myth relates that Athena was born in an instant, by springing forth from the head of Zeus, or Jupiter, fully armed. It is believed that in this sculpture she was represented a moment after birth when she appeared in full, colossal majesty, shouting her war-cry and waving her lance—something as these lines represent the scene :

"Wonder strange possessed
The everlasting gods, that shape to see
Shaking a javelin keen, impetuously
Rush from the crest of ægis-bearing Jove.
Fearfully Heaven was shaken, and did move
Beneath the might of the Cærulean-eyed
Earth dreadfully surrounded far and wide,
And lifted from its depths; the sea swelled high
In purple billows."

It is very important, when considering the sculpture at Athens, to know something about the character of this goddess whose power and influence was so great there. I shall give an extract from an English writer on Greek sculpture, Mr. Walter Copeland Perry:

"It is a very remarkable fact, and one which gives us a deep insight into the character of the Athenians, that the central figure in their religion, the most perfect representative of their feelings, thoughts, and aspirations, was not Zeus or Hera (Juno), nor the most popular gods of all times and nations, Ares (Mars) and Aphrodite (Venus), but Athena, the virgin, the goddess of wise counsel and brave deed! She was enthroned in the very heart of their citadel; and she stood in colossal grandeur on the battlements to terrify their foes, and to give the first welcome to the mariner or the exile when he approached his divine and beautiful home, which reposed in safety under the protection of her lance and shield."

The attributes of this goddess, as given in Greek literature and shown forth in Greek art, are very varied and hard to be understood as belonging to one person. She is the patroness of war, and in Homer's Iliad she is represented as rushing into battle in this wise:

"The cuirass donn'd of cloud-compelling force
And stood accoutred for the bloody fray.
Her tasselled ægis round her shoulders next
She threw, with terror circled all around,

And on its face were figured deeds of arms
And Strife and Courage high, and panic Rout.
There too a Gorgon's head of monstrous size
Frown'd terrible, portent of angry Jove.
. . . . . . . In her hand
A spear she bore, long, weighty, tough, wherewith
The mighty daughter of a mighty sire
Sweeps down the ranks of those her hate pursues."

But this warlike goddess is also represented as the wise counsellor who restrains Achilles from rash action; and though she does not shrink from war and danger, yet the most precious gift to her people was not the war-horse, but the olive, the emblem of peace, and to her honor was this sacred tree planted. "She stands in full armor, with brandished lance, on the highest point of the Acropolis, and yet she is the patroness of all household and female work, in which she herself excels."

It is very interesting to notice that in the early representations of Athena, while she is very warlike in her bearing and raises her lance in her right hand, she also carries in her left the distaff and the spindle and the lamp of knowledge. In the later art of Phidias she is still stern and severe, but her face also expresses dignity and grandeur of thought and character. Later still, her warlike attributes are made less prominent: the shield rests on the ground, and the lance is more like a sceptre, until, in the decline of art, she is represented as lovely and gentle, and all her grand power is lost, and she is not above a great number of other goddesses who are attractive for their soft, lovely grace, but have no selfhood, no individuality to command our admiration or respect.

We come now to speak of the Elgin marbles from the frieze of the Parthenon. It was about thirty-five feet above the floor, three feet three inches broad, and about five hundred and twenty-two feet long. It represented a continuous procession, and the subject is called the great Panathenaic Procession. About four hundred feet of this frieze remains, so that a good judgment can be formed of it. First I must tell you what this procession means. The festival of the Panathenæa was the most important of all the splendid pomps which were celebrated at Athens. It is probable that this festival was held every year about the middle of August, but *the great Panathenaic* occurred only in the third year of each olympiad; an olympiad was a period of four years, extending from one celebration of the Olympic games to another, which was an event of great importance in reckoning time with the Greeks; thus we see that the great procession represented on the frieze occurred once in every four years. This festival continued several days, and all were filled with horse-racing, cock-fighting, gymnastic and musical contests, and a great variety of games; poets also recited their verses, and philosophers held arguments in public places.* But the most important day was that on which a procession went up to the Parthenon and carried the peplos, or garment for the great goddess, which had been woven by the maidens of Athens. This peplos was made of crocus-colored stuff, on which the figures of the gods engaged in their contests with the giants appeared in beautiful, rich embroidery. In later years, after the Athenians had fallen from their first high-minded simplicity, they sometimes embroidered on the peplos the likeness of a man whom they wished to flatter, as thus placing him in the company of the gods was a very great compliment.

The procession of the peplos was formed at daybreak in the Potters' Quarter of the city, and passed to the Dromos, then to the market-place, onward to the temple

* In the Persian invasion of Greece by Xerxes, B.C. 480, that monarch was surprised to learn that the Olympic games were not suspended at the approach of his army.

of Demeter, round the Acropolis along the Pelasgic wall, through the Propylæa to the temple of Athena Polias. The procession was as splendid as all the wealth, nobility, youth and beauty of Athens could make it. Of the vast multitude which joined it some were in chariots, others on horses and almost countless numbers on foot. After the most important officers of the government come the envoys of the Attic colonies with the noble Athenian maidens, the basket-bearers, the aliens who resided in Athens dressed in red instead of white, and a chosen company of aged men bearing branches of the sacred olive.

The peplos was not borne by hands, but was suspended from the mast of a ship, upon wheels, which some writers say was moved by machinery placed underground. When the temple was reached the splendid garment was placed upon the sacred statue, which was believed to have fallen from heaven. During the festival of the Panathenæa prisoners were permitted to enjoy their freedom, men whose services to the public merited recognition received gifts of gold crowns, and their names were announced by heralds in public places, and many interesting ceremonies filled up the time. We do not know the exact order in which all these things happened; but it is believed that the procession of the peplos was the crowning glory of it all, and was celebrated on the final day.

The plan of the Parthenon frieze which represented this great procession was as follows: On the eastern side above the main entrance to the temple there were two groups of the most important and powerful of the many gods of the Greek religion. Each of these groups had six gods and an attendant, so that there were seven figures in each of these groups, as you will see by the illustration (Fig. 27).

There has been much study of these sculptures, and many scholars have written about them. There is still a difference of opinion as to which gods are here represented,

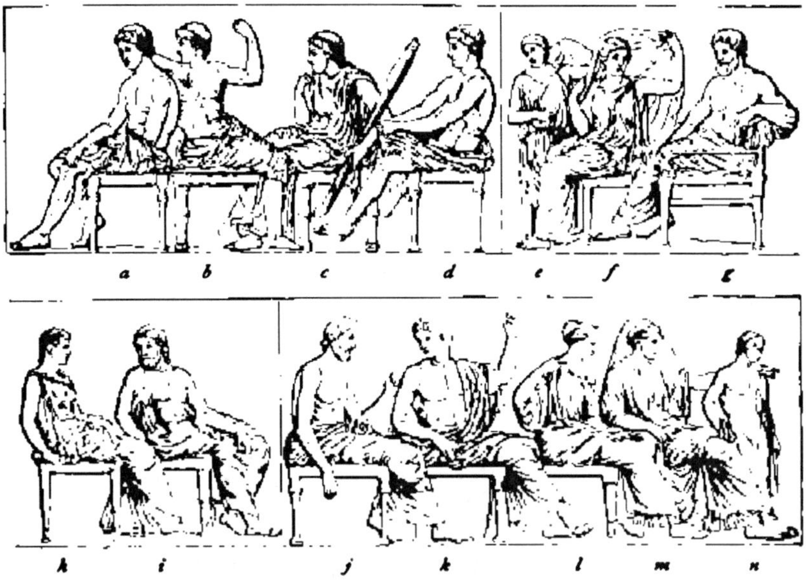


FIG. 27.

but I shall give you the most generally accepted opinion, which calls *a*, Hermes, or Mercury, the messenger of the gods; *b*, Apollo; *c*, Artemis, or Diana; *d*, Ares, or Mars; *e*, Iris, who is attending upon *f*, Hera, or Juno; *g*, Zeus, or Jupiter; *h*, Athena, Minerva, or Pallas; *i*, Hephæstus, or Vulcan; *j*, Poseidon, or Neptune; *k*, Dionysus, or Bacchus; *l*, *m*, *n* are more doubtful, but are probably Aphrodite, or Venus, Demeter, or Ceres, and Triptolemus, the boy who was a favorite with Ceres, who invented the plough and first sowed corn.

Now, these two groups of divinities were divided by a very singular group containing five figures (Fig. 28).

There has been much controversy as to these figures and what they are doing. They seem to be unconscious of the great gods who are near to them on either side. The greater number of critics consider that the two maidens, *c* and *d*, are of the number who have embroidered the peplos ; the central figure, *c*, a priestess of Athena ; *a*, the Archon Basileus ; and *b*, a consecrated servant-boy, who is delivering up the peplos. Other critics believe, however, that these figures are all preparing for the sacred ceremonies about to begin, and that the priest is giving the boy-servant a garment which he has taken off. Other theories may arise, and we can only listen to them all, and yet not know the truth ; but the more we study the more we shall admire these exquisite figures.

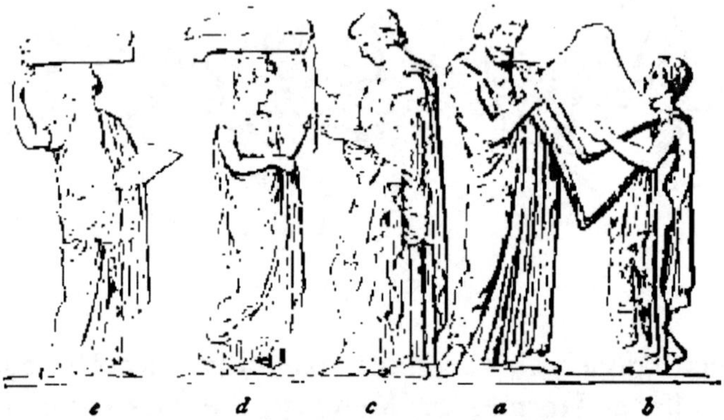


FIG. 28.—THE FIVE CENTRAL FIGURES.

Just here I will call your attention to one feature of these antique bas-reliefs which is called *Isocephalism*, and means that all the heads are at an equal height. You will see that all figures, whether standing or sitting, walking, in chariots, or on horseback, have the heads on the same level.

These three groups, the five central figures and the two groups of gods, are approached on each side by long, continuous processions, and these processions each start out from the south-west corner of the Parthenon, so that one branch goes along the south and a part of the east side, and the other and longer division marches on the whole of the west and north, and a portion of the east side. I shall give here a series of pictures which are all explained by their titles, and will give you an excellent idea of this magnificent frieze, and doubtless many of my readers have studied or will study and admire it in the British Museum (Figs. 29, 30, 31, 32, 33, 34, 35).

Though all this frieze was the conception of the great Phidias, it must have been the work of many hands, and close examination shows that some portions of it are done much better than others. These sculptures have a double value; for while they are so priceless as treasures of art, they tell us much of that prosperous, glorious Athens of which we love to read and hear stories. These figures show us how the people dressed and moved, and we see in them the "stately magistrates and venerable seers of Athens, the sacred envoys of dependent states, the victors in their chariots drawn by the steeds which had won for them the cheap but priceless garland, the full-armed warriors, the splendid cavalry, and the

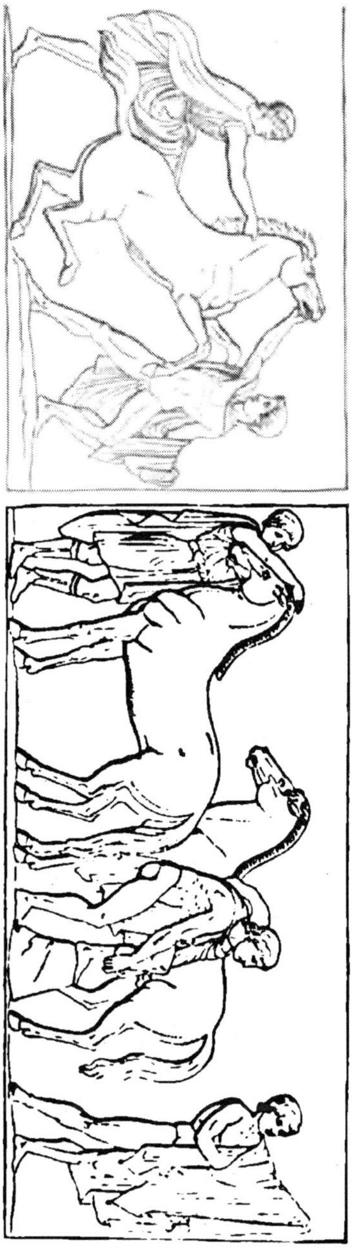

Fig. 29.—Youths Preparing to Join the Cavalcade.

FIG. 30.—HORSEMEN STARTING.

FIG. 31.—PROCESSION OF CAVALRY.

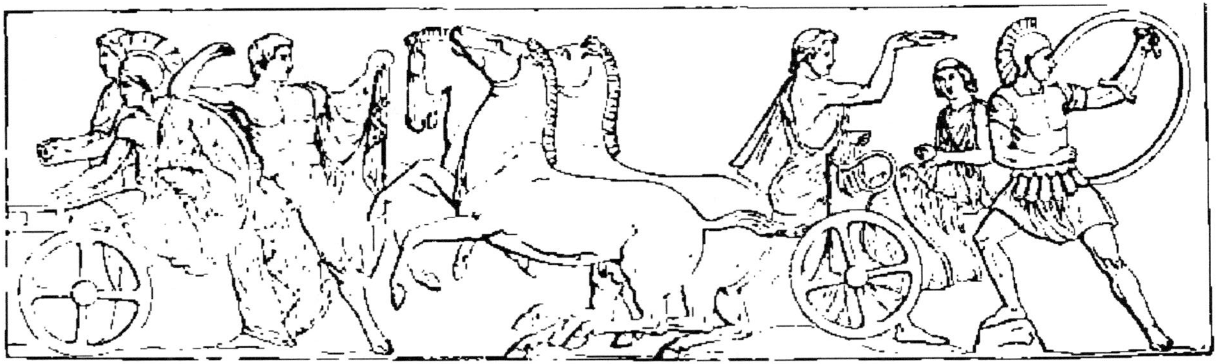

Fig. 32.—Procession of Chariots.

Fig. 33.—Train of Musicians and Youths.

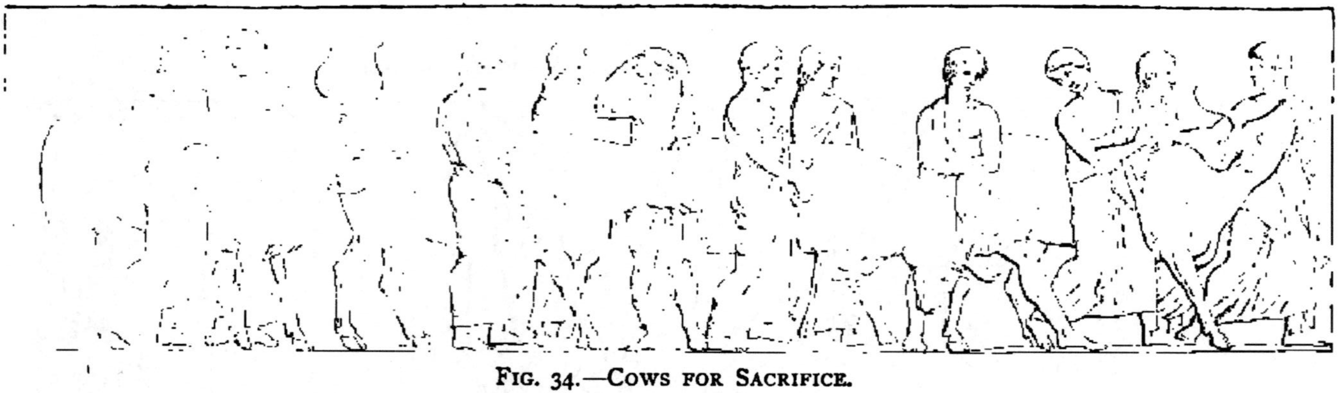

Fig. 34.—Cows for Sacrifice.

Fig. 35.—Train of Noble Maidens.

noble youths of 'horse-loving' Athens on their favorite steeds, in the flush and pride of their young life; and last, not least, the train of high-born Athenian maidens, marching with bowed heads and quiet gait, for they are engaged in holy work, with modest mien, and gentle dignity and grace. All that was sacred, powerful, and grand—all that was beautiful, graceful, and joyous in Athenian life, is represented there, in ideal form, of course, but in strict conformity with the realities of life. . . . It is by the study of such works as these that we get the clearest insight into the essence and spirit of classical antiquity;" and they help us better to understand all that we may read in history or poetry concerning the ancient, classic Greeks.

We must now leave Phidias and speak of other sculptors who were his contemporaries and pupils. Among the last ALCAMENES was the most celebrated. He was born in Lemnos, but was a citizen of Athens; so he is sometimes called an Athenian, and again a Lemnian. His statues were numerous, and most of them represented the gods. One of Hephæstus, or Vulcan, was remarkable for the way in which his lameness was concealed so skilfully that no deformity appeared.

His most famous statue was a Venus, or Aphrodite, concerning which it is related that Agoracritus, another celebrated pupil of Phidias, contended with Alcamenes in making a statue of that goddess. The preference was given to Alcamenes, and Agoracritus believed this to have been done on account of his being an Athenian citizen, and not solely for the merit of the statue. The Venus of Alcamenes stood in a temple of that goddess in a garden beyond the eastern wall of Athens. This statue was very much praised for its beauty by ancient writers, who all mention with especial pride the *eurythmy* of the action of the wrist. This is a term frequently used in regard to sculpture, and is somewhat difficult to explain. It means a harmony and proportion of action which corresponds to rhythm in music. When a statue has the effect it should have it appears as if the motion of the figure was arrested for a moment, and would be resumed immediately. That is what we mean when we say a statue has life; and, as in life, the motion of a statue may be awkward or it may be graceful; it may be harmonious to the eye, just as music is harmonious to the ear, or it may seem out of tune and time, just as inharmonious sounds are to a correct ear for the rhythm of sound; so when we speak of the eurythmy of sculpture we mean that its apparent motion is in accord with the laws of proportion, and is harmonious and graceful to the eye.

While Alcamenes had this power of imparting grace to his statues, he also approached Phidias in majesty and a divine sweetness, which was the sweetness of great strength. In truth, he is recognized as the sculptor who most nearly approached the great Phidias. He represented also for the first time the god Asclepius, or Æsculapius, who was very important to the Greeks, who placed great value upon physical health. Alcamenes represented him as a sort of humanized Zeus or Jupiter. Of the Asclepius heads found at Melos we may regard this one given here as a free copy of the type of god which this great sculptor represented the god of medicine and health to be (Fig. 36).

FIG. 36.—HEAD OF ASCLEPIUS.
*In the British Museum.*

Alcamenes was also the principal assistant of Phidias in

his decoration of the temple of Jupiter at Olympia, and is said to have himself executed the relief upon the western pediment, in which the battle of the Centaurs and Lapithæ was represented with great spirit.

AGORACRITUS of Paros, who has been mentioned as the rival of Alcamenes, is called the favorite pupil of Phidias, and it is said that the master even gave Agoracritus some of his works, and allowed the pupil to inscribe his name upon them. For this reason the ancient writers were often in doubt as to the authorship of the statues called by the names of these sculptors. It is said that when the Venus of Alcamenes was preferred before that of Agoracritus the latter changed his mark, and made it to represent a Nemesis, or the goddess who sent suffering to those who were blessed with too many gifts. It is said that this statue was cut from a block of marble which the Persians brought with them to Marathon for the purpose of making a trophy of it which they could set up to commemorate the victory they felt so sure of gaining; in their flight and adversity it was left, and at last served a Greek sculptor in making a statue of an avenging goddess. This seems to be a striking illustration of "poetic justice."

Agoracritus sold the Nemesis to the people of Rhamnus, who had a temple dedicated to that goddess, and made a condition that it should never be set up in Athens. In the museum of the Lateran at Rome there is a small but very beautiful antique statue of Nemesis, which is thought to be a copy of this famous work. As Nemesis was the goddess who meted out fortune according to her idea of right, a measure was her symbol, and the Greek measure of a cubit was generally placed in her hand. The word cubit means the length of the forearm from the elbow to the wrist, and in this statue of which we speak this part of the arm is made very prominent, and the measure itself is omitted.

The sculptor Myron also had pupils and followers who

executed many works, and of this school was CRESILAS of Cydonia, in Crete. We are interested in him because two copies from his works exist, of which I give pictures here. Pliny, in speaking of the portrait statue of Pericles, said it was a marvel of the art "which makes illustrious men still more illustrious." The cut given here is from a bust in the British Museum. There is reason to believe that

FIG. 37.—A WOUNDED AMAZON.
*Cresilas.*

FIG. 38.—STATUE OF PERICLES.
*Cresilas.*

Cresilas excelled Myron in the expression of his faces (Figs. 37, 38).

CALLIMACHUS is an artist of whom we know little, but that little is interesting. We do not know where he was born, but as he was employed to make a candelabra for the eternal lamp which burned before the sacred statue of Athena Polias, we may suppose that he was an Athenian.

Some writers say that he invented a lamp which would burn a year without going out, and that such an one made of gold was the work he did for the temple of Minerva. Callimachus lived between B.C. 550 and 396, and is credited with having invented the Corinthian capital in this wise: A young girl of Corinth died, and her nurse, according to custom, placed a basket upon her grave containing the food she had loved best in life. It chanced that the basket was put down upon a young acanthus plant, and the leaves grew up about the basket in such a way that when Callimachus saw it the design for the capital which we know as Corinthian was suggested to him, and was thus named from the city in which all this had occurred.

While the plastic art of Athens, or the Attic school of sculpture, reached its greatest excellence in Phidias, there was in the Peloponnesus another school of much importance. Argos was the chief city of this school, and its best master was POLYCLEITUS of Sicyon, who was born about B.C. 482. He was thus about twelve years younger than Phidias. Polycleitus was held in such esteem that many of the ancient writers couple his name with that of Phidias. He was employed in the decoration of the Heraion, or temple of Hera, at Argos. But his greatest work was a statue of Hera, or Juno, for a temple on Mount Eubœa, between Argos and Mycenæ. This statue was chryselephantine, and as Juno was the majestic, white-armed, ox-eyed goddess consort of Jupiter, it is a striking coincidence that Phidias at Olympia and Polycleitus on Mount Eubœa should have made from ivory and gold two famous statues of this renowned pair, who reigned over the mythical world of the Greek religion. There are several copies of heads of Juno in various museums, and some of them have been ascribed to Polycleitus; but the proof of the truth of this is far from being satisfactory. This master made other statues of divinities, but he excelled in representing athletes; and however fine his other works may have been, it was in the reproduction of strong, youthful, manly beauty that he surpassed other sculptors. Some of his statues of this sort, especially a Doryphorus, or spear-bearer, were considered as models from which all other artists could work.

Polycleitus is said to have written a treatise in which he gave exact rules for the proportions of the different parts of the body. This was called "the canon" of Polycleitus, and there is good reason to believe that the Doryphorus was called by the same name, "the canon," because it was fashioned according to the rules laid down by Polycleitus in his treatise. His pupils and followers are mentioned with honor by the Greek authors of his time, but I need not mention them here.

The art of Phidias and Polycleitus was the art of Greece at its best period. After the close of the Persian wars the people of Greece were a religious and patriotic people. The Persian wars developed the best quality of character, for these wars were waged against a foreign foe, and the Greeks were defending their freedom and their civilization, and at the end of the struggle Pericles, who guided them to their greatest prosperity, was a statesman and a man of high aims; he was a gentleman as well as a strong ruler. The Peloponnesian war, on the contrary, was a civil war, and it divided the Greeks among themselves and roused the evil passions of friend against friend all over their country. It was the cause of selfishness, treachery, and immorality, and one of its worst effects was seen in the loss of religious tone among the people: their old contented simplicity of life and thought was gone; every man thought only of himself, and the nation began to sink into the condition which at last made it an easy prey to the Macedonians. We have studied all these wars in our histories, but perhaps we have not thought how much they affected sculpture and the other arts, and brought them down from the lofty heights of the Periclean age.

But there were still men who strove to be great and grand in morals and in intellect, and perhaps strove all the more earnestly for this on account of the decline they saw about them. Few countries in any age have had more splendid men than Socrates, Plato, Euripides, Aristophanes, Pelopidas, Epaminondas, Demosthenes, Dion, and Timoleon, and these all lived between the Peloponnesian and the Macedonian wars. And while the arts were less grand than before, they did not fall into decline for some years, though they took on new features. The gods who had been mostly represented were less often the subjects of the sculptor, and when they were so they were softened and made less awful in their effect. Other gods were more freely taken for models, such as came nearer to human life and thought, because less sublime in their attributes and characters. Among these were Venus as a lovely woman rather than as the great mother of all living creatures, and Eros, or Love; while Plutus, or Wealth, and satyrs, nymphs, and tritons were multiplied in great numbers.

When the gods who were represented were more like human beings in their character, it followed that the statues of them more nearly resembled men and women, and gradually the old grandeur and sublimity were changed to grace, beauty, and mirth. Many people would prefer these works because they come nearer to the every-day life of the world; but earnest, thoughtful minds look for something more noble in art—something that will not come down to us as we are, but will help us to rise above ourselves and to strive after better things.

CEPHISODOTUS was a sculptor who lived until about B.C. 385, or a little later, and stood between the old and the new schools of Greek art. The cut given here is from a group at Munich, which is believed to be a copy of a work by him, and it is a combination of the simple dignity of the art of Phidias (which is seen in the flowing drapery and the wavy edge of its folds) and the later Attic style (which is seen in the dreamy, gentle air of the face of the nurse of the little god). (Fig. 39.) We know very little of the life of Cephisodotus, and as little is said of his works by ancient writers.

FIG. 39.—EIRENE AND THE YOUNG PLUTUS. *Cephisodotus.*

SCOPAS of Paros was one of the greatest sculptors of the later Attic school. The island of Paros, where he was born, was the place where the finest Greek marble was found; but he worked so much at Athens that he is spoken of as an Athenian. He was an architect as well as a sculptor, and he superintended the erection of some splendid structures, which he also ornamented with his sculptures. I shall speak especially of the tomb of Mausolus, the King of Caria. Scopas executed the sculptures of the east side, and as he was the best artist of the sculptors employed there, it is probable that he had much to do with the design for all the work. This mausoleum was reckoned as one of the "seven wonders of the world," and has given a name to fine tombs the world over.

The most interesting of the sculptures from this tomb which are now in the British Museum seems to me to be the statue of Mausolus himself. It is plainly intended to be an exact portrait of the king, and it is so designed and executed that we feel sure it must show him to us just as he was when alive, more than twenty-two hundred years ago (Fig. 40).

Fig. 40.—Portrait of Mausolus.

A part of the frieze upon the mausoleum showed the battle of the Greeks and the Amazons, and this illustration from it gives an idea of the boldness of action and the correctness of the design (Fig. 41). This picture is from a slab in the possession of the Serra family in Genoa. On the right a warrior holds down an Amazon whom he has forced to her knees and is about to kill, while she stretches out her right hand in supplication. The figures to the left are full of spirit, and absolutely seem to be in motion. We do not know that any of these figures were executed by the hand of Scopas, but it is probable that they were, and they give us an idea of the art of his time.

Scopas also carved one of the splendid pillars of the temple of Diana at Ephesus, and did much architectural decoration, as well as to execute many statues and groups of figures. The ancient writers say very little of the art of Scopas, but when all that we can learn is brought together, it shows that he had great fertility in expressing his own ideas, that his genius was creative and his works original. He represented the gods which the earlier sculptors had shown in their works in quite a new manner, and he was the

FIG. 41.—FROM THE FRIEZE OF THE MAUSOLEUM.

first to show the goddess Venus in all the beauty which imagination could attribute to her. His representations of nymphs of wood and sea, of monsters, and all sorts of strange, imaginary beings were numberless, and he made his sculptured figures to express every emotion that can be fancied or felt, from the tenderest and sweetest affection to the wildest passions of the soul.

His works were always representations of gods or of sentiments as shown by some superhuman beings; he never portrayed a hero, with the exception of Hercules, and was ever busy with the ideal rather than with realities about him. He worked in marble only, which is far more suited to the elegant beauty of his style than are bronze and gold or ivory.

We are accustomed to call PRAXITELES the greatest sculptor of the second school of Greek art, just as we give that place to Phidias in the first. We have no fixed dates concerning Praxiteles. We know that he was the son of a Cephisodotus, who was a bronze worker, and was thought to be a son of Alcamenes, thus making Praxiteles a grandson of the latter. Praxiteles was first instructed by his father. Later he came under the influence of Scopas, who was much older than he; and by Scopas he was persuaded to give up working in bronze and confine himself to marble. Perhaps the most authentic date we have concerning him is that given by Pliny, who says that he was in his prime from B.C. 364–360.

It is impossible to praise a sculptor more than Praxiteles was praised by the Greek authors; and, although Athens was the place where he lived and labored most, yet he was known to all Greece, and even to other countries, and the number of his works was marvellous. There are trustworthy accounts of forty-seven groups, reliefs, and statues by his hand, and it is not probable that these are all that he executed.

Praxiteles represented youth and beauty and such subjects as are most pleasing to popular taste. Thus it happened that his male figures were the young Apollo, Eros, and youthful satyrs, while a large proportion of his statues represented lovely women. Venus was frequently repeated by him, and there is a story that he made two statues of her, one being draped and the other nude. The people of Cos bought the first, and the last was purchased by the Cnidians, who placed it in the midst of an open temple, where it could be seen from all sides. It became so famous that many people went to Cnidos solely for the purpose of seeing it, and the "Cnidian Venus" acquired a reputation wherever art was known. When the oppressor of the Cnidians, King Nicodemus of Bithynia, offered to release them from a debt of one hundred talents (about $100,000) if they would give him the Venus, they refused, and declared that it was the chief glory of their State.

Another story relates that Phryne, a friend of Praxiteles, had been told by him that she could have any work which she might choose from his workshop. She wished to have the one which the artist himself considered the best. In order to find out which he so esteemed she sent a servant to tell him that his workshop was on fire. He exclaimed, "All is lost if my Satyr and Cupid are not saved!" Then Phryne told him of her trick, and chose the Cupid, or Eros, for her gift. Phryne then offered the statue to the temple of Thespiæ, in Bœotia, where it was placed between a statue of Venus and one of Phryne herself. This Cupid was almost as celebrated as the Cnidian Venus, and was visited by many people. The head given here (Fig. 42), which was found in Centocelle by Gavin Hamilton, and is now in the Vatican, is thought by many to be a copy of a Cupid by Praxiteles, and even of the Thespian statue; but we have no proof of this. The Cupid, or Eros, of the art of Scopas and Praxiteles is not the merry little creature who bears that name in later art; he is a youth just coming into manhood, with a dreamy, melancholy face, the tender beauty

FIG. 42.—THE EROS OF CENTOCELLE.

of which makes him one of the most attractive subjects in sculpture. Caligula carried the Thespian Cupid to Rome; Claudius restored it to its original place, but Nero again bore it to Rome, where it was burned in a conflagration in the time of Titus.

I shall say no more of Praxiteles personally, because I wish to describe to you the largest and grandest group of Greek statues which exists, or, as I should say, of which we have any copies. We do not know whether Scopas or Praxiteles made these famous figures, since they are attributed to both these sculptors; perhaps we can never positively know to whom to ascribe the fame of this marvellous work. The historian Pliny tells us that they stood in the temple of Apollo Sosianus at Rome. Sosius was the legate of Antony in Syria and Cilicia; he erected this temple in his own honor, and brought many beautiful works from the East for its decoration. It is believed that he brought the Niobe group from Cilicia, and displayed it when celebrating his victory over Judea, B.C. 35.

In A.D. 1583 a large number of statues representing this subject were found in Rome, and were purchased by the Grand Duke of Tuscany, who placed them in the Villa Medici. In 1775 they were removed to the Palace of the Uffizi, in Florence, where an apartment was assigned to them. The figures were restored, and each one placed on its own pedestal, which work was not completed until 1794.

The group must have had originally seventeen figures—Niobe and fourteen children, a pedagogue and a female nurse. Now there are but twelve—Niobe, six sons, four daughters, and the pedagogue. At first it was supposed that these figures ornamented the temple pediment, but it is now thought that they stood on an undulating rocky base, with a background at a little distance. Niobe is the central figure, in any case, and the children were fleeing toward her from either side; she is the only one represented in such a way as to present the full face to the beholder (Fig. 43). But we shall better understand our subject if I recount as concisely as possible the story of Niobe, which,

FIG. 43.—NIOBE AND HER YOUNGEST DAUGHTER.

as you know, is a Grecian myth. Niobe was the daughter of Tantalus, and was born on Mount Sipylus. When a child Niobe played with Lato, or Latona, who afterward married the great god Jupiter, or Zeus. Niobe became the wife of Amphion, and had a very happy life; she was the mother of seven sons and seven daughters, and all this prosperity made her forget that she was mortal, and she dared to be insolent even to the gods themselves. Lato had but two children, the beautiful Apollo and the archer-queen of heaven, called Diana, or Artemis.

Amphion and Niobe were the King and Queen of Thebes, and when the worship of Lato was established in that city Niobe was very angry. She thought of Lato as her playmate and not a goddess, and was so imprudent as to drive in her chariot to the temple and command the Theban women not to join in this worship. Niobe also asserted that she was superior to this Lato, who had but two children, while she had fourteen lovely sons and daughters, any one of which was worthy of honor. All this so enraged Lato that she begged Apollo, who was the god of the silver bow, and Diana, her huntress daughter, to take revenge on Niobe. Obedient to her commands, Apollo and Artemis descended to earth, and in one day slew all the children of Niobe. Then this proud mother, left alone, could do nothing but weep, and this she did continually

FIG. 44.—BROTHER AND SISTER.

until Jupiter took pity on her and turned her into stone, and whirled her away from Thebes to Mount Sipylus, the scene of her happy childhood. In this picture of Niobe she clasps her youngest child, who has fled to her for protection.

I cannot give pictures of all the figures, but one of the most interesting is this brother and sister. She is wounded, and he endeavors to raise his garment so as to shield her and himself from the deadly arrows which pursue them (Fig. 44).

FIG. 45.—THE ELDEST DAUGHTER.

This figure of the eldest daughter is very beautiful. An arrow has pierced her neck, and the right hand is bent back to the wound. The face is noble and simple, and has been a favorite model to Guido Reni and other Italian masters (Fig. 45).

Fig. 46 shows one of the older sons, who, though wounded and fallen on one knee, still looks toward his slayer with an air of defiance. There is a world of interest connected with these statues, and they move us with a variety of emotions. The poor mother, so prosperous a moment before, and now seeing her children dying around her, slain by the sure arrows of the unseen gods—how can we pity her enough! and then the brave son who tries to shield his sister while he is dazed by the suddenness of the misfortunes which he cannot account for; the old pedagogue, to whom the youngest boy has run for protection—and, indeed, all demand our sympathy for their grief and our admiration for their beauty, which is still theirs in spite of their woe.

One of the young sculptors who was employed with Scopas in the work on the mausoleum was LEOCHARES. We read of several statues of Zeus and Apollo by this master, but his most celebrated work was the group of Ganymede borne upward by the eagle of Zeus. There are several copies of this sculpture, but that given here, from the Vatican figure, is the best of all, and is very beautiful. We know very few facts concerning Leochares, and cannot even say whether he was an Athenian or not (Fig. 47).

FIG. 46.—A NIOBID.

There is still standing at Athens, in its original place, the Choragic monument of Lysicrates; and though we do not know the names of the architects and sculptors who made it, there are traces upon it which indicate that it belonged to the school of Scopas (Fig. 48).

This monument was erected B.C. 334, when Lysicrates was *choragus*—that is, when it was his office to provide the chorus for the plays represented at Athens. This was an expensive office, and one that demanded much labor and care. He had first to find the choristers, and then bring them together to be instructed, and provide them with proper food while they studied. The choragus who gave

FIG. 47.—GANYMEDE. *After Leochares.*

the best musical entertainment received a tripod as his reward, and it was the custom to build a monument upon which to place the tripod, so that it should be a lasting honor to the choragus and his family. The street in which these monuments were erected was called "the street of the Tripods."

FIG. 48.—MONUMENT OF LYSICRATES. *Athens.*

It was also the custom to dedicate each tripod to some special divinity, and this of Lysicrates was dedicated to Bacchus, and had a frieze with sculptures telling the story of that god and the Tyrrhenian robbers who bore him off to their ship. In order to revenge himself he changed the oars and masts into serpents and himself into a lion ; music was heard, and ivy grew all over the vessel ; the robbers went mad and leaped into the sea, and changed into dolphins.

In the frieze, however, it is represented that the god is on shore quietly amusing himself with the lion (Fig. 49), while satyrs and sileni punish the robbers by beating them with sticks and chasing them with fury, while they are turning gradually into dolphins and rushing into the sea. The design is so fine that it might easily be attributed to one of the best sculptors ; but the execution is careless, and this is not strange when we remember that it was all done at the expense of one man, and he a private citizen.

We will return now to the Peloponnesian school, of which Polycleitus was the head in its earliest period. After his time the sculptors of his school continued to prefer the subjects in which he excelled, and represented youthful heroes and victors with as much industry as the artists of Athens bestowed upon their statues of womanly grace and beauty. The subjects of the Peloponnesian school were especially suited to the use of bronze, and the chief

FIG. 49.—BACCHUS AND LION. *From the Lysicrates Monument.*

sculptor of his time, LYSIPPUS, whose works are said to have numbered fifteen hundred, worked entirely in bronze. In order to keep a record of the number of his works, he adopted the plan of putting aside one gold coin from the price of every statue, and at his death his heirs are said to have found the above number of these coins thus laid away. His home was at Sicyon, and his time of work is given as B.C. 372–316. This seems a long period for active employment as a sculptor; but the number of his works accords well with this estimate of his working years.

Lysippus cannot be said to have followed any school; he was original, and this trait made him prominent, for he was not bound by old customs, but was able to adapt himself to the new spirit of the age, which came to Greece with the reign of Alexander. This sculptor made a great number of statues of Hercules; and as Alexander loved to regard himself as a modern Hercules, Lysippus also represented the monarch in many different ways, and with much the same spirit as that he put into the statues of the hero-god. For example, he made a statue of "Alexander with his Spear," "Alexander at a Lion Hunt," "Alexander as the Sun-God," and so on through many changes of expression and attributes, but all being likenesses of the great king. There is in the Capitol at Rome a head of Alexander called *Helios*, which is thought by many critics to be the best bust of him in existence. There are metal rays fastened to the head; it has a wild, Bacchus-like air, and the hair is thrown back, as if he had shaken his head furiously; and the defect of a wry neck, which the monarch had, is cleverly concealed by this motion. Alexander was a very handsome man, his

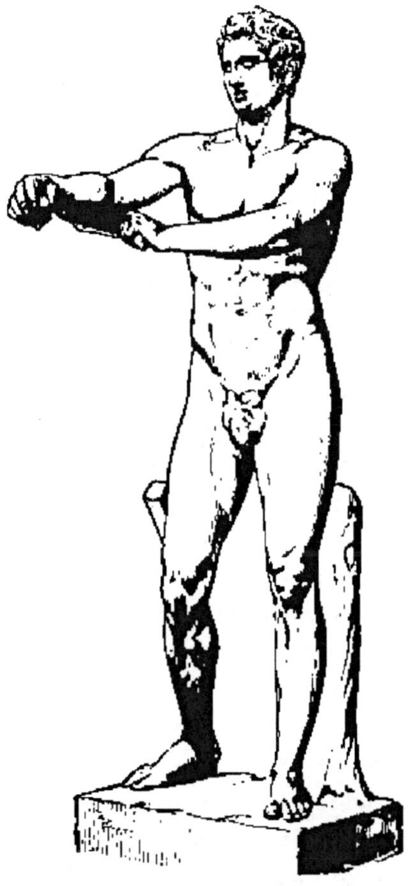

FIG. 50.—THE APOXYOMENOS OF LYSIPPUS.

faults being this twist in his neck and a peculiar shape of the eye.

We cannot here give the long list of works by Lysippus, but will speak of that which interests us most, because we have a beautiful copy of it. I mean the Apoxyomenos, which is in the Vatican. It represents a youth scraping himself (as the name denotes) with the strigil after a contest in the arena (Fig. 50). The Vatican copy was found in the Trastevere at Rome in 1849, and is well preserved. Without doubt it is a faithful reproduction of the original, which was probably brought from Greece to Rome by Agrippa, who set it up in front of his public baths. Here it became such a favorite with the people that when Tiberius removed it to his own house there was a demonstration in the theatre, and so violent a demand was made for its restoration that the cunning emperor dared not refuse. This statue may be called an example of a grand *genre* style. It represents a scene from common life in Greece, but it is so simply natural, so graceful and free from restraint, that one could not weary of it. The expression of the face is that of quiet content—his task has been faithfully done, and the remembrance of it is pleasant. The hair is finely executed ; this was a point in which Lysippus excelled ; but the great charm of the whole is in the pose of the figure. In his occupation of scraping one portion of the body after another he must constantly change his position, and this one, in which he can rest but a moment, seems to have the motion in it which he must almost instantly make, while it is full of easy grace in itself. The art of Lysippus was not as elevated as that of Phidias, who tried to represent the highest ideal which a mortal may form of a god ; but there was nothing mean or vulgar in the works of the former ; on the contrary, it was with a pure and noble spirit that he endeavored to represent the perfections of youthful, manly beauty, and his naturalism was of a healthy and dignified sort.

The most important pupil of Lysippus was CHARES OF LINDOS, who was prominent not only on account of his own works, but also because he introduced the art of Sicyon into his native island of Rhodes. This island is but forty-five miles long and twenty miles wide at its broadest part, and yet its art became second only to that of Athens.

At the city of Rhodes alone there were three thousand statues, besides many paintings and other rare and beautiful objects. Chares is best known for the sun-god which he erected here; it was called the "Colossus of Rhodes," and was reckoned as one of the seven wonders of the world. One hundred statues of the sun were erected at Rhodes, and Pliny says that any one of them was beautiful enough to have been famous; but that of Chares was so remarkable that it overshadowed all the rest.

It stood quite near the entrance to the harbor of Rhodes, but we have no reason to believe that its legs spanned the mouth of the port so that ships sailed between them, as has often been said, although its size was almost beyond our imagination. The statue was one hundred and five feet high, and few men could reach around one of its thumbs with their arms, while each finger was as large as most statues. Twelve years were occupied in its erection, from B.C. 292 to 280, and it cost three hundred talents, or about $300,000 of our money, according to its usual estimate, though there are those who name its cost as more than four times that amount. The men of Rhodes obtained this great sum by selling the engines of war which Demetrius Poliorcetes left behind him when he abandoned the siege of Rhodes in B.C. 303. We have no copy of this statue, but there are coins of Rhodes which bear a face that is believed with good reason to be that of the Colossus.

Fifty-six years after its completion, in B.C. 224, the Colossus was overthrown by an earthquake, and an oracle forbade the restoration of it by the Rhodians. In A.D. 672, nearly a thousand years after its fall, its fragments were sold to a Jew of Emesa by the command of the Caliph Othman IV. It is said that they weighed seven hundred thousand pounds, and nine hundred camels were required to bear them away. When we consider what care must have been needful to cast this huge figure in bronze, and so adjust the separate parts that the whole would satisfy the standard of art at Rhodes, we are not surprised that it should have been reckoned among the seven wonders, and that Chares should have become a famous master.

Chares also founded a school of art which became very important, and, indeed, it seems to have been the continuance of the school of the Peloponnesus; for after the time of Lysippus the sculpture of Argos and Sicyon came to an end, and we may add that with Lysippus and his school the growth of art in Greece ceased; it had reached the highest point to which it ever attained, and all its later works were of its decline, and foreshadowed its death.

The reign of Alexander the Great was so brilliant that it is difficult to realize that it was a time of decline to the Greeks; and during the life of Alexander perhaps this does not appear with clearness; but at the close of his reign there arose such contentions and troubles among his generals that everything in Greece suffered, and with the rest Greek art was degraded. In the time of Pericles it was thought to be a crime in him that he permitted his portrait to be put upon the shield of the Parthenon, and he was prosecuted for thus exalting himself to a privilege which belonged to the gods alone. Alexander, on the contrary, claimed to be a god, and was represented by painters and sculptors until his portraits and statues were almost numberless.

Soon after the death of Alexander the humiliation of Athens and its old Periclean spirit was complete. If you read the history of Demetrius Poliorcetes, who was even allowed to hold his revels in the most sacred part of the Parthenon—the temple of Minerva—you will see that Athens was enslaved and her people no longer worthy to lead the world in the arts of peace, as they were no longer the brave men who could stand first in war. In their degraded state the Athenians suffered three hundred and sixty statues to be erected to Demetrius Phalereus, and these were destroyed to make way for the golden images of the conquering freebooter Poliorcetes. This last was hailed by the debased people as a god and a saviour. His name and that of his father, Antigonus, were woven into the sacred peplos.

At length, under the Diadochi, or successors of Alexander, order was restored, and Antigonus, Ptolemy, Seleucus, and Lysimachus divided the kingdom of Alexander into four Græco-Oriental monarchies. The dynasty of the Ptolemies in Egypt was the most reputable of these, and gave much encouragement to art and letters. But the sacred fire seems to have died out, or did not burn clearly when transplanted from Athens to Alexandria. The Alexandrines seem to have been mere imitators of what had gone before, and there is nothing to be said of them that is of importance enough for us to linger over it. Very few works remain from this Diadochean period. The Metope of Ilium, which Dr. Schliemann has in his garden in Athens, the Barberini Faun, in the Glyptothek at Munich, and the Nile of the Vatican are the most important remnants of Alexandrine sculpture.

Amid all the confusion and strife which followed the death of Alexander the island of Rhodes remained undisturbed, and when the division of the monarchies was made the Rhodians still retained their independence. They were neutral, and so had a commerce with all the monarchies, and thus gained great wealth; and theirs was the only independent State of the old Hellenic world which was able to found and maintain a school of art. Among the great works of the Rhodian artists none is more familiar to us than the group of the Laocoon.

In the time of Pliny this work stood in the palace of Titus, and the historian called it "preferable to all other works of pictorial or plastic art." There is a difference of opinion as to the period when it was made, and many date it in the time of Titus, who lived A.D. 40 to 81. But the weight of argument seems to me to rest with those who believe that it was made at Rhodes in the time of the Diadochi.

The group in the Vatican is probably a copy, because Pliny says that the original was made of one block, and that of the Vatican is composed of six pieces. Pliny also tells us that the Laocoon was the work of three sculptors, AGESANDER, POLYDORUS, and ATHENODORUS. The Vatican group was found in 1506 in the excavation of the Baths of Titus, in Rome, and was placed in its present position by Pope Julius II. (Fig. 51). The right arm of Laocoon was missing, and Michael Angelo attempted to restore it, but left it incomplete; Montorsoli made an unsatisfactory attempt for its restoration, and the arm as it now is was made by Cornacini, and more straight than it should be.

The story which these statues illustrate is told in the second book of the Æneid, and says that Laocoon was a priest of Apollo at Troy, who, when the Greeks left the wooden horse outside the city and pretended to sail away, warned the Trojans against taking the horse inside the walls; he also struck his spear into the side of the monster. But Sinon, who had been left behind by the Greeks, persuaded the Trojans that the horse would prove a blessing to them, and they drew it into the city, and ordered feasts and sacrifices to be celebrated to do honor to the occasion. Laocoon had much offended Pallas Athene by his words and acts, and when he went to prepare a sacrifice to Neptune that goddess sent two huge serpents up out of the sea to destroy him and his two sons, who were with him by the altar. When the three victims were dead the fearful creatures went to the Acropolis and disappeared.

FIG. 51.—THE LAOCOON GROUP.

In the Laocoon group it appears that the eldest son will save himself, and in certain minor points the sculptors seem not to have followed the account of Virgil; but we see that it must be the same story that is illustrated, and we know that it was told with some variation by other poets. This group is a wonderful piece of sculpture, but it is not of the highest art, and it is far from pleasant to look at. The same is true of another famous group which is in Naples, and which is also from the Rhodian school.

I mean the Farnesian Bull, or the Toro Farnese. This group was made by APOLLONIUS and TAURISCUS, who are believed to have been brothers. It was probably made at Tralles, in Caria, which was their native place, and sent by them to Rhodes, the great art-centre; from Rhodes it was sent to Rome, where it was in the possession of Asinius Pollio. This splendid group, which is probably the original work, was found in the Baths of Caracalla, in 1546, and was first placed in the Farnese Palace, from which it was removed to the National Museum in Naples, in 1786 (Fig. 52).

This group tells a part of the story of Dirce, who had incurred the hatred and displeasure of Antiope, the mother of Amphion, who was King of Thebes and the husband of Niobe. In order to appease the wrath of his mother, Amphion, with the aid of his twin-brother Zethus, bound Dirce to the horns of a wild bull to be dashed to pieces. All this takes place on Mount Cithæron, and it is said that after Dirce had suffered horrible agonies the god Dionysus changed her into a fountain, which always remains upon this mountain.

In this piece of sculpture, dreadful as the idea is, there is less of horror than in the Laocoon, for the reason that the moment chosen is that just before the climax of the catastrophe, while in the Laocoon it is in its midst. The latter group is made to be seen from but one side, and was probably intended for a niche; but the Farnese Bull is perfect, and presents a finished aspect on all sides and from every point of view. There are numerous accessories and much attention to detail, while the rocky base represents Mount

Cithæron and the wildness of the scene in a manner not before known in sculpture. The group has been much restored, but its excellences support the theory of its being the original work of the Greek artists, and the skill with

FIG. 52.—THE FARNESE BULL.

which the various figures are brought into one stupendous moment is such as commands great praise and admiration; it is doubtful if any other work of sculpture tells its story with power equal to that of this celebrated group.

After the art of Rhodes that of Pergamon was important. When Attalus I., King of Pergamon, gained his victory over the Gauls, in B.C. 229, the Greek artists were aroused to new efforts to record in sculpture the great deeds of Attalus and to place him on a level with the glorious heroes of their nation who had preceded him. It is recorded that the conqueror himself offered four groups of statues at Athens, and that they stood on the southern wall of the Acropolis. The subjects were: "The Battle of the Gods and Giants," "The Battle of Athenians and Amazons," "The Battle of Marathon," and "The Destruction of the Gauls in Mysia by Attalus." Thus the different epochs of Greek history were represented, and Attalus placed himself near the other great warriors who had preserved the honor and freedom of their nation. These groups consisted of many figures, and are estimated to have been from sixty to eighty in number. It is believed that at least ten of them are now in European collections—that is, three in Venice, four in Naples, one in Paris, one in the Vatican, and the last in the Castellani collection in Rome. This picture of one of those in Venice seems to represent a warrior who has been suddenly thrown down; his weapons and shield—which last was probably held in the left hand—have been dropped in the violence of the shock which has prostrated him (Fig. 53). His face and hair are of the barbarian type, and the power and elasticity of his powerful frame are manifest

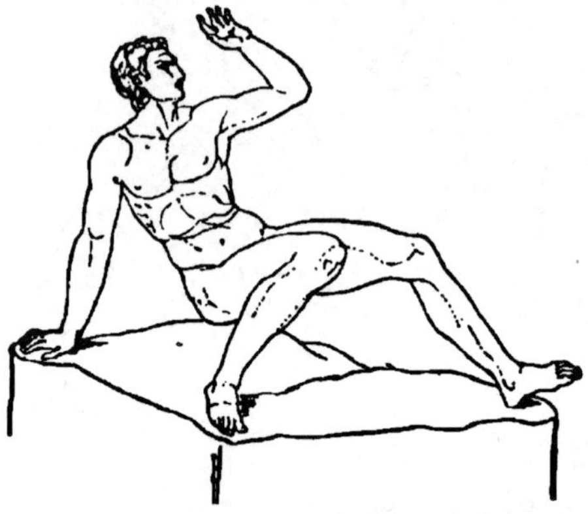

FIG. 53.—GALLIC WARRIOR. *Venice.*

even in this moment of his defeat. He is yet unwounded, but the weapon of his adversary may be before his eyes, and in another moment he may sink back in the agony of death.

It is now believed that the statue of the Dying Gaul, often called the Dying Gladiator, was the work of a sculptor of Pergamon, and represents a Gaul who has killed himself rather than submit as a slave to his conquerors. The moment had come when he could not escape, and he chose death rather than humiliation. We learn from his-

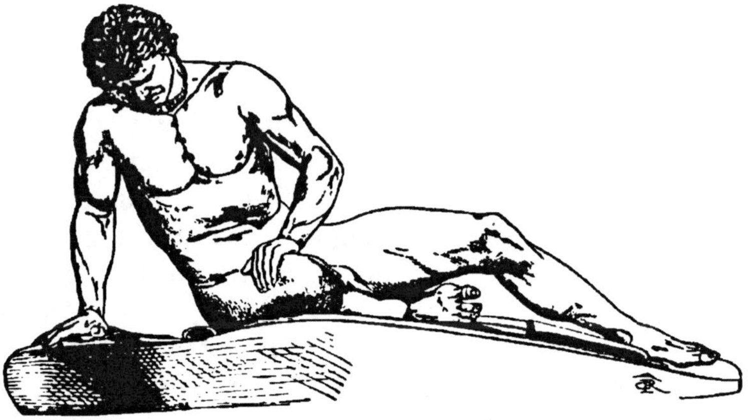

FIG. 54.—THE DYING GAUL.

tory that when these barbarians saw that all was lost they frequently slew their wives and children and then themselves, to avoid being taken as prisoners, which really meant being made slaves. This warrior has thrown himself upon his shield ; his battle-horn is broken, and the sword which has given him the freedom of death has fallen from his hand. His eye is already dim, his right arm can scarce sustain him, his brow is contracted with pain, and it seems as if a sigh escaped his lips. He has not the noble form of the Greeks ; we do not feel the exalted spirit which is shown in the death scenes of some of the Periclean statue heroes; here it is only a rude, barbarous Gaul, suffering death as a brute might; it is very realistic, and when we are near the marble itself we see the coarseness of the skin, the hardened soles of the feet, the coarse hand, and we are sure the artist must have made a true representation of this wild, savage man, who yet had the nobility of nature which would not live to be enslaved (Fig. 54).

These illustrations and remarks will give you some idea of the art of Pergamon, and I shall now leave the subject of Greek sculpture after some account of BOETHUS OF CHALCEDON. His date is very uncertain, though we have accounts of his works by ancient writers. Some scholars believe that he lived about B.C. 275. Many works in chased silver made by Boethus were in the temple of Athena in Lindus in the time of the historian Pliny; there are accounts of a figure of a boy made in gold and one of the youthful Asclepius; but the Boy Strangling a Goose, in the gallery of the Louvre, is his most interesting work for us (Fig. 55). You will remember that even the ancient Egyptians made caricatures and playful, mocking pictures not unlike some of our own day. This boy and goose are of the same spirit, and is intended as a parody on the representations of Hercules struggling with the Nemean lion, which had been represented many times, by Greek artists. The boy seems to be working as hard as any giant could do. The execution of this work is fine. It was probably made for a fountain, the water coming through the beak of the goose. There are several works of ancient sculpture which are of the same spirit, and

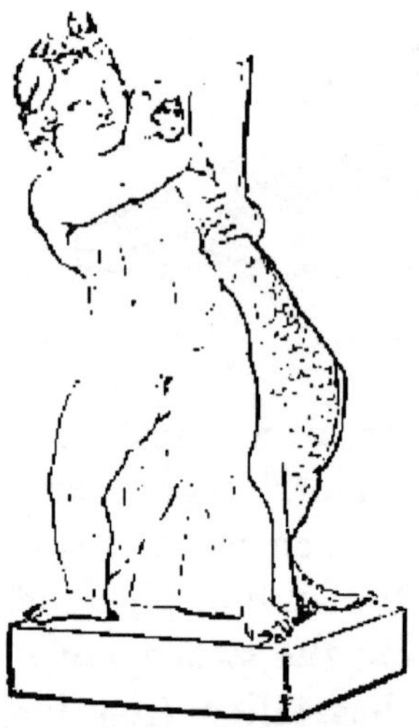

FIG. 55.—BOY AND GOOSE.

for this reason are attributed to Boethus. The Spinario, or Thorn-extractor, in the museum of the Capitol, at Rome, is one of the most charming pieces of *genre* statuary in existence (Fig. 56).

FIG. 56.—SPINARIO.

It represents a boy taking a thorn from his foot. His attitude is natural and graceful, and the purity and simplicity of its style places it on an equality with works of the best period of sculpture. The expression of the face is that of perfect absorption in what he is doing, and is given with great skill and truthfulness. The treatment of the hair is like that of the archaic period, and there will always be some critics who cannot think that such perfection could exist in the sculpture of what we call the Alexandrian age.

## CHAPTER III.

### ANCIENT ITALIAN SCULPTURE.

ANCIENT Italian sculpture was essentially Greek in its spirit, and originated with the Etruscans, a very ancient people in Italy. There are traces of an Oriental influence in the art of Etruria — a suggestion of the sculpture of Egypt and Assyria, just as there is in Greek archaic art; but the real feeling and spirit of it is Greek, and must have been borrowed from Greece in some way.

The different theories and opinions about the Etruscans and their origin do not concern us here; we have to do only with their sculpture as it is seen in the remnants of it now in existence. In the beginning the Etruscans made their statues of clay; marble was very rarely used. Later on they learned the art of working in bronze, and carried it to great perfection. Their bronze works were so numerous that in B.C. 295 Fulvius Flaccus is said to have carried away two thousand statues from Volsinii alone. Some of their figures were colossal, but the greater number were statuettes.

There are some Etruscan bronzes remaining in the museums of Europe. The Etruscans always were copyists rather than original artists; but they copied such excellent things, and did it so well, that their productions are by no means to be despised, and the skill which they acquired caused their bronze and metal work to be highly valued, even in Athens itself.

The Etruscans were physically a more luxurious people than the Greeks, as may be seen in the pictures of them which still remain in the tombs of Corneto and other places. They gave much attention to luxury of living, and the richly decorated goblets and other articles of table furniture which they made may be seen in the Vatican and British Museum, while the delicate and artistic gold work of their personal ornaments is still much admired and copied diligently.

The Romans as a people were patrons of art rather than artists. They seem from very early days to have admired the plastic art of other nations; but of Romans themselves there were very few sculptors; their artists were architects of grand structures rather than workers in the lesser monuments of artistic skill and genius. At first, as we have said, they relied upon the Etruscans, who built their earliest temples and adorned them with sculptures, and the first record which we have of Greek artists working in Rome gives us the names of Damophilus and Gorgasus, who decorated the temple of Ceres with paintings and sculptures. This temple was consecrated in B.C. 493; if its adornment was of the same date, the knowledge of Greek art was brought to Rome at a very early period—at least fifty-six years before the completion of the Parthenon.

But the means by which the whole Roman people were made familiar with the beauties of Greek art are to be found in another direction. It was not the building of their own temples, or any work done by Greek artists in Rome, that gave the Romans their love and appreciation for art; it was rather the art spoils seized by their victorious leaders and brought home to adorn and beautify every portion of the Eternal City. In B.C. 212 Marcellus carried to Rome the spoils he had taken at Syracuse; he exhibited them in his triumphal procession, and afterward consecrated them in the temple of Honor and Valor which he built.

From this time it was the fashion to bring home all the choice things that Roman conquerors could seize, and the number of beautiful objects thus gained for Rome was marvellous.

When Flaminius defeated Philip of Macedon it required two days to gather up the spoils. After Fulvius Nobilior conquered the Ætolians he brought Greek artists to Rome to arrange his festivities, and he exhibited five hundred and fifteen bronze and marble statues which he had taken from the defeated people. When Perseus of Macedon was overcome by Æmilius Paulus it required two hundred and fifty wagons to remove the pictures and statues alone which he displayed in his triumphal procession; among these treasures there was a statue of Athena by Phidias himself. This work of spoiling the Grecian cities which came into their power was diligently carried on by Mummius, Sulla, and others, until at length the Emperor Augustus removed many of the archaic sculptures to Rome. But the works which best pleased the Romans were those of the later school of Athens. The ruling gods at Rome were Mars, Bacchus, and Venus, and the statues of these deities were much valued.

So far, to the time of Augustus, the statues and other objects removed had been the spoils of war; but Caligula and Nero did not hesitate to go in times of peace and act the part of robbers. The first sent a consul in A.D. 31 with orders to bring the best works of art from Greece to Rome to adorn his villas; Nero went so far as to send his agents to bring even the images of the deities from the most sacred temples, together with the offerings made to them, for the decoration of his Golden House; it is said that from Delphi alone he received five hundred statues of bronze.

At first the larger number of these art spoils were so placed as to be constantly seen by the whole Roman people, and there is no doubt that their influence was very great and went far to refine their ideas and to prepare the way for the polish and grace of the Augustan age. Very soon the individual desire for works of art was felt, and wealthy men began to decorate their homes with pictures and statues; and at last these things were thought to be necessary to the proper enjoyment of life.

From all these causes there came about a revival of Greek art under the Romans, and in it many beautiful works were produced. Indeed, the greater portion of the sculptures which are now the pride of the collections all over Europe belong to this period. It cannot be said that the artists of this date originated much, but they followed the greatest masters that ever lived; and if they repeated their subjects they so changed them to suit the spirit of their time that they gave their works a certain effect of being something new, and threw their own individuality about them.

The list of names which can be given as belonging to Greek sculptors who worked at Rome is long, and would have little interest here. Instead of speaking of the artists I shall speak of the most famous works of the time which remain; most of these are so placed that they are seen by travellers, and have become familiar to all the world.

The beautiful statue which is known as the Venus de' Medici is so called because after its discovery it rested for a time in the Medici Palace in Rome. It was found in the seventeenth century in the Portico of Octavia at Rome, and was broken into eleven fragments. The arms from the elbows down are restored; when it was found it had traces of gilding on the hair; the ears are pierced, as if gold rings had sometimes been placed in them. In 1680 Duke Cosmo III. removed it to Florence, where it is the chief glory of the famous Tribune of the Uffizi Gallery. Many persons believe this to have been a copy of the renowned Cnidian Venus by Praxiteles, of which I have told you.

This Venus de' Medici was the work of an Athenian artist named Cleomenes. He was the son of Apollodorus, a sculptor who lived in Rome in the first or second century of the Christian era. (Fig. 57.)

The aim of the sculptor was not to make a goddess, and his work lacks the dignity which was thrown around the more ancient statues of Venus. Cleomenes endeavored to produce a lovely woman in the youth of her beauty. Some critics believe that this Venus is intended to represent the moment when that goddess stood before Paris for judgment. If this story is not well known I will tell how when Peleus and Thetis were married they invited all the gods to their wedding save the goddess Discordia, and she was so offended by this slight that she threw into the midst of the assembly a golden apple on which were the words, "To the fairest." Juno, Minerva, and Venus all claimed it, and Jupiter sent Mercury to conduct these three beautiful goddesses to Paris, that he might decide to which it belonged. His decision gave the apple to Venus; and this so excited the jealousy and hatred of the others that a long list of serious troubles arose until Paris was driven out of Greece, and, going to the house of Menelaus, he saw and loved Helen, carried her off to Troy, and thus brought on the Trojan war of which the world has heard so much ever since. If I were writing a Sunday-school book I could draw many lessons from this story; but as I am only writing about art, I will go back and remind you that many persons try to study these old

FIG. 57.—VENUS DE' MEDICI.

statues and to find out exactly what they mean; some such students say that the moment when Paris pronounced Venus to be the most lovely of the goddesses is the time represented by the sculptor of the Venus de' Medici.

As Venus was the goddess of Love and Beauty, it was natural that statues of her should be multiplied. The Chigi Venus in the Vatican has much the same pose as the Venus de' Medici, but she holds the end of a fringed garment in her hand. The Venus of the Capitol, in Rome, is larger than these; the Venus Callipiga, which was found in the Golden House of Nero, and is now in the Museum of Naples, is also worthy of being mentioned in company with these other exquisite sculptures.

However, there is yet another Venus more admirable and more praised than these. She is called the Venus of Milo, or Melos, and is in the gallery of the Louvre, at Paris. This statue is probably of a later date than those of which we have spoken, and is thought to be the work of Alexandros, the son of Menides of Antiocheia, or one of those sculptors who are called Asiatic Greeks. It is said that the base of this statue with the name of the artist upon it was destroyed, for the purpose of leading the King of France to believe it to be more ancient than it really is (Fig. 58, *frontispiece*).

This magnificent statue was discovered in 1820 by a peasant of the town of Melos, or Milo, on the island of the same name. It was in a niche of a wall which had long been buried. The Marquis of Rivière, who was the French Ambassador at Constantinople, purchased it and presented it to King Louis XVIII., who placed it in the Louvre. It is made from two blocks of marble joined above the drapery which envelops the legs. As the statue now stands it has the tip of the nose and the foot which projects beyond the drapery as they have been restored by modern artists.

This is the only Venus which has come down to us from

the past which represents a goddess rather than a beautiful woman. The form has beauty of the highest type, but it has a grandeur which exalts it far above mere beauty. The pure, majestic expression of the head and face speak the calm dignity of a superior being. I shall quote from Perry, who says: "The Venus de Milo is justly admired, not only for the grandeur of its design, the perfection of its proportion, and the exquisite moulding of the superb and luxuriant form, but for the vivid freshness of the flesh and the velvet softness of the skin, in which it stands unrivalled in ancient and modern art. The extraordinary skill with which minute details, such as the folds of the skin in the neck, are harmonized with the ideal beauty of the whole is beyond all imitation and all praise. The life-like effect of this wonderful masterpiece is greatly enhanced by the rare and perfect preservation of the epidermis and by the beautiful warm, yellowish tinge which the lapse of centuries has given to the marble."

In the Museum at Naples is the Farnesian Hercules, which was found in the Baths of Caracalla, in Rome, in 1540. It was first placed in the Farnese Palace, and from that circumstance received the name by which it is known. It is the work of Glycon, an Athenian, and his name is inscribed upon it. There is little doubt that this is a copy of a more ancient statue by the great Lysippus; that master created representations of Hercules in all ages and forms. Glycon probably worked in the time of Hadrian; and though he copied the design and form of Lysippus, he exaggerated some points so as to injure the effect of the whole. For example, the head is small in proportion to the breadth of the breast and shoulders; and because Hercules was a swift runner the sculptor has made the legs too long to be natural. It is in such particulars as these that the decline of art may be traced, even in works that command admiration (Fig. 59).

The moment in which the god is represented is that which immediately followed his securing the apples of the Hesperides, the wedding present of Ge to Juno. Of all the labors of Hercules, perhaps this was the most arduous. Juno had left these apples with the Hesperides for safe-keeping. These goddesses lived on Mount Atlas, and the serpent Ladon helped them to guard their precious trust. Hercules did not know just where the apples were kept, and this made his task all the more difficult. When, therefore, he arrived at Mount Atlas he offered to hold up the world for Atlas if he would go and fetch the apples. This Atlas did, but refused to take the weight from Hercules again. However, Hercules took the apples and hastened to his master, Eurystheus, with them. While performing this labor he had a terrible struggle with Ladon, and some accounts say that he killed the monster.

FIG. 59.—THE FARNESIAN HERCULES.

Now, the statue represents the god with the apples in his right hand, the world held on his back, while he leans heavily on his club covered with a lion's skin. All the muscles of his body are swollen from his struggle; his head droops, his whole expression of face and form is that of sadness and weariness. The youthfulness and strength with which the older sculptors invested him is not here. It is a splendid work, but it is not of the best; it belongs to an age when there was too much straining after effect, when the moderation of the best Greek masters did not satisfy the spirit of the time; and no sculptor lived whose power equalled that of Phidias or Lysippus.

There are some reliefs and vases of this Roman period that are very interesting. I shall speak of but one relief—the Sacrifice of Iphigenia, which is in Florence. It is called the work of Cleomenes, and his name is inscribed upon it; but there is some doubt as to the genuineness of the inscription. This relief is very beautiful. It represents a priest cutting off the hair of the lovely maiden as a preparation for her sacrifice.

FIG. 60.—THE APOLLO BELVEDERE.

The story runs that Iphigenia was the daughter of Agamemnon, who killed a hart sacred to Diana. To revenge this act the goddess becalmed the Greek fleet on its way to Aulis. The seer Calchas advised Agamemnon to sacrifice his daughter to appease Diana; this he consented to do, but Diana put a hart in the place of the maiden, whom she bore to Tauris and made a priestess. In this relief the maiden has an air of resigned grief; her father stands by himself with his head covered. The sculptor of this relief was not the first who had represented Agamemnon thus, for a painter, Timanthes, had made a picture of this subject about B.C. 400, and in describing it Quintilian said that "when he had painted Calchas sad, Ulysses sadder, and had represented in the face of Menelaus the most poignant grief that art can express, having exhausted the deepest feelings and finding no means of worthily portraying the countenance of *the father*, he covered his head and left it to every man's own heart to estimate his sufferings."

FIG. 61.—HEAD OF APOLLO BELVEDERE.

I come now to the Apollo Belvedere, one of the most celebrated of all the statues in the Vatican, and the best known and most universally admired of all the ancient statues which remain to us. It was found at about the end of the fifteenth century at the ancient city of Antium, where it probably made one of the ornaments of the Imperial Palace. The authorities upon such subjects have never yet agreed as to whether the marble from which it is cut is a marble of Greece or of Italy (Fig. 60).

FIG. 62.—THE STEINHÄUSER HEAD.

This statue has been lauded in all tongues of the civilized world, and nothing could be added to what has been said in its praise; and yet all who see it wish to exalt it still higher if possible. A few years ago another head of Apollo, of Greek marble, was found in a magazine in Rome, by Herr Steinhäuser, by whose name it is known; it is now in the museum at Basle (Figs. 61, 62).

Though this statue has been so much studied and admired it has never yet been satisfactorily explained, and there are several important questions about it which cannot be answered with certainty. Nothing is known of its age or of the name of its sculptor. It is not described by any ancient writer, neither can any one say whether it is an original or a copy; and above all in importance is the question of what this beautiful young god is doing—what is the meaning of it?

The answers of the authorities to these queries vary so much that here I shall only mention the theory which I love, and which is accepted by many. When the statue was found the left hand was missing, and a bow was believed to have been the article which it held; and it was said that Apollo had just shot an arrow on some dreadful flight, and was watching for its effect. This theory was the principal one until 1860, when a scholar, Stephani, called attention to the fact that in St. Petersburg there is a bronze statuette, less than two feet high, which is almost exactly the same as the Apollo Belvedere—too nearly the same to be an accidental likeness. Now, as this is an antique bronze, it seems to prove that both it and the marble of the Vatican are copies of an ancient work. The statuette is called the Stroganoff Apollo, because it belongs to the collection of a nobleman of that name. It is believed to be one of a number of bronzes which were found near Janina in 1792, and given

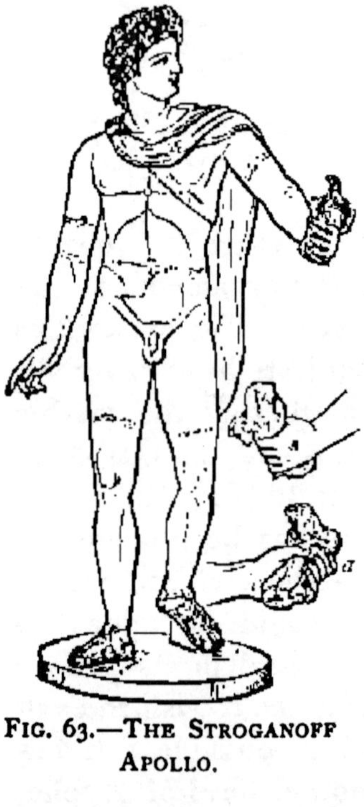

FIG. 63.—THE STROGANOFF APOLLO.

by the son of Ali Pasha to his physician, Dr. Frank (Fig. 63).

The chief importance of this discovery was the fact that the left hand was perfect, and did not hold a bow, but some soft, elastic substance which Stephani believes to be the ægis, or shield, of Jupiter, on which was the head of Medusa. The sight of this shield paralyzed those who saw it; and though it belonged to Jupiter and Minerva, Jupiter sometimes lent it to his son Apollo to aid him in his warfare; such instances are recorded by Homer. After Stephani had told his idea of it, the German scholar Ludwig Preller pointed out what seems to be the true meaning of it by suggesting that Apollo was extending this dreadful *ægis* before the sight of the Gauls at Delphi, in B.C. 279. History relates that when the Gauls approached Delphi the people asked the oracle if they should carry away and conceal the treasures of the temple. The oracle replied, "I myself and the White Maidens (meaning Athena and Artemis) will take care of that." Then four thousand Greeks stood by ready to defend the sacred place; but in the midst of the battle the youthful god came down through the roof of the temple, and the White Maidens left their own altars to aid him in driving back the barbarous foe. A great tempest arose, and rocks fell from Parnassus on the heads of the Gauls, and it seemed as if all the powers of heaven and earth had united to sustain the Greeks against their enemies. It is also written that the spectres of Greek heroes who had long been dead were seen in the midst of the battle dealing death upon the Gauls. But above all the fury of the tempest and the noise of war the clashing of the shield and spear of Athena and the twanging sound of the oft-discharged bow of Artemis were heard, while the flash of the awful shield of Apollo was seen to be even more vivid and terrific than the forked lightnings themselves.

It is recorded that after this victory two statues of

Apollo and one each of Athena and Artemis were offered in the temple of Apollo as thank-offerings for its preservation and the victory over the Gauls. It is delightful to regard the Apollo Belvedere as a copy of one of these, and this view of it is most satisfying. Lübke, in speaking of this theory, says: "Not till now have we understood the Apollo Belvedere. In unveiled beauty we see the elegant form of the slender figure, the left shoulder only being covered by the chlamys, which falls down over the arm, which, far outstretched, holds the ægis with its Medusa head. The right arm is slightly turned aside, but both hands have been unskilfully restored. The attitude of the god is full of pathos, and is conceived at a dramatic moment. Ardently excited and filled with divine anger, with which is mingled a touch of triumphant scorn, the intellectual head is turned sideward, while the figure, with elastic step, is hastening forward. The eye seems to shoot forth lightning; there is an expression of contempt in the corners of the mouth, and the distended nostrils seem to breathe forth divine anger. It is a bold attitude thus transfixed in marble, full of life-like and excited action."

In the Iliad Homer describes the scene when Jupiter gave the ægis to Apollo, that he might put the Achæans to flight with it. In connection with the Apollo Belvedere it is well to recall that description which is thus translated by Lord Derby

> "While Phœbus motionless his ægis held,
> Thick flew the shafts, and fast the people fell
> On either side; but when he turned its flash
> Full in the faces of the astonished Greeks,
> And shouted loud, their spirits within them quailed,
> Their fiery courage borne in mind no more."

It is very interesting to know that many who believe that the Apollo Belvedere represents that god when terrifying the Gauls, believe also that the statues of the " White Maidens" rushing forth from their temples to aid him are in existence, the Artemis being the statue at the Louvre known as "*Diane à la Biche*," and the Minerva being the Athena with spear and shield in the museum of the Capitol at Rome.

This statue of Artemis, or Diana, has been in France since the time of Henry IV. Formerly it was at Versailles, but is now one of the treasures of the Louvre. The left hand with the bow is restored. The effect of the figure is that of lightness combined with strength. She is going forward rapidly, with her eyes fixed on some distant object, and draws an arrow from her quiver even as she flies. This figure corresponds to the Apollo Belvedere in its spirit and apparent earnestness of purpose; it is of the same proportions, and in such details of treatment as the rich sandals it plainly belongs to the time and the school of the Apollo—indeed, there is no reason why it might not have formed a part of a group in which the Apollo stood. (Fig. 64.)

FIG. 64.—DIANE À LA BICHE.

If we think of this Diana simply as an ideal huntress hastening to the chase the statue is very beautiful, and a remarkable example of such a subject; but when she is regarded as one of the " White Maidens" rushing forth to aid her brother in defending his temple against a barbarous enemy she is invested with a deeper interest; she becomes an important actor in a terrible drama, and those of us who could have no sympathy with her love for hunting are roused to an enthusiastic hope that she will succeed in doing her part to turn the savage foe away from the sacred hill of Pytho, and thus preserve its temple and its treasures.

FIG. 65.—ATHENA OF THE CAPITOL.

The statue of Athena, advancing with spear and shield, is supposed to be a third member of the group which commemorated the victory over the Gauls. The position of the two goddesses would indicate that they were represented as hastening from opposite directions toward the Apollo Belvedere, the central figure of the whole. The whole bearing of this statue carries out the impression which Homer gives of the delight with which Athena led the Greeks to battle; she is full of eagerness, and rushes forward with the undaunted vigor of the confidence and courage of one who goes to fight for a just and holy cause (Fig. 65).

Whether this "Gallic theory," as it is called, concerning the Apollo, Diana, and Athena be correct or no, it is the most satisfactory in sentiment of any that has been advanced, and certainly, when we consider the three statues in this connection, there is nothing inharmonious in the supposition that they made the important parts of a whole which may have had many other figures of lesser importance in it.

There are many other statues of the Roman period in various museums, but I shall leave this part of our subject here, and speak briefly of the historical sculpture in the reliefs upon the triumphal arches of the Eternal City. In an age when martial glory was the chief desire of man, and among a people who accorded to successful generals the highest honors, it was most natural that the conquerors should desire to place some monument of their exploits where it would be constantly before the eyes of the people, and thus keep in perpetual remembrance their valiant deeds and their great successes.

We read that pictures of the foreign scenes of sieges and battles were displayed in public places in Rome at a very early date. We cannot find records of plastic works of this

FIG. 66.—TRIUMPHAL PROCESSION FROM ARCH OF TITUS.

sort before the time of the emperors, but after such sculptures came into favor they were multiplied rapidly. The principal historical reliefs in Rome were upon the arches of

Claudius, Titus, Trajan, Marcus Aurelius, and Septimius Severus, and on the architrave of the temple of Minerva in the Forum.

Of the arch of Claudius there are some remaining fragments of sculpture, now in the Villa Borghese. The arch of Titus was erected to celebrate the taking of Jerusalem in A.D. 70. It was restored in 1822. The frieze represents both a triumphal procession and one of sacrifice. The picture we give here shows a company of warriors in the dress of peace, who bear articles of booty taken from the conquered city. They have the candelabra with seven branches, the table of the shew-bread, the silver trumpets, etc. This will give you a good idea of these reliefs. (Fig. 66.)

The arch of Trajan no longer stands, and its reliefs are now on the arch of Constantine ; but Trajan's Pillar is one of the best preserved of all the antique monuments of Rome, and with some account of this column and a picture from it we will leave the historical sculptures of Rome. The Senate and people of Rome decreed that this column should be erected to the memory of Trajan, and it was in the centre of the Forum which bore the same name—the Forum Trajani. The column is about one hundred and six feet high, and originally was surmounted by a bronze statue of Trajan, which was replaced by one of St. Peter by Pope Sixtus V. A band of reliefs runs around this pillar in a spiral form ; this band is six hundred feet long, and the sculptures represent Trajan's campaign against the Dacians. Many of the figures lose their effect on account of the height at which they are placed. There are more than a hundred scenes upon it, in which are about twenty-five hundred human figures, besides many horses and other objects. The whole is executed with the greatest care.

The real object of the whole work was to glorify the Emperor Trajan, and he is represented in many of the scenes ; sometimes he is conducting engagements, storming a fort, or encouraging his troops; again he is holding an audience, protecting the women of a conquered city, or sitting in judgment on captives. Fig. 67 represents the Dacians assaulting a Roman fort. It is winter, and while some have crossed the ice in safety, others have broken through. Everything about it is represented in the most life-like and matter-of-fact manner, and this shows distinctly the principal difference between the Greek and the Roman art when the latter was not influenced by the former. It is pure, realistic, historical sculpture, and this pillar shows this at its very best estate; it is a splendid specimen of this kind of art. In all these many scenes there are but two mythological figures: one is Selene, used to represent Night, and the other is *Jupiter tonans*, who indicates Storm. But the correctness and elegance of the sculptures show what the Greek teaching did for the Romans; for it was to the Greeks that the latter owed their knowledge of the human form and their power to render it properly in sculpture.

FIG. 67.—FROM THE RELIEFS OF TRAJAN'S COLUMN.

The last sort of ancient sculpture of which I shall speak is portrait sculpture, and perhaps this belongs also to historical sculpture, for it is by means of statues and busts that we know the faces and forms of many of the great men and women who hold their places in the regard of the world through all the centuries, because they were concerned in the events which make up what we call the history of the world. We have said that in Greece in very early times there were no portrait sculptures; gradually they were introduced until, in the time of Alexander, portrait statues were almost numberless, and these and busts were used for the decoration of libraries and public buildings, as well as for the adornment of squares and places of resort in the open air.

The finest life-size statue which remains from the Greeks is that of Sophocles, of which we give a picture (Fig. 68). It was not found until about 1839, and was presented to Pope Gregory XVI. by Cardinal Antonelli; it is in the museum of the Lateran. This engraving from it shows its beauties so well that it is scarcely needful to speak of it in detail. This statue is valuable not only as a portrait of Sophocles, but as a representation of a true product of the highest and best of Athenian civilization and culture; of an elegant, aristocratic man who was trained in gymnastic and warlike exercises which developed his physical parts, as well as in science, philosophy, and music—in various deep studies and lighter accomplishments which rendered him profound and scholarly, and at the same time elegant and graceful. "The attitude, though simple, is well chosen to show the most graceful lines of the figure; and the position of the arms—the one gracefully enveloped in the himation, and the other firmly planted on the hip—gives to the whole form an air of mingled ease and dignity. The face is handsome and full of winning grace, and bears the stamp not only of the creative genius of the poet, but of the experience of the active citizen; of one who has felt both the joys and the sufferings of human lot, and preserved amid them the constitutional calmness, the gentle benevolence, the tranquil, meditative piety for which he was renowned and loved by the people among whom he lived and sang."

FIG. 68.—PORTRAIT STATUE OF SOPHOCLES.

Among the Romans portrait sculpture held a position of importance. This people had always placed great value upon the likenesses of the dead, and from the earliest times had used different means of making them. In the very early days of the nation the custom prevailed of making masks of the faces of the dead in wax, and these masks were worn in the funeral procession by one of the mourners, who also wore the dress and insignia of the departed. The first aim in these masks was to have an exact resemblance to the dead; and this idea was carried on through all the eras of Roman art, and is a strong distinguishing feature between Greek and Roman sculpture; for while the Greeks wished to reproduce the face of one of whom they made a bust or statue, they did not hesitate to idealize that face; but the Romans labored to make an exact likeness of the man, leaving him in his statue as nothing more than he looked to be. This manner of portraiture often does great injustice to its model, for the changing expressions which come with emotions and with conversation often illuminate the plainest faces with a rare beauty; therefore the aim of portraiture should be to give the very most and best that can be imagined as coming to the face which is reproduced.

Fig. 69.—Statue of Augustus.

I can speak of but a few of the almost numberless Roman portrait sculptures.

This statue of Augustus was found in 1863 in a villa built by his wife, Livia, about nine miles from Rome, at Porta Prima. It is a noble work, and every minute detail of the ornamentation has a force and meaning that can be explained. At the same time the whole work is full of strength and dignity, which comes from the character of the man himself, and is in no sense dependent on all the emblems of his rank and power, with which the dress is loaded (Fig. 69). This statue is in the Vatican, and there one can compare it with the exquisite bust known as the "Young Augustus" and with the statue of the emperor when aged, in which he is veiled as a priest. The study of these three sculptures, thus fortunately near each other, is most interesting.

The Roman women who held important positions were frequently honored with statues. Among those that remain none is more interesting than this of the elder Agrippina. She was a woman of great strength and equally great purity of character, and as we study this statue we can easily understand that she could perform the duties of a general when occasion demanded this service, and when that neces-

FIG. 70.—AGRIPPINA THE ELDER.

sity was past could nurse the sick and wounded with all the tenderness of a true womanly nature. It is in every way a noble work of art, combining grace, dignity, and the aristocratic refinement of a high-born lady. The drapery of this and other similar statues is very beautiful, and fully satisfies all artistic demands. We have full proof that such garments were in actual use by the women of Greece and Rome (Fig. 70).

It was not unusual for the great men and women of Rome to be represented in portrait statues with the attributes of gods and goddesses. Livia appears as Ceres, Julia as Flora, and so on; and during the best days of Roman art these statues were very beautiful. But at last they, like all other sculptures, grew less and less worthy, until they became positively absurd, and lacked any power to command our admiration.

What is thus true of portrait sculpture is true of all Roman art. Its decline kept step with the decline of the nation, and both fell at length into a pitiable state of feebleness and corruption. From this we are glad to turn to the study of Christian art, which, even in its primary struggles, when groping its way through ignorance and helplessness, was still a living thing, and held the promise of a new life—a *renaissance* of that which had gradually died in Greece and Rome.

## CHAPTER IV.

### MEDIÆVAL SCULPTURE, FROM THE FIFTH TO THE FIFTEENTH CENTURY.

THE ancient or classic Italian sculpture of which we have spoken may be said to have extended to about the middle of the fourth century of the Christian era. The arch of Constantine was one of its latest works, and is interesting as an example of the decline of art. The sculptures upon it, which were taken from the arch of Trajan, executed two centuries earlier, are so superior to those that were added in the time of Constantine, that nothing could give one a clearer idea of the decadence of sculpture than seeing the works of two periods thus placed side by side.

After the time of Constantine, when the Christians were no longer forced to hide their art in the catacombs, they began to have a sculpture of their own. The first Christians in Rome were brought into contact with the worship of Isis and Pan, Venus and Apollo, and were filled with horror at the sight of the statues of these divinities. They believed that any representation of the human form was forbidden by the commandment which says, "Thou shalt not make to thyself any graven image, nor the likeness of anything that is in the heaven above, or in the earth beneath, or in the water under the earth." Thus it happened that when the early Christians desired to represent the Saviour they employed painting, such as is found in the catacombs, rather than sculpture, and separate statues are the rarest remains of early Christian art.

The oldest Christian statue which is known in marble is that of St. Hippolytus, which is in the Museum of the Lateran Palace, where there are also two small statues of Christ as the Good Shepherd, which were found in the catacombs.

FIG. 71.—STATUE OF ST. PETER.

The most important statue of this period is that of St. Peter, which is held in great reverence by Roman Catholics, who kiss its toe as they enter the church of St. Peter's at Rome, and press their foreheads against the extended foot. The statue is of bronze, and some antiquarians believe that it is the Jupiter of the Capitol changed so as to answer for a statue of St. Peter ; others say that it was cast from the metal of the statue of Jupiter ; and the usual belief is that it was made by the order of Pope Leo I. about the middle of the fifth century as a thank-offering for the deliverance of Rome from the barbarian Attila by the miraculous protection of St. Peter and St. Paul. This statue is too rude to belong to classic art, though it is of remarkable excellence for a work of the fifth century (Fig. 71).

The principal use of sculpture by the early Christians was for the decoration of the sarcophagi, or burial-cases. These were cut in bas-reliefs after the manner of the ancients, the subjects being taken from the life of Christ ; the ornaments were the Christian emblems, such as the lamb, cross, vine, palm, dove, and the monogram of Christ. As time passed the designs were more and more elaborate ; stories from the Old Testament were frequently illustrated, and numerous figures were crowded together, with many symbols ingeniously inserted to make the meaning of the whole more clear.

The largest number and the best of these sarcophagi are now in the museums of the Lateran and the Vatican. In the centre of one of the finest of these is a shell, in which are the half figures of the two who were buried in this sarcophagus. At the upper left hand is the Saviour before the tomb of Lazarus ; one of the sisters of the dead man kisses the hand of Jesus ; next to this is the Denial of Peter ; nearest the shell Moses reaches up to receive the Table of the Law. On the right of the shell, in the upper row, is the Sacrifice of Isaac and the Washing of Pilate's Hands. On the lower row, beginning at the left, is Moses causing the Water to flow from the Rock ; next is the Apprehension of Peter, and next, Daniel in the Lions' Den.

Besides these there are the Healing of the Blind and the Miracle of the Loaves and Fishes. This will show how elaborate the carving is on these burial-cases, and how the subjects from the Old and New Testaments are mingled without order or apparent reason. These sarcophagi have been found in various parts of Italy and in France, and are seen in many museums.

In no part of the Roman Empire was sculpture as favorably regarded by the early Christians as at Byzantium. Several attempts to adorn the city with statues and other works of art were made there, and many of the Greek sculptures which had been carried to Rome were again borne off to decorate this new Capitol. The Emperor Constantine there erected a column a hundred feet high, and placed his statue on it; Theodosius also erected a column and an obelisk; but Justinian excelled all these, and about 543 A.D. set up a monument with a colossal equestrian statue of himself in bronze upon it. The column which supported this statue was of brick masonry covered with plates of bronze. From the accounts we have of it we conclude that this was a fine work for its time; it was called the Augustio, and was placed on the Augusteum near the church of St. Sophia; in the sixteenth century it had been overthrown and broken in pieces, and the metal was then melted down. The artist who executed the Augustio was Eustathius of Rome, who was sent to Byzantium for this purpose.

But the Byzantine Christians soon grew into a fixed disapproval of statues, and favored only the lesser works of art. Ivory-carving, which long before had been brought from the East by the Greeks, now came into special favor, and the Byzantine artists devoted all their talent to making beautiful works of this sort. The most important of these carvings which remains is in the cathedral of Ravenna. It is the episcopal chair or cathedra of Maximianus, and was made between 546 and 552 (Fig. 72).

This chair is composed entirely of carved plates of ivory ; scenes from the life of Joseph and other similar designs are represented, and these are surrounded by a great variety of small figures, which form a sort of framework around the principal parts ; for example, animals and birds among vine-branches, and all arranged in a life-like and artistic manner. So large a work as this chair in ivory is unusual. The greater number of ivory carvings are upon small objects, such as drinking-cups and other vessels, book-covers and diptychs, or tablets for writing, of which fine specimens remain and are seen in art collections.

Fig. 72.—From the Cathedra of Maximianus.

Diptychs were carved ivory tablets, with the inner surface waxed for writing, and were used by the early Christians, as they had been by the ancients. The illustration given here is from the diptych of the Consul Areobrudus, and belongs to the year 506 (Fig. 73). The whole design upon it represents a contest with lions and bears ; the scene is where—the circus gates being thrown open—the animals rush into the arena to be slain by the gladiators. Some diptychs are ornamented with subjects from the life of Christ and other religious themes.

About the beginning of the tenth century ivory-carving was much used for church purposes. The smaller altars were covered with it, the vessels used for the Holy Sacrament were made of it, magnificent covers for church books were carved, and as much thought seems to have been given to the designs upon these small objects as had formerly been devoted to the splendid temples of the ancients. Ivory-carving extended from Byzantium into Germany and

FIG. 73.—DIPTYCH. *Zurich.*

other Western countries, and along with it went the working in rich and precious metals, which had also been practised somewhat by the earlier Christians.

During the tenth century the metal works were very costly, and the different cathedrals and churches rivalled each other in possessions of this sort. Altar tables were covered with embossed metal plates, which were extended down from the top of the table to the floor, forming antependiums, as they are called, in the same way that those of cloth are now used. These plates of metal were worked into designs in relief, ornamented with delicate filigree work, with paintings in enamel, and even with rare antique cameos and exquisite gems. Crucifixes were also made of metals and richly adorned, as well as all the vessels and smaller articles used in the service and ceremonials of the church—incense-burners, candlesticks, tabernacles and reliquaries, or caskets for preserving relics. In the sacristies of many old churches and in art collections these rare, costly articles are still preserved, and are of great interest in the study of art.

Many of the designs used on these objects were quaint and even grotesque, while the drawing of the figures and the arrangement of the subjects is often done in the crudest and most inartistic manner. Vessels for church use were made in the shapes of griffins, dragons, cranes, lions, and other curious birds and beasts, while the human faces represented sometimes had enamelled or jewelled eye-balls. In one case the eyes of the Saviour were made of large carbuncles; you can understand that this would give an expression quite the opposite of that gentleness and peace which we look for in the face of the Redeemer. In truth, there is so much of the grotesque and even barbarous element in many of these works, that we can but ridicule while we recognize the industry and care which was expended upon them. It is also difficult to understand how the feeling for art and the practice of it which had attained to such perfection among the ancients could have died out of the world so completely, for in these mediæval days it existed nowhere on the face of the earth.

About the beginning of the eleventh century bronze casting came to hold an important place in the art of Germany, and as architecture now received more attention, and bronze gates, and occasionally bronze figures of bishops and other church dignitaries, were used for the decoration of church buildings, we may say that bronze works made the medium through which sculpture in connection with architecture was again brought into use. At Hildesheim there is still a bronze gate at the principal entrance to the cathedral, which was cast in 1015, and in various places in Germany, France, and Northern Italy works of this kind are seen which belong to the eleventh century, while a bit of stone or wood sculpture of this period is very rarely met.

The twelfth century brought about a great change in sculpture and its uses. This century was a period of remarkable activity in every department of human life. The Crusades were then preached, and armies of zealous Christians went forth to redeem Jerusalem from the power of the Pagans; in this century all the institutions of chivalry flourished; the nations of the world had more intercourse with each other than had before existed; commerce was extended into new channels; men were more individual and thought more independently for themselves than they had done hitherto; and, in short, human intellect all over the Western world seemed to be awakening from a long, deep sleep, and to be inspired with strength and activity.

With all the other changes there came revivals of architecture and sculpture, which went hand in hand, and in the beginning can scarcely be separated from each other. The early Christians had been content with the decoration of interiors; now the exteriors received much attention, and the portals or entrances to the churches were richly decorated with statues and other sculptured ornaments, and the exterior decoration soon extended to many portions of the edifices. In the interiors, too, the altars, fonts, choir-screens, and other objects were made of carved stone or of stucco, which hardened like stone, and were all richly ornamented with sculpture. A completely new spirit seemed to possess the artists, who thus found a satisfactory field for their labors, and the period known as the *Romanesque* was thus ushered in.

We cannot claim that the works of the twelfth century were free from the faults of the preceding eras, or were satisfactory to our artistic sense; but we may say that they show

FIG. 74.—FROM THE FAÇADE OF CHARTRES CATHEDRAL.

the effect of the new life which had come into the world, and give unerring promise of the progress which followed. The same improvement is seen in bronze-casting as in sculpture; and though to our eyes it still remains crude and ungraceful, yet by comparing it with the work of the previous century we mark a hopeful and important change.

Germany, in its different provinces, took the lead in this artistic progress; but France was not far behind; and, indeed, in the cathedral of Chartres the first promise was given of the splendid church portals of the early Gothic style of architecture which followed the Romanesque. In this cathedral, too, we see for the first time an attempt to make the head and face a reproduction of nature rather than a repetition of the classic head, which had come to be so imperfectly copied that it had degenerated into a caricature. (Fig. 74.)

Other cathedrals at St. Denis, Le Mans, Bourges, and Paris are splendid examples of the art of this time; and when we remember how Italy took the lead of these northern countries in later days, it seems strange that at this era she was far behind them. It is even true that the first works in Northern Italy which indicated that the awakening which had come north of the Alps had reached that country were executed wholly or in part by German artists; but by the end of the twelfth century both the sculpture and bronze-casting of Italy gave promise of the great revival of true art which was to come in that home of the arts.

However, it is not possible to connect the art of Italy with that of any other country in any comprehensive sense. Italian art may be said to have died out more completely in the beginning of the middle ages than did the art of northern nations; its period of decline, too, was longer; but when its awakening came it aroused itself and took on new strength by a method of its own, and may be said to have been distinct from northern art in every respect, and divided from it by its different spirit as clearly as Italy was divided from other lands by the towering summits of the Alps.

About the beginning of the thirteenth century there dawned upon the northern nations a new era in literature. Hitherto the written language had been the monkish Latin; now the poets began to use their own tongues. This new writing may be said to have commenced with the Provençal poets, who were followed by those of Northern France; but it was in Germany that such song broke forth as showed how the national feeling had been repressed, and how, now that it had burst its bonds, it resembled the freshets of spring when they escape from the icy hand of Winter and rush from one point to another, brushing aside every obstacle which lies in their way. I cannot here speak in detail of these poets and their works, but Hartmann of Aue, Walther von der Vogelweid, Wolfram and Gottfried of Strasburg are names which grow brighter with passing centuries.

At the same time with this advance in letters there came, in North-eastern France, the new Gothic style of architecture, which had the effect to revive sculpture and in a degree restore to it the importance it had in classic days. Now, the same artist was both architect and sculptor, and the result was that architecture was so arranged as to afford an honorable place to sculpture, which, in its turn, added much to the grand and full effect of architecture.

Artists now began to study nature and the life about them in preference to the antique, and the sculptors of the thirteenth century were fortunate in living in a time when costumes were picturesque and suited to artistic representations. The dress of a knight was as graceful as one could wish, with its flowing lines and the mantle clasped at one side of the neck, or thrown loosely over the arm and shoulder; and the costume of the other sex, with the full folds of the lower garment fastened by the girdle, and veiling without hiding the movement of the figure, was scarcely less fitting for the artist's use than were the classic robes of the Greeks.

The effect of the sculpture of this period was frequently heightened by the use of color. The draperies were enriched by gold ornaments, and painted in rich blue and red, while the flesh parts were delicately tinted. Colors were used with care, and often served to conceal the defects in the sculpture itself, and were thus of great advantage. Color was most frequently used in interior decoration, but it was not unknown upon exterior portals, and porches were introduced to protect this polychromy, as the painting of sculpture was called.

The subjects now represented in sculpture were far more numerous than formerly. While the life of Christ and the Virgin still made the central and most important topic, there were added scenes from the lives of the saints, those who were regarded as the patrons of the city or those to whom the edifice was dedicated being most frequently chosen. New symbolic designs were made showing the flight of time by seasons and months; others represented the virtues, and even the customs and habits of the people were sometimes introduced. There were also humorous representations, even on sacred edifices. Water-pipes and gutter-spouts were ended with the heads of monsters and curious animals, and even with grotesque faces; in short, the smaller details of the architecture of this period show the vividness of the imagination of the time. For example, the leaf-work which was used in the ornamental portions of sculpture had hitherto copied the antique acanthus leaf; now the flowers and leaves native to France were the models of the sculptors, and a charming variety of life-like ornament was the result.

The church of Ste. Chapelle, at Paris, completed about 1248, was the first edifice in which this style was seen in its full development. Here, for the first time, the statues were not placed in the stiff, perpendicular posture, but, by being inclined to different positions, had a light appearance and an air of movement, which was a great relief from the rigidity which had ruled up to this time.

The cathedral at Rheims, however, shows the perfection of thirteenth-century art. It is conceded to be the best example of church building of its time, and its façade the most beautiful structure of the Middle Ages. Its wealth of sculpture is wonderful; its three great portals, the buttresses, the space above the great window and various other portions are so much ornamented that the whole effect is that of a forest of sculpture, and it is difficult to turn from it to consider the architecture of the edifice. It naturally follows that in this vast amount of artistic work there is no equality of excellence; some of the statues are like those of an earlier date: some are too tall and awkward; others too short and rotund; but there are many elegant figures, full of grace and dignity, with the drapery falling in natural folds, and an air of life and freedom of movement about the heads quite unknown before this time.

In one of the side portals of this cathedral there is a figure of Christ which was not surpassed by any work of this period. The study of every portion of the figure is so perfect as to surprise us when we remember that anatomy was not then studied by artists as it had been in classic times or as it has been in more recent days. This statue holds an orb in the left hand, and the right hand is uplifted; not only the nails of the fingers, but the structure of all the joints is skilfully indicated.

It frequently happens that the reliefs are far more excellent than the statues of mediæval date. This is so noticeable that it would seem as if the best sculptors preferred to make the reliefs, and that the figures were left to those of less talent. On the pediment at Rheims the Last Judgment is represented in five divisions, and these reliefs are among the most beautiful sculptures of this century. The scene of the Resurrection of the Dead is arranged in two rows of figures; a section of it is here given (Fig. 75).

There are twenty-nine of these little figures in the whole subject, and the variety of positions and the naturalness of the various expressions are all that could be desired in any age of art. The forms are in good proportions, and the faces are filled with fear, surprise, hope, and supplication. A volume might be written upon the sculptures of the Rheims Cathedral which would be full of interest to the student of mediæval art.

FIG. 75.—FROM THE NORTH TRANSEPT OF RHEIMS CATHEDRAL.

Critics have compared the progress and life which pervaded the art of the thirteenth century with the spirit of the age of Phidias. The two periods are alike in the fact that the artists of each broke away from the traditions of those who had preceded them, and took up their work with a desire to come nearer to nature. They were alike, too, in the union of architecture and sculpture, and in the fact that all kinds of sculpture were required for the adornment of a single structure. Colossal and full-sized statues, statuettes, reliefs, and a great variety of simply ornamental designs were lavished upon the Christian cathedral, as they had been upon the Greek temple; and in one case as in the other the various groups and scenes represented were intended to show forth religious mysteries, and to illustrate the working of the supreme power which controls the world in relation to human beings.

But I must leave this part of our subject and speak of the monumental sculpture of the thirteenth century. While many of the tomb statues still retained a general resemblance to those of the past, there were many examples of new strength and progress. In a church near Le Mans the statue of Berengaria, the wife of Richard Cœur de Lion, who died in 1219, was made with open eyes; this gives a very life-like appearance to the face, and the whole head is as noble as that of an antique statue; the drapery is full and free; the feet rest upon a dog, which is the emblem of fidelity, and in the hands is a casket. There is something about this statue which appeals to us—a human element which had been sadly wanting in the monumental statues of the preceding centuries.

But the series of reliefs which were made for the Cathedral of St. Denis were the most important tomb sculptures of this period. They were sixteen in number, and represented princes of the early lines of French sovereigns down to the thirteenth century. Of course those of the Merovingians and Carlovingians could not be portrait statues, and the heads of both kings and queens are all of the same type until those of Philip the Bold, who died in 1285, and his wife, Isabella of Aragon, who died in 1271, are reached. These two are intended to be portraits, and they show the individual characters of these royal personages. In all France there is no more interesting succession of monuments than these.

In Germany the Romanesque style of architecture and the sculpture which went with it held their sway much longer than in France, and the new Gothic style made its way very slowly in the countries north of France. Slight traces of its influence in one way and another may be found about the middle of the thirteenth century; but it was not until the very end of this period that the Gothic style had affected German art, except in the south-western portions of the country. These provinces bordered upon France, and formed a sort of middle ground between the two nations. In Strasburg, at the end of the century, a cathedral was built which was one of the most splendid examples of a union of the two styles that could be produced. The sculptures show the effect of the new French manner in

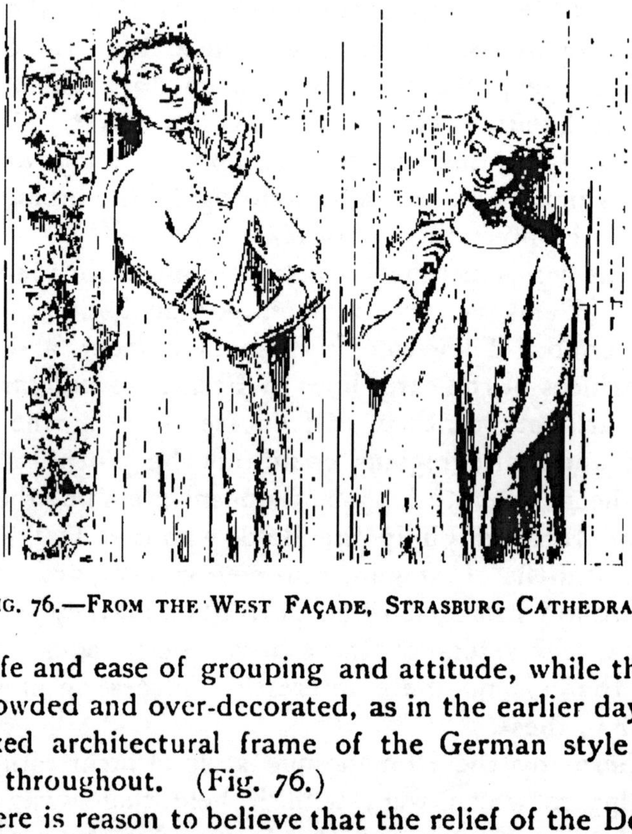

FIG. 76.—FROM THE WEST FAÇADE, STRASBURG CATHEDRAL.

their life and ease of grouping and attitude, while they are still crowded and over-decorated, as in the earlier days, and the fixed architectural frame of the German style is preserved throughout. (Fig. 76.)

There is reason to believe that the relief of the Death of the Virgin, at Strasburg, was the work of Sabina von Steinbach, a daughter of the architect of the west façade of the cathedral. The grouping is fine, and the transparent drapery, which reminds us of the same effects in antique sculpture, is beautifully executed.

In the Cathedral of Freiburg, the nave of which was completed in 1270, there are some very fine sculptures, which are like the Rheims works in spirit and execution; a figure of the Madonna is one of the best statues of the time in any country. There is much to admire in the whole of this cathedral. Here and there in Germany there are some tomb-sculptures of the thirteenth century, which are simple, noble, and individual; but the progress of art here was much less rapid than in France.

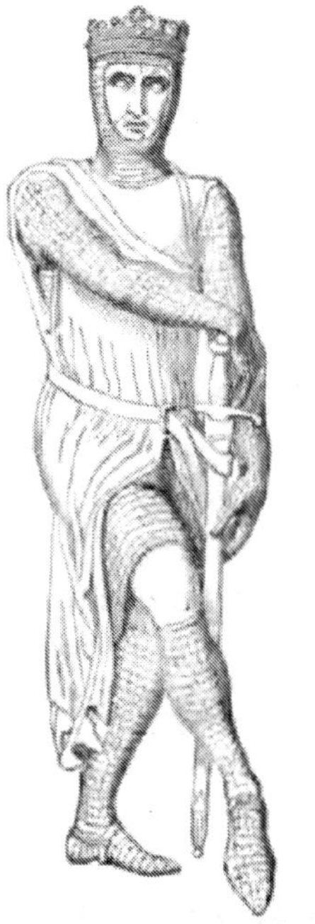

FIG. 77.—DUKE ROBERT OF NORMANDY.

Another marked event in the art history of the thirteenth century was the introduction of sculpture into England. The few pieces of plastic art which existed in that country before this date were not sufficient in number or excellence to merit the name of English sculpture.

The first important step was made about the end of the twelfth century, when Guillaume de Sens, a French architect, was employed to build a new choir to Canterbury Cathedral. Not long after this the Temple Church was erected; then Westminster Abbey followed, and at length, under Henry III., all the arts were rapidly advanced in his kingdom. This king summoned artists and skilled workmen from different countries, and portrait-sculpture received especial attention in the England of that day. By comparing English tomb-sculpture with that of other countries, it is seen that the aim of the artists was to make the statues resemble those whose memories they honored, far more than other nations had done. The illustration given here, with its air of life—almost of motion--is a good example of what I mean (Fig. 77).

The sculptures upon the English exteriors, and, indeed, upon the interiors of edifices, were far less lavish than on the Continent; but in Wells Cathedral, completed before 1250, there is a wealth of sculpture for an English church of this date, and from this time forward the plastic arts were of great importance in Great Britain.

With the beginning of the fourteenth century there were great changes in the religious and political affairs of all Europe. The Pope no longer held the supreme authority that had belonged to his office, and the imperial power was also much shaken. We cannot speak of these subjects in detail here, but the result to art of these changes was seen in a development of individualism, and the effects of it did not show an improvement when considered as a whole, though it has some new features which were attractive.

In these days of which we now speak the word citizen had a far deeper meaning than ever before, and the growth of wealth and prosperity in the citizen classes gave a new impulse to all the activities of life, and to art along with others.

This new life and spirit gave more freedom to artists, and they attempted new effects, so that a far greater variety was made in their works. The statue of the Madonna, for example, was so often repeated that it afforded an opportunity for all sorts of experiments, by which the sculptors tried to add to the deep feeling and the devotion that had already been expressed in the representations of the sweet Mother of Christ. But just here they failed; the new era brought more realism, more likeness to nature, more freedom to the artist to put something of himself into his work; but much of the deep thought and the devout feeling of the thirteenth century was lost, and it cannot be said that art was elevated in its tone.

There were influences, too, in the new state of society which permitted details to be introduced into religious subjects which were far from suitable or devotional; sometimes they were even comic in their effects. For example, such scenes as allowed the representation of evil spirits or devils were made to serve for all sorts of coarse, grotesque, and burlesque side-play, and the little figures which represented these powers were made to do all kinds of ridiculous capers side by side with such serious subjects as the Last Judgment or the death scenes of eminent men. This makes us feel, when we study the fourteenth century, that the sculpture of the Middle Ages reached its highest point in the thirteenth century, and soon after began to decline.

In Germany the most important sculptures of this period were executed at Nuremberg. The Church of St. Laurence, that of St. Sebald, the Frauenkirche, or the Church of Our Lady, are all great monuments to the art of this city and the calm dignity and grace which marked the works of the Nuremberg sculptors.

At the close of the century, between 1385 and 1396, Master Heinrich den Balier erected the "Beautiful Fountain," which is still the pride of the city and a splendid monument of the time. In Nuremberg many of the dwelling-houses were decorated with sculptures, and it is now one of the most interesting places in all Germany to the student of ancient art.

We have not the space to speak in detail of the sculpture of the time; Augsburg, Prague, Stuttgart, Bamberg, Würzburg, Cologne, and many other German towns and cities have rich treasures of its work, but its character is everywhere much the same, and great activity, with a tendency toward decline, are its prominent features.

In Germany in this century ivory-carving was much

practised and used for a great variety of purposes. In these smaller works the life and freshness, the grace and spirit of the manner of the time were very attractive (Fig. 78).

FIG. 78.—IVORY RELIEF. HUNTING SCENE.

In France the fourteenth century was much less productive of works of art than the preceding one had been. The fact that so much had been done in the thirteenth century—so many new churches built and so many older ones remodelled—is one reason for this change. In this direction there was very little left to be done. Then, too, the country was so disturbed by wars with England that the arts of peace suffered neglect. However, there was still much to be done to complete the grand works already begun, and during the early part of this century a great deal was accomplished by way of interior decoration in edifices not yet completed, and in the making of monuments in memory of persons of rank and importance. Those in the Cathedral of St. Denis were much increased in number, and in all parts of France these works were multiplied.

During this century many artists from the Netherlands were employed in France; and in the city of Dijon, which was the residence of the dukes of Burgundy, the works of Flemish artists were very numerous.

Perhaps the most skilful of these masters was CLAUX SLUTER, who was the favorite of Philip the Bold, and executed the splendid monument to that duke which is now in the Museum at Dijon. He was also the sculptor of the Moses Fountain, the decorations of the Carthusian chapel, and other works which still remain to show how fine a sculptor he was. Sluter had a great influence upon art, and, in fact, may be said to have established a school the effects of which endured long after his time.

In England sculpture made no progress during the fourteenth century. Large architectural sculptures were neither numerous nor fine. Tomb-sculptures and monuments with portrait reliefs and statues were the principal plastic works of the time. The habit of erecting monuments to the dead now extended to all classes, whereas it had formerly been confined to noble and distinguished people. The result was that the monuments of the higher classes were more and more splendid in order to mark the differences of rank, and much grand effect was thus produced; but the merits of the sculpture was less than formerly, and the monuments of this age are wanting in spirit, stiff and unattractive. The costume of the time, too, was so ugly that it served to give a grotesque air to many figures, and thus added to the general appearance of decline which marked the English tomb-sculpture of the fourteenth century. It compares unfavorably with the German monuments of the same period, and the realistic portrait element which ruled it makes it seem like a monotonous and feeble system of mechanics rather than a style of art.

As we have said, the sculpture of Italy was quite different from that of the more northern countries of Europe. One great reason for this was that individualism in art was a strong power in Italy much earlier than in more northern countries. In Germany the early sculptors of the Middle Ages did not put their names upon their works; they practised their art as a religious service, and their pious devotion made them forget themselves. Not so in Italy: there each artist wished to be known in his works, and regarded them as works of art, done for the sake of art, and not as acts of piety. One result of this difference was that the northern sculptures had more of deep feeling and profound thought in them, while the Italian works had more perfection of form.

In Italy sculpture held the second place in the decoration of churches. Painting was preferred before it, and in spite of the influence of the Gothic style, which extended south of the Alps, the Italians would not give up their large wall-spaces and the splendid Christian paintings which were their glory. They built their edifices with this end in view, and as the same person was frequently an architect, painter and sculptor, he knew how to arrange his plans so as to suit his ideas of the merits of each art.

So it happened that the principal works which the sculptors did for the church were separate objects, such as altar-pieces, fonts, pulpits, and tombs. It rarely occurred that whole fronts of churches were covered with sculptures, as in Germany or France, and there were few richly sculptured portals of churches in Italy. The material mostly used for Italian sculpture was fine white marble, which was very rarely colored; sometimes a little gilding was used; but as a rule painting and sculpture were not united, as they had been north of the Alps.

However, the sculptors of Italy had a wider range in art than in other lands; for being less devoted to the service of the church, they were employed for more secular works. It is true that the separate statues of the Madonna were very numerous, and that tomb-sculpture was important; but added to these there were civil monuments to show forth the glory of the cities and their great men, and there were public fountains and other sculptures which told of the splendor and fame of each one of the many petty powers into which the whole country was divided. The council-halls of the free cities were very fine, and gave great opportunity to Italian artists to give variety to their works, and the sculptors very early excelled in reliefs, which told historical stories with great clearness.

As early as the beginning of the thirteenth century we can trace the progress of Italian sculpture by telling the story of the lives of separate artists. The first man of importance who thus claims our attention is NICOLA PISANO, who was born at Pisa between 1205 and 1207, and who, according to the custom of his time, was both architect and sculptor. When he was but fifteen years old he received an appointment as architect to Frederic II., with whom he went to Naples; he served this sovereign ten years, and then went to Padua, where he was employed as the architect of the Basilica of St. Anthony.

In 1237 Nicola made his first essay in sculpture, and executed a relief representing the Deposition from the Cross, which still remains in its place over one of the side doors of the Cathedral of San Martino at Lucca. This work was most excellent as the attempt of a young artist, and it was also excellent when compared with the work of other Italian sculptors who had preceded him. (Fig. 79.)

During the twelve years following this time Nicola Pisano was chiefly employed as an architect, and it was not until 1260 that he established his fame as a sculptor; but

FIG. 79.—RELIEF BY NICOLA PISANO. *Lucca.*

when we consider the pulpit for the Baptistery of Pisa, which he now did, it is plain that he must have given much thought and study to sculpture since his first work at Lucca; and this last work has such qualities as indicate that he had studied the sculpture of classic days. The work upon this pulpit is a wonderful advance upon the sculpture of the period; and though there are marks of his inexperience in its arrangement, as a whole it is above criticism when the time to which it belonged and the circumstances of its sculpture are taken into account. (Fig. 80.)

Nicola went next to Bologna to make a sarcophagus to contain the remains of St. Dominick, who had died there in 1221. This burial-case was completed in 1267, and is very interesting as an illustration of the art of the thirteenth century. The next work of this sculptor was a pulpit for the Cathedral of Siena. When he undertook this work he agreed to live at Siena until it was completed, with the exception of short visits to Pisa—four in each year. He had assistants in this work, and it was completed in about a year and a half. Meantime he exerted a great influence upon the sculpture of Siena, which up to this time had amounted to little more than good stone-cutting. Indeed, Nicola Pisano had an effect upon the art of all Italy: in the north at Padua, in the south at Naples, and in Central Italy at Pisa, Lucca, and Siena.

In 1269 he was commissioned to build a convent and an abbey at La Scorgola, which are now in ruins. In 1274 Nicola commenced his last work, the Fountain of Perugia. He did not remain constantly in that city, but after making the plans he left his son Giovanni in charge of the work, while he returned to Pisa and occupied himself with making the figures for its decoration. This fountain was held in such esteem that laws were enacted for its preservation, and it was called the most valuable possession of the city,

FIG. 80.—RELIEF FROM THE PULPIT AT PISA. *Nicola Pisano.*

while some went so far as to say that it could not be surpassed in the world. Even now, after all it has suffered from time and weather, it commands our admiration.

In 1278 Nicola died, after a life of great achievements. He left an untarnished name, too, for he had been loved and respected by all his associates, and as patron, friend, and servant had done all his duty. Mr. Perkins, in his "Tuscan Sculptors," says of him : "Inestimable were the services rendered to art by this great man. He gave the death-blow to Byzantinism and barbarism ; established new architectural principles ; founded a new school of sculpture in Italy, and opened men's eyes to the degraded state of art by showing them where to study and how to study ; so that Cimabue, Guido da Siena, the Masuccios and the Cosmati all profited by his pervading and enduring influence. Never hurried by an ill-regulated imagination into extravagances, he was careful in selecting his objects of study and his methods of self-cultivation ; an indefatigable worker, who spared neither time nor strength in obedience to the numerous calls made upon him from all parts of the peninsula ; now in Pisa, then in Naples, Padua, Siena, Lucca, or Florence ; here to design a church, there to model a bas-relief, erect a pulpit, a palace or a tower ; by turns architect and sculptor, great in both, original in both, a reviver in both, laying deep and well the foundations of his edifices by hitherto unpractised methods, and sculpturing his bas-reliefs upon principles evolved from the study of antique models long unheeded. Ever respected and esteemed by the many persons of all classes with whom he came in contact, he was truly a great man—one to whom the world owes an eternal debt of gratitude, and who looms up in gigantic proportions through the mist of five centuries, holding the same relation to Italian art which Dante holds to Italian literature."

FRA GUGLIELMO D'AGNELLO (1238–1314?), also a Pisan, was a pupil of Nicola Pisano, and worked with him at Bologna. There is little to be said of his works after his master's death.

GIOVANNI PISANO (about 1240–1320) was born at Pisa, and though a pupil of his father and a co-worker with him, he seems to have fallen under some other and a very different influence. In architecture he preferred the Gothic style, and in sculpture he was fond of all sorts of fantastic action and expression; his works were full of exaggeration. He was an architect as well as sculptor, and was a master in his own right when twenty years old, and in 1268 he went to Naples to design a church for the Franciscans; he was also the architect of the episcopal palace there.

After the death of his father the Pisans were anxious to retain Giovanni in their service; he first transformed an old church into a new one in the pointed style of architecture. It was named Santa Maria della Spina, because a rich merchant had presented one of the thorns from the crown of Christ to it. This was the first building in Italy of this style of architecture. Giovanni next built the Campo Santo of Pisa. Many shiploads of earth had been brought from Palestine to Pisa in order to make a burial-place in which Christians could be laid in the sacred earth. Giovanni Pisano inclosed the spot where this earth was laid with walls and arranged the interior of the inclosure in such a way that it could be extensively decorated with works of art. He made it the most beautiful Campo Santo in Italy. Many of the sculptures are by his own hand. (Fig. 81.)

This allegorical representation of Pisa was the first attempt at making large statues in Italy since the days of the Emperor Constantine. The city stands alone, and is a proud princess with a diadem, holding in her arms two infants to indicate her fruitfulness. Below her are four statues of the cardinal virtues, Temperance being a nude figure. It is a very strange work, and in some respects not attractive, but it shows the originality of the sculptor; the principal figure has much intensity of expression.

From this monument and his other works in Pisa, Gio-

FIG. 81.—CAMPO SANTO OF PISA. *Giovanni Pisano.*

vanni became famous, and was called to Siena to build the front of the cathedral. The people of Siena held out every inducement to him to make his home there, by freeing him from taxes for life ; but after three years he went to Perugia, where he erected a monument which has been destroyed. After this time he devoted himself entirely to sculpture, and executed a variety of works at Arezzo, Pistoja, Florence, Perugia, and Cortona. In 1312 he commenced the rebuilding of the cathedral at Prato.

We have not the space to speak of his works in detail. The Campo Santo has more of interest than the others, and is Romanesque in its character; and yet it is true that he employed Gothic forms far more than any other. Some authors credit Giovanni with having introduced an independent art into Italy; but let that be as it may, he had not the feeling for beauty, neither had he the repose which was such a charm in the works of his father. At the same time his works are full of life and dramatic action, and could never have been designed or executed by any man who had not an uncommon genius.

ARNOLFO DI CAMBIO (1232–1310) was also a pupil of Nicola Pisano, and though eight years older than Giovanni Pisano he did not become an independent master until after Giovanni had won much fame. There are some works in Rome which are attributed to Arnolfo, but as there are uncertainties about his being their author, it is not best for us to discuss them here. He erected at Orvieto, in the church of San Domenico, a monument to the Cardinal de Braye. It was a very elaborate work, and the statue of the Madonna, which is placed above that of the cardinal, is full of majestic spirit and dignified repose. This is the only well-authenticated sculptural work by Arnolfo, but this is one of the most finished monuments of the art of the Pisan school, and is quite sufficient to bring his name through the centuries with honor.

ANDREA PISANO (1270–1345) is principally famous as a bronze-caster, and his chief work was the making of the gates to the Baptistery of Florence, which have since been replaced by those of Ghiberti. When these gates were finished, in 1339, the Signory went in procession to view them; this proves in what esteem they must have been held, for the Signory never left the Palazzo Vecchio in a body except on the most important occasions. After examining the gates they conferred the honor of citizenship upon the sculptor. These gates told the story of John the Baptist, and the work is full of sentiment, beauty, and simplicity, while the design is pure, the draperies full of elegant grace, and the execution of the whole almost perfect.

NINO PISANO was the son of the latter. The time of his birth is not known; he died before 1361. His works are pleasing, and he especially excelled in drapery. They are not numerous, and are seen in the churches of Pisa.

But by far the most important pupil of Andrea Pisano, and, indeed, the most important Tuscan master of the end of the fourteenth century, was ANDREA ARCAGNUOLO DI CIONE, commonly called ANDREA ORCAGNA (1329–1376?). This artist was the son of Maestro Cione, a goldsmith of Florence. Orcagna was an architect, goldsmith, sculptor, painter, mosaist, and poet. Painting is the art by which he is best known and of which he executed the greatest number of interesting works. In this place we shall speak of his most important work as a sculptor, which was the tabernacle in the church of Or San Michele, in Florence, made to hold the picture of the Madonna painted by Ugolino da Siena. This tabernacle is of white marble in the Gothic style. It rises from the centre high up toward the roof of the church, and has sculptures in bas-relief, statuettes and busts, all illustrating the life of the Virgin from her birth to her death. It is also enriched with mosaics, intaglios, enamels, gilded glass, *pietra dura*, and all of these arranged in a whole which is quite unique in art. It may be regarded as a piece of architecture or as a sculptural work, and it is full of symbolism; and whatever view is taken of it, it commands admiration for the artist who conceived and executed so difficult a task.

During the later years of the fourteenth century there were many sculptors in Italy of whom we know very little more than their names. They did a vast amount of work in all parts of the country, much of which is still to be seen.

One of these, of whom few personal facts are known, exerted a large influence in Florence, where the fruits of his industry were almost marvellous. He was called PIETRO DI GIOVANNI and PIETRO TEDESCO, or "the German." The time and place of his birth are not known, but the records show that he worked on the Cathedral of Florence from 1386 to 1399. He worked in true German style; wherever scroll-work and simple ornamental designs were required he mingled a variety of leaves and flowers where the acanthus alone had before been used. He also made fantastic little human beings, dwarfs and grotesque beings of different sorts, and exhausted the animal world in his designs. Lions, bears, apes, dogs, lizards, crabs, birds and fish, bees, butterflies, and all manner of insects may be seen nestling among vines and branches, while angels play on pipes and violas. The whole effect of these works is cheerful and natural, and would be as suitable to decorate a music hall or a theatre as they are for a church.

The works of this master are too extreme in the realistic element to be taken as a fair example of the Italian sculpture of this time, but NICCOLÒ OF ARREZZO, the MASSEGNE, and the BON or BUONI family, and many others in different portions of the country contributed to put aside the stiff, formal manner of the past, and to bring in the more sympathetic and natural one of the fifteenth century. In truth, the last decades of the fourteenth century were a transition period, when art was bursting its bonds, and was preparing for the glorious works of the golden days of sculpture in Italy.

## CHAPTER V.

### ITALIAN SCULPTURE IN THE FIFTEENTH CENTURY.

THERE was no one great influence or circumstance which led up to the revival of art and letters which took place in the fifteenth century, and which is known under the general name of the Renaissance. Its causes were many, and may be traced in every department of the life of the Middle Ages—in religion, politics, learning, and the habits of the people. This is far too great a topic for us to enter on here, and we must keep to the one matter which we have in hand.

In Italy, heretofore, as we have shown, sculpture had been almost entirely separated from other arts, and stood by itself. Its works had been the smaller objects of which we have spoken; and though these were oftentimes splendid in their design and execution, they did not afford the sculptor the same broad field for his work as he has when his productions are combined with architecture. Now all this was changed. The French and German artists had brought out a style of architecture of their own, the Italians pursued another course, and went back to classic art for their teaching, and now every opportunity was given for sculpture to assume its utmost importance; and the art of ancient Greece was studied with all the enthusiasm of the Italian nature.

The masters of Florence, or, rather, of Tuscany, were of great importance in the beginning of the new movement, and I shall speak first of them. FRANCESCO SQUARCIONE, who lived from 1396 to 1474, was a painter, and travelled into Greece to collect antique objects, and made many drawings from the monuments which he saw. He established a school in Padua, and his museum was of advantage to sculptors as well as to painters. Other Tuscan artists who were in love with classic art wandered among its remains in Rome and other parts of Italy, and brought back to their homes a greater knowledge of sculpture, as well as the drawings which they had made; and in this part of Italy the Renaissance early made itself a living, active power.

Among the very first of these sculptors was JACOPO DELLA QUERCIA (1374–1438), who was so called from the little market town of Quercia, near Siena, in which he was born. His father was a goldsmith, and instructed his son in his art; but the boy loved sculpture, and studied it under one Luca di Giovanni. When but nineteen years old he made an equestrian statue of wood, and covered it with cloth, and painted it to represent marble in a manner which proved him to be an artist. About this time he left his home, and the next that we know of him was about ten years later, when his design for the gates of the Baptistery of Florence was pronounced to be next in merit to those of Ghiberti and Brunelleschi.

In 1408 Quercia went to Ferrara, where he did several works. While there he was called by the Signory of Siena to make a new fountain in the Piazza del Campo. This was a beautiful work, and even in this century, though much injured, its remaining sculptures prove that it must have been a wonder in its day. It has been restored after the original model by Quercia, who was often called Jacopo della Fonte on account of this work. He executed some sculptures in Lucca, but his masterpiece was the decoration of the great portal of the Basilica of San Petronio, at Bologna. (Fig. 82.)

The fifteen reliefs here represent the history of Adam and Eve, and other stories from the creation to the deluge. They show the full freedom and power of Quercia's style, and are among the most attractive of all the Tuscan sculptures of this period. During the last years of his life this artist was employed as superintendent of the works upon the Cathedral of Siena, in which city he died.

FIG. 82.—RELIEF BY JACOPO DELLA QUERCIA. *Bologna.*

We come now to speak of the famous LORENZO GHIBERTI (1378–1455), who was born in Florence, and was both a goldsmith and sculptor; and though his fame rests upon his bas-reliefs, yet the exquisite detail and careful finish in them came from his practice of the goldsmith's art. In 1398 a plague broke out in Florence, and Ghiberti fled to Rimini for safety. While there he painted a few pictures; but his name is so linked with the splendid gates which he made for the Baptistery of Florence that it is of those that one naturally thinks when his name is heard.

We have spoken of the gates which Andrea Pisano had made to this Baptistery long before; these were for the south side; and when, in 1400, the plague again visited Florence the people believed that the wrath of Heaven should be appeased by a thank-offering. Accordingly the

Guild of Wool-merchants promised to add gates on the north and east of the Baptistery of St. John the Baptist.

A time was appointed for the examination of designs, and many artists entered into the competition, and sent in their drawings and models. A great number of these represented the Sacrifice of Isaac. At length all the models were set aside but two, and these were made by Brunelleschi and Ghiberti; then the former declared that he thought his rival's design the best, thus showing a nobility of character which cannot be too much praised.

The commission was thus given to Ghiberti, who first executed the northern gates. He began them in 1403, and finished them twenty-one years later. They illustrate the life of Christ in twenty scenes; they have also the figures of the evangelists and the four Fathers of the Church in a beautiful frame-work of foliage, animals, and other ornamental figures, which divides and incloses the larger compositions. These gates are done in a manner much in advance of that of Pisano, and yet they retain some features of an earlier style which are not found in Ghiberti's later works. But from the first he showed original talent, as one may see by his model of the Sacrifice of Isaac, which is preserved in the Museum of the Bargello, beside that of Brunelleschi.

These northern gates are very beautiful, but those on the east are far more so; it is of these last that Michael Angelo declared, "They are worthy to be the gates of Paradise!" These are divided into ten compartments, representing: 1, Creation of Adam and Eve; 2, History of Cain and Abel; 3, Noah; 4, Abraham and Isaac; 5, Jacob and Esau; 6, History of Joseph; 7, Moses on Mount Sinai; 8, Joshua before Jericho; 9, David and Goliath; 10, Solomon and the Queen of Sheba (Fig. 83).

This sculptor showed great skill for one in his age, but to us there is some disappointment in them on account of the crowded appearance of the figures. Familiarity with them, however, reveals their beauty, and we find that, in truth, the stories Ghiberti wished to tell are brought out with much distinctness. They will ever remain one of the great monuments of the sculpture of the Renaissance.

Ghiberti endeavored to introduce fine backgrounds to his reliefs, which gave him an opportunity to add figures illustrating other incidents than the principal one of the work. His sculptures show the influence of the Gothic style, the study of nature and that of the antique all combined; with these are united his own power of conception, his ability in design, and his wonderful delicacy of execution. These gates have been continually studied by the artists of his own and succeeding generations.

The next work of importance by Ghiberti is the sarcophagus of St. Zenobius in the Cathedral of Florence. Other lesser sculptures are in other churches in Florence and in the Cathedral of Siena.

We come now to one of the most interesting sculptors of the fifteenth century. DONATELLO he was called, but his real name was DONATO DI BETTO BARDI (1386–1468). He was born in Florence, and from his boyhood was a member of the family of the rich banker Ruberto Martelli, who was the firm friend of the sculptor for life, and when he died he provided in his will that the works by Donatello which he bequeathed to his family should never be pledged, sold, or given away, but kept as a perpetual inheritance for his heirs. Donatello was a realist, and followed nature with great exactness. This was not always productive of beauty in his works; indeed, some of them are very ugly, and a story which illustrates this is told of himself and Brunelleschi. Donatello had made a crucifix, carved from wood, for the Church of Santa Croce, and when it was finished he asked Brunelleschi's opinion of it. This latter artist was principally an architect; but as he had learned the gold-

FIG. 83.—FROM THE EASTERN GATES. *Showing compartments* 6, 8, *and* 10.

smith's trade, he executed some sculptures, and a close friendship existed between himself and Donatello. Relying on their love for each other, Brunelleschi frankly told Donatello that his crucifix was very ugly, and his figure of Christ like that of a day-laborer, whereas it should represent a person of the greatest possible beauty.

Donatello was very angry at this, and exclaimed, "It is easier to criticise than to execute; do you take a piece of wood and make a better crucifix!" Brunelleschi determined to do this, and when his work was finished he invited Donatello to sup with him. He placed the crucifix in a conspicuous place in his house, and then took Donatello with him to the market to buy their food. He gave the parcels to Donatello, and asked him to go before to the house, saying that he would soon follow. When Donatello entered and saw the crucifix he was so delighted at the sight that he forgot everything else, and dropped the eggs, cheese, and all on the floor, and stood gazing at the carving as motionless as if he were a statue himself. When Brunelleschi came he said, "What are we to do now? You have spoiled all the dinner!"

"I have had dinner enough for to-day," replied Donatello. "You may have a better appetite. To you, I confess, belongs the power of carving the figure of Christ; to me that of representing day-laborers."

This famous crucifix by Brunelleschi is now in the Gondi Chapel of the Church of Santa Maria Novella; that by Donatello is in the chapel of Saints Ludovico and Bartolommeo in the Church of Santa Croce.

The Annunciation cut from sandstone, which is in Santa Croce, is one of his earliest works, and is full of grace and nobleness (Fig. 84). He made some beautiful groups of dancing children, which are now in the Uffizi Gallery; but he considered his David, which is in the same gallery, as his masterpiece. He was so proud of it that he swore by it, saying, "By the faith I have in my Zuccone!" This word means bald-head, and had come to be used as the usual name for the David.

FIG. 84.—THE ANNUNCIATION. *By Donatello.*

But in spite of his liking for the David, it is generally thought that his St. George, on the exterior of the Church of Or San Michele, is far better. The German art-writer Grimm thus speaks of this work: "What a man is the St. George in the niche of the Church of Or San Michele! He stands there in complete armor, sturdily, with his legs somewhat striding apart, resting on both with equal weight, as if he meant to stand so that no power could move him from his post. Straight before him he holds up

FIG. 85.—STATUE OF ST. GEORGE.
*By Donatello.*

his high shield; both hands touch its edge, partly for the sake of holding it, partly in order to rest on it; the eyes and brows are full of expectant boldness. . . . We approach this St. George, and the mere artistic interest is transformed suddenly into a more lively sympathy with the person of the master. . . . Who is it, we ask, who has placed such a man there, so ready for battle?" (Fig. 85.)

Donatello's impetuosity led him into many rash acts. Among other instances of this it is related that a rich Genoese merchant gave an order for a portrait bust of himself in bronze; when it was finished the great Duke Cosimo de' Medici, who was a friend of Donatello, admired the work so much that he placed it on his balcony, so that all Florentines who passed by could see it. When the merchant was given the price of the bust he objected to it, and it was referred to Duke Cosimo for settlement. In the conversation the Genoese said that the bust could be made in a month, and that he was willing to pay the artist a dollar a day for his time and labor.

When Donatello heard this he exclaimed, "I know how to destroy the result of the study of years in the twinkling of an eye!" and he threw the bust into the street below, where it was broken into fragments. Then the merchant was deeply mortified, and offered the sculptor double the price he had asked if he would repeat the work; but though Donatello sadly needed the money he would not do this, and persisted in his refusal, even when Cosimo de' Medici tried to persuade him to consent.

When Donatello was old Duke Cosimo gave him an allowance which would support himself and four workmen; but in spite of this Donatello wore such shabby clothes that Cosimo sent him a red surcoat, a mantle and hood. These Donatello returned, saying they were far too fine for him. When the sculptor at length became feeble and bed-ridden his benefactor had died, but Piero de' Medici, the son of Cosimo, was careful to keep him in comfort; and when he died his funeral was attended with much ceremony. He was buried near Duke Cosimo, in the Church of San Lorenzo.

Several of Donatello's works are in this church, and are a more suitable monument to his memory than any that could be made by other hands.

The works of Donatello are numerous, both in marble and bronze, and in both these substances he made statues and reliefs. We cannot speak in detail of all that he accomplished; but as he lived in an age when every advance in art was an event in history, we must not forget to say that he made the first equestrian statue which had been produced since the time of the Romans. This statue is in Padua, in front of the Church of San Antonio; it is of colossal size, and represents the Venetian General Gattamelata; and though it does not satisfy our conception as an equestrian statue, it is worthy of some praise when we remember all the circumstances of its origin. It is not probable that Donatello had ever seen an antique equestrian statue, unless it might have been that of Marcus Aurelius, which was found in the Forum in 1187; no modern statues existed as examples for him; he was not familiar with the modelling of horses, and for every reason it was a bold thing for him to undertake such a work.

Donatello had more influence upon the art of his time than any other Tuscan sculptor, with the single exception of Michael Angelo. As a man he was honest, simple, and upright in all his dealings; as a friend he was loyal and faithful; as a Christian he was humble and charitable, and left behind him a name which has been handed down through more than four centuries with respect and honor.

LUCA DELLA ROBBIA (1400–1481) is another native of Florence, whose name is widely known. Like many others, he began life as a goldsmith, and in this way gained a mastery over detail and a finish of style that are remarkable in all his works. He turned his attention to sculpture early in life, and was so enthusiastic in his pursuit of this art that he worked night and day, minding neither cold nor hunger and fatigue; in the beginning he made numerous wax models, which have perished, and with all his industry we have no work of his before he was forty-five years old, except the reliefs of Music, Philosophy, Geometry, Grammar and Astronomy, Plato and Aristotle, Ptolemy and Euclid, and a man playing a lute, which are set into the side of the Campanile at Florence, and two scenes from the life of St. Peter, which are in the Uffizi.

In the same gallery are also the series of reliefs which Luca began when forty-five years old for the balustrade of an organ in the cathedral. These reliefs represent boys singing, dancing, and playing on musical instruments (Fig. 86). The attitudes are so graceful and so varied, and the expressions on the faces are so many, that there is much to admire in a subject which in unskilful hands would be very monotonous.

FIG. 86.—DANCING BOYS. *By Luca della Robbia.*

No sculptures since the classic days represent child-life with such freshness and charming qualities, and these alone would have raised Luca to a high rank as a sculptor. In the Uffizi one is able to examine these works closely, and they gain by this nearness to the eye, which enables one to see the minuteness of his finish. There are various works of his in bronze and marble still to be seen in the churches of Florence, but the special art to which he gave his attention was to the perfecting of enamel upon terra-cotta—on the making of what is known as the Robbia ware. In this he achieved a great success, and his bas-reliefs are very beautiful. At first he used but few colors, but later he increased their number, and was able to produce a combined effect of painting and relief that is very pleasing.

These works were used for altar-pieces, medallions on exteriors, fountains, wall decoration, and a great variety of purposes. Twelve medallions representing the months, which are in the South Kensington Museum, are said to have been made by Luca to decorate a writing cabinet for one of the Medici.

Luca worked with his nephew, Andrea, who had four sons; and when Luca died his secrets belonged to them, and made their fortunes. They were occupied eleven years in making a frieze to a hospital in Pistoja; it represented the Seven Acts of Mercy. One of them went to France and decorated the Château of Madrid for Francis I. Pope Leo X. employed another to pave the Loggie of the Vatican with Robbia tiles, and these wares, in one form and another, were used in numberless ways, both useful and decorative.

The Robbia family was followed by other workers in glazed ware, and during about a century it was a prominent feature in art, and then was gradually given up.

The most noted pupil of Donatello was ANDREA DEL VEROCCHIO (1432–1488). He was born at Florence, and was early apprenticed to a goldsmith called Verocchio, from whom the sculptor took his surname. It is said that this name came from the fact that the elder Verocchio had remarkable exactness of sight.

Neither the metal works nor the paintings which Verocchio did remain, and after about 1466 he devoted himself entirely to sculpture. It is difficult to associate him with

Donatello; his execution is finished like most sculptors who were also metal-workers; his nude parts are true to nature, but not graceful or attractive, and his draperies are in small folds, which give a tumbled, crumpled effect rather than that of the easy, graceful falling of soft material.

His best works are a David in the Museum of the Bargello, Florence; a bronze Genius pressing a Dolphin to itself on a fountain in the court of the Palazzo Vecchio (Fig. 87); an equestrian statue of Colleoni before the Church of San Giovanni e Paolo, Venice (Fig. 88); and a group of St. Thomas examining the Wounds of Christ at the Church of Or San Michele, Florence. This last work is in his best and latest manner; the expression is powerful, but the drapery is still very faulty.

FIG. 87.—BOY WITH DOLPHIN. *By Verocchio.*

Although this equestrian statue is called by Verocchio's name, he did not live to see it completed; and though it was without doubt made from his design, still some credit for its execution is due to Alessandro Leopardo, who finished it. When Colleoni died he left all his large fortune to the Republic of Venice on condition that they should erect an equestrian monument to him in the square of St. Mark. As it was forbidden by the laws of Venice to place such things in the Piazza of St. Mark, it was placed in its present position, before the Church of San Giovanni e Paolo, on the square of the School of St. Mark, and it was thought that this answered the requirements of the will.

FIG. 88.—STATUE OF COLLEONI. *By Verocchio.*

When Verocchio had gone to Venice and had modelled the horse, he was told that the Signory intended to have the rider made by another sculptor. He felt this to be an insult, and broke off the head and legs of the horse, and left Venice for Florence. The Signory issued a decree forbidding him to set foot again on Venetian soil under pain of death. The sculptor replied that he should not take the risk, as he well knew that the Signory could take off his head, and he could not put it on, while he could replace his horse's head with a better one. The Venetians knew that this was true, and repealed their decree, and doubling his pay, asked him to come to complete his work. Verocchio consented to do so, but had not been long in Venice when he died. Verocchio is said to have spent much time in drawing from the antique, and his works prove him to have been diligent and painstaking; these qualities made him the sculptor that he was; but we see no traces in his work of the heaven-born genius which makes the artist great, and so inspires himself that his works fill all beholders with an enthusiasm in a degree akin to his own; the works of such artists as Verocchio, who have only the excellencies which come from patient industry, interest us, but they cannot move our hearts.

It often happened in Italy that a number of artists belonged to the same family, as in the case of the Robbias. One such family had the name of GAMBARELLI, but were known in art as the ROSSELLINI. There were five sculptors of this name, all brothers. Two of them had great ability, Bernardo and Antonio. Bernardo was most distinguished as an architect, and some very celebrated edifices were built from his designs; he also executed some excellent sculptures, among which are the fine monument of Lionardo Bruni in the Church of Santa Croce, and that of the Beata Villana in Santa Maria Novella, Florence. The first is one of the best monuments in Tuscany. In the Uffizi are a bust of St. John, a charming work, and a portrait bust of Battista Sforza.

ANTONIO ROSSELLINO (1427–1490), called PROCONSOLO, from the quarter of Florence in which he was born, was by far the best sculptor of the family. He is called a pupil of Donatello, but his work very closely resembles that of Ghiberti. Among his best works are the monument to

Cardinal Portogallo, in the Church of San Miniato, near Florence; that of Mary of Aragon in Monte Oliveto at Naples; a relief of the Nativity in the same church, and a relief of the Adoring Madonna in the Uffizi Gallery. His characteristics were grace, delicacy of treatment, sweetness of expression, and all these combined with a noble dignity.

Other Tuscan sculptors of this period were DESIDERIO DA SETTIGNANO, MINO DA FIESOLE (1400–1486), ANDREA FERRUCCI (1465–1526), and BENEDETTO DA MAJANO (1442–1498), who was eminent as an architect as well as for his sculpture. His father was a stone-cutter, and two other sons in the family were artists. Benedetto began life as a worker in wooden mosaics, or intarsiatore, as it is called. He made two beautiful inlaid chests, and carried them to Hungary as a gift to King Matthias Corvinus, whose fame as a patron of art had reached his ears. But the young artist was doomed to a dreadful disappointment, for when he unpacked his chests in the presence of the king it was found that the sea-damp had spoiled them, and the mosaics had fallen apart. Benedetto then determined to work in more durable materials, and executed some sculptures in marble and terra-cotta while he remained in Hungary.

After his return to Florence, Benedetto worked as an architect, and the Strozzi Palace was built after his design. His masterpiece in sculpture was the monument to Filippo Strozzi, in the Strozzi Chapel in Santa Maria Novella, and it also merits mention among the best works of the fifteenth century. A pulpit in Santa Croce, by Benedetto, is also very fine, and his skill was shown here in his supporting the pulpit against a column and putting the staircase by which the pulpit is entered inside the column; thus it was concealed, and the building in no wise weakened, while the pulpit is far more beautiful than it would be were the staircase in sight.

Benedetto was summoned to Naples by the Duke of Calabria, who gave him commissions which occupied him for two years. Few Tuscan sculptors have produced more pleasing works than Benedetto's; though not profound they are pleasing and unaffected, and in whatever frame of mind one may be, they do not disturb, but rather soothe and charm, as they could not do if they were false in sentiment or executed in an affected manner.

MATTEO CIVITALI DI GIOVANNI (1435–1501) was born in Lucca, but studied art in Florence. His statue of St. Sebastian in the Cathedral of Lucca was so much admired by the painter Perugino that he copied it in his picture of the Entombment.

Civitali's chief work in sculpture was the tomb of Pietro da Noceto in the same cathedral. In Genoa, in the Chapel of St. John the Baptist, he executed six statues and five bas-reliefs. A bas-relief of Faith by Civitali in the Uffizi Gallery is a fine work, full of earnestness and deep religious feeling.

Civitali was also an accomplished architect, and did much to improve the style of building in Lucca. The beautiful temple of the Volto Santo in the cathedral was designed by him.

This sculptor may be said to have had four different styles of work. The St. Sebastian was in his earliest manner, and is simply realistic; his second manner was the best; it is pure and dignified in conception, while deep feeling pervades all; the tomb of Noceto was in this second style; his third manner was more free and less pure, while the fourth, as seen in his work at Genoa, is full of extravagant exaggeration.

Next to the sculptors of the Tuscan or Florentine school of this period were those of Venice in importance and independence of manner. This school was much influenced by that of Tuscany because of the nearness of the two cities and the constant communication between them, as well as by the fact that Tuscan sculptors were more or less employed in Venice. One of the earliest Venetian sculptors was ANTONIO GIOVANNI BREGNO, called ANTONIO RIZZO or RICCIO (about 1430–1498 ?). Although he was born in Verona, and there had the opportunity to study the Roman ruins which are the pride of the city, he is yet essentially an artist of Venice, since he spent most of his life there, and was even at the head of the workshop for the sculptors who worked upon the palace. One little episode in the life of this artist was an expedition to Scutari with the Venetian soldiers, who went to its defence against the Turks. Rizzo showed himself so brave in action, and was so severely wounded, that after his return to Venice the Senate gave him a pension which lasted through twenty years. Rizzo so won the confidence of the Venetians that he was appointed to important offices with large salaries, and it is sad to be forced to add that he proved to be a dishonest man, and when his accounts were examined he fled to Foligno, where he soon died. We will not speak of him as an architect ; as a sculptor he is known by statues of Adam and Eve in niches opposite the Giant's Staircase in the Ducal Palace, and by sepulchral monuments in the Church of the Frari. While his works cannot be highly praised for beauty, they do show the style of the Renaissance distinctly.

LOMBARDO is the family name of three sculptors of this period in Venice. They were PIETRO and his two sons, TULLIO and ANTONIO, and the three together are spoken of as the Lombardi. Pietro, the father, was as much an architect as a sculptor, and the works of the father and son are so associated that it is difficult to speak of them separately. We know that Tullio was the superior artist of the three, but there are no works of theirs that command a detailed description here. The monument to the Doge Pietro

Mocenigo, in the Church of SS. Giovanni e Paolo, the angels of the font in San Martino, an altar-relief in the altar of San Giovanni Crisostomo, reliefs on the front of the Scuola di San Marco, and two reliefs in the Church of San Antonio at Padua, are the principal sculptures of the Lombardi.

ALESSANDRO LEOPARDO, who flourished about 1490, was the most eminent bronze-caster of his time, and was distinguished for the happy manner in which he adapted classic ideas to his needs in his works.

Very little is known of the life of this sculptor, and that little is not to his credit. He lived in Venice, and had a studio in the Piazza del Cavallo, and in 1487 committed a forgery, for which he was banished from the city. But when Verocchio died, leaving the Colleoni statue unfinished, the Senate desired to have it completed by Leopardo, so they sent him a safe-conduct for six months, and he returned to Venice. As there is no account of his again leaving the city, it is supposed that he was allowed to remain as long as he chose. There has been much difference of opinion as to which artist—Verocchio or Leopardo—should be credited with the excellence of the Colleoni statue. The truth, as near as it can be told, seems to be that Verocchio designed and modelled it, that Leopardo completed and cast it, and made the lofty pedestal upon which it stands, and which, taken by itself, is a splendid work. It is of fine proportions, and has six Corinthian columns, in the capitals of which there are dolphins, while the frieze is composed of trophies and marine animals, all of which are symbols of the City on the Sea which erected the monument.

After the Colleoni statue was unveiled the Senate gave Leopardo an order for three standard bases of bronze to be placed in the Piazza of St. Mark's. He also made three splendid candelabra for the Venetian Academy. Leopardo was also an architect. The time of his death is very uncertain, but a writer speaks of him in 1541 as "the new glory of our age, who shines like a star in the Venetian waters."

Although an immense amount of sculpture of this period remains in various parts of Italy, it is very difficult to trace the story of separate artists and to give a satisfactory account of those whose works are worthy of high praise. There is scarcely an Italian city of any size which has not some splendid remains of this morning of the Renaissance. In Ancona there are the portal of San Francesco and the

FIGS. 89, 90.—TERRA-COTTAS FROM THE OSPEDALE GRANDE. *Milan.*

front of Mercanzia, with which the name of Giorgio da Sebenico is associated. At Rimini the Church of San Francesco, with its wealth of plastic ornament, cannot be ascribed to any one artist or to any number with surety; it is in the style of Luca della Robbia and Donatello, but in the execution does not reach their standard. In Cesena, Padua, and Verona there are fifteenth-century sculptures, and in the Milanese territory the plastic art of this period is very interesting.

In Milan, in the Church of Santa Maria delle Grazie, in

the Ospedale Grande, and in the cathedral there is a wealth of sculpture to reward the student of this art who visits them; and in the Museum of the Breda there are many interesting works. The terra-cotta decoration of the Ospedale excels all other works of this sort in upper Italy, and the immense façade of this edifice is a marvel in its way (Figs. 89, 90). The differences between this hospital and the wonderful Milan Cathedral afford a remarkable contrast in works of the same period.

GIOVANNI ANTONIO AMADEO, or OMODEO (1447–1520), was born on a farm near the Certosa of Pavia. When but nineteen years old his name appears as one of those who were employed upon this splendid edifice, and the records of his payments show that his work was well considered, even then. Omodeo was undoubtedly the best sculptor of his time in all Lombardy, and his sculptures in the Colleoni Chapel at Bergamo would be sufficient to make any artist famous. The whole work may be called his, for he designed the building and the sculptures of the façade, which are in the richest style of the Renaissance; there are statuettes, colonettes, busts, medallions, and bas-reliefs, and wherever a flat surface exists it is divided into diamond-shaped slabs of colored marbles. The portal is very much ornamented: on each side of the rose window above this entrance there are busts of Cæsar and Augustus in contrast with numbers of angels' heads not far away. There are bas-reliefs representing children playing upon musical instruments, and the whole front of the chapel, with its numerous pilasters and colonettes, has been compared to a gigantic organ, by Mr. Perkins, in his "Italian Sculptors."

Of the interior decoration we can only say that it is much in Omodeo's style, though the monument to Colleoni, the founder of the chapel, is said to be the work of German sculptors, and to have been done after Omodeo left Bergamo.

At Pavia, Omodeo succeeded Guiniforte as chief architect of the Certosa, and designed the façade, which was made by him and his successors. The bas-relief of the Deposition from the Cross, which is on the front of the high-altar here, is the work of Omodeo. At Cremona and at Isola Bella he executed some monuments, but at length, in 1490, he began his work on the Cathedral of Milan. Here a cupola was commenced after his model and under his direction; but when it was partly done doubts of its solidity were expressed, and Omodeo was commanded to leave it and design the north door to the cathedral. He also constructed the spiral staircase leading to the roof through an elegant Gothic turret, where the medallion portrait of Omodeo may be seen. It has since been proved that the cupola of Omodeo was solid enough, for it has sustained the spire which was put upon it in 1772; but he was tormented concerning it in many ways, and died without justification.

Omodeo stands at the head of northern Italian sculptors in his dexterous use of his chisel; his ease in composition and his skill in the management of drapery would have made him eminent; but the effect of all these good qualities was injured by his mannerism, and the fact that his standard of beauty was not a high one. This may be partly accounted for by the fact that in Lombardy an artist had no opportunity to study the remains of classic art, and this one circumstance very largely excuses the inferiority of the northern sculptors to those of Tuscany, whose taste had been much improved by close study of ancient plastic art.

There are many sculptors mentioned as having done some part of the work upon the Milan Cathedral, but very few are known, except by casual remark. CRISTOFORO SOLARI, called "IL GOBBO, or DEL GOBBO," was one of the most prominent, and yet we know almost nothing of his history until, in 1490, he was so disappointed when Omodeo was made architect of the cathedral instead of himself that he went to Venice, and remained there during several years.

After a time Solari was appointed ducal sculptor to Ludovico Moro, and the monument which he erected to Beatrice d'Este was one of his principal works. When Ludovico lost his power Solari went to Rome, and remained until he was recalled to Milan to execute sculptures for the cathedral. He was very independent in his reply, and refused to go unless his conditions were complied with; one of these conditions was that he should not be under the direction of any one, but should select his marbles and his subjects to please himself. The statues he made are not as fine as we might expect them to be after this beginning; however, he was at length appointed head architect. Soon after this he was engaged in making a new model for a cupola, and then suddenly his name ceases to appear upon the registers.

The Cathedral of Como is another of those vast edifices which afforded opportunities for artists to make themselves famous. The principal part of the façade to this cathedral was ornamented by TOMMASO and JACOPO RODARI. The first was at one time architect of the cathedral, and together they executed a large portion of the sculptures. Their best work was in the ornamental parts.

In the southern parts of Italy, both in the states of the Church and in Naples, there are many works of the fifteenth century which were executed by artists from Florence and other parts of Italy. Thus there is nothing new to be said concerning sculpture in Southern Italy during this period, since the works which are not by foreign artists are in the same style as theirs; for the native sculptors copied those from Central and Northern Italy, and no great progress or original manner can be found in these southern districts.

## CHAPTER VI.

### SCULPTURE IN GERMANY, FRANCE, ENGLAND, AND SPAIN, FROM 1450 TO 1550.

IN Italy, as we have seen, the sculpture of the Renaissance was much advanced by the fact that in the beginning of its growth the architecture of the country was largely an imitation of Greek architecture; and as the same artist was frequently an architect, sculptor, and painter, edifices were designed with the purpose of placing the works of the sculptor in the most favorable positions.

In the countries north of Italy sculpture had no such aid or advantages. The Gothic style of architecture was a hindrance to the sculptor, whose works were combined with it. The Gothic construction afforded no broad, generous spaces for sculpture; all plastic work must be confined in limited spaces between columns and baldachins, or in arched niches, or between narrow flutings; and though something had been done to vary the upright stiffness of the statues of its earliest days, there was no freedom for the realistic and natural tendencies of the Renaissance art to develop in.

Another advantage on the side of Italian art was the fact that Italy was a land of grace and beauty; its people were more refined in manner, more elegant and picturesque in their costumes than were those of Northern Europe, and all the influences surrounding the Italian artist were far more favorable to a development of his artistic nature than were those of France or Germany. Then, too, the remains of antique art which were within reach of the Italian sculptor were quite shut off from others. For all these and other reasons the sculpture of the north was more tardy in taking on the better spirit and form of the Renaissance, and as a whole it never became as pleasing to most people as was the sculpture of Italy.

In a former chapter we have spoken of the sculptor Claux Sluter and his work at Dijon in the fourteenth century; the desire which he showed to make his figures like the men they represented, and a general study of nature rather than of older works of sculpture, had much effect upon the sculpture of his time, and gradually became much exaggerated. German sculptors tried not only to make exact portraits of the faces and heads of their figures, but they gave the same attention to imitating every detail of costume and every personal peculiarity of the model from which they worked. This tended to weaken and narrow their own designs, and the whole effect of their work is fantastic and exaggerated—an effect quite opposed to the noble and harmonious treatment of the whole which the best Italian masters strove to attain.

The attempt to produce startling effects in German art made such subjects as the Passion of Christ, the Temptation of St. Anthony, and the Martyrdoms of the Saints to be constantly repeated, and many reliefs are overloaded with such details as may very properly be used in painting, and which belong to *picturesque* art, but which take away the dignity and calm grandeur which should make the spirit of sculpture. But there is one feature of German sculpture at this time which appeals to our sympathy—that is, the deep, earnest feeling which pervades it, and which constantly tried new methods of expression.

In Germany there were guilds or trade-associations, and the members of these guilds were allowed to work in the special branch only of sculpture which belonged to their company, so that this art was divided by more fixed lines than in Italy, where, in truth, at the period of which we speak, the Florentine school was a supreme power, and its sculptors, as we have seen, worked in as many sorts of sculpture as pleased them.

The schools of Germany were far more independent of each other, and the entire organization of art in Germany was very different from that of Italy.

One of the most prominent effects of the architecture of Germany was to drive the sculptors to seek for such work as had no relation to architecture, and an important result from this was the great attention which they paid to wood-carving; indeed, this was the favorite pursuit of the German sculptors for many years. About the middle of the fifteenth century the importance of this art in Germany was far greater than those of bronze-casting or stone sculpture.

The principal works in wood-carving were the altars, which finally came to be colossal in size, and with their multitude of reliefs, statuettes, and ornaments were marvellous monuments to the industry and skill of the wood-carvers. The reliefs in these works are usually arranged on landscape backgrounds, and so much resemble pictures in many ways that the colors and gilding which were freely used on them do not seem out of place, and it appears to be quite natural that wood-carvers should often have been painters also.

The Swabian school, the principal seat of which was Ulm, was the earliest to adopt the new, realistic style. There are works by Swabian artists which show this tendency as early as 1431. JÖRG SYRLIN, who flourished during the last half of the fifteenth century, was an eminent wood-carver, and as he did not color his works he can be better judged as a sculptor than he could be if the effect of the whole depended partly upon painting. The choir-stalls in the Cathedral of Ulm and the fountain in the market-place, called "Fischkasten," are his most important works; but a singing-desk, now in the museum, and other lesser pieces are also excellent examples of his style. The choir-stalls have an immense number of figures and a mass of ornament, which made them far richer than any such work of an earlier date, and none that have since been made have equalled them. It is almost incredible that they were completed in four years, and yet there are no marks of haste upon the work. The figures are dignified and graceful, the faces delicate and expressive, the hands well formed, and a beauty of design and execution marks the whole. The lower figures, which come nearest the eye, are finer than those which are higher up, so that a unity of effect is preserved throughout the whole. He sometimes took occasion to give touches of humor in his works, and in these stalls he introduced his own portrait and that of his wife.

The "Fischkasten" is sculptured in stone, and has three knights upon it which appear to be boldly advancing, as if about to step off and walk away. Other works by this master are less important, and it is doubtful if all that are called by his name are really his own. Jörg Syrlin, the younger, trained by his father, adopted his style, and became an excellent artist.

We have not space to speak of the Swabian sculptures in detail. Fine works exist in Tiefenbronn, Rothenburg, Blaubeuren, Herrenberg, Gmünd, Ravensburg, and many other places.

The influence of the Swabian school was very wide; it can be traced in many parts of Germany, in Hungary and Transylvania, and even in Switzerland, Austria, and Bavaria. Swabian artists were often summoned to adjacent provinces, and thus did much work away from their homes. The reliefs upon the door of the Cathedral of Constance were executed by Simon Hayder, a Swabian, in 1470. The altar of the cathedral at Chur was the work of Jacob Rösch, another Swabian master, who thus labored on the very boundary of Italy. The school at Augsburg was the second Swabian school in importance, and much influence went out from that centre, though its sculptures were not as fine as those of Ulm.

In some cases fine old sculptures still exist in the churches and other places for which they were intended. Again we find them either whole, or in parts, in museums to which they have been removed when they were no longer required for the uses for which they were made, or when they were replaced by more modern works. So few facts are known concerning them that it is almost impossible to do more than repeat descriptions of the subjects they represent; and this is neither profitable nor entertaining in a book of this kind; therefore I shall now speak only of such artists as have left some record behind them, and of works whose authorship can be given.

VEIT STOSS, who flourished about the middle of the fifteenth century, was an eminent wood-carver. Very little is known about him. His name is sometimes said to be Wit Stwosz, and Cracow and Nuremberg both claim to have been his birthplace. But it is now believed that he was born in Nuremberg, as it is known that in 1477 he gave up his citizenship there and went to Cracow, and in 1496 he paid a small sum to be again made a citizen of Nuremberg.

We also know that his reputation as a man was not good. In a Nuremberg decree he is called a "reckless and graceless citizen, who has caused much uneasiness to the honorable council and the whole town." He was convicted of crimes for which he should have suffered death, but the sentence was changed, and he was branded: both cheeks were pierced with a hot iron. After this he broke the oath he had taken to the city, and joined her enemies in plotting against her; he was subsequently imprisoned, and at his death, in 1533, he was very old and perfectly blind.

It seems almost like a contradiction to say that this master was one of the most tender in feeling of all the wood-carvers of his time. He was especially successful in representing the purity of the Madonna and of youthful saints. His principal works are in the churches of Cracow and Nuremberg. In the Frauenkirche at Cracow the high-altar, a part of the stalls in the choir, and some other sculptures are his. In Nuremberg his best works are a bas-relief of the Crowning of the Virgin, which is preserved in the Burgkapelle; the great Madonna statue, which was placed in the Frauenkirche in 1504; and the colossal Angel's Salutation, which is suspended in the choir of the Church of St. Laurence. This last is an unusual and important work. The angel appears as if flying, and the drapery is much inflated; the Virgin is queenly and majestic, yet graceful; all around are medallions in which are represented the Seven Sorrows of the Virgin. The style of these reliefs is charming if we except the drapery; that has the faults of the time, and is bad in style; but the female heads are all that we could ask; the whole design is distinct, and few reliefs could surpass these in simple beauty and genuine artistic feeling.

Another remarkable work of his is a panel of roses, now in the Burgkapelle. The panel is seven feet high by five wide; more than half of this is covered by a wreath of roses; there are besides four rows of small half-length figures arranged round a cross of St. Anthony, a representation of the Last Judgment, scenes in the history of man from the creation to the death of the Virgin, and many other saints and like subjects in bits of reliefs, which fill up all spare spaces. The style is very distinct, and the draperies better in this work than in others from his hand.

There are other works in Nuremberg and elsewhere

which are attributed to Veit Stoss, but these that are known to be his are quite enough to establish his fame as a gifted artist and a remarkable sculptor for his time.

Though Stoss is among the early masters of Nuremberg, it is yet true that others had been at work while he was in Cracow, and the way had been prepared for him and his work when he returned to his native city in 1496. Among the most active artists in Nuremberg was MICHAEL WOHLGEMUTH (1434–1519), who is generally considered as a painter only; but we know that he made contracts for entire works in which sculpture and painting are combined, and must have had the oversight of the whole; and in this view it is proper to mention this master's name. The altars at Haller Cross Chapel, Nuremberg, one at Zwickau, another at Schwabach, and that of the Heilsbronn Monastery, near Nuremberg, are all ascribed to Wohlgemuth.

ALBRECHT DÜRER (1471–1528), who was one of the great masters of the world, was an architect, painter, and sculptor. He was a pupil of Michael Wohlgemuth, and sculpture was less practised by him than other arts; yet the few works of his which remain are much valued.

Dürer probably executed his carvings about 1510–1520. In the British Museum there is a relief of the Birth of St. John the Baptist, which was purchased in the Netherlands more than eighty years since for $2500. It is cut in a block of cream-colored stone, seven and one half by five and one half inches in size, and is a wonderful work. The companion piece, which represents the same saint Preaching in the Wilderness, is in the Brunswick Museum, where there is also an "Ecce Homo" carved in wood.

Dürer executed many little carvings in stone, ivory, and boxwood, and the existing ones are seen in various collections in Germany. It is quite probable that others are in private hands.

There are in Nuremberg many most excellent wood-carvings by unknown masters; one who cares for this art is well repaid for a visit to this old city, and, indeed, this is true of other old German towns. Bamberg, Marburg, Frankfort-on-the-Main, Dortmund, Halle, and many other towns have riches in this kind of art.

The stone sculpture of Germany in the fifteenth century was of less importance than the wood-carving until toward the close of the period. The exteriors of the churches and other edifices erected at this time had but little sculptural ornament, and that consisted principally of traceries and figures in geometric designs. Some small detached works, such as fonts, pulpits, or fountains, were made in stone, but the chief use of stone sculpture was for monuments to the dead.

ADAM KRAFFT (about 1430–1507), of whose early history almost nothing is known, is a very important master of this time, and his principal works add another charm to the city of Nuremberg. A remarkable series of works by Krafft are the Seven Stages, or seven bas-reliefs placed on the way to the Johannis Cemetery, the designs representing the seven falls of Christ on his way to Golgotha.

These reliefs are much crowded, and the only part that is at all idealized is the figure of Christ; that is noble and calm in effect, and the drapery is simple and dignified. The other figures are coarse and dressed like the Nurembergers of the time in which Krafft lived.

In the churches of St. Sebald and St. Laurence and in the Frauenkirche there are other splendid works of Krafft, and in some dwelling-houses of Nuremberg there are sculptures of his. A Madonna on the houses, 1306, in the Hirschelgasse, is one of the finest, perhaps the very best in all Germany. We do not know whether this was by Krafft or not, but it has a purity and nobleness that scarcely any other German sculptor attained.

That Krafft had a sense of humor is shown by a bas-relief above the entrance to the Public Scales. The weigher stands observing the beam, and beneath it is written, "To thyself as to others." Another man adds a weight to one scale, and the man who is to be taxed puts his hand into his money-bag very reluctantly.

Perhaps his most artistic work was the tabernacle in the Church of St. Laurence. It is sixty-four feet high; the lower part is supported by the kneeling figures of Krafft and two of his associates. Above this rises a slender Gothic pyramid ornamented with bas-reliefs and statuettes. He was employed upon this tabernacle from 1496 to 1500. It is believed that a "Burial of Christ," in the chapel of the Johannis Cemetery, was his latest work, and executed in 1507, the year in which he died, in the hospital of Schwabach. Krafft led a most industrious life, and was so skilful a workman that he could work with his left hand as readily as with his right.

TILMAN RIEMENSCHNEIDER was an important sculptor, born at Osterode, in the Hartz Mountains, probably about 1460. In 1483 he went to Würzburg, and was elected to one honorable office after another, until, in 1520, he was head burgomaster. After the Peasants' War, in 1525, he was deprived of his office; he lived but six years after this, and kept himself in close retirement, not even practising his art.

His sculptures are mostly in stone, and are quite numerous in Würzburg and its vicinity. His monument to the Knight Eberhard von Grumbach, in the church at Rimpar, was probably his earliest important work. In it he has contrived to express strength and bravery of character in spite of the stiff costume, every detail of which is worked out (Fig. 91).

In 1495 Riemenschneider received the important commission to erect in Bamberg Cathedral a splendid monument to the Emperor Heinrich II. and his wife Kunigunde.

**Fig. 91.—Count Eberhard von Grumbach.** *Rimpar.*

This occupied him until 1513, and is a splendid example of his skill. The figures of the two royal personages lie upon a large sarcophagus; the statues are more than life-size, and are dressed in the fantastic costume of the fifteenth century. Upon the sides of the sarcophagus are five reliefs, representing as many scenes from the lives of the emperor and empress. The monuments and religious subjects executed by this sculptor are very numerous. In the church at Maidbrunn there is a relief representing the "Lamentation over the Dead Body of Christ," which is probably his latest work. It is cut from sandstone, and the figure of Nicodemus is believed to be the sculptor's own portrait.

We give here four figures from the portal of the cathedral at Berne, in Switzerland. The really splendid sculptures were the work of Nicolaus Künz, and from their style seem to belong to about 1520. They show the influence of

FIG. 92.—JUSTICE.

FIG. 93.—THE THREE WISE VIRGINS.

such artists as the painters Nicolaus Manuel (1484–1531) and Hans Holbein (about 1459–1524). The statues of the Wise and Foolish Virgins are fine, and that of Justice, whose pose is full of grace, and whose almost transparent garment is an exquisite work, affords an excellent illustration of the most pleasing sculpture of this period (Figs. 92, 93).

Another art, which had its headquarters at Nuremberg in the fifteenth century, is bronze-casting, and its chief master was the famous PETER VISCHER, who was the son of another brasier, HERMANN VISCHER. The date of Peter Vischer's birth is given as 1460, and he was admitted to be a master in his art in 1489. Five years later than this he was summoned to Heidelberg together with a sculptor, Simon Lamberger, to aid the Elector Philip with advice and skill. Nothing is known of any work which Vischer did there.

Vischer's foundry at Nuremberg enjoyed a great fame, and orders were sent to it from far and near. No doubt a great many monuments were cast here which were not designed by Vischer at all. His works were numerous, but I shall only describe his masterpiece, which was the shrine or tomb of St. Sebald, and occupied Peter Vischer from 1508 to 1519, he being assisted by his five sons. The son Peter was admitted as a master in the thimble trade in 1527. Hans was called "the caster," and seems to have superintended the carving of models; Hermann went to Italy and brought home designs and models; and Jacob and Paul seem to have had no special departments. Between 1495 and 1508 so little was recorded of Peter Vischer that it leads to the belief that these years must have been given to study and to the improvement which the tomb of St. Sebald shows over the work of the monument to Archbishop Ernst, in the Magdeburg Cathedral, which was done in 1495.

The bones of St. Sebald had been inclosed in a sarcophagus of the Middle Ages, and the work required of Vischer was a fitting tomb for such precious and honored relics, for St. Sebald is the special patron saint of Nuremberg, and dwelt in a cell near that city. His legend relates that he was the son of a Danish king, who came to Germany as a missionary and settled at Nuremberg, where he did many miraculous works of charity. On one occasion,

FIG. 94.—TOMB OF ST. SEBALD. *By Peter Vischer. Nuremberg.*

during very cold weather, he is said to have found a family nearly frozen and without fuel; he commanded them to bring the icicles hanging from the roof and make a fire of them. They obeyed, and were thus warmed. Many such wonders are told of him, and Vischer in his statue makes him to appear as a pilgrim, with shell in hat, staff, rosary and wallet, while in his hand he holds a model of a church intended to represent that in which the tomb is erected. This Church of St. Sebald is now used for the Lutheran service, and the shrine still stands in the centre of the choir. (Fig. 94.)

The architecture of this remarkable work is of the richest style of Gothic, and the whole of it is in bronze, except that the oaken sarcophagus is encased in silver plates. This rests beneath a fret-work canopy supported on slender pillars. There is an abundance of ornament everywhere, but the close examination of its detail shows beauty and fitness in every part. For example, if we compare the statue of the saint, of which we have spoken, which stands at the end of the shrine most exposed, with the statue of Vischer himself, which is at the opposite end, we shall see how the saint, with his symbols and his flowing drapery, is an ideal work, and seems to be advancing with authority and the air which befits the son of a king, while Vischer, with his round cap, leather apron, and German face, is simply the representation of a worker bent upon doing his best (Fig. 95).

FIG. 95.—PETER VISCHER'S STATUE.

The sarcophagus rests upon a base on which are four reliefs of scenes from the life of the saint, all in the purest manner of the time. One of these represents the burning of the icicles recounted above (Fig. 96).

This base and sarcophagus and the fret-work above it form the centre of the tomb. Then outside of this are eight pillars supporting a baldachin, or canopy, in the richly ornamented Romanesque style, and the combinations of the Gothic and the decorative architecture are so skilfully made as not to offend our taste. But it is generally acknowledged that the chief beauty of this work is the series of the figures of the apostles, which are upon the pillars. They are slender in proportion, gracefully draped, and bear their distinctive symbols. They are perfectly free from the realism of the earlier works of Vischer, and have more of the purity

FIG. 96.—ST. SEBALD AND THE BURNING ICICLES. *Vischer.*

and nobleness of the works of Ghiberti than are seen in the statues of any other German artist of this age (Figs. 97, 98).

Above the apostles are figures of prophets and other Biblical personages ; Perseus and Hercules are also represented, and other statues typify Strength, Justice, Prudence, and Moderation. The figure of the Infant Christ is upon the centre of the highest, or middle dome. Between the pillars at their bases stand graceful candelabra, and the base itself rests upon snails. Besides all these principal figures there are almost numberless others and many ornamental designs. There are harpies, sirens, satyrs, fawns, and all sorts of fantastic creatures. The whole work is full of the deep feeling of the north and the beauty and richness of the south, and is a most remarkable production.

We are told that Vischer was but poorly paid for this labor, with all its thought and skill. He inscribed upon it these words: ". . . He completed it for the praise of God Almighty alone, and for the honor of St. Sebald, Prince of Heaven, by the aid of pious persons, paid by their voluntary contributions." There is a satisfaction in remembering that Vischer lived ten years after this tomb was completed, and must have heard many praises of his work.

FIG. 97.—PETER. FIG. 98.—JOHN.
*By Peter Vischer.*

The later works of Vischer were a few reliefs and two important monuments at Aschaffenburg and Wittenberg. His sons Hans and Hermann executed a few monuments, which are done in the manner of their father, but do not equal him in design or finish. There are numerous works which must be regarded as productions of Vischer's studio and foundry of which we cannot give clear accounts, not knowing whether they were the earlier works of the father, or were executed by the sons or other pupils, of which he had many.

PANKRAZ LABENWOLF was one of Vischer's pupils, and completed the splendid lattice-work over the Town-hall which the master left unfinished; Labenwolf added some ornaments and coats-of-arms to it. In 1550 he cast the fountain in the court-yard of the same building, which is a graceful and creditable work; but another fountain in the vegetable market, behind the Frauenkirche, is truly original; the water flows from the mouths of two geese held under the arms of a peasant; the whole effect is droll and unique (Fig. 99).

FIG. 99.—MAN AND GEESE.
*By Labenwolf.*

You will remember how, about 1390, Claux Sluter, by his works in Dijon, had a great influence upon French sculpture. A century and more later this art in France was largely under the influence of Italian masters, who had been called into France by Francis I. and other patrons of art. Splendid works of sculpture were also imported from Italy, and the effect of the Italian Renaissance, which was so plainly seen upon the painting of France, was also at work upon its sculpture.

Where the sculptures were a part of an architectural decoration, as in the case of the choir screen in the cathedral at Amiens, and other like works, the change was not as complete as in cases where the work was one of independent sculpture, as in monuments and statues to commemorate the dead, or in portrait sculpture.

The wealth and power of the nobility of France at this period enabled them to gratify their desire to leave fine monuments of themselves, in order to keep their names in memory in future centuries. In these the Italian manner was adopted, and the works when completed were far more splendid and elegant than were the corresponding works in Germany. But they have a grave fault, which makes them much less interesting than are the German sculptures: they are more conventional, less expressive, and far less artistic in spirit. They impress one as if the soft, luxurious court atmosphere had passed over them, and taking away their strong points, had left them only a general air of being well-bred and well-kept persons, of little importance to the real life of the world.

In the Louvre, in the Museum of Modern Sculpture, all this change can be traced, and the traveller in France may see such monuments as we refer to in all the cathedrals and most of the churches all over the country. Many of them cannot be traced to any one master. A fine specimen is the Amboise Monument in Rouen Cathedral, which is said to have been the work of one Roulland de Roux and his assistants.

JEAN JUSTE of Tours was one of the best French artists of his day. In the Cathedral of Tours is a monument to two young children of Charles VIII., which proves him to have had much delicacy and tenderness of execution. The sarcophagus is covered with graceful designs, and on the lid lie the two babies, for the eldest was but three years old. The whole work is exquisite, and gives one a feeling of satisfaction.

About 1530 Juste erected the splendid monument to Louis XII. and Anne of Brittany in the Church of St. Denis. While the general form of the monument is much like that of the Visconti in the Certosa at Pavia, the figures of the dead couple are quite different from the Italian manner. Below on a bier the two nude bodies are stretched in all the realism possible, and the heads are noble and touching in expression. Above, on the upper part of the monument, where in Italy the patron saint or some other figure usually is placed, the king and queen again appear; they are kneeling, with full drapery about them, while the faces are characteristic and very expressive. This monument, taken all in all, is in the perfection of the French art of the time. Another work by Juste now in the Louvre is the monument to Louis de Poncher, one of the ministers of Francis I., and his wife, Roberta. These statues are in alabaster, and were formerly in the Church of St. Germain l'Auxerrois, which was built by Poncher.

PIERRE BONTEMPS must have been a famous sculptor, as he was chosen to erect the monument to Francis I., his wife Claude and their three children. This is also at St. Denis, and is even more grand than that to Louis XII. On the upper platform the five figures are kneeling; they are noble and simple, with an air of great repose. These examples serve to give an idea of the religious sculpture of the time.

Secular subjects were unusual. A house in Bourges is decorated with the figures of the master and mistress above the entrance, as if they would speak a welcome, while reliefs of industrial scenes, such as might be seen outside and inside of the house, are placed in various positions over the building and in the court-yard. Something of a like sort is upon the Hotel Bourgtheroulde at Rouen, where the friezes show scenes between Francis I. and Henry VIII. Biblical scenes are also distributed over the building.

Bruges is almost the only city of the Netherlands that has any sculptures of this period of which one would speak. Just at this time the art of that country was painting preeminently, and the Van Eycks and their followers had done such things as held the attention of all to the neglect of other arts. At Bruges in the cathedral, the Church of St. Jacques, and the Liebfrauenkirche there are some fine monuments, and the Palais de Justice has a carved chimney-piece which is magnificent, and a work of the highest rank.

In England sculpture was of less account even than in the Netherlands. One circumstance is worthy of notice. Pietro Torrigiano, after quarrelling with Michael Angelo and breaking his nose, fled to England, and his monument of Henry VII. and his queen in Westminster Abbey, erected in 1519, marks the introduction of the style of the Italian Renaissance into England. The structure is of black marble; the statues of the king and queen are in gilt bronze, and are grandly noble in design and finished in execution. The smaller figures and all the details of the monument are fine. The master received £1000 for this work. Torrigiano executed other works, and entered into an agreement to make a monument to Henry VIII. and Catherine of Aragon, but for some reason he went to Spain in 1519 and never returned, as he was destroyed by the Inquisition three years later.

It is probable that Torrigiano may have been led to Spain by hearing of the revival of art which was taking place there. Flemish and Italian artists went there, and the influence of their styles was felt by the native masters. The result was that they brought forth a manner of their own, combining certain features of northern and of southern art, and used to express the thoughts of the Spaniards themselves. The carved altars of Seville, Toledo, and Burgos show how splendid this art was; and though we cannot trace the lives and works of Spanish sculptors as we should like to do, we can be sure that there were men among them equal to any demand that could be made upon decorative sculptors.

This is proved by the portals and fronts of the churches, by the highly ornamented chapels, the wall niches and choir screens of the interiors, while the monuments are also equal to those of other nations. That of Ferdinand and

Isabella in the Church of the Guardian Angel, at Granada, is noble and magnificent. It is believed to have been erected before the death of Ferdinand in 1516, and was probably the work of an Italian sculptor. This monument has a large marble sarcophagus, with a structure above it in the Renaissance style. At the corners of the sarcophagus there are griffins of excellent workmanship, and on the sides reliefs and statuettes of the Four Fathers of the Church; on the lid repose the figures of the royal pair, executed in a grand and dignified simplicity.

# CHAPTER VII.

## ITALIAN SCULPTURE IN THE SIXTEENTH CENTURY—CELLINI, MICHAEL ANGELO, AND OTHERS.

BY the beginning of the sixteenth century sculpture occupied a different place with relation to architecture from that which it had held in the previous centuries which we have just considered. The architecture of Italy became much more plain, and its union with sculpture in any large degree was rare.

Painting, too, had now an effect to lessen the sphere of sculpture. This art was always preferred by the Christians, as has been shown before, and now, when it had reached most satisfactory heights, it was used in many places where sculpture had before been placed. One important example of this is seen in the decoration of altars; where bas-reliefs had been used paintings were now preferred, and the end of all was that sculpture was limited to monuments and to separate pieces—reliefs or single statues or groups of figures.

In some ways this separation of the arts was a benefit to all. Under the old rule sculptors had often been forced to sacrifice their design to the needs of the architecture their work adorned. At other times they were compelled to put aside their own feeling and their artistic ideas as to how a subject should be treated, and suit themselves to such forms as were approved by the particular priest or bishop whose church they decorated. Now, when left to itself, sculpture became more individual in its expression, and far more free and interesting in itself. In the beginning of the sixteenth century the works of Italian sculpture were splendid in the extreme. It was delicate and beautiful; the drapery was made to show the figure and its natural motion, while it added an exquisite grace to the whole; many works of this period were fine in conception, good in their arrangement, and executed in a noble, spirited manner. Some critics believe that during the first four decades of this era Italian sculpture equalled the antique art of the Romans. Others make 1520, or the time of Raphael, the limit to the best epoch of this art; but it is scarcely possible thus to fix an exact bound; the important point is that this excellence was reached, and the regret follows that it could not endure for a longer period.

A far greater variety of subjects was represented in this age of sculpture than before. Formerly the rule was the production of religious effects. Scenes from the life of Christ and his disciples, others from those of the saints, or the illustration of scriptural stories, with the portrait tomb-sculpture, had been the sculptor's work. Now all the stories of mythology were studied as diligently as they had been in classic days, and artists studied to clothe the pagan personages with new forms; and in all this effort much appeared that was original. It is easy to see that such sculpture from the hand of a Christian artist must lack the important element of pure sincerity. An artist who believed in Jesus Christ could not conceive a statue of Jupiter, with all the glorious attributes, that an ancient Greek would have given to his god of gods. In this view the sculpture of classic subjects of this sixteenth century may be said to have been two-sided—the work illustrated a religion in which the artist pleased his imagination, but for which he had no reverence or love. But in spite of all it was a golden age, and many of its works are a "joy forever."

Although the first public work which Leonardo da Vinci did at Milan was to model an equestrian statue, we can scarcely speak of him as a sculptor. But the first Florentine of this period whom I shall mention is GIOVANNI FRANCESCO RUSTICI (1476–1550), who was a fellow-pupil with Leonardo under Verocchio. Very few works by this master remain, but a prominent and important one is the bronze group above the northern portal to the Baptistery at Florence. It represents the "Preaching of St. John the Baptist," and is grand in the free action of its figures. The drapery is in a pure style, very much like that of Ghiberti (Figs. 100, 101). This work was ordered by a guild of merchants, and they failed to pay the price which had been fixed for it. Rustici was so embarrassed by this that he undertook no more large works, and after the Medici were expelled from Florence he went into the service of Francis I. In France he had executed various works, and was finally commissioned to model an equestrian statue of the king in colossal size, when the sovereign died. Rustici survived but three years, and we are told that he only executed small works, and those "for the most part for the sake of kindness."

FIG. 100. PHARISEE. FIG. 101. LEVITE.
*By Rustici.*

ANDREA CONTUCCI DAL MONTE SAN SAVINO, called SANSOVINO (1460–1529), was a very important sculptor, because large works were committed to him, and his name must remain associated with them. Like Giotto, Sansovino was a shepherd-boy, and drew pictures upon the stones of the fields. Like Giotto, too, he was sent to Florence to study, and in the school of Pallajuolo made good progress. When thirty years old he was appointed architect and sculptor to the King of Portugal. After an absence of ten years he returned to Florence, and later to Rome, where Pope Julius II. commissioned him to erect monuments to the Cardinals Rovere and Sforza, in the Church of Santa Maria del Popolo.

These monuments were his best works, but they cannot be praised. The statues are in positions which seem to be uncomfortable, and there is such a mass of ornament and so many statuettes that the whole has an effect of confusion.

In 1513 Leo X. sent Sansovino to Loreto to adorn the temple which incloses the "Casa Santa" with bas-reliefs. This Casa Santa is believed to be the house in which the Virgin Mary was born at Nazareth; and when the Saracens invaded the land four angels are said to have borne the house to the coast of Dalmatia, and later to a spot near Loreto; but here some brigands entered it, and again it was removed to its present position in the Church of Loreto; this is said to have been done in 1295. Naturally this "Casa Santa" is a sacred object to all Roman Catholics, and it is visited by thousands and thousands of pilgrims each year.

The decoration of this shrine was very important, and an honorable work for any artist. Sansovino did not execute all the reliefs, and the highest praise that can be given to those he did is to say that they are superior to the others that are beside them. He was a most skilful workman, and it seems as if marble became like wax under his hand; but this very skill led him to multiply his ornaments, and to repeat acanthus leaves and honeysuckle vines until the whole was a weariness and confusion, and conveyed no meaning or sentiment whatever.

Sansovino's most important pupil was JACOPO TATTI, who, on account of his master, is called JACOPO SANSOVINO (1477-1570). He was born at Florence, and when Andrea Sansovino returned from Portugal Jacopo became his pupil. Early in life he went to Rome, and there studied and copied the works of antiquity; among other things he made a copy of the Laocoon, which was cast in bronze at a later time. Soon after his return to Florence, in 1511, Jacopo received orders for some works, but the most important statue which he made about this time is the Bacchus, now in the Uffizi. In this work he showed how completely he was in sympathy with the classic spirit; this Bacchus is a triumph in this manner, and has been called "the most beautiful and spirited pagan statue of the Renaissance period." It is full of gladness, and is simple, delicate, and beautiful. The young god is advancing and holding up a cup, which he regards with an expression of delight; in his right hand he has a bunch of grapes, from which a Pan is eating stealthily (Fig. 102).

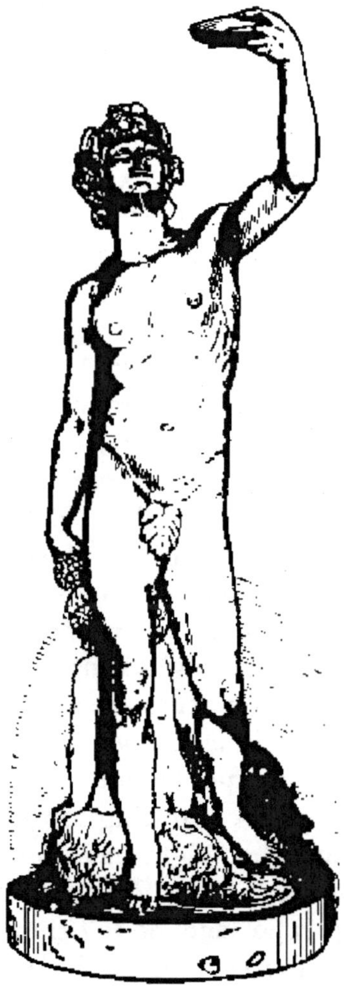

FIG. 102.—BACCHUS.
*By Jacopo Sansovino.*

In 1514 Jacopo Sansovino was employed upon the decorations for the visit of Leo X. to Florence. Soon after this he went again to Rome and submitted plans for the Church of San Giovanni de' Fiorentini, which the Florentines were about to erect—for this master was an architect as well as a sculptor. The taking of Rome by Constable de Bourbon, in 1527, drove Sansovino away; he went to Venice, intending to go to France, but Venice charmed him, and his work pleased the Venetians, and the result was that from 1529 he served the Venetians as long as he lived. He was appointed Protomastro of the Republic of Venice, and had the care of St. Mark's, the Campanile, the Piazza, and the surrounding buildings. He received a good salary, and was provided with a handsome house to live in.

He first restored the cupolas of St. Mark's; then completed the Scuola della Misericordia; he next made the interior of San Francesco della Vigna: then the Zecca, the Fabbriche Nuove, and the Loggietta of the Campanile. He also erected other churches and palaces, besides smaller sculptural works. But his architectural masterpiece was the Library of St. Mark's. The bronze gate to the Sacristy of St. Mark's was one of his principal works. It is subject to criticism as being too crowded; but it is a fine work and full of strong feeling.

His statues are numerous and seen all over Venice; indeed, it is proper to speak of him as a Venetian, so thoroughly did he adopt that city, and so industriously did he work for it during forty years. Had he remained in Florence he might have been a better artist; the splendor and luxury of the Venetians brought out corresponding traits in Jacopo, and he fell short of the purity which the influence of Florence might have given him. He is one of the masters in whom the sensual influence of the study of pagan art was fully manifested. Many of his subjects were mythological; among them were the story of Phrixos and Helle, Mercury, Apollo, Pallas, Mars, and Neptune, the last two being colossal figures on the steps of the Doge's Palace.

Among the pupils and associates of Sansovino were NICCOLO BRACCINI (1485–1550), called IL TRIBOLO, and FRANCESCO SANGALLO (1498–1570), neither of whom were important artists, though many works by them are seen in various places in Italy.

BENVENUTO CELLINI (1500–1572) is a far more interesting study than were many sculptors of his time. His life was an eventful one, and his own account of it is one of the most interesting books of its class in existence. His statement of the origin of his family is that "Julius Cæsar had a chief and valorous captain named Fiorino da Cellino, from a castle situated four miles from Monte Fiascone. This Fiorino having pitched his camp below Fiesole, where Florence now stands, in order to be near the river Arno, for the convenience of the army, the soldiers and other persons, when they had the occasion to visit him, said to each other, 'Let us go to Fiorenza,' which name they gave to the place where they were encamped, partly from their captain's name of Fiorino, and partly from the abundance of flowers which grew there; wherefore Cæsar, thinking it a beautiful name, and considering flowers to be of good augury, and also wishing to honor his captain, whom he had raised from an humble station, and to whom he was greatly attached, gave it to the city which he founded on that spot."

When this artist was born his father was quite old, and named him Benvenuto, which means welcome, on account of his pleasure in the child of his old age. The father had a passion for music, and from the first wished that his son should study this art; but the boy loved drawing, and was determined to be an artist; thus his time was divided between these two pursuits until he was fifteen years old, when he was apprenticed to a goldsmith.

Benvenuto had a fiery temper, and when still very young he became involved in so serious a quarrel that he was obliged to flee from Florence. He went first to Siena, and thence to Bologna, and at last back to Florence, where he resumed his work. It was not long, however, before he became angry again because his best clothes were given to his brother, and he walked off to Pisa, where he remained a year. He had even then become so skilful in his art that some of his works done there have never been excelled either in design or execution.

When Cellini was eighteen years old Torrigiano came to Florence to engage artists to go to England to aid him in some works he was to execute. He wished to have Cellini in the number; but Torrigiano so disgusted Benvenuto by his boasting of the blow that he had given Michael Angelo, that though he had the natural youthful desire to travel, he refused to be employed by such a man as Torrigiano. We can safely assume that this predisposed Michael Angelo in Cellini's favor, and was the foundation of the friendship which he afterward showed to the younger sculptor.

From his eighteenth to his fortieth year Cellini lived mostly at Rome. He was employed by Pope Clement VII., the cardinals and Roman nobles. The Pope desired to have a cope button made and a magnificent diamond set in it. This jewel had cost Julius II. thirty-six thousand ducats. Many artists sent in designs for this button, and Clement chose that by Cellini. He used the diamond as a throne, and placed a figure of the Almighty upon it; the hand was raised as if in blessing, and many angels fluttered about the folds of the drapery, while various jewels were set around the whole. When other artists saw the design they did not believe that it could be executed successfully; but Cellini made it a perfect work of art and of beauty.

Cellini writes of himself as being very active in the siege of Rome, May 5th, 1527. He says that he killed the Constable de Bourbon, who led the siege, and that he wounded the Prince of Orange, who was chosen in Bourbon's place.

No one else saw him perform these feats. Cellini went to the Pope, who was in the Castle of St. Angelo, and he there rendered such services to the cause of the Church that the Holy Father pardoned him for all the sins into which his temper had led him—"for all the homicides he had committed or might commit in the service of the Apostolic Church." A few years later, when Cellini was called upon to take part in the defence of his own city, he put all his property into the care of a friend, and stole away to Rome.

In 1534 Cellini killed a fellow-goldsmith, called Pompeo; Paul III. was now Pope; and as he needed the services of Benvenuto very much he pardoned him. But the sculptor felt that he was in ill favor with all about him, and went to France. In about a year he returned to find that he had been accused of stealing some jewels which the pope had commanded him to take out of their settings. Cellini was held a prisoner nearly two years, but his guilt was never proved.

At the end of this time the Cardinal Ippolito d'Este obtained his release in order that he might go to France to execute some work for Francis I. Cellini remained in France five years, and received many honors and gifts; but as Madame d'Étampes and other persons to whose advice the king listened were enemies of Cellini, he never was treated as his artistic qualities merited. Francis I. really admired Cellini, and presented him with the Hôtel de Petit Nesle, which was on the site of the present Hôtel de la Monnaie; he also made him a lord, and on one occasion expressed his fear of losing him, when Madame d'Étampes replied, "The surest way of keeping him would be to hang him on a gibbet."

Of all the objects which Cellini made during his five years in France but two remain. One is a splendid salt-cellar, and the other is a nymph in bronze, which was made for the Palace of Fontainebleau, and is now in the Renaissance Museum of the Louvre. This salt-cellar is now in the Ambraser Gallery at Vienna. The frieze around the base has figures in relief which represent the hours of the day and the winds. The upper part is made like the surface of the sea, and from it rise figures of Neptune and Cybele. The first is a symbol of the salt of the sea, and the second of the spices which the earth gives. The god is placing his arm on a small ship intended for the salt, and a vessel for pepper, in the form of a triumphal arch, is near the goddess. All this is made of fine embossed gold, and has some touches of enamel-work. It is one of the finest pieces of the goldsmith's art which remains from the sixteenth century.

In 1545 Cellini returned to Florence, and remained there, with short absences, until his death. Duke Cosmo de' Medici became his patron, and commissioned him to make a statue of Perseus for the Loggia de' Lanzi. The ambition of the artist was much excited by the thought of having his work placed by those of Donatello and Michael Angelo, and all care was taken from his mind, as the Duke provided him with a comfortable house and gave him a salary sufficient for his support.

It was nine years before the statue was completed and in its place, and in this time Cellini had suffered much. Baccio Bandinelli and others were his enemies, and at times the Duke had been under their influence, and would not furnish the money necessary to the work. But at last all was ready for the casting; and just at this unfortunate moment for Cellini to leave it he was seized with a severe illness; he was suffering much, and believed himself about to die, when some one ran in shouting, "Oh, Benvenuto, your work is ruined past earthly remedy!"

Ill as he was he rushed out to the furnace, to find that the fire was too low, and the metal, being cool, had ceased flowing into the mould. By almost superhuman efforts he remedied the evil, and again the bronze flowed; he prayed earnestly, and when the mould was filled he writes: "I fell on my knees and thanked God with all my heart, after which I ate a hearty meal with my assistants, and it being then two hours before dawn, went to bed with a light heart, and slept as sweetly as if I had never been ill in all my life."

FIG. 103.—PERSEUS. *By Benvenuto Cellini.*

When the statue was unveiled Cellini's prediction that it would please all the world except Bandinelli and his friends was fulfilled. Perseus is represented just at the moment when he has cut off the head of Medusa, who was one of the Gorgons, and had turned to stone every one who looked at her. (Fig. 103.)

After the completion of the Perseus, Cellini went to Rome for a short time. While there he made a bust of Bindo Altoviti; when Michael Angelo saw this he wrote: "My Benvenuto, I have long known you as the best goldsmith in the world, and I now know you as an equally good sculptor, through the bust of Messer Bindo Altoviti." Cellini did no more important works, though he was always industrious. He made a crucifix which he intended for his own grave, but he gave it to the Duchess Eleanora; this was afterward sent to Philip II. of Spain, and is now in the Escurial.

Cellini's life was by no means a model one, but he had his good qualities. He took a widowed sister with six children to his home, and made them welcome and happy. At his death he was buried in the Church of the Annunziata, beneath the chapel of the Company of St. Luke, and many honors were paid to his memory.

His autobiography was so rich in its use of the Florentine manner of speech and so fine in its diction that it was honored as an authority by the Accademia della Crusca. He also wrote valuable works on the goldsmith's art and on bronze-casting and sculpture. He wrote poems and various kinds of verses, but his large acquaintance with popes, cardinals, kings, artists, and men of letters makes his story of his life far more interesting than his other writings.

The artists of Upper Italy were much influenced by Florentine art, as they had formerly been, and we can speak of no very great sculptor of this century who belonged to this part of the country. ALFONSO LOMBARDO (1488–1537) was a native of Lucca; his principal works are seen in Ferrara, Bologna, and Cesena.

PROPERZIA DE' ROSSI (1490–1530) was born at Bologna, and is interesting as the one Italian sculptress of that time. She was born about a year after her father had returned from the galleys, where he had worked out a sentence of eighteen years for the crime of manslaughter. Properzia seems to have inherited her father's violent temper, and was twice arraigned in court. She was very beautiful in person, and had a devoted lover in Antonio Galeazzo Malvasia de' Bottigari, who did not marry until many years after the death of Properzia.

Properzia studied drawing under Marc Antonio Raimondi, the famous engraver. She first devoted herself to the cutting of intaglios, which demanded an immense amount of patient labor. There is in the cabinet of gems in the Uffizi Gallery, at Florence, a cherry-stone carved by Properzia, on which sixty heads may be counted ; the subject is a Glory of Saints. Other like works of hers exist in the Palazzo Grassi, in Bologna. Her next work was in arabesques, marble ornaments, lions, griffins, vases, eagles, and similar objects.

Finally she essayed a bust of Count Guido Pepoli ; it is now in the Sacristy of San Petronio, in Bologna. In the same place are two bas-reliefs by her hand, Solomon receiving the Queen of Sheba, and Joseph and Potiphar's Wife. In the chapel Zambeccari in San Petronio there are two large figures of angels by Properzia, which are near the Ascension of the Virgin by Il Tribolo. Her manner was much influenced by her contact with this sculptor. Properzia was employed, with other artists, to finish the sculpture of the portal of San Petronio, left unfinished by Jacopo della Quercia.

ANTONIO BEGARELLI (1499-1565), called also ANTONIO DA MODENA, from the place of his birth, was a celebrated modeller in clay. It is said that when Michael Angelo visited Modena in 1529 he saw Begarelli and his works, and exclaimed, "Alas for the statues of the ancients, if this clay were changed to marble!" Begarelli had a school for teaching design and modelling, and he greatly influenced the manner of the Lombard school of painting. Its foreshortening, its relief and grace are largely due to him and his teaching.

Begarelli and Correggio were fast friends, and resembled

each other in their conception of the grand and beautiful. When Correggio was decorating the cupola of the Cathedral of Parma, Begarelli was at work in the same place, and made many models from which Correggio painted his floating figures. Some works by Begarelli may be seen in the Berlin Museum. His Descent from the Cross, in the Church of San Francesco, at Modena, is one of his best works. He was also employed in the Church of San Benedetto, in Mantua, and in San Giovanni, at Parma.

During the sixteenth century the works at the Certosa at Pavia and in various edifices in Milan were constantly carried on. Frequently the same sculptors worked in both cities, but there is no one artist of great excellence among them of whom we can give an account. The same is true of the works in Venice and in Southern Italy. The traveller sees many pieces of sculpture belonging to this period, but there are no great and interesting men whose story we can tell in connection with them, and I shall now pass to an account of the great Florentine.

MICHAEL ANGELO BUONARROTI (1475–1564) was born in the Castle of Caprese, where his father, Ludovico Buonarroti, was stationed at that time, holding the office of Podesta, or Governor, of the towns of Caprese and Chiusi. The Buonarroti family held good rank in Florence, and the mother of the great artist was also a woman of good position. When his father returned to Florence the child Michael was left at Settignano upon an estate of the family, and was in the care of the wife of a stone-mason. As soon as the boy could use his hands he drew pictures everywhere that it was possible, and his nurse could show many of these childish drawings with which he adorned the walls of her house.

At a proper time Michael Angelo was removed to Florence and placed in a school, where he became intimate with Francesco Granacci, who was a pupil of the artist

Ghirlandajo. Michael Angelo's father and his uncles were firmly opposed to his being an artist; they wished him to follow the traditions of his family, and carry on the silk and woollen trade. But the boy was firm in his determination, and after many trials was at length, in 1488, apprenticed to the Ghirlandaji for three years.

Domenico Ghirlandajo was at this time engaged in the restoration of the Church of Santa Maria Novella, and Michael Angelo came into the midst of great artistic works. One day at the dinner hour he drew a picture of the scaffolding and all its belongings, with the men at work on it; it was a remarkable drawing for a boy, and when the master saw it he exclaimed, "He understands more than I do myself!" The master really became jealous of his pupil, more especially when Michael Angelo corrected the drawings which Ghirlandajo gave his scholars for models.

About this time Michael Angelo was brought to the notice of Lorenzo de' Medici, who was at that time at the head of the government of Florence, and from him the boy-artist obtained admission for himelf and Granacci to study in the gardens of San Marco. The art treasures of the Medici were placed in these gardens; works of sculpture were there, and cartoons and pictures were hung in buildings erected for the purpose, and art-students were admitted to study there and proper instructors provided for them.

The master in sculpture was old Bertoldo, and Michael Angelo, forsaking painting, obtained some instruments and a piece of marble, and copied a mask of a faun. He changed his own work somewhat from the model, and opened the mouth so that the teeth could be seen. When Lorenzo saw this he praised the work, but said, "You have made your faun old, and yet you have left all his teeth; you should have known that at such an age there are generally some teeth wanting." When he came again he saw that a gap had been made in the teeth, and so well done that he was delighted. This work is now in the Uffizi Gallery.

Very soon Lorenzo sent for Michael Angelo's father, who had been sad enough at the thought that his son might be a painter, and was now in despair when he found that he inclined also to be a stone-mason. At first he refused to see the duke, but Granacci persuaded him to go. He went with a firm determination to yield to nothing, but once in presence of Lorenzo he yielded everything, and returned home declaring that not only Michael, but he himself, and all that he had were at the nobleman's service.

Lorenzo at once took Michael Angelo into his palace; he clothed the boy properly, and gave him five ducats a month for spending money. Each day Lorenzo gave an entertainment, and it was the rule that the first person who came should sit next the duke at the head of the table. Michael Angelo often had this place, and he soon became a great favorite with Lorenzo, and obtained besides the greatest advantages from the life in the palace; for many eminent men from all parts of the world came to visit there, and all sorts of subjects were discussed in such a manner that a young man could learn much of the world and what was in it, and acquire a feeling of ease with strangers and in society such as few young persons possess.

Michael Angelo was but seventeen years old when Poliziano advised him to attempt an original work, and gave him the marble for a relief of the contest between Hercules and the Centaurs. This work surprised every one, and is still preserved in the collection of the Buonarroti family. In the year 1492 he also made a relief of the Madonna Suckling the Child Jesus, which is also in the same place. In the same year Lorenzo de' Medici died, and Michael Angelo, full of grief, went to his father's house and arranged a studio there. After a time Piero de Medici invited him to come back to the palace, and he went; but it was

FIG. 104.—MICHAEL ANGELO'S ANGEL. *Bologna.*

no more the same place as formerly, and he was unhappy there. Soon political troubles drove the Medici from power, and in 1494, in the midst of the confusion, Michael Angelo escaped to Venice. There he made friends with Gian Francesco Aldovrandi of Bologna, and was persuaded by that nobleman to accompany him to his own city.

While at Bologna he executed an angel holding a candelabra, which is one of the most lovely and pleasing things he ever made (Fig. 104). When he received the commission to ornament the sarcophagus which contained the remains of San Domenico in the Church of San Petronio, the Bolognese artists were so angry at being thus set aside for a stranger, and a youth of twenty, that they threatened vengeance on him, and he returned to Florence.

It was at this time that he executed a Cupid, which was the means of leading him to Rome. The story is that when he had the statue completed Lorenzo de' Medici, a relative of his first patron, advised him to give it the appearance of an antique marble, and added that he would then sell it in Rome and get a good price for it. Michael Angelo consented to this plan, and in the end he received thirty ducats for the work. The secret of its origin was not kept, and the cardinal who had bought it sent an agent to Florence to find out the truth about it. This agent pretended to be in search of a sculptor; and when he saw Michael Angelo he asked him what works he had done. When he mentioned a Sleeping Cupid, and the agent asked questions, the young sculptor found that the cardinal had paid two hundred ducats for it, and that he had been greatly deceived when attempting to deceive others.

Michael Angelo consented to go to Rome with this man, who promised to receive him into his own house, and assured him that he would be fully occupied in the Eternal City. The oldest writing by the hand of Michael Angelo is the letter which he wrote to Lorenzo telling him of his

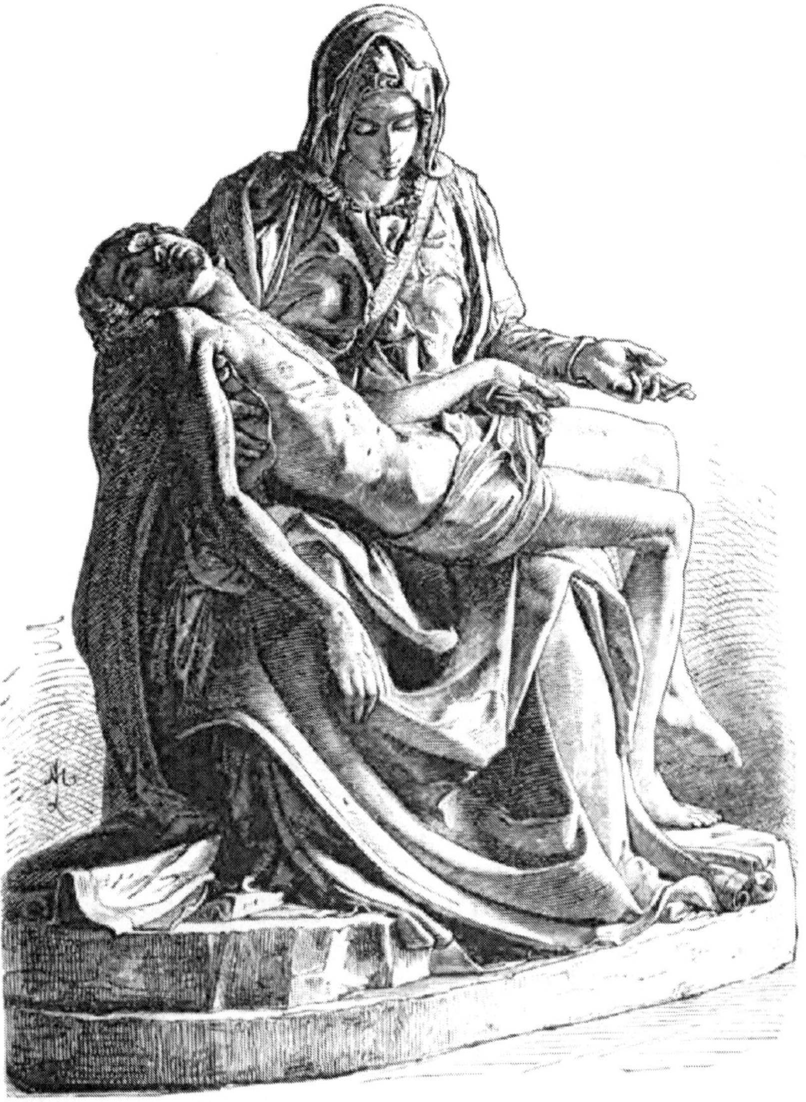

FIG. 105.—PIETÀ. *By Michael Angelo.*

arrival in Rome; when this was written he was twenty-one years old. The first work which he did after he reached Rome was the "Drunken Bacchus," now in the Uffizi Gallery; it shows a great knowledge of anatomy in one so young, and the expression of drunkenness is given in the most natural manner.

But the work that established his fame as a great sculptor is the Pietà, now in St. Peter's at Rome (Fig. 105). He was twenty-five years old when he executed this work, and from that time was acknowledged to be the greatest sculptor of Italy—a decision which has never been reversed.

Soon after this Michael Angelo returned to Florence, and his first important work was a Madonna, now at Bruges; it is life-size, and one of his finest sculptures. There was at this time an immense block of marble which had lain many years in the yard to the workshops of the cathedral. Several sculptors had talked of making something from it, and now Michael Angelo was asked by the consuls to make something good of it. He had just taken an order for fifteen statues for the Piccolomini tomb at Siena; but when he saw the immense block he gave up the Siena work, and contracted to make a statue in two years. He was to be paid six gold florins a month, and as much more as could be agreed upon when the work was done. He first made a model in wax of his David; it was very small, and is now in the Uffizi. In the beginning of 1504, after about two years and a half had been spent upon it, the work was done, and a discussion then arose as to where it should be placed.

At length it was decided to put it where Michael Angelo himself wished it to be, next the gate of the palace where the Judith of Donatello then stood. The statue weighed eighteen thousand pounds, and its removal was a work of great importance. I shall not give all the details of it here, but shall quote what Grimm says: "The erection of this

David was like an occurrence in nature from which people are accustomed to reckon. We find events dated so many years after the erection of the giant. It was mentioned in records in which there was not a line respecting art."

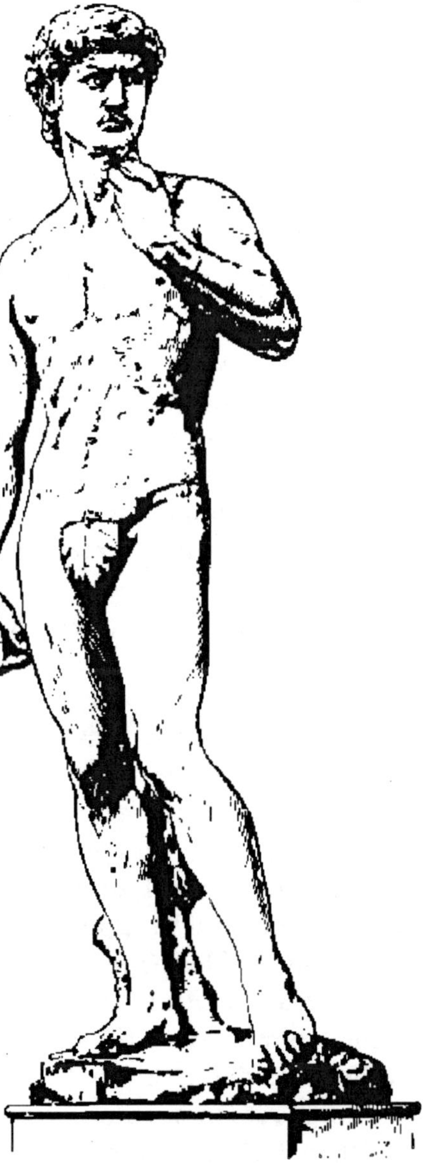

FIG. 106.—MICHAEL ANGELO'S DAVID

In 1527 the statue was injured by a stone thrown in a riot. At length it began to show the effect of time and weather, and the people of Florence talked of removing it for better preservation. There was much feeling against this; the Florentines feared that misfortunes would fall upon them if this great work were disturbed; but at last, in 1873, it was placed in the Academy of Fine Arts. It represents the youthful David at the moment when he declares to Goliath, "I come unto thee in the name of the Lord of

Hosts." The beautiful figure is muscular and pliant, and the face is full of courage. (Fig. 106.)

About the beginning of the year 1505 Pope Julius II. summoned Michael Angelo to Rome, and after a time gave him a commission to build a colossal mausoleum to be erected for himself. The design was made and accepted, and then Michael Angelo went to Carrara to select marble; after much trouble he succeeded in getting it to Rome, where all who saw it were astonished at the size of the blocks. Pope Julius was delighted, and had a passage made from the palace to the workshop of the sculptor, so that he could visit the artist without being seen. Other sculptors now became jealous of Michael Angelo, and when he went a second time to Carrara, Bramante persuaded the pope that it was a bad sign to build his tomb while he was still living. When Michael Angelo returned and the workmen he had hired arrived from Florence, he found the pope much changed toward him. He no longer hastened the work, neither would he furnish money to carry it on.

Michael Angelo sought the pope for an explanation, and was refused an audience. He wrote a letter thus: "Most Holy Father, I was this morning driven from the palace by the order of your Holiness. If you require me in future you can seek me elsewhere than in Rome." He ordered a Jew to sell all he possessed in Rome, and started for Florence, and stopped not until he was on the ground of Tuscany. The pope sent after him, but as he was a citizen of Florence he threatened the messengers if they touched him. He said he had been treated as a criminal, and he considered himself free from his engagements, and would not return then or ever.

When he reached home a letter came to the Signory of Florence urging his return, and saying that he should be safe. But Michael waited until the third letter was received, and only consented to go when it was arranged that he should be sent as an ambassador of Florence, and be under the protection of the Florentine Republic.

In November, 1506, when the pope had taken Bologna, he sent for Michael Angelo to come to him there. Michael Angelo had not yet seen the pope since he left Rome in anger. When he reached Bologna he went first to San Petronio to hear mass. A servant of the pope recognized him and led him to his Holiness. Julius was at table, but ordered that Michael Angelo should come in, and said to him, "You have waited thus long, it seems, till we should ourselves come to seek you." Michael Angelo kneeled down and begged his pardon, but added that he had remained away because he had been offended. The pope looked at him doubtfully, when one of the priests, fearing what would happen, advised the pope not to judge an ignorant artist as he would another man. Then the pope turned upon him in great anger, and declaring that he himself was ignorant and miserable, ordered him out of his sight. The poor ecclesiastic was so terrified that the attendants were obliged to carry him out, and then the pope spoke graciously to the sculptor, and commanded him not to leave Bologna without his permission. The pope soon gave him an order for a colossal statue in bronze to be erected in Bologna.

The first cast of this statue failed, and the work was not ready to be put in its place until February, 1508. This being done, Michael Angelo returned to Florence, where he had much to do; but Julius soon sent for him to go to Rome, and insisted that he should paint the roof of the Sistine Chapel, which occupied him a long time.

In 1513 Julius II. died, and Michael Angelo resumed his work upon his mausoleum. The pope had mentioned it in his will, and his heirs wished it to be completed. At this time he probably worked upon the statue of Moses and upon the two chained youths. He devoted himself to the mausoleum during three years.

Leo X., who was now pope, demanded the services of Michael Angelo to erect a façade to the Church of San Lorenzo in Florence. The artist objected to this great work, and declared that he was bound to complete the tomb for which he had already received money. But Leo insisted upon his going to Florence. He had much trouble to get his marble from the quarries—the men were ill there. He was ill himself, and he passed a year of great anxiety and trouble, when there came word from Rome that the work must be given up; the building was postponed, and no payment was made to Michael Angelo! He was much disheartened, but returned to his work on the mausoleum.

About 1523, when, after many changes, Cardinal Medici was pope, the work at San Lorenzo was resumed. But in 1525 the pope again summoned Michael Angelo to Rome. The heirs of Julius were complaining of delay, but at last the pope insisted upon his great need of the artist, and again he was sent back to Florence, where the cupola of the new Sacristy to San Lorenzo was soon finished. Great political confusion now ensued, and little can be said of Michael Angelo as a sculptor until 1530, when he again resumed his work on the Sacristy.

He worked with the greatest industry and rapidity, and in a few months had nearly finished the four colossal figures which rest upon the sarcophagi of Lorenzo and Giuliano de' Medici. The pope was forced to command the sculptor to rest. His health was so broken by the sorrow which the political condition of Florence caused him, and by his anxiety about the mausoleum of Julius, that there was much danger of his killing himself with work and worry. He went to Rome, and matters were more satisfactorily arranged. He returned to Florence, and labored there until 1534, when Clement VII. died, and Michael Angelo left

FIG. 107.—GIULIANO DE' MEDICI. *By Michael Angelo.*

his work in San Lorenzo, never to resume it. Unfinished as these sculptures are, they make a grand part of the wonderful works of this great man. The statues of the two Medici and those of Morning, Evening, Day, and Night would be sufficient to establish the fame of an artist if he had done nothing more. (Fig. 107.)

Under the new pope, Paul III., he was constantly employed as a painter, and architectural labors were put upon him, so that as a sculptor we have no more works of his to mention except an unfinished group which was in his studio at the time of his death. It represents the dead Christ upon his mother's lap, with Joseph of Arimathea standing by. This group is now in the Church of Santa Maria del Fiore, or the Cathedral of Florence. The mausoleum of Julius II. caused Michael Angelo and others so much trouble and vexation that the whole affair came to be known as the "tragedy of the sepulchre." When Julius first ordered it he intended to place it in St. Peter's, but in the end it was erected in the Church of San Pietro in Vincoli, of which Julius had been the titular cardinal. Of all the monument but three figures can really be called the work of Michael Angelo. These are the Leah and Rachel upon the lower stage, and the Moses, which is one of the most famous statues in the world. Paul III., with eight cardinals, once visited the studio of the sculptor when he was at work upon this statue, and they declared that this alone was sufficient for the pope's monument (Fig. 108).

The life of Michael Angelo was a sad one; indeed, it is scarcely possible to recount a more pathetic story than was his. The misfortunes which came to the Medici were sharp griefs to him, and his temperament was such that he could not forget his woes. His family, too, looked to him for large sums of money, and while he lived most frugally they spent his earnings. In his old age he said, "Rich as I am, I have always lived like a poor man."

FIG. 108.—STATUE OF MOSES. *By Michael Angelo.*

In 1529, when Florence was under great political excitement, Michael Angelo was appointed superintendent of all the fortifications of the Florentine territory. In the midst of his duties he became aware of facts which determined him to fly. He went to Venice, and was proscribed as a rebel. We cannot stay here to inquire as to his wisdom in this, but must go on to say that at length he was so much needed that he was persuaded to return. Then he had the dreadful experiences of hope and fear, sickness and famine, and all the horrors of a siege, only to see his beloved home deprived of its freedom, and in the possession of those whom he despised and hated. To Michael Angelo this was far more bitter than any personal sorrow; he never recovered from its effects, and it was immediately after this that he worked in the Sacristy of San Lorenzo as if trying to kill himself.

He was bold as he was angry. He was treated kindly, and advised to forget the past; but he never concealed his views. When his statue of Night was exhibited, verses were put upon it, according to the custom of the time; one verse read, "Night, whom you see slumbering here so charmingly, has been carved by an angel, in marble. She sleeps, she lives; waken her, if you will not believe it, and she will speak."

To this Michael Angelo replied, "Sleep is dear to me, and still more that I am stone, so long as dishonor and shame last among us; the happiest fate is to see, to hear nothing; for this reason waken me not. I pray you, speak gently." He had great courage to speak his anger thus publicly in the midst of those who could easily destroy him.

In 1537 or 1538 his father died, and the artist suffered terribly from his grief. He wrote a sonnet beginning:

"Already had I wept and sighed so much,
I thought all grief forever at an end,
Exhaled in sighs, shed forth in bitter tears."

The religious views of Michael Angelo were very broad, and he had a trustful and obedient dependence upon God, in whose mercy and love he gratefully rested with the simple faith of a child. It was not far from the time when his father died that Michael Angelo first met Vittoria Colonna. He was now more than sixty years old ; and though his poems show that he had loved children and women all his life, yet he had allowed himself no attachments ; his life had been lonely and alone. Now, at this late hour, he yielded his heart to this beautiful, gifted woman, who returned his friendship with the fullest esteem. During these years he was happier than he had ever been. But in 1541 she fell under the suspicion of the Inquisition, and was obliged to leave Rome.

During two years they wrote constantly to each other, and each sent to the other the sonnets they wrote. At this time all Italy read the poems of Vittoria, and those of Michael Angelo still stand the test of time. In them he shows the blessed effect of her influence over him. At length she returned to Rome and entered a convent, where she died in 1547. Michael Angelo was with her to the last, and years later he declared that he regretted nothing so much as that he had only kissed her hand, and not her forehead or cheeks in that last hour. His loss was far too great to be told. (An engraving of a portrait of Michael Angelo can be seen in Mrs. Clement's "Painting," p. 95.)

In the year following Vittoria's death all the hopes which he had cherished for the freedom of Florence were crushed. High honors were offered him to induce him to return there, but he would not go. His health failed, his sadness increased, and his writings show how constantly he mourned for Vittoria. After this he did much work as an architect, and held the post of director of the building of St. Peter's. He superintended the erection of the statue of Marcus Aurelius, and completed the Farnese Palace, and had many improvements in mind.

Now, in his old age, he was authority itself in Rome. He had no rival, and his advice was sought by artists as well as others. He lived very simply: he dined alone, and received his visitors in the plainest manner. Anatomy, which had always been a passion with him, was now his chief pursuit. He made many dissections of animals, and was grateful when a human subject could be allowed him.

When he could not sleep he would get up at night and work upon the group of which we have spoken; he had a cap with a candle in it, so that it cast a light upon his work. Vasari once entered when he was at work upon this group, and had a lantern in his hand; he dropped it purposely, so that the sculpture should not be seen, and said: "I am so old that death often pulls me by the coat to come to him, and some day I shall fall down like this lantern, and my last spark of life will be extinguished."

There are many very interesting circumstances told of his last years and his strength of mind, and the work which he did was wonderful; but we have not space to recount it here.

At length, in February, 1564, when almost ninety years old, he died. He had asked to be buried in Florence. His friends feared that this would be opposed, so they held burial-services in Rome, and his body was afterward carried through the gates as merchandise. In Florence the body was first laid in San Piero Maggiore, and on Sunday, at evening, the artists assembled, and forming a procession, proceeded to Santa Croce, where he was buried. The younger artists bore the bier upon their shoulders, and the older ones carried torches to light the way. A great multitude followed the procession, and in the Sacristy of Santa Croce the coffin was opened; though three weeks had passed since his death, his face appeared as if he had just died; the crowd was very great, but all was quiet, and before morning it had dispersed. The Duke had thought that a public funeral would recall old memories, and might cause a disturbance ; but Michael Angelo had left Florence thirty years before his death, and his connection with the city was forgotten by many.

The July following was appointed for a memorial service in his honor ; San Lorenzo was splendidly decorated ; Varchi delivered an oration. Leonardo, his nephew, erected a monument to him in Santa Croce, for which the Duke gave the marble. His statue stands in the court of the Uffizi with those of other great Florentines, but with no especial prominence. His house in the Ghibelline Street is preserved as a museum, and visitors there see many mementos of this great man.

In 1875 a grand festival was held in Florence to celebrate the four hundredth anniversary of his birth. The ceremonies were impressive, and certain documents relating to his life which had never been opened, by command of the king, were given to suitable persons for examination. Mr. Heath Wilson, an English artist, then residing at Florence, wrote a new life of Michael Angelo, and the last signature which Victor Emmanuel wrote before his death was upon the paper which conferred on Mr. Wilson the Order of the *Corona d'Italia*, given as a recognition of his services in writing this book.

The national pride in Michael Angelo is very strong. "All Italians feel that he occupies the third place by the side of Dante and Raphael, and forms with them a triumvirate of the greatest men produced by their country—a poet, a painter, and one who was great in all arts. Who would place a general or a statesman by their side as equal to them ? It is art alone which marks the prime of nations."

The genius of Michael Angelo and his spirit were powerful forces. They pervaded the whole art of Italy to such an extent that it may be said that all sculptors were his imitators, both while he lived and after his death. He loved to treat strong subjects, such as demanded violent movement and unusual positions. It was only a man of his genius who could raise such subjects above grotesqueness and the one effect of strange and unnatural exaggeration. As we look over all his works it seems as if the idea of beauty and such things as are pleasing to the ordinary mind rarely, if ever, came to his mind. Noble feeling, depth of thought, strength, and grandeur are the associations which we have with him, and in the hands of weaker men, as his imitators were, these subjects became barren, hollow displays of distorted limbs and soulless heads and faces.

The result is, that there is little to be said of the immediate followers of this great man. GUGLIELMO DELLA PORTA was one of his most able scholars, and his chief work was a monument to Pope Paul III. in the Church of St. Peter's. The figure of the pope is in bronze, is seated, and holding the right hand in benediction. It is dignified and well designed. The figures of Justice and Prudence are not as good, and two others, Peace and Abundance, which were a part of this work, but are now in the Farnese Palace, lack power, and show an attempt at a representation of mere physical beauty.

BACCIO BANDINELLI (1487–1559) is more noticeable for his hatred of Michael Angelo than for any other characteristic. He was a native of Florence and a friend of Leonardo da Vinci. He was powerful in his design and bold in his treatment of his subjects, but he was full of affectation and mannerisms in his execution of his works. He was false and envious, and his one good quality was that of industry. His best works are on the screen of the high-altar in the Cathedral of Florence, a relief on a pedestal in the Piazza of San Lorenzo, in Florence, and a group in the Church of the Annunziata, which he intended for his own monument; the subject is Nicodemus supporting Christ, and the Nicodemus is a portrait of Bandinelli himself.

# CHAPTER VIII.

## EUROPEAN SCULPTURE FROM MICHAEL ANGELO TO CANOVA.

NOT only Italian artists attempted to follow the great sculptor of Italy, but those of other nations flocked to Rome, and whatever ideas they may have had before reaching that city they seemed to lose them all and to aim simply at one thing—to be Michaelangeloesque.

GIOVANNI DA BOLOGNA (1529–1608) was born in Douai, in Flanders, and was called Il Fiammingo for this reason. Giovanni was intended for a notary by his father, who planned his education with that end in view; but the boy's passion for sculpture was so great that the father was obliged to yield to it, and placed him under the instruction of a sculptor named Beuch, who had studied in Italy. Later Giovanni went to Rome, and finally settled in Florence, where his most important works remain.

He was an imitator of Michael Angelo, and one of his best imitators; but when his works are compared with those of the great master, or with the masterpieces of the fifteenth century, we see a decline in them. In religious subjects Giovanni was not at home; his most successful works were those which represented sentiment or abstract ideas, because on them he could lavish his skill in execution, and use ornaments that did not suit the simplicity of religious subjects. In the Loggia de' Lanzi, at Florence, there are two groups by him, the Rape of the Sabines and Hercules and Nessus. In the Piazza della Signoria is his excellent statue of Duke Cosmo I., and in the Uffizi Gallery a bronze statue of Mercury. The Rape of the Sabines is his masterpiece, and the Mercury is one of the best works of its kind since the days of classic art. It is the favorite Mercury of the world, and has been frequently copied. It is seen in many galleries and collections in its original size, and a small copy is much used in private houses. (Fig. 109.)

Giovanni was especially happy in his designs for fountains, and that which he erected in Bologna, in 1564, in front of the Palazzo Pubblico, is a splendid work of this kind. The statue of Neptune at its summit is stately and free in its action; the children are charming and life-like, and the Sirens at the base give an harmonious finish and complete the outline with easy grace.

He also erected a magnificent fountain in the island of the Boboli Gardens. In the Palazzo Vecchio is a marble group by Giovanni representing Virtue conquering Vice. At Petraja there is a beautiful Venus crowning a fountain remarkable for grace and delicacy, and, all in all, his works prove him to have been the best sculptor of his own time. Tuscany may claim him and be proud of him, for he was far more her son than that of his native Flanders.

Giovanni da Bologna was far less successful in reliefs than in statues, as may be seen in the bronze gates to the Cathedral of Pisa, which he made in the last years of his life. In his character this master was attractive and much beloved by his friends. One of them wrote of him: "The best fellow in the world, not in the least covetous, as he shows by his poverty; filled with a love of glory, and ambitious of rivalling Michael Angelo."

Giovanni decorated a chapel in the Church of the Annunziata with several reliefs in bronze and with a crucifix;

FIG. 109.—MERCURY. *By Giovanni da Bologna.*

he not only wished to be buried here himself, as he was, but he also desired to provide a place of burial for any of his countrymen who might die in Florence. The chapel is called that of the Madonna del Soccorso.

The decline of sculpture in Italy at this period makes its study so unpromising that it is a pleasure to turn to France, where the works of JEAN GOUJON show that he had the true idea of sculpture in relief. From 1555 to 1562 this sculptor was employed on the works at the Louvre, and during the massacre of St. Bartholomew he was shot while on a scaffold quietly working at a bas-relief on that palace.

Goujon was an architect as well as a sculptor, and also a medal engraver, as is shown by the curious and rare medal which he made for Catherine de' Medici. Many of his works are preserved in different parts of France, and some bas-reliefs in the Museum of the Louvre are excellent specimens of his style.

One also sees in France many works by GERMAIN PILON, who died in 1590. He executed the monument to Francis I., and took a part in that of Henry II. and Catherine de' Medici at the Church of St. Denis. He was the sculptor of the group of the three Graces in the Louvre, which formerly bore an urn containing the heart of Henry II., and was in the Church of the Celestines.

But the sculptors of France at this time are not of such interest as to hold our attention long. There was a certain amount of spirit in their decorations of palaces and tombs, but there were no men of great genius, and no splendid works upon which we can dwell with pleasure or profit.

In Germany, too, while there was much activity in sculpture, and public fountains and luxurious palaces and rich ornaments employed many artists, yet there was no originality or freshness in these works, and they fell below those of the past. Bronzes are still made at Nuremberg, but they only serve to make one regret that they are so inferior to those of earlier days ; and nowhere in all Germany does any one artist stand out and present a man to be studied in his works or remembered as one of the gifted of the earth. And yet a list of the names of German sculptors of this time would be very long, for all over the land churches were being decorated, monuments built, and statues and fountains erected.

In England the best sculpture of the sixteenth century was seen in the portrait statues on monuments, and we find no great artists there of whom to give an account.

In Spain ALONSO BERRUGUETE (1480–1561), who was the most eminent artist of his time, had introduced the Italian manner. He went to Italy about 1503, and studied

FIG. 110.—RELIEF BY BERRUGUETE. *Valladolid.*

in Rome and Florence during seventeen years. This was at the time when Italian sculpture was at the height of its excellence ; and Berruguete returned to Spain filled with the purest and best conceptions of what art should be, and the ends it should serve. He has been called the Michael Angelo of Spain, because he was an architect, painter, and sculptor.

Upon his return to Spain he was appointed painter and sculptor to Charles V. Among his most celebrated works in sculpture are the reliefs in the choir of the Cathedral at Toledo; the altar in the Church of San Benito el Real at Valladolid (Fig. 110), for which he was paid forty-four hundred ducats, and his sculptures in the Collegio Mayor at Salamanca. His final work was a monument to the Cardinal and Grand Inquisitor, Don Juan de Tavera, which is in the Church of the Hospital of St. John at Toledo. The sarcophagus is ornamented by reliefs from the story of John the Baptist, which are executed in an excellent manner, simple and expressive.

Other Spanish sculptors were ESTEBAN JORDAN, an eminent wood-carver, GREGORIO HERNANDEZ (1566–1636), who has been called "the sculptor of religion." His works are so full of a spirit of devotion that they seem to have been executed under an inspiration. Hernandez was very devout in his life, and did many works of charity; he often provided decent burial for the very poor who died without friends who could bury them.

Many of his works have been removed from the chapels for which they were designed, and are now in the Museum of Valladolid, where they are not as effective as when placed in their original positions. He is superior to other Spanish sculptors in his representation of nude figures and in the grandeur of his expression.

JUAN DE JUNI (died 1614) studied in Italy, and acquired much mannerism; his works are seen in Valladolid.

JUAN MARTINEZ MONTAÑES (died 1650) was a famous sculptor, and excelled in figures of children and cherubs. His conceptions had much beauty and depth of feeling, and his draperies were most graceful; and to this power of thinking out clearly and well the subject he wished to represent he added the ability to do his work in an artistic manner, and to give it an elegance of finish without taking away its strength. A Conception by him, in the Cathedral of Seville, is a noble work, and in the university church of the same city there is an altar which is one of his important works. Other sculptures by Montañes are in the Museum of Seville.

The great ALONSO CANO (1601–1667) was a pupil of Montañes in sculpture, and, like so many other artists of his time, was a painter and architect as well as a sculptor. His personal history is very peculiar. He was a man of violent temper, and was often involved in serious quarrels. He was obliged to flee from Granada to Madrid on account of a duel, and when his wife was found murdered in her bed he was suspected of the crime. In spite of all this he took priest's orders, and was appointed to a canonry in the Cathedral of Granada; but on account of his temper he was deprived of this office by the chapter of the cathedral. He was so angry at this that he would do no more work for the cathedral.

He devoted the remainder of his life to religious and charitable works. He gave away the money he earned as soon as he received it, and when he had no money to give away he was in the habit of making drawings, which he signed and marked with a suitable price; these he gave to the person he desired to assist, and recommended some person to whom application to buy the work could be made. After his death a large number of these charitable works was collected.

He hated Jews with such hatred that he could not endure to look at one, and many strange stories are told of him in connection with these people.

He loved his chisel better than his brush, and was accustomed to say that when weary he carved for rest. One of his pupils expressed great surprise at this, when Cano answered, "Blockhead, don't you perceive that to create form and relief on a flat surface is a greater service than to fashion one shape into another?"

The most beautiful sculpture by Cano which remains is a Virgin about a foot high in the Sacristy of the Cathedral of Granada, where there are several other statuettes by him. These are colored in a manner which the Spaniards call "estofado;" it has the effect to soften the whole appearance of the works, like an enamel. At the entrance of the choir of the cathedral there are two colossal busts by Cano; they are grand works, and are called Adam and Eve.

PEDRO ROLDAN (1624–1700), born at Seville, is an interesting sculptor because of his work, and on account of his being the last one whose manner was like that of Juni and Hernandez. His first celebrated work was the high-altar in the chapel of the Biscayans in the Franciscan convent. When the Caridad, or Hospital of Charity, was restored, Roldan executed the last great work in painted sculpture; it was an immense piece for the centre of the retablo of the high-altar of the church, and represented the Entombment of Christ.

Seville abounds in his works, and he executed bas-reliefs in stone for the exterior of the Cathedral at Jaen. He was so devoted to his art that he felt every moment to be lost that was not spent in its service. He married a lady of good family, and lived in the country; when obliged to go to Seville he was accustomed to carry a lump of clay, and model from it as he rode along. Roldan was not by any means the best of Spanish sculptors, but he had great skill in the composition of his works, and the draperies and all the details were carefully studied. His daughter, Doña Luisa Roldan, studied sculpture under her father's instruction, and became a good artist; he was accustomed to allow her to superintend her studio and his pupils. She often aided him by her suggestions, and on one occasion, when a statue that he had made was rejected, she pointed out to him certain anatomical defects, which he remedied, and the whole appearance of the work was so changed that it was thought to be new, and was accepted for the place for which it had been ordered.

The works executed by Doña Luisa were principally small figures of the Virgin, the Adoration of the Shepherds, and kindred subjects. Several of these were presented to King Charles II., and he was so pleased by them that he ordered a life-size statue of St. Michael for the Church of the Escorial. She executed this to his satisfaction, and he then appointed her sculptress in ordinary to the king. She died at Madrid in 1704, surviving her father but four years. She left works in various convents and churches.

In Italy at the beginning of the seventeenth century a new era in sculpture was inaugurated. Art was now required to serve the Church in the way of appealing to sentiments and feeling in a far coarser and more sensational a manner than formerly. Painting was suited to these purposes far more than sculpture, and it had been raised to great heights, in Spain, by Murillo, in the North by Rubens and his followers, and in Italy by numerous masters.

Lübke says of this period: "All that was now demanded of art was effect and feeling at any price. The one was attained through the other. A passionate excitement pulsates throughout all artistic works; the ideal repose of the former altar-pieces no longer satisfied. Longing, devotional ardor, passionate rapture, enthusiastic ecstasy—these are the aims of the new art. No longer the solemn dignity of the saint, but the nervous visions of enraptured monks, are its ideal. It delights in thrilling delineations of martyrdom, seeking to render such scenes as effective and touching as possible. A desire for substantial power, a political-religious tendency, had taken possession of art, and had adapted it to its own objects. That, under such circumstances, painting reaches a new and truly artistic importance may be traced above all to the great masters who now cultivated the art, and still more to the tone of the age, which promoted it in a rare measure. . . . The same spirit, however, which imparted such genuine importance to painting produced the ruin of sculpture. This epoch, more than any other, is a proof that the greatest men of talent, appearing in a perverted age, are carried by their very genius all the more certainly to ruin. All that, in a more favorable period, would have raised them to be stars in the art firmament, now made them fall like some *ignis fatuus*, the brilliant light of which owes its illusory existence only to miasma. This striking fact appears, at first sight, inexplicable ; but it is easy to understand, if we consider the different character of the two arts. Plastic art had formerly emulated painting, and thus, especially in relief, had suffered unmistakable injury to its own peculiar nature. At that time, however, painting itself was full of architectural severity and plastic nobleness of form. Now, when everything depended on striking effect and speaking delineation of passionate emotions, it was compelled to have recourse to naturalistic representation, to freer arrangements and to more striking forms that emulated reality. If, however, sculpture, which could not keep pace with its rival in the enamelled coloring and mysterious charm of the *chiaro-oscuro* which it brought into the field, would, in anywise, do the same as painting, it was compelled to plunge regardlessly into the same naturalism of forms and into the same bold display of passion with which painting produced such grand effects. And this sculpture did without the slightest scruple, and in this lack of an artistic conscience its whole glory perished. It is true in this passion for excited compositions an excess of splendid works were produced ; it is true immense resources were expended, and able artists were employed ; but such inner hollowness stares at us with inanimate eye from the greater number of these works that we turn from them with repugnance, and even often with disgust."

The artist who first met this new demand upon sculpture, and may be called the founder of a new style, was GIOVANNI LORENZO BERNINI (1598–1680), a very gifted man. When but ten years old this remarkable genius was known as a prodigy in art, and it was at this early age that his father took him to Rome. Pope Paul V. was soon interested in him, and Cardinal Barberini assisted him in his studies ; from this fortunate beginning all through his life good fortune attended his steps. He lived through the pontificate of nine popes, and was always in favor with the reigning head of the Church. This gave him the opportunity to fill Rome with his works, and he imprinted himself upon the art of the Eternal City ; no artist since the time of Michael Angelo held such sway, and Bernini acquired his power easily, while the grand Michael Angelo was disputed at every step, and fought a long, hard battle before he was allowed to take the place which was so clearly his by right.

The fame of Bernini extended to other lands, and he was invited to France, where he went when sixty-eight years old, accompanied by one of his sons and a numerous retinue. He was loaded with favors, and received large sums of money and many valuable presents. In Rome, too, he was much favored ; he held several church benefices, and his son was made a Canon of Santa Maria Maggiore ; and it was in this church that Bernini was buried with great magnificence, as became his position and his wealth, for he left the immense fortune of four hundred thousand Roman crowns.

Bernini had great versatility of talent, a remarkable imagination and power of conceiving his subjects clearly, and, more than all, he had marvellous power of execution and compelling his marble to show forth his thought. It has been said that marble was like wax or clay beneath his hand. He was subject to no rules; indeed, he believed that an artist must set aside all rules if he would excel. This sounds very fascinating, but a study of Bernini's works will show that it is a deceitful maxim. A man of small talent could do nothing in this way, and even Bernini, who without doubt had great gifts, often failed to make up in any way for the sins against rules of which he was guilty. Westmacott, in his writing upon sculpture, says it would have been better for art if Bernini had never lived; and it is true that in his struggle for effect he was an injury rather than a benefit to the art of his own day and the succeeding years.

The worst defect in the sculpture of Bernini is his treatment of the human body. At times he exaggerates the muscular power beyond all resemblance to nature, and again he seems to leave out all anatomy and soften the body to a point that far exceeds possibility. This softness is seen in his Apollo and Daphne, which shows the moment when she is suddenly changed into a laurel-tree in order to escape the pursuit of the young god. This group is in the Villa Borghese, at Rome; it was executed when Bernini was but eighteen years old, and near the close of his life he declared that he had made little progress after its production.

But he reached the height of this objectionable manner in his representation of the Rape of Proserpine, which is in the Villa Ludovisi. The Pluto is a rough, repulsive man, with whom no association of a god can be made, and the Proserpine is made a soulless, sensual figure, so far from attractive in a pure sense that we are almost willing that Pluto should carry her to some region from which she is not likely to come back. At the same time we are sorry not to provide her with an ointment for the blue marks which the big hands of Pluto are making on her soft flesh. The plain truth is, that this work makes a low and common thing of a subject which could be so treated as to be a "thing of beauty" in a charming sense. (Fig. 111.)

FIG. 111.—RAPE OF PROSERPINE.
*By Bernini.*

Bernini executed a statue of St. Bibiana for the church of that saint at Rome, and one of St. Longinus in one of the niches to the dome of St. Peter's; he also made the designs for the one hundred and sixty-two statues in the colonnades of St. Peter's, and for the decorations of the bridge of St. Angelo; in such works, almost without exception, he chose some moment in the lives of the persons represented that called for a striking attitude and gave an opportunity for an effect that is often theatrical. As a mere decoration such statues have a certain value of an inferior sort; but as works of art, as intellectual efforts, they are worthless. However, this decorative effect, as it is seen on the façade of the Lateran, where the figures stand out against the sky, or on the bridge of St. Angelo, is not by any means to be despised; only we cannot call a sculptor a great artist when he can do nothing finer than this.

Some of Bernini's works in which he shows intense suffering have more genuine feeling, and are finer in artistic qualities. One of these is Pietà, in the chapel of St. Andreas Corsini in the Lateran. But he frequently goes beyond the bounds of good taste, as, for example, on the monument to Pope Urban VIII., in St. Peter's, where he represents Death with his bony hand writing the inscription on the panel; this is truly terrible, and not less so is another Death upon the monument of Alexander VII., raising the marble curtain before the entrance to the vault, as if he were inviting one to walk in. Many objections can be made to his draperies. He exaggerated the small curtains seen on some ancient tombs until they were huge objects of ugliness; the drapery upon his figures is so prominently treated that instead of being a minor object it sometimes seems like the principal one; it no longer serves to conceal forms, and at the same time show their grace and motion, but it is inflated, fluttering, grotesque in form and quite absurd when compared with statues in which it answers its true purpose.

Charles I. of England heard so much of Bernini that he desired to have a statue of himself executed by this sculptor; three of Vandyck's portraits of the king were sent to him, and the likeness of the statue was so satisfactory to the monarch that he sent the artist six thousand crowns and a ring worth as much more.

Bernini executed a colossal equestrian statue of Constantine for the portico of St. Peter's; he made another of Louis XIV., which was changed into a Marcus Curtius, and sent to Versailles. He also executed the fountain in the Piazza Navona, at Rome, which is one of his exaggerated works.

FRANÇOIS DUQUESNOY (1594–1646) was born at Brussels, and was known in Rome as Il Fiammingo. The Archduke Albert sent him to Rome to study, and he was a contemporary of Bernini. When his patron died Duquesnoy was left without means, and was forced to carve small figures in ivory for his support. His figures of children, which were full of life and child-like expression, became quite famous. An important work of his in this way is the fountain of the Manneken-Pis, at Brussels.

His masterpiece is a colossal statue of St. Andrew in the Church of St. Peter's; it occupied him five years, and is one of the best works of modern art. His statue of St. Susanna in the Church of Santa Maria di Loreto, in Rome, is simple and noble, and is much admired. Little is known of this artist's life, and it is said that he was poisoned by his brother when on his way to France.

There was a goodly company of sculptors following Bernini, but none whose works or life was of sufficient importance or interest to demand our attention here, and we will pass to the sculpture of France, where the arts were less devoted to the service of the Church and more to the uses of kings, princes, and noblemen. The court of France was devoted to pomp and pleasure, and sculpture was used for the glorification of the leaders in all its follies. In one sense this is more agreeable than the art in Italy which we have been considering, for nothing can be more disagreeable than a false religious sentiment in art; it is only when the artist is filled with true devotion and feels deeply in his own soul all that he tries to express in his work that religious representations can appeal to us agreeably or benefit us by their influence.

SIMON GUILLAIN (1581–1658) is especially interesting as the sculptor of the statue of Louis XIV. as a boy, which is in the Louvre; those of his parents are also there; formerly they decorated the Pont au Change. Other works by this master are in the same museum.

JACQUES SARRAZIN (1588–1660) is only known by his works, which are now in the Louvre, of which a bronze bust of the Chancellor Pierre Séguier is worthy of notice.

François Anguier (1604–1669) was born at Eu, in Normandy, and was the son of a carpenter, who taught his son to carve in wood at an early age. When still quite young François went to Paris to study, and later to Rome. He became one of the first artists of his time in France, and was a favorite of the king, Louis XIII., who made him keeper of the gallery of antiquities, and gave him apartments in the Louvre. Most of his important works were monuments to illustrious men. His copies of antique sculptures were very fine.

Michel Anguier (1612–1686) was a brother of the preceding, with whom he studied until they both went to Rome. Michel remained there ten years, and was employed with other artists in St. Peter's and in some palaces. In 1651 he returned to Paris, and assisted François in the great work of the tomb of the Duke de Montmorenci at Moulins.

Michel executed a statue of Louis XIII., which was cast in bronze. He adorned the apartments of Queen Anne of Austria in the Louvre, and for her executed the principal sculptures in the Church of Val de Grace; a Nativity in this church is his best work. His sculptures are seen in various churches, and he also executed statues of ancient gods and vases for garden ornaments. He was a professor in the Academy of Arts in Paris, and wrote lectures on sculpture.

François Girardon (1630–1715), born at Troyes, was a *protégé* of the Chancellor Séguier. Louis XIV. gave him a pension, by which he was enabled to study in Rome, and after his return to France the king gave him many commissions. The monument to Cardinal Richelieu in the Church of the Sorbonne is from the hand of this sculptor. Perhaps his best-known work is the Rape of Proserpine at Versailles. He made an equestrian statue of Louis XIV., which was destroyed in the Revolution; a model of it in bronze is in the Louvre. His bust of Boileau is a strong, fine work. Many of his sculptures were destroyed by the revolutionists.

A devoted follower of Bernini was PIERRE PUGET (1622–1694). His works are seen at the Louvre and at Versailles. His group of Milo of Crotona endeavoring to free himself from the claws of the lion is full of life and is natural, but the subject is too repulsive to be long examined ; his Perseus liberating Andromeda is more agreeable, and is noble in its forms and animated in expression. His Alexander and Diogenes is in relief, and is effective and picturesque.

ANTOINE COYSEVOX (1640–1720) was born at Lyons, and manifested his artistic talent very early in life. Before he was seventeen years old he had distinguished himself by a statue of the Virgin, and progressed rapidly in his studies, which he made in Paris. In 1667 he was engaged by Cardinal Furstenburg to go to Alsace to decorate his palace ; this occupied him four years. When he again went to Paris he became a very eminent artist. He executed a statue of Louis XIV., and received a commission from the province of Bretagne for an equestrian statue of the same monarch.

Among his best works are the tomb of Cardinal Mazarin ; the tomb of the great Colbert in the Church of St. Eustache ; the monument of Charles le Brun in the Church of St. Nicolas ; the statue of the great Condé ; the marble statue of Louis XIV., in the Church of Notre Dame, and others. In the tomb of Mazarin he showed fine powers of construction and excellence of design. The kneeling figure of the minister is a dignified statue and well executed ; the statues in bronze of Prudence, Peace, and Fidelity, and the marble figures of Charity and Religion are each and all noble works, and free to a remarkable degree from the mannerisms and faults of his time.

NICOLAS COUSTOU (1658–1733) was a nephew and pupil of Coysevox. He took the grand prize at Paris, and went to Rome to study when he was twenty-three years old. He made many copies of the antique. After his return to France he was much employed. His chief work was a colossal representation of the Junction of the Seine and the Marne. He also made for the city of Lyons a bronze statue representing the river Saone. Some of his sculptures are in the Church of Notre Dame.

GUILLAUME COUSTOU (1678–1746), brother of Nicolas, also gained the grand prize and went to Rome, and on his return made a fine reputation. Much of his best work was for the gardens of Marly; he executed a bronze statue of the Rhone at Lyons; a bas-relief of Christ with the Doctors, at Versailles, and statues of Louis XIV. and Cardinal Dubois, in the Museum of French Monuments.

JEAN BAPTISTE PIGALLE (1714–1785) is the last French sculptor of whom I shall speak here. He was born in Paris, and gained his first fame by a statue of Mercury; but his masterpiece was the tomb of Marshal Moritz of Saxony, in the Church of St. Thomas, at Strasburg. The soldier is represented in his own costume, just as he wore it in life, about to enter a tomb, on one side of which stands a skeleton Death, and on the other a mourning Hercules. A statue representing France tries to hold him back, and a Genius attends on him with an inverted torch. There are many accessories of military emblems and trophies. There have been several engravings made from this tomb, the best part of which is the figure of the Marshal.

Pigalle was a favorite with Mme. Pompadour, of whom he made a portrait statue. She employed him to do many works for her. His best monument in Paris is that of the Comte d'Harcourt, in the Church of Notre Dame.

In the Netherlands, as in Italy, the painting of the time had a great effect upon sculpture, and it was full of energy, like the pictures of the Rubens school; at the same time there remained traces of the traditions of former days, and while a great change had come since the days of Vischer, there was still a firm adherence to nature, and no such affectations and mannerisms existed here as were seen in the works of Bernini and his followers in Italy and France.

One of the ablest sculptors of his day was ARTHUR QUELLINUS, who was born at Antwerp in 1607. He studied under Duquesnoy, and was especially happy in his manner of imagining his subjects, and of avoiding the imitation of others or a commonplace treatment of his own. The magnificent Town Hall of Antwerp was commenced in 1648, and Quellinus received the commission to decorate it with plastic works. His sculptures are numerous, both on the interior and exterior of the edifice. In the two pediments he introduced allegorical representations of the power of the city of Antwerp, especially in her commerce. These compositions are picturesque in their arrangement, but the treatment is such as belongs to sculpture; in one of these a figure which represents the city is enthroned like a queen, and is surrounded by fantastic sea-gods, who offer their homage to her. (Fig. 112.)

FIG. 112.—CARYATIDE. *Quellinus.*

We cannot give a list of many detached works by Quellinus, but one of the best of the old monuments in Berlin is attributed to him. It is the tomb of Count Sparr in the Marienkirche.

At the present day Berlin is a city of much artistic importance, and the beginning of its present architectural and sculptural prominence may be dated at about the end of the seventeenth century, not quite two hundred years ago. One of the most influential artists of that time was ANDREAS SCHLÜTER (1662–1714), who was born in Hamburg. His father was a sculptor of no prominence, but he took his son with him to Dantzig, where many Netherlandish artists were employed upon the buildings being constructed there. Andreas Schlüter was naturally gifted, and he devoted himself to the study of both architecture and sculpture, at home and later in Italy. Before he was thirty years old he was employed in important affairs in Warsaw, and in 1694

FIG. 113.—HEADS OF DYING WARRIORS. *By Schlüter.*

he was summoned to Berlin, where he executed the plastic ornaments of the Arsenal ; the heads of the Dying Warriors above the windows in the court-yard are remarkable works. They are very fine when regarded only as excellent examples of good sculpture, and they are very effective placed as they are, for they seem to tell the whole tragic story of what a soldier's life and fate must often be (Fig. 113).

However, the masterpiece of this sculptor is the equestrian statue of the Great Elector for the long bridge at Berlin, which was completed in 1703 (Fig. 114). Lübke says of this: "Although biassed as regards form by the

FIG. 114.—THE GREAT ELECTOR. *By Schlüter.*

age which prescribed the Roman costume to ideal portraits of this kind, the horseman on his mighty charger is conceived with so much energy, he is filled with such power of will, he is so noble in bearing and so steady in his course, that no other equestrian statue can be compared with this in fiery majesty. Equally masterly is the arrangement of the whole, especially the four chained slaves on the base, in whom we gladly pardon a certain crowding of movements and forms."

Schlüter also made a statue of the Elector Frederic III., which is now in Königsberg. Besides his works in sculpture he was the architect of the royal palaces at Potsdam, Charlottenburg, and Berlin, and there are many sculptures by him at these places. When he was thus in an important position and at the height of professional prosperity he met with a sad misfortune, from the effects of which he never recovered. A chime of bells had been purchased in Holland, and Schlüter was commissioned to arrange an old tower for their reception. He carried it higher than it had been, and was proceeding to finish it, when it threatened to fall, and had to be pulled down. On account of this Schlüter was dismissed from his position as court architect; and though his office of sculptor was left to him his power was gone, and he was broken down in spirit. He was called to St. Petersburg by Peter the Great, and died soon after. Now, the verdict of judges is that he was one of the greatest artists of his age, and that his works, both in sculpture and architecture, belong to the noblest productions of his century.

## CHAPTER IX.

### CANOVA, THORWALDSEN, AND OTHER RECENT SCULPTORS.

IN the middle of the eighteenth century the arts had fallen into such a feeble state that a true artistic work—one conceived and executed in an artist spirit—was not to be looked for. As in the Middle Ages, too, thought seemed to be sleeping. Both art and letters were largely prostrated to the service of those in high places ; they were scarcely used except for the pleasure or praise of men whose earthly power made them to be feared, and because they were feared they were flattered openly and despised secretly.

But about the end of the century another spirit arose ; a second Renaissance took place, which may be traced in literature and in art, as it may be in the movement of political events and an independence of thought everywhere.

Naturally the question as to where artists could turn for their models was an important one, and as before in various epochs in art the antique had been the "only help in time of trouble," so it proved again. In 1764 Winckelmann published his "History of Ancient Art," in which the rich significance of classic art was clearly placed before the student. The service which this author rendered to art can scarcely be over-estimated, coming, as it did, at a time when the genius of art seemed to have turned his back upon the world, and all true inspiration was lost. At about the same time the monuments of Athens were recalled to the European world by Stuart and Revett in their architectural designs, and by the end of the century the study of the antique had done its transforming work, and artists were striving for more worthy ends than the favor of kings and powerful patrons. This new study of classic art did not show its full and best results until the Danish sculptor Thorwaldsen executed his works; but before his time others were striving for that which it was his privilege to perfect.

Among the earliest and most famous of these eighteenth-century reformers was the Venetian, ANTONIO CANOVA (1757–1822). He was born in Possagno, and was the son and grandson of stone-cutters. His father died when he was very young, and he was thus left to the care and instruction of his grandfather, the old Pasino Canova, who lost no time in accustoming the boy to the use of the chisel, for there are cuttings in existence which were executed by Canova in his ninth year. Signor Giovanni Faliero dwelt near Possagno, and was in the habit of employing Pasino Canova frequently; he entertained such respect for the old stone-cutter that he sometimes asked him to spend a few days at his villa. On these visits the old man was accompanied by Antonio, who soon became a favorite with all the family of Faliero, and a friend of the young Giuseppe.

On one occasion when Pasino and the boy attended a festival at Villa Faliero, the ornament for the dessert was forgotten. When the servants remembered it at the last moment they went to the old Pasino in distress, and begged him to save them from the displeasure of the master. The old man could do nothing for them, but the young Tonin, as he was called, asked for some butter, and from it quickly carved a lion. At table this strange ornament attracted the attention of all the guests, and Tonin was called in to receive their praises; from this time the Senator Faliero became his patron, and he placed the boy under the instruction of Giuseppe Bernardi, called Toretto, a Venetian sculptor who had settled at Pagnano.

At this time Canova was twelve years old ; he studied two years under Toretto, and made many statues and models, which are still preserved by the Faliero family, or in other collections. His first really original work was the modelling of two angels in clay ; he did these during an absence of his master's ; he placed them in a prominent place, and then awaited Toretto's opinion with great anxiety. When the master saw them he was filled with surprise, and exclaimed that they were truly marvellous ; from these models the grandfather cut two angels in *pietra dura* for the high-altar at Monfumo. At this same period Canova made his first representations of the human form ; he was accustomed to make small statues and give them to his friends.

When he was fifteen years old Faliero sent for him, and received him into his own family. Canova wished to earn something for himself, and engaged to work half of the day for Giuseppe Ferrari, who was a nephew of his former master, Toretto. Of this time Canova afterward wrote : "I labored for a mere pittance, but it was sufficient. It was the fruit of my own resolution, and, as I then flattered myself, the foretaste of more honorable rewards." This circumstance proves how remarkable he must have been ; it is unusual for a boy of fifteen to be paid for work instead of paying for instruction. In Venice he was able to learn much from observation. He divided his time systematically, spending his mornings in the Academy or some gallery, his afternoons in the shop where he was employed, and his evenings in studies for which he had had no opportunity as a child.

The first commission which was given to Canova was from the Commendatore Farsetti for a pair of baskets filled with fruit and flowers, to be sculptured in marble, and placed on a staircase which led to the picture gallery in the Farsetti Palace, where Canova spent much time in study. These works have no special excellence.

After a year in Venice he went to Asolo with the Faliero family. Some time before this his patron had asked Canova to make for him a group of Orpheus and Eurydice, taking the moment when Eurydice beholds her lover torn away from her forever. Canova had been busy with this in his leisure hours in Venice, and he took with him to Asolo everything necessary to the work. He completed the Eurydice in his sixteenth year; it was life-size, and cut from *pietra di Costosa.*

With this first attempt Canova became convinced that the small models such as were in use by sculptors were quite insufficient to good work, and he determined that his models should be of the size which the finished work would have, even when colossal.

After this time he had his studio in a cell of the monastery of the Augustine friars attached to the Church of San Stefano, in Venice. During the next three years he was occupied with his Orpheus and a bust of the Doge Renier. At this time he studied entirely from nature; he devoted himself to the pursuit of anatomy, and after a time was accustomed to make dissections in order to sketch or model from important parts or some conformations that he desired in particular instances.

In 1776 his Orpheus was finished and exhibited, and it chanced to be at the annual festival of the Ascension, when the opera of Orpheus was brought out in Venice. Canova was accustomed to say that the praise he then received was "that which made him a sculptor;" and so grateful was he for it that later, when he became Marquis of Ischia, he chose for his armorial ensigns the lyre and serpent which are the mythological symbols of Orpheus and Eurydice. The

Senator Grimani ordered a copy of the Orpheus, and this was the first work of Canova in Carrara marble.

He soon found his workshop too small, and removed to one in the street of San Maurizio, where he remained until he left his native country. His next work was a statue of Æsculapius, larger than life ; a short time before his death, when he saw this statue, he sorrowfully declared that "his progress had by no means corresponded with the indications of excellence in this performance of his youth." About this time he executed an Apollo and Daphne which was never entirely finished, and when twenty-two years old he completed a group of Dædalus and Icarus for the Senator Pisani. This was intended for an exterior decoration of his palace ; but when it was done Pisani considered it worthy of a place in his gallery, already famous on account of the painting of Darius and his Family, by Paul Veronese, and other fine works. This may be called Canova's last work in Venice, as he went to Rome soon after his twenty-third birthday.

The Cavaliere Zuliani was then the representative of Venice in Rome, and Faliero gave Canova letters to him. Zuliani was an enlightened patron of art, and he received the young sculptor with great kindness, and soon arranged to have his model of Dædalus and Icarus exhibited to the best artists and judges of art in Rome. We can fancy the anxiety with which Canova went to this exhibition ; but the praise which he there received secured for him a place among the artists then in Rome.

Canova had a great desire to undertake a group of some important subject, and Zuliani was his friend in this ; for he gave him the marble, and promised if no other purchaser appeared to give him the full value of the work when completed. He also gave him a workshop in the Venetian Palace, to which no one had access, where he could be entirely free and undisturbed. The subject chosen for the group was Theseus vanquishing the Minotaur, and the size was to be colossal. Canova now worked with untiring devotion; he was often seen before the statues on Monte Cavallo, with sketch-book in hand, as soon as it was light enough for him to see, and he studied faithfully in the museums and galleries of Rome. His friends in Venice had secured for him a pension of three hundred ducats, which placed him above want, and he was free to devote himself to his Theseus, although while at work on that he made a statue of Apollo, which was exhibited with Angelini's Minerva, and received much praise.

Meantime no one knew of the Theseus save the ambassador. When it was finished Zuliani prepared it for exhibition, and invited all the most distinguished men in Rome to an entertainment. A model of the head of Theseus was put in a prominent place, and the guests were busy in discussing it; they asked questions and expressed opinions, and when their interest was well awakened Zuliani said: "Come, let us end this discussion by seeing the original," and the statue was unveiled before their eyes. Canova often declared that death itself could not have been more terrible to him than were those moments. But he and all else were forgotten in the surprise and admiration which the group excited; in that hour the artists who afterward hated him gave him their sincere praise. From that day the fame of Canova was established.

Very soon he was selected to erect a monument to Clement XIV. This pope was a famous man; he was the collector of the Clementine Museum, the author of the elegant letters known by his family name of Ganganelli, and, above all, he was the suppressor of the Jesuits. While Canova felt the honor that was thus offered him he also thought himself bound to consult those who had conferred his pension upon him, and thus helped him to become the artist that he was. He went, therefore, to Venice and

Fig. 115.—The Three Graces. *By Canova.*

sought direction from the Senate; he was told to employ his time as should be most profitable to himself. He therefore gave up his studio in Venice, and as his patron, Zuliani, had now left Rome, he fitted up the studio in the Strada Babbuino, which became so well known to lovers of art of all nations who visited Rome. In 1787 the above monument was exhibited, and was much admired. An engraving was made from it and dedicated to Zuliani; but Canova desired to do something more worthy for his patron, and made a statue of Psyche as a gift to him; Zuliani hesitated to accept it, but finally consented to do so if Canova would in turn accept a number of silver medals with the Psyche on one side and a head of Canova on the other, which he could give to his friends. In the midst of all this Zuliani died, and his heirs were so angry because he had left works of art to the Public Library that they refused to carry out his plans. In the end the Psyche was bought by Napoleon and presented to the Queen of Bavaria.

Canova executed a second papal monument to Pope Clement XIII. It was erected in St. Peter's by his nephews. The mourning genius upon it is frequently mentioned as one of Canova's happiest figures. The execution of these two monuments occupied almost ten years of the best part of this sculptor's life.

Canova's fame had extended over all Europe, and he was asked to go to St. Petersburg, and offered most advantageous terms if he would do so; but he declined, and executed the monument of Admiral Emo, on a commission from the Venetian Senate. For this work he received a gold medal and an annuity for life.

In 1798, during the revolutionary excitement at Rome, Canova went to Possagno, his native town. Here, in his retirement, he painted more than twenty pictures, which were by no means to be despised. His masterpiece represented the Saviour just taken from the cross, and surrounded by the Marys, St. John, Nicodemus, and Joseph of Arimathea. This was the first of the many gifts which he made to this little church, by which it became a splendid temple and the expression of Canova's love for his birthplace and early home.

After he returned to Rome his health was not sufficient to allow of his usual close application to work, and he went to Berlin and Vienna in company with Prince Rezzonico, and this so benefited him that he was able to resume his labors with new energy. He soon achieved a proud triumph, for his Perseus was placed in one of the Stanze of the Vatican by a public decree; this was the first modern work which had been thus honored.

In 1802-1803 Napoleon requested Canova to go to Paris to model a portrait bust for a colossal statue; the work was finished six years later. In 1805 the artist went again to Vienna, where he modelled a bust of the Emperor of Austria; in 1810 again to Paris to prepare a model for the statue of Maria Louisa. With the exception of these short journeys he was constantly at work in his Roman studio until 1815, when he was sent in an official capacity to France by the pope, for the purpose of reclaiming the works of art which had been carried from Italy in times of war, and which really belonged to the patrimony of the Church. Canova executed his commission with rare judgment, and then continued his journey to England. In London he received many honors; the king gave him an order for a group, held several conversations with him, made him valuable gifts, and intrusted him with a private letter to the pope.

Canova returned to Rome on January 5th, 1816. His entry might almost be called a triumphal one, for the people of Rome were so grateful for the restoration of their treasures that they expressed their joy in demonstrations to Canova. He had been President of St. Luke's Academy before ; he was now made President of the Commission to purchase works of art, and of the Academy of Archæology. In full consistory of all the high officers of the Church, the pope caused his name to be inscribed upon the "golden volume of the Capitol," and conferred upon him the title of Marquis of Ischia, with a pension of three thousand crowns a year.

Canova now determined to execute a colossal statue of Religion, which should commemorate the return of the pope from banishment. He endeavored to persuade the authorities to decide where it should be placed ; this was not done, and he was much grieved at his failure to carry out the idea. But he determined that from this time he would devote his life and fortune to religion, and resolved to erect a church at Possagno, to adorn it with works of art, and to make it his own burial-place.

On July 8th, 1819, Canova assembled his workmen in his native town, and gave them a *fête ;* many peasant girls joined in the festivities and assisted in the breaking of the ground ; at evening, as they all passed before Canova to bid him farewell, each one received a gift from him. Three days later the religious ceremony of laying the corner-stone of the future church took place. An immense number of people from the surrounding country and from Venice were present ; Canova, in his robes as a Knight of Christ, and wearing the insignia of other orders, led the procession ; all who had seen Canova when a poor boy in their midst were much impressed by this occasion. Here, in a public manner, he consecrated his life and fortune to the service of God and the benefit of his birthplace. Every autumn Canova went to Possagno to encourage the workmen and to give directions as to how the whole should be done. Between these visits he worked devotedly, for he was forced to earn all he could in order to pay for his great undertaking.

At this time he executed a statue of Washington, and was making an equestrian statue of Ferdinand of Naples, and in the month of May, 1822, went to that city, where he fell ill; he returned to Rome, and revived somewhat, and resumed his work. On September 17th he went to Possagno, in October to Villa Faliero, where, fifty years before, he had spent such happy days. From here he went to Venice, and on the 13th of the same month he died.

Solemn services were held in the cathedral, and his remains were then intrusted to the priests of Possagno, who bore them to their temple, where he was buried on the 25th of the month; the crowd was so great that the oration was delivered in the open air. Canova's heart was given to the Academy of Venice, and an elegant little monument was erected in the Palace of Arts to contain this relic of the sculptor. The Venetian artists arranged to erect to him a monument, and chose the design which he himself had made for the tomb of Titian; it is in the Church of Santa Maria de' Frari. In Rome a statue was decreed to him, and he was declared the perpetual President of her chief academy.

In personal appearance Canova was not grand or very attractive. His head was remarkably well placed upon his shoulders, and the loose manner in which he dressed his neck allowed this to be seen; his forehead was a noble one, his hair black, and his whole manner and dress was modest and simple. His habits were very orderly and quiet; he rose early to work, and went little into public society; but he welcomed a few friends to dinner almost daily. He entertained them cordially, but without display, and led the conversation to light, cheerful topics that did not touch upon art, or demand mental exertion. At eleven o'clock he retired to his own room and amused himself with a book or pencil before sleeping. Some of his best drawings were made at this hour, and have been published with the title of

FIG. 116.—HEBE. *By Canova.*

"Pensieri," or thoughts. To describe one day was to give a picture of all, so regular were his habits of life.

In his professional life he was just and generous to others, and though he would have no pupils, he would leave everything to advise an artist or visit his works. He was also a patron of art, and had executed, at his own expense, the numerous busts of distinguished persons in the Capitoline Museum.

There is a story of a romance in his life. It is said that when he first arrived in Venice he fell in love with a beautiful girl who was older than himself, who went to draw in the Farsetti Gallery. Day by day he watched her until she came no more; at length her attendant returned, and Canova inquired for her mistress; she burst into tears and answered, "La Signora Julia is dead." He asked no more, and never knew who Julia was or any circumstances of her history; but all his life he treasured her image, and when he endeavored to unite the purity of an angel with the earthly beauty of a woman, the remembrance of Julia was always in his mind.

Canova was one of the few artists who received their full merit of praise and the benefits of their labors while alive. Without doubt he was a great sculptor, and coming as he did, at a time when art was at its worst, he seemed all the more remarkable to the men around him. But the verdict of to-day would not exalt him as highly as did his friends and patrons. His statues lack the repose which makes the grandest feature of the best sculpture; his female figures have a sentimental sort of air that is not all we could wish, and does not elevate them above what we may call pleasing art. His male figures are better, more natural and simple, though some of his subjects bordered on the coarse and brutal, as in the two fencers, Kreugas and Damoxenes, or Hercules and Lichas. But in his religious subjects he is much finer, and in some of his monuments he shows dignity and earnestness, while his composition is in the true artistic spirit. Taken on the whole, he was a wonderful artist and a man of whom his century might well be proud.

Other sculptors of this period and of different nations studied at Rome, and devoted themselves to the antique with enthusiasm. One of these was ANTOINE DENIS CHAUDET (1763–1810), who was born at Paris. His talent was so early developed that he was admitted to the Royal Academy when fourteen years old, and when twenty-one he gained the first prize, and with the royal pension went to Rome, where he remained five years. He soon took good rank among artists of that time, for he was a designer and painter as well as sculptor. He adhered strictly to the antique style, and attained much purity, though he was always cold in treatment. He was made a Professor of Sculpture in the French Academy, and made valuable contributions to the "Dictionary of Fine Arts."

Chaudet's principal works in sculpture were the silver statue of Peace in the Tuileries ; a statue of Cincinnatus in the Senate Chamber ; a statue of Œdipus ; a bas-relief of Painting, Sculpture, and Architecture, in the Musée Napoléon, and many busts and smaller works.

He also designed numerous medals and some of the illustrations for a fine edition of Racine, and painted a picture of Æneas and Anchises in the Burning of Troy.

JOHANN HEINRICH DANNECKER (1758–1841) was born at Stuttgart. By a statue of Milo he gained the prize of the academy founded by Duke Charles Eugene, and with the royal pension he went first to Paris and then to Rome, where he studied seven years. He then returned to Würtemberg, and was made Director of the Royal Academy, with a salary of fifteen thousand francs a year. During fifteen years Dannecker maintained a high rank in his art, but his health became so feeble that he was forced to see others excel him. One of his works has a wide reputation, and is known to many people the world over, through the generosity of Herr Bethmann of Frankfort, who admits visitors to his gallery, and from the models and pictures which have been made from it ; it is the Ariadne on a Panther (Fig. 117).

Dannecker had a delicate feeling for nature ; his figures were light and graceful, and his heads were noble in expression. He labored eight years upon a figure of Christ, which belongs to the Emperor of Russia ; in Stuttgart a nymph pouring water on Neckar Street and two nymphs on a reservoir in the palace garden show his fine taste in architectural sculpture. Among his other works are a statue of Alexander, a monument to Count Zeppelin, a Cupid, and a Maiden lamenting a Dead Bird. Some of his works are among the very best productions of modern sculpture ; his portraits are noble and true to nature ; the works named here are by no means all that he did, and we should add

FIG. 117.—ARIADNE AND THE PANTHER. *By Dannecker.*

that his efforts in religious subjects exhibit a pure sense of the beautiful, and a true conception of Christian ideas.

We come now, for the first time, to a great English sculptor. JOHN FLAXMAN (1755–1826) was born in York, but while he was still an infant his father removed to London, where he kept a plaster-cast shop. The boy began to draw and even to model very early; when but five years old he kept some soft wax, with which he could take an impression from any seal or ring or coin which pleased him. He was very delicate in health, and was once thought to be dead, and was prepared for burial, when animation returned; his parents tried to gratify all his wishes, and while a child he modelled a great number of figures in wax, clay, and plaster.

By the time he was ten years old he was much stronger, and was able to use the activity which corresponded to his enthusiastic feeling and imagination. About this time he read "Don Quixote," and was so moved by the adventures of that hero that he went out early one morning armed with a toy sword and bent upon protecting some forlorn damsel; he went to Hyde Park and wandered about all day, not finding any one who was in need of his services. At night he returned home, very hungry and weary, to find his family in great alarm over his unusual absence.

He now spent all his time in drawing and modelling, and never had more than two lessons from a master; at eleven years of age he began to gain various prizes, and at fourteen was admitted to study at the Royal Academy, and gained the silver medal there that same year. About this time he made some friends who aided him to study the classics and to learn more of history, all of which was of great use to him in his art. He was also fortunate in having the friendship of Mr. Wedgwood, for whom he made many models. He also painted a few pictures in oil.

Among his earliest sculptures were a group of Venus

and Cupid and a monument to Mrs. Morley, who, with her baby, died at sea. Flaxman represented the mother and child rising from the sea and being received by descending angels.

In 1782 Flaxman married Miss Ann Denman, whose intelligence and love of art were of great assistance to her husband. In 1787 he went to Rome, where he remained seven years. During this time he made a group for Lord Bristol, representing the Fury of Athamas, from the Metamorphoses of Ovid ; this work cost him much labor, for which he received but small pay ; it was carried to Ireland and then to Ickworth House, in Suffolk, where but few people see it. In Rome Flaxman also made a group of Cephalus and Aurora for Mr. Thomas Hope, and the designs from Homer, Æschylus, and Dante, which have such a world-wide fame.

In 1794 he returned to England, where he was constantly employed on important works until his death. We cannot give a list of his numerous works. Many of his monuments are seen in the churches of England. In Glasgow are his statues of Mr. Pitt and Sir John Moore, in bronze ; in Edinburgh is that of Robert Burns. Flaxman executed much sculpture for the East Indies, one of these works being unfinished when he died. Some critics consider his Archangel Michael and Satan his best work ; it was made for the Earl of Egremont, who had his life-size Apollo also.

In 1797 Flaxman was elected an Associate of the Royal Academy, in 1800 an Academician, and in 1810, when a Professor of Sculpture was added to the other professors of the Academy, he was appointed to the office. His lectures have been published. The friezes on the Covent Garden Theatre were all designed by Flaxman, and he executed the figure of Comedy himself. His last work was making designs for the exterior decoration of Buckingham Palace, which would have been entirely under his direction and partly executed by him if he had lived.

His wife died in 1820, and her loss was a grief from which he could not recover; she had been a great advantage to him, and he had depended much upon her sympathy and counsel. Flaxman was a singularly pure man, and so attractive in manner that he was the friend of old and young alike.

Sir Richard Westmacott succeeded Flaxman as Professor at the Royal Academy; he said: "But the greatest of modern sculptors was our illustrious countryman, John Flaxman, who not only had all the fine feeling of the ancient Greeks (which Canova in a degree possessed), but united to it a readiness of invention and a simplicity of design truly astonishing. Though Canova was his superior in the manual part, high finishing, yet in the higher qualities, poetical feeling and invention, Flaxman was as superior to Canova as was Shakespeare to the dramatists of his day."

But the perfection of the results of the study of Canova and others who endeavored to raise sculpture to its ancient glory was seen in the Dane, BERTEL THORWALDSEN (1770–1844), who was born in Copenhagen. The descent of this artist has been traced to memorable sources in two quite distinct ways. Those who claim that the Norsemen discovered America relate that during their stay upon this coast a child was born, from whom Thorwaldsen's descent can be distinctly followed. The learned genealogists of Iceland say that his ancestors were descended from Harald Hildetand, King of Denmark, who, in the eighth century, was obliged to flee, first to Norway and then to Iceland, and that one of his descendants, Oluf Paa, in the twelfth century, was a famous wood-carver. But this much is certain: in the fourteenth century there lived in Southern Iceland a wealthy man, whose family and descendants were much honored. One of these, Thorvald Gottskalken, a pastor, had two sons and but a small fortuhe ; so he sent his sons to Copenhagen, where one became a jeweller and died young; the other, who was a wood-carver, was the father of the artist, whose mother was Karen Gröulund, the daughter of a Jutland peasant.

The father was employed in a shipyard, and carved only the rude ornaments of vessels and boats ; but these served to lead the mind of the little Bertel to the art he later followed. His father could not have dreamed of such a future as came to his son, but he was wise enough to know that the boy might do more and better than he had done, and he sent him, when eleven years old, to the free school of the Royal Academy to study drawing; and very soon the works of the father showed the gain which the son had made, for his designs were those now used by the old wood-carver.

Bertel was also sent to study his books at the school of Charlottenburg, and here he was so far from clever that he was put in the lowest class. When Bertel gained his first prize at the academy the chaplain of the school at Charlottenburg asked him if the boy who had taken the prize was his brother. He looked up with surprise, and blushing, said, "It is myself, Herr Chaplain." The priest was astounded at this, and said, "Herr Thorwaldsen, please to pass up to the first class."

The boy was amazed at these honors, and from this day retained the title of "Herr," which gave him much distinction. When, after many years, the sculptor had been loaded with honors, and stood on the heights of fame, he was accustomed to say that no glory had ever been so sweet to him as that first rapture which came from the words of the Chaplain Höyer when he was seventeen years old and a poor school-boy.

The effect of this first prize seemed to be to rouse his

ambition, and he worked with the greatest diligence and earnestness. Two years later he made a bas-relief of Love in Repose, which took the large silver medal. His father now thought him prepared to enter on the life of a ship's carver, and Bertel made no objection to doing so ; but the painter Abildgaard, who had been his teacher in the academy, had grown very fond of him, and saw how much talent he had, and could not think of his being but a common tradesman without deep regret. He went, therefore, to the old carver, and after some difficulty obtained his consent that his son should spend half his time in study at the academy; and the other half in the earning of his daily bread at his father's side.

In 1790, when twenty years old, Thorwaldsen made a medallion of the Princess of Denmark, which was so good a likeness that a number of copies was sold. A year later he gained the small gold medal of the academy by a bas-relief of the Expulsion of Heliodorus from the Temple. The Minister of State now became interested in the young artist, and measures were taken to aid him to go on with his studies. His patrons desired him to study the subjects of the antique sculptures, and he chose that of Priam begging the Body of Hector from Achilles. Later in life he repeated this subject, and it is interesting to notice the strength and grandeur of the second when compared with the weakness of the first. And yet it was from the latter that predictions were made of Thorwaldsen's future greatness. In 1793 he gained the prize which entitled him to travel and study three years at the expense of the academy. The work he presented was a bas-relief of Saint Peter healing the Paralytic. In these works this sculptor already showed two qualities which remained the same through his life ; in his subjects from antiquity he showed a Greek spirit, which has led some writers to speak of him as a "posthumous Greek," or a true Greek artist born after other Greek artists had died ; on the other hand, when he treated religious subjects his spirit was like that of the best masters of the Renaissance, and these works remind us of Raphael. All this excellence came entirely from his artistic nature, for outside of that he was ignorant ; he knew nothing of history or literature, and was never a man of culture as long as he lived. Outside of the work connected with his profession Thorwaldsen was indolent, and only acquired knowledge of other matters through observation or from the conversation of others.

Although he gained the prize which allowed him to travel in 1793, he did not leave Copenhagen until May, 1796. In the mean time he had done what he could to earn something : he had made designs for book-publishers, given lessons in drawing and modelling, and made some bust and medallion portraits, reliefs, and so on. The vessel in which the young sculptor sailed for Naples was called the Thetis, and the captain engaged to watch over him ; the voyage was long, and all on board became fond of Thorwaldsen, though the captain wrote, "He is an honest boy, but a lazy rascal." This opinion is very amusing when we know what an enormous amount of labor he performed. At Naples he remained for some time, and saw and admired all its works of art. He did not reach Rome until about nine months after leaving Copenhagen, but from that time his whole thought and life were changed. He was accustomed to say, "I was born on the 8th of March, 1797 ; before then I did not exist."

While in Naples Thorwaldsen had been ill, and suffered from a malarial affection, which compelled him to be idle much of the time. But he was always studying the antique statues, and made many copies. Some of the first original works which he attempted were failures, when, at last, he modelled a colossal statue of Jason, which was well received by those who saw it, and made him somewhat famous in Rome (Fig. 118). Canova praised it, and other critics did the same; but Thorwaldsen had no money; the academy had supported him six years; what could he do? Quite discouraged, he was engaged in his preparations for leaving Rome, when Mr. Thomas Hope, the English banker, gave him an order for the Jason in marble. In an hour his life was changed. He was living in Rome not as a student on charity, but as an artist gaining his living. We are forced to add that Mr. Hope did not receive this statue until 1828, and Thorwaldsen has been much blamed for his apparent ingratitude; but we cannot here give all the details of the unfortunate affair.

FIG. 118.—JASON. *By Thorwaldsen.*

Thorwaldsen had a true and faithful friend in Rome, the archæologist Zoëga; at his house the young Dane had met a beautiful Italian girl, Anna Maria Magnani, whom he loved devotedly. She was too ambitious to marry a poor sculptor, so she married a rich M. d'Uhden; but she persuaded Thorwaldsen to sign an agreement by which he bound himself to take care of her if she should not agree with her husband and should leave him; this was just what happened in 1803, and the sculptor received her into his house, where she remained sixteen years, when she disappears from his life. He provided an honorable marriage for their daughter.

In 1803 Thorwaldsen also made the acquaintance of the Baron von Schubart, the Danish Minister, who presented the sculptor to Baron von Humboldt; and through the friendship of these two men, and the persons to whom they presented him, Thorwaldsen received many orders. In 1804 his fame had become so well established that he received orders from all countries, and from this time, during the rest of his life, he was never able to do all that was required of him. He was much courted in society, where he was praised for his art and beloved for his agreeable and pleasing manner. In this same year he was made a Professor of the Royal Academy of Florence; and though the Academy of Copenhagen expected his return, they would not recall him from the scene of his triumphs, and sent him a gift of four hundred crowns. A few months later he was made a member of the Academy of Bologna and of that of his native city, in which last he was also appointed a Professor.

Many circumstances conspired to increase his popularity and to excite the popular interest in him, when, in 1805, he produced the bas-relief of the Abduction of Briseis, which still remains one of his most celebrated works. His Jason had put him on a level with Canova, who was then at the height of his fame; now the Briseis was said by many to excel the same type of works by Canova, and there is no question that in bas-relief the Dane was the better sculptor of the two. This relief and his group of Cupid and Psyche, which was completed in 1805, mark the era at which Thorwaldsen reached his full perfection as a sculptor. In this same year he modelled his first statue of Venus; it was less than life-size; and though two copies of it were finished in marble, he was not pleased with it, and destroyed the model: later he made the same statue in full size.

In 1806 he received his first commission for religious subjects, which consisted of two baptismal fonts for a church in the island of Fionia. But he was devoted to mythological subjects, and preferred them before all others, and in this same year modelled a Hebe while engaged upon the fonts. His industry was great, but he found time to receive many visitors at his studio, and went frequently into society. At the house of Baron von Humboldt, then Prussian Ambassador at Rome, Thorwaldsen was always welcome and happy; here he met all persons of note who lived in or who visited Rome.

It was at this period that the young Prince Louis of Bavaria entered into a correspondence with Thorwaldsen, which ended only with the sculptor's life. Louis was collecting objects for his Glyptothek at Munich, and he frequently consulted Thorwaldsen in these matters; his advice was of value, and he more than once saved Louis from imposition by dealers. Louis gave the sculptor the order for the fine Adonis, now in the Glyptothek; it was modelled in 1808, but was not completed until 1832; this splendid work was executed entirely by Thorwaldsen's own hands. In 1808 he also received the order for four bas-reliefs to be used in the restoration of the Palace of Christiansborg, which had been injured by fire. This was the year, too, when he was made an honorary member of the Academy of St. Luke.

The year 1809 brought deep sorrows to Thorwaldsen in the death of his two friends, Stanley and Zoëga. He interested himself in the settlement of the affairs of the latter, and had much trouble and anxiety; but he managed to accomplish the modelling of six bas-reliefs in this year, in spite of the disturbed state of Rome on account of the pope's departure, and in spite of the hindrances in his own life.

In 1810 the King of Denmark made Thorwaldsen a Knight of Danebrog, and he was then known in Italy as the *Cavaliere Alberto*. His work this year was in bas-reliefs, and in 1811 he modelled a colossal statue of Mars, the bust of Mademoiselle Ida Brun, a lovely statue of Psyche, and his own portrait as a colossal Hermes.

The people of Denmark were growing very impatient at the prolonged absence of their artist. He had left home a mere boy, and was now famous over all the world. They wished for his return ; a marble quarry had been discovered in Norway, and even Prince Christian Frederick wrote to Thorwaldsen to urge his going home. The sculptor wished to go, and even made some preparations to do so, when he received so important a commission that it was impossible to leave Rome. This new work was a frieze for one of the great halls in the Quirinal Palace. He chose the Entrance of Alexander the Great into Babylon for his subject, and it proved to be one of the most important works of his life. It was completed in June, 1812 ; and though it had been somewhat criticised as too rough in its finish, when it was elevated to its proper height it was all that had been expected by the artist's friends ; later he repeated this frieze for his own countrymen. In Rome he was now frequently called the "Patriarch of Bas-relief." Soon after this he was made a member of the Imperial Academy of Vienna.

In 1813 Thorwaldsen was again a victim of malignant fever, and visited the baths of Lucca, in company with the Baron and Baroness von Schubart, for the benefit of his health. He met many people and received much honor, especially from the Grand Duchess of Tuscany. His health was improved, but his old and tried friend, the Baroness von Schubart, died the winter following ; he felt her loss deeply, for she had been his friend and confidante from the time of his arrival in Rome.

He was always busy, and one after another of his almost numberless works was finished. In 1815 he made the Achilles and Priam, a relief which is sometimes called his masterpiece ; in the same year he made the famous and familiar medallions of Night and Morning ; it is said that he conceived the first while awake in a sleepless, restless condition, and modelled it entirely on the following day; these medallions have been reproduced in all possible forms—in engravings, on cameos, gems, in metals, and a variety of marble, plaster, and porcelain.

About this time Thorwaldsen removed to a spacious studio with gardens, and received pupils, and was overwhelmed with orders, so that he could not yet go to Denmark, in spite of the urgent letters he received. He executed many important original works, and also restored the marbles of Ægina, now at Munich; this was a great task, but his study of the antique had made him better able to do it than was any other modern sculptor.

FIG. 119.—GANYMEDE AND THE EAGLE.
*By Thorwaldsen*

The exquisite group of Ganymede and the Eagle (Fig. 119) shows the effect of his study of the antique, and the same may be said of his statue of Hope, a small copy of which was afterward placed above the tomb of the Baroness von Humboldt. The Three Graces (Fig. 120) belongs to the year 1817; the Mercury was of about this date, as well as the elegant statue of the Princess Baryatinska, which is his finest portrait statue.

After an absence from Denmark of twenty-three years he left Rome in July, 1819, and turned his face toward home. His model for the famous Lion of Lucerne had already been sent on before him, and the work commenced by one of his pupils, Bienaimé. Thorwaldsen first went to Lucerne, where he gave all necessary advice in this work, and then proceeding on his journey reached Copenhagen on the 3d of October. Apartments had been prepared for him in the Academy of Fine Arts, and as soon as it was known that he was there he was the centre of attraction and importance. Crowds went to welcome him to his home. A great reception and a grand banquet were given in his honor, and he was lauded to the skies in speeches, and was made a Counsellor of State, in order that he might sit at table with the royal family and not violate the court etiquette.

FIG. 120.—THE THREE GRACES.
*By Thorwaldsen.*

All this must have gratified the artist, who had earned such proud honors by the force of his genius ; but it interests us much more to know that he received commissions for some very important works, among which those of the Church of Our Lady are very interesting. The orders for all the work which he did here were not given at once, but in the end it became a splendid monument to this sculptor, and embraces almost all his religious works of any importance. There are the figures of Christ and the Twelve Apostles; the Angel of Baptism, which is an exquisite font; the Preaching of St. John the Baptist, which is a group in terra-cotta on the pediment of the church; a bas-relief in marble of the Institution of the Lord's Supper; another in plaster of Christ's Entry into Jerusalem; one of Christ Bearing the Cross; one of the Baptism of Christ; another of the Guardian Angel, and one of Christian Charity.

He did not remain very long in Denmark, but went to Warsaw, where he had been summoned to arrange for some important works. He was presented to the Emperor Alexander, who gave him sittings for a portrait bust; this was so successful that for some years Thorwaldsen employed skilled workmen to constantly repeat it, in order to fill the demand for it which was made upon him. While at Warsaw he received an order for a monument to Copernicus, which was dedicated in 1830; other important commissions were given him, and after visiting Cracow, Troppau, and Vienna, he reached Rome in December, 1820, where he was heartily welcomed by the artists, who gave him a banquet, on which occasion the Prince Royal of Denmark sat next to the sculptor.

Before this a correspondence had established a friendship between Thorwaldsen and Prince Louis of Bavaria; but from the year 1821 intimate personal relations existed between them. He took up work with great energy; he had returned to Rome with so much to do that he required much room, and employed a large company of workmen. In the summer of 1822 he was able to secure a large building which had been used for a stable to the Barberini Palace, and here he was able to set up all his large models.

In 1824 Thorwaldsen was summoned by the Cardinal Consalvi, who gave him the commission for the monument to Pius VII., now in the Clementine Chapel of St. Peter's at Rome; this work was not completed when the cardinal himself died, and his own monument by Thorwaldsen was placed in the Pantheon before that of Pius VII. was put in its place. He also made a cross for the Capuchins for which he would accept no reward, though they were entirely satisfied with it.

In 1825 Thorwaldsen was elected President of the Academy of St. Luke with the advice and consent of Pope Leo XII., who paid him a visit in his studio. Many delays occurred, and the monument to Pius VII. was not erected until 1831.

The works upon which the artist and his assistants were engaged were far too numerous to be mentioned; he was at the very height of fame and popularity, and was forced to refuse some of the commissions sent him. In 1830 he went to Munich to superintend the setting up of his monument to Eugène Beauharnais, the Duke of Leuchtenberg. This gave Louis of Bavaria an opportunity to show his regard for the sculptor, which he did in every possible way. Soon after the monument was unveiled Thorwaldsen received the cross of an officer of the Legion of Honor.

Thorwaldsen's place in Rome was a very important one, not only as an artist, but as a man. He had the respect and esteem of many good men of all nations; he also suffered some things from the envy of those who were jealous of him, as is the case with all successful men; but he was a fearless person, and did not trouble himself on account of these things. The frequent agitations of a political nature, however, did disturb him, and he began to think seriously of returning to Denmark. In 1837, when the cholera broke out in Rome, he determined to leave; his countrymen were delighted, and a government frigate was sent to take him home; he sailed from Leghorn in August, 1838. His arrival was hailed with joy in Denmark, and wherever he went his progress was marked by tokens of the pride which his countrymen felt in him. As soon as it was known in Copenhagen, on September 17th, that the "Rota," which brought the sculptor, was in the harbor, a flag was run up from St. Nicolas Church as a signal for the beginning of the festivities which had been arranged.

Although it rained heavily, boats filled with artists, poets, students, physicians, mechanics, and naval officers went out to meet him; each boat had a flag with an appropriate device, that of the artists having Thorwaldsen's Three Graces, the poets, a Pegasus, and so on. The meeting with his friends on the deck of the ship was a pleasant surprise to the artist, who was hurried ashore amid the firing of salutes and all sorts of joyous demonstrations, a vast number of boats rowing after that in which he was seated. His carriage was drawn by the people from the quay to Charlottenburg, where a vast crowd assembled to get a sight at him. His form was tall and erect, his step firm; his long white hair fell on his shoulders, and his clear eye and benevolent face beamed with intelligence and sympathetic interest in all around him. He was led out on a balcony, where, uncovered, he saluted the people, who greeted him with wild applause. Thorwaldsen smiled and said, "Would not any one think that we were in Rome, and I were the pope about to give the benediction *urbi et orbi* from the balcony of St. Peter's?"

One ovation after another followed, day by day, and such crowds of visitors went to see him that he was unable to unpack and arrange his possessions which he had brought from Italy, or to work at all, which was worse to him. At last he began to do as he had done in Rome, and to receive his friends with his chisel or modelling-stick in hand. He lived frugally, and continued many of his Roman habits of life; but he was forced to dine out every evening.

He was now sixty-eight years old, but he did a vast amount of work in one way and another, and was so pursued by all sorts of people who wished to engage his attention in a variety of projects, that he seriously considered the question of leaving Copenhagen. He became very fond of certain families where he visited, among which was that of the Baron von Stampe, who, with his wife and children, were soon treated by the sculptor as if they were his own kindred. He went with them to their summer home at Nysoë, and while there the baroness persuaded him to model his own statue. He did this imperfectly, as he had no suitable workshop; and when the baroness saw his difficulty in working in an ordinary room she had a studio built for him in a garden near the castle. She took the time to do this when Thorwaldsen was absent for eight days, and in this short space the whole was completed, so that when he returned it seemed to him like magic. This studio was dedicated in July, 1839.

He then began the proper modelling of his own statue, and was progressing very well when he received a letter from the poet Oehlenschlaeger, who was in great haste to have a portrait bust made of himself. Thorwaldsen felt that he ought not to make his own statue when thus wanted for other work, and he threw down his tools, and would have broken the model. But the baroness succeeded in getting him away, and locked the studio, keeping the key. However, no argument or entreaty would move the sculptor, and she could do nothing with him until she happened to think of crying. When she began to weep and to accuse him of having no affection for her, and reminded him of the proofs of her devotion which she had given him, he was taken in by her mock tears, and exclaimed, "Well, they may think what they like. My statue is not for posterity, but I cannot refuse it to a friend to whom it will give such pleasure." He then resumed his work, and completed his statue in seventeen days. He represented himself standing with one arm resting upon his statue of Hope.

After this summer Thorwaldsen divided his time between Copenhagen and Stampeborg, and worked with the same industry in one place as in the other. The life in the country was a great delight to him; he played games, listened to fairy tales from the poet Andersen, or to music from the young girls of the house, all with equal pleasure; and if he were allowed to have his mornings for work he would spend the rest of the day in the woods or pay visits, and was perfectly happy in this succession of labor and leisure.

Baroness Stampe did not stop at one trick upon the old artist, for she found it more easy to gain a point in this way than by argument. He had promised to execute a statue of Christian IV. for Christian VIII., the reigning king; he put it off until the king was impatient. One day, when he had gone for a walk, the baroness went to the studio and began a sketch in clay as well as she could. When Thorwaldsen returned he asked what she was doing, and she answered, "I am making the statue of the king. Since you will not do it, and I have pledged my word, I must do it myself." The artist laughed, and began to criticise her work; she insisted it was all right, and at last said, "Do it better, then, yourself; you make fun of me; I defy you to find anything to change in my work." Thorwaldsen was thus led on to correct the model, and when once he had begun he finished it.

It would be impossible to give any account here of the numerous incidents in the later years of the life of this sculptor; of the honors he received, of the many works he was consulted about and asked to do, of the visits he paid and received from persons of note; few lives are as full as was his, and the detailed accounts of it are very interesting.

He had always desired to go again to Rome, and in 1841, when the Baron von Stampe decided to go there with his family, Thorwaldsen travelled with them. They went through Germany, and were everywhere received as honorably as if he were a royal person: he was invited to visit royal families; court carriages were at his service; Mendelssohn gave a musical *fête* for him; in all the great cities he was shown the places and objects worthy of his attention; poets and orators paid him respect, and nothing that could be done to show appreciation of his genius and his works was omitted.

In Rome it was the same; he remained there almost a year, and upon his arrival at Copenhagen, in October, 1842, he experienced the crowning glory of his life. During his absence the Thorwaldsen Museum had been completed, and here, the day after he reached home, he was received. The building was decorated with garlands, and he went over the whole of it; at last he entered the inner court, where he was to be buried; here he stood for some time with bowed head, while all about him kept silence. Can any one fancy the thoughts that must have come to him? Here he must be buried, and yet here would he live in the works of his hand which would surround him and remain to testify to his immortal powers.

He lived three years more, and was always busy. His mind was strong and his conceptions of his subjects had lost nothing, but his ability to execute his works was less; his hand had lost somewhat of its cunning. He went much into society, was fond of the theatre, and under the devoted care of his servant, Wilkens, he enjoyed all that was possible to a man of his age. On the 24th of March, 1844, the Baroness von Stampe went to ask him to dine at her house ; he said he was not well and would not go out ; but as his daughter was to be there and expected him he decided to go. He was modelling a bust of Luther, and threw down before it a handful of clay and stuck a trowel in it ; just so, as he left it, this now stands in the museum, preserved under glass, with the print of his hand in the clay.

He was merry at dinner, and in speaking of the museum said he could die now, whenever he chose, since the architect Bindesböll had finished his tomb. After dinner he went to the theatre, and there it was seen that he was really ill ; he was taken out with haste and laid upon a sofa, when it was found that he was already dead. The Charlottenburg joined the theatre, and there, in the hall of antique sculpture, he was laid. He was first buried in the Frue Kirke, which he had so splendidly decorated ; four years later he was borne to the vault in the centre of the Thorwaldsen Museum, where above him grows the evergreen ivy, a fitting emblem of his unfading fame.

Thiele, in his splendid book called "Thorwaldsen and his Works," gives a list of two hundred and sixty works by this master ; and as one journeys from Rome, where are some of his sculptures in St. Peter's and the Quirinal, to Copenhagen, with the Frue Kirke and the Museum, one passes through few cities that are not adorned by his statues and reliefs. Among his most important works are the frieze of Alexander's entrance into Babylon, at the Quirinal ; the Lion of Lucerne ; the many statues, groups, and bas-reliefs in the Frue Kirke ; more than thirty sepulchral and commemorative monuments in various cities and countries ; sixteen bas-reliefs which illustrate the story of Cupid and Psyche ; twenty bas-reliefs of Genii ; twenty-two figures from antique fables, and many portrait busts and statues, and various other subjects.

Thorwaldsen was a very remarkable man. No circumstance of his youth indicated his success, and a certain indolence which he had would have seemed to forbid it; but the power was within him, and was of that genuine quality which will declare itself; and a man who has it becomes great without intending to be so, and almost without believing that he is remarkable beyond others. The true antique spirit seems to have been revived in him. His characteristics as a sculptor are severe simplicity, perfect beauty in form, distinctness, and repose. Thiele says of him: "He has challenged and has received the decision of the world's Supreme Court, that his name shall stand on the rolls of immortality. And if his life might be embodied in a single emblem, perhaps it should be that of a young lion, with an eye that glows and flashes fire, while he is bound with ivy and led by the hand of the three graces."

The sculpture of Germany in the last part of the eighteenth and the early years of the present century was very interesting. The architect Schinkel was a great lover of antique art, and he had much influence over all arts, as well as in his special department. Thorwaldsen himself so admired the sculptor JOHN RUDOLPH SCHADOW (1786–1822) that when the King of Prussia gave him a commission for a statue he replied: "Sire, there is at this moment in Rome one of your faithful subjects who is more capable than I of performing to your satisfaction the task with which you deign to honor me; permit me to solicit for him your royal favor." The commission was given to Schadow, and he made his charming work, The Spinner. John Rudolph was the son of JOHN GOTTFRIED SCHADOW (1764–1850), who was court sculptor, and long survived his gifted son. The chief works of the father were the statues of Count von der Mark, at Berlin; that of Frederick the Great, at Stettin; Luther's monument in the market-place at Wittenberg, and Blücher's statue at Rostock.

John Rudolph Schadow studied under both Canova and

Thorwaldsen, and was a very gifted artist. He was engaged upon a group of Achilles protecting the body of Penthesilea at the time of his death; it was finished by Wolff.

CHRISTIAN FREDERIC TIECK (1776–1851) was an eminent sculptor of his time, and decorated with sculpture some of the fine edifices erected at Berlin by Schinkel. He was very active in establishing a gallery of models from the antique at Berlin, and was a Director of the Sculptures in the Museum as well as a member of the Academy. His most successful original works were portrait busts, and he had many notable people among his sitters. Among them were the Emperor of Germany, the King of Bavaria, Schelling, Goethe, Lessing, and many others.

CHRISTIAN RAUCH (1777–1857). This eminent sculptor was born at Waldeck, and followed the manner of Schadow,

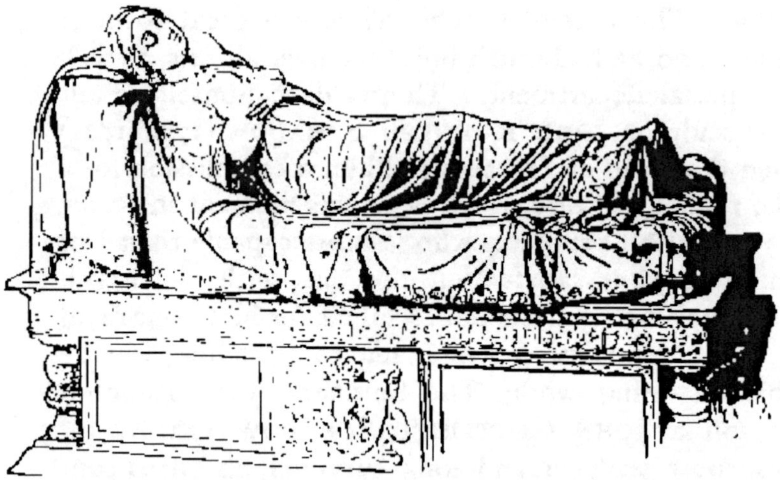

FIG. 121.—STATUE OF QUEEN LOUISE. *By Rauch.*

which he carried to its perfection. His statue of Queen Louise (Fig. 121) is one of the finest works of modern sculpture, and his statues of the Generals Scharnhorst and Bülow, in Berlin, are very fine; the reliefs upon the pedestals are of classic beauty. But his masterpiece is the grand Friedrichs monument. Rauch executed many excellent busts; he made good portraits, and yet he elevated the character of his subjects to the greatest nobleness of which they were capable. As a rule Rauch avoided religious subjects, but late in life he modelled the group of Moses supported in prayer by Aaron and Hur.

Among his important works are the statue of Blücher, at Breslau; that of August Hermann Franke, at Halle; Dürer, at Nuremberg; monument to Maximilian I., at Munich; and six marble Victories for the Walhalla. His works are numerous, and in them we feel that this artist had not a great imaginative power; he rarely conceived imaginary subjects, but he took some fact or personality as his motive, and elevated it to the highest point to which it could be brought, and under his masterly style of execution produced splendid results.

ERNST RIETSCHEL (1804–1860) was a gifted pupil of Rauch. After spending some time in Rome he settled in Dresden, and executed the statue of Friederich August of Saxony, for the Zwingerhof, when but twenty-seven years old. His chief excellence was in portrait statues, and those of Lessing and Luther are remarkable for their powerful expression of the intellectual and moral force of those men. His religious subjects were full of deep feeling, and his lighter works have a charming grace about them.

LUDWIG SCHWANTHALER (1802–1848) studied much in Rome, and was as devoted to the antique as was Thorwaldsen. He executed many works in Munich, the principal ones being the interior decoration of the Glyptothek; also that of the Königsbau and two groups for the Walhalla. A prominent work by this master is the bronze statue of Bavaria, which is fifty-four feet high and stands in front of the Ruhmeshalle. He also made twelve gilt-bronze statues of Bavarian sovereigns. Schwanthaler had remarkable powers of invention and a fruitful imagination; in these points he ranks with the first of modern sculptors; but his works rarely rise above what we call decorative art, and in spite of his excellent gifts he lacked the power to arouse any enthusiasm for his statues.

There are many other names that might be mentioned in connection with modern sculpture in Germany. Nowhere have the monuments and portrait statues and busts reached a higher excellence than in what we may call, in general terms, the Berlin school. Profound attention has been given to the proper reproduction of the individual characters of its subjects, while the art has not been allowed to sink into caricature or commonplaceness. Nowhere does the traveller better appreciate the art of our own day than in the sculpture of Germany.

But there are exceptions to this rule; some such artists as THEODORE KALIDE and LUDWIG WICHMANN are wanting in the serious qualities of Schadow, Rauch, and their followers, and sometimes fall into a coarse realism; but in spite of this, the revival of love for the antique, which began with Canova and his time, has borne rich fruit in the works of modern German sculptors.

In France the spirit of modern sculpture has been largely that of the severe classic style, and it has shown many of the same qualities that we have seen in modern German sculpture; but the different characteristics of the two nations have had their influence here as in everything else. In France the artist has aimed at a fine effect—flowing outline and dazzling representations of dramatic motives—far more than the northern sculptors have done. There is less thought and depth of feeling, more outward attraction and striking effect. The classic taste which asserted itself in the time of Canova was adopted in France, but in a French manner; and one of the earliest artists who showed its effects was FRANÇOIS JOSEPH BOSIO (1769–1845), who was much honored. He was made a member of the Institute of France and of the Royal Academy of Berlin ; he was chief sculptor to the King of France, and executed

FIG. 122.—NYMPH. *By Bosio.*

many public works. He made many portrait busts of the royal family and other prominent persons, but his chief works were the reliefs on the column of the Place Vendôme, the Chariot on the arch of the Place du Carrousel, the monument to the Countess Demidoff, and statues of mythological heroes and heroines. For the Chapelle Expiatoire, Bosio executed a group representing Louis XVII. receiving comfort from an angel; the design is not as good as in some of his classic works, but the conception is pure and noble.

JAMES PRADIER (1790–1832), though born in Geneva, was essentially a French sculptor, and excelled the artists of his day in his representations of feminine beauty. His masterpiece is a fountain at Nimes, in which the figures are fine and the drapery noble and distinct in treatment. The serious and comic Muses of the Fountain Molière are excellent works. He made several separate statues which are well known; his Psyche has a butterfly poised on the upper part of the arm; Atalanta is fastening her sandals; Sappho is in despair. His Niobe group showed his power to represent bold action, and his Prometheus chained, erected in the garden of the Tuileries, is grand and spirited.

We could name a great number of French sculptors belonging to this period whose works are seen in many public places which they adorn, but whose genius was not sufficient to place them in the first ranks of the world's artists, or make the accounts of them anything more than a list of works which has little meaning, except when one stands before them. Perhaps no one man had so wide an influence upon this art as had PIERRE JEAN DAVID (1793–1856), who is called David of Angers, which was his birthplace, in order to distinguish him from Jacques Louis David, the great painter, who was like a father to this sculptor, though in no way connected with him by ties of kindred, as far as we know. But when the sculptor went to Paris, a very poor boy, David the painter, whose attention was called to him in some way, was his friend, and gave him lessons in drawing and aided him in other ways. In 1811 David of Angers obtained the prize which enabled him to go to

Rome, and after his return to Paris he was constantly employed. The amount of his work was enormous; many of his statues were colossal, and he executed a great number of busts and more than ninety medallions.

He made the statue of Mme. de Staël; one of Talma for the Théâtre Français; the colossal statue of King René at Aix; monument to Fénelon at Cambray; the statue of the great Condé at Versailles; the Gutenberg memorial at Strasburg, which is one of his most successful works, and a large number of other sculptures.

His chief characteristic is realism, and he carried this so far that it frequently became coarseness. David designed the relief for the pediment of the Pantheon. The inscription on the building declares that it is dedicated by a grateful country to its great men, and the sculptor seems to have had this in mind, for he represented in his group a figure of France surrounded by those who had been great in its times of war and days of peace. It is too realistic to be pleasing, and is far less creditable to the sculptor than are many of his less prominent works.

If little can be said of the modern French sculpture prior to our immediate time, there is still less to be told of that of England. There are many public monuments there, but they do not show forth any high artistic genius or rise above the commonplace except in very rare instances. There is but one English sculptor of whom I shall speak. JOHN GIBSON (1791–1866) was born near Conway, in Wales. When he was nine years old his parents went to Liverpool with the intention of sailing for America; but they gave up the idea, and the boy was sent to school in Liverpool. Before this he had been in the habit of drawing and of making sketches of anything that he saw and was pleased with; he now studied the prints in the shop windows, and made pictures, which he sold to his fellow-pupils. He attracted the attention of a print-seller, who was so interested in him that he allowed him to draw from studies and casts from the antique which he had. When fourteen years old the boy was apprenticed to a cabinet-maker, but after a year he persuaded his employer to allow him to leave his shop, and was then apprenticed to a wood-carver. He did not stop at this, however, for when he became acquainted with the Messrs. Francis, who had a marble-yard, he persuaded his second master to release him, and was apprenticed for the third time, and in this case to the occupation which he had determined should be that of his life.

He was now very happy, and his improvement in drawing, modelling, and working in marble was very rapid. After a few months he made the acquaintance of William Roscoe, who became his friend and patron. He remained in Liverpool until he was twenty-seven years old ; he had improved every advantage within his reach, but he was very desirous of travelling. In 1817, armed with a few letters of introduction, he went to London, where he obtained several orders, and in October of that year went to Rome.

He had a letter to Canova, who took him under his care and gave him admission to the classes in the Academy, in which he could draw from living models. In 1819 he received his first important commission ; it was from the Duke of Devonshire for a group of Mars and Cupid. From this time he advanced steadily in his profession, and was always busy. He lived twenty-seven years in Rome, and passed his summers in Innsbrück.

In 1844 he went to Liverpool to oversee the erection of his statue of Mr. Huskisson ; he was received with enthusiasm, and when he went to Glasgow to superintend the placing of his statue of Mr. Finlay in the Merchants' Hall his reception was even more flattering, as it was given him simply as an artist, and not connected with any former associations, as in Liverpool. During this visit to England Gibson was summoned to Windsor to make a statue of

Queen Victoria, which he completed after his return to Rome. The queen was represented in a classical costume, and the diadem, sandals, and borders of the drapery were colored. This was very much criticised and much was written and said about it; Gibson took little notice of all this, and simply answered it by saying, "Whatever the Greeks did was right."

In 1851 Gibson sustained a great loss in the death of his brother Ben, who had lived with him in Rome for fourteen years. Five years later, when in perfect health, the sculptor was attacked by paralysis, and lived but a short time. He was buried in the English cemetery at Rome, and Lord Lytton wrote the inscription upon his monument. It says: "His native genius strengthened by careful study, he infused the spirit of Grecian art into masterpieces all his own. His character as a man was in unison with his attributes as an artist—beautiful in its simplicity and truthfulness, noble in its dignity and elevation." A monument was also raised to Gibson in the church at Conway.

The master left the models of all his works and the larger part of his fortune to the Royal Academy in London. Among his works are Mars and Cupid, at Chatsworth; Psyche borne by Zephyrs, in the Palazzo Torlonia, at Rome, and a replica at St. Petersburg; Hylas surprised by Nymphs, in the National Gallery, London; Sleeping Shepherd Boy, in the Lenox collection in New York; Cupid disguised as a Shepherd, which he often repeated; portraits of Queen Victoria, at Buckingham Palace and Osborne; Sir Robert Peel, in Westminster Abbey; George Stephenson, in St. George's Hall, Liverpool; eighteen portrait busts; sixteen bas-reliefs of ideal subjects and sixteen others for monuments to the dead. A large part of these are in the chapel of the Liverpool Cemetery. He modelled a bas-relief of Christ blessing little children.

Gibson found his entire happiness in his art. In his

own words, he worked on "happily and with ever new pleasure, avoiding evil and with a calm soul, making images, not for worship, but for the love of the beautiful. The beautiful elevates us above the crowd in this world; the ideal, higher—yes, higher still, to celestial beauty, the fountain of all. Socrates said that outward beauty was the sign of the inward; in the life of a man, as in an image, every part should be beautiful."

He was never elated by praise; he was glad of tributes which proved that he was respected, but he received all honors with a simplicity of self-respect which spoke the sincere nobility of his nature.

There are many amusing anecdotes told of his absent-mindedness about everything not connected with his art. Miss Harriet Hosmer was his only pupil, and she said of him: "He is a god in his studio, but God help him when he is out of it." He never could master the ins and outs of railroad travelling, and even when put in the right train at the right time he would be sure to get out at the wrong place at the wrong time.

On one of his journeys, when he supposed he was at the right place, he got out and asked the porter to show him the way to the cathedral. In his own account he said: "But the scoundrel would have it there was no cathedral in the place, and at last had the impudence to ask me if I knew where I was. Then I discovered that instead of being in Chichester, where I had a particular appointment with the dean and chapter, I was safe in Portsmouth, where there was no cathedral at all."

The time has not come for any comprehensive estimate of the sculpture of our own country. So many of our artists are still living that it would be unjust to speak of them in connection with those whose work is complete and whose rank is fixed as a matter of history. We have no right to say of one who is still working that he has reached his full height, and even after death a certain period must elapse before the true merit of an artist can be established and his name written in its just place upon the roll of fame. So, in leaving this subject, we will turn again to the land of which we first spoke in considering modern sculpture. In Italy this art has not risen above the elevation to which Canova and Thorwaldsen brought it; for though the last was a Dane, his work may truly be said to belong to the Roman school. We must regard Italy as the land of art in a peculiar sense, but it is easy to understand that under the political misfortunes which she has suffered an advance in artistic life could not be made. Now, when a new spirit is active there, and a freer thought prevails in other directions, may we not believe that in the arts there will be a revival of the best inspiration that has ever come to that home of grace and beauty?

As we glance over the entire civilized world of to-day we find an immense activity in all matters pertaining to the fine arts. Schools and academies are multiplied everywhere, and the interest in works of art is universal. Many a private gentleman is to-day as liberal a patron of artists as were the princes and nobles of the past. It is as if there were a vast crucible in which artists of all nations are being tested, and from this testing of their metal it would seem that much pure gold must come forth.

As we review the history of sculpture from its earliest days to the present, we are compelled to linger lovingly with the Greek or classic art. The period in which it existed was a blessed period for the sculptor. We all know that the best foundation for the excellence of art is the study and reproduction of *nature*, and in the times of the Greeks there was no reason why the human form, the most beautiful object in nature, should not be used by the sculptor for the decoration of the temple, for the statues of the public square or theatre, or for any position in which sculpture could be used at all. The customs of modern life are opposed to this free exhibition of nude forms, and the difficulties that are thrown in the way of the sculptor by this one fact are almost more than we can realize; and the task of draping a figure and yet showing its shape and indicating its proper proportions and action is one before which even a Greek sculptor would have reason to doubt himself.

On the other hand, when a sculptor does succeed in producing a draped figure which satisfies artistic taste, he has achieved much, and merits the highest praise. A drapery which has gracefully composed masses and flowing lines adds great dignity to the figure of a patriarch or a prophet, and there are numerous subjects, religious and monumental, in which a full, graceful drapery is requisite; but when, as is often the case, the sculptor is required to reproduce the actual costume of the day, what can we look for? The truth is, it has no grace in itself; what, then, must it be when put into the fixedness of bronze or marble? Yet where is the remedy for this? We do not wish to see the men whom we have known and who have moved among us in the dress of other men put into an antique disguise by the sculptor; the incongruity of this is too apparent. Much has been written and said upon these points, and no solution of the difficulty has been found; but it is only just that when we judge of the statues made under such difficulties, we should remember them and give the artist the benefit of the consideration of all the hindrances that exist for him.

Westmacott, in his "Handbook of Sculpture," gives as his "Conclusion" an account of the mechanical methods of the sculptor, and I believe that I can add nothing here which will be of greater use to my readers than a quotation from that author.

"The artist, having invented or conceived his subject, usually begins by making a small sketch of it in some soft and obedient substance, as clay or wax. He can change or alter this at his pleasure till he is satisfied with the lines and masses of the composition, and the proportions it will command of light and shadow. He then proceeds to copy this small but useful sketch, as his guide, in its general arrangement, for his full-sized model. Before commencing the larger model it is necessary to form a sort of skeleton or framework of iron and wood, with joints made of wire, to support the great mass of clay in which the figure or group is now to be executed. This iron frame is firmly fixed upon a turning bench, or banker, so that the model may be constantly moved without difficulty, so as to be seen in different lights and in various points of view. As the clay is likely to shrink as it gets dry, it is necessary occasionally to wet it. This is done by sprinkling water over it with a brush, or from a large syringe, and by laying damp cloths upon it. This is the ordinary process for making a model in the 'round.'

"In modelling in *rilievo* of either kind, *alto* or *basso*, a plane or ground is prepared upon which the design is, or should be, carefully drawn. This may be made of clay floated or laid upon a board, or the ground may be of slate, or even of wood, though the latter is objectionable, in large works especially, from its liability to shrink and to be warped by the action of damp or moisture. The clay is then laid in small quantities upon this ground, the outline being bounded by the drawing, which should be carefully preserved; and the bulk or projection of the figures is regulated by the degree of relief the sculptor desires to give to his design.

"If the final work is to be baked in clay (*terra-cotta*) there must be no iron or wooden nucleus, as it would interfere with the model drying regularly and uniformly, and probably cause it to crack in shrinking. The model is therefore prepared for drying without such support. When perfectly free from moisture the model is placed in an oven and baked slowly, by which it acquires great hardness and the peculiar brownish-red color seen in these works. This art has been brought to great perfection in England in modern days.

"If the final work is to be in marble, or bronze, or only in plaster, the next process after finishing the model is to mould it, in preparation for its being reproduced in a material that will bear moving about without risk of injury to the design. This is done by covering it with a mixture of plaster of Paris with water, which quickly sets or becomes consistent, forming a hard and thick coating over the whole. The clay is then carefully picked out, and an exact matrix, or form, remains. This is washed clean, and the interior is then brushed over with any greasy substance, usually a composition of soap and oil, to prevent the plaster with which it is next to be filled adhering too firmly to it. The fresh plaster is mixed to about the consistency of cream and then poured into the mould, which is gently moved about till the inner surface is entirely filled or covered, so that all parts may be reached. The thickness or substance of the coating depends upon the size of the work and the degree of strength required.

"When the newly introduced plaster is set the mould is carefully knocked away with chisels, and a true cast appears beneath, giving an entire fac-simile of the original model. Some skill is required in making moulds, in order to provide for projecting parts and under-cuttings; practice alone can teach the artist how to deal with those difficulties when they occur. The above general instructions sufficiently explain the ordinary processes of moulding and casting in plaster.

"In metal-casting or founding great attention must be paid to the strengthening of the parts to bear the weight of the metal; but the principle described in plaster-moulding applies also to the preparation for metal-casting. The mixture of metals to form bronze, the proper heating of the furnace, burning and uniting parts, chasing and other processes of founding cannot be fully described in this place. They belong to a distinct practice, and to be well understood must be studied in the foundry.

"If the model—now reproduced in plaster—is to be copied in marble or stone, the first step is to procure a block of the required size. Two stones, called *scale-stones*, are then prepared, upon one of which the model or plaster cast is placed, and upon the other the rough block of marble. The fronts of these stones have figured marks or 'scales,' to use the technical term, exactly corresponding. An instrument capable of being easily moved, and which is fitted up with socket-joints and movable arms, is then applied to the scale-stone of the model, and a projecting point or 'needle' is made to touch a particular part of the model itself. This is carefully removed to the scale-stone of the rough block, and the marble is cut away till the 'needle' reaches so far into the block as to correspond with the 'point' taken on the model. A pencil-mark is then made to show that the *point* is found and registered. This process is repeated all over the model and block, alternately, till a rough copy or shape of the model is entirely made. These 'pointing' machines are not always precisely alike in their forms, but the principle upon which they act is exactly similar in all. The statue being thus rudely shaped out, the block is placed in the hands of a superior workman, called a 'carver,' who, having the plastic model near at hand to refer to, copies the more minute portions of the work by means of chisels, rasps, and files, the pencil-marks made by the 'pointer' showing him the precise situation of the parts and the limit beyond which he is not to penetrate into the marble. When the carver has carried the work as far as the sculptor desires, he proceeds himself to give it the finishing touches, improving the details of form and expression, managing the different effects produced by two different materials—one, the plastic model, being opaque; the other, the marble, being considerably diaphanous; giving the proper varieties of texture in the flesh, hair, and drapery, and, more especially, harmonizing the whole.

"The rich quality of surface that appears more or less in works of marble is produced by rubbing with fine sand or pumice-stone and other substances, and the ancients appear to have completed this part of their work by a process which is called '*circumlitio,*' and may mean not only rubbing or polishing, but applying some composition, such as hot wax, to give a soft, glowing color to the surface. Many of the ancient statues certainly exhibit the appearance of some foreign substance having slightly penetrated the surface of the work to about one eighth of an inch, and its color is of a warmer tint than the marble below it; a process, be it observed, quite distinct from and not to be confounded with *polychromy*, or what is usually understood by painting sculpture with various tints, in imitation of the natural color of the complexion, hair, and eyes. Its object, probably, with the ancients as with modern sculptors, has been simply to get rid of the glare and freshness of appearance that is sometimes objected to in a recently finished work, by giving a general warmth to the color of the marble."

# INDEX.

FIG. I.—THE PYRAMIDS OF GHIZEH.

PART III.

# ·ARCHITECTURE·

# CONTENTS.

## CHAPTER I.



## CHAPTER II.



## CHAPTER III.

# LIST OF ILLUSTRATIONS.

# ARCHITECTURE.

## CHAPTER I.

### ANCIENT OR HEATHEN ARCHITECTURE.

3000 B.C. TO A.D. 328.

RCHITECTURE seems to me to be the most wonderful of all the arts. We may not love it as much as
's, when we are young perhaps we cannot do so,
ise it is so great and so grand; but at any time of life
an see that in Architecture some of the most marvel-
achievements of men are displayed. The principal
ı for saying this is that Architecture is not an imita-
rt, like Painting and Sculpture. The first picture that
ver painted was a portrait or an imitation of some-
that the painter had seen. So in Sculpture, the first
or bas-relief was an attempt to reproduce some being
iect that the sculptor had seen, or to make a work
combined portions of several things that he had
ed; but in Architecture this was not true. No
's or tombs or palaces existed until they had first
form in the mind and imagination of the builders,
're created out of space and nothingness, so to speak.
'ainting and Sculpture are imitative arts, but Archi-
is a constructive art; and while one may love pict-

this pyramid has from one to four Fellahs or Arabs, who pull him forward or upward by his arms, or push him and lift him from behind, and finally drag him to the top (Fig. 2). When he thinks of all the weary months and days of the twenty years during which it is said that those who built it worked, cutting out the stone in the quarries, moving it to the spot where it was required, and then raising it to the great heights and fitting it all in place, he regards his fatigue in its ascent as a little thing, though at the time it is no joke to him.

FIG. 2.—THE ASCENT OF A PYRAMID.

Many of the pyramids were encased in stone taken from the Mokattam Mountains, which were somewhat more than half a mile distant; but the pyramid of Cheops was covered with the red Syenite granite, which must have been quarried in the "red mountain," nearly five hundred miles away, near to Syene, or the modern Assouan. The interior of the pyramid is divided into chambers and passages (Fig. 3), which are lined with beautiful slabs of granite and con-

:ucted in such a way as to prove that at the remote time which the pyramids were built Egyptian architects and ›rkmen were already skilled in planning and executing :at works. Of the seventy pyramids known to have ex-ed in those early days, sixty-nine had the entrance on the rth side, leaving but single exception to s rule; all of them re situated on the stern side of the er Nile, just on the e of the desert, be-d the strip of cul-.ble ground which lers the river.

Near the pyramids e are numerous bs, which are built ewhat like low ies, having several tments with but entrance from the de. The walls of : apartments are ıed with pictures ır to this one of a erer's shop (Fig. hey represent the ers and customs of ıncient Egyptians great exactness.

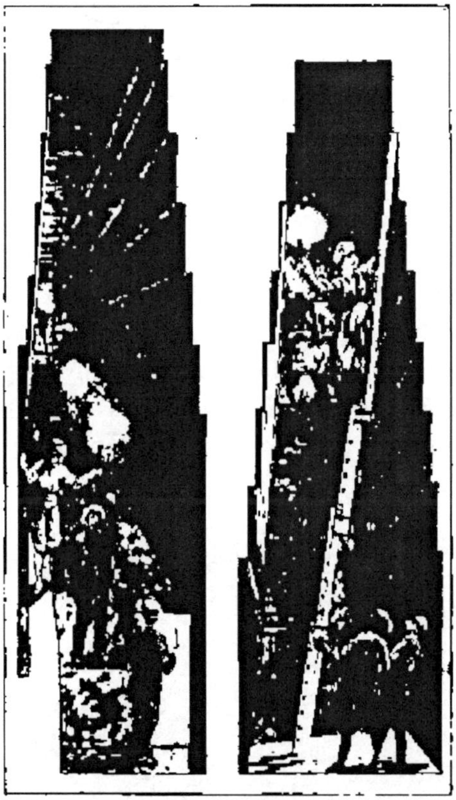

FIG. 3.—VIEW OF GALLERY IN THE GREAT PYRAMID.

ıe tombs at Beni-Hassan are among the most ancient of Egypt, and are very interesting (Fig. 5). They nade between 2466 and 2266 B.C. They are on the n bank of the Nile, and are hewn out of the solid

FIG. 4.—POULTERER'S SHOP.

rock; they are ornamented with sculptures and pictures which are full of interest; it has been said that these tombs were built by the Pharaoh, or king, of Joseph's time, and one of the paintings is often spoken of as being a representation of the brethren of Joseph; but of this there is no proof. The colors of the pictures are fresh and bright, and they show that many of the customs and amusements of that long, long ago were similar to our own, and in some cases quite the same. The manufactures of glass and linen, cabinet work, gold ornaments, and other artistic objects are pictured there; the games of ball, draughts, and *morra* are shown, while the animals, birds, and fishes of Egypt are all accurately depicted.

FIG. 5.—ROCK-CUT TOMB, BENI-HASSAN.

An interesting thing to notice about these tombs is the

y in which the epistyle—the part resting upon the umns—imitates squarely-hewn joists, as if the roof were wood supported by a row of timbers. When we come the architecture of Greece we shall see that its most portant style, the Doric, arose from the imitation in ne of the details of a wooden roof, and from a likeness ween these tombs and the Doric order, this style has n named the Proto-Doric.

The tombs near Thebes which are called the "Tombs of Kings," and many other Egyptian tombs, are very inter-ng, and within a short time some which had not before n observed have been opened, and proved to be rich in orations, and also to contain valuable ornaments and ks of art, as well as papyri, or records of historical value.

The most magnificent of all the Egyptian tombs is that King Seti I., who began to reign in 1366 B.C. He was l of splendid buildings, and all the architects of his time : very busy in carrying out his plans. His tomb was discovered until 1817, and was then found by an Italian eller, whose name, Belzoni, has been given to the tomb. staircase by which it is entered is twenty-four feet long, opens into a spacious passage, the walls of which are tifully ornamented with sculptures and paintings. is succeeded by other staircases, fine halls, and cor-s, all of which extend four hundred and five feet into nountain in which the tomb is excavated, making also dual descent of ninety feet from its entrance. It is a erful monument to the skill and taste of the architects lived and labored more than three thousand years ago.

he two principal cities of ancient Egypt were Memphis Thebes. The first has been almost literally taken to s and carried away, for as other more modern cities been built up near it, the materials which were first in the old temples and palaces have been carried here here, and again utilized in erecting new edifices.

Thebes, on the contrary, has stood alone during all the centuries that have passed since its decline, and there is now no better spot in which to study the ancient Egyptian architecture, because its temples are still so complete that a good idea can be formed from them of what they must have been when they were perfect. The ruins at Thebes are on both banks of the Nile, and no description can do justice to their grandeur, or give a full estimate of their wonders; but I shall try to tell something of the palace-temple of Karnak, which has been called "the noblest effort of architectural magnificence ever produced by the hand of man."

The word palace-temple has a strange sound to us because we do not now associate the ideas which the two words represent. Many palaces of more modern countries and times have their chapels, but the union of a grand temple and a grand palace is extremely rare, to say the least. Perhaps the Vatican and St. Peter's at Rome represent the idea and spirit of the Egyptian palace-temples as nearly as any buildings that are now in existence.

The Egyptian religion controlled all the affairs of the nation. The Pharaoh, or king, was the chief of the religion, as well as of the State. When a king came to the throne he became a priest also, by being made a member of a priestly order. He was instructed in sacred learning; he regulated the service of the temple; on great occasions he offered the sacrifices himself, and, in fact, he was considered not only as a descendant of gods, but as a veritable god. In some sculptures and paintings the gods are represented as attending upon the kings, and after the death of a king the same sort of veneration was paid to him as that given to the gods. This explains the building of the palace and temple together, and shows the reason why the gods and the kings, and the affairs of religion and of government, could not be separated. As we study the arts of different countries we are constantly reminded that the religion of a

:ople is the central point from which the arts spring forth. 'om its teachings they take their tone, and adapt their rms and uses to its requirements. I refer to this fact ›m time to time because it is important to remember that underlies much of the art of the world.

It may be said that all the art of Egypt was devoted to : service of its religion. Of course this is true of that :d in the decoration of the temples ; it is also true of all t did honor to the kings, because they were regarded as red persons, and all their wars and wonderful acts which represented in sculpture and painting, and by statues l obelisks, are considered as deeds that were performed the sake of the gods and by their aid.

It was also the religious belief in the immortality of the l that led the Egyptians to build their tombs with such :, and to provide such splendid places in which to lay body, which was the house of the spirit.

[n the study of Architecture it will also be noted that a ıtry which has no national religion—or one in which the :rnment and the religion have no connection with each r—has no absolutely national architecture. It will have ıin features which depend upon the climate, the build-naterials at command, and upon the general customs of ›eople ; but here and there will be seen specimens of xisting orders of architecture, and buildings in some :e representing the art of all countries and periods; architecture is known by the term composite, because :omposed of portions of several different orders, and o absolutely distinct character.

his palace-temple of Karnak is made up of a collection urts and halls, and it is very difficult to comprehend ze of all these parts which go to make up the enor-whole. The entire space devoted to it is almost as large as the whole area of St. Peter's at Rome, and times as great as any of the other cathedrals of

Europe ; a dozen of the largest American churches could be placed within its limits and there still be room for a few chapels. All this enormous space is not covered by roofs, for there were many courts and passages which were always open to the sky, and one portion was added after another, and by one sovereign and another, until the completion of the whole was made long after the Pharaoh who commenced it had been laid in one of the tombs of the kings.

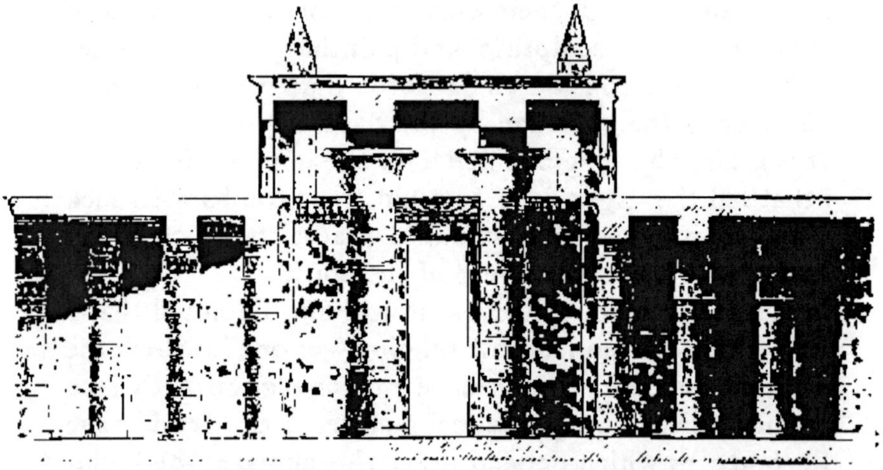

FIG. 6.—THE HALL OF COLUMNS AT KARNAK.

The most remarkable apartment of all is called the great Hypostyle Hall, which high-sounding name means simply a hall with pillars (Fig. 6). This hall and its two pylons, or entrances, cover more space than the great cathedral of Cologne, which is one of the largest and most famous churches of all Europe.

This splendid hall had originally one hundred and thirty-four magnificent columns, of which more than one hundred still remain ; they are of colossal size, some of them being sixty feet high without the base or capital, which would increase them to ninety feet, and their diameter is twelve eet. This large number of columns was necessary to ıphold the roof, as the Egyptians knew nothing of the ırch, and had no way of supporting a covering over a space vider than it was possible to cover by beams. The hall vas lighted by making the columns down the middle half ıs high again as the others, so that he roof was lifted, and the light ame in at the sides, which were eft open.

As I must speak often of colımns, it is well to say here that he column or pillar usually consists of three parts—the base, the shaft, and the capital (Fig. 7). The ase is the lowest part on which the shaft rests. Sometimes, as in the Grecian Doric order, the base is eft out. The capital is the head of the column, and is usually the nost ornamental part, giving the nost noticeable characteristics of he different kinds of pillars. The shaft is the body of the pillar, beween the base and capital, or all elow the capital when the base is omitted.

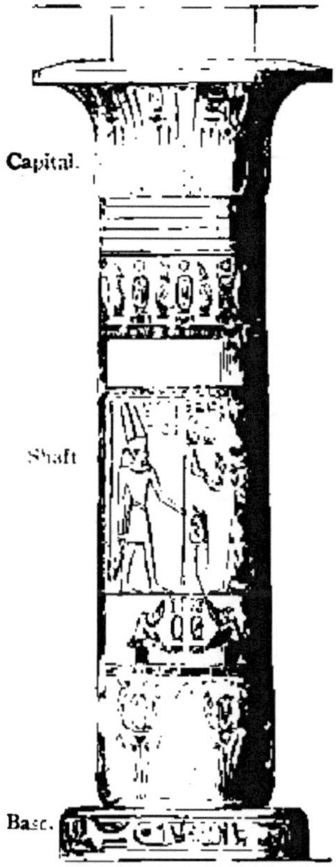

FIG. 7.—PILLAR FROM THEBES.
Showing the three parts.

The Egyptian pillars seem to have grown out of the square stone piers which at first were used for support. The square corners were first cut off, making an eight-sided pier ; then some architect carried the cutting farther, and by slicing off each corner once more gave the pillar sixteen sides. The advantage of the octagonal piers over the square ones was that the cutting off of sharp corners made it easier for people to move about between them, while the play of light on the sides was more varied and pleasant to the eye. The sixteen-sided pillar did not much increase the first of these advantages, while the face of its sides became so narrow that the variety of light and shade was less distinct and attractive. It is probable that the channelling of the sides of the shaft was first done to overcome this difficulty, by making the shadows deeper and the lights more striking; and we then have a shaft very like that of the Grecian Doric shown in the picture in Fig. 40, or the Assyrian pillars in Figs. 29 and 30. In the Egyptian pillars it was usual to leave one side unchannelled and ornament it with hieroglyphics. In time the forms of the Egyptian pillars became very varied, and the richest ornaments were used upon them. The columns in the hall at Karnak are very much decorated with painting and sculptures, as Fig. 6 shows. The capitals represent the full-blown flowers and the buds of the sacred lotus, or water-lily. In other cases the pillars were made to represent bundles of the papyrus plant, and the capitals were often beautifully carved with palm leaves or ornamented with a female head. (See Figs. 8, 9, and 10).

FIG. 8.—SCULPTURED CAPITAL.

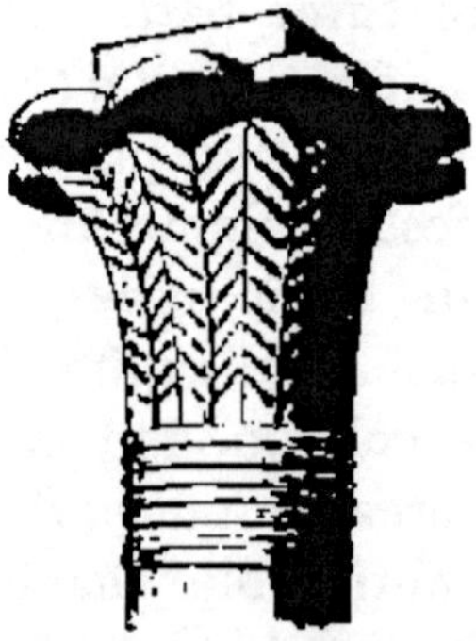

FIG. 9.—PALM CAPITAL.

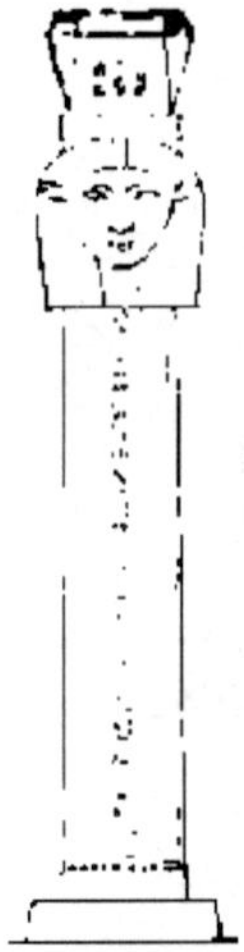

FIG. 10.—PILLAR FROM SEDINGA.

The whole impression of grandeur made by the Temple of Karnak was increased by the fact that the Temple of

,uxor, which is not far away, is also very impressive and eautiful, and was formerly connected with Karnak by an venue bordered on each side with a row of sphinxes cut ut of stone. These were a kind of statue which belonged ɔ Egyptian art, and originated in an Egyptian idea, lthough a resemblance to it exists in the art of other ncient countries (Fig. 11).

FIG. 11.—THE GREAT SPHINX.

Before the Temple of Luxor stood Colossi, or enormous statues, of Rameses the Great, who built the temple, and not far distant were two fine obelisks, one of which is now in Paris.

There was much irregularity in the lines and plan of Egyptian palaces and temples. It often happens that the side walls of an apartment or court-yard are not at right angles; the pillars were placed so irregularly and the decorations so little governed by any rule in their arrangement, that it seems as if the Egyptians were intentionally regardless of symmetry and regularity.

The whole effect of the ancient Thebes can scarcely be imagined; its grandeur was much increased by the fact that its splendid buildings were on both banks of the Nile, which river flowed slowly and majestically by, as if it borrowed a sort of dignity from the splendid piles which it reflected, and which those who sailed upon its bosom regarded with awe and admiration. There are many other places on the Nile where one sees wonderful ruins of ancient edifices, but we have not space to describe or even to name them, and Thebes is the most remarkable of all.

"Thebes, hearing still the Memnon's mystic tones,
Where Egypt's earliest monarchs reared their thrones,
Favored of Jove! the hundred-gated queen,
Though fallen, grand; though desolate, serene;
The blood with awe runs coldly through our veins
As we approach her far-spread, vast remains.
Forests of pillars crown old Nilus' side,
Obelisks to heaven high lift their sculptured pride;
Rows of dark sphinxes, sweeping far away,
Lead to proud fanes and tombs august as they.
Colossal chiefs in granite sit around,
As wrapped in thought, or sunk in grief profound.

"The mighty columns ranged in long array,
The statues fresh as chiselled yesterday,
We scarce can think two thousand years have flown
Since in proud Thebes a Pharaoh's grandeur shone,
But in yon marble court or sphinx-lined street,
Some moving pageant half expect to meet,
See great Sesostris, come from distant war,
Kings linked in chains to drag his ivory car;
Or view that bright procession sweeping on,
To meet at Memphis far-famed Solomon,
When, borne by Love, he crossed the Syrian wild,
To wed the Pharaoh's blooming child."

The obelisks of ancient Egypt have a present interest hich is almost personal to everybody, since so many of ιem have been taken away from the banks of the Nile and ι placed that they now overlook the Bosphorus, the Tiber, ιe Seine, the Thames, and our own Hudson River; in

FIG. 12.—CLEOPATRA'S NEEDLES.

truth, there are twelve obelisks in Rome, which is a larger number than are now standing in all Egypt.

The above cut (Fig. 12) shows the two obelisks known as Cleopatra's Needles, as they were seen for a long time at Alexandria. They have both crossed the seas; one was presented to the British nation by Mehemet Ali, and the other, which now stands in Central Park, was a gift to America from the late Khedive of Egypt, Ismail Pasha.

The obelisks were usually erected by the kings to express their worship of the gods, and stood before the temple bearing dedications of the house to its particular deity; they were covered with the quaint, curious devices which served as letters to the Egyptians, which we call hieroglyphics, and each sovereign thus recorded his praises, and declared his respect for the special gods whom he wished to honor. They were very striking objects, and must have made a fine effect when the temples and statues and avenues of sphinxes, and all the ancient grandeur of the Egyptians was at its height; and these grave stone watchmen looked down upon triumphal processions and gorgeous ceremonials, and kings and queens with their trains of courtiers passed near them on their way to and from the temple-palaces.

It is always interesting to study the houses and homes of a people—domestic architecture, as it is called; but one cannot do that in Egypt. It may almost be said that but one ancient home exists, and as that probably belonged to some royal person, we cannot learn from it how the people lived. There were many very rich Egyptians outside of the royal families, and they dwelt in splendor and luxury; on the other hand, there were multitudes of slaves and very poor people, who had barely enough to eat to keep them alive and enable them to do the work which was set them by their task-masters.

The house of which we speak is at Medinet Habou, on the opposite side of the Nile from Karnak (Fig. 13). It has three floors, with three rooms on each floor, and is very irregular in form. But if we have no ancient houses to study in Egypt, we can learn much about them from the paintings which still exist, and we may believe that the cities which surrounded the old temples fully displayed the

alth and taste of the inhabitants. These pictures show
e houses in the midst of gardens laid out with arbors,
vilions, artificial lakes, and many beautiful objects, such
we see in the fine gardens of our own day.

FIG. 13.—PAVILION AT MEDINET HABOU.

After about 1200 B.C. there was a long period of decline in the architecture of Egypt; occasionally some sovereign tried to do as the older kings had done, but no real revival of the arts occurred until the rule of the Ptolemies was established; this was after 332 B.C., when Alexander the Great conquered the Persians, who had ruled in Egypt about one hundred and ninety-five years.

Under the Ptolemies Egypt was as prosperous as she had been under the Pharaohs, but the arts of this later time never reached such purity and greatness as was shown in the best days of Thebes; the buildings were rich and splendid instead of noble and grand, or, as we might say, "more for show" than was the older style.

It is singular that, though the Egypt of the Ptolemies was under Greek and Roman influence, it still remained essentially Egyptian. It seems as if the country had a sort of converting effect upon the strangers who planned and built the temples of Denderah, and Edfou, and beautiful Philæ, and made them try to work and build as if they were the sons of the pure old Egyptians instead of foreign conquerors. So true is this that before A.D. 1799, when scholars began to read hieroglyphics, the learned men of Europe who studied art believed that these later temples were older than those of Thebes.

Outside of Thebes there is no building now to be seen in Egypt which gives so charming an impression of what Egypt might be as does the lovely temple on the island of

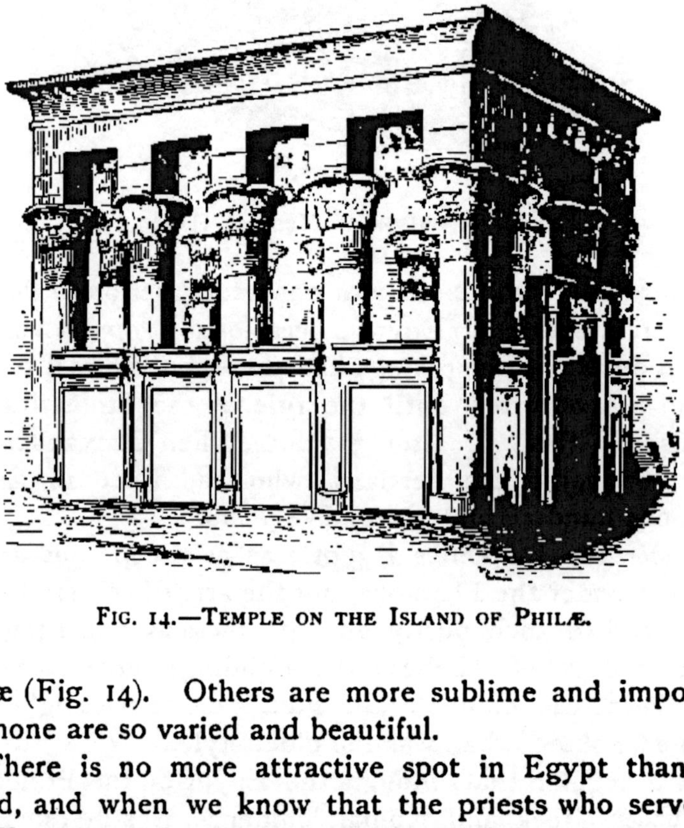

FIG. 14.—TEMPLE ON THE ISLAND OF PHILÆ.

Philæ (Fig. 14). Others are more sublime and imposing, but none are so varied and beautiful.

There is no more attractive spot in Egypt than this island, and when we know that the priests who served in the Temple of Isis here were never allowed to leave the island, we do not feel as if that was a misfortune to them. It was a pity, however, that none but priests were allowed to go there, and in passing I wish to note the fact that this ıs the most ancient monastery of which we know ; for at it was in simple fact, and the monks lived lives of strict :votion and suffered severe penance.

The buildings at Philæ, as well as most of those of the tolemaic age, had the same irregularity of form of which e have spoken before ; their design, as a whole, was fine, ut the details were inferior, and it often happens that the :ulpture and painting which in the earlier times improved nd beautified everything, lost their effect and really injured he appearance of the whole structure.

At first thought one would expect to be able to learn nuch more about the manners and customs of the later :han of the earlier days of Egypt, and to find out just how :hey arranged their dwellings. But this is not so, for history tells us of nothing save the superstitious religious worship of the conquerors of Egypt. There are no pictures of the houses, or of the occupations and amusements of the people ; no warlike stories are told ; we have no tombs with their instructive inscriptions ; not even the agricultural and mechanical arts are represented in the ruins of this time. The fine arts, the early religion, the spirit of independence and conquest had all died out ; in truth, the wonderful civilization of the days of the pyramid-builders and their descendants was gone, and when Constantine came into power Egypt had lost her place among the nations of the earth, and her grandeur was as a tale that is told.

The weakness of Egyptian architecture lay in its monotony or sameness. Not only did it not develop historically, remaining very much the same as long as it lasted, but the same forms are repeated until, even with all their grandeur, they become wearisome. The plan of the temples varies little ; the tendency toward the shape of the pyramid appears everywhere ; while the powerful influence of the ritual of the Egyptian religion gives a strong likeness among all the places of worship. The Greeks performed the most important parts of their service in the open air before their temples, and almost all their care was lavished on exteriors ; the Egyptians, on the other hand, elaborated the interior with great abundance of ornaments, yet without that power of adaptation which gave so great an air of variety and grace to Grecian art.

A second and even more serious fault in Egyptian architecture is a want of proportion. In natural organized objects there is always a fixed proportion between the parts, so that if a naturalist is given a single bone of an animal he can reproduce with considerable exactness the entire beast. In art it is necessary to follow this principle of adapting one part to another, and without this both grace and refinement are wanting. The Egyptian temples are often too massive, so that they impress by their size simply, and not by any beauty of plan or arrangement.

Yet for grandeur and impressiveness no nation has ever excelled the Egyptians as builders. One may prefer the style and the ornamentation of the Greeks, or the forms and arrangement of the Gothic order ; but, taken as a whole, the combination of architecture, sculpture, painting, and hieroglyphics which goes to make up an Egyptian temple, with the addition of the obelisks, the avenues of sphinxes and the Colossi, which all seemed to belong together—these, one and all, result in a whole that has never been surpassed in effect during the thirty centuries that have rolled over the earth since Cheops built his magnificent tomb on the great desert of Egypt.

## ASSYRIA.

Our knowledge of Egyptian history is more exact than that of some other ancient nations, because scholars have been able to read Egyptian hieroglyphics for a much longer time than they have read the cuneiform or arrow-headed inscriptions which are found in Assyria, Babylon, and Persia. But we know a great deal about the ruins of Assyria, and especially of the cities of Nineveh and Khorsabad, where there are wonderful architectural remains.

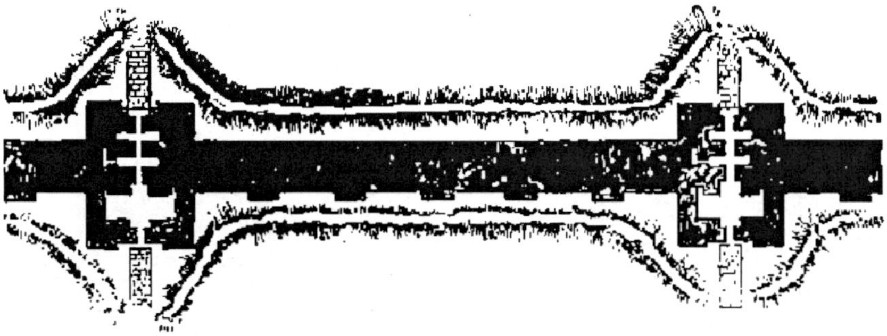

FIG. 15.—GATEWAYS IN WALLS OF KHORSABAD.

The walls which surrounded Nineveh are an important part of its ruins. It is said that in the days of the earliest sovereign these walls were one hundred feet high, and so broad that three chariots could drive abreast on their top. This story does not seem unreasonable, for all the years that have passed, and all the dust and deposit of these ages that are collected about the foot of the walls, still leave some places where they are forty-six feet high and from one to two hundred feet wide. The lower portion was of limestone, and the upper of sun-dried bricks ; the blocks of stone were neatly hewn out and smoothly polished. The walls surrounded the city, which was so large that one hundred and seventy-five thousand people could live there, and we know that its inhabitants were very numerous. The gates which opened through the walls were surmounted by lofty towers, and it is supposed that shorter towers were built upon the walls between the gateways (Fig. 15).

The above plans show the arrangement of gateways which have been excavated. It seems that there were four separate gates, and between them large chambers which may have been used by soldiers or guards. The two outer gates were ornamented by sculptured figures of colossal bulls with human heads and other strange designs ; but the inner gates had a plain finish of alabaster slabs. It is thought that arches covered these gateways like some representations of gates which are seen on Assyrian bas-reliefs. Within the gates there is a pavement of large slabs,

FIG. 16.—ENTRANCE TO SMALLER TEMPLE, NIMRUD

in which the marks worn by chariot wheels are still plainly seen.

We learn that the Assyrians made their religion a prominent part of their lives. The inscriptions of the kings begin and end with praises and prayers to their gods, and on all occasions religious worship is spoken of as a principal duty. We know that the monarchs devoted much care to the temples, and built new ones continually; but it also appears from the excavations that have been made that they devoted the best of their art and the greatest sum of their riches to the palaces of their kings. The temple was far less splendid than the palace to which it was attached as a sort of appendage. This was undoubtedly due to the fact that the Assyrian kings received more than the monarchs of any other ancient people divine honors while still living; so that the palace was regarded as the actual dwelling of a god. The inner ornamentation of the temples was confined to religious subjects represented on sculptured slabs upon the walls, but no large proportion of the wall was decorated, and the rest was merely plastered and painted in set figures. The gateways and entrances were guarded by sacred figures of colossal bulls, or lions (Fig. 16), and covered with inscriptions; there was a similarity between the palace entrances and those of the temples.

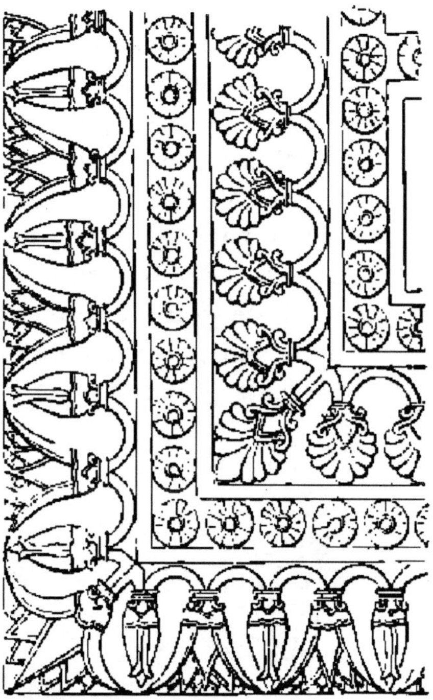

FIG. 17.—PAVEMENT SLAB FROM KOYUNJIK.

The palaces were always built on artificial platforms, which were made of solid brick or stone, or else the outside walls of the platforms were built of these substances and the middle part filled in with dirt and rubbish. Sometimes the platforms, which were from twenty to thirty feet high, were in terraces and flights of steps led up and down from one to another. It also happened that more than one palace was erected on the same platform ; thus the size and form of the platforms was much varied, and when palaces were enlarged the platforms were changed also, and their shape was often very irregular. The tops of the platforms were paved with stone slabs or bricks, the last being sometimes as much as two feet square ; the pavements were frequently ornamented with artistic designs (Fig. 17), and inscriptions are also found upon them.

At the lower part of the platform there was a terrace on which several small buildings were usually placed, and near by was an important gateway, or, more properly, a propylæum, through which every one must pass who entered the palace from the city. The next cut (Fig. 18) shows one of these grand entrances decorated with the human-headed bulls and the figure of what is believed to be the Assyrian Hercules, who is most frequently represented in the act of

FIG. 18.—REMAINS OF PROPYLÆUM, OR OUTER GATEWAY, KHORSABAD.

strangling a lion. Much rich ornament was lavished on these portals, and the entrance space was probably protected by an arch.

Below these portals, quite down on a level with the city, there were outer gateways, through which one entered a court in front of the ascent to the lower terrace.

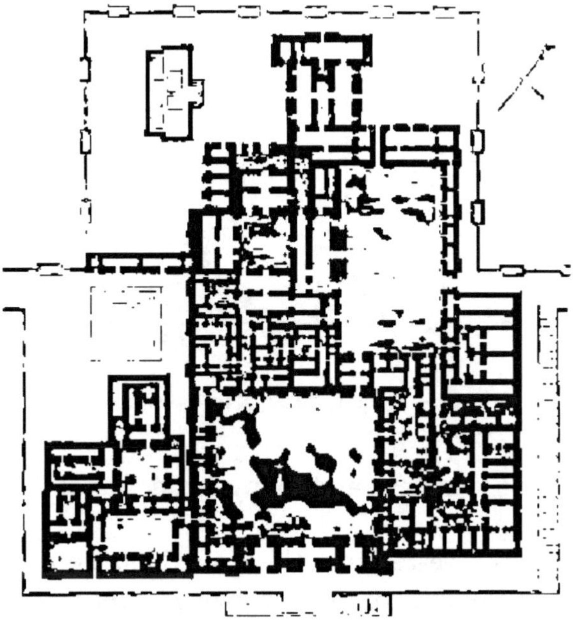

FIG. 19.—PLAN OF PALACE, KHORSABAD.

The principal apartments of the palaces were the courts, the grand halls, and the small, private chambers. The fine palaces had several courts each ; they varied from one hundred and twenty by ninety feet, to two hundred and fifty by one hundred and fifty feet in size, and were paved in the same way as the platforms outside (Fig. 19).

The grand halls were the finest portions of these splendid edifices ; here was the richest ornament, and the walls were lined with sculptured slabs, while colossal bulls, winged genii, and other figures were placed at the entrances. Upon the slabs the principal events in the lives of the monarchs were represented, as well as their portraits, and religious

FIG. 20.—RELIEF FROM KHORSABAD. A TEMPLE.

ceremonies, battles, and many incidents of interest to the nation (Fig. 20).

The slabs rested on the paved floors of the halls and reached a height of ten or twelve feet; above them the walls were of burnt brick, sometimes in brilliant colors; the whole height of the walls was from fifteen to twenty feet. The smaller chambers surrounded these grand halls, and the number of rooms was very large; in one palace which has been but partially explored there are sixty-eight apartments, and it is not probable that any Assyrian palace had less than forty or fifty rooms on its ground floor. Of all the palaces which have been examined that of Khorsabad is best known and can be most exactly described. It is believed that Sargon, a son of Sennacherib, built it, and it is very splendid.

After entering at the great portal one passes through various courts and corridors; these are all adorned with sculptures such as have been described above; at length one reaches the great inner court of the palace, which was a square of about one hundred and fifty feet in size. This court had buildings on two sides, and the other sides extended to the edge of the terrace of the platform on which the palace was built, and commanded broad views of the open country. On one side the buildings contained the less important apartments of the officers of the court; the grand state apartments were on the other side. There were ten of these at Khorsabad; five were large halls, four were smaller chambers, and one a long and narrow room. Three of the large halls were connected with one another, and their decorations were by far the most splendid of any in the palace. In one of them the sculptures represented the king superintending the reception and chastisement of prisoners, and is called the "Hall of Punishment." The middle hall has no distinguishing feature, but the third opened into the "Temple Court," on one side of which the small temple was situated. The lower sculptures of the middle and third halls represented the military history of Sargon, who is seen in all sorts of soldier-like positions and occupations; some of the upper sculptures represent religious ceremonies.

On one side of the Temple Court there were several chambers called Priests' Rooms, but the temple itself and the portions of the palace connected with it are not as well preserved as the other parts, and have nothing about them to interest us in their study.

The palaces of Nineveh are much less perfect than the palace-temples of Thebes, and cannot be described with as much exactness. There is no wall of them still standing more than sixteen feet above the ground, and we do not even know whether they had upper stories or not, or how they were lighted—in a word, nothing is positively known about them above the ground floors, and it is very strange that the sculptures nowhere represent a royal residence. But what we do know of the Assyrians proves that they equalled and perhaps excelled all other Oriental nations as architects and designers, as well as in other departments of art and industry.

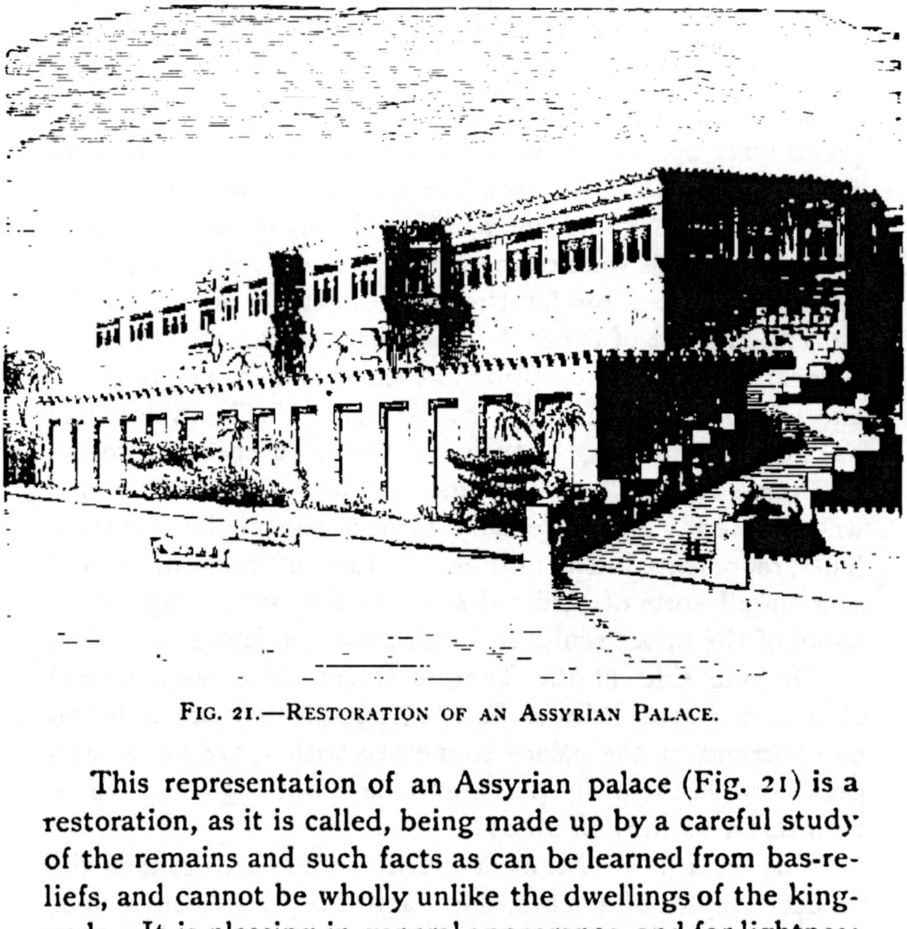

FIG. 21.—RESTORATION OF AN ASSYRIAN PALACE.

This representation of an Assyrian palace (Fig. 21) is a restoration, as it is called, being made up by a careful study of the remains and such facts as can be learned from bas-reliefs, and cannot be wholly unlike the dwellings of the king-gods. It is pleasing in general appearance, and for lightness and elegance is even to be preferred to Egyptian architecture, though it is far inferior in dignity and impressiveness.

The Assyrians knew the use of both column and arch, but never developed either to any extent. They also employed the obelisk, and it is noticeable that instead of terminating it with a pyramid, as was the case in Egypt, they capped it with the diminishing terraces, which is the fundamental form which underlies all the architecture of the country, as the smooth pyramid is the most prominent element in the architecture of Egypt.

## BABYLON.

It is probable that Babylon was the largest and finest of all the ancient cities. The walls which surrounded it, together with its hanging gardens, were reckoned among the "seven wonders of the world" by the ancients. Its walls were pierced by a hundred gates and surmounted by two hundred and fifty towers; these towers added much to the grand appearance of the city; they were not very high above the walls, and were probably used as guard-rooms by soldiers.

The River Euphrates ran through the city. Brick walls were built upon its banks, and every street which led to the river had a gateway in these walls which opened to a sloping landing which extended down to the water's edge; boats were kept at these landings for those who wished to cross the stream. There was also a foot-bridge across the river that could be used only by day, and one writer, Diodorus, declares that a tunnel also existed which joined the two sides of the river, and was fifteen feet wide and twelve feet high in the inside.

The accounts of the "Hanging Gardens" make it seem that they resembled an artificial terraced mountain built upon arches of masonry and covered with earth, in which grew trees, shrubs, and flowers. It is said by some writers that this mountain was at least seventy-five feet high, and occupied a square of four acres; others say that in its highest part it reached three hundred feet; but all agree that it was a wonderful work and very beautiful.

In the interior of the structure machinery was concealed

which raised water from the Euphrates and filled a reservoir at the summit, from which it was taken to moisten the earth and nourish the plants. Flights of steps led up to the top, and on the way there were entrances to fine apartments where one could rest. These rooms, built in the walls which supported the structure, were cool and pleasant, and afforded fine views of the city and its surroundings. The whole effect of the gardens when seen from a distance was that of a wooded pyramid. It seems a pity that it should have been called a "Hanging Garden," since, when one knows how it was built, this name is strangely unsuitable, and carries a certain disappointment with it.

The accounts of the origin of this garden are interesting. One of them says that it was made by Semiramis, a queen who was famous for her prowess as a warrior, for having conquered some cities and built others, for having dammed up the River Euphrates, and performed many marvellous and heroic deeds. It is not probable that any woman ever did all the wonders which are attributed to Semiramis, but we love to read these tales of the old, old time, and it is important for us to know them since they are often referred to in books and in conversation.

Another account relates that the gardens were made by Nebuchadnezzar to please his Median queen, Amytis, because the country round about Babylon seemed so barren and desolate to her, and she longed for the lovely scenery of her native land.

What we have said will show that the Babylonians were advanced in the science of such works as come more properly under the head of engineering; their palaces were also fine, and their dwelling-houses lofty; they had three or four stories, and were covered by vaulted roofs. But the Babylonians, like the Egyptians, lavished their best art upon their temples. The temple was built in the most prominent position and magnificently adorned. It was usually within a walled inclosure, and the most important temple at Babylon, called that of Belus, is said to have had an area of thirty acres devoted to it. The chief distinguishing feature of a Babylonish temple was a tower built in stages (Fig. 22).

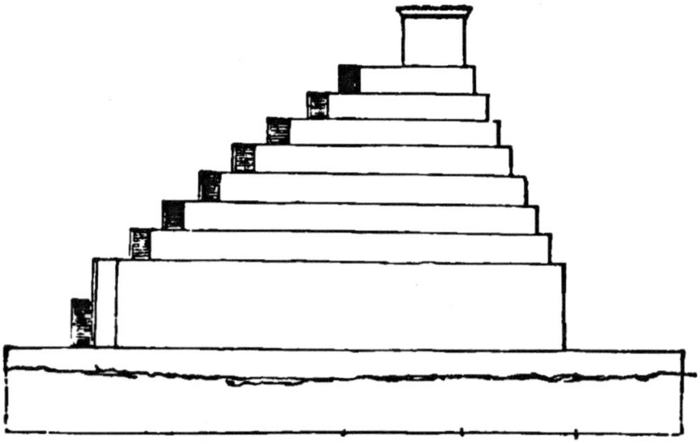

FIG. 22.—ELEVATION OF THE TEMPLE OF THE SEVEN SPHERES AT BORSIPPA.

The number of the stages varied, eight being the largest. At the summit of the tower there was a chapel or an altar, and the ascent was by steps or an inclined plane which wound around the sides of the tower. The Babylonians were famous astronomers, and it is believed that these towers were used as observatories as well as for places of worship. At the base of the tower there was a chapel for the use of those who could not ascend the height, and near by, in the open air, different altars were placed, for the worship of the Babylonians included the offering of sacrifices.

Very ancient writers describe the riches of the shrines at Babylon as being of a value beyond our belief. They tell of colossal images of the gods of solid gold; of enormous lions in the same precious metal; of serpents of silver, each of thirty talents' weight (a talent equalled about two thousand dollars of our money), and of golden tables, bowls, and drinking-cups, besides magnificent offerings of many kinds which faithful worshippers had devoted to the gods. These great treasures fell into the hands of the Persians when they conquered Babylon.

The Birs-i-Nimrud has been more fully examined than any other Babylonish ruin, and a description of it can be given with a good degree of correctness. As it now stands, every brick in it bears the name of Nebuchadnezzar; it is believed that he repaired or rebuilt it, but there is no reason to think that he changed its plan. Be this as it may, it is a very interesting ruin (Fig. 23). It was a temple raised on a platform and built in seven stages; these stages represented the seven spheres in which the seven planets moved (according to the ancient astronomy), and a particular color was assigned to each planet, and the stages colored according to this idea. That of the sun was golden; the moon, silver; Saturn, black; Jupiter, orange; Mars, red; Venus, pale yellow, and Mercury, deep blue.

It is curious to know how the various colors were obtained. The lower stage, representing Saturn, was covered with bitumen; that of Jupiter was faced with bricks burned to an orange color; that of Mars was made of bricks from a bright red clay and half burned, so that they had a blood-red tint; the stage dedicated to the sun was probably covered with thin plates of gold; that of Venus had pale yellow bricks; that of Mercury was subjected to intense heat after it was erected, and this produced vitrification and gave it a blue color; and the stage of the moon was coated in shining white metals.

Thus the tower rose up, all glowing in colors and tints as cunningly arranged as if produced by Nature herself. The silvery, shining band was probably the highest, and had the effect of mingling with the bright sky above. We can scarcely understand how glorious the effect must have been, and when we try to imagine it, and then think of the present wretched condition of these ruins, it gives great force to the prophecies concerning Babylon which foretold that her broad walls should be utterly broken down, her gates burned with fire, and the golden city swept with the besom of destruction.

FIG. 23.—BIRS-I-NIMRUD, NEAR BABYLON.

We know so little of the arrangement of the palaces of Babylon that we cannot speak of them in detail. They differed from those of Assyria in two important points: they are of burnt bricks instead of those dried in the sun which the Assyrians used, and at Babylon in the decoration of the walls colored pictures upon the brick-work took the place of the alabaster bas-reliefs which were found in the palaces of Nineveh.

These paintings represented hunting scenes, battles, and other important events, and were alternated with portions of the wall upon which were inscriptions painted in white on a blue ground, or spaces with a regular pattern of rosettes or some fixed design in geometrical figures. A sufficient number of these decorations have been found in the ruins of Babylon to prove beyond a doubt that this was the customary finish of the walls. We also know that the houses of Babylon were three or four stories in height, but were rudely constructed and indicate an inferior style of domestic architecture.

## PERSIA.

The Persians were the pupils of the Assyrians and Babylonians in Art, Learning, and Science, and they learned their lessons so well that they built magnificent palaces and tombs. Temples seem to have been unimportant to them, and we know nothing of any Persian temple remains that would attract the attention of travellers or scholars.

The four most important Persian palaces of which we have any good degree of knowledge are that of Ecbatana, the ruins of which are very imperfect ; a second at Susa, of which the arrangement is known ; a third at Persepolis, which is not well enough preserved for any exact description to be given ; and a fourth, the so-called Great Palace, near Persepolis, in which the latest Persian sovereigns lived. This magnificent palace was burned by Alexander the Great before he or his soldiers had seen its splendor. The story is that he made a feast at which Thais, a beautiful and wicked woman, appeared, and by her arts gained such power over Alexander that he consented to her proposal to fire the palace, and the king, wearing a crown of flowers upon his head, seized a torch and himself executed the dreadful deed, while all the company followed him with acclamations, singing, and wild shouts. At last they surrounded and danced about the dreadful conflagration.

The poet Dryden wrote an ode upon "Alexander's Feast" in 1697 which has a world-wide reputation. I quote a few lines from it:

> "'Twas at the royal feast for Persia won
>   By Philip's warlike son:
> Aloft, in awful state,
> The godlike hero sate
>   On his imperial throne;
> His valiant peers were placed around,
> Their brows with roses and with myrtles bound
> (So should desert in arms be crowned);
>   The lovely Thais by his side
>   Sate, like a blooming Eastern bride,
> In flower of youth and beauty's pride.
>   Happy, happy, happy pair!
>     None but the brave,
>     None but the brave,
> None but the brave deserves the fair.
>
> "Behold how they toss their torches on high,
>   How they point to the Persian abodes,
> And glittering temples of their hostile gods!
> The princes applaud with a furious joy,
> And the king seized a flambeau with zeal to destroy;
>     Thais led the way
>     To light him to his prey,
> And, like another Helen, fired another Troy."

Much study and time has been given to the examination of the ruins of Persepolis, and the whole arrangement of the city has been discovered and is made plain to the student of these matters by means of the many charts, plans, and photographs of it which now exist. I shall try to tell you something of the Great Palace of Persepolis, and the other palaces near it and on the platform with it, for the Persians, like the Assyrians and Babylonians, built their palaces upon platforms. This one of which we speak was distinct from the city, but quite near it, and is in almost perfect condition.

It is composed of large masses of hewn stone held together by clamps of iron or lead. Many of the blocks in this platform wall are so large as to make their removal from the quarries and their elevation to the required height a difficult mechanical task, which could only have been performed by skilled laborers with good means for carrying on their work. The wall was not laid in regular blocks, but was like this plate (Fig. 24).

FIG. 24.—MASONRY OF GREAT PLATFORM, PERSEPOLIS.

The platform was not of the same height in all its parts, and seems to have been in several terraces, three of which can still be seen. The buildings were on the upper terrace, which is about forty-five feet above the plain and very large; it is seven hundred and seventy feet long and four hundred feet wide. The staircases are an important feature of these ruins, and when all the palaces were in perfection these broad steps, with their landings and splendid decorations, must have made a noble and magnificent effect. The ascent of the staircases was so gradual and easy that men went up and down on horseback, and travellers now ascend and descend in this way.

There is little doubt that the staircases of Persepolis were the finest that were ever built in any part of the world, and on some of them ten horsemen could ride abreast. The broadest, or platform staircase, is entirely without ornament ; another which leads from the platform up to the central or upper terrace is so elaborately decorated that it appears to be covered with sculptures. There are colossal representations of lions, bulls, Persian guardsmen, rows of trees, and continuous processions of smaller figures. In some parts the sculptures represent various nations bringing tributes to the Persian monarch ; in other parts all the different officers of the court and those of the army are seen, and the latter appear to be guarding the stairs. (See Fig. 25.)

FIG. 25.—PARAPET WALL OF STAIRCASE, PERSEPOLIS (RESTORED).

In a conspicuous position on this ornamental staircase there are three slabs ; on two there is no design of any sort ; on the third an inscription says that this was the work of "Xerxes, the Great King, the King of Kings, the son of King Darius, the Achæmenian." This inscription is in the Persian tongue, and it is probable that it was the intention to repeat it on the slabs which are left plain in some other languages, so that it could easily be read by those of different nations ; it was customary with the ancients to repeat inscriptions in this way.

The other staircases of this great platform are all more or less decorated with sculptures and resemble that described ; they lead to the different palaces, of which there are three. The palaces are those of Darius, Xerxes, and Artaxerxes Ochus, and besides these there are two great pillared halls ; one of these is called the "Hall of One Hundred Columns," and the other *Chehl Minar*, or the "Great Hall of Audience."

This view of the palace of Darius gives an idea of the appearance of all these buildings. A description of them

FIG. 26.—RUINS OF THE PALACE OF DARIUS, PERSEPOLIS.

would be only a wordy repetition of the characteristics of one apartment and hall after another, and I shall leave them to speak of the magnificent halls which are the glory of the ruins of Persepolis, and the wonders of the world to those who are acquainted with the architectural monuments of the Turkish, Greek, Roman, Moorish, and Christian nations. (See Fig. 26.)

The Hall of a Hundred Columns was very splendid, as one may judge from this picture of its gateway (Fig. 27) ; but the *Chehl Minar*, or Great Hall of Audience, which is also called the Hall of Xerxes, was the most remarkable of all these edifices. Its ruins occupy a space of almost three hundred and fifty feet in length and two hundred and forty-six feet in width, and consist principally of four different kinds of columns. One portion of this hall was arranged in a square, in which there were six rows of six pillars each,

FIG. 27.—GATEWAY OF HALL OF A HUNDRED COLUMNS.

and on three sides of this square there were magnificent porches, in each of which there were twelve columns; so that the number of pillars in the square was thirty-six, and that of those in the three porches was the same. These porches stood out boldly from the main building and were grand in their effect.

The columns which remain in various parts of this hall

Fig. 28.—Double Horned Lion Capital.

are so high that it is thought that they must originally have measured sixty-four feet throughout the whole building.

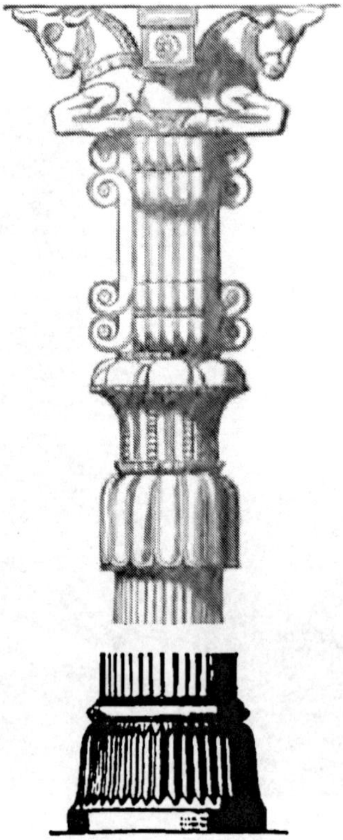

Fig. 29.—Complex Capital and Base of Pillars, Persepolis.

The capitals of the pillars were of three kinds: the double Horned Lion capital (Fig. 28) was used in the eastern porch, and was very simple; in the western porch was the double Bull capital, which corresponded to the first in size and general form, the difference being only in the shape of the animal.

The north porch faced the great sculptured staircase, and was the real front of the hall. On this side the columns were much ornamented. The following plates show the entire design of them, and it will be seen that the bases were very beautiful (Figs. 29 and 30).

Fig. 30.—Base of Another Pillar, Persepolis.

The capitals have three distinct parts; at the bottom is a sort of bed of lotus leaves, part of which are turned down, and the others standing up form a kind of cup on which the next section above rests. The middle section is fluted and has spiral scrolls or volutes, such as are seen in Ionic capitals, only here they are in a perpendicular position instead of the customary horizontal one. The upper portion had the same double figures of bulls as were on the columns of the western colonnade. The decoration on the bases was made of two or three rows of hanging lotus leaves, some round and others pointed in form. The shafts of these pillars were formed of different blocks of stone joined by iron cramps ; they were cut in exact and regular flutings, numbering from forty-eight to fifty-two on each pillar.

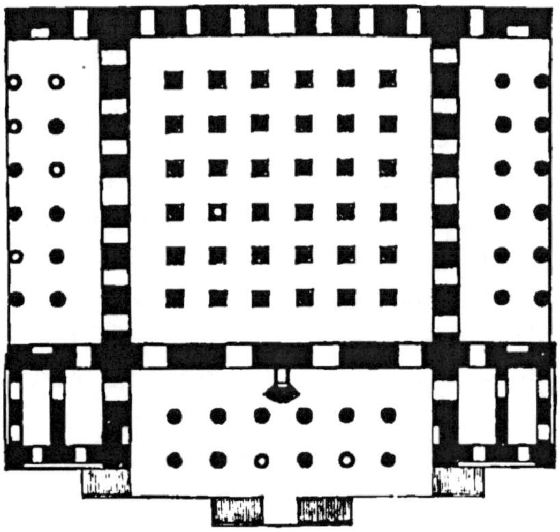

FIG. 31.—GROUND PLAN (RESTORED) OF HALL OF XERXES, PERSEPOLIS.

This plan of the Hall of Audience will help you to understand its arrangement more clearly (Fig. 31).

The square with the thirty-six columns, and the three porches with twelve columns each, are distinctly marked. The most ornamental pillars were on the side with the entrance or gateway. The two small rooms on the ends of the main portico may have been guard-rooms.

We can only regret that, while we know certain things about this hall, there is still much of which we know nothing. However, there are many theories concerning it. Some authorities believe that it was roofed, while others think that it was open and protected only by curtains and hangings, of which the Persians made much use. As we cannot know positively about it, and Persepolis was the spring residence of the Persian kings, it is pleasant to fancy that this splendid pillared hall was a summer throne-room, having beautiful hangings that could be drawn aside at will, admitting all the spicy breezes of that sunny land, and realizing the description of the palace of Shushan in the Book of Esther, which says, "In the court of the garden of the king's palace; where were white, green, and blue hangings, fastened with cords of fine linen and purple to silver rings and pillars of marble; the beds were of gold and silver, upon a pavement of red, and blue, and white, and black marble."

Here the king could receive all those who sought him; the glorious view of the plains of Susa and Persepolis, the breezes which came to him laden with the odors of the choicest flowers would soothe him to content, and realize his full desire for that deep breath from open air which gives a sense of freedom and power. We know that no Oriental, be he monarch or slave, desires to live beneath a roof or within closed doors.

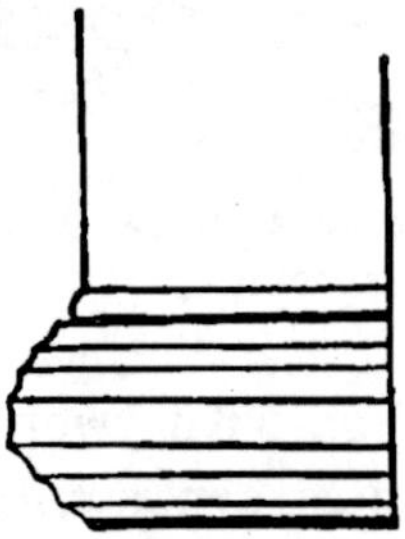

FIG. 32.—PART OF A BASE OF THE TIME OF CYRUS, PASARGADÆ.

The column was in Persia developed with a good deal of originality and much artistic feeling; and one fine base of the time of Cyrus is especially interesting for its close resemblance to the base of certain Ionic pillars afterward made in Greece (Fig. 32).

The tombs of the royal Persians were usually hewn out of the solid rock; the tomb of Cyrus, only, resembles a little house; this plate gives a representation of it (Fig. 33).

The one apartment in this tomb is about eleven feet

FIG. 33.—THE TOMB OF CYRUS.

long, seven feet broad, and seven feet high; it has no window, and a low, narrow doorway in one of the end walls is the only entrance to it. Ancient writers say that the body of Cyrus in a golden coffin was deposited in this tomb.

Seven other tombs have been explored; they are excavations in the sides of the mountains high enough to be prominent objects to the sight, and yet difficult of approach. The fronts of these tombs are much ornamented, and the internal chambers are large; there are recesses for the burial-cases, and these vary in number, some having only space for three bodies. The tomb of Darius had three recesses, in each of which there were three burial-cases; but this was an unusually large number. The tombs near Persepolis are the finest which have yet been examined.

The most noticeable characteristic of Persian architecture is its regularity. The plans used are simple, and only straight lines occur in them; thus, all the angles are right angles. The columns are regularly placed, and the two sides of an apartment or building correspond to each other. The magnificent staircases, and the abundance of elegant columns which have been called "groves of pillars" by some writers, produced a grand and dignified effect. The huge size of the blocks of stone used by Persian builders gives an impression of great power in those who planned their use, and demands for them the respect of all thoughtful students of these edifices.

The faults of this architecture lay in the narrow doorways, the small number of passages, and the clumsy thickness of the walls. But these faults are insignificant in comparison with its beauties, and it is all the more to be admired that it was invented by the Persians, not copied from other nations, and there is little doubt that the Greeks profited by its study to improve their own style, and through this study substituted lightness and elegance for the clumsy and heavy effect of the earliest Grecian architecture.

## JUDEA.

There is so much of religious, historical, romantic, and poetical association with the land of Judea, that it is a disappointment to know that there are no remains of Judean architecture from which to study the early art-history of that country; it is literally true that nothing remains.

The ruins of Jerusalem, Baalbec, Palmyra, Petra, and places beyond the Jordan are not Jewish, but Roman remains. The most interesting remnant is a passage and gateway which belonged to the great temple at Jerusalem. This passage is situated beneath the platform of the temple; it is called "The Gateway Huldah." The width of it is forty-one feet, and at one point there is a magnificent pillar, called a monolith, because it is cut from a single stone. This pillar supports four arches, which divide the passage into as many compartments, each one of which has a flat dome. On these domes or roofs there were formerly beautiful ornamental designs, one of which remains, and is like this picture (Fig. 34). Its combination of Oriental and Roman design proves that it cannot be very old, but must have been made after the influence of the Romans had been felt in Judea.

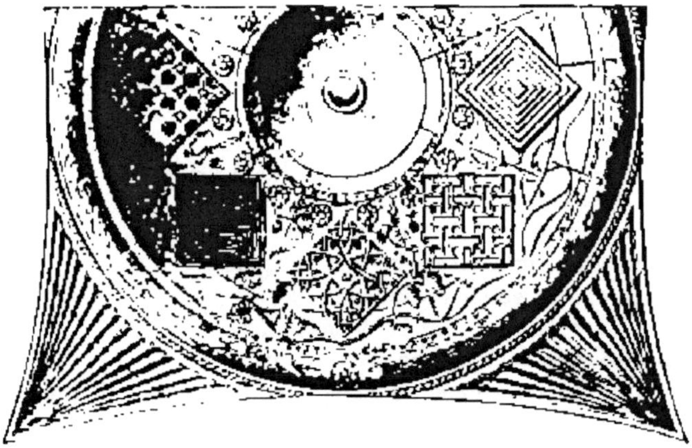

FIG. 34.—ROOF OF ONE OF THE COMPARTMENTS OF THE GATE HULDAH.

Since the excavations in Assyria, and through the use of the knowledge obtained there and in other ancient countries, and by comparing this with the descriptions of the Bible and the works of Josephus, some antiquarians have made plans and drawings of what they believe that the temple at Jerusalem must have been at the time of the Crucifixion. The result of this work has little interest, for two reasons: first, because we do not know that it is correct; second, because even at the time to which it is ascribed, it was not the ancient temple of Solomon. That had been destroyed, and after the return of the Jews from the Captivity, was rebuilt; again, it had been changed and restored by the Romans under Herod, so that it had little in reality, or by way of association, to give it the sacred and intense interest for us which would belong to the true, ancient temple at Jerusalem.

"Lost Salem of the Jews, great sepulchre.
Of all profane and of all holy things,
Where Jew and Turk and Gentile yet concur
To make thee what thou art, thy history brings
Thoughts mixed of joy and woe. The whole earth rings
With the sad truth which He has prophesied,
Who would have sheltered with his holy wings
Thee and thy children. You his power defied;
You scourged him while he lived, and mocked him as he died!

"There is a star in the untroubled sky,
That caught the first light which its Maker made,—
It led the hymn of other orbs on high;
'Twill shine when all the fires of heaven shall fade.
Pilgrims at Salem's porch, be that your aid!
For it has kept its watch on Palestine!
Look to its holy light, nor be dismayed,
Though broken is each consecrated shrine,
Though crushed and ruined all which men have called divine."

## GREECE.

The earliest history of Greece is lost in what we may call the Age of Legend. From that period have come to us such marvellous stories of gods and goddesses, and all sorts of wonderful happenings and doings, that even the most serious and wise scholars can learn little about it, and it remains to all alike a kind of delightful fairy-land.

Back to that remote age one can send his fancy and imagination to feast upon the tales of wondrous bravery, passionate love, dire revenge, and supernatural occurrences of every sort until he is weary of it all. Then he is glad to come back to his actual life, in which cause and effect are so much more clearly seen, and which, if more matter-of-fact, is more comfortable than the hap-hazard existence of those remarkable beings who were liable to be changed into beasts, or trees, or almost anything else at a moment's notice, or to be whisked away from the midst of their families and friends and set down to starve in some desolate place where there was nothing to eat, and no one to listen to complaints of sorrow or hunger.

This legendary time in Grecian history begins nobody knows when, and ends about one thousand years before the birth of Christ. Our only knowledge of it comes from the mythology which we have inherited from the past, and the two poems of Homer, called the "Iliad" and the "Odyssey."

The "Iliad" recounts the anger of Achilles and all that happened in the Trojan War; the "Odyssey" relates the wonderful adventures of Ulysses. Probably Homer never thought of such a thing as being an historian—he was a poet—much less did he dream of being the only historian of any certain time or age; but since, in the course of his poems, he refers to the manners and customs of the years that had preceded him, and gives accounts of certain past events, he is, in truth, the prime source from which we learn the little that we know of the prehistoric days in Greece.

It is believed that Homer wrote about 850 B.C., and after that date we have nothing complete in Greek literature until the time of Herodotus, who is called the "Father of History" and was born in 484 B.C. Thus four centuries between Homer and Herodotus are left with no authoritative writings.

The legendary or first period of Greek history was followed by five hundred years more of which we have no continuous history; but facts have been gathered here and there from the works of various authors which make it possible to give a reliable account of the Greece of that time. For our purpose in this book we go on to a still later time, or a third period, which began about 500 B.C., in which the architecture and art which we have in mind, when we use the general term Greek Art, originated.

It is true that before this temples had been erected of which we have some knowledge, and the elegant and ornate articles which Dr. Schliemann has found in his excavations at Troy and Mycenæ prove that the art of that remote time reached a high point of excellence. The temples and other buildings of which we know anything, and which belonged to the second period, were clumsy and rude when compared with the perfection of the time which we propose to study.

Before we speak of any one edifice it is best to understand something of the various orders of Greek architecture, more especially as the terms which belong to it and had their origin in it are now used in speaking of architecture the world over, and from being first applied to Greek art have grown to be general in their application.

In the most ancient days of Greece the royal fortresses were the finest structures, but in later days the temple became the supreme object upon which thought and labor were lavished. The public buildings which served the uses of the whole people were second in consideration, while the private dwellings were of the least importance of all. The Greek temple was built upon a raised structure like those of Assyria and other Oriental nations, but the Greek temple was much smaller, and by a dignified and simple elegance in detail, and a harmony in all its parts, it expressed a more noble religious sentiment than could be conveyed by all the vast piles of massive confusion that had abounded in more Eastern lands.

FIG. 36.—TEMPLE OF DIANA, ELEUSIS.

The earliest and simplest Greek temples were merely small, square chambers made to contain an image of a god, and in later times, when the temples came to be splendid

FIG. 35.—GRAVESTONE FROM MYCENÆ (SCHLIEMANN).

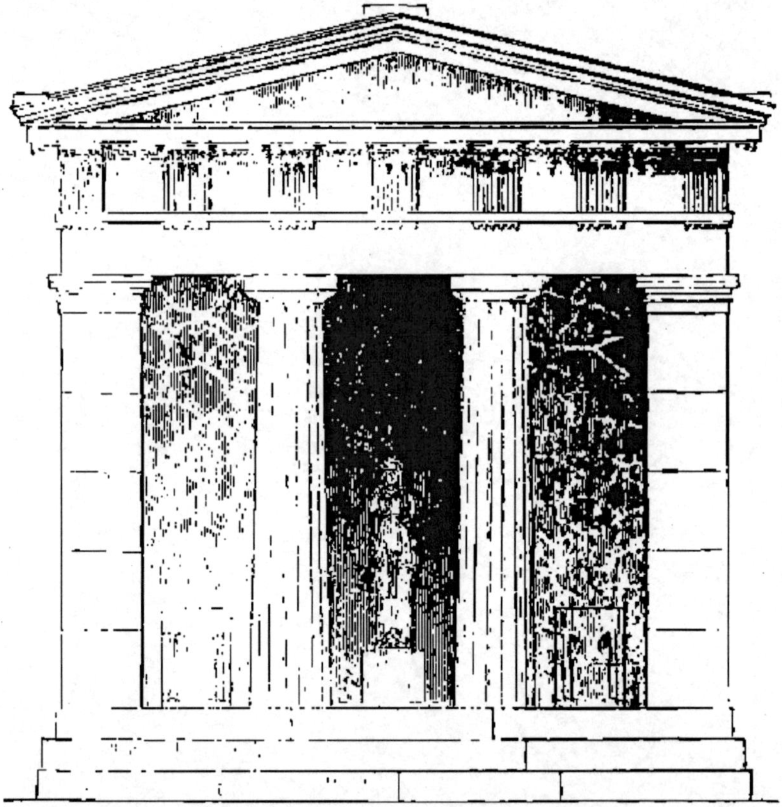

FIG. 37.—SMALL TEMPLE AT RHAMNUS.

and grand, the apartment containing the sacred image was still called the *cella* or cell, as it had been named from the first. The simplest form of temple was like the little cut (Fig. 36), and had two pillars in the centre of the front and two square pilasters at the front end of the side walls. These pilasters are called *antæ*, and the whole style of the building is called *distyle in antis;* the word distyle denotes the two pillars, and the expression means two pillars with antæ.

The above picture shows the next advance that was made in form (Fig. 37). A porch was added to the cell,

FIG. 39.—THE PARTHENON. *Athens.* (RESTORED.)

the two parts being separated by a wall with a doorway in it. After a time the number of pillars in front was increased to six, and the two outer ones were the first of a row which extended along the entire length of the sides of the temple, thus forming a peristyle, or a row of columns entirely around the cell; the cell itself remained, according to the original plan, in the centre of the building. The ground plan of such a temple is given in the next wood-cut (Fig. 38).

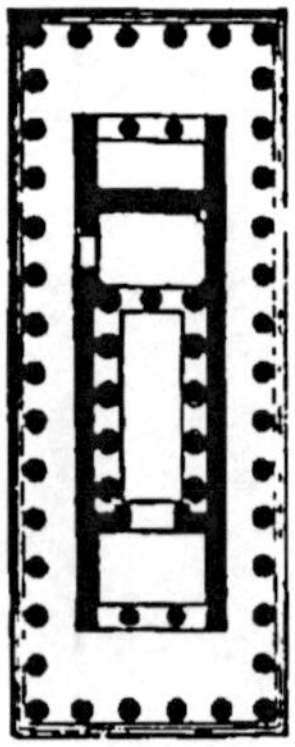

FIG. 38.—PLAN OF TEMPLE OF APOLLO, BASSÆ.

A large proportion of the Greek temples were built in this manner, and were called *hexastyle* from the six columns on the front.

The different orders of ancient Greek architecture are called the Doric, the Ionic, and the Corinthian. The Greeks were very fond of the Doric order, and used it so extensively as to make it almost exclusively their own. The picture of the Parthenon will help you to understand the explanations of the characteristics of the Doric order (Fig. 39).

As you see, the pillars had no base, but rested directly on the upper plinth of the foundation of the building. The shaft of the column is cut in flutings, and the number of them varies from sixteen to twenty; the latter number being most frequently used. The capital of the column is divided into two portions; the lower one is called the *echinus*, and projects beyond the shaft and supports a square tile or block which is called the *abacus*, and this is the architectural name for the upper member of all capitals to columns. The *architrave* or principal beam above these columns rests directly on the capitals and runs around the building. This architrave is made of separate blocks of marble or stone, and is finished at the top by a small strip of the same materials, which is called a *tenia*. This cut, which gives a section of the Parthenon on a larger scale than the last picture, will enable you to find the different portions more easily (Fig. 40).

Above the architrave and resting on it is the *frieze;* this is ornamented with fluted spaces called *triglyphs*, because they are cut in three flutings. The spaces between the

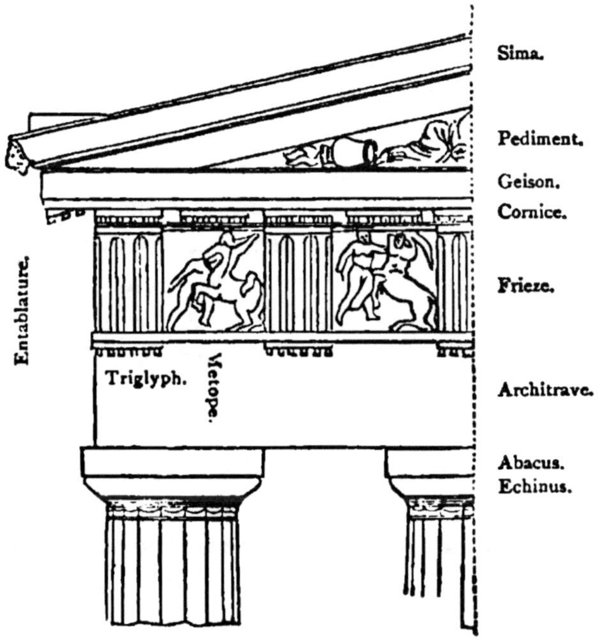


FIG. 40.—FROM THE PARTHENON, ATHENS.

triglyphs are called *metopes*, and sometimes left plain, and sometimes ornamented with sculptures, as is the case in the frieze of the Parthenon. Under the triglyphs six little blocks, or drops, are placed so that they lay over the architrave. Above the frieze there is another narrow strip, or tenia, like that upon the architrave. Above all this rests the *cornice*, and underneath the cornice are one or more rows of the small, drop-like blocks such as make the lower finish of the triglyphs; in the lower band of the cornice separate blocks are placed over each triglyph and each metope, with a small space between.

It is important to know that the architrave, frieze, and cornice, all taken together, form what is called the *entablature;* and the entablature occupies the whole of the broad space between the top of the capitals of the pillars and the lower edge of the roof.

The triangular space formed by the sloping of the roof upon the ends of a building is called the *pediment*, and, as you will see in the picture of the Parthenon, its pediment was ornamented with elaborate sculptures which are spoken of in the volume of this series which is devoted to that art. It was customary to thus ornament the pediment and to paint the walls of the cella and other portions of the building, so that while the pure Doric style seems at first sight to be stiff and straight in its effect, it becomes rich and ornamental by the use of sculpture and painting, and yet remains solid and stable.

The Doric style may be regarded as a native growth in Greece, as almost every detail of its construction and its ornaments may be traced back to the early wooden buildings of the people, as the architecture of the tombs of Beni-Hassan had been. The triglyphs, for instance, represent the ends of the beams upon which the rafters rested, while the bas-reliefs between took the place of the votive offerings which in the primitive temples were placed in the open spaces between the beams. It is not necessary here to go into all the particulars of this resemblance, which perhaps learned men have sometimes carried too far, and which are rather difficult to understand ; it is enough to say that there are excellent reasons for regarding the theory as, upon the whole, sound, although, of course, the Grecian architects modified and enriched the forms which the simple timber work had suggested.

The next great order was called the Ionic, and has a

close relation with certain forms found in Asia Minor. This picture of an Ionic capital and entablature is taken from the Temple of Athena at Priene (Fig. 41). Its scroll-like capital recalls those of the pillars in the Great Hall of Xerxes at Persepolis, shown in Figs. 28 and 29, and many examples of even closer resemblance might be given. The order differed from the Doric principally in the ornamentation of its capitals and in the fact that the columns have bases. These cuts show different kinds of bases belonging to the Ionic order. The first is from the temple at Priene (Fig. 42), and the second is the form known as the Attic base (Fig. 43). The third is especially interesting from its close resemblance to the ancient Persian base shown in Fig. 32, and is another illustration of the Eastern origin of this order (Fig. 44).

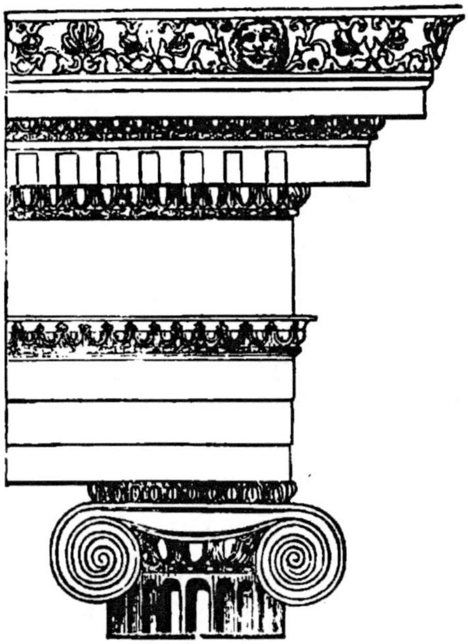

FIG. 41.—IONIC ARCHITECTURE.

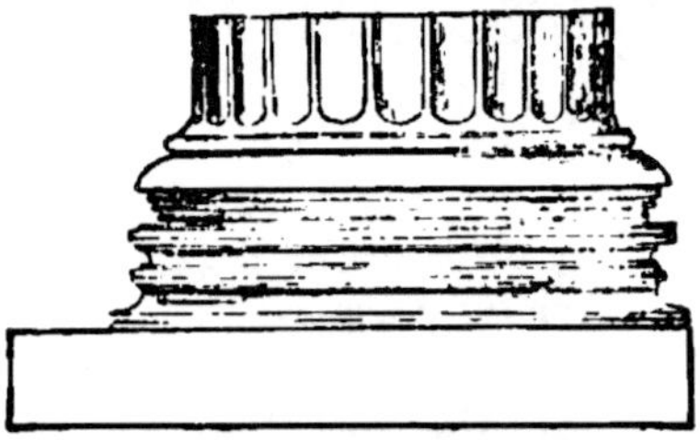

FIG. 42.—IONIC BASE, FROM PRIENE.

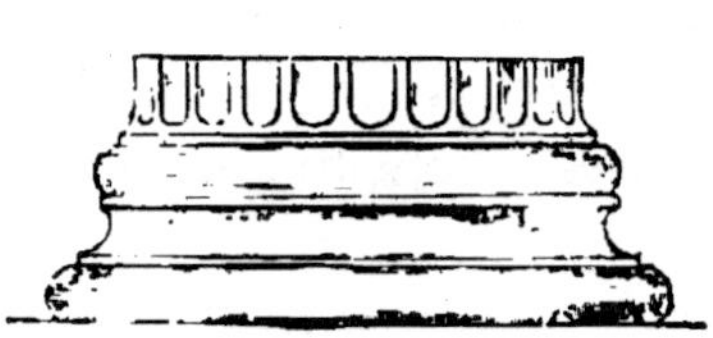

FIG. 43.—ATTIC BASE.

The Ionic capital is very easily recognized by its spiral projections, or scrolls, which are called volutes (Fig. 45).

These are so placed that they present a flat surface on the opposite sides of the capital, like the picture below (Fig. 46); sometimes the volutes are finished by a rosette in the centre.

FIG. 44.—BASE FROM TEMPLE OF HERA, SAMOS.

The shaft of the Ionic column is sometimes plain and sometimes fluted; the flutings number twenty-four, and are separated by a narrow, plain band or fillet. In some ancient examples of the Ionic order the entire entablature is left plain, but in many instances there are bands of carvings, as in the first Ionic example given above; in some modern Italian architecture even more ornament has been added.

The three, or sometimes two, layers or bands of stone which form the Ionic architrave project a little, each one more than the other, and the ornamented band above it serves to separate it from the frieze so as to make these two portions of the entablature quite distinct from each other. The frieze is never divided into set spaces as in the Doric order, but when ornamented has a continuous design in relief.

FIG. 45.—IONIC CAPITAL (FRONT VIEW).

FIG. 46.—IONIC CAPITAL (SIDE VIEW).

The lower part of the cornice is frequently cut in little pieces or dentals which form what is called the "tooth-like ornament ;" these have the effect of hanging from underneath the cornice. There is a certain pleasing effect in Ionic architecture which, perhaps, appeals to our taste at first sight more forcibly than does the severe elegance of the Doric order. Nevertheless, the latter is a higher type of art, and it is not probable that it can ever be superseded by any new invention or lose the prestige which it has held so long.

That which is called the Corinthian order differs very little from the Ionic except in the capital, but as this was so prominent a member of the Ionic style, the difference seems greater than it really is. It is therefore not necessary to speak of its parts in detail. The Choragic Monument of Lysicrates at Athens is as good a specimen of the order as remains at this time, and of this we give an illustration (Fig. 47).

FIG. 47.—FROM MONUMENT OF LYSICRATES, ATHENS.

The Corinthian order of architecture does not belong to the early period of art in Greece. It came after the influence of Oriental architecture had been shown in the Ionic style ; and perhaps the beautiful Corinthian capital may have been suggested by the palm-leaf and lotus capitals of Egypt. What has been said of other orders will help you in understanding this ; but I shall tell you especially about its capital, as that is its distinguishing feature. The form of the capital may be called bell-shaped, and it is set round with two rows of leaves, eight in each row ; above these is a third row of leaves, or of a sort of small twisted husks, which supports eight small volutes. The abacus or top portion of the capital is cut out at the corners so that sharp projections are made, called horns, and one volute comes directly under each horn of the abacus. This cut (Fig. 48) gives a more distinct idea of the capital than does that above, and you will see that four of the volutes really form the upper corners of the capital. The four other volutes meet on two opposite sides of the capital ; sometimes they are interwoven, and a flower, or rosette, or some other ornament is placed above them and lays up over the abacus. Different kinds of leaves are used in making this capital ; olive, water plant, and acanthus are all thus employed ; there is a very pretty legend as to its origin which makes the acanthus seem to be the only one which belongs to it, and is as follows :

FIG. 48.—CORINTHIAN ORDER.

It was the custom in Greece to place a basket upon the new-made graves in which were the viands which those there buried had preferred when in life. About 550 B.C. a lovely virgin died at Corinth, and her nurse arranged the basket with care and covered it with a tile. It happened that the basket was set directly over a young acanthus plant, and the leaves grew up about it in such a manner that the sculptor Callimachus was attracted by its grace and beauty, and conceived the idea of using it as a model for a new capital in architecture. I have always been sorry that it was not named for the beautiful maiden rather than for the city in which she was buried.

Another feature of Greek architecture is the use of the Caryatid, or a human figure standing upon a base and supporting the capital of a column upon the head, or, to put it more plainly, a human figure serving as the shaft to a column. These figures are usually females, and this picture of one from the Erechtheium at Athens shows how they are placed (Fig. 49). Sometimes the figures of giants, called *Telamones*, were used in the same way.

FIG. 49.—CARYATID.

In Oriental art such figures are numerous; they are used to support platforms and the thrones of kings; their position is sometimes varied by making the uplifted hands bear the weight instead of the head (Fig. 50). In any case this feature in architecture is tiresome, and its use is certainly questionable as a matter of good taste.

FIG. 50.—STOOL, OR CHAIR, KHORSABAD.

Having given a general outline of the characteristics of Greek architecture, I will speak of some remarkable edifices which are beautiful in themselves and have an interest for us on account of their associations with the history of the world, as well as with that of art.

The Temple of Diana at Ephesus, of which nothing now remains, was the largest and most splendid of all the Greek temples. It was four hundred and twenty-five feet long by two hundred and twenty wide.

The ancients counted this temple as one of the Seven Wonders of the World, and when we know that its pillars were sixty feet high, and that the beams of the architrave which had to be lifted up above the pillars to be put in place were each thirty feet long, we can readily understand that the building of it was a wonderful work. This was not the first temple that had stood on the same spot, for we know that one had been burned on the night in which Alexander the Great was born, 356 B.C. It was set on fire by Herostratus; he was tried for this crime and was put to the torture to make him declare his motive for doing such a dreadful deed; he gave as his only reason his desire to have his name handed down through all ages, and he believed that by burning the temple he should accomplish his object—as, indeed, he did, for every historian repeats the story of his crime, and his name stands as a synonym for wicked ambition.

After this destruction the temple was rebuilt on a most magnificent scale, and was not finished until two hundred and twenty years had passed. Diana was a great and powerful goddess, and all the nations of Asia united in gifts for the adornment of her shrine; the women even gave their personal ornaments to be sold to increase the fund to be spent upon it.

This temple was four times as large as the Parthenon at Athens, and had one hundred and twenty-seven splendid columns, thirty-six of which were finely carved and were the gifts of various sovereigns. The grand staircase was made from the wood of a single Cyprian vine. But great as was the temple itself, its adornments of statues by the sculptor Praxiteles, and the vast treasures of ornaments and rare objects by which it was enriched made it even more famous. The Temple of Diana was robbed by Nero and burned by the Goths, but its final destruction probably occurred after A.D. 381, when the Emperor Theodosius I. issued an edict forbidding all the ceremonies of the pagan worship.

Many beautiful objects were taken away to adorn the mediæval churches of other religions than that of the Ephesians. Some of its green jasper columns were used to support the dome of St. Sophia at Constantinople, and other parts of it are seen in the cathedrals of Italy.

There is scarcely a more desolate spot in the world than is the Ephesus of to-day. No remaining ruins are so preserved as to afford the visitor any satisfaction. The marbles and stone have been used to build other towns, which in their turn have been destroyed. The inhabitants are a handful of poor Greek peasants; wolves and jackals from the neighboring mountains roam about; and though an abundance of myrtle and some lovely groves relieve the gloominess of the scene, it is impossible when there to recreate in imagination the splendid Ephesian city, with its wharves and docks, its temples, theatres, and palaces, which were so famous as to cause it to be spoken of with wonder throughout the ancient world.

We often hear of the glory of the Periclean age at Athens, and it is true that under the leadership of Pericles Athens reached its greatest prosperity. This picture shows the Acropolis as it appeared at that time (Fig. 51).

In these best days of Athens the whole Acropolis was consecrated to religious worship and ceremonials, and its entire extent was occupied by temples and statues of the gods. The fact that I have before mentioned, that the religion of a country moulds its art, is especially true of the art of Greece; figures of the gods and bas-reliefs of the ceremonies of the Grecian worship form a large and most important part of the work of the Greek artists, and the splendid temples were raised to be the sacred homes of the statues of the great gods, to which the people could come with offerings and prayers.

The Acropolis was also a sort of fortress, because it was an eminence, and its sides of craggy rock allowed of but one ascent; thus it could be easily defended. Then, when all the wonders and riches of art had been collected there, the pure white marble, the sculpture and painting, and the ornaments of shining metals which glistened in the sun, while brilliant colors added their rich effect, it might be called a gorgeous museum, such as has never since been equalled in the history of the world.

It is important to know that the Athenians worshipped three different goddesses, all called by the one name of Athene or Athena. The most ancient and most sacred of these was Athena Polias, whose statue, made of olive-wood, was believed to have fallen from heaven. The Erechtheium was dedicated to this goddess, and there this holy, heaven-sent figure was kept, with other sacred objects of which I shall speak in their place.

The Athena next in importance was the goddess of the Parthenon, or the "House of the Virgin," as the word signifies, for this Athena Parthenos is the same as the goddess Minerva, who is said never to have married or known the sentiment of love; she was the goddess of war, prudence, and wisdom. The third Athena was called Promachos, which means the champion. Phidias made of her one of his splendid statues, standing erect, with helmet, spear, and shield.

In describing the Acropolis we shall begin with the Propylæa, or the entrances, which occupy the centre of our picture and to which the steps lead, showing the passage between the pillars, three being left on each side. This magnificent series of entrances—as the whole ascent

from the outer gate in the wall, up the steps, and through the passage between the pillars may be called—was erected about 437 B.C., and cost two thousand talents of gold, which is equal to about two millions of our dollars. The fame of the Propylæa was world-wide, and together with the Parthenon it was considered the architectural glory of the Periclean age. The style in which they are built is a splendid example of the combination of the Doric and the Ionic orders, for while the exterior is almost pure Doric, the interior is made more cheerful by the use of the Ionic columns and ornamentation.

High up at the right of the picture stands the Parthenon. Its architecture, which is Doric, has been described. We do not know when this temple was begun, but it is probably on the site of an older one. It was finished 438 B.C., and the general care of its erection was given to Phidias, the most famous of all sculptors. The marble of which the Parthenon was built was pure Pentelic, and as it rested on a rude basement of limestone the contrast between the two made the marble of the temple seem all the finer. Within and without this temple abounded in magnificent sculptures executed by Phidias himself or under his orders.

The Erechtheium, which is only partly visible at the back on the left of the picture, was the most sacred temple of Athens. It was the burial-place of Erechtheus, who was regarded not only as the founder of this temple, but also of the religion of Athena in Athens. Beside the heaven-descended statue of Athena Polias which was kept here, there was the sacred olive-tree which Athena had called forth from the earth when she was contending for the possession of Attica; here, too, was the well of salt water which Poseidon (or Neptune) made by striking the spot with his trident, and several other sacred objects (Fig. 52).

This beautiful temple was built in the Ionic style, and is very interesting because it is so different in form from every other Greek temple of which we know. This is partly due to the fact that it was built where the ground was not level, one portion of it being eight feet higher than another. A second reason for its irregularity may be that it required to be divided into more cells or apartments than other Greek temples in order to arrange the different sacred objects within its walls. A very considerable portion of this temple is still standing. The frieze, of which but little remains, was of black marble, upon which there were figures in white marble.

The Erechtheium is certainly a splendid example of the Attic-Ionic style, and the eye rests upon it with admiration; but its half-pillars and caryatides, its various porches and luxuriant detail of form and ornament, are less effective as a whole than is the Parthenon in its pure Doric architecture.

An interesting fact about Greek architecture is that the marbles used were painted in high colors. There is a theory, which may or may not be true, that the custom first arose in the same way as the shape of the Doric entablature, from the imitation of wooden buildings. The wood was painted to preserve it, and when stone began to be substituted, the architects, accustomed to bright effects, colored the marbles to look like wood. Whether this is the true origin of the custom or not, it is certain that the custom prevailed. The lower parts of the pillars of a Doric temple were usually stained a light golden-brown tint; the triglyphs and the mutules, or brackets beneath the cornices, were a rich blue; the trunnels, or wooden pins, were red or gilded; the metopes had a dark red background, against which the bas-reliefs with which they were ornamented stood out in strong contrast, while the frieze and cornice were richly painted with garlands and leaves. So highly colored a building would seem less out of place amid the varied landscape of Greece than under our colder skies, and

FIG. 52.—THE ERECHTHEIUM, *Athens.* (RESTORED.)

it is difficult for us to form any just idea of the splendid appearance it must have presented.

One of the most wonderful things about Greek architecture is the way in which allowance was made for the deception of the eye by certain forms and lines. It is not easy to explain this fully, but it is too remarkable to be wholly passed over. If a column were cut so as to diminish regularly from the bottom to the top it would seem to the eye to hollow in, and to correct this the clever Greek architect made his columns swell out a little at the middle. This is called *entasis*, and is the best known of the means taken to make forms look as they should. Another case is that of long horizontal lines. If they are really level they appear to sag at the centre, therefore in Greek temples they are delicately rounded up a little, and so have the effect of being perfectly straight. These two examples may serve to show what I mean by saying that architectural forms were made one way so as to look another, and in nothing did the Greek architecture show more marvellous skill and taste than in this.

In other Grecian cities the architecture differed but little from that of Athens, and, indeed, the influence of Athenian art and artists was felt all over the Eastern world; it is therefore not necessary for our purpose to speak further of Greek temples.

Next in importance were the municipal buildings, of which we find but few traces at Athens. The monument of Lysicrates is so beautiful that it gives us a most exalted idea of what the taste in such edifices must have been (Fig. 53).

This monument was erected in the year 334 B.C. when Lysicrates was *choragus*; this officer provided the chorus for the plays represented at Athens for the year. It was expensive to hold this position, and its duties were arduous; the choragus had to find the men for the chorus, bring them together, and have them instructed in the music, and also provide proper food for them while they studied. It was customary to present a tripod to the *choragus* who provided the finest musical entertainment, and also to build a monument upon which the tripod was placed as a lasting honor to him who had received it. There was a street at Athens called the "Street of the Tripods" because it passed a line of choragic monuments. These monuments were dedicated to different gods; this of Lysicrates was devoted to Bacchus, and was decorated with sculptures representing scenes in the story of that god, who was regarded as the patron of plays and theatres; indeed, the Greek drama originated in the choruses which were sung at his festivals.

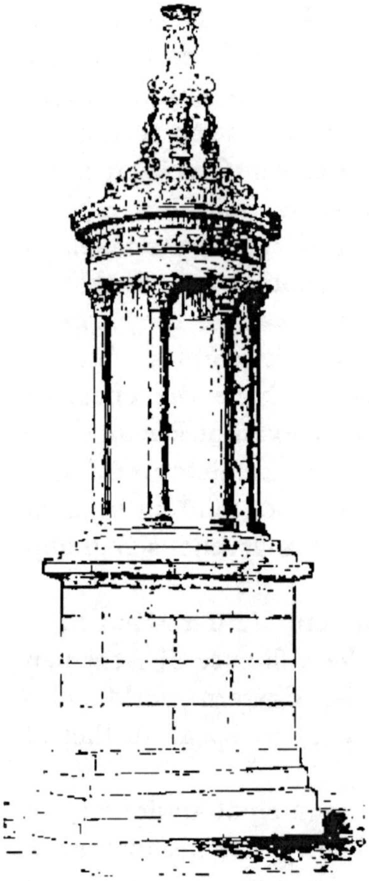

FIG. 53.—CHORAGIC MONUMENT OF LYSICRATES. *Athens.*

The Greek theatres were very large and fine; the seats were ranged in a half circle, but as none remain in a sufficient state of preservation to afford a satisfactory picture, it would be impossible to give a clear description of them here.

The ancient Greeks were not tomb-builders, and we know little of their burial-places. However, the Mausoleum built at Halicarnassus by Artemisia, in memory of her husband, Mausolus, was so important as to be numbered among the seven wonders of the world (Fig. 54).

FIG. 54.—THE MAUSOLEUM AT HALICARNASSUS (RESTORED).

Mausolus was the King of Caria, of which country Hali-
nassus was the chief city. He died about 353 B.C., and
wife, Artemisia, gradually faded away with sorrow at
death, and survived him but two years. But during
time she had commenced the erection of the Mauso-
n, and the artists to whom she intrusted the work were
ithful in completing it as though she had lived, for the
of their own fame as artists. This magnificent tomb
be described as an example of architecture as a fine art

exclusively, for it cannot be said to have been useful, since the body of Mausolus was burned according to custom, and certainly a much smaller tomb would have been sufficient for the remaining ashes.

The whole height of the Mausoleum was one hundred and forty feet; the north and south aisles were sixty-three feet long, and the others a little less. The burial vault was at the base, and the whole mass above it was ornamented with magnificent designs splendidly executed. Above the whole was a quadriga, or four-horse chariot, in which it is said that a figure of Mausolus was placed so that from land or sea it could be seen at a great distance. It is not strange that this tomb was called a wonder in its day, and from it we still take our word "mausoleum" for all burial-places which merit so distinguished a name.

Writers of the twelfth century speak of the beauty of this tomb, but in A.D. 1402, when the Knights of St. John took possession of Halicarnassus, it no longer remained, and a castle was built upon its site. The tomb had been buried, probably by an earthquake, and the name of the place was then changed to Boodroom.

In the year 1522 some sculptures were found there, but it was not until 1856 that Mr. Newton, an Englishman, discovered that these remains had belonged to the Mausoleum. A large collection of reliefs, statues, and other objects, more or less imperfect, was taken to London and placed in the British Museum, where they are known as the "Halicarnassus Sculptures."

As other temples were influenced by the example of the Athenian builders, so many other tombs resembled that of Mausolus in greater or less degree, although none approached it in grandeur and magnificence.

Of the domestic architecture of the Greeks we know very little. Almost all that is said of it is chiefly speculation, as even the descriptions of Grecian palaces and houses which are given by the classic writers are imperfect. The life of the Greek was passed largely in public, at the temple, the theatre, or the baths, or at least in the open air, and comparatively little attention was given to the building of the private houses; but in the ruins of the temples and other monuments which still exist we have sufficient proof that no art has surpassed that of ancient Greece in purity, elegance, and grandeur of style.

## ETRURIA.

Since the Etruscans were an earlier Italian nation than the Romans, and Rome, in her primal days, was ruled by Etruscan kings, it is here fitting to speak of this remarkable old people.

FIG. 55.—TOMBS AT CASTEL D'ASSO.

As Rome increased the Etruscans disappeared, and the younger power came to have so mighty an influence in the world that it absorbed the consideration of all nations as much as if no other had ever ruled in Italy.

No Etruscan temple now remains, but we know that they were not splendid like those of Greece. They were of two forms, one being circular and dedicated to a single deity, while others were devoted to three gods and had

FIG. 56.—PRINCIPAL CHAMBER IN REGULINI-GALEASSI TOMB.

three cells; their walls were built at right angles, thus making their shape regular.

The theatres and amphitheatres of the Etruscans were nearly circular and much like those of the later Italians, but not one remains except that at Sutri, which, being cut in the rock, does not afford a good example of the usual arrangement of these edifices.

In fact, the only important remains of Etruscan architecture are the tombs, of which there are many. These are of two kinds; the first are cut in the rocks and resemble the Egyptian tombs at Beni-Hassan, reminding one of little houses (Fig. 55).

FIG. 57.—ARCH AT VOLTERRA.

The second and most numerous class are mounds of earth raised above a wall at the base. These were called "Tumuli," and some of them had fine, well-furnished apartments in their midst. The next cut shows such a room as it appeared when first opened; in it were found bedsteads, biers, shields, arrows, a variety of vessels, and several kinds of useful utensils (Fig. 56).

FIG. 58.—GATEWAY. *Arpino.*

These tombs are in truth more connected with other arts than with architecture, and many beautiful articles have been found in them. The most interesting feature of Etruscan architecture is the arch, which was first brought into general use by the Romans, but is found in Etruscan remains (Fig. 57), both in the semi-circular and pointed forms. The principle of the arch had been known to several Oriental nations, but it had been applied only to short spaces and comparatively unimportant uses, such as windows and doorways (Fig. 58).

There is no doubt that many of the earliest works of the Romans were executed under the direction of Etruscan architects. Among these was the great Cloaca Maxima, or

FIG. 59.—ARCH OF CLOACA MAXIMA. *Rome.*

principal drain of ancient Rome. This was a wonderful achievement; it is probable that the oldest arch in Europe is that of this sewer, and the fact of its still remaining proves how well it must have been built in order to last so long (Fig. 59).

## ROME.

The early works of Rome, which were largely executed by the Etruscans, were principally those useful, semi-architectural objects necessary in the making of a city, such as aqueducts and bridges. These belong quite as much to civil engineering as to architecture, and we shall not speak of them.

In studying Roman architecture one is surprised at the number of uses to which it was applied, for not only do the temples, tombs, theatres, and monuments such as we have found in other countries exist in Rome, but there are also basilicas, baths, palaces, triumphal arches, pillars of victory, fountains, and various other objects suited to the wants of a great people.

No truly pure, national order of architecture existed at Rome. The union of the arch of the Etruscans with the columns of the Greeks enabled the Romans to change the forms of their edifices and to produce a great variety in them. They employed the Doric, Ionic, and Corinthian orders, but they rarely used one of these alone; they united them in endless combinations, and introduced a capital of the order which is called the Composite (Fig. 60). It consists of the lower part of the Corinthian and the upper part of the Ionic capital; this was very rich in ornament, but the line where the two orders were joined was always a defect, and it never came into general favor.

FIG. 60.—COMPOSITE ORDER, FROM THE ARCH OF SEPTIMIUS SEVERUS. *Rome.*

The Romans also introduced what is called the Tuscan order, which is usually mentioned with the Doric, Ionic,

Corinthian, and Composite, as being one of the five classic orders of architecture, although it is really little more than a variety of the Doric, as the Composite is of the Corinthian order. It differed from the Doric in having a base, while its frieze was simple and unadorned, the cornice also being very plain. The shaft of the Tuscan column was never fluted.

The Romans also used an arcade which was a combination of Greek and Etruscan art, like this cut (Fig. 61); thus showing a power of adapting forms which already existed in new combinations and for new purposes, rather than an originative genius.

FIG. 61.—DORIC ARCADE.

A very important advance made by the Romans was the improvement of interior architecture. The halls and portions of edifices to be used were more cared for than ever before; this was sometimes done at the expense of the exteriors, to which the Greeks had devoted all their thought. In fact, many ancient Roman temples were inferior to other edifices which they built. The Pantheon is the only one existing in such a state as to be spoken of with satisfaction.

This ground-plan (Fig. 62) shows that the Pantheon is circular with a porch. Taken separately, the rotunda and the porch are each fine in their own way, but the joining of the circular and angular forms has an effect of unfitness which one cannot forget even when looking at that which we regard with reverent interest. The central portion was at first a part of the Baths of Agrippa, but on account of its great beauty it was changed by Agrippa himself into a temple, by the addition of a row of Corinthian columns around the interior. (See Fig. 63.)

Taken all in all, the effect of the Pantheon is that of grandeur and simplicity. When we remember that sixteen hundred and eighty-eight years have passed since it was

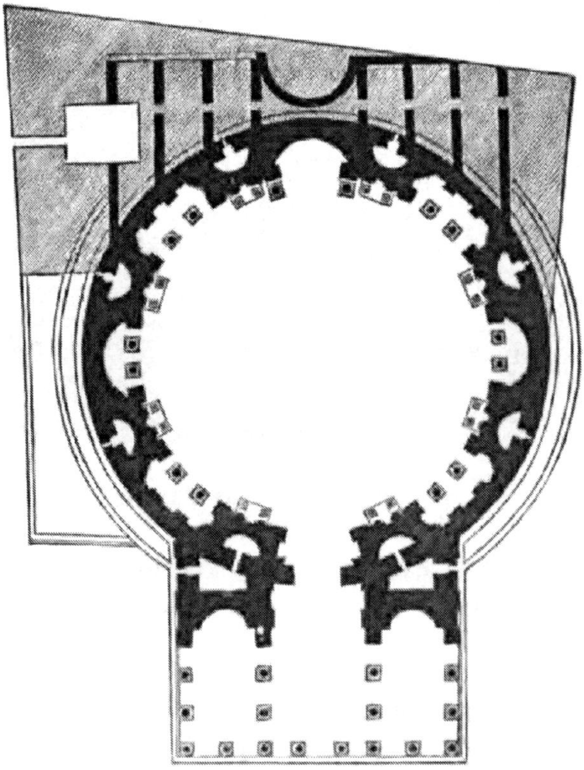

FIG. 62.—GROUND-PLAN OF PANTHEON. *Rome.*

repaired by Septimius Severus, we wonder at its good preservation, though we know that it has been robbed of its bronze covering and other fine ornaments. An inscription still remaining on its portico states that Marcus Aurelius and Septimius Severus repaired this temple ; history says that Hadrian restored it after a fire, probably about the

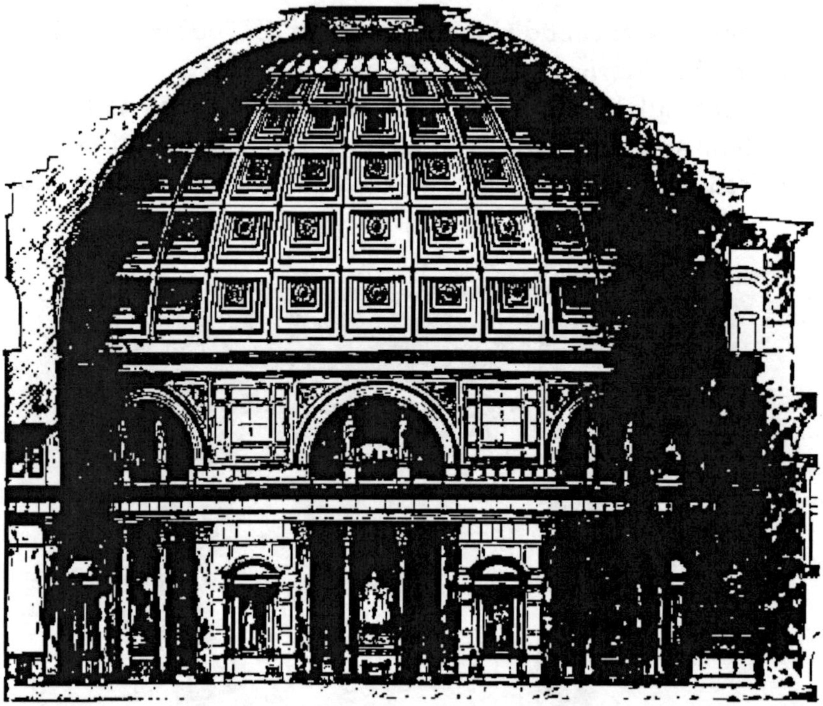

FIG. 63.—INTERIOR OF THE PANTHEON.

year 117, and it is even said that Agrippa, who died A.D. 13, added the portico to a rotunda which existed before his time.

The objects now in the interior of the Pantheon are so largely modern that they do not belong to this portion of our subject, but there is much interest associated with this spot, and it is dear to all the world as the burial-place of Raphael, Annibale Caracci, and other great artists.

Next to the temples of Rome came the Basilicas, of which there were many before the time of Constantine. The word basilica means the royal house, and these edifices were first intended for a court-room in which the king administered his laws; later they became markets, or places of exchange, where men met for business transactions.

The ruins of the Basilicas of Trajan and Maxentius, two of the finest of these edifices, are in such condition that their plans can be understood (Fig. 64). They were large, and divided into aisles by rows of columns; at one end there was a semi-circular recess or apse, in which was a raised platform, approached by steps, also semi-circular in form. Upon this platform the king or other exalted officer had his place, while those of lesser rank were on the steps below, on either side. Fronting the apse was an altar upon which sacrifices were offered before commencing any important business.

FIG. 64.—LONGITUDINAL SECTION OF BASILICA OF MAXENTIUS.

The principal reason for speaking of basilicas is that by the above cut you may see the great change made in architecture about this time by the use of columns, only half the height of the building, which were united by arches. This was a very important step, and is, in truth, one of the principal features that mark the progress of the change from ancient to Gothic architecture—a change not fully developed until the twelfth century.

I shall not say much of the theatres, amphitheatres, and baths of ancient Rome, because it is not easy to treat them in the simple manner suited to this book; they were magnificent and costly, and made an important part of Roman architecture; they were probably copied from the public buildings of the Etruscans.

Marcus Scaurus built a theatre in 58 B.C. which held eighty thousand spectators; it had rich columns and statues, and was decorated with gold, silver, and ivory. The first stone theatre in Rome was built in 55 B.C., and was only half the size of that of Marcus Scaurus. Parts of the theatre of Marcellus still remain in the present Orsini Palace in Rome, and serve to give an idea of the architecture of the period immediately before the birth of Christ.

The Emperor Augustus boasted that he had found a city of brick and had changed it to one of marble, but after his time architecture suffered a decline, and its second flourishing period may be dated from A.D. 69. To this time belongs the Colosseum, also called the Flavian Amphitheatre; it covers about five acres of ground, and is sufficiently well preserved for a good idea to be formed of what it must have been when in its best estate. The enormous size of these ancient Roman edifices is almost too much for us to imagine, and the most extensive of them all were the *Thermæ*, or public baths.

The Baths of Diocletian, built A.D. 303, were the largest of all; they had seats for twenty-four hundred bathers. These baths were in reality a group of spacious halls of varied forms, but all magnificent in size. The great hall of the Baths of Diocletian was three hundred and fifty feet long by eighty feet in width and ninety-six feet high; it was converted into a church by Michael Angelo and is called S. Maria Degli Angeli, or Holy Mary of the Angels. Many splendid pictures which were once in St. Peter's are now in this church, and copies of them made in mosaic fill the places where they were originally hung.

The Baths of Caracalla were built in A.D. 217, and though they had seats for but sixteen hundred bathers, they were much more splendid than the Baths of Diocletian.

They were surrounded by pleasure gardens, porticoes, and a stadium or race-course, where all sorts of games were held. Some beautiful mosaic pavements have been taken from these baths, and are now in the Lateran and the Villa Borghese palaces; there was a Pinacotica, or Fine Art Gallery here, in which were some of the greatest art treasures of the world, such as the Farnese Hercules, the Farnese Bull, the two Gladiators, and other famous statues, besides cameos, bronzes, and sculptures, almost without end. The granite basins in the Piazza Farnese, and some green basalt urns now in the Vatican Museum, were taken from the Baths of Caracalla, and, indeed, all over Rome there are objects of more or less beauty which were found here.

Formerly the site of these baths was like a beautiful Eden where Nature made herself happy in luxuriant growths of all lovely things. The poet Shelley was very fond of going there, and wrote of it, "Among the flowery glades and thickets of odoriferous blossoming trees, which are extended in ever-winding labyrinths upon its immense platforms and dizzy arches suspended in the air," by which we know that the ruins were covered with a soil which was fruitful in flowers, vines, and trees; but all these have been torn away in order to make the excavations which were necessary for the exploration of these wonderful baths, and now the parts which remain stand fully exposed to the view of the curious traveller.

The Roman Triumphal Arches were one of the characteristic outgrowths of the Imperial period. These splendid works were designed to perpetuate the fame of the emperors and to recall to the people the important acts of their lives. The arch of Constantine given below is one of the most famous arches in Rome (Fig. 65). It is believed that parts of it were in an arch of Trajan's time, and some even go so far as to say that it was originally dedicated to the earlier emperor and adopted by Constantine as his own. It is remarkably well preserved, and this is undoubtedly due to the fact of its being dedicated to the first Christian sovereign of Rome. The other most famous arches in the city are that of Titus, which dates from A.D. 81, and that of Septimius Severus, which was erected in honor of him and

FIG. 65.—ARCH OF CONSTANTINE. *Rome.*

of his wife, Julia, by the silversmiths and merchants of the Forum Boarium, in which spot the arch was raised.

These triumphal arches existed in all the countries where Rome held sway, and, indeed, this is true of all kinds of Roman architectural works.

This Arch of Beneventum was erected in the second century after Christ, by Trajan, when he repaired the

Appian Way. It is one of the most graceful and best preserved of all the arches of Italy (Fig. 66).

All these arches had originally groups of statuary upon them, for which they served merely as the pedestals. Their taking the form of an arch was due to their being placed in the public way, where it was necessary to leave a passage

FIG. 66.—ARCH OF TRAJAN. *Beneventum.*

for the street. Sometimes they were placed where two roads met, and a double arch was then made. Elaborate as the arches often were, you must keep in mind that they are only a part of the entire design, and that the least important part; the statuary, which has been destroyed by time, being really the more striking feature of the whole.

The tombs of Rome were very numerous, and were an

important element in Roman architecture. The tomb of Cecilia Metella is of importance because it is the oldest remaining building of Imperial Rome and the finest tomb which has been preserved (Fig. 67).

FIG. 67.—TOMB OF CECILIA METELLA.

As you see, the tomb is a round tower. In the thirteenth century it was turned into a fortress, and so much dust has been deposited on its summit in the passing of time that bushes and ivy now grow there. Many writers describe it, and Byron in his "Childe Harold" spoke of it in some verses, of which the following is the beginning :

> "There is a stern round tower of other days,
> Firm as a fortress, with its fence of stone,
> Such as an army's baffled strength delays,
> Standing with half its battlements alone,
> And with two thousand years of ivy grown,
> The garland of eternity, where wave
> The green leaves over all by time o'erthrown ;—
> What was this tower of strength ? within its cave
> What treasure lay so lock'd, so hid ?—a woman's grave."

The tomb of Hadrian, now known as the Castle of St. Angelo, is very interesting, and is one of the most prominent and familiar objects in Rome at the present day. But the tombs called Columbaria were much in use in ancient Rome, and differed essentially from those of which we have spoken, inasmuch as they were usually below the ground, and externally had no architecture. They consisted of oblong or square apartments, the sides of which were filled with small apertures of the proper size to hold an urn which contained the ashes that remained after a body had been burned, according to the Roman custom. Some of these apartments, especially when they belonged to private families, were adorned with pilasters and decorated with colors. (See Fig. 68.)

FIG. 68.—COLUMBARIUM NEAR THE GATE OF ST. SEBASTIAN. *Rome.*

The sepulchres of Rome were gradually enlarged, until, in the days of Constantine, they were frequently built like small temples above the ground, with crypts or vaults beneath them.

So little now remains of the ancient domestic architecture of Rome that one is forced to study this subject from written descriptions collected from the works of various historians, poets, and other writers. But from what we know we may conclude that the villas and country-houses were so constructed as to be full of comfort, and suited to the uses for which they were built, without too much regard to the symmetry of the exteriors. The interior convenience was the chief thing to be considered, and when finished they must have often resembled a collection of buildings all joined together, of various heights and shapes ; but within they were adapted to the different seasons, as some rooms were made for being warm, while others were arranged for coolness ; the views from the windows were also an important feature, and, in short, the pleasure of the people living in them was made the first point to be gained, rather than the impression upon the eye of those who saw them from without.

There was great luxury and elegance in the palaces of the noble classes in ancient Rome. The home of Diocletian at Spalatro was one of the most famous Roman palaces, and its ruins show that it was once magnificent. This palace was divided by four streets which ran through it at right angles with each other and met in its centre. Its entrances were called the Golden, Iron, and Brazen Gates. Its exterior architecture was simple and massive, as it was necessary that it should serve as a fortress in case of an attack. Its principal gallery overlooked the sea ; it was five hundred and fifteen feet long and twenty-four feet wide, and was famous for its architectural beauty and for the views which it commanded.

# CHAPTER II.

## CHRISTIAN ARCHITECTURE.

### A.D. 328 TO ABOUT 1400.

I HAVE written more in detail concerning Ancient architecture than I shall do of that of later times, because it is best to be thorough in studying the beginnings of things; then we can make an application of our knowledge which helps us to understand the results of what has gone before, just as we are prepared for the full-blown rose after we have seen the bud. Or, to be more practical, just as we use the simplest principles of arithmetic to help us to understand the more difficult ones; sometimes we scarcely remember that in the last lessons of the book we unconsciously apply the first tables and rules which were so difficult to us in the beginning.

I shall not try, because I have not space, to give a connected account of Christian architecture, but I shall endeavor to give such an outline of its rise and progress in various countries as will make a good foundation for the knowledge you will gain from books which you will read in future.

The architecture of Italy in the period which followed the conversion of the Emperor Constantine is called the Romanesque order. As the Christians were encouraged under Constantine and became bold in their worship, many basilicas were given up for their use. The bishops held the

FIG. 69.—INTERIOR OF BASILICA OF ST. PAUL'S. *Rome.*

principal place upon the platform formerly occupied by the king and his highest officers, and the priests of the lower orders were ranged around them. The same altars which had served for the heathen sacrifices were used for the worship of the true God, and from this cause the word basilica has come to signify a large, grand church, in the speech of our time.

Among the early basilicas of Rome which still remain none are more distinguished than that of *San Paolo fuori della Mura*, or St. Paul's without the Walls. It was ancient, and splendid in design and ornament. In 1823 it was burned, and has been rebuilt with great magnificence, but the picture above shows it as it was before the fire (Fig. 69). It was built about 386 A.D. under the Emperors Valentinian II. and Theodosius.

This basilica had four rows of Corinthian columns, twenty in each row ; many of these pillars were taken from more ancient edifices, and were composed of very beautiful marbles, forming by far the finest collection of columns in the world. The bronze gates were cast at Constantinople ; the fine paintings and magnificent mosaics with which it was decorated added much to its splendor. Tradition taught that the body of St. Paul was buried beneath the high altar.

Before the Reformation the sovereigns of England were protectors of this basilica just as those of France were of St. John Lateran ; this gives it a peculiar interest for British people, and the symbol of the Order of the Garter is still seen among its decorations. On account of its associations, San Paolo was the most interesting, if not the most beautiful, of the oldest Christian edifices in Rome.

In the early days there were many circular churches throughout Italy ; some of these had been built at first for tombs. The Christians used churches of this form for baptisms, for the sacrament for the dying, burials, and sometimes for marriage.

The circular temple of Vesta is very beautiful. It had originally twenty Corinthian columns ; nineteen of which still remain. This temple is not older than the time of Vespasian, and is not the famous one mentioned by Horace and other ancient writers, in which the Palladium was preserved—that temple no longer exists. It is probable that many of the earliest churches built by Christians in Italy were circular in form, and numbers of these still remain in various Italian cities ; but they differed from the ancient temples of this form in their want of exterior decoration. The ancient Romans had used columns, peristyles, and porticoes ; the Christians used the latter only in a few instances, but even these were soon abandoned.

The beautiful Baptistery at Florence was originally the

cathedral of the city. It is octagonal, or eight-sided, and this form is not infrequent in buildings of the fourth and following centuries. It is said that this Baptistery was built by Theodolinda, who married Autharis, King of the Lombards in 589.

This king had proposed to Garibald, King of Bavaria, for the hand of his daughter, and had been accepted. Autharis grew impatient at the ceremonies of the wooing, and escaping from his palace joined the embassy to the King of Bavaria.

When they reached the court of Garibald and were received by that monarch, Autharis advanced to the throne and told the old king that the ambassador before him was indeed the Minister of State at the Lombard Court, but that he was the only real friend of Autharis, and to him had been given a charge to report to the Italian king concerning the charms of Theodolinda. Garibald summoned his daughter, and after an admiring gaze the stranger hailed her Queen of Italy and respectfully asked that she should, according to custom, give a glass of wine to the first of her future subjects who had tendered her his duty. Her father commanded her to give the cup, and as Autharis returned it to her he secretly touched her hand and then put his finger on his own lips. At evening Theodolinda told this incident to her nurse, who assured her that this handsome and bold stranger could have been none other than her future husband, since no subject would venture on such conduct.

The ambassadors were dismissed, and some Bavarians accompanied the Lombards to the Italian frontier. Before they separated Autharis raised himself in his stirrups and threw his battle-axe against a tree with great skill, exclaiming, "Such are the strokes of the King of the Lombards!" Then all knew the rank of this gallant stranger. The approach of a French army compelled Garibald to leave his

FIG. 70.—THE CATHEDRAL OF CHARTRES.

capital; he took refuge in Italy, and Autharis celebrated his marriage in the palace of Verona; he lived but one year, but in that time Theodolinda had so endeared herself to the people that she was allowed to bestow the Italian sceptre with her hand. She had converted her husband to the Catholic faith. She also founded the cathedral of Monza and other churches in Lombardy and Tuscany, all of which she dedicated to St. John the Baptist, who was her patron saint.

The cathedral of Monza is very interesting from its historical associations. Here is deposited the famous iron crown which was presented to Theodolinda by Pope Gregory I. This crown is made of a broad band of gold set with jewels, and the iron from which it is named is a narrow circlet inside, said to have been made from one of the nails used in the crucifixion of Christ, and brought from Jerusalem by the Empress Helena. This crown is kept in a casket which forms the centre of the cross above the high altar in the cathedral of Monza; it was carried away in 1859 by the Austrians; at the close of the Italo-Prussian war, in 1866, the Emperor of Austria gave it to Victor Emmanuel, then King of Italy. This crown has been used at the coronation of thirty-four sovereigns; among them were Charlemagne, Charles V., and Napoleon I. The latter wore it at his second coronation as King of the Lombards in 1805. He placed it on his head himself, saying, "God has given it to me, woe to him who touches it!"

There are few secular buildings of this period remaining in Italy, and Romanesque architecture endured but a short time, for it was almost abandoned at the time of the death of Gregory the Great, in 604. During the next four and a half centuries the old styles were dying out and the Gothic order was developing, but cannot be said to have reached any high degree of perfection before the close of the eleventh century.

## GOTHIC ARCHITECTURE.

It is difficult to speak concisely of Gothic architecture because there is so much that can be said of its origin, and then it has so extended itself to all parts of the world as to render it in a sense universal. Perhaps Fergusson makes it as simple as it can be made when he divides Europe by a line from Memel on the shores of the Baltic Sea to Spalatro on the Adriatic, and then carries the line westward to Fermo and divides Italy almost as the forty-third parallel of latitude divides it. He then says that during the Middle Ages, or from about the seventh to the fifteenth centuries, the architecture north and west of these lines was Gothic; south and east it was Byzantine, with the exception of Rome, which always remained individual, and a rule unto herself.

There was a very general belief in all Christian lands that the world would end in the year 1000 A.D., and when this dreaded period had passed without that event happening, men seem everywhere to have been seized with a passion for erecting stone buildings. An old chronicler named Rodulphe Glaber, who died in 1045 A.D., relates that as early as the year 1003 A.D. so many churches and monasteries of marble were being erected, especially in France and Italy, "that the world appeared to be putting off its old dingy attire and putting on a new white robe. Then nearly all the bishops' seats, the churches, the monasteries, and even the oratories of the villages were changed for better ones."

Such a movement could not fail to have a great influence upon architecture, and it was at this time that the Gothic style began to be rapidly developed; and, indeed, so far as any particular time may be fixed for the beginning of the Gothic order, it would fall in the tenth and eleventh centuries. The classic forms, with their horizontal cornices and severe regularity, were then laid aside, and a greater freedom and variety than had ever obtained before began to make itself felt in all architectural designs.

We must first try to understand what are the distinguishing features of Gothic architecture. Perhaps the principal one may be called constructiveness; which is to say, that in Gothic architecture there is far greater variety of form, and the power to make larger and more complicated buildings than had been possible with the orders which preceded it. During the Middle Ages the aim was to produce large edifices, and to build and ornament them in a way that would make them appear to be even larger than they were. The early Gothic buildings are so massive as to have a clumsy effect, because the architects had not yet learned how to make these enormous masses strong and enduring, and yet so arranged as to be light and graceful in their appearance.

A second striking difference between the ancient orders and the Gothic, is that in the former enormous blocks of stone or marble were used and great importance was attached to this. Many ancient works are called Cyclopean for this reason. It does not make a building more beautiful to have it massive, but it does make it grand. Even in a less colossal mode of building a column is more effective when it is a monolith, and an architrave more beautiful when its beams are not joined too frequently. But in the Gothic order the use of massive blocks is largely given up, and the endeavor is to so arrange smaller materials as to display remarkable constructive skill.

A third and a very important feature of the Gothic order is the use of the arch. The much-increased constructive power of which we have spoken depended very largely upon this. The ancients knew the use of the arch, but did not like it because they thought that it took away from the

FIG. 71.—CHURCH OF ST. NICHOLAS. *Caen.*

repose of a building. Even now the Hindoos will not use it; they say, "An arch never sleeps," and though the Mohammedan builders have used it in their country, the Hindoos cannot overcome their dislike of it. In the Gothic order, however, the use of arches, both round and pointed, is unending. The results are very much varied, and range all the way from a grand and impressive effect to a sort of toy-like lightness which seems more suited to the block-houses made by children than to the works of architects. The earlier Gothic arches were round, although pointed

Fig. 73.—Clustered Pillar.

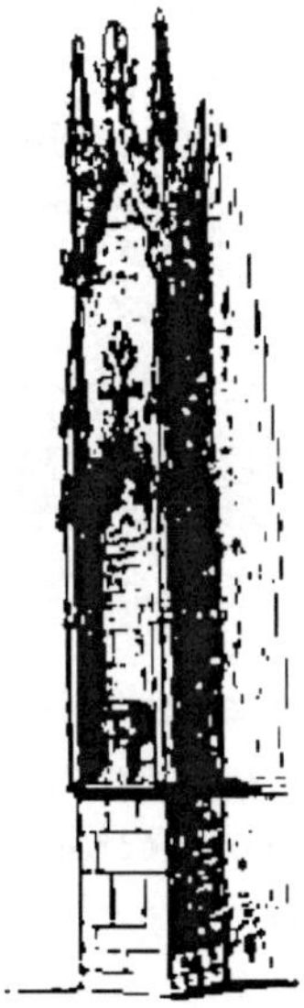

Fig. 74.—Buttress.

Fig. 75.—Hinge.

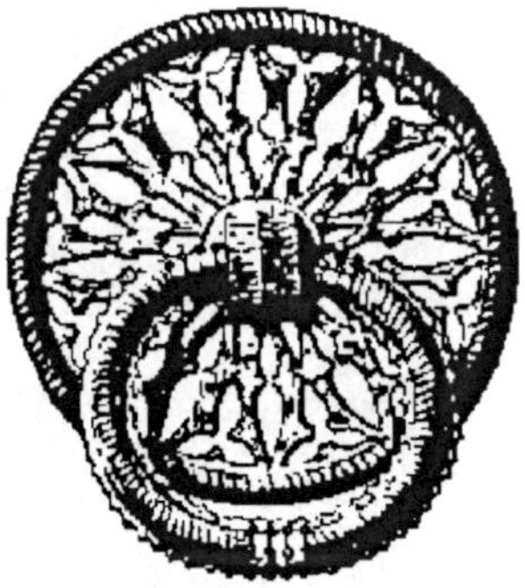

Fig. 77.—Iron-work.

Fig. 78.—Gargoyle.

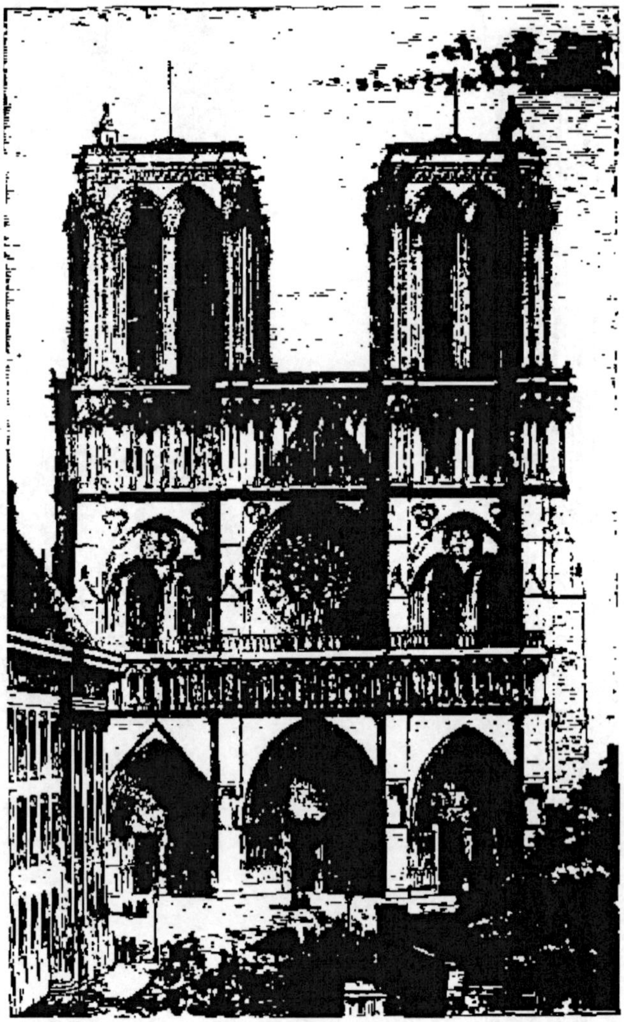

FIG. 72.—FAÇADE OF CATHEDRAL OF NOTRE DAME. *Paris.*

arches are occasionally found in very ancient buildings. The picture (Fig. 71), however, gives a just idea of the form of arch most used until the introduction of the pointed arch, which occurred in France during the twelfth century. Of this form the doorways of the next cut present a fine example (Fig. 72).

FIG. 73.—CLUSTERED PILLAR.

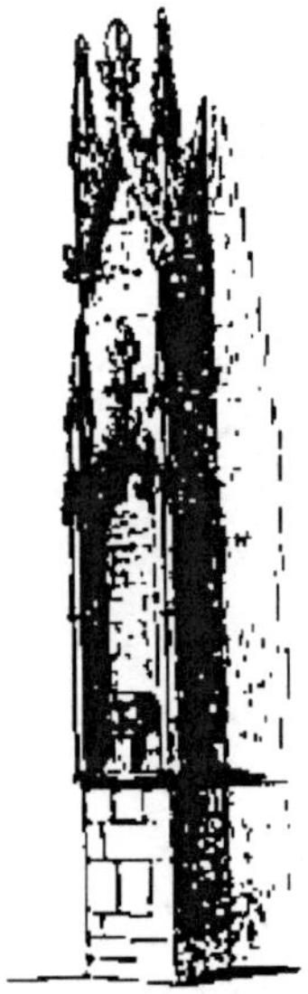

FIG. 74.—BUTTRESS.

FIG. 75.—HINGE.

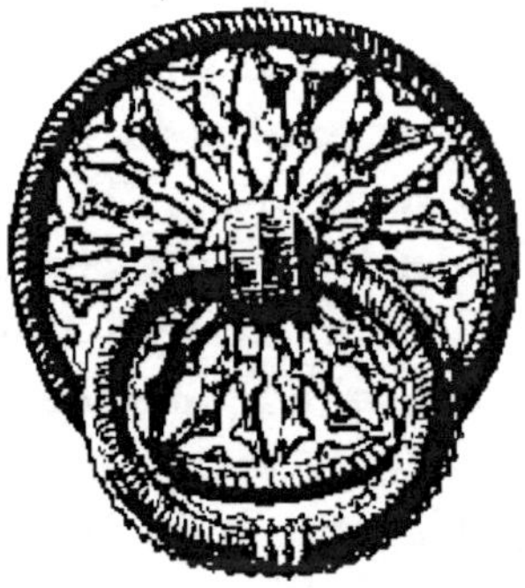

FIG. 77.—IRON-WORK.

FIG. 78.—GARGOYLE.

An important characteristic of Gothic architecture was the fact that every part of the building was so made as to show its use. Instead of hiding the supports they were made prominent. If a pier or buttress was to stand a perpendicular strain, even the lines of decoration were generally made to run in that direction; if extra supports were needed, they were not concealed, but built in so as to show, and even to be prominent. In the details the same feeling was often shown in a very marked degree; the hinges and nails and locks of Gothic buildings were made to be seen, and whatever was needed for use was treated as if it were of value as an ornament. The spouts by which the water was carried over the eaves were made bold and comparatively large, and carved into those curious shapes of animals and monsters called gargoyles, which are seen on so many mediæval edifices. Many of these details of Gothic buildings are very elegant, and serve to-day as models for modern workmen. (See Figs. 73, 74, 75, 76, 77, 78, 79.)

FIG. 76.—NAIL-HEAD.

Among the inventions of Gothic architects the division of the interior into three aisles, with the centre one much the highest, was very important. By this arrangement the space was made to appear longer and higher than it really was, and what was lost in the effect of width was more than made up in a certain elegance of form which is very pleasing. The three central aisles of the next cut illustrate this arrangement (Fig. 80).

FIG. 79.—SCROLL.

The Gothic builders gave loftiness to their edifices by the use of spires and towers. They became very skilful in constructing them with buttresses below and pinnacles above, so that the spires should not detract from the apparent size of the buildings to which they were attached (Fig. 81).

In the matter of design in ornament the Gothic order had no fixed method, except so far as its forms were symbolic. Every form of vegetable design was employed ; vines and leaves were abundant. As a rule the use of human forms or animals as supports to columns or other weights

FIG. 80.—SECTION OF CHURCH. *Carcassone.* WITH OUTER AISLES ADDED IN FOURTEENTH CENTURY.

was avoided. If they were introduced the animals were not reproductions of such as exist, but the imaginary griffin or other monster, and at times dwarfs or grotesque human beings, were represented as if for caricatures.

Sculptured figures were usually placed upon a pedestal either with or without niches for them, and were not made to appear to be a part of the building itself. The deep recesses of Gothic portals, the pinnacles and niches gave

FIG. 81.—SPIRES OF LAON CATHEDRAL.

opportunities to display exterior sculpture to great advantage (Fig. 82). The interiors were also appropriate for any amount of artistic ornament in bas-reliefs or figures that could be lavished upon them.

The most original and effective feature of ornament, however, which was introduced by Gothic architects is that of painted glass. To this they devoted their best talent. It is not necessary to say how beautiful and decorative it is; we all know this, and our only wonder is that it was left for the Gothic architects to apply it to architectural uses. We do not know precisely when stained or painted glass was invented, but we know that it existed as early as 800, and came into very general use in the eleventh and twelfth centuries.

Before painted glass was used windows were made very small, and it was some time before the large, rich style was adopted. The following cut from Notre Dame, at Paris, gives the three stages of the change, and it is interesting to see them thus in one church (Fig. 83).

On the left are the undivided windows without mullions or dividing supports ; next, at the right, the upper window shows the form with one perpendicular mullion and a circular or rose window above the centre ; lastly, on the right of the lower story we see a full traceried window.

The window became one of the most important and characteristic features of Gothic buildings. These large

FIG. 82.—PORTAL OF THE MINORITES' CHURCH. *Vienna.*

open spaces gave opportunity for elegant shapes and splendid colors, both the form of the opening and the dividing ribs, or tracery, as it was called, being made with the utmost beauty and grace. The round windows, called rose windows and wheel windows, were often exquisitely designed, as the following example shows (Fig. 84).

FIG. 83.—EXTERNAL ELEVATION, CATHEDRAL OF PARIS.

The window is illustrative of the influence which climate may have on the development of architectural style. In warm countries where spaces were left open, window forms and painted glass were, of course, never employed ; but in more northern lands they became one of the most marked features in important edifices.

A whole book might be written about these windows and be very interesting also, but we can give no more space to them here.

Gothic architecture gradually extended from the centre of Italy to the most northern bounds of civilization, and though practised by so many nations, was as much the architectural expression of a religion as the architecture of a single ancient nation had been the outgrowth of its peculiar religious belief. During the Middle Ages the priests and monks preserved learning in the midst of general darkness and ignorance, and were the chief patrons of all art which survived the decline of the time. They built up the Christian faith by every means in their power. The monks were missionaries. They went to various countries, and selecting favorable spots they founded abbeys ; around these abbeys a poor population settled ; gradually churches were built, and it frequently happened that the monks not only planned the work to be done, but also executed it with their own hands. Many of them were masons and builders, and several bishops were architects. St. Germain, Bishop of Paris, designed the church in that city now called by his name, and was also sent to Angers to build another church, and to Mans to erect a monastery.

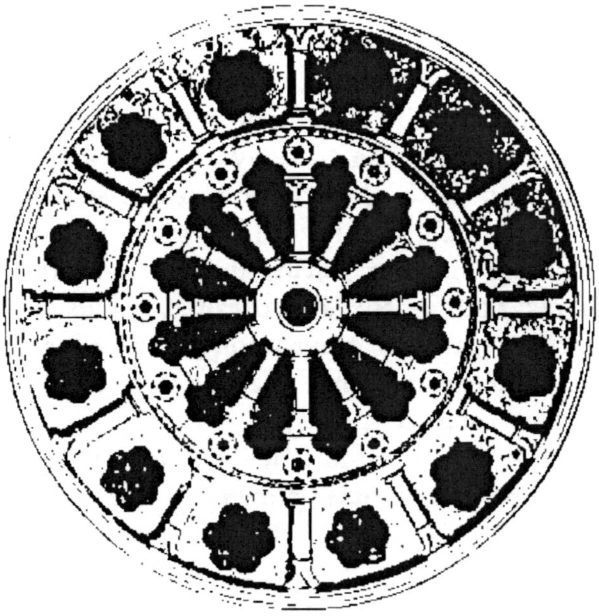

FIG. 84.—WHEEL WINDOW, FROM CATHEDRAL. *Toscanella.*

The finest buildings being thus made for religious purposes and under the direction of the clergy, they must have been as full an expression of Christianity as were the temple-palaces of Egypt an expression of the religion of Osiris and Isis, when the kings were both priests and sovereigns, and dwelt in these palaces. And this was true as long as Gothic art was in the hands of the clergy and used almost entirely for religious purposes.

Later on, when it was employed for civic edifices erected under the direction of laymen, it became an expression of political independence also. The freedom of thought which came with the decline of the feudal system inspired new aspirations and imaginations in the hearts and minds of men, and these found expression in all the arts, and very especially in architecture. If we cannot always admire the manner in which Gothic art was made to express these lofty desires, we can fully sympathize with the sentiment which was behind it.

The Gothic order held undisputed sway west and north of the geographical line of which we have spoken until the fifteenth century. Then a revival of classical literature took place, and with this there arose also a revival of classic art and architecture; this revival is known as the Renaissance, or the new birth, and the period of time is spoken of as that of the Renaissance. The effect of this classic reaction was very great upon all the educated classes of Europe, and its influence may be said to have endured through about three centuries.

Again, during the eighteenth century, Gothic art was revived. A reverence has grown up for the good that wrestled with the darkness of the Middle Ages and survived all their evils. The rough, strong manhood of that time is now justly appreciated. Perhaps the feeling in this direction is too much exaggerated. While our regard for a rude and weather-stained monument of the spirit and architecture of the past may be natural and proper, the imitation of it which is made in our day may easily become absurd, and is very rarely suited to our purposes.

Spain is one of the countries which are on the Gothic side of the geographical line we have drawn, and among the many splendid edifices in that country some of the finest are of the Gothic order. There is no national architecture there, for though the Spaniards love art and its expression

FIG. 85.—COLLEGIATE CHURCH, TORO. *From Villa Amil.*

passionately, they have themselves invented almost nothing which is artistic.

But while it is true that the Spaniards invented no styles, they did modify those which they adopted, and there are peculiarities in the Spanish use and arrangement of the Gothic order which give it new elements in the eyes of those who understand architecture scientifically. To the uneducated also it appears to have a personality of its own, something that is suited to Spain and the Spaniards; so that, while we know that Spanish Gothic architecture was borrowed from France and Germany, we yet feel that if the cathedrals of Paris and Cologne were to be put down in Valencia or Madrid they would look like strangers, and not at all well-contented ones at that; and if the churches of Toledo or Burgos were copied precisely in any other country, they would have an air of being quite out of keeping with everything around them (Fig. 85).

We call the architecture of Spain before 1066 the "Early Spanish," and from that time the Gothic order prevailed during nearly three centuries.

FIG. 86.—ST. PAUL. *Saragossa.*

Meantime in the south of Spain the Moresco or Moorish order had sprung up, of which Fig. 86 gives an example. It was gradually adopted to a limited extent, until finally some specimens of it existed in almost every province of the country. The Gothic order was affected by it, inasmuch as the richness of ornament of the Moorish order so pleased the taste of the Spaniards that their architects allowed themselves to indulge in a certain Moorish manner of treating the Gothic style. We cannot describe these differences in words, but Figs. 86 and 87 will make it plain.

As has been said, the interior decoration of all Gothic churches was very rich and abundant. It is also true that all church furniture was made with great care; the matter of symbolism was carefully considered, and each design made to indicate the use of the article for which it was intended. No altar, preaching-desk, stall, chair, or screen was made without due attention to every detail, and the endeavor to have it in harmony with its use and its position in the church. The following cut shows a rood-screen, which was the kind of screen that was placed before the crucifixion over the high altar (Fig. 88).

The fantastic sculptures and wealth of ornament in Gothic decorations produce a confusing effect on the brain and the eye if we look at the whole carelessly; but when we remember that each separate design has its especial meaning we are interested to examine them, and we find that the variety of forms is almost innumerable. Where there are trailing vines and lions, faith is indicated; roses and pelicans are the symbols of mercy and divine love; dogs and ivy, of truth; lambs, of gentleness, innocence, and submission; fishes are an emblem of water and the rite of baptism; the dragon, of sin and paganism; a serpent, too, typifies sin, and when wound around a globe it indicates the power of evil over the whole world; a hind or hart signifies solitude; the dove, purity; the olive, peace; the palm, martyrdom; the lily, purity and chastity; the lamp, lantern, or taper, piety; fire and flames, zeal and the suffer-

FIG. 87.—CLOISTER. *Tarazona.*

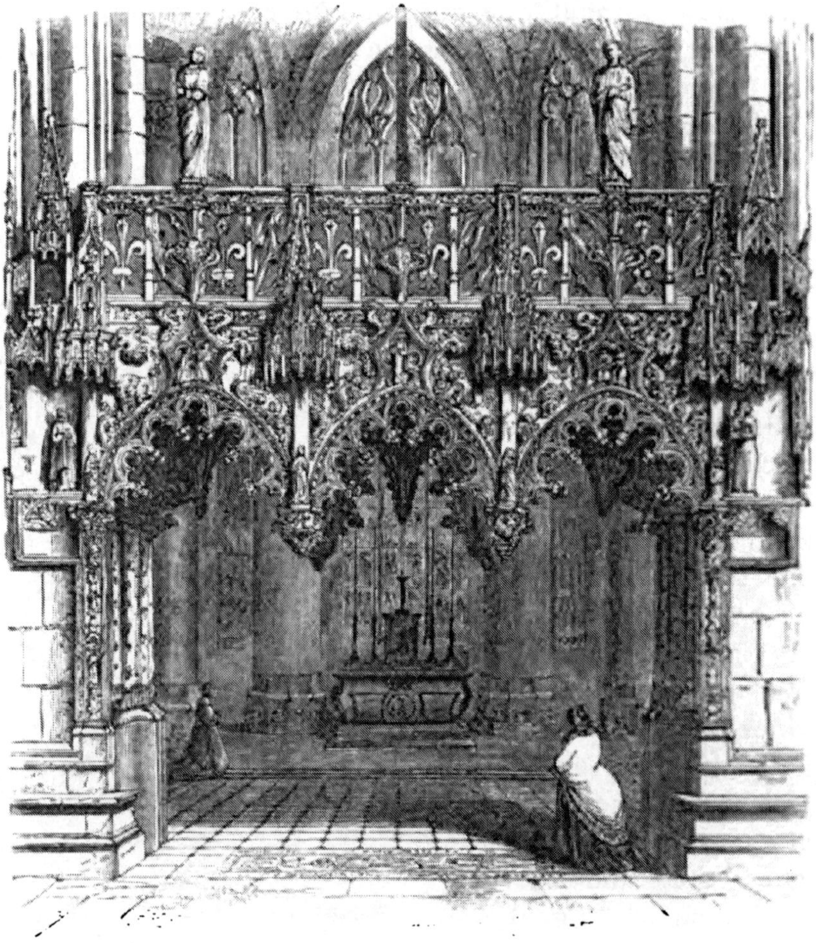

FIG. 88.—ROOD-SCREEN, FROM THE MADELEINE. *Troyes.*

ings of martyrdom; a flaming heart, fervent piety and spiritual love; a shell, pilgrimage; a standard or banner, victory; and so on, and on, we find that meaning and thought were worked out in every bit of Gothic ornament, and that what at first appears so wild and hap-hazard is full of a method which well repays one for the study of it.

The Gothic order was also used in building municipal

Fig. 89.—Palace of Wartburg.

edifices, palaces, and even for the purposes of domestic architecture. The finest remains of this kind are in Germany, the most interesting of them all being the castle on the Wartburg. This castle is large, grand, and imposing. It is also well preserved. A few years ago it was discovered that many windows and arched galleries, of very beautiful style, had been filled up, and that frescoes and other decorations had been covered. The Grand Duke of Saxe-Weimar caused its restoration, and the ancient halls are now quite in their original state. (See Fig. 89.)

There are very interesting legends and historical facts connected with this castle of Wartburg. As early as 1204 to 1208, when Hermann, Count of Thuringia, dwelt there with his wife, the Countess Sophia, it is related that the "War of the Minstrels" occurred. This was a contest between several of the wandering minstrels or Minnesingers of that time as to who should excel, and he who failed was to suffer death. The penalty fell on Henry of Ofterdingen; in his despair he begged the Countess to gain him a respite so that he could go for his master, Klingsor. Her prayer was granted, and in the end Henry of Ofterdingen saved his head, though the legend says that Satan aided him. This story is without doubt founded on truth, but has much of fancy mingled with it.

The next remarkable story connected with Wartburg is the residence here of St. Elizabeth of Hungary, as she is called. This wonderful woman was the daughter of the King of Hungary, and when four years old she was betrothed to Prince Louis, son of Count Hermann, mentioned above. At this tender age she was given to his family. Her life at Wartburg was very remarkable, and I advise you to read about it, for it is too long to be given here. At last, her husband having died in Jerusalem, where he had gone with the Crusaders, his brother Henry drove her out with her children to seek a home where she could. She suffered much, and supported herself by spinning wool. But when the knights who had gone with her husband returned, they obliged Henry to give the son of Elizabeth his rights. She received the city of Marburg as her dower, but she did not live long. Miraculous things are told of her, and she is often represented by painters and sculptors.

Again, Wartburg was the residence of a remarkable

person ; for Luther dwelt there after escaping from the Diet at Worms. He was called Ritter George, and the room where he wrote and spent much of his time is shown to travellers who visit the castle.

We come back now to Italy, the country we left when we passed from the Romanesque to Gothic architecture. In the north of Italy where the Gothic order had prevailed after the eleventh century, it had been modified by the Romanesque influences and Roman traditions, in some such degree as the Moors had influenced the Gothic order in Spain. But, on the whole, the mediæval buildings of Northern Italy were Gothic in style.

Rome, as we said, was individual, and her art remained Roman or Romanesque up to the date of the Renaissance. In Southern Italy, as we shall see, the architecture was of the Byzantine order.

Among the most interesting edifices of the Middle Ages are the Italian towers. They were frequently quite

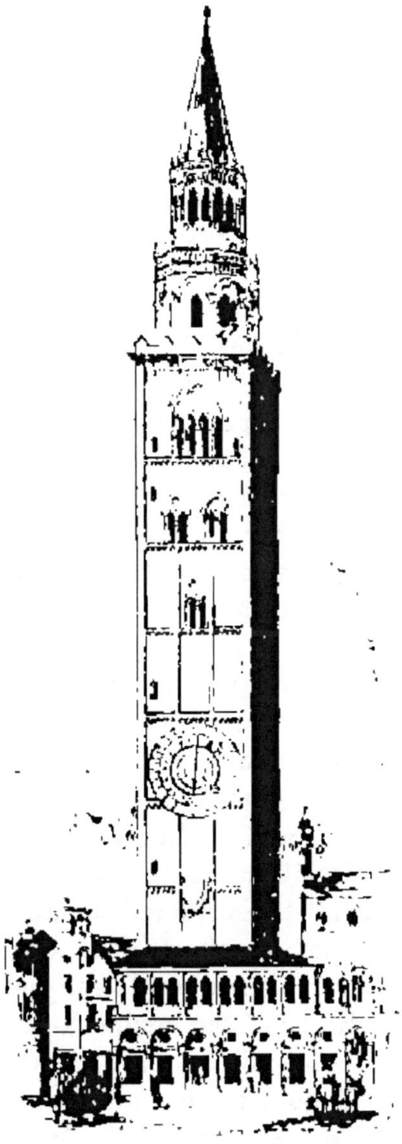

FIG. 90.—TOWER OF CREMONA.

separate from the churches and were built for various purposes. Some of them were bell towers, and such a tower was called a *campanile.* Others were in some way associated with the civic power of the cities which built them ; but the largest number were for religious uses.

The *campanile* is always square at the bottom and for some distance up, and then is frequently changed to an octagonal or circular form and finished with a slender spire or ornamental design.

Fig. 90 shows one of the finest square towers in all Italy. It was built in 1296 to commemorate a peace after a long war. It is three hundred and ninety-six feet high. It has little beauty in the lower two thirds ; above that it is more pleasing, but the two parts do not look as if they belonged together. The tower of Italy, however, which is most beloved and most famous is that of Giotto, beside the cathedral of Florence. (See Fig. 102.)

Another striking feature of Gothic art in Northern Italy is seen in the porches attached to the churches. They are commonly on the side, and as they were usually added after the rest of the church was finished, and frequently do not correspond to the rest in style, they look as if they were parts of some other churches and had come on a visit to those beside which they stand. In Italy the main portion of these porches always rested on lions.

A porch at Bergamo is one of the finest, and certainly its details are exquisite, and the whole structure is beautiful when it is considered separately ; but as a part of the church it loses its effect, and seems to be pushed against it as a chair is placed beside the wall of a room.

Some of the mediæval town-halls are still well preserved, and a few of them are truly beautiful. Perhaps the Broletto at Como is as fine a remnant of civic architecture as exists in Northern Italy. It is not very large and is faced with party-colored marbles.

The architecture of Venice and the Venetian Province must be treated almost as if it were outside of Italy, because it differs so much from that of other portions of that country. During the Middle Ages it was the most prosperous portion of Italy. Its architecture was influenced by the Byzantine and Saracenic orders, but is not like them; neither is it like that of Northern Italy; in fact, it is Venetian, being Gothic in principle, but treated with Eastern feeling and decorated in Oriental taste; and this was quite natural since the Venetians had extensive traffic and intercourse with the nations of the East.

There are few places in the world, of no greater extent, about which so many interesting associations cluster as about the Piazza of St. Mark's in Venice. On one side stands the great basilica, and not far away are the *campanile* and the clock-tower; the ancient Doge's Palace, and the beautiful Library of St. Mark, of later date, are near by, with their treasures of art and literature to increase the value of the whole. It is a spot dear to all, and especially so to English-speaking people, since the poetry of Shakespeare has given them a reason for personal interest in it under all its varying aspects. At some hours of the day St. Mark's seems as if it were the very centre of the earth, to which men of all nations are hastening; again this bustle dies away, and one could fancy it to be forgotten and deserted of all mankind, though its silence is eloquent in its power to recall the great events of the Venice of the past. (See Figs. 91, 105, and 106.)

St. Mark's Basilica is called Byzantine in its order, and in a general way the term is applicable to it; but on careful examination there are so many differences between it and a purely Byzantine church that it would be more properly described by the name Italian or Venetian Byzantine. Its five domes were added to its original form late in the Middle Ages, and though there are many Eastern mosques with this number, they are not arranged like those of St. Mark's, and so have quite a different appearance. The portico with its five entrances is not European in form, but the details of these deep recesses are more like the Norman architecture than like anything Byzantine.

It is scarcely profitable to carry this examination farther, for, in a word, the whole effect of St. Mark's is very impressive from the exterior, and the interior is so beautiful in its subdued light and shadow that one is satisfied to enjoy it without criticising it, and many critics consider it one of the finest interiors of Western Europe.

FIG. 92.—SECTION OF SAN MINIATO. *Near Florence.*

The same difficulty which one finds in defining or classing the architecture of Venice is met in that of Southern Italy, which is Byzantine and not Byzantine, but, in fact, is that order so changed that the name of Byzantine-Romanesque seems better suited to it than any other term could be. We shall mention but a single example of this order, and pass to the true Byzantine style.

The church of San Miniato, which overlooks the city of Florence, was built in 1013, and is one of the most perfect as well as one of the earliest of the churches of the Byzantine-Romanesque order in Italy. It is not large, but the

FIG. 93.—SAN GIOVANNI DEGLI EREMITI. *Palermo.*

proportions are so good as to make it very pleasing; the pillars are so nearly classic in design that they were probably taken from some earlier building, and the effect of colored panelling both within and without is very satisfactory to the eye. (See Fig. 92.)

There arose in Sicily in the eleventh century, and after the Norman Conquest, a remarkable style of architecture. It belongs to Christian art because it was used by Christians to construct places of Christian worship; but, in truth, it was a combination of Greek spirit with Roman form and Saracenic ornament. It makes an interesting episode in the study of architecture. I shall give one picture of a church built by King Roger for Christian use as late as 1132, which, except for the tower, might well be mistaken for a purely Oriental edifice (Fig. 93).

## BYZANTINE ARCHITECTURE.

This term strictly belongs to the order which arose in the East after Constantinople was made the Roman capital. It is especially the order of the Greek Church as contrasted with the Latin or Roman Church. It would make all architectural writing and talking much clearer if this fact were kept in mind ; but, unfortunately, wherever some special bit of carving in an Oriental design or a little colored decoration is used—as is frequently done in the modern composite styles of building—the term Byzantine is carelessly applied, until it is difficult for one not learned in architecture to discover what the Byzantine order is, or where it belongs.

We have spoken of its influence and partial use in Italy. Now we will consider it in its home and its purity. Before the time of Constantine the architecture used at Rome was employed at Jerusalem, Constantinople, and other Eastern cities which were under Roman rule and influence. Between the time of Constantine and the death of Justinian, in A.D. 565, the true ancient Byzantine order was developed. The church of St. Sophia, at Constantinople, was the greatest and the last product of the pure old Byzantine style.

From that time the order employed may be called the Neo-Byzantine. This was a decline of art as much as the history of Greece and the Eastern Empire during the same period (about 600 to 1453) was the history of the decline and extinction of a power that had once been as great among governments as St. Sophia (Fig. 94) was among churches.

The chief characteristic of Byzantine architecture is the use of the dome, which is the most important part of its

FIG. 94.—CHURCH OF ST. SOPHIA. *Constantinople. Exterior View*

design. A grand central dome rises over the principal portion of the edifice, and just as in other orders courts and colonnades were added to the simpler basilica form in the ground plan of the churches, so in the Byzantine order lesser domes and cupolas were added above until almost any number of them was admissible, and they were placed with little attention to regularity or symmetry of arrangement.

Fgi. 95.—Lower Order of St. Sophia.

As domes were the chief exterior feature, so the profuse ornamentation was most noticeable in the interior. The walls were richly decorated with variegated marbles; the vaulted ceilings of the domes and niches were lined with brilliant mosaics; the columns, friezes, cornices, door and window-frames, and the railings to galleries were of marbles, and entirely covered with ornamental designs (Figs. 95 and 96).

The historian Gibbon describes the building of St. Sophia and its decorations. He tells us that the emperor went daily, clad in a linen tunic, to oversee the work. The architect was named Anthemius; he employed ten thousand workmen, and they were all paid each evening. When it was completed and Justinian was present at its consecration, he exclaimed, "Glory be to God, who hath thought me worthy to accomplish so great a work; I have vanquished thee, O Solomon!"

Paul Silentiarius was a poet; he saw St. Sophia in all its glory and describes it with enthusiasm. It was very rich in variegated marbles. He mentions the following: 1. *The Carystian*, pale with iron veins. 2. *The Phrygian*, two sorts, both of a rosy hue; one with a white shade, the other purple with silver flowers. 3. *The Porphyry of Egypt*, with small stars. 4. *The green marble of Laconia.* 5. *The Carian*, from Mount Iassis, with oblique veins, white and red. 6. *The Lydian*, pale, with a red flower. 7. *The African or Mauritanian*, of a gold or saffron hue. 8. *The Celtic*, black, with white veins. 9. *The Bosphoric*, white, with black edges. There were also the *Proconnesian*, which made the pavement; and the *Thessalian* and *Molossian* in different parts.

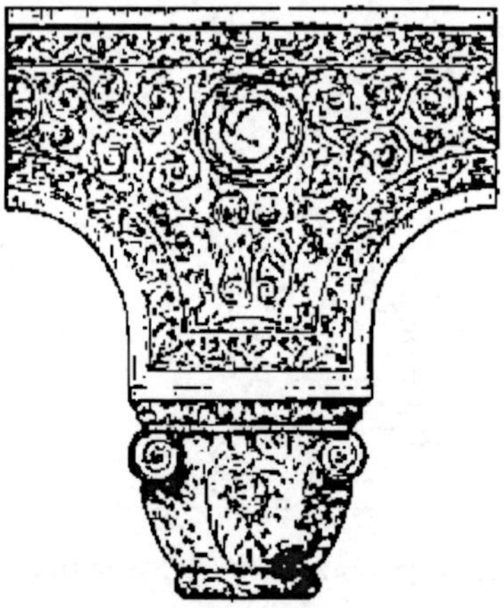

FIG. 96.—UPPER ORDER OF ST. SOPHIA.

This array of marbles was made even more effective by the beautiful columns brought from older temples. The mosaics were rich in color, and numerous, and many parts of the church were covered with gold, so that the effect was dazzling.

Those objects that were most sacred were of solid gold and silver, while such as were less important were only covered with gold-leaf. In the sanctuary there was altogether forty thousand pounds of silver; the vases and vessels used about the altar were of pure gold and studded with gems. Its whole cost was almost beyond belief. At the close of his description Gibbon says: "A magnificent

Fig. 97.—Interior View of Church of St. Sophia.

temple is a laudable monument of taste and religion, and the enthusiast who entered the dome of St. Sophia might be tempted to suppose that it was the residence or even the workmanship of the Deity. Yet how dull is the artifice, how insignificant is the labor, if it be compared with the formation of the vilest insect that crawls upon the surface of the temple!"

Of course, individual taste must largely influence the opinion regarding the beauty of any work of art, but to me St. Sophia, which is the chief example of Byzantine architecture, is far less beautiful and less grand than the finest Gothic cathedrals. Comparatively little attention was paid to the elegance and decoration of the exterior in the Eastern edifices, while the interiors, in spite of all their riches, have a flat and unrelieved effect. Probably the chief reason for this is that color is substituted for relief—that is to say, in Gothic architecture heavy mouldings and panellings, though of the same color as the walls themselves, yet produce a marvellous effect of light and shadow, and even lend an element of perspective to various parts of the building. In the place of these mouldings flat bands of color are often used in the Byzantine order, and the whole result is much weakened, though a certain gorgeousness comes from the color. Another cause of disappointment in St. Sophia is the absence of painted glass. At the same time, and in spite of these defects, St. Sophia is grand and beautiful—but not solemn and impressive in comparison with the dim cathedral aisles of many Gothic churches in other parts of the world. (See Fig. 97.)

The Romanesque and Byzantine styles came at last to be so mingled that it would be folly to attempt to separate their influence, but the Byzantine had much more originality, and left a far wider mark.

Among the most noted examples of the latter style, beside St. Sophia and St. Mark's, are the church of St.

Vitale at Ravenna, the cathedral at Aix-la-Chapelle, supposed to have been built by Charlemagne about 800 A.D., and the church of the Mother of God at Constantinople.

## SARACENIC ARCHITECTURE.

In speaking of Saracenic architecture I will first explain that it is one with the Moresco or Moorish order of which I spoke in connection with Spain. The only difference is that the earliest Mohammedan conquerors of Spain are said to have come from ancient Mauri or Mauritania and were called Moors, while the name of *Saraceni*, which means "the Easterns," was also given to them. Thus the Mohammedan architecture in Spain is called both Moresco, or Moorish, and Saracenic. Again, it is also called Arabian, but I think this is the least correct, since the Easterns who went to Spain were not so universally Arabian as to warrant this name. When we speak of Moresco or Moorish architecture we speak of Spain; but the term Saracenic is used for Mohammedan architecture in all countries where it is found, and is a just term, for they are Eastern or Oriental lands.

In absolute fact, Saracenic architecture is that of the followers of "the Prophet," as Mohammed is called, and would be more suitably named if it were called Mohammedan architecture, or the architecture of Islam.

Mohammed was born at Mecca A.D. 570, but it was not until 611 that he was commissioned, as he believed, to build up a new faith and a new church. At first his followers were so few and so mingled with other sects and tribes in their outward life that they had no distinctive art. It was not until A.D. 876, when the ruler Ibn-Touloun commenced his splendid mosque at Cairo, that the Mohammedans could claim any architecture as their own. It is very interesting to know that there were pointed arches in this mosque, probably two centuries, at least, earlier than they were used in England, for it is generally believed that they were first used there in the rebuilding of Canterbury Cathedral after it was burned in 1174. When, however, the Saracenic order was fully established it was so individual and so different from all other architecture that there is no mistaking it for that of any other religion or nation than that of Mohammed and his followers.

FIG. 98.—MOSQUE OF KAITBEY.

FIG. 99.—THE CALL TO PRAYER.

The picture of the mosque of Kaitbey shows one of the finest and most elegant mosques of the East. It is just outside the walls of Cairo, and is quite modern, having been built in 1463. This view of it gives an excellent idea of the appearance of a fine mosque and shows the minaret or tower, which is so important in a mosque, to good advantage (Fig. 98).

These minarets are constantly used for the many calls to prayer which are made throughout the day and night. The person who makes these calls is styled " the Muezzin," and is usually blind. Several times during the day he ascends the minaret and calls out in a loud and melodious tone, "God is most great; there is no God but Allah, and I testify that Mohammed is Allah's prophet! Come to prayer! Come to security! Prayer is better than sleep!" This is several times repeated and is called the *Adan.*

The form of words used for the night varies a little, ending, "There is no God but Allah. He has no companion! To Him belongs dominion, etc.;" this is called the *Ula.* The call made an hour before day is the *Ebed,* and praises the perfection of God. When one is sleeping near enough to a minaret to hear the muezzin's voice it is a pleasant sound and helps one to realize that the care of God is ever about him; the clear, Christian bell can be heard by more people, and this was originally intended as a call to prayer. (See Fig. 99.)

The principal homes of Saracenic architecture are Syria, Egypt, Mecca, Barbary, Spain, Sicily, Turkey, Persia, and India. There are many very interesting mosques and minarets that might be mentioned had we space, but I can speak only of the mosque of Cordova, which is universally admitted to be the finest Saracenic edifice in the world (Fig. 100), and shall quote a part of the interesting description of it given by De Amicis in his delightful book called "Spain and the Spaniards."

This mosque was commenced by the Caliph Abd-er-Rahman in 786, and was completed by his son Heshâm, who died 796. The great Caliph declared that he would build a mosque which should exceed all others in the world and be the Mecca of the West. De Amicis, after describing the garden which surrounds the mosque, enters, and then goes on as follows: "Imagine a forest, fancy yourself in the thickest portion of it, and that you can see nothing but the trunks of trees. So, in this mosque, on whatever side you look, the eye loses itself among the columns. It is a forest of marble whose confines one cannot discover. You follow with your eye, one by one, the very long rows of columns that interlace at every step with numberless other rows, and you reach a semi-obscure background, in which other columns still seem to be gleaming. There are nineteen naves, which extend in every direction, traversed by thirty-three others, supported (among them all) by more

FIG. 100.—EXTERIOR OF THE SANCTUARY IN THE MOSQUE OF CORDOVA.

than nine hundred columns of porphyry, jasper, breccia, and marbles of every color. Each column upholds a small pilaster, and between them runs an arch (see plate above), and a second one extends from pilaster to pilaster, the latter placed above the former, and both of them in the shape of a horseshoe ; so that, in imagining the columns to be the trunks of so many trees, the arches represent the branches, and the similitude of the mosque to a forest is complete. . . . How much variety there is in that edifice which at first sight seems so uniform! The proportions of the columns, the designs of the capitals, the forms of the arches change, one might say, at every step. The majority of the columns are old, and were taken from the Arabs of Northern Spain, Gaul, and Roman Africa, and some are said to have belonged to a temple of Janus, on the ruins of which was built the church that the Arabs destroyed in order to erect the mosque. Above several of the capitals one can still see traces of the crosses that were cut on them, which the Arabs broke with their chisels. . . . I stopped for a long time to look at the ceiling and walls of the principal chapel, the only part of the mosque that is quite intact. It is a dazzling gleam of crystals of a thousand colors, a network of arabesques, which puzzles the mind, and a complication of bas-reliefs, gildings, ornaments, minutiæ of design and coloring, of a delicacy, grace, and perfection sufficient to drive the most patient painter distracted. . . . You might turn a hundred times to look at it, and it would only seem to you, in thinking it over, a mingling of blue, red, green, gilded and luminous points, or a very intricate embroidery changing continually, with the greatest rapidity, both design and coloring. Only from the fiery and indefatigable imagination of the Arabs could such a perfect miracle of art emanate. . . . Such is the mosque of to-day. But what must it have been in the time of the Arabs? It was not surrounded by a wall, but open, so that one could catch a glimpse of the garden from every part of it; and from the garden one could see to the end of the long naves, and the air was full of the fragrance of oranges and flowers. The columns which now number less than a thousand were then fourteen hundred; the ceiling was of cedar-wood and larch, sculptured and enamelled in the finest manner; the walls were trimmed with marble; the light of eight hundred lamps, filled with perfumed oil, made all the crystals in the mosaics gleam, and produced on the pavements, arches, and walls a marvellous play of color and reflection. 'A sea of splendors,' sang a poet, 'filled this mysterious recess; the ambient air was impregnated with aromas and harmonies, and the thoughts of the faithful wandered and lost themselves in the labyrinth of columns which gleamed like lances in the sun.'"

The famous palace of the Alhambra is so well known that I cannot leave this part of our subject without one picture and one bit of description of it from the same author, De Amicis.

The Alhambra was built about four centuries ago, and the wall which inclosed it was four thousand feet long by twenty-two hundred feet wide. Within this there were gardens, fountains, kiosks, and many beautiful, fanciful structures, all of which doubtless cost as much as the more necessary parts of the edifice. The roofs of the different parts of the palace were supported by forty-three hundred columns of precious marbles; eleven hundred and seventy-two of these were presented to Abd-er-Rahman (for he was also the founder of the Alhambra) by sovereigns of other countries, or else brought by him from distant shores for the decoration of this splendid, fairy-like place. All the pavements were of beautiful marbles; the walls, too, were of the same material, with friezes arranged in splendid colors; the ceilings were of deep blue color, with figures in gilding and interlacing designs running over all. In truth, nothing that could be imagined or wealth buy to make this palace beautiful was left out; and yet we are told that the palace of Zahra which was destroyed was still finer. All this leads one to almost believe that the "Arabian Nights" are no fanciful tales, but quite as true as many more serious sounding stories.

The Court of the Lions is called "the gem of Arabian art in Spain," and of this our author says: "It is a forest of columns, a mingling of arches and embroideries, an indefinable elegance, an indescribable delicacy, a prodigious richness, a something light, transparent, and undulating like a great pavilion of lace; with almost the appearance of a building which must dissolve at a breath; a variety of lights, views, mysterious darkness, a confusion, a capricious disorder of little things, the majesty of a palace, the gayety of a kiosk, an amorous grace, an extravagance, a delirium, the fancy of an imaginative child, the dream of an angel, a madness, a nameless something—such is the first effect produced by the Court of the Lions!" (Fig. 101.)

This court is not large; the ceiling is high, and a light portico runs round it upheld by white marble columns in clusters of two, three, or more, so arranged as to resemble trees coming up from the ground. Above the columns the designs almost resemble curtains, and there are little graceful suggestions like ribbons and waving flowers. "From the middle of the shortest sides advance two groups of columns, which form two species of square temples of nine arches each (see cut) surmounted by as many colored cupolas. The walls of these little temples and the exterior of the portico are a real lace-work of stucco, embroideries, and hems, cut and pierced from one side to the other, and as transparent as net-work, changing in design at every step. Sometimes they end in points, in crimps, in festoons, sometimes in ribbons waving round the arches, in kinds of stalactites, fringes, trinkets, and bows which seem to move and mingle with each other at the slightest breath of air. Large Arabic inscriptions run along the four walls, over the arches, around the capitals, and on the walls of the little temples. In the centre of the court rises a great marble basin, upheld by twelve lions (see cut), and surrounded by a little paved canal. . . . At every step one takes in the court that forest of columns seems to move and change place, to form again in another way; behind one column, which seems alone, two, three, or a row will spring out;

Fig. 101.—Court of the

others separate, unite, and separate again. . . . We remained for more than an hour in the court, and it passed like a flash ; I, too, did what almost all people do, be they Spanish or strangers, men or women, poets or not. I ran my hand along the walls, touched all the little columns, and passed my two hands around them, one by one, as around the waist of a child ; I hid among them, counted them, looked at them on a hundred sides, crossed the court in a hundred ways, tried if it were true that in saying a word, *sotto voce*, into the mouth of one lion, one could hear it distinctly from the mouths of all the others ; I looked on the marbles for the spots of blood of poetic legends, and wearied both brain and eye over the arabesques. . . . In all my life I have never thought, nor said, nor shall I say, so many foolish, stupid, pretty, senseless things as I said and thought in that hour."

The study of Saracenic architecture in Turkey, Persia, and India is very interesting, but our space warns us that we must hasten to leave this dreamy, fairy-like part of our subject and come down to later times and more realistic matters.

## CHAPTER III.

### MODERN ARCHITECTURE.

### 1400 A.D. TO THE PRESENT TIME.

ALL Architecture since the time of the Renaissance is called Modern Architecture; this term, therefore, embraces all edifices erected during nearly four centuries.

When I first spoke of Architecture I said that it was a constructive art, and not imitative like Painting and Sculpture. In its earlier history this was true, but the time came when it also became an imitative art and had no true or original style. The Gothic order was the last distinct order which arose, and since its decline, at the beginning of the Renaissance, all architecture has been an imitation because it is a reproduction of what existed before; at times some one of the older orders has been in favor and closely imitated, and again, parts of several orders are combined in one edifice. Since the time of the Reformation it has been true, almost without exception, that every building of any importance has been copied from something belonging to a country and a people foreign to the land in which it was erected.

When the revival of Classic Literature began, Rome was the first to feel its influence. It was welcomed there with open arms, just as we might receive the early history and literature of our country if it had all been lost and was found again; for this was precisely what it meant to the

Romans, when, after the Dark Ages, the works of Livy, Tacitus, and Cæsar were in their hands, and they read of the history, art, and literature of their past. They were enthusiastic, and their feeling soon spread over all Italy.

France was the next to adopt the newly-revived ideas, for that country looked to Rome as the source of true religion, and a model in all things. Spain was then in an unsettled state, and welcomed the revival of classic art as heartily as it had already embraced the Church of Rome.

In Germany the love of the classics was enthusiastic, but that nation was more taken up with literature and slower in adopting the revival of the arts than were the more southern peoples, and the fifteenth and sixteenth centuries are a barren period in the history of German architecture.

In England, too, the Renaissance made slow progress. It was not until the time of Charles I. that any influence was felt in Great Britain from the revival of classic taste which was so well established on the Continent.

As it is true that no new order of Architecture has arisen since the time of those of which I have already told you, I shall try to make you understand something of Modern Architecture by speaking of certain important edifices in one country and another, with no attempt at any more detailed explanation of it.

## ITALY.

We cannot say that the art of the Renaissance originated in one city or another, because the movement in the revival of art was so general throughout Italy; but Florence has a strong claim to our first consideration from the fact that Filippo Brunelleschi was a Florentine and did his greatest work in his native city, and on account of it has been called "the father of the Art of the Renaissance." He was born in 1377, and from his early boyhood was inclined to be an architect. The cathedral of Florence (Fig. 102), which is

also called the church of Sta. Maria del Fiore, had been built long before, but had never been finished by a roof or dome.

Brunelleschi was possessed with but one desire, which was to complete this cathedral. He went to Rome and diligently studied the remains of classic art which he found there, and especially the dome of the Pantheon. Returning to Florence he took measures to bring his plans before the superintendents of the cathedral works; he was ridiculed and discouraged on every hand, but he never gave up his hopes nor lessened his study of the ways and means by which the dome could be built. Thus many weary years passed by; Brunelleschi made drawings in secret, and from these he constructed models in order to convince himself of what he could do.

At last those who had authority in the matter were ready to act, and a convention was called, before which the architects of different nations appeared and were requested to explain their theories of what could be done to cover the cathedral. Many artists were assembled and various plans were shown, but after all had been examined the work was given to Brunelleschi, and he was happy in finding that the years he had devoted to the study of the dome had not been spent in vain.

It was on this occasion that Brunelleschi refused to show his models, and when the other architects blamed him for this he asked that some eggs should be brought, and proposed that he who could make an egg stand upright on a smooth piece of marble should be the builder of the dome. The others tried to do this and failed; at last Brunelleschi brought his egg down on the marble with a sharp tap and left it standing erect. Then all exclaimed, "Oh, we could have done that if we had known that was the way," to which Brunelleschi replied, "So you could have built a dome if I had shown you my models."

This story is often told of Columbus, but as Brunelleschi was much older than Columbus, and the fact is related by Florentine writers of his time, it is probable that Columbus had heard of it from the geographer Toscanelli, who was a great admirer of Brunelleschi and a friend of Columbus also. In building the dome, Brunelleschi encountered great difficulties, but he lived to be assured of his success, for at his death, in 1444, it lacked but little of completion, and all the parts essential to its perfection and durability were finished.

This is the largest dome in the world, for though the cross on the top of St. Peter's is farther from the ground than that of Florence, the dome itself above the church is not as large as the dome of Sta. Maria del Fiore.

This work made Brunelleschi's greatest fame, but he was the architect of many other fine churches and of secular buildings also ; among the last the Pitti Palace, in which is the famous Pitti Gallery, is one of the most important. When you go to Florence you will see a statue of Filippo Brunelleschi, which is very interesting, on account of the way in which it is represented and the position in which it is placed. It is on one side of the Piazza of the cathedral ; he is calmly sitting there with a plan of the church spread before him on his lap, while he lifts his head to look at the great dome as it stands out against the sky, the realization of all his thought and labor during so many years.

The church of St. Peter's at Rome, which is the largest and most magnificent of all Christian temples, was begun about 1450, and was not brought into its present form until about 1661, or more than two centuries later (Fig. 103).

The history of its building is largely a story of contentions and troubles between popes, architects, and artists of different kinds. As it now stands it is as much the work of Michael Angelo as of any one man, but several other architects left their imprint upon it, both before and after

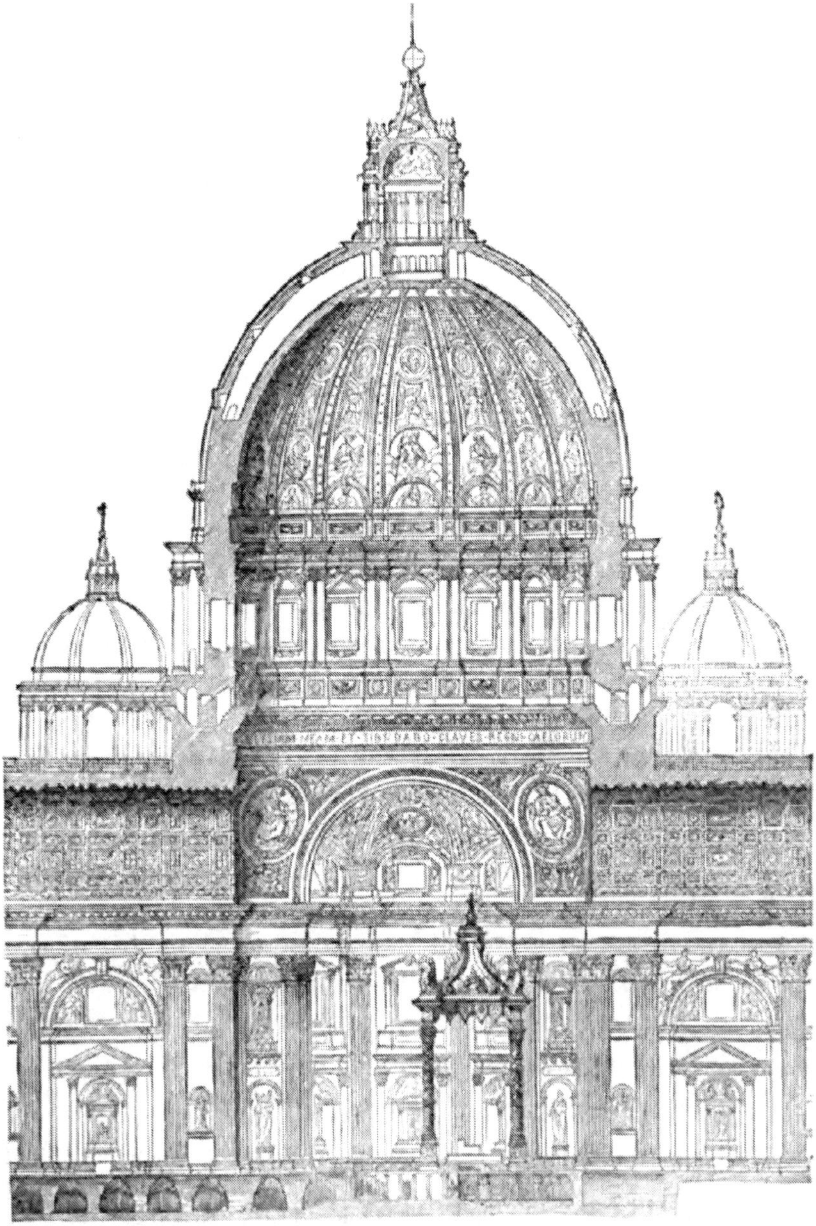


FIG. 104.—SECTION OF ST. PETER'S.

his time ; and all who aided in its construction were eminent men, in their way. Michael Angelo was in his seventy-second year when he took up the task of completing St. Peter's. Bramante, Raphael, and Peruzzi had preceded him as architects of the church ; Michael Angelo designed the dome, and when he was ninety it was nearly finished ; the models for its completion which he made were not followed after his death ; his plan would have made the church more harmonious with the dome, in size, than it now is. Money was sent in large sums, from all Europe, to carry on this work ; the finest materials were used in building it, and the most gifted artists were employed in its decoration ; it is now the vast home of multitudes of treasures. "I have hung the Pantheon in the air!" Michael Angelo is said to have exclaimed, while looking at the splendid dome of St. Peter's ; and no dome in the world has a more imposing effect, although its harmony with the rest of the building is injured by the change of the plan from that of a Greek cross which was made after his death.*

In spite of all this the critics of architecture are never weary of pointing out the defects of St. Peter's ; but to those who cannot apply to it the test of strictly scientific rules, its interior is sublime in its effect, and has few rivals —perhaps but one—in the world, and that is the great Hypostyle Hall at Karnak, of which we spoke when writing of Egyptian architecture. But even here the difference is almost too great to admit of comparison ; the spirit of the two is so unlike—St. Peter's is complete and Karnak is a ruin—so, after all, it must be admitted that the interior of St. Peter's is superior to all other edifices of which we know (Fig. 104).

* The interior diameter of the dome of St. Peter's is one hundred and thirty-nine feet ; that of St. Sophia, one hundred and fifteen feet, and that of Sta. Maria del Fiore, at Florence, one hundred and thirty-eight feet, six inches.

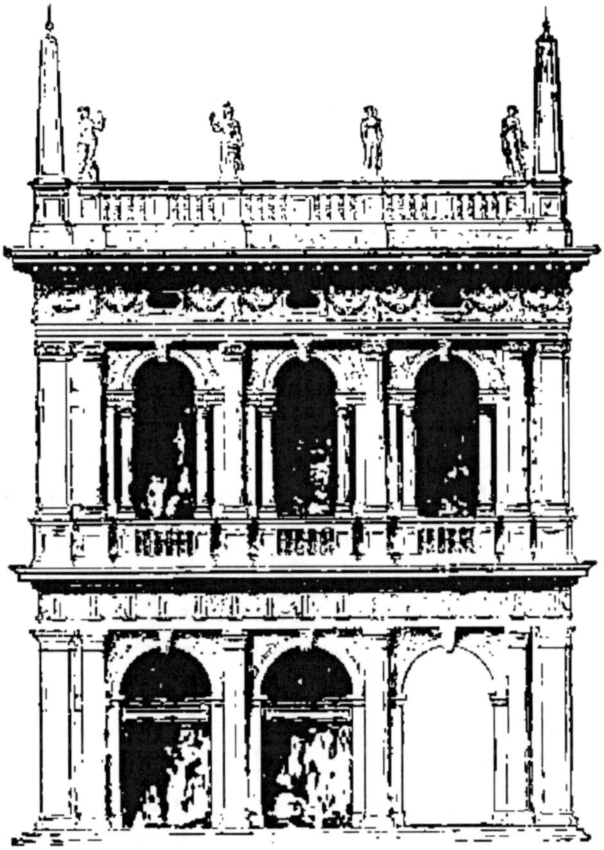

FIG. 105.—EAST ELEVATION OF LIBRARY OF ST. MARK. *Venice.*

From the time of the beginning of the Renaissance, about 1420, to about 1630, the architecture of Venice was going through a change, and finally reached such perfection that during the next half century the most magnificent style of architecture prevailed which has ever been known there. We mean to say that the whole effect was the grandest, for, while it is true that the edifices of that time are stately and striking in their appearance, it is equally true that their form and ornamentation are not as much in keeping with their use as they had been in older edifices.

Sansovino, who lived from 1479 to 1570, was an important architect and had great influence upon modern Venetian architecture. His masterpiece was the Library of St. Mark, of which the preceding cut gives one end (Fig. 105). It is a very beautiful structure, and is made more interesting from the fact that it stands directly opposite to the Doge's Palace, and in the midst of all the interest which centres about the Piazza of St. Mark.

The Ducal Palace at Venice is called by John Ruskin, the great English critic, "the central edifice of the world." It is divided into three stories, of which the uppermost occupies rather more than half the height of the building. The two lower stories are arcades of low, pointed arches, supported on pillars, the one beneath being bolder and heavier in character than the second. The capitals of the columns are greatly varied, no two in the upper arcade being exactly alike. Above the arches of the middle story was a row of open-work spaces, of the form called quatrefoil; while the third story is faced with alternating blocks of rose-colored and white marble, and is pierced with a few large pointed windows. The whole front, or façade, is crowned by an open parapet made up of blocks of stone carved into lily-like forms alternating with lance-shaped leaves. The whole effect is one of great richness and beauty, especially since time has mellowed its color, and softened without destroying the whiteness of its marbles (Fig. 106).

During the time of the Renaissance there were churches, palaces, museums, hospitals, and other large buildings erected in all the important cities of Italy. There are but few of these which have such special features as entitle them to be selected for description here. The reason for this has been given already—viz.: there was nothing new in them; they were all repetitions of what has been described in one form or another. Perhaps the next cut gives

FIG. 106.—THE DOGE'S PALACE. *Venice.*

Fig. 107.—Great Court of the Hospital of Milan.

as good an example of secular architecture in this age as any that could be selected (Fig. 107).

Indeed, it is one of the most remarkable buildings of its class in any age. It was commenced by Francesco Sforza and his wife, Bianca, in 1456. They died long before its completion, and one part and another have been changed from time to time, but its great court, which was designed by Bramante, still remains, the finest thing of its kind in all Italy.

I shall now leave Italy with saying that the early days of the Renaissance were the best days of Italian Architecture, and, indeed, of Italian Art. The period made sacred by the genius and works of Michael Angelo, Bramante,

Sangallo, Leonardo da Vinci, and Raphael was a golden era, and still sheds its lustre over the land of their nativity. These artists followed the highest ideal of Art, and their errors were superior to the so-called successes of less gifted men.

The Italian Art of the fifteenth century was individual and grand; in the sixteenth century it became formal and elegant; in the seventeenth century it was bizarre, over-ornamented, and uncertain in its aim and execution; since then it has been comparatively unimportant, and its architecture scarcely merits censure, and certainly cannot be praised.

## SPAIN.

From the time of the fall of Granada, in 1492 to 1558, Spain was the leading nation of Europe. The whole country had been united under Ferdinand and Isabella, and their reign was a glorious period for their country. The importance of the nation was increased by the discovery of the New World, and so many great men were in her councils that her eminence was sure, and almost undisputed. Thus it followed that during the first half of the sixteenth century the Architecture of Spain gave expression to the spirit by which the nation was then animated.

This did not long continue, however, for the iron, practical rule of Philip II. crushed out enthusiasm and was fatal to artistic inspiration. This sovereign desired only to extend his kingdom; the priests, who acquired almost limitless power under his reign, aimed only to strengthen their authority, while the people were wildly pursuing riches in the New World which opened up to them a vast and attractive field. Thus no place or time was left to the cultivation of Art, and the only noteworthy period of Spanish Architecture since the beginning of the Renaissance was the sixty years which we have mentioned.

The Modern Architecture of Spain has been divided into three eras, each of which was distinguished by its own style. The first extends from the beginning of the Renaissance down to that of the abdication of the great Emperor Charles V. in 1555; the manner of this period is called Platerisco, or the silversmith's style, on account of the vast amount of fine, filigree ornament which was used. The second period is from the above date to about 1650, and its art is called the Græco-Roman style because it is an attempt to revive the Classic Art of the ancient Greeks and Romans. The third period comes from 1650 to about a century later, and the Spaniards call its manner the Churrigueresque, which difficult name they take from that of Josef de Churriguera, the architect who invented this style. Since 1750 we may almost say that no such thing as Spanish Architecture has existed.

The cathedrals of Granada, Jaen, and Valladolid, and the churches of Malaga and Segovia, with many other ecclesiastical edifices, are among the chief monuments of Spanish Renaissance Architecture, but we shall pass on to a little later period and speak of but one great achievement, the famous Escurial, which is of much historic interest.

This combination of basilica, palace, monastery, and college was begun in 1563 by Philip II., in accordance with a vow which he made to St. Lawrence at the battle of St. Quentin. This battle was fought in 1557 under the walls of the French town of St. Quentin, by the French and the Spaniards, and the latter were completely victorious.

This cut gives an idea of how grand and impressive this collection of walls, towers, courts, and edifices must be, all crowned with the dome of the basilica. It is almost like a city by itself, and all who visit it agree that it is a gloomy and depressing place in spite of its grandeur (Fig. 108).

The front has three imposing entrances, with towers at the corner angles. Within the inclosure are a college,

FIG. 108.—THE ESCURIAL. *Near Madrid.*

monastery, palace with state apartments, the church, numerous courts, gardens, and fountains. The front is injured by the great number of small windows, which divide it into such numberless sections as to become very tiresome to the eye, while they take away the noble elegance of larger spaces and the air of repose which such spaces give. The angle towers are not as rich in effect as they should be, and the side walls have been compared to those of a Manchester cotton-mill; thus the exterior, which is effective from its size and general air, has not the beauty of detail which satisfies a close observer.

The effect of the interior, as one goes in by the central entrance, is all that can be desired. The court leads directly to the square before the church ; as one passes to it he has the college on one side, the monastery on the other, farther on the palace, with the whole culminating in the grand state apartments and the basilica. The various courts are striking in their arrangement, and the church with its dome and towers gives a supreme glory to the whole. Gardens, fountains, and many other fine objects add their effect to the richness and beauty of the whole ; but all are insignificant beside the basilica, which merits a place in the foremost rank of the churches of the Renaissance. Indeed, the Escurial is a marvellous place, and is often called "the eighth wonder of the world." The richest marbles, splendid pictures, and many magnificent objects help to make it one of the grandest works of modern architecture.

It is also true that it is one of the gloomiest places visited by travellers, and I shall quote a few lines from De Amicis to show the depressing effect which it has upon those who go there.

"The first feeling is that of sadness ; the whole building is of dirt-colored stone, and striped with white between the stones ; the roofs are covered with strips of lead. It looks like an edifice built of earth. The walls are very high and bare, and contain a great number of loopholes. One would call it a prison rather than a convent. . . . The locality, the forms, the colors, everything, in fact, seems to have been chosen by him who founded the edifice with the intention of offering to the eyes of men a sad and solemn spectacle. Before entering you have lost all your gayety ; you no longer smile, but think. You stop at the doors of the Escurial with a sort of trepidation, as at the gates of a deserted city ; it seems to you that, if the terrors of the Inquisition reigned in some corner of the world, they ought to reign among those walls. You would say that therein one might still see the last traces of it and hear its last echo. . . . The royal palace is superb, and it is better to see it before entering the convent and church, in order not to confuse the separate impressions produced by each. This palace occupies the northeast corner of the edifice. Several rooms are full of pictures, others are covered from floor to ceiling with tapestries, representing bull-fights, public balls, games, fêtes, and Spanish costumes, designed by Goya; others are regally furnished and adorned; the floor, the doors, and the windows are covered with marvellous inlaid work and stupendous gilding. But among all the rooms the most noteworthy is that of Philip II.; it is rather a cell than a room, is bare and squalid, with an alcove which answers to the royal oratory of the church, so that, from the bed, by keeping the doors open, one can see the priest who is saying mass. Philip II. slept in that cell, had his last illness there, and there he died. One still sees some chairs used by him, two little stools upon which he rested the leg tormented with gout, and a writing-desk. The walls are white, the ceiling flat and without any ornament, and the floor of brick. . . . In the court-yard of the kings you can form a first idea of the immense frame-work of the edifice. The court is inclosed by walls; on the side opposite the doors is the façade of the church. On a spacious flight of steps there are six enormous Doric columns, each of which upholds a large pedestal, and every pedestal a statue. There are six colossal statues, by Battiste Monegro, representing Jehoshaphat, Ezekiel, David, Solomon, Joshua, and Manasseh. The court-yard is paved, scattered with bunches of damp turf. The walls look like rocks cut in points; everything is rigid, massive, and heavy, and presents the fantastic appearance of a Titanic edifice, hewn out of solid stone, and ready to defy the shocks of earth and the lightnings of heaven. There one begins to understand what the Escurial really is.

"One ascends the steps and enters the church. The interior is sad and bare. . . . Beside the high altar, sculptured and gilded in the Spanish style, in the inter-columns of the two royal oratories, one sees two groups of bronze statues kneeling, with their hands clasped toward the altar. On the right Charles V. and the Empress Isabella, and several princesses; on the left, Philip II. with his wives. . . . In a corner, near a secret door, is the chair which Philip II. occupied. He received through that door letters and important messages, without being seen by the priests who were chanting in the choir. This church, which, in comparison with the entire building, seems very small, is nevertheless one of the largest in Spain, and although it appears so free from ornamentation, contains immense treasures of marble, gold, relics, and pictures, which the darkness in part conceals, and from which the sad appearance of the edifice distracts one's attention. . . . But every feeling sinks into that of sadness. The color of the stone, the gloomy light, and the profound silence which surrounds you, recall your mind incessantly to the vastitude, unknown recesses, and solitude of the building, and leave no room for the pleasure of admiration. The aspect of the church awakens in you an inexplicable feeling of inquietude. You would divine, were you not otherwise aware of it, that those walls are surrounded, for a great distance, by nothing but granite, darkness, and silence; without seeing the enormous edifice, you feel it; you feel that you are in the midst of an uninhabited city; you would fain quicken your pace in order to see it rapidly, to free yourself from the weight of that mystery, and to seek, if they exist anywhere, bright light, noise, and life. . . . One goes to the convent, and here human imagination loses itself; . . . you pass through a long subterranean corridor, so narrow that you can touch the walls with your elbows, low enough almost to hit the ceiling with your head, and as damp as a submarine grotto; you reach the end, turn, and you are in another corridor. You go on, come to doors, look, and other corridors stretch away before you as far as the eye can reach. At the end of some you see a ray of light, at the end of others an open door, through which you catch a glimpse of a suite of rooms. . . . You look through a door and start back alarmed; at the end of that long corridor, into which you have glanced, you have seen a man as motionless as a spectre, who was looking at you. You proceed, and emerge on a narrow court, inclosed by high walls, which is gloomy, overgrown with weeds, and illumined by a faint light which seems to fall from an unknown sun, like the court of the witches described to us when we were children. . . . You pass through other corridors, staircases, suites of empty rooms, and narrow courts, and everywhere there is granite, a pale light, and the silence of a tomb. For a short time you think you would be able to retrace your steps; then your memory becomes confused, and you remember nothing more; you seem to have walked ten miles, to have been in that labyrinth for a month, and not to be able to get out of it. You come to a court and say, 'I have seen it already!' but you are mistaken; it is another. . . . You seem to be dreaming; catch glimpses of long frescoed walls ornamented with pictures, crucifixes, and inscriptions; you see and forget; and ask yourself, 'Where am I?' . . . On you go from corridor to corridor, court to court; you look ahead with suspicion; almost expect to see suddenly, at the turning of a corner, a row of skeleton monks, with their hoods drawn over their eyes and their arms folded; you think of Philip II., and seem to hear his retreating step through dark hallways; you remember all that you have read of him, of his treasures, the Inquisition, and all becomes clear to your mind's eye; you understand everything for the first time; the Escurial *is* Philip II., he is still there, alive and frightful, and with him the image of his terrible God. . . . The Escurial surrounds, holds, and overwhelms you ; the cold of its stones penetrates to your marrow ; the sadness of its sepulchral labyrinths invades your soul ; if you are with a friend you say, 'Let us leave ;' if you were alone you would take to flight. At last you mount a staircase, enter a room, go to the window, and salute with a burst of gratitude the mountains, sun, freedom, and the great and beneficent God who loves and pardons. What a long breath one draws at that window !

"An illustrious traveller said that after having passed a day in the convent of the Escurial, one ought to feel happy throughout one's life, in simply thinking that one might still be among those walls, but is no longer there. This is almost true. Even at the present day, after so great a lapse of time, on rainy days, when I am sad, I think of the Escurial, then look at the walls of my room, and rejoice !"

During the sixteenth century there were many palaces erected in Spain, but nothing can be added to the impressions you will get from the descriptions we have quoted of the cheerful, gay Alhambra, and the gloomy, sad Escurial.

The domestic architecture of Spain is unattractive. There are no fine *châteaux*, as in France, or elegant parks, as in England. Ford compares the front of the residence of the Duke of Medina to "ten Baker-street houses put together," and this is true of many so-called palaces. This state of modern Spanish architecture is fully accounted for by the following quotation from Fergusson, the learned writer on architecture :

"On the whole, perhaps, we should not be far wrong in assuming that the Spaniards are among the least artistic people in Europe. Great things have been done in their country by foreigners, and they themselves have done creditable things in periods of great excitement, and under the pressure of foreign example ; but in themselves they seem to have no innate love of Art, no real appreciation for its beauties, and, when left to themselves, they care little for the expression of beauty in any of the forms in which Art has learned to embody itself. In Painting they have done some things that are worthy of praise ; in Sculpture they have done very little ; and in Architectural Art they certainly have not achieved success. Notwithstanding that they have a climate inviting to architectural display in every form ; though they have the best of materials in infinite abundance ; though they had wealth and learning, and were stimulated by the example of what had been done in their own country, and was doing by other nations—in spite of all this, they have fallen far short of what was effected either in Italy or France, and now seem to be utterly incapable of appreciating the excellencies of Architectural Art, or of caring to enjoy them."

## FRANCE.

After the reigns of Charles VIII. and Louis XII. the French people became somewhat familiar with Italian Art, and at length, during the reign of Francis I., from 1515 to 1546, everything Italian was the fashion in France. Francis invited such artists as Leonardo da Vinci, Benvenuto Cellini, Primaticcio, and Andrea del Sarto to come to France and aid him in his works at Fontainebleau and elsewhere.

It was not long before the Gothic architecture which had been so much used and improved in France was thought to be inferior in beauty to the Italian architecture as it existed in the sixteenth century, and very soon the latter style was adopted and considered as the only one worthy of admiration. But the French architects had been so trained to the Gothic order that it was not easy for them to change their habits of design, and the result was that new edifices were largely of the Gothic form, but were finished and ornamented like the Italian buildings; by this means the effect of the whole, when completed, was such as is seen in this picture of the church of St. Michael at Dijon (Fig. 109). In these days no one approves of this union of Gothic design and Italian decoration, but when it was the fashion it was thought to be very beautiful by French architects.

Francis I., who was so anxious to introduce Italian art into France, erected edifices of a very different sort from those which he attempted to imitate. In Italy, the principal buildings of the Renaissance were churches or convents, or such as were in some way for religious uses. Francis I. built palaces like that of Fontainebleau, and splendid châteaux like those of Chambord, or Chenonceaux, and the Italian style of architecture could not be readily adapted to the lighter uses of the French kings. The splendid massive Pitti Palace, built after the design of the great Brunelleschi, would scarcely have harmonized with the river banks and the lovely undulating meadows around a country villa or château. So it gradually happened that French Architecture was more graceful, light, and elegant than the architecture of the churches, monasteries, and other religious edifices of Italy, and at the same time the Italian feeling and influence can easily be traced in the French buildings of the time of which we speak.

In Italy the Pope and the Church governed in Art, and considered it only as a religious means of glorifying the Church and impressing its doctrines upon the whole people. In France the sovereigns held the leading place, and in the midst of their ambitions and their gayeties they found little time to consider the matter of church architecture. Though the church of St. Eustache was erected at Paris, and other churches were restored, it was not until 1629, when Cardinal Richelieu ordered the building of the church

FIG. 109.—FAÇADE OF THE CHURCH OF ST. MICHAEL. *Dijon.*

finest domical edifices in Europe, and a most satisfactory example of the architecture of its class (Fig. 110).

Directly underneath this dome is the crypt in which is the sarcophagus which contains the remains of Napoleon Bonaparte. On the door which leads to the crypt are inscribed the following words, taken from the will of the exile at St. Helena: "I desire that my ashes may rest on the banks of the Seine, in the midst of the French people whom I have loved so well."

This tomb is said to have cost nearly two millions of dollars, and though it is beautiful, and in good taste in its details, yet one can but regret that all this expense should not have erected a splendid mausoleum, such as would have dignified the monumental art of France.

The church of St. Genevieve, or the Pantheon, as it is usually called, is a very important architectural work. It was twenty-six years in building, and was not completed until after the death of its architect, Soufflot, which occurred in 1781 (Fig. 111).

It is said that this church was begun as the fulfilment of a vow made by King Louis XV. when he was ill, but as the French Revolution was in progress when it was completed, it was dedicated to the "*Grands Hommes*," or the great men of France, and not to God or the sweet St. Genevieve, who was one of the patron saints of Paris.

The dome of the Pantheon is elegant and chaste, but not great in design or effect, and the whole appearance of the church is weakened by the extreme width of the spaces between the front columns; this makes the entablature appear weak, and is altogether a serious defect. Another striking fault is the way in which a second column is placed outside at each end of the portico; one cannot imagine a reason for this, and it is confusing and unmeaning in the extreme. The interior of the Pantheon is superior to the exterior, and many authorities name it as the most satis-

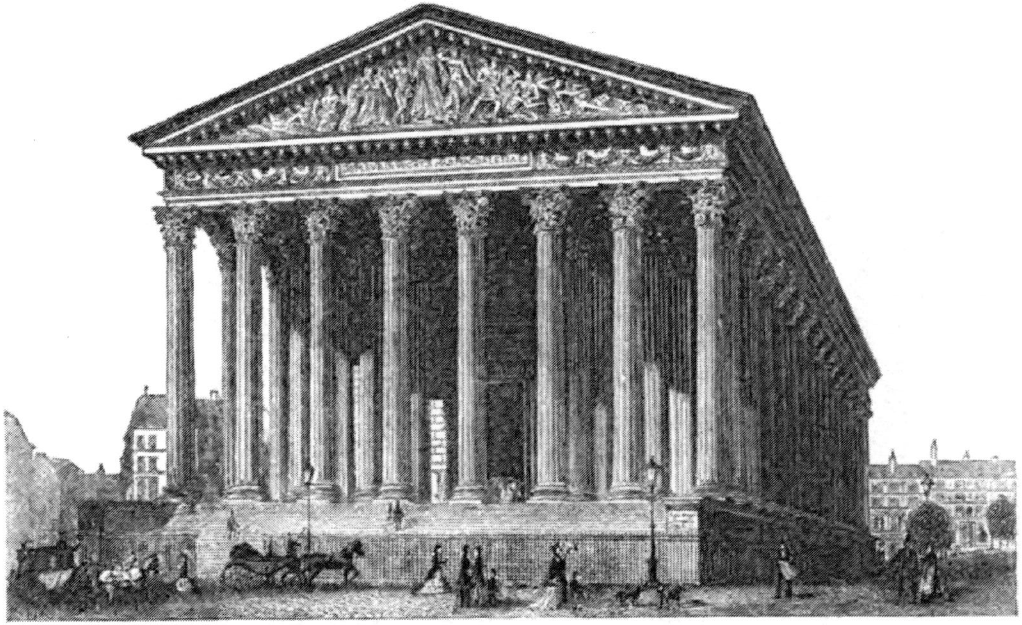

FIG. 112.—THE MADELEINE. *Paris.*

factory of all modern, classical church interiors; when it was built it was believed to be as perfect an imitation of antique classical architecture as could be made, and all the world may be grateful that it escaped the fate prepared for it by the Communists. This was averted by the discovery and cutting of the fuse which they had prepared for its destruction on May 24th, 1871; the fuse led to the crypts beneath the church, where these reckless men had placed large quantities of powder.

In the beginning of the present century French architects believed it best to reproduce exactly ancient temples which had been destroyed. According to this view the church of the Madeleine was begun in 1804, after the designs of Vignon. Outwardly it is a temple of the Corinthian order, and is very beautiful, though its position greatly lessens its effect. If it were on a height, or standing in a large square by itself, it would be far more imposing (Fig. 112).

The church of the Trinity and that of the Augustines, at Paris, are important church edifices of the present day, but though much thought and time have been lavished on them, they are not as attractive as we could wish the works of our own time to be; and they seem almost unworthy of attention when we remember that in the same city there are so many examples of architecture that have far more artistic beauty, as well as the additional charms of age and the interest of historical associations.

We have already spoken of the sort of building in which Francis I. delighted. Of all his undertakings the rebuilding of the Louvre was the most successful. Its whole design was fine and the ornaments beautiful; many of these decorations were made after the drawings of Jean Goujon, who was an eminent master in such sculptures. The court of the Louvre has never been excelled in any country of Europe; it is a wonderful work for the time in which it

FIG. 113.—PAVILION DE L'HORLOGE AND PART OF THE COURT OF THE LOUVRE.

was built, and satisfies the taste of the most critical observers (Fig. 113).

We cannot give space to descriptions of the châteaux built by Francis I., but this picture of that of Chambord affords a good example of what these buildings were (Fig. 114).

From the time of the reign of Charles IX. (1560) to the close of the reign of Louis XIII., the style of architecture which was used in France was called the "style of Henry IV.;" this last-named king ruled before Louis XIII., and during his time architecture sank to a very low plane—there was nothing in it to admire or imitate. Under Louis XIII.

it began to improve, and in the days of Louis XIV., who is called the "*Grand Monarque*," all the arts made great progress and received much patronage from the king, and all the people of the court, for whom the king was a model. Louis XIV. began a revival of Roman classical architecture, and there is no doubt that he believed that he equalled, or perhaps excelled, Julius Cæsar and all other Roman emperors as a patron of the Fine Arts.

But we know that this great monarch was deceived by his self-love and by the flatteries of those who surrounded him and wished to obtain favors from him. His architectural works had so many faults that it is very tiresome to read what is written about them, and in any case it is pleasanter to speak of virtues than of faults. The works of Louis XIV. were certainly herculean, and when we think of the building of the palace of Versailles, the completion of the Louvre, and the numberless hôtels, châteaux, and palaces which belong to his reign, we feel sure that if only the vastness of the architectural works of his time is considered, he well merits the title of the Great Monarch. But these important edifices require more time and space if spoken of in detail than we can give, and I pass to some consideration of the works of our own time.

The architecture of the reign of Napoleon III. requires the space of a volume, at least, were it to be clearly described, for during that reign there was scarcely a city of France that did not add some important building to its public edifices. First, the city of Paris was remodelled and rebuilt to a marvellous extent, and as in other matters Paris is the leader, so its example was followed in architecture. The new Bourse in Lyons, the Custom House at Rouen, and the Exchange at Marseilles are good specimens of what was done in this way outside the great metropolis.

During the reign of Louis Philippe, and a little later, French domestic architecture was vastly improved, and

FIG. 114.—CHÂTEAU OF CHAMBORD.

since then much more attention has been given by Frenchmen to the houses in which they live. The appearance of the new Boulevards and streets of Paris is picturesque, while the houses are rich and elegant. Many portions of this city are more beautiful than any other city of Europe; and yet it is true that the architecture of forty years or so ago was more satisfactory than that of the present time.

FIG. 115.—PORTE ST. DENIS. *Paris.*

The French are an enthusiastic people, and have been very fond of erecting monuments in public places which would remind them continually of the glories of their nation, the conquests of their armies, and the achievements of their great men. Triumphal Arches and Columns of Victory are almost numberless in France; many of them are impressive, and some are really very fine in their architecture. Since the Porte St. Denis was (Fig. 115) erected, in

FIG. 116.—ARC DE L'ÉTOILE. *Paris.*

1672, almost every possible design has been used for these monuments, in one portion of France or another, until, finally, the Arc de l'Étoile (Fig. 116) was built at the upper end of the Champs Elysées, at Paris. This is the noblest of all modern triumphal arches, as well as one of the most splendid ornaments in a city which is richly decorated with architectural works of various styles and periods—from that of the fine Renaissance example seen in the west front of the Louvre, built in 1541, down to the Arc de l'Étoile, the Fontaine St. Michel, and the Palais du Trocadéro of our own time.

The French architecture of the present century is in truth a classic revival; its style has been called the *néo-*

*Grec*, or revived Greek, and the principal buildings of the reign of Napoleon III. all show that a study of Greek art had influenced those who designed these edifices.

## ENGLAND.

We may say that England has never had an architecture of its own, since it has always imitated and reproduced the orders which have originated in other countries. The Gothic order is more than any other the order of England, and, in truth, of Great Britain. All English cathedrals, save one, and a very large proportion of the churches, in city and country, are built in this style of architecture.

It is also true that during the Middle Ages, when the Roman Catholics were in power in England and made use of Gothic architecture, they built so many churches, that, during several later centuries, it might be truly said that England had no church architecture, because so few new churches were required or built.

It is so difficult to trace the origin and progress of the Classical or Renaissance feeling in English architecture that I shall leave it altogether, and passing the transition style and period, speak directly of the first great architect of the Renaissance in England, Inigo Jones, who was born in 1572 and died in 1653. He studied in Italy and brought back to his native country a fondness for the Italian architecture of that day. He became the favorite court architect, and there are many important edifices in England which were built from his designs. His most notable work was the palace of Whitehall, though his design was never fully carried out in it; had it been, this palace would have excelled all others in Europe, either of earlier or later date. Among the churches designed by Inigo Jones that of St. Paul's, Covent Garden, is interesting because it is probably the first important Protestant church erected in England which still exists. It is small and simple, being almost an exact reproduction of the early Greek temples called *distyle in antis*, such as I described when speaking of Greek architecture (Fig. 117).

FIG. 117.—EAST ELEVATION OF ST. PAUL'S. *Covent Garden.*

Inigo Jones made many designs for villas and private residences, and perhaps he is more famous for these works than for any others. Among them are Chiswick and Wilton House, and many others of less importance.

After Jones came Sir Christopher Wren, who was the architect of some of the finest buildings in London. He was born in 1632 and died in 1723. The great fire, in 1666, when he was thirty-four years old, gave him a splendid opportunity to show his talents. Only three days after this fire he presented to the king a plan for rebuilding the city, which would have made it one of the most convenient as well as one of the most beautiful cities of the world.

Sir Christopher Wren is most frequently mentioned as the architect of St. Paul's Cathedral. This was commenced nine years after the great fire, and was thirty-five years in building. St. Paul's is the largest and finest Protestant cathedral in the world, and among all the churches of Europe that have been erected since the revival of Classical architecture, St. Peter's, at Rome, alone excels it (Fig. 118).

Although so many years were consumed in the building of St. Paul's, Sir Christopher Wren lived to superintend it

FIG. 118.—ST. PAUL'S, LONDON. *From the West.*

all, and had the gratification of placing the topmost stone in the lantern of this splendid monument to his genius.

The western towers of Westminster Abbey are said to have been built after a design by Wren, but of this there is a doubt. Among his other works in church architecture are the steeple of Bow Church, London ; the church of St. Stephen's, Walbrook ; St. Bride's, Fleet Street, and St. James's, Piccadilly.

The royal palaces of Winchester and Hampton were designed by Wren, and many other well-known edifices, among which is Greenwich Hospital. He made some signal failures, but it is great praise to say, what is undoubtedly true, that, though he was a pioneer in the Renaissance architecture of England, ana died a century and a half ago, no one of his countrymen has surpassed him, and we may well question whether any other English architect has equalled him.

FIG. 119.—ST. GEORGE'S HALL. *Liverpool.*

Churches, palaces, university buildings, and fine examples of municipal and domestic architecture are so numerous in England and other portions of Great Britain that we cannot speak of them in detail. The culmination of the taste for the imitation of Classical architecture was reached about the beginning of the present century, and among the most notable edifices in that manner are the British Museum, Fitzwilliam College, Cambridge, and St. George's Hall, Liverpool (Fig. 119).

A revival of Gothic Architecture has taken place in England in our own time. The three most prominent secular buildings in this style are Windsor Castle, the Houses of Parliament, and the New Museum, at Oxford. Of course, in the case of Windsor Castle, the work was a remodelling, but the reparations were so extensive as to almost equal a rebuilding. Sir Jeffry Wyatville had the superintendence of it, and succeeded in making it appear

FIG. 120.—WINDSOR CASTLE.

like an ancient building refitted in the nineteenth century—that is to say, it combines modern luxury and convenience in its interior with the exterior appearance of the castellated fortresses of a more barbarous age (Fig. 120).

In the Houses of Parliament there was an attempt to carry out, even to the minutest detail, the Gothic style as it existed in the Tudor age, when there was an excess of ornament, most elaborate doorways, and the fan-tracery vaultings were decorated with pendent ornaments which look like clusters of stalactites. Sir Charles Barry was its architect. The present school of artists in England are never weary of abusing it ; they call it a horror and declare its style to be obsolete. In fact, it is not the success at which Barry aimed ; but it excels the other efforts to revive the Gothic in this day, not only in England, but in all

FIG. 121.—THE HOUSES OF PARLIAMENT. *London.*

Europe, and has many points to be admired in its plan and its detail, while the beauty of its sky-line must be admitted by all (Fig. 121).

In the New Museum of Oxford, the Gothic is that of Lombardy, rather than the Early English. It is an example of the result of the teaching of Mr. Ruskin. It does not realize the expectations of those who advocated this manner of building, and has proved a great disappointment to the advanced theorists of a quarter of a century ago.

English architecture of the present day may be concisely described by saying that it is Gothic for churches, parsonage-houses, school-houses, and all edifices in which the clergy are interested or of which they have the oversight. On the other hand, palaces, town-halls, municipal buildings, club-houses, and such structures as come within the care of the laity, are almost without exception in the Classic style.

Neither of these orders seems to be exactly suited to the climate of England or to the wants of its people; therefore, neither would satisfy the demands of the ancients, who taught that the architecture of a nation should be precisely adapted to its climate and to the purposes for which the edifices are intended. In fact, the ancients carried their ideas of fitness so far that one could tell at a glance the object for which a structure had been designed; we know that it is not possible to comply with this law in this day, although it is doubtless in accord with the true ideal of what perfect architecture should be. At the present day there is little doubt that the edifices of the Church and clergy are far more praiseworthy and true architecturally than are those for secular and domestic uses.

## GERMANY.

I shall not speak of the period of the Renaissance in Germany, but shall go forward to the time of the Revival of Classic Architecture, which dated about 1825. During the eighteenth century the discoveries which were made in Greece were of great interest to all the world, and the drawings which were made of the temples and monuments, as well as of the lesser objects of art which existed there, were sent all over Europe, and had such an effect upon the different nations, that with one accord they began to adopt the Greek style of architecture, whenever any important work was to be done. This effect was very marked in Germany, and the German architects tried to copy every detail of Greek architecture with great exactness.

When we begin to speak of modern German architecture at this point, we do not omit anything important, for the struggles of the Reformation, and the results of the Thirty Years' War were such, that no great architectural advances were attempted for a long time. Again, the division of Germany into many small principalities, and the establishment of many little courts so divided the wealth of the German people into small portions, that no one was rich enough to undertake large buildings. There was no one great central city as in France and England, and no one sovereign was rich enough to adorn his capital with splendid edifices or to be a magnificent patron of art and artists after the fashion of the "*Grand Monarque*" in France.

Before taking up the Revival, however, I wish, for two reasons, to givè a picture of the Brandenburg Gate, at Berlin. This gate was erected between 1784 and 1792. It is important because such monuments are more rare in Germany than in other European countries, especially of the time in which this was built, and because it is one of the best imitations of Greek art that exists in any nation (Fig. 122).

It is interesting to remember that when Napoleon entered Berlin as a conqueror, after the Battle of Jena, he sent the Car of Victory, which surmounts this gate, to Paris, as a trophy of his prowess. After his abdication it was returned to its original position.

The effect of the German revival of Greek art is more plainly seen in Munich than in any other city. It is the capital of Bavaria, and one of its kings, Louis I., while he was young and had not yet become king, resided at Rome; he was a passionate lover of art, and he resolved that when he came to the throne he would make his capital famous for beautiful things. Above all, he desired to imi-

FIG. 122.—THE BRANDENBURG GATE. *Berlin.*

tate all that he had most admired in the countries he had visited, and also the art of the ancients as he knew it from models and pictures. For this reason it happens that Munich is a collection of copies of buildings which have existed in other countries and in past ages, and as these buildings, which were first made in marble and stone, are mostly copied in plaster in Munich, much of their beauty is lost; and since these copied buildings are not used for the same purposes for which the ancient ones were intended, the whole effect of them is very far from pleasing or satisfactory. In fact, the result is just such as must always follow the imitation of a beautiful object, when no proper regard is paid to the use to be made of it. If, for example, a fine copy of a light and airy Swiss châlet should be made in the United States of America, and placed on some business street in one of our cities, and used for a bank building, we could not deny that it was an exact copy of a building which is good in its way; but it would be so unsuited to its position and its uses, that the man who built it there would be counted as insane or foolish. And this is the effect of the modern architecture of Munich; it seems as

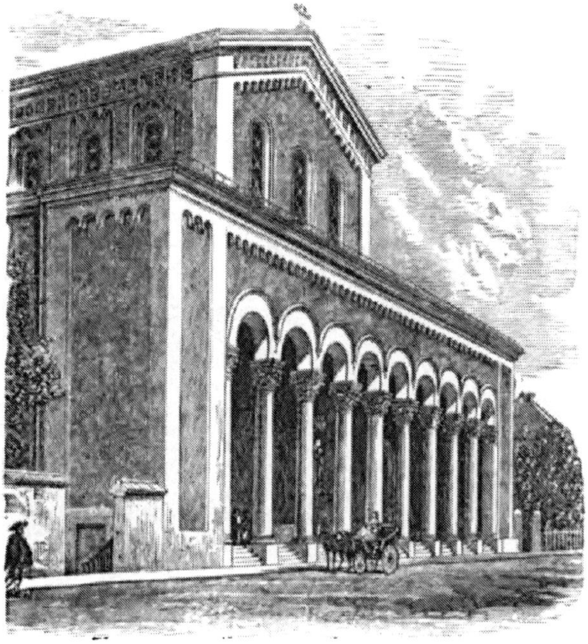

FIG. 123.—THE BASILICA AT MUNICH.

if King Louis must have been a madman to expend so much time and money in this absurd kind of imitative architecture, and yet it is very interesting to visit this city and see these edifices.

Of the Munich churches erected under Louis I. that of St. Ludwig is in the Byzantine order; the Aue-Kirche is in the pointed German Gothic, and the Basilica is like a Roman basilica of the fifth century. It resembles that of

St. Paul's-without-the-Walls; it was begun in 1835 and completed in 1850. In a vault beneath this basilica Louis and his Queen, Theresa, are buried. The picture given here shows its extreme simplicity; its whole effect is solemn and satisfactory; still one must regret that since it is so fine up to a certain point, it should not have been made still finer (Fig. 123).

The Ruhmeshalle, or Hall of Fame, at Munich, is an interesting and somewhat unique edifice. It is a portico

FIG. 124.—THE RUHMESHALLE. *Near Munich.*

of marble with forty-eight Doric columns, each twenty-six feet high. Against the walls are brackets holding busts of celebrated Germans who have lived since 1400. In front of the portico stands the colossal bronze statue of Bavaria. She is represented as a protectress with a lion by her side; in the right hand she holds a sword, and a chaplet in the left; it is sixty-one and a half feet high, and the pedestal raises it twenty-eight and a half feet more; inside, a staircase leads up into the head, where there are seats for eight persons. The view from the top of this statue is fine, and so extensive that in a favorable atmosphere the heights of the Alps can be discerned. The hill upon which the Ruhmeshalle is built is to the south of Munich, and is called the Theresienhöhe. The grand statue is intended to be the principal object of interest here, and the portico is made so low as to throw the figure out and show it off to advantage ; altogether it is one of the most successful architectural works in Munich (Fig. 124).

The Glyptothek, or Sculpture Gallery, the Pinakothek, or Picture Gallery, the Royal Palace, the Public Library,

FIG. 125.—THE MUSEUM. *Berlin.*

the War Office, the University, Blind School, other palaces and secular buildings, all belong to the time of the Revival in Germany. The Ludwig Strasse, which King Louis fondly hoped to make one of the most beautiful avenues in the world, is—with its Roman arch at one end, and a weak copy of the Loggia dei Lanzi at the other—a tiresome, meaningless, architectural failure.

The Museum of Berlin is a striking result of the same Revival of Classic architecture, and is far more splendid than anything in Munich (Fig. 125).

In Dresden the most important works in this style are the New Theatre and Picture Gallery. The last is almost an exact reproduction of the Pinakothek of Munich. All over Germany the effects of this Revival are more or less prominent, but I shall speak of but one other edifice, the Walhalla (Fig. 126).

This is also a Temple of Fame, and is situated about six miles from Ratisbon. It overlooks the River Danube from a height of more than three hundred feet. It was begun in 1830, and was twelve years in building, costing eight millions of florins. It is of white marble, and on the exterior

FIG. 126.—THE WALHALLA.

is an exact reproduction of the Parthenon at Athens. The interior is divided into two parts by an entablature, which supports fourteen caryatides, made from colored marbles. These figures in turn support a second entablature, on which is a frieze in eight compartments, on which is sculptured scenes representing the history of Germany from its early days to the time of the introduction of Christianity. Along the lower wall there are one hundred busts of illustrious Germans who had lived from the earliest days of Germany down to those of the poet Goethe.

The grounds about the Walhalla are laid out in walks, and from them there are fine, extensive views. Taken by itself there is much to admire in the Walhalla. The sculptures arouse an enthusiasm about Germany, her history, and the men who have helped to make it, in spite of the strange unfitness with which the artists have mingled Grecian myths and German sagas. But aside from this sort of interest the whole thing seems incongruous and strangely unsuited to its position ; one writer goes so far as to say of it that " Minerva, descending in Cheapside to separate two quarrelling cabmen, could hardly be more out of place." And yet it is true that the Walhalla is the only worthy rival to St. George's Hall, Liverpool, as an example of the possible adaptability of Greek or Roman Architecture to the needs and uses of our own days.

## THEATRES AND MUSIC HALLS.

In speaking of theatres I will first give a list of the most important ones in Europe, as they are given by Fergusson in his " History of Modern Architecture."

| | Depth from Curtain to back of Boxes. | Depth of Stage. |
|---|---|---|
| | feet. | feet. |
| La Scala, Milan | 105 | 77 |
| San Carlo, Naples | 100 | 74 |
| Carlo Felice, Genoa | 95 | 80 |
| New Opera House, Paris | 95 | 98 |
| Opera House, London (old) | 95 | 45 |
| Turin Opera House | 90 | 110 |
| Covent Garden, London | 89 | 89 |
| St. Petersburg, Opera | 87 | 100 |
| Académie de Musique, Paris | 85 | 82 |
| Parma, Opera | 82 | 76 |
| Fenice, Venice | 82 | 48 |
| Munich Theatre | 80 | 87 |
| Madrid Theatre | 79 | 55 |

The Opera House of La Scala, at Milan, is generally said to be the finest of all for seeing and hearing what goes on upon the stage: it was begun in 1776 and finished two years later. San Carlo, Naples, holds the second place, and was first erected in 1737, but was almost destroyed by fire in 1816, and was afterward thoroughly rebuilt.

The new Opera House of Paris is interesting to us because it has been built so recently and so much written and said of it that we are familiar with it. Any description

FIG. 127.—THE NEW OPERA HOUSE. *Paris.*

that would do it justice would occupy more space than we can afford for it, but this cut (Fig. 127) gives an excellent idea of its size and exterior appearance. It is distinguished by great richness of material and profusion of ornament, its interior decorations being especially splendid. It has been criticised as lacking repose and dignity, but its elegance and magnificence compel admiration.

Music halls are only another sort of theatre, and have come into great favor in recent days, especially in England.

The Albert Hall, South Kensington, is the finest music hall that has been erected. It seats eight thousand people, besides accommodating an orchestra of two hundred and a chorus of one thousand singers ; it is one hundred and thirty-six feet from the floor to the highest part of the ceiling. This hall has some defects, but is so far successful as to prove that a theatre or music hall could be so constructed as to seat ten thousand persons and permit them to hear the music as distinctly as it is heard in many halls where only two or three thousand can be comfortable.

## UNITED STATES OF AMERICA.

When we remember that we have been able to give some account of architecture as it existed thousands of years before Christ, and to speak of the temples and tombs of the grand old nations who laid the foundation of the arts and civilization of the world—and then, when we remember the little time that has passed since the first roof was raised in our own land, we may well be proud of our country as it is—and at the same time we know that its architecture may in truth be said to be a thing of the future.

It is but a few years, not more than seventy, since any building existed here that could be termed architectural in any degree. To be sure, there were many comfortable, generous-sized homes scattered up and down the land, but they made no claim to architectural design, and were not such edifices as one considers when speaking or writing of architecture.

The first buildings to which much attention was given in the United States were the Capitols, both State and National, and until recently they were in what may be called a Classic style, because they had porticoes with columns and certain other features of ancient orders ; but when

Fig. 128.—The United States Capitol. *Washington.*

the cella, as is the case in America, is divided into two or more stories, with rows of prosaic windows all around, and chimneys, and perhaps attics also added, the term Classic Architecture immediately becomes questionable, and it is difficult to find a name exactly suited to the needs of the case; for it is still true that from a distance, and in answer to a general glance, they are nearer to the Classic orders than to anything else.

The National Capitol at Washington, which is the principal edifice in the United States, was begun in 1793, when General Washington laid the foundation-stone; the main portion was completed in 1830; two wings and the dome have since been added, and its present size is greater than that of any other legislative building in the world, except the British Houses of Parliament (Fig. 128).

The dome, and the splendid porticoes, with the magnificent flights of steps leading up to them, are the fine features of the Capitol. The dome compares well with those that are famous in the world, and taken all in all the Wash-

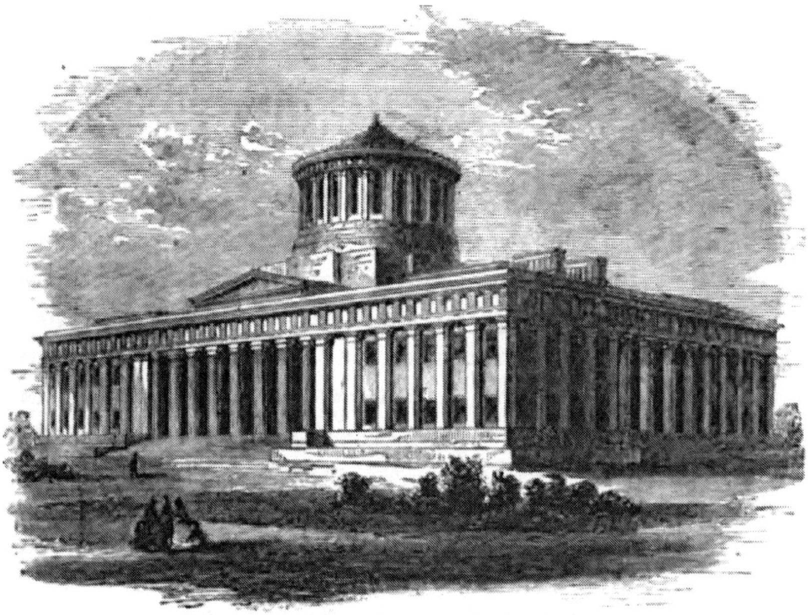

FIG. 129.—STATE CAPITOL. *Columbus, Ohio.*

ington Capitol is more stately than the Houses or Parliament, and is open to as little criticism as buildings of its class in other lands.

Several of the State Capitols illustrate the manner of building which I described above. This cut of the Capitol of Ohio is an excellent example of it (Fig. 129).

In domestic architecture, while there has been no style so original and absolutely defined as to be definitely called

American, we may roughly classify three periods—the Colonial, the Middle, and the Modern. These terms have no close application, and you must understand that I use them rather for convenience than because they accurately, or even approximately, indicate particular styles. The mansions of the Colonial period are, perhaps, most easily recognized, and in some respects were the frankest and most independent class of houses ever built in this country. The early settlers took whatever suited them from all styles, and instead of imitating the English, the Dutch, or the French manner of building, mingled parts of all, with especial reference to the needs of their climate and surroundings.

This fine old house (Fig. 130) shows the plain, homely, yet quaint style of many of the mansions of the Colonial period. It was built near the beginning of the last century, and occupied by Sir William Pepperell until his death. Its interior, with heavy wainscoting of solid mahogany, was more imposing by far than the exterior. The Van Rensselaer homestead at Albany is an excellent example of a more stately house, possessing much dignity and impressiveness.

The Middle period was a time when domestic architecture, still without any originality and losing much of the independence of the Colonial, copied more closely from foreign models. Some fine old mansions belong to this period, which covered the last years of the last century and the first half of this. The celebrated Cragie House at Cambridge, occupied by the poet Longfellow; "Elmwood," the home of James Russell Lowell; "Bedford House," in Westchester County, New York, the home of the Hon. John Jay, are to be referred to this period; and so is the imposing "Old Morrisania," at Morrisania, New York, the old Morris mansion (Fig. 131).

It is modelled after a French château, and was erected by General Morris after his return from France in 1800. It

FIG. 130.—SIR WILLIAM PEPPERELL'S HOUSE. *Kittery Point, Maine.*

is one of the most striking among the mansions of its time, and both its interior and exterior are highly interesting.

These views serve to illustrate the want of anything like a regular style, of which I spoke above; but they show how many different forces were at work to influence building in the Modern period. This division is meant to extend to and include the present time, and so great is the diversity of styles now employed that in a work like this it would be idle to attempt anything like an enumeration of them, and still less to try and determine their origin and importance. I can only give you one example of the handsome and costly homes which are being built to-day, and leave you to observe others as you now see them everywhere about the country (Fig. 132). A modern writer on American architecture claims that in private dwellings an American order is gradually being developed by the changes made to adapt foreign forms to our climate, and especially to the brilliancy of the sunlight here. All this is so difficult to define, however, that it would be impossible to show it clearly in the limits of a book like this, even if it exists.

What is called the "Queen Anne" style, modelled upon the English fashion of the time of that monarch, is very widely used in country houses at the present time, sometimes in conjunction with the Colonial, which also exists as an independent style. The tendency of domestic architecture is to make everything quaint and picturesque, though this is not so far carried to extremes as was the case a few years since.

In public buildings many splendid edifices have been erected of late years. The imitation of classic forms which was formerly the fashion, and which is so strikingly exhibited by Girard College, Philadelphia, is now almost entirely laid aside. A lighter, less constrained style, which may be called eclectic—which means selecting—because it takes freely from any and all styles whatever suits its pur-

pose, is arising; and as this selecting is being every year more and more intelligently done, and as original ideas are constantly being incorporated with those chosen, the prospects for architecture are more promising than ever before in this country. The Casino, at Newport, is a fine example of a modern building; and the still more recent Casino in New York shows a fine example of the adapting of ideas from Saracenic architecture to American uses. The Capitol at Albany has many fine features, but it is the work of several designers who did not harmonize. Memorial Hall, at Cambridge, is one of the more striking of modern American buildings, but its sky-line—that is, its outline as seen against the sky—lacks simplicity and repose.

The churches in this country exhibit the widest variety of style. Trinity Church in New York was the first Gothic church erected in America, and Trinity Church in Boston, one of the latest churches of importance, is also Gothic, though of the variety called Norman Gothic, and considerably varied. The Roman Catholic Cathedral of New York, and many others of less magnitude, might be cited as a proof that American architecture is advancing, and that we may speak hopefully of its future.

Railroad depots and school-houses of certain types are among the most distinctive and characteristic American edifices. The first, especially, are being constructed more nearly in accordance with the ancient principle of suiting the structure to its uses than are any other buildings that are worthy to be considered architecturally. Art museums and public libraries, too, now form an important feature in both town and country, and, in short, the beginning of American architecture, for that is all that can be claimed for what as yet exists, is such as would be the natural outcome of a nation such as ours—varied, restless, bold, ugly, original, and progressive. All these terms can be applied to American art, but in and through it all there is a prom-

ise of something more. As greater age will bring repose and dignity of bearing to our people, so our Fine Arts will take on the best of our characteristics ; as we outgrow our national crudities the change will be shown in our architecture, and we may well anticipate that in the future we shall command the consideration and assume the same importance in these regards that our excellence in the Useful Arts has already won for us in all the world.

## GLOSSARY OF TECHNICAL TERMS.

*Abacus.*—The uppermost portion of the capital of a column, upon which rested the weight above.

*Aisle.*—The lateral divisions of a church ; more properly, the side subdivisions.

*Amphitheatre.*—A round or oval theatre.

*Apse.*—The semi-circular or polygonal termination to the choir or aisles of a church.

*Arcade.*—A series of arches supported on piers or columns.

*Arch.*—A construction of wedge-shaped blocks of stone or of bricks, of curved outline, spanning an open space.

*Architrave.*—(1) The lowest division of the entablature, in Classic architecture resting on the abacus. (2) The moulding used to ornament the margin of an opening.

*Base.*—The foot of a column or wall.

*Basilica.*—Originally a Roman hall of justice ; afterward an early Christian church.

*Buttress.*—A projection built from a wall for strength.

*Byzantine.*—The Christian architecture of the Eastern church, sometimes called the round arched ; named from Byzantium (Constantinople).

*Capital.*—The head of a column or pilaster.

*Caryatid.*—A statue of a woman used as a column.

*Cathedral.*—A church containing the seat of a bishop.

*Cella.*—That part of the temple within the walls.

*Chamfer.*—A slope or bevel formed by cutting off the edge of an angle.

*Column.*—A pillar or post, round or polygonal; the term includes the base, shaft, and capital.

*Composite Order.*—See *Order.*

*Corinthian Order.*—See *Order.*

*Cornice.*—The horizontal projection crowning a building or some portion of a building. Each classic order had its peculiar cornice.

*Crypt.*—A vault beneath a building.

*Dome.*—A cupola or spherical convex roof.

*Doric Order.*—See *Order.*

*Entablature.*—In classic styles all the structure above the columns except the gable. The entablature had three members, the architrave or epistyle, the frieze, and the cornice.

*Entasis.*—The swelling of a column near the middle to counteract the appearance of concavity caused by an optical delusion.

*Epistyle.*—See *Architrave.*

*Façade.*—The exterior face of a building.

*Frieze.*—The middle member of an entablature.

*Gable.*—The triangular-shaped wall supporting the end of a roof.

*Gargoyle.*—A projecting water-spout carved in stone or metal.

*Hexastyle.*—A portico having six columns in front.

*Intercolumniation.*—The clear space between two columns.

*Ionic Order.*—See *Order.*

*Metope.*—The space between the triglyphs in the frieze of the Doric Order.

*Minaret.*—A slender tower with balconies from which Mohammedan hours of prayer are called.

*Mosaic.*—Ornamental work made by cementing together small pieces of glass, stone, or metal in given designs.

*Nave.*—The central aisle of a church ; the western part of the church occupied by the congregation.

*Obelisk.*—A quadrangular monolith terminating in a pyramid.

*Order.*—An entire column with its appropriate entablature. There are usually said to be five orders : Tuscan, Doric, Ionic, Corinthian, and Composite ; the first and last are, however, only varieties of the Doric and Corinthian developed by the Romans. The peculiarities of the orders have been described in the body of the book. When more than one order was used in a building, the heavier and plainer, the Doric and Tuscan, are placed beneath the others.

*Pediment.*—In classic architecture what the gable (which see) was in later styles.

*Peristyle.*—A court surrounded by a row of columns ; also the colonnade itself surrounding such a space.

*Pier.*—A solid wall built to support a weight.

*Pilaster.*—A square column, generally attached to the wall.

*Pillar.*—See *Column.*

*Plinth.*—A square member forming the lower division of the base of a column.

*Polychrome.*—Many-colored; applied to the staining of walls or architectural ornaments.

*Quatrefoil.*—A four-leaved ornament or opening.

*Shaft.*—The middle portion of a column, between base and capital.

*Story.*—The portion of a building between one floor and the next.

*Triglyph.*—An ornament upon the Doric frieze consisting of three vertical, angular channels separated by narrow, flat spaces.

# INDEX.

Lightning Source UK Ltd.
Milton Keynes UK
UKOW03f0936270415

250400UK00010B/313/P

9 781174 442179